THE ART OF
THE WAR OF THE REALMS

ASSISTANT EDITOR
CAITLIN O'CONNELL

ASSOCIATE MANAGING EDITOR
KATERI WOODY

EDITOR, SPECIAL PROJECTS
MARK D. BEAZLEY

SENIOR EDITOR
JENNIFER GRÜNWALD

VP PRODUCTION & SPECIAL PROJECTS
JEFF YOUNGQUIST

SVP PRINT, SALES & MARKETING
DAVID GABRIEL

DIRECTOR, LICENSED PUBLISHING
SVEN LARSEN

EDITOR IN CHIEF
C.B. CEBULSKI

CHIEF CREATIVE OFFICER
JOE QUESADA

PRESIDENT
DAN BUCKLEY

EXECUTIVE PRODUCER
ALAN FINE

SPECIAL THANKS TO **JAMES HARROLD & WIL MOSS**

THE ART OF WAR OF THE REALMS. First printing 2019. ISBN 978-1-302-91764-7. Published by MARVEL WORLDWIDE, INC., a subsidiary of MARVEL ENTERTAINMENT, LLC. OFFICE OF PUBLICATION: 135 West 50th Street, New York, NY 10020. Copyright © 2019 MARVEL No similarity between any of the names, characters, persons, and/or institutions in this magazine with those of any living or dead person or institution is intended, and any such similarity which may exist is purely coincidental. **Printed in Canada.** DAN BUCKLEY, President, Marvel Entertainment; JOHN NEE, Publisher; JOE QUESADA, Chief Creative Officer; TOM BREVOORT, SVP of Publishing; DAVID BOGART, SVP of Business Affairs & Operations, Publishing & Partnership; DAVID GABRIEL, SVP of Sales & Marketing, Publishing; JEFF YOUNGQUIST, VP of Production & Special Projects; DAN CARR, Executive Director of Publishing Technology; ALEX MORALES, Director of Publishing Operations; DAN EDINGTON, Managing Editor; SUSAN CRESPI, Production Manager; STAN LEE, Chairman Emeritus. For information regarding advertising in Marvel Comics or on Marvel.com, please contact Vit DeBellis, Custom Solutions & Integrated Advertising Manager, at vdebellis@marvel.com. For Marvel subscription inquiries, please call 888-511-5480. **Manufactured between 3/8/2019 and 4/9/2019 by SOLISCO PRINTERS, SCOTT, QC, CANADA**

10 9 8 7 6 5 4 3 2 1

THE ART OF THE WAR OF THE REALMS

WRITTEN BY

JESS HARROLD

book design by

RODOLFO MURAGUCHI

thor created by

STAN LEE, LARRY LIEBER & **JACK KIRBY**

INTRODUCTION

As soon as I got the gig as the Mighty Thor's main saga chronicler back in 2012, I knew right away I had a stellar artist by my side in Esad Ribić, and I very quickly came up with a notebook full of hammer-swinging story ideas, some of which we're only just now getting to. But there was one important ingredient for Thor success that I still didn't have.

I didn't know Niffleheim from Nidavellir.

I didn't know where the Elves lived or the Dwarves called home. I didn't know which land was made of ice and which was all fire.

I didn't know the realms.

The Nine Realms of Norse mythology. Well, there were nine back in 2012, but since then we've gone and added a tenth one.

When I first started working on Thor, I couldn't name all those realms or tell you how one was different from the other. And the more I dug into it, I became worried that not many Thor readers could tell you much about them either.

Those realms are the beat that Thor walks as a hero. They're one of the unique characteristics that sets the God of Thunder apart from the other heroes of the Marvel U. Spider-Man has the Five Boroughs. Thor has the Ten Realms.

In other words, the realms are important, in my mind, to what makes the Thunder God so thunderously exciting. But they hadn't always been utilized in major ways story-wise over the years. I wanted to change that. During my tenure writing the character, I wanted to take Thor to each of those realms, to flesh them out, nail down who lives there, do a bit of world-building, have a bunch of maps drawn up (because the more fantasy maps the better!), give each realm

their own kind of shark (sorry, that's one of my things) and just generally make the Ten Realms interesting locales that readers would know and understand and hopefully want to go back to again and again.

But how to do that? How to craft a Thor story that takes us from realm to realm? A road trip, maybe? A *Cannonball Run* but with gods? No. Something bigger.

How about a war?

Not long after I began my run on *Thor,* his old foe Malekith the Accursed re-emerged and sparked a conflict that began to rage across all of creation. Since then, thousands of Elves have died. Maybe millions. Dwarves have burned inside their mountains. Rainbow Bridges have shattered. Gods have wept. Thors have fallen.

All because I wanted to take you on a sightseeing tour.

And Odin's beard, what sights we've seen.

And hopefully had some fun along the way.

The fun part for me has been getting to work with the thunderer's row of talented artists you'll see featured in this book, from the ink-slinging berserker known as Esad Ribić to the golden god of designs and fine lines named Russell Dauterman and every last amazing artist in between. Each of them did the work of an All-Father to bring the Ten Realms and their inhabitants to life in the grandest and most wildly imaginative fashion. And then together…we set it all on fire and watched it burn.

That fire has been raging for seven years and around 87 issues. And now at long last, it's time for the final conflagration. I'm thankful we get to enjoy the last few flames of this war together, my friends.

For we may never war this way again.

JASON AARON
Somewhere along the
shores of Midgard
March 2019

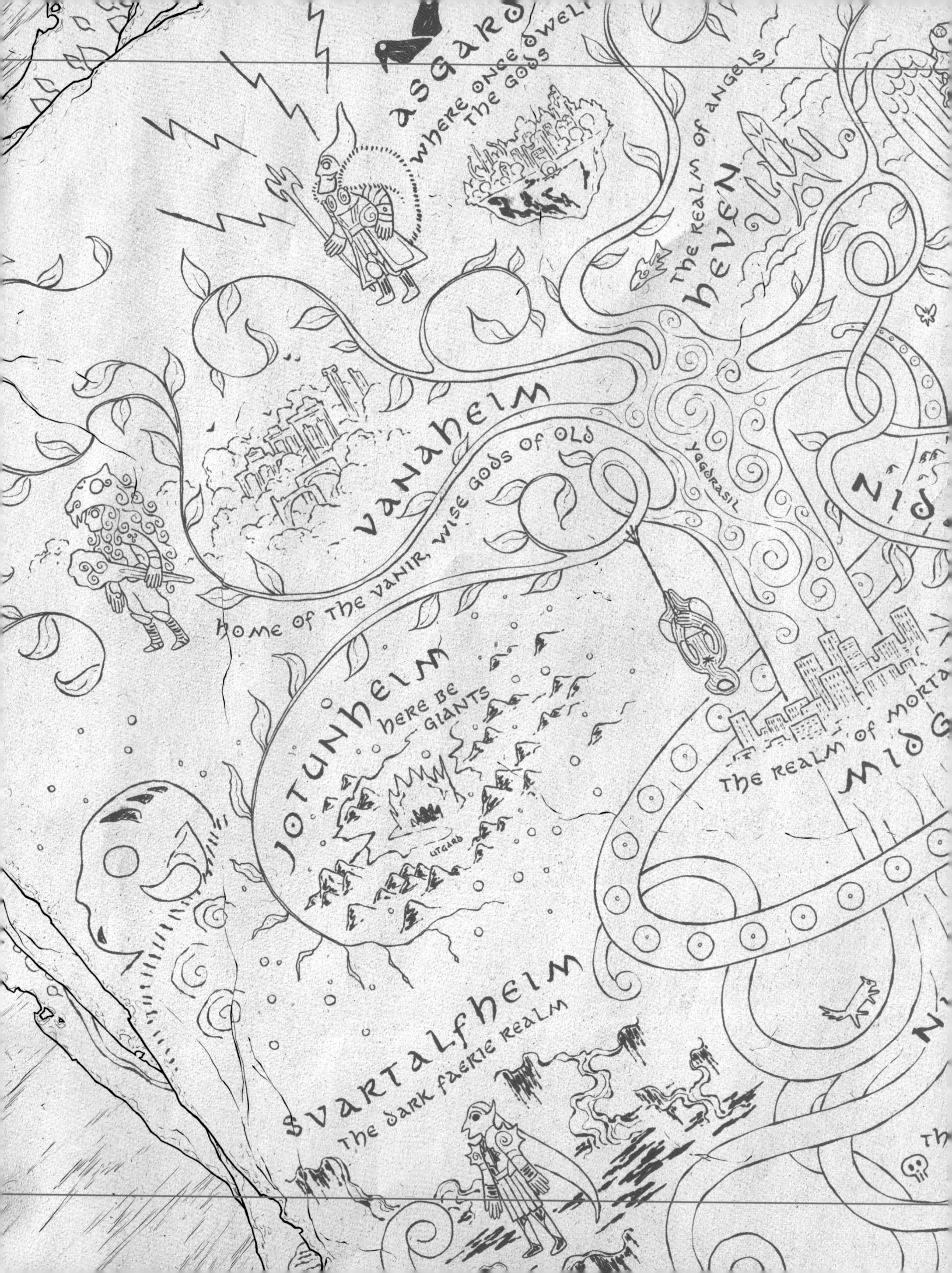
ASGAR
WHERE ONCE DWEL
THE GODS
THE REALM OF ANGELS
HEVEN
VANAHEIM
HOME OF THE VANIR, WISE GODS OF OLD
YGGDRASIL
NID
JOTUNHEIM
HERE BE GIANTS
UTGARD
THE REALM OF MORTA
MIDG
SVARTALFHEIM
THE DARK FAERIE REALM

THERE IS A STORY, STILL UNFOLDING.

IT IS A STORY OF WAR ACROSS ALL THE REALMS — NINE YOU
MAY ALREADY KNOW, AND A TENTH YOU MAY YET NOT.

OF GODS AND MONSTERS, ELVES AND TROLLS,
DWARVES AND GIANTS, ANGELS AND DEMONS.

OF ONE DARK SORCERER WHO WOULD RULE
THEM ALL...OR WATCH THEM BURN.

AND A BRAVE HAMMER WIELDER WHO FIGHTS FOR
ALL WORLDS...WHOEVER HE OR SHE MAY BE.

IT IS A STORY OF EVERLASTING IMMORTALITY...
AND ALL-TOO-FLEETING MORTALITY.

ONE OF PAST, PRESENT AND FAR FUTURE.

OF BEING WORTHY...AND HAVING WORTHINESS
SLIP THROUGH YOUR FINGERS.

OF WHAT IT TRULY MEANS TO BE A GOD.

THIS IS NOT THAT STORY.

BUT IT IS, PERHAPS, THE STORY OF THAT STORY.

THE TALE OF A SCRIBE WHO WOULD MAKE LEGENDS...
AND THE PANTHEON OF ARTISTS THAT BRINGS HIS WORDS TO LIFE.

THIS IS

THE ART OF
THE WAR OF THE REALMS

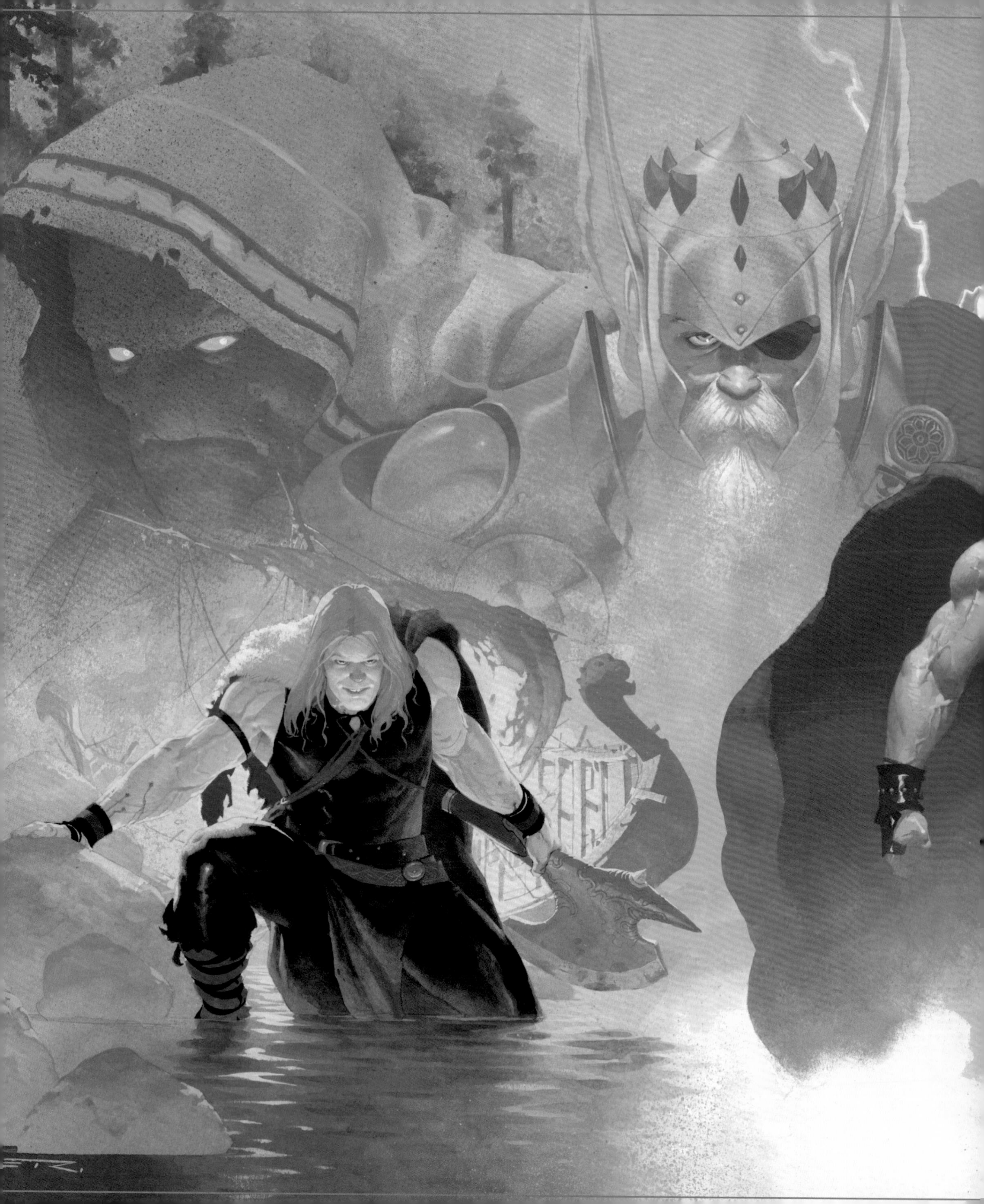

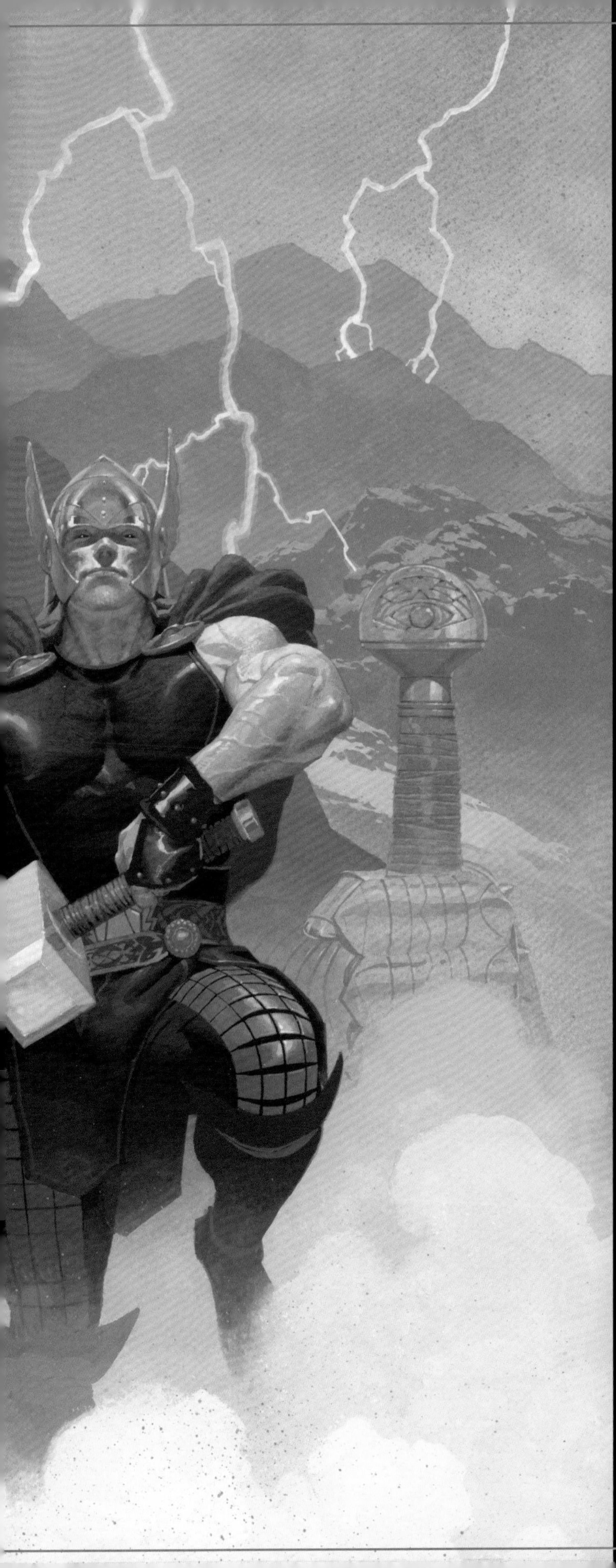

chapter one:

THE GOD BUTCHER

"I've seen war in the heavens.
I've seen gods suffer and bleed...
I've seen hel itself.
But I've never seen anything like
the **horror** in this god's eyes."
— Thor

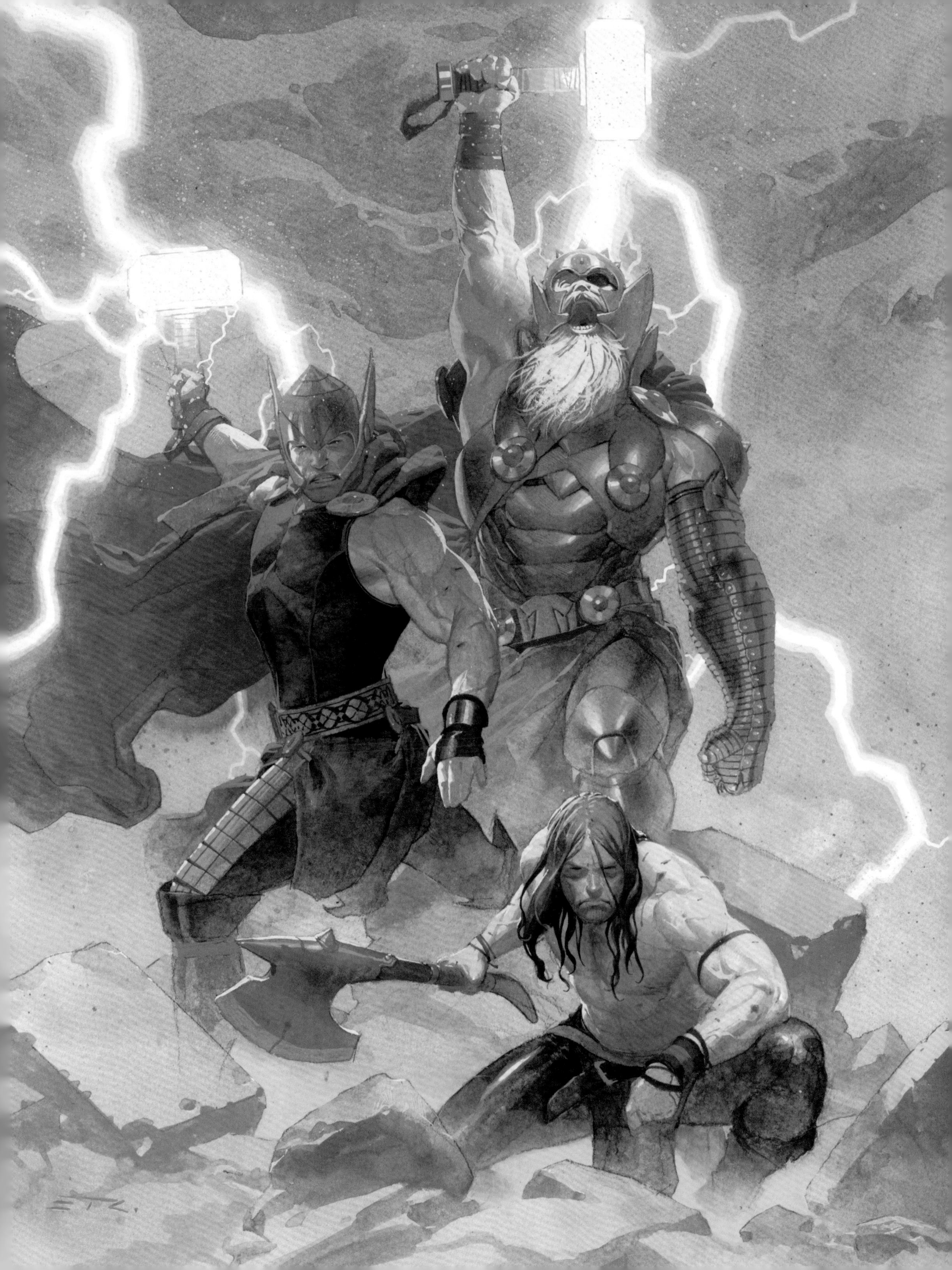

T he road to war began not with one God of Thunder, but with three. As Jason Aaron commenced his soon-to-be-legendary run alongside artist Esad Ribić on the relaunched and retitled *Thor: God of Thunder*, he took inspiration from his cherished *Conan the Barbarian* novels and the storytelling techniques of their author, Robert E. Howard. "One of the things I always loved about the Howard stories is how he skipped around all throughout Conan's timeline," Aaron says. "We got to see adventures of young Conan and also of grizzled old King Conan. I wanted something that was so huge and epic — a story you could only do with Thor. So the idea of having one villain that he encountered over the course of thousands and thousands of years I thought was fun."

Aaron's initial arc, "The God Butcher," features a young Thor, not yet worthy of lifting Mjolnir, who lives to fight, drink and carouse with Vikings; the present-day Thor, warrior of Asgard and Avenger of Earth; and millennia into the future, an old, grizzled Thor, who has lost an arm and an eye and sits alone on the throne of Asgard as the last of the gods. Uniting them across the eras is a foe unlike any Thor has battled before — a relentless, remorseless, seemingly unstoppable serial killer of deities. The God Butcher himself — Gorr! The story depicts Thor's long-forgotten first encounter with Gorr, from which the young Thunder God barely escapes with his life, as well as today's Thor scouring the galaxy in search of missing gods, which leads to another savage showdown. And centuries from now, the long-suffering old King Thor grows weary of battle with Gorr's monstrous Black Berserkers. But these three Thors would not be separated by centuries for long. "The bonus of introducing those different versions of Thor was having them team up," Aaron says. "The idea of present-day Thor having to team up with his arrogant young self and some surly older self, who has basically become his dad, made for a lot of fun."

"The God Bomb," in issues #7-11, unites this trio of Thunder Gods in brutal, final conflict with Gorr as he seeks to trigger his titular bomb and wipe out all deities across time and space. The thrilling climax sees Thor in his prime — "our" Thor — with a Mjolnir in each hand, doing the impossible as only the greatest of all gods can. The two arcs compose a single tale that is epic in every sense — one that weaves between the frozen landscapes of ninth-century Northern Europe; the future ruins of Asgard; and the science-fiction settings of Omnipotence City, nexus of the gods, and Chronux, palace of infinity. Only one artist could possibly capture a story told on this scale: Ribić, who had worked previously with Aaron on *Dark Reign: The List — Wolverine* and *X-Men: Battle of the Atom #2* and had demonstrated his flair for Asgardian lore on 2004's *Loki*, written by Robert Rodi.

"I was thrilled to get to work with him again," Aaron says. "Esad is a guy who can draw pretty much anything, the crazier the better. Esad was perfect to launch the book with — that dark-fantasy-mixed-with-sci-fi kind of tale. Knowing Esad was doing it helped me shoot for the stars in wanting to do this big, sprawling eleven-issue opening arc to take us to different eras of Thor and lean into what made Thor different from everybody else in the Marvel Universe. He is a god, and I wanted to lean hard into that godhood. I like exploring what it means to be a god in the Marvel Universe. I love the idea of a Thor who wakes up every morning, looks at the hammer and does not know if he'll be able to lift it."

PREVIOUS PAGES: *THOR: GOD OF THUNDER #1-2* INTERLOCKING COVERS BY ESAD RIBIĆ

LEFT: *THOR: GOD OF THUNDER #9* COVER BY ESAD RIBIĆ

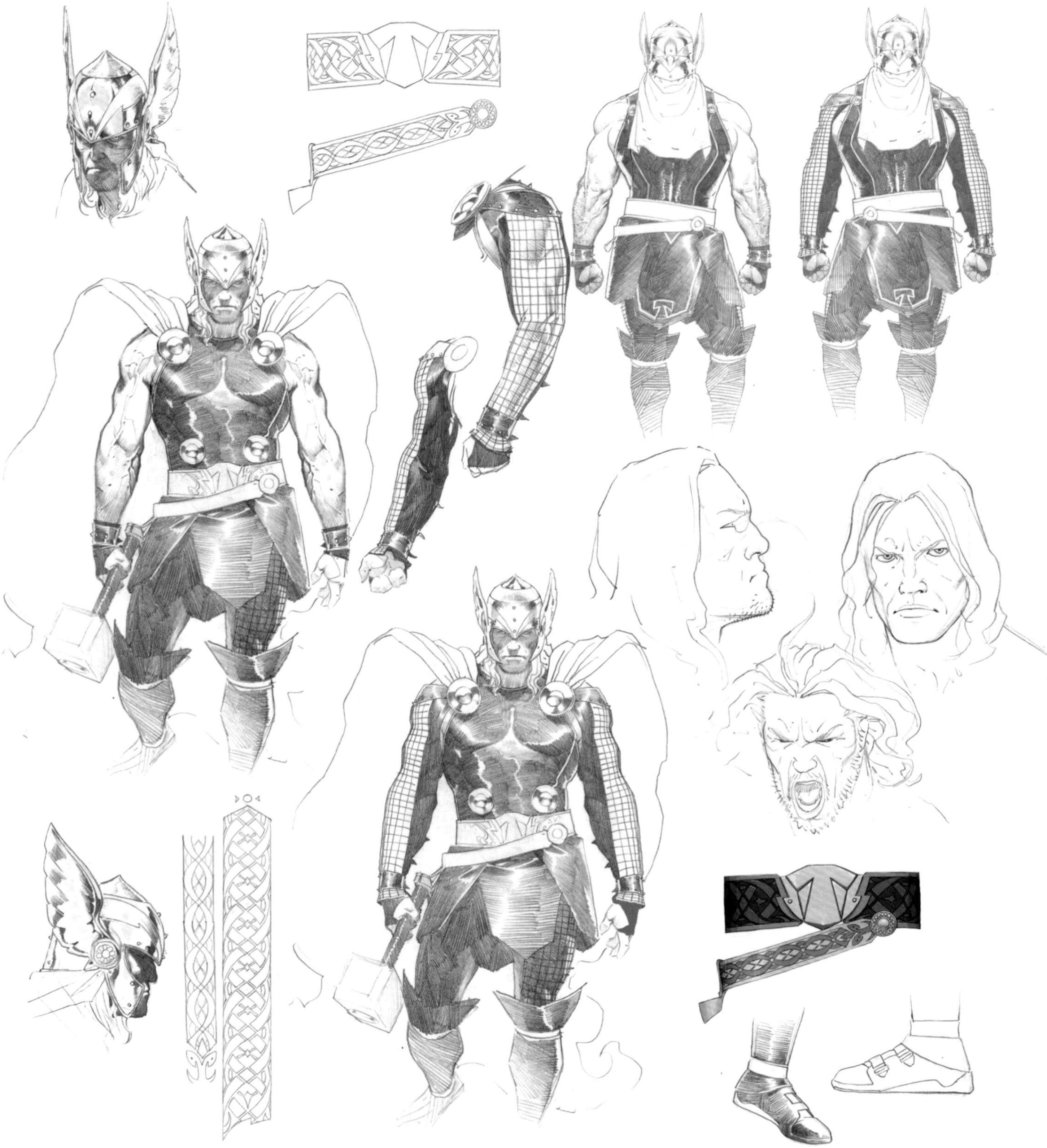

"I wanted to make Thor more like what Vikings would imagine their gods to be. I didn't want to have stuff that looks too much like a costume — there is a difference between a suit and a costume. I was really trying as much as possible to make them feel like just clothes to wear instead of elaborate costumes. Whatever you do, you have to retain the recognizable look, so you can't move away too far. But the thing with Thor is, you know, long hair, huge hammer, muscles and a cape — everything else you can do almost whatever you want with and you still have a recognizable character. So that's not really that much of a problem — more a problem for me was how realistic I wanted it to look compared to Norse mythology and what the Nordic people would have imagined. How far do I go?"
— ESAD RIBIĆ

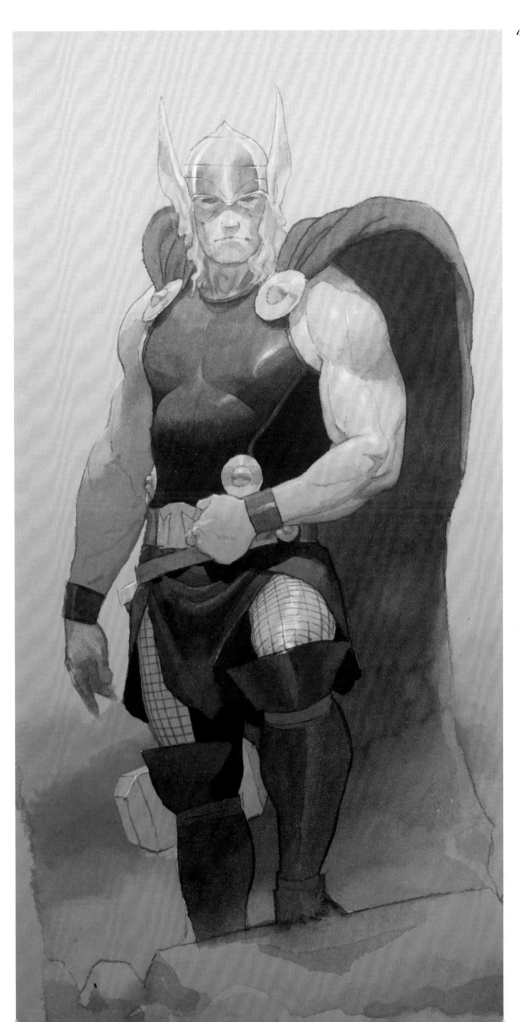

"If you do a helmet that they [actually] had in that time, that is not recognizable as Thor's helmet. His helmet is pure sci-fi — none of the historical helmets from that era looked like that. When I was doing *Loki*, because Loki had a huge set of horns and I needed something to give it balance, I just added something at the back that made it more stable, like a counterweight. So I decided to keep on using that in *God of Thunder* for Thor's helmet too."

— ESAD RIBIĆ

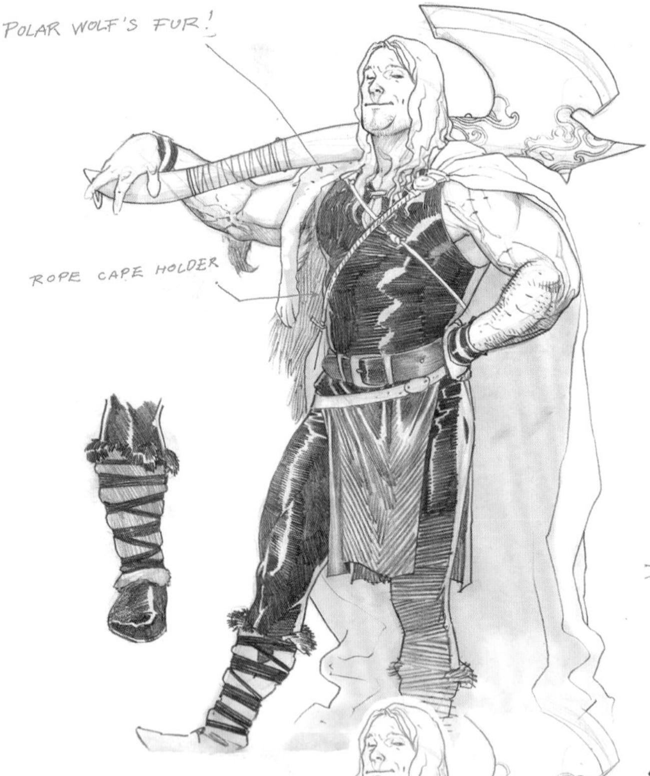
POLAR WOLF'S FUR!
ROPE CAPE HOLDER

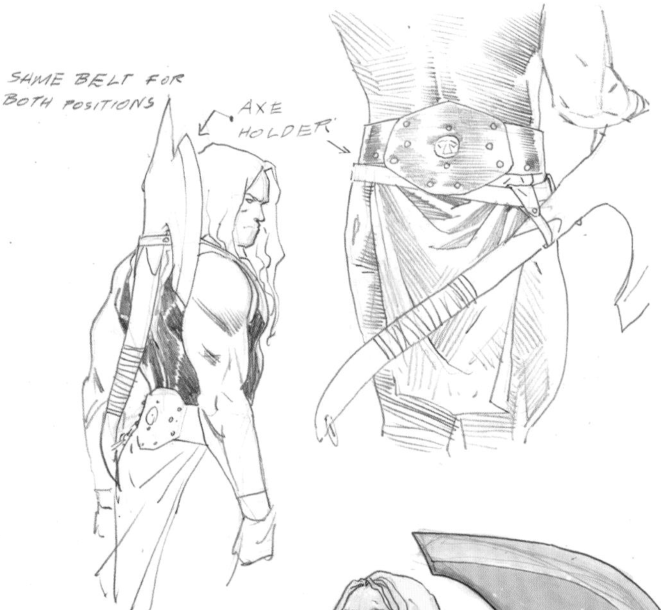
SAME BELT FOR BOTH POSITIONS
AXE HOLDER

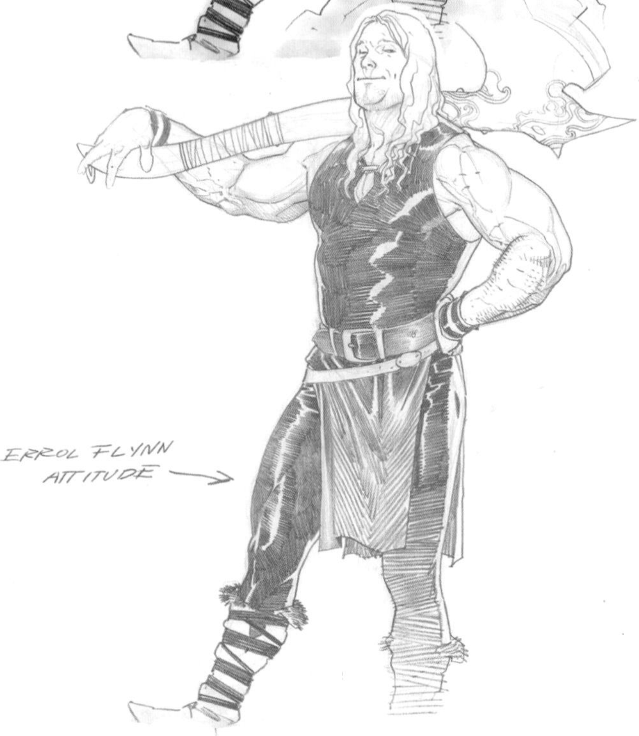
ERROL FLYNN ATTITUDE

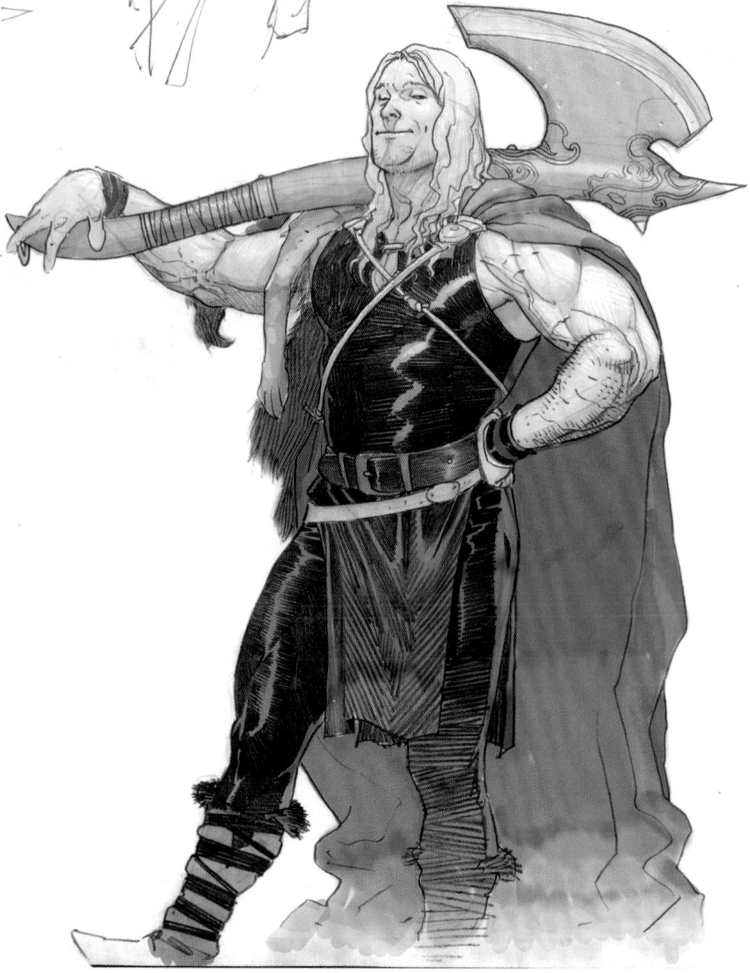

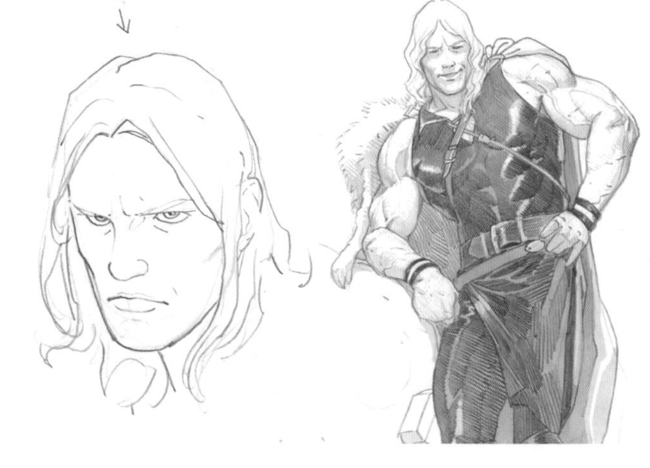
YOUNG THOR

"Young Thor is just what I imagined a ninth-century Viking god to look like. What they would imagine would be down to what they see in the world, so Thor can't have something on him that Vikings would not see in their reality. The basic idea was I wanted to make him more the warrior, avoid the 'costume.'"
— **ESAD RIBIĆ**

“One thing I decided to do with Old Thor was that he constantly wears armor. That was basically chosen because what it subliminally tells you when someone constantly wears armor is that they are more vulnerable. I wanted to have him look like a huge, hulking guy — but when you put that kind of armor on him, it suggests he needs it and he is past his prime.

I made a point of doing armor that doesn’t look like Odin’s armor. It’s more realistic armor — let’s say fourteenth-century armor — so still I went with historically informed design.”

— ESAD RIBIĆ

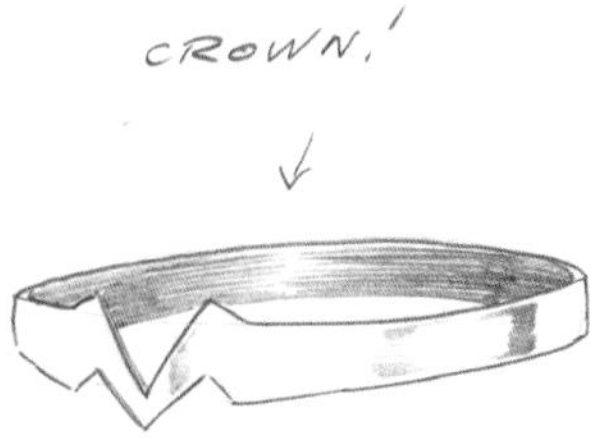
CROWN!

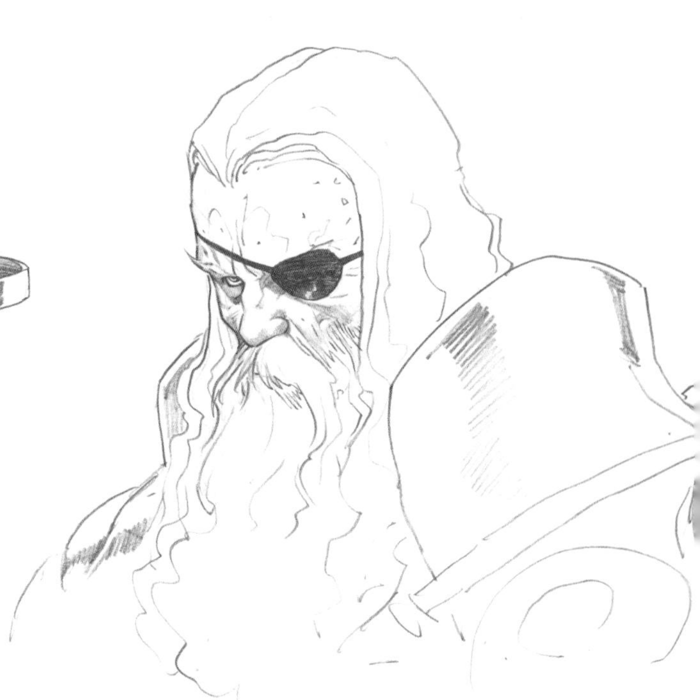

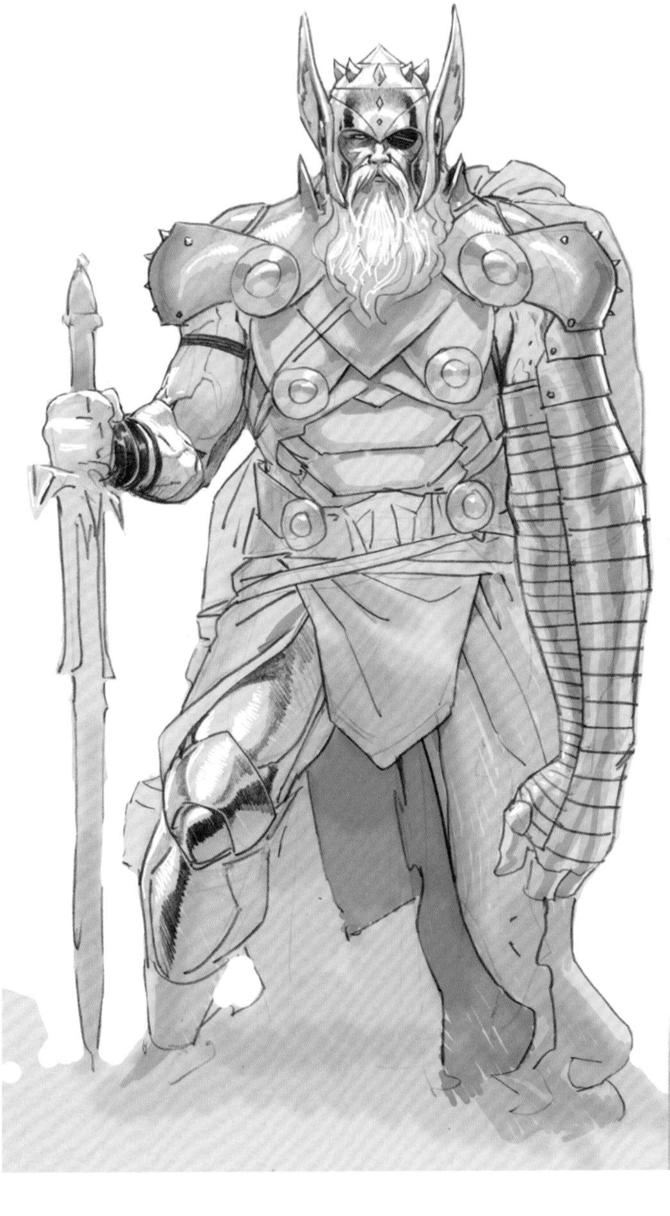

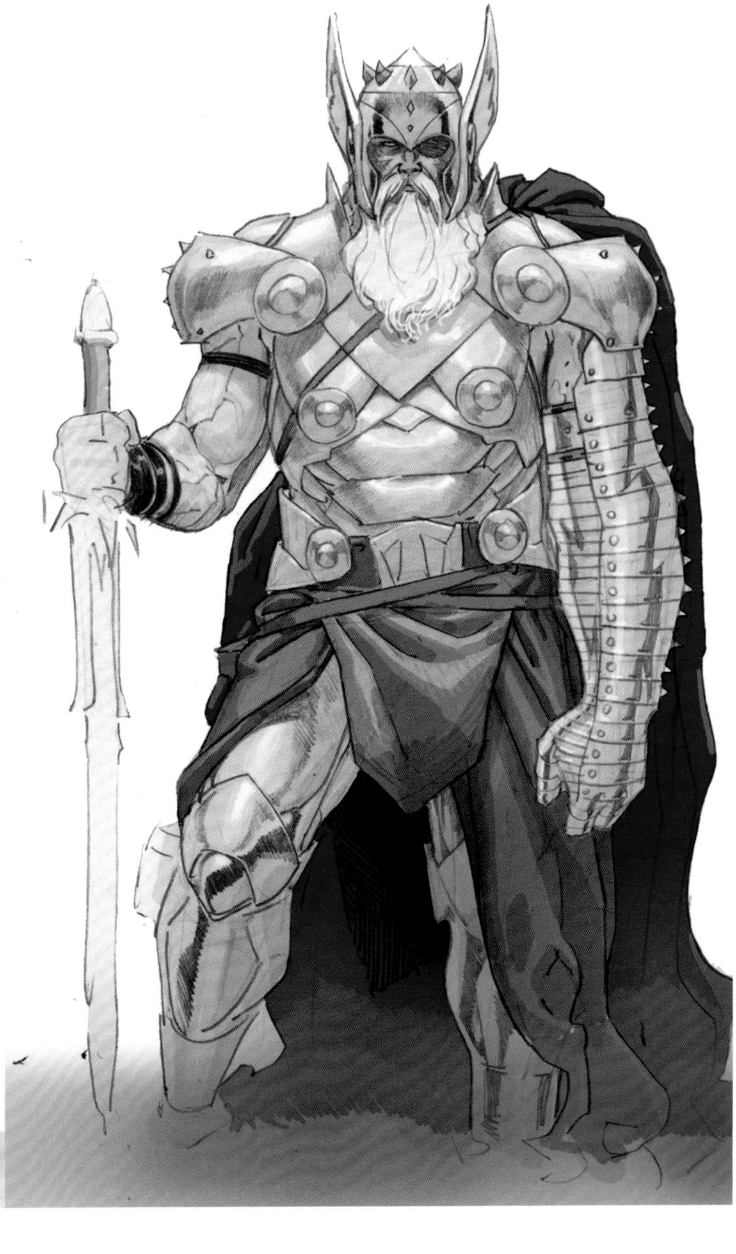

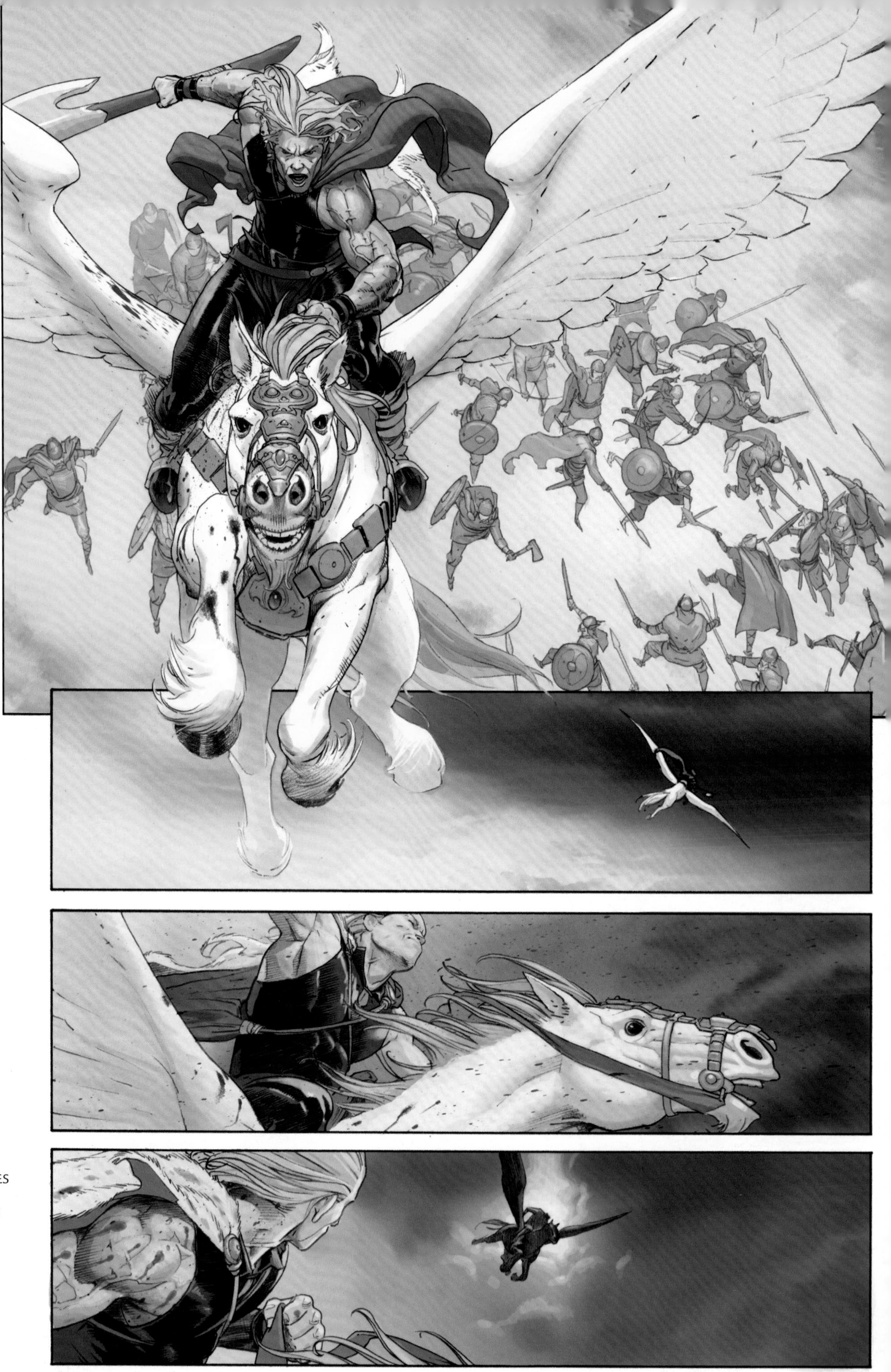

YOUNG THOR — WIELDING HIS AX, JARNBJORN — TAKES FLIGHT ON THE WINGED HORSE OF THE DEAD SLAVIC GOD PERUN.

***THOR: GOD OF THUNDER* #2** INTERIOR ART BY ESAD RIBIĆ AND COLOR ARTIST IVE SVORCINA

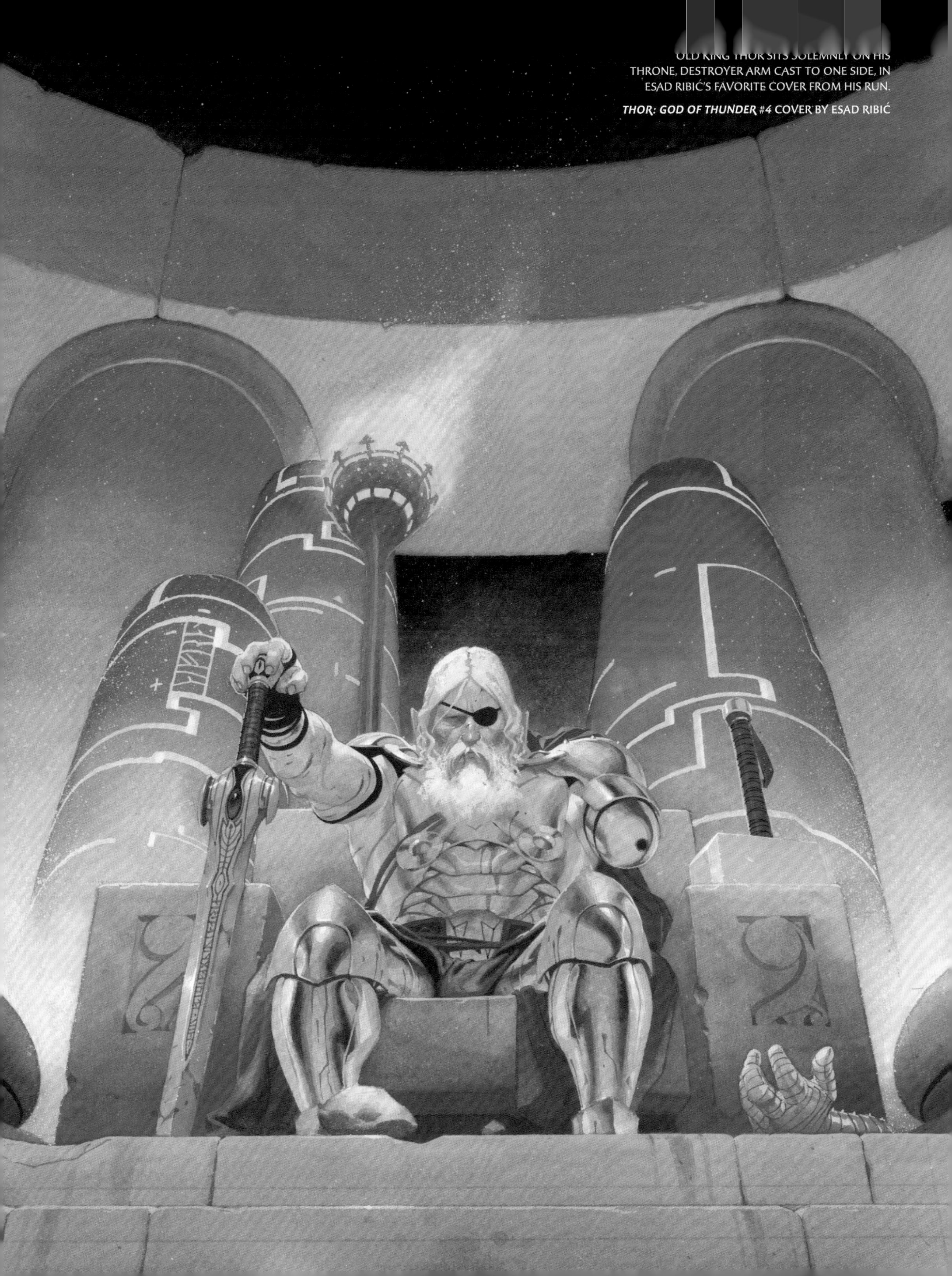

OLD KING THOR SITS SOLEMNLY ON HIS THRONE, DESTROYER ARM CAST TO ONE SIDE, IN ESAD RIBIĆ'S FAVORITE COVER FROM HIS RUN.

***THOR: GOD OF THUNDER* #4** COVER BY ESAD RIBIĆ

THE MODERN-DAY THOR ARRIVES IN THE FAR FUTURE.

THOR: GOD OF THUNDER #5 INTERIOR ART BY ESAD RIBIĆ AND IVE SVORCINA

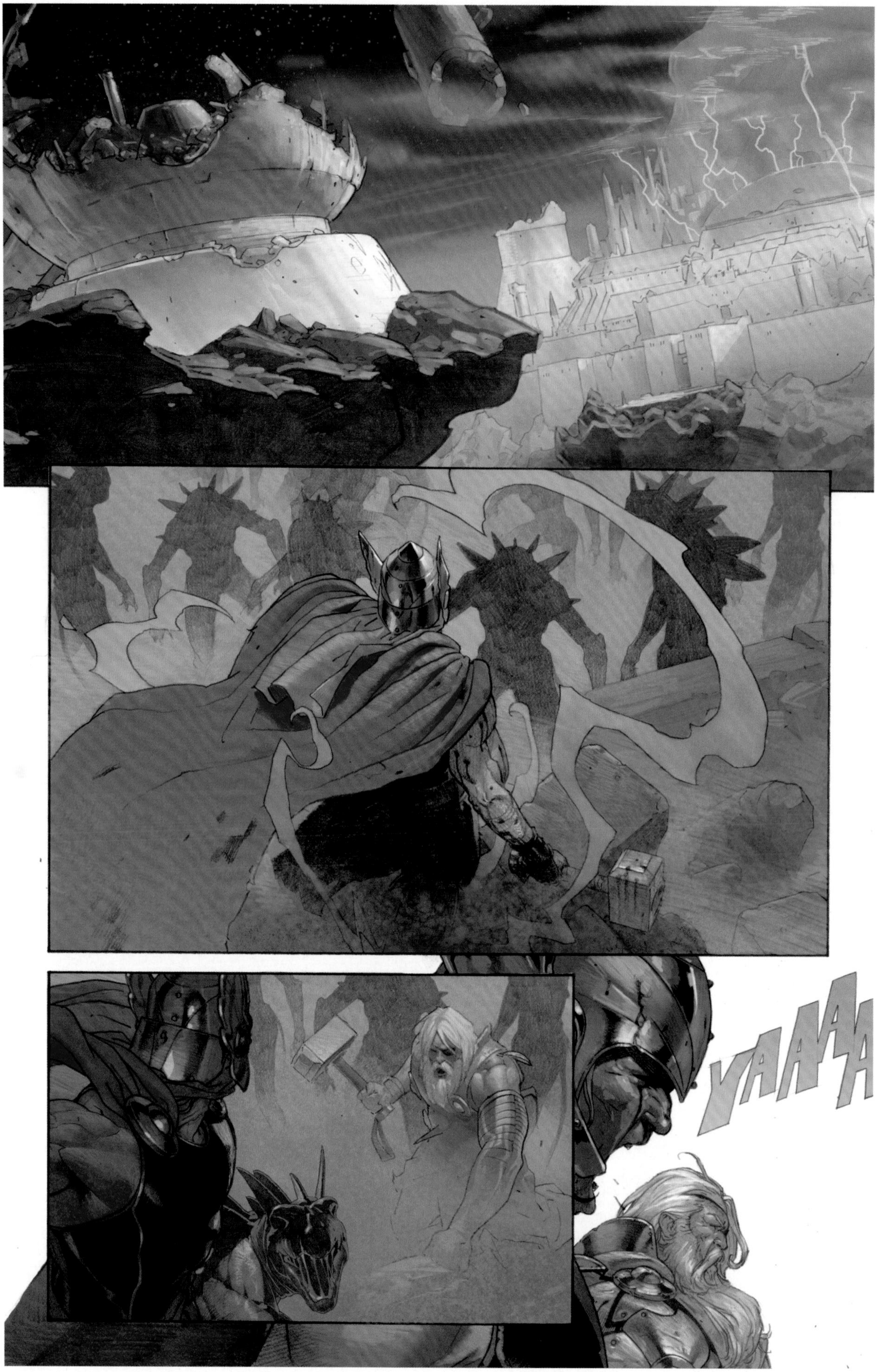
YAAAA

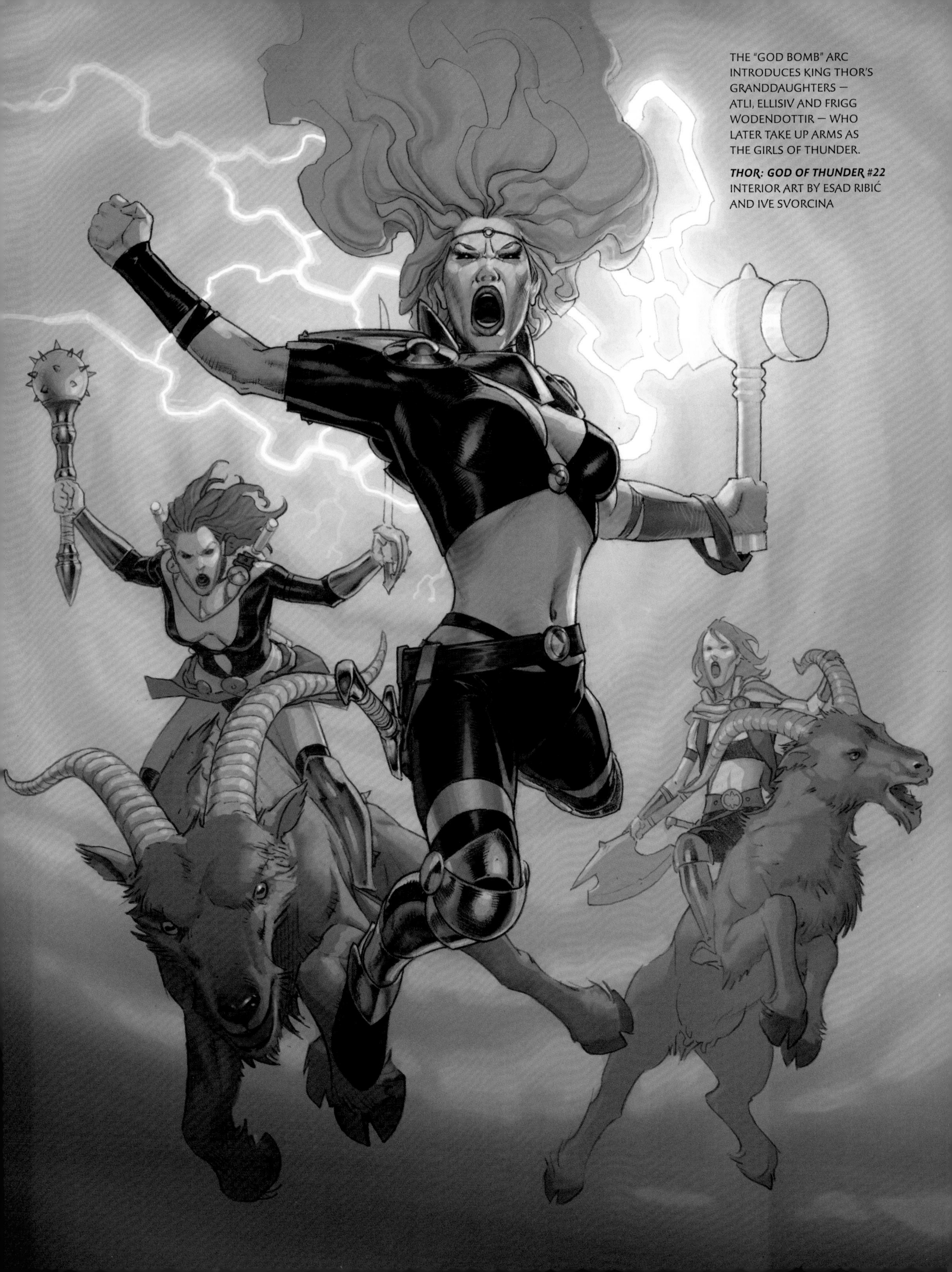

THE "GOD BOMB" ARC INTRODUCES KING THOR'S GRANDDAUGHTERS — ATLI, ELLISIV AND FRIGG WODENDOTTIR — WHO LATER TAKE UP ARMS AS THE GIRLS OF THUNDER.

***THOR: GOD OF THUNDER* #22**
INTERIOR ART BY ESAD RIBIĆ AND IVE SVORCINA

"Jason sent me the concept for [Gorr], and the result is basically the first thing I came up with, five seconds after seeing his description. I live in Croatia, and there are a lot of different folk tales. I saw a movie, made in the 1970s, based on a folk tale about a devil who decides to go out in the world. Basically, he cuts off his horns, he hides his appearance — everything apart from one goat leg that he just cannot hide. So he always has a cloak to hide the goat leg and he is limping. I just loved that. One thing you cannot really do in a comic book is show a character limping, so I hope that people got that from his lack of symmetry, him not having the same legs. He obviously needed to have some alien face. I added tentacles like thorns, which are poisonous so he can kill you like a snake. Jason had this idea for just a black cloak, but I also went in another direction and had his skin very white as a contrast. The thing is the character is very black-and-white philosophically, and so the point is that he is the biggest contrast anywhere on the pages when he shows up, because everything else is not black and white."

— ESAD RIBIĆ

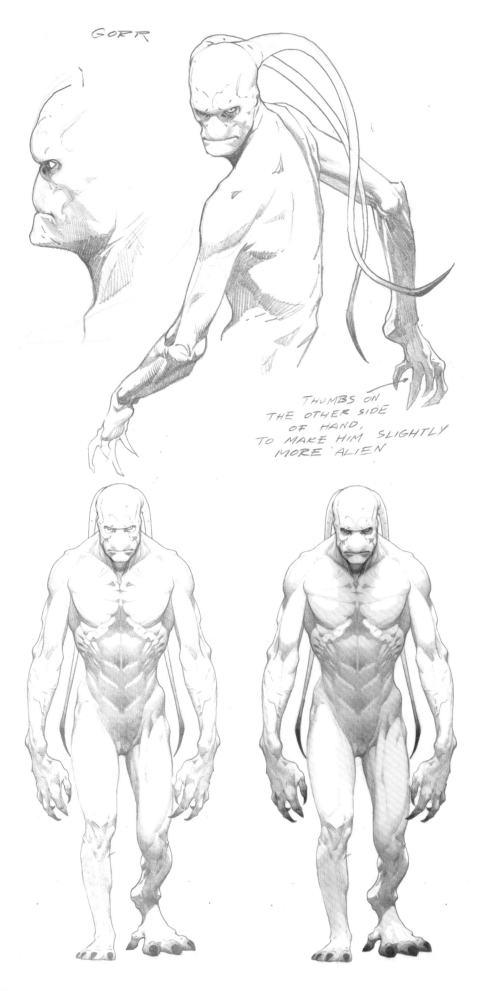

GORR

THUMBS ON THE OTHER SIDE OF HAND, TO MAKE HIM SLIGHTLY MORE ALIEN

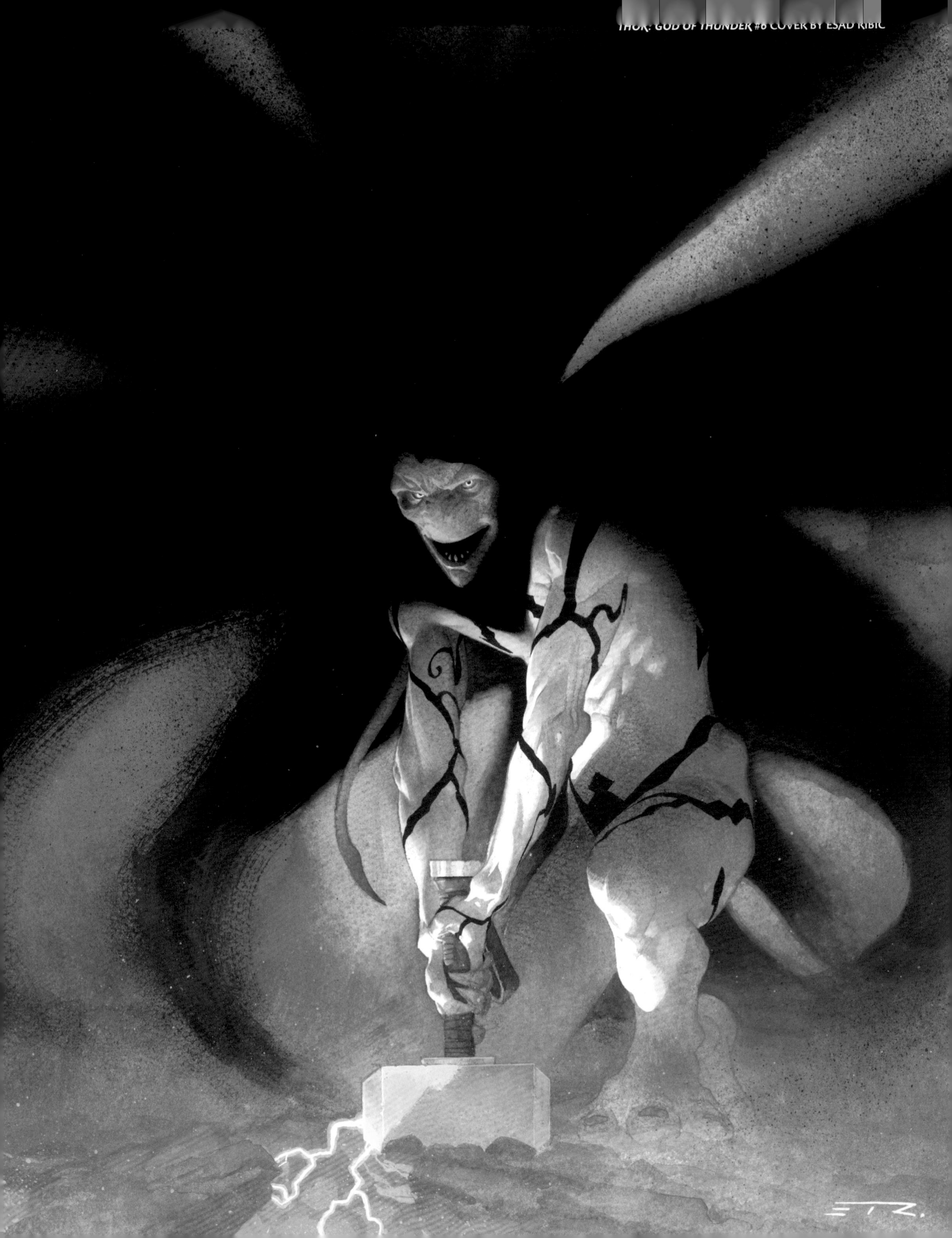

THOR: GOD OF THUNDER #6 COVER BY ESAD RIBIC

THOR WITNESSES THE FULL HORROR OF GORR'S WORK.

***THOR: GOD OF THUNDER* #1** INTERIOR ART BY ESAD RIBIĆ AND IVE SVORCINA

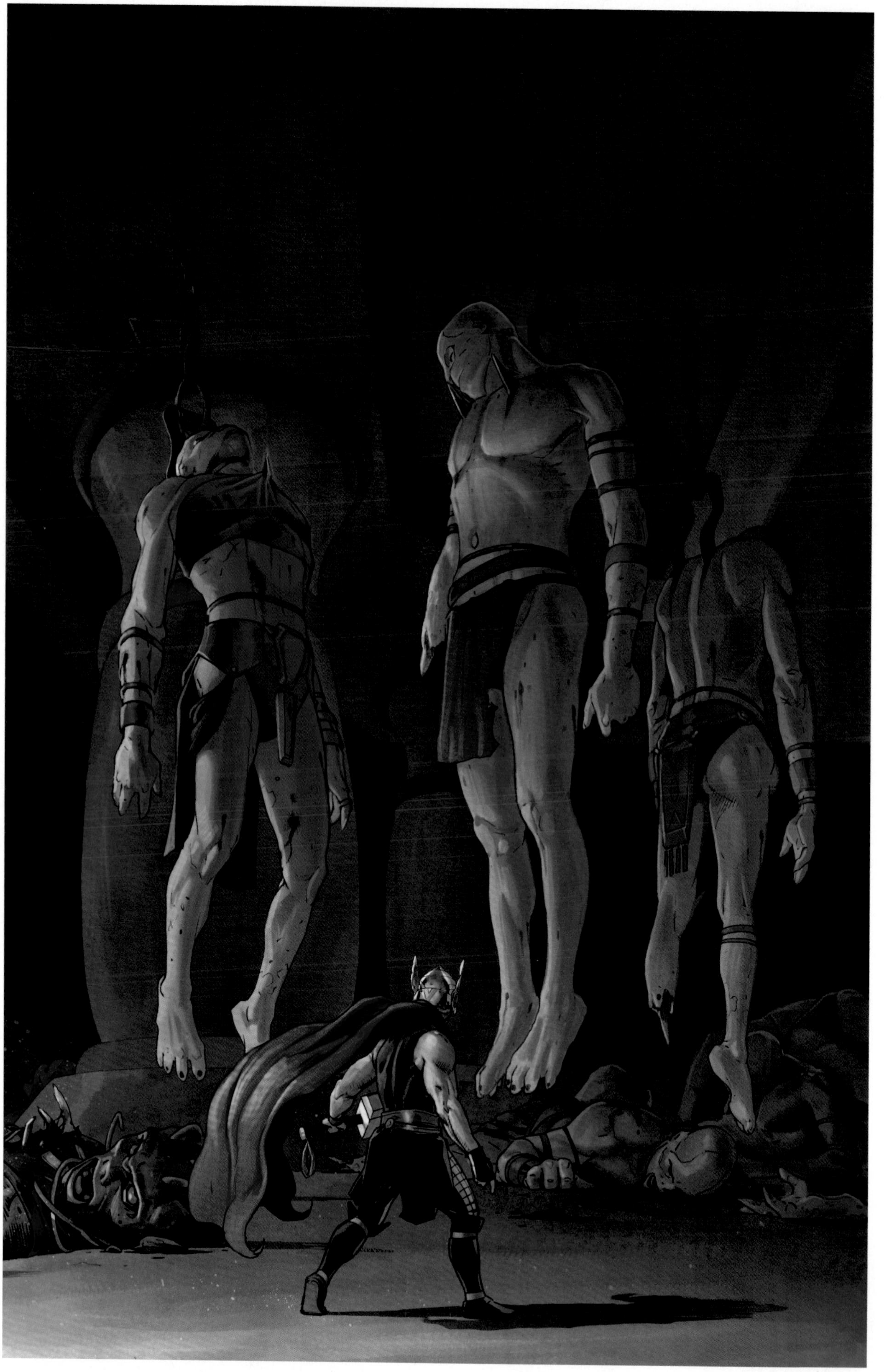

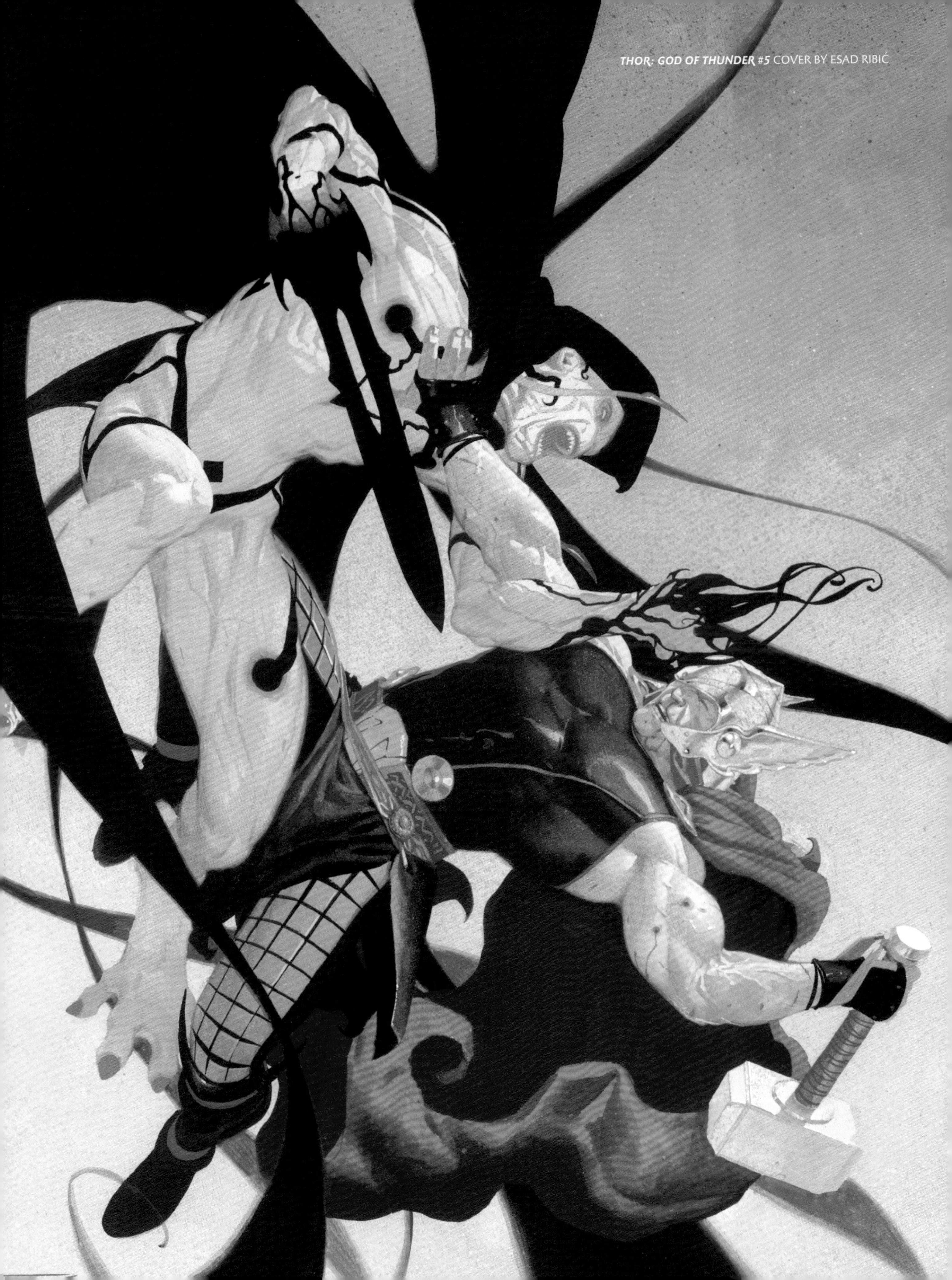

THOR: GOD OF THUNDER #5 COVER BY ESAD RIBIĆ

IN FINAL BATTLE
WITH GORR, THOR
— WIELDING TWO
MJOLNIRS — STEALS
THE SOURCE OF THE
GOD BUTCHER'S
POWER, AN
ANCIENT WEAPON
NAMED ALL-BLACK
THE NECROSWORD.
IT IS THE SLICER
OF WORLDS...THE
ANNIHILABLADE...
AND WHILE GORR'S
LIFE COMES TO AN
END, ITS STORY IS
JUST BEGINNING!

**RIGHT AND
OPPOSITE:** *THOR:
GOD OF THUNDER
#11* INTERIOR ART
BY ESAD RIBIĆ AND
IVE SVORCINA

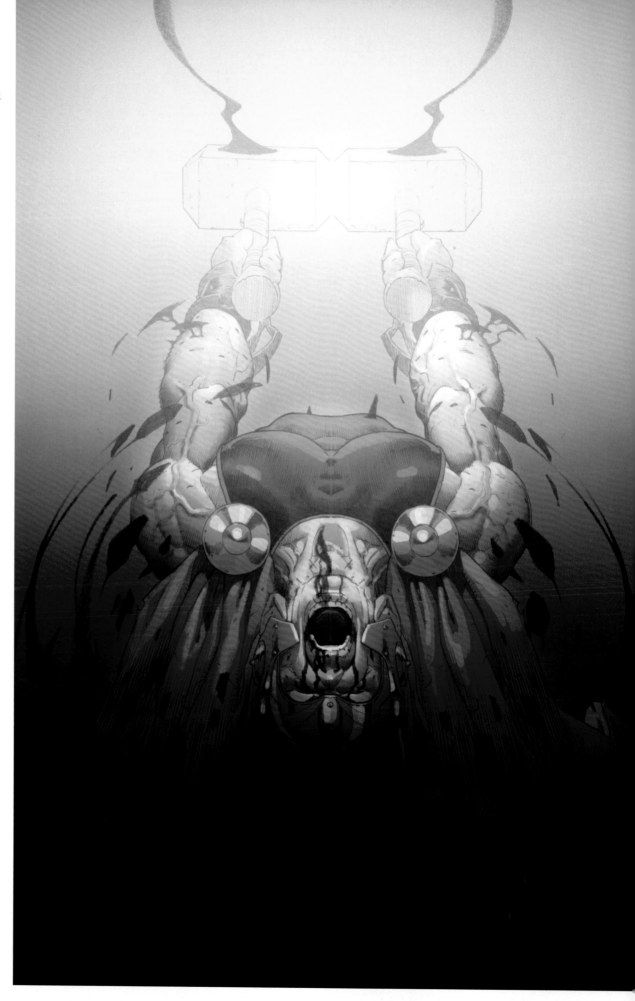

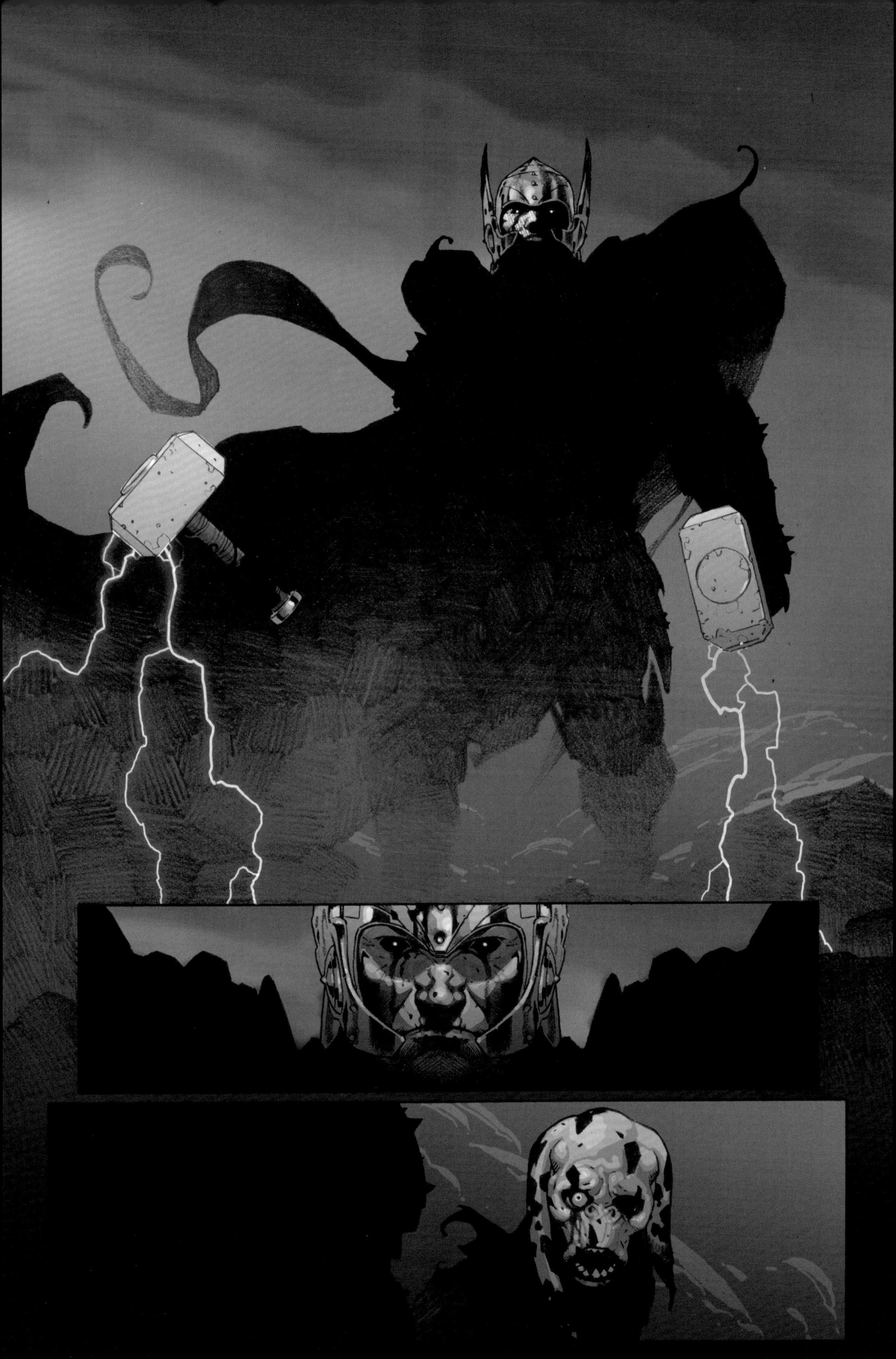

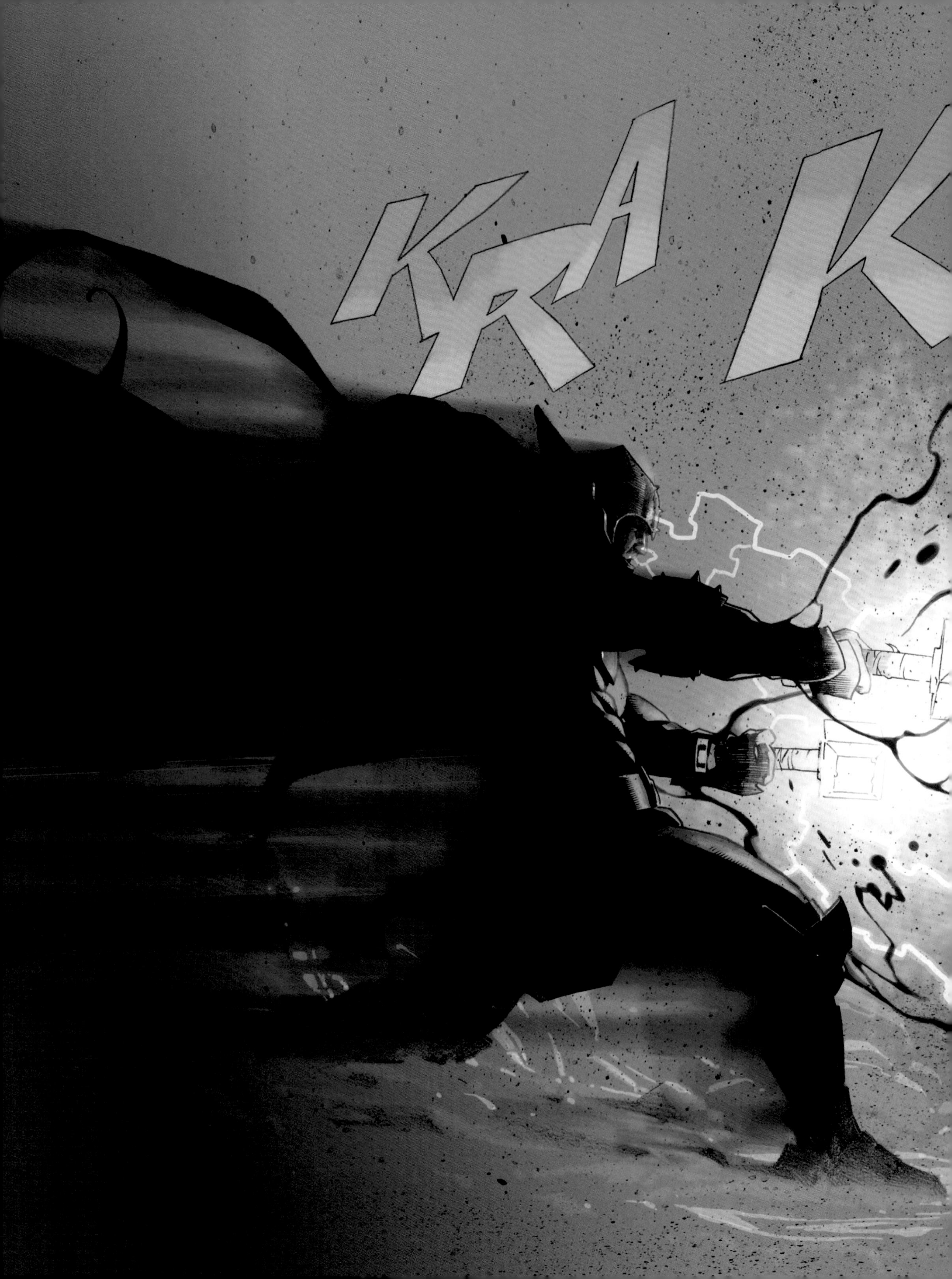
KRAK

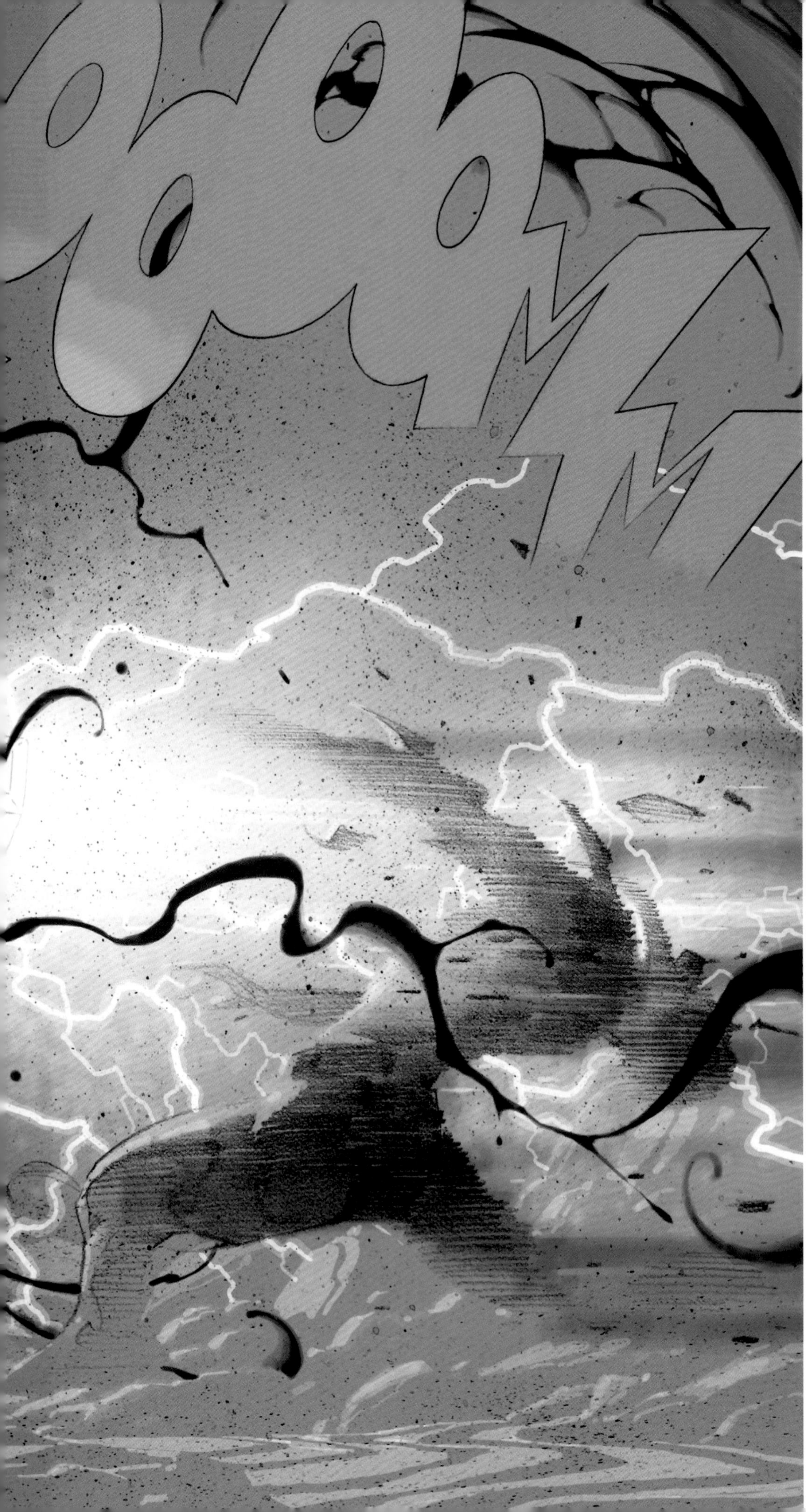

***THOR: GOD OF THUNDER* #11**
INTERIOR PENCILS BY ESAD RIBIĆ

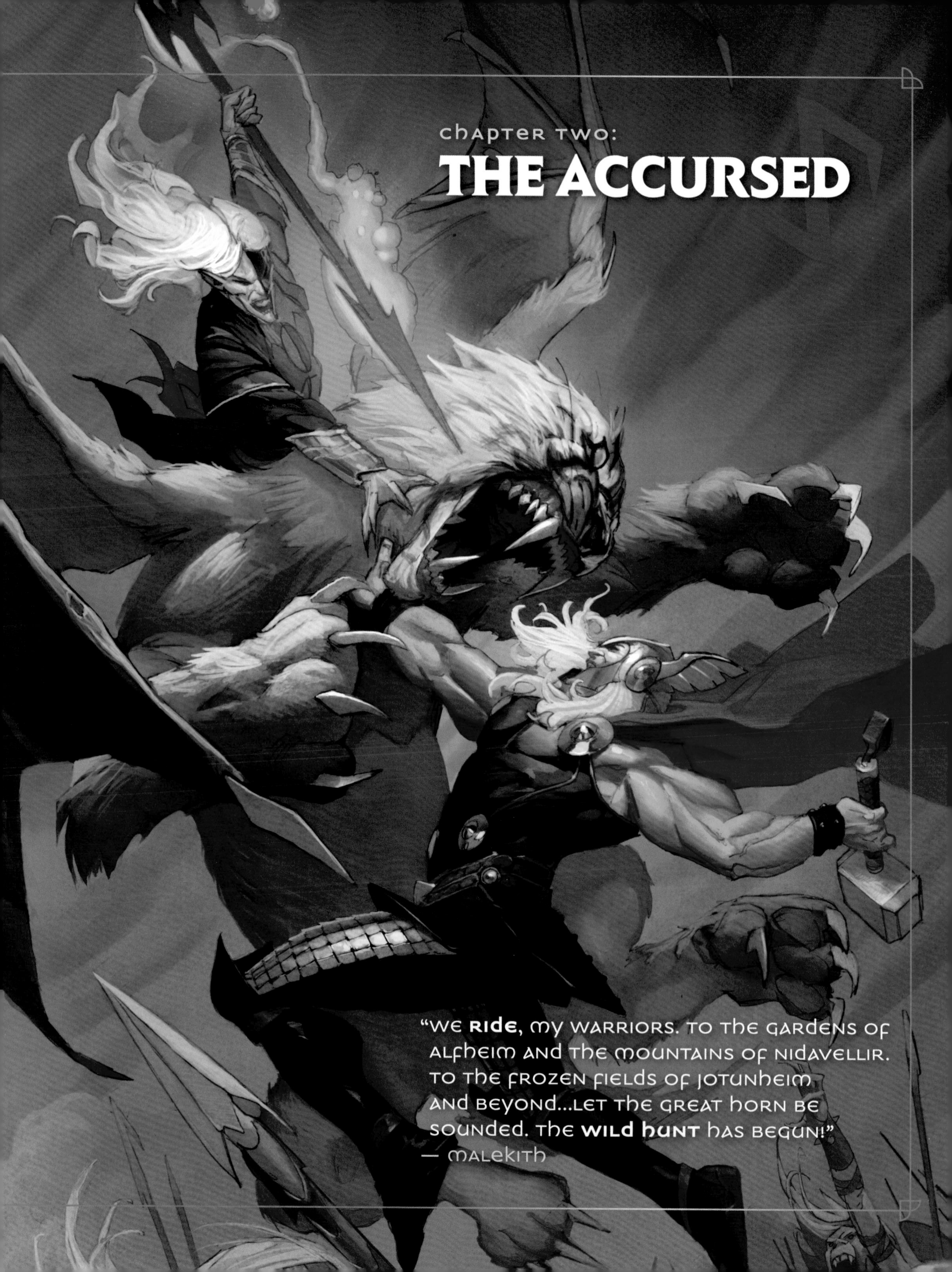

chapter two:

THE ACCURSED

"We **ride**, my warriors. To the gardens of Alfheim and the mountains of Nidavellir. To the frozen fields of Jotunheim and beyond...Let the great horn be sounded. The **Wild Hunt** has begun!"
— Malekith

For his opening act on *Thor: God of Thunder*, Jason Aaron had removed Thor from his usual surroundings and closest allies, choosing to shine the spotlight on the Thunder God himself. But as Aaron began his second year on the book, he returned his title character to the gleaming city of Asgardia — hovering, as it was, in the skies above Broxton, Oklahoma — to begin a new tale steeped in the comic book lore. "This is the story of those Nine Worlds," Aaron wrote, "and of the one mighty god who bestrode them all."

Such a mighty god called for another detestable villain to once again test him to his limits. This time, Aaron found the ideal foe in Walter Simonson's legendary 1980s *Thor* run: the wicked Malekith. The Dark Elf sorcerer had for years been banished to the hellish Hall of Nastrond in frozen Niffleheim — a prison for the most fearsome of dishonored dead. Deep in a pit, guarded by monstrous spiders and venomous snakes, Malekith lay rotting — until now. A group of Dark Elf loyalists achieves the impossible and frees their former king — all but one laying down their lives in the process. The sole survivor, Scumtongue, sacrifices the body part that earned him his name; he now serves silently at his master's side as Malekith the Accursed begins to plot.

"I wanted to bring Malekith — one of the main bad guys from Walt's run — back as a major player, which fit with my idea of starting to explore those different realms. The realm of the Dark Elves was a good place to start. I remember vividly writing issue #13, which felt for the first time like I was really diving deep into the fantasy aspects of the character. I loved writing all that: this group of Dark Elves drinking magic potions, hitting the frozen beach in Hel and sneaking into a prison filled with giant spiders to sneak out Malekith. It was drawn by Ron Garney, whom I'd done a lot of stuff with, including *Wolverine*. It was cool to see him go from the gritty real-world stuff we'd done to drawing a lot of these fantastic creatures."

The liberated Malekith seeks to take back his throne — by slaughtering those of his own race who would oppose him. As Dark Elves flee across the realms, Malekith's "Wild Hunt" takes him from his former kingdom of Svartalfheim to Alfheim, Nidavellir, Jotunheim and beyond — all in search of Alflyse, Svartalfheim's current queen. Naturally, Thor seeks to rally his allies to stop his enemy — but the Congress of Worlds, an oftentimes fractious political assemblage consisting of representatives from each of the realms, forbids unilateral Asgardian action in such affairs. A united response is required — and so is born the League of Realms, an unlikely group of reluctant allies. Their squabbles, fights and other interactions offer a sense of the historical rivalries between these races — and their ultimately futile struggles to thwart Malekith fully set in motion the War of the Realms.

"With this arc we bring in the Dwarves and the Light Elves and the Giants and characters from a lot of different realms," Aaron says. "We wanted to clean a lot of that stuff up and define it, because there hadn't really been set definitions for a lot of the realms. They had kind of changed over time. I wanted to try to nail all that down. Six years later, I'm still working on that!"

OPPOSITE:
***THOR: GOD OF THUNDER** #13*
COVER BY RON GARNEY
AND IVE SVORCINA

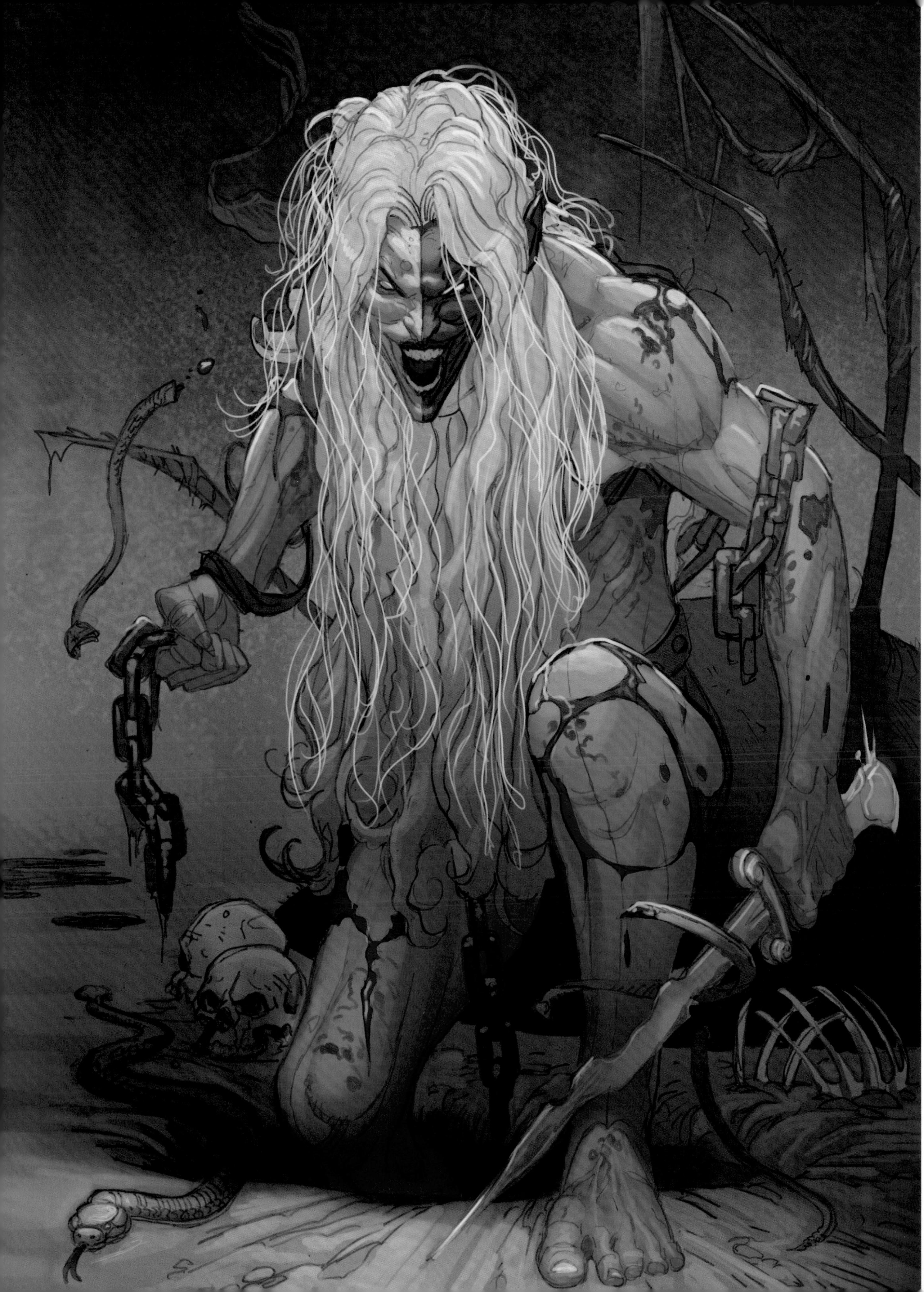

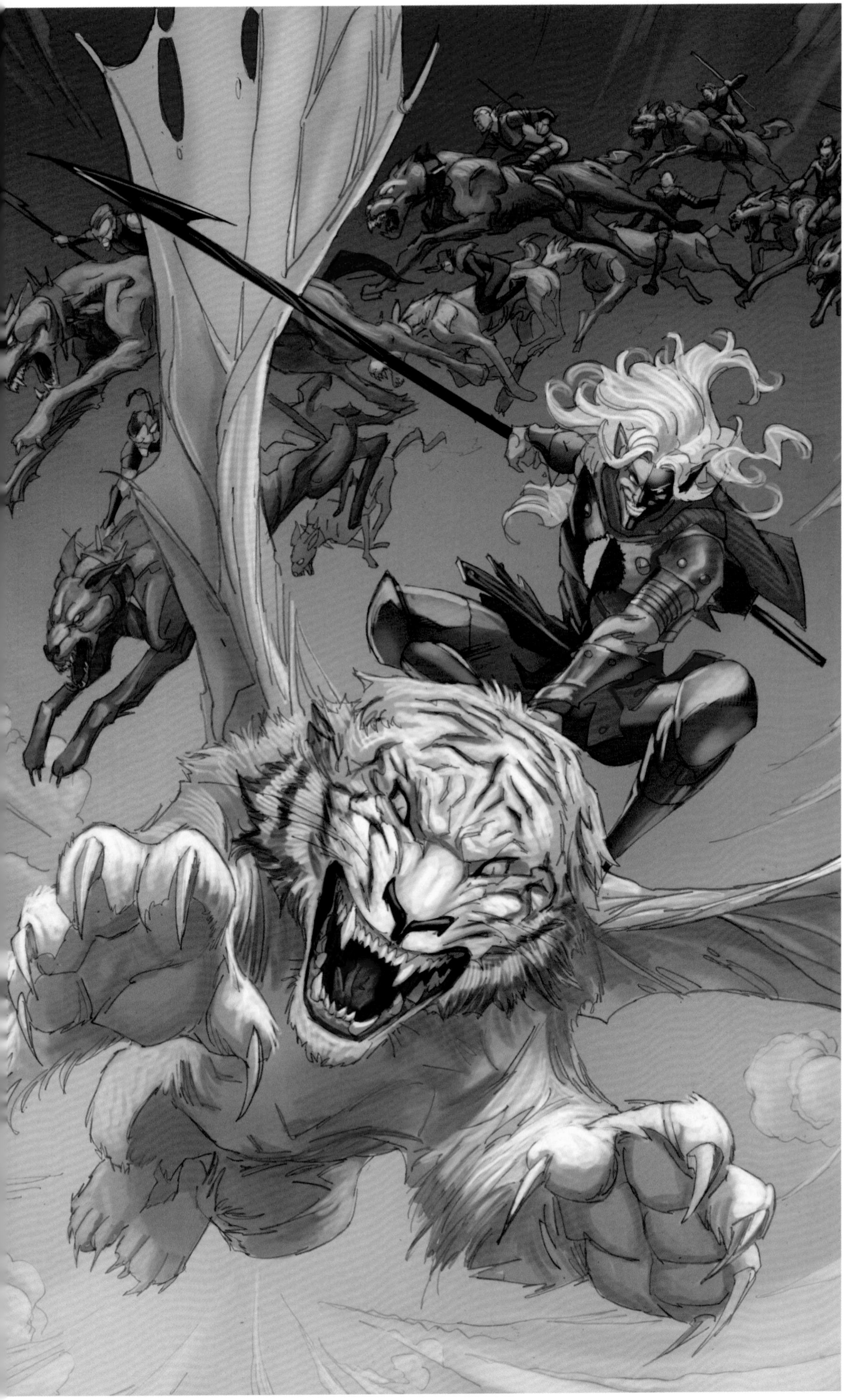

"Before I fell into comics I was planning to be a fantasy illustrator, à la Boris Vallejo or Frank Frazetta. I had tons of paintings I had done that were all stolen out of my old apartment, sadly. *Thor: God of Thunder* definitely scratched that itch, and I would love to do something in that genre again someday. I actually think I may paint Malekith riding a flying tiger as an oil painting at some point."
— RON GARNEY

LEFT AND OPPOSITE:
THOR: GOD OF THUNDER #13
INTERIOR ART BY RON GARNEY AND IVE SVORCINA

"I wanted to do the Dark Elves from one of the Norse worlds — I thought that would be cool. I did a bunch of reading at the time about the Celtic fairy faith in Great Britain and Northern Europe, discovering things like iron is inimical to elves, so I thought about all that. I needed a voice for the Dark Elves to personify them, so I made up a bad guy and made him one of Surtur's allies. As for the name itself, there was an English writer named Katharine Mary Briggs who wrote several popular books about elves and fairy folklore that I really enjoyed. There was one story about a girl named Malekin. I turned that over and made it a guy: Malekith. I liked it as a name because 'mal' as a root word often means 'evil' — or 'ill' in French — while 'kith and kin' as a phrase means your relatives. So the Elves are not so far removed from humans. He was kind of a smart-ass as a character, so his costume had echoes of old jester costumes. I split him down the middle, half light-skinned and half black. I'm not sure if I had any really heavy meaning in that — I just thought it was a cool look. It probably had a little to do with old theatrical masks. He doesn't have a split face in that sense — one side's not frowning, one side's not grinning — but that kind of duality I thought was neat. That was really the origin for the character."

— WALTER SIMONSON

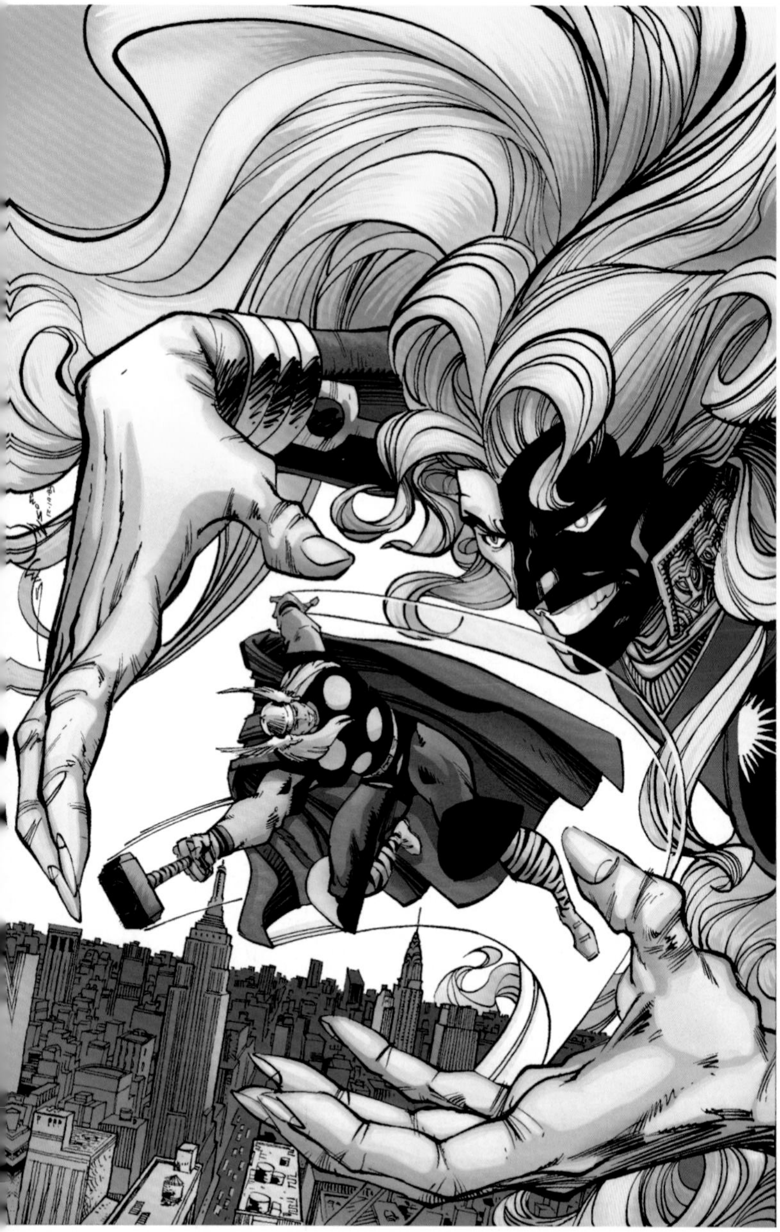

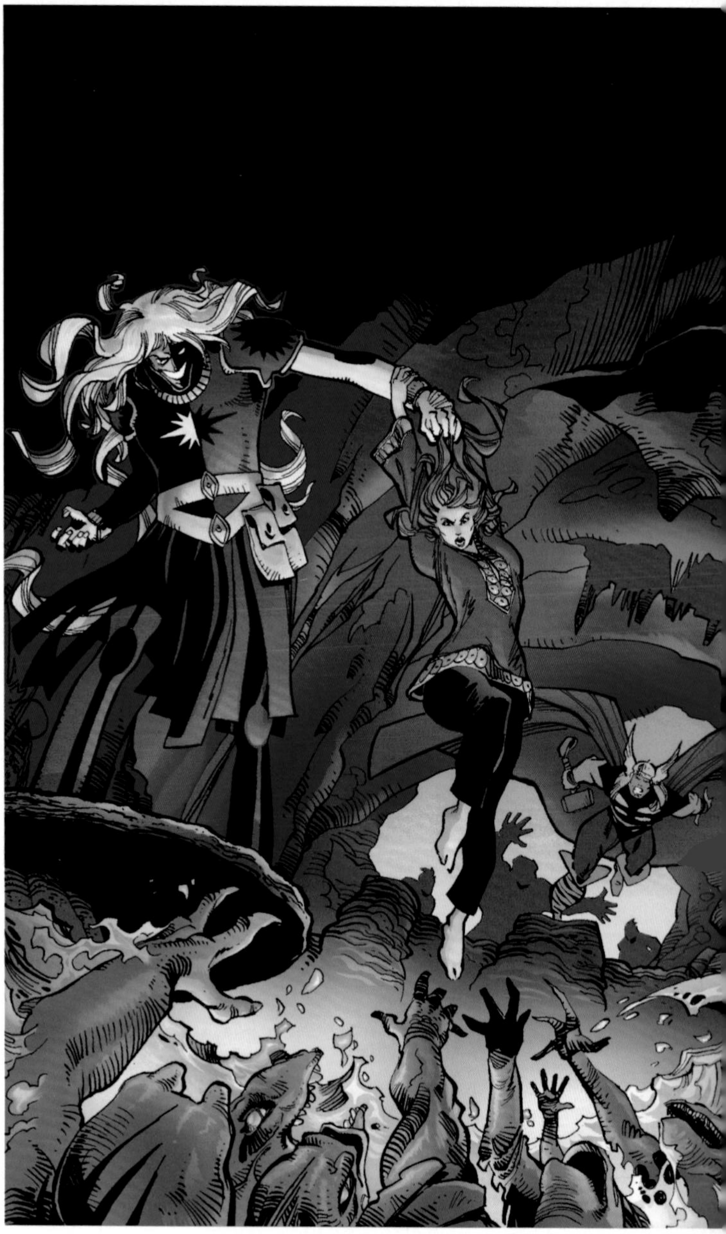

AFTER HIS BRIEF FIRST APPEARANCE IN ***THOR (1966) #344***, MALEKITH QUICKLY MADE LIFE DIFFICULT FOR THE MIGHTY THOR.

THOR (1966) #345 AND ***#347*** COVERS BY WALTER SIMONSON

"I gush every time I'm around Walt, to the point I embarrass him, I think. He was probably one of the big reasons I got so pumped to do this. I used to take his *Thor* every month and sit under a tree at the park and just lose myself in his stories, particularly the Surtur saga. I love his art — then and now. It was a joy to draw Malekith due in no small part to the fact that I got to draw what Walt did."
— RON GARNEY

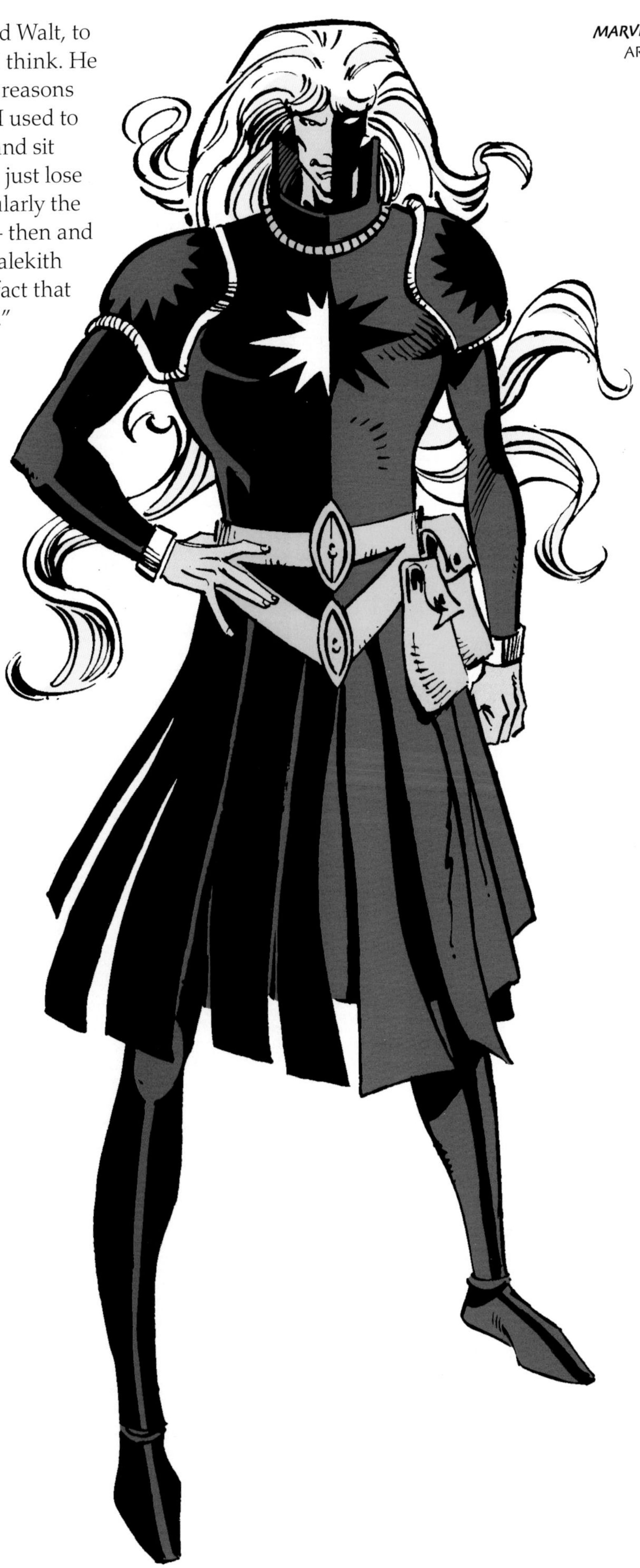

OFFICIAL HANDBOOK OF THE MARVEL UNIVERSE – DELUXE EDITION
ARTWORK BY WALTER SIMONSON AND JOSEF RUBINSTEIN

"Svartalfheim is a tough place to grow up. The Dark Elves were always fighting with somebody. They were very much a war-ravaged people. That's where Malekith grew up, and it's a very tragic childhood tale. You would think he would be the opposite of what he is — that he would want to eradicate war. Instead, in his mind, that would make his life and his suffering meaningless. He's got to continue that war — if anything, ramp it up and spread it everywhere."

— JASON AARON

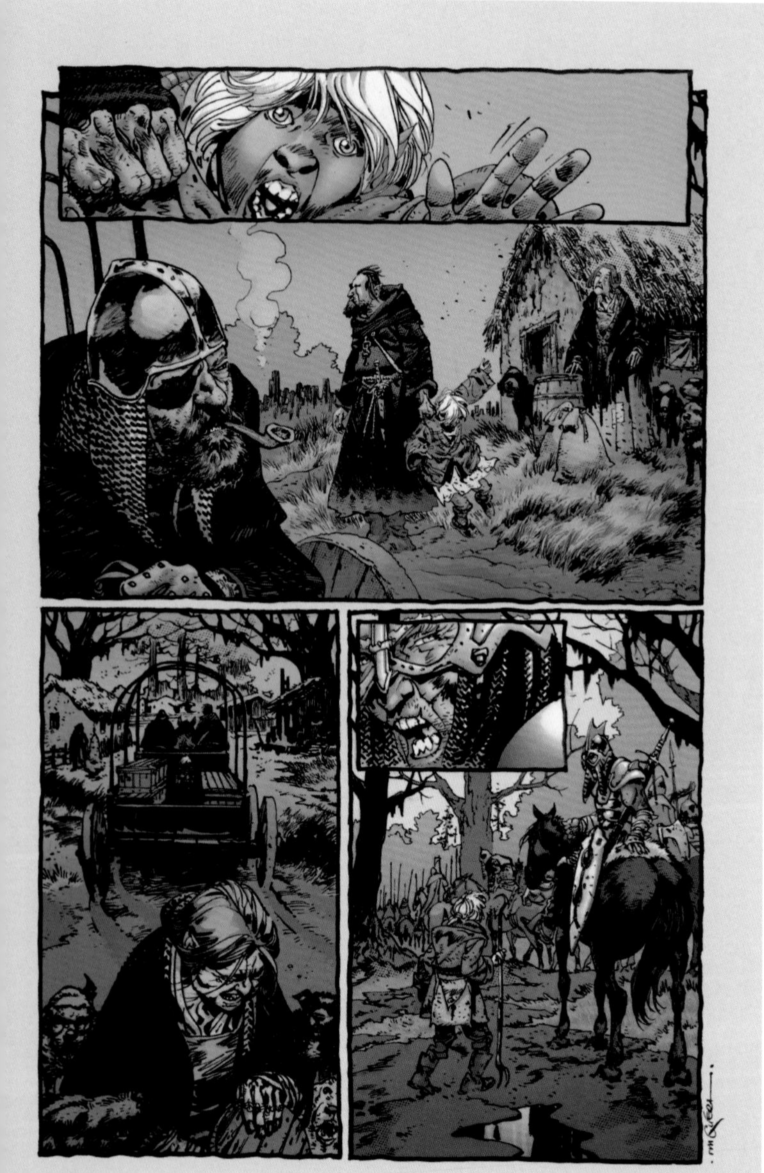

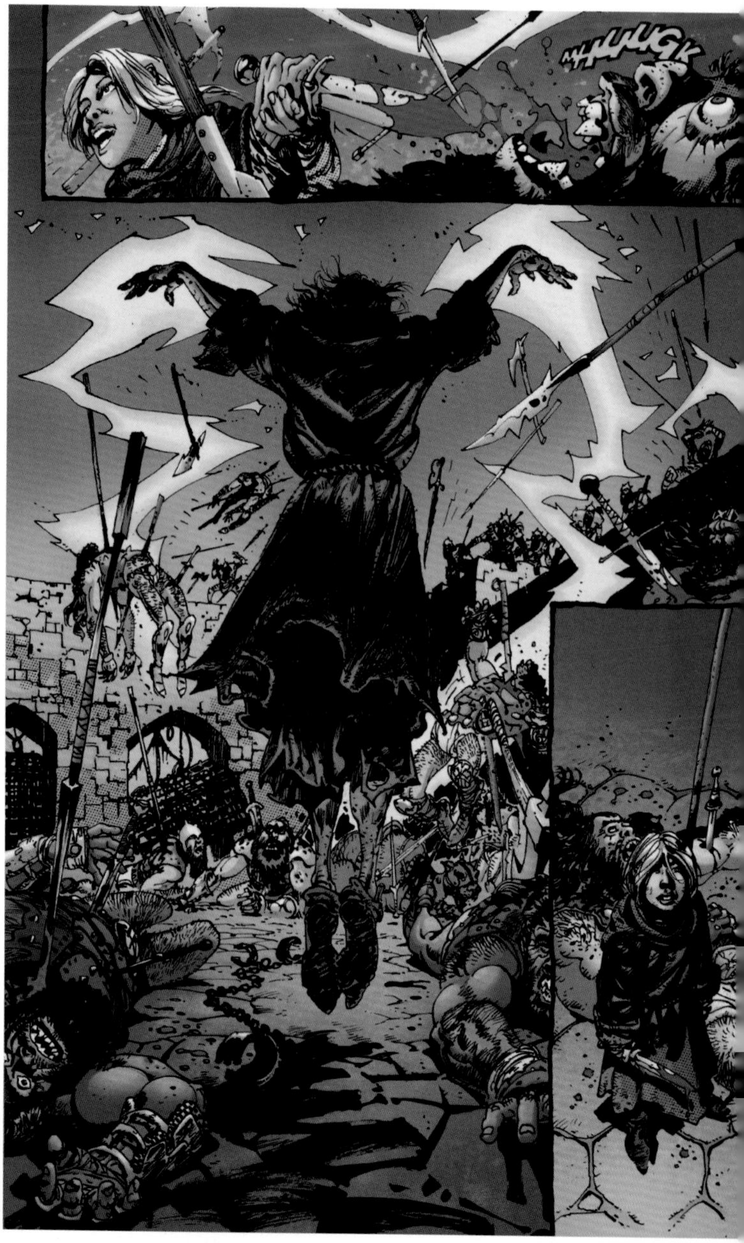

THE DARK AND BLOODY ORIGIN OF MALEKITH IS REVEALED AT LAST!

ABOVE AND OPPOSITE: ***THOR: GOD OF THUNDER #25*** INTERIOR ART BY R.M. GUERA AND GIULIA BRUSCO

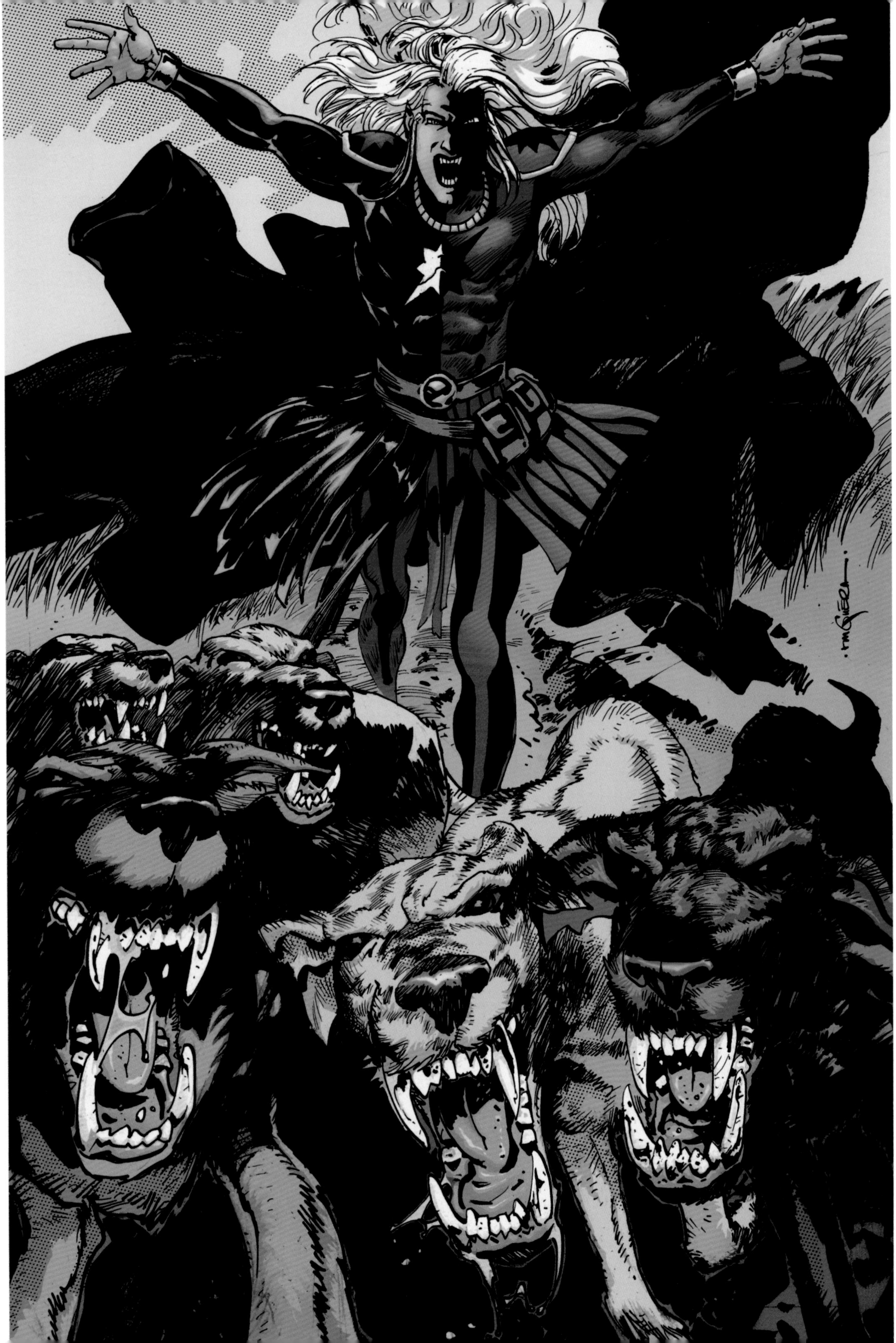

"The League of Realms [was full of] all-new characters. That's part of the fun — the world-building of all these different worlds. I liked the idea of doing the Avengers of the different realms, and we can certainly expect to see them again."
— JASON AARON

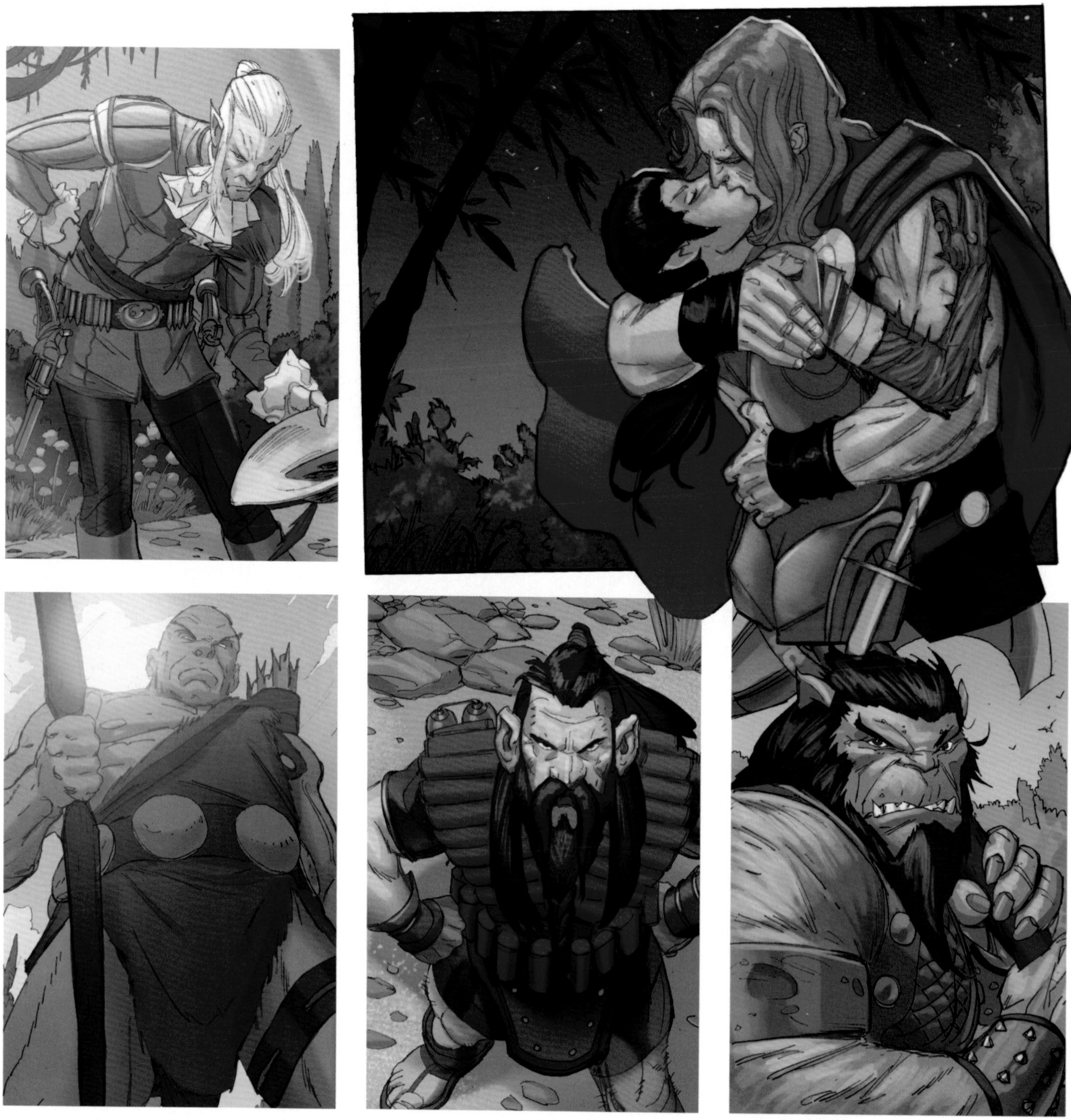

LEAGUE OF REALMS ASSEMBLE! COUNTERCLOCKWISE, FROM TOP LEFT: SIR IVORY HONEYSHOT OF THE LIGHT ELVES OF ALFHEIM. OGGMUNDER DRAGGLEVLADD VINNSUVIUS XVII — "OGGY" FOR SHORT — OF THE LONGSTOMP TRIBE FROM THE HILLS OF JOTUNHEIM. SCREWBEARD, SON OF NO-EARS, SON OF HEADWOUND, OF THE DYNAMITE DWARVES OF NIDAVELLIR. UD THE TROLL. AND THOR'S CLOSEST...ALLY...AMONG THEM, LADY WAZIRIA OF THE DARK ELVES OF SVARTALFHEIM!

ABOVE: ***THOR: GOD OF THUNDER #14*** AND ***#15*** INTERIOR ART BY RON GARNEY AND IVE SVORCINA

OPPOSITE: ***THOR: GOD OF THUNDER #15*** COVER BY RON GARNEY AND IVE SVORCINA

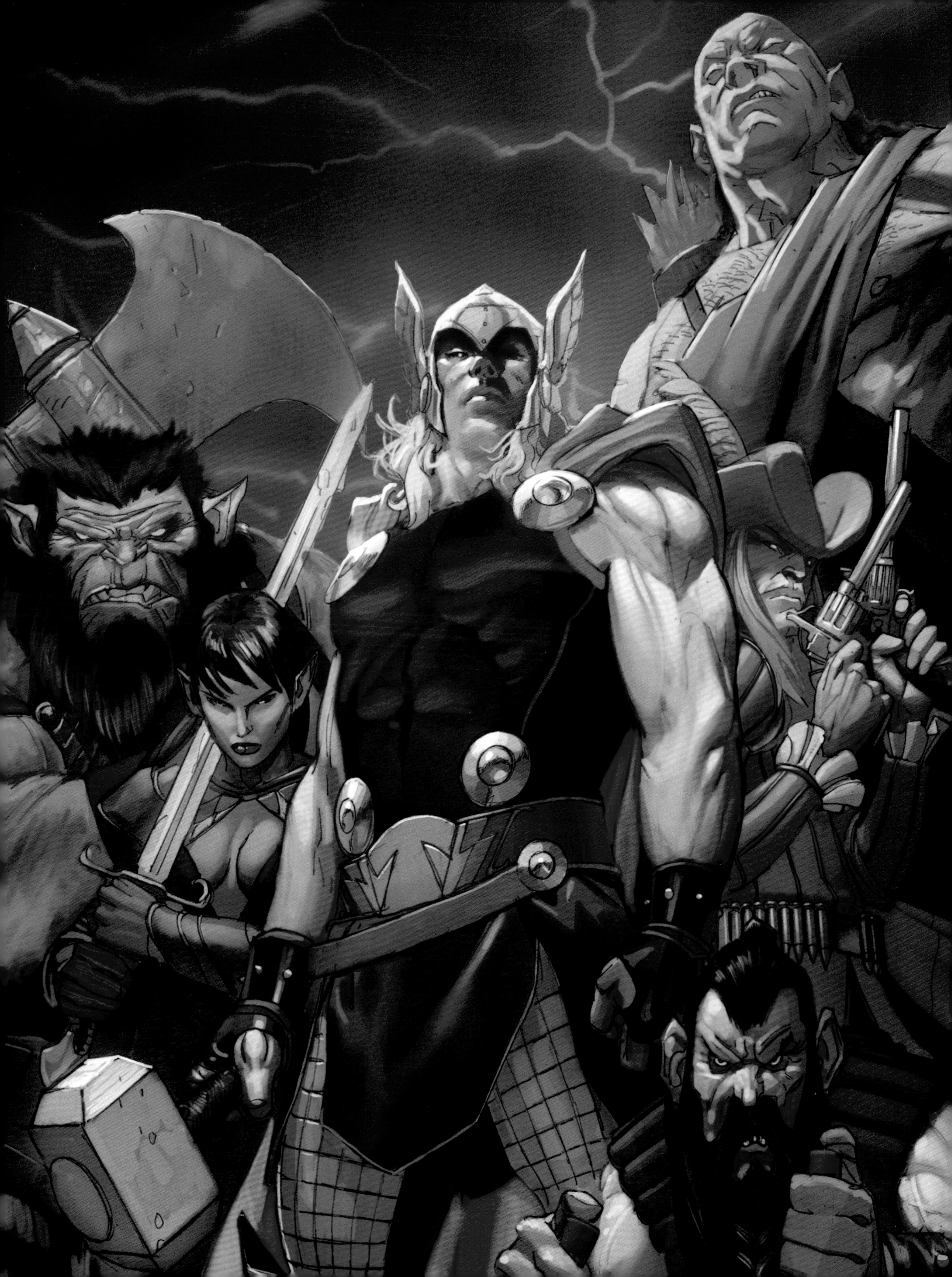

"Volume three was a fantasy story, a map-making story, that served to define the wondrous landscape of the series' overall setting and to foreshadow something big and dark and epically deadly that awaits us in the future. You know, like fantasy stories do."
— JASON AARON

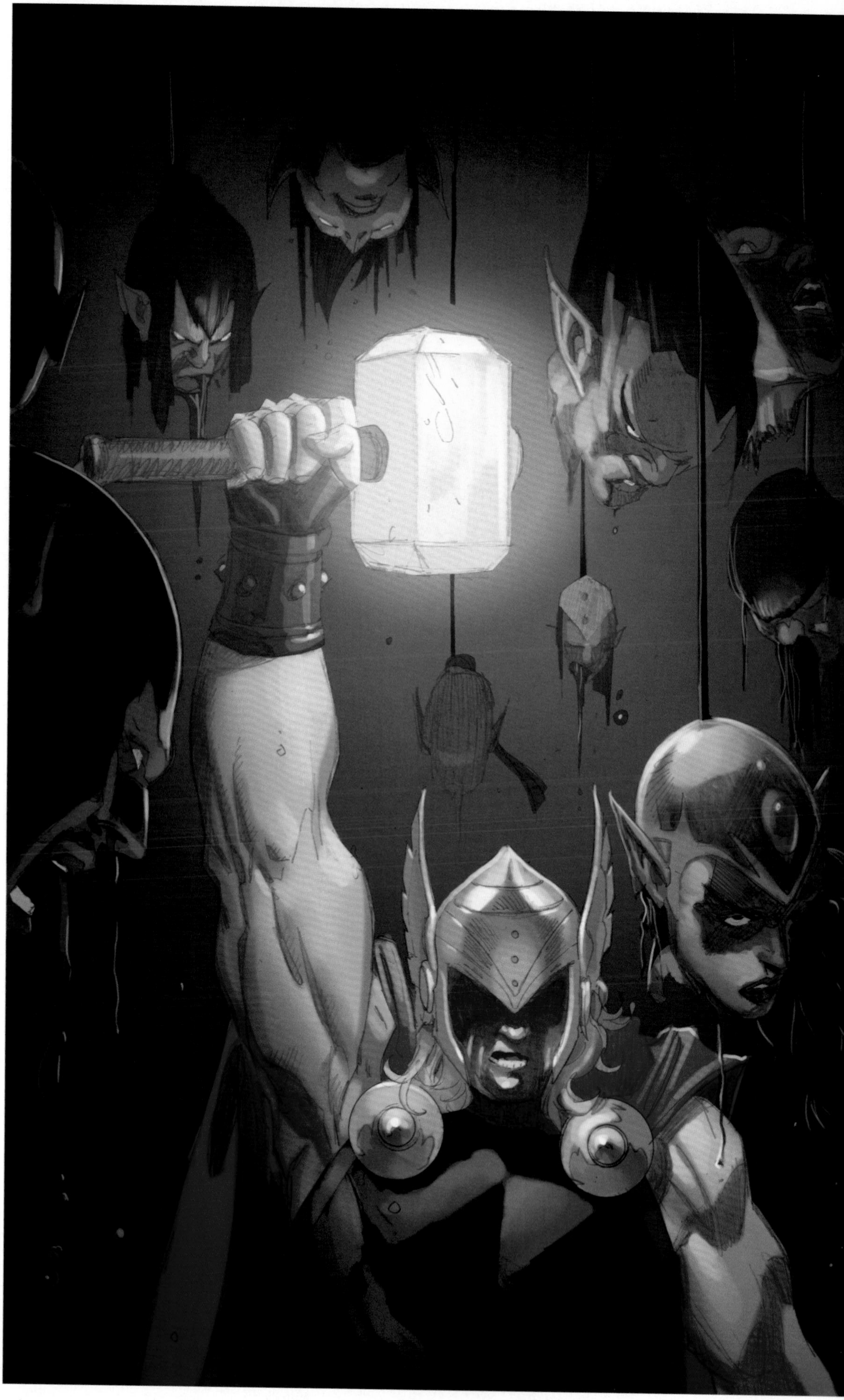

MALEKITH'S FULL BRUTALITY IS LAID BARE WITH THE SLAUGHTER OF QUEEN ALFLYSE AND HER SUPPORTERS, AND HIS DARK ALLIANCES BEGIN WITH THE FROST GIANTS.

RIGHT AND OPPOSITE: ***THOR: GOD OF THUNDER #14-15*** INTERIOR ART BY RON GARNEY AND IVE SVORCINA

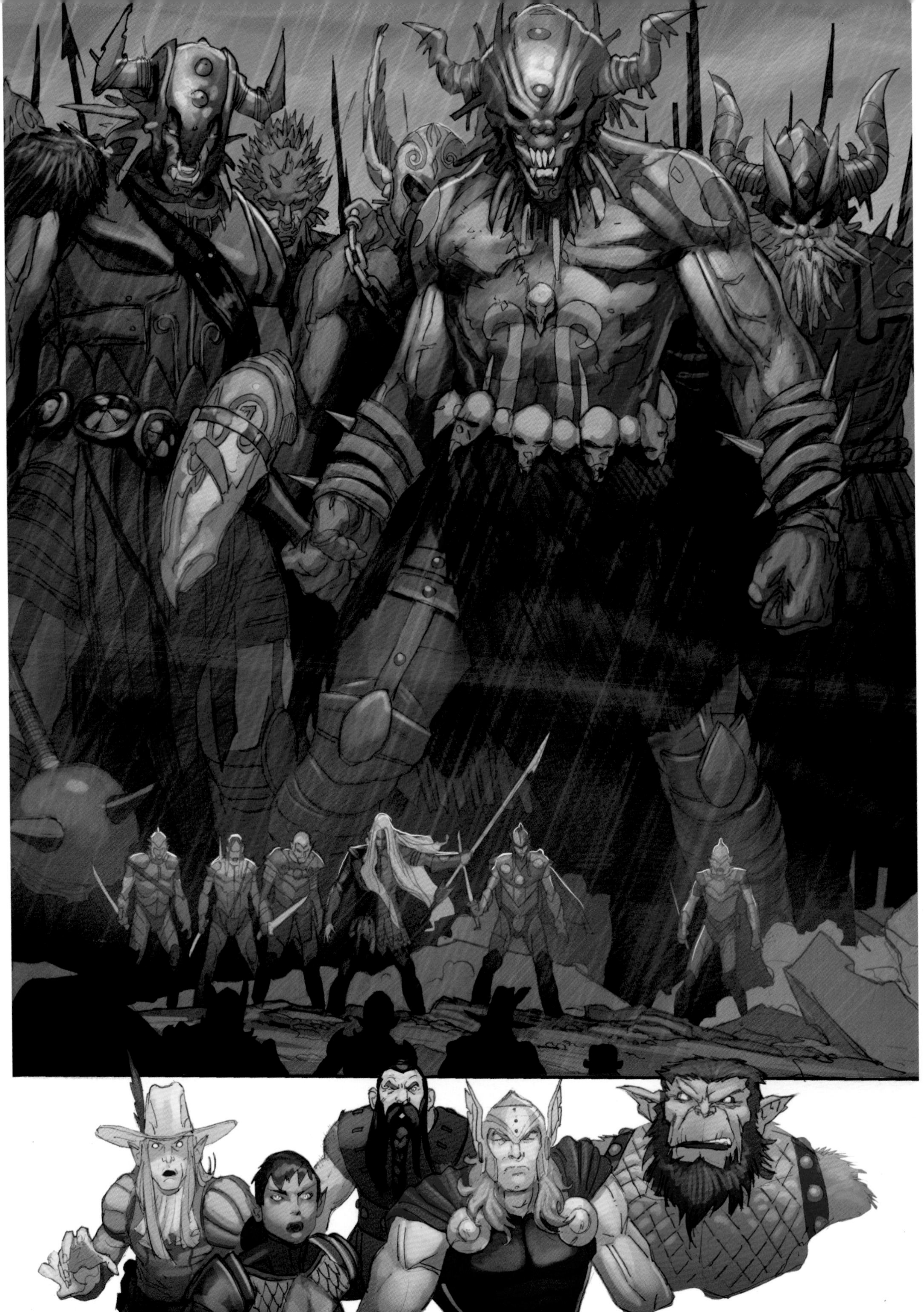

OGGY THE GIANT IS THE FIRST OF THE LEAGUE OF REALMS TO FALL TO THE RUTHLESS MALEKITH.

***THOR: GOD OF THUNDER* #15**
INTERIOR ART BY RON GARNEY AND IVE SVORCINA

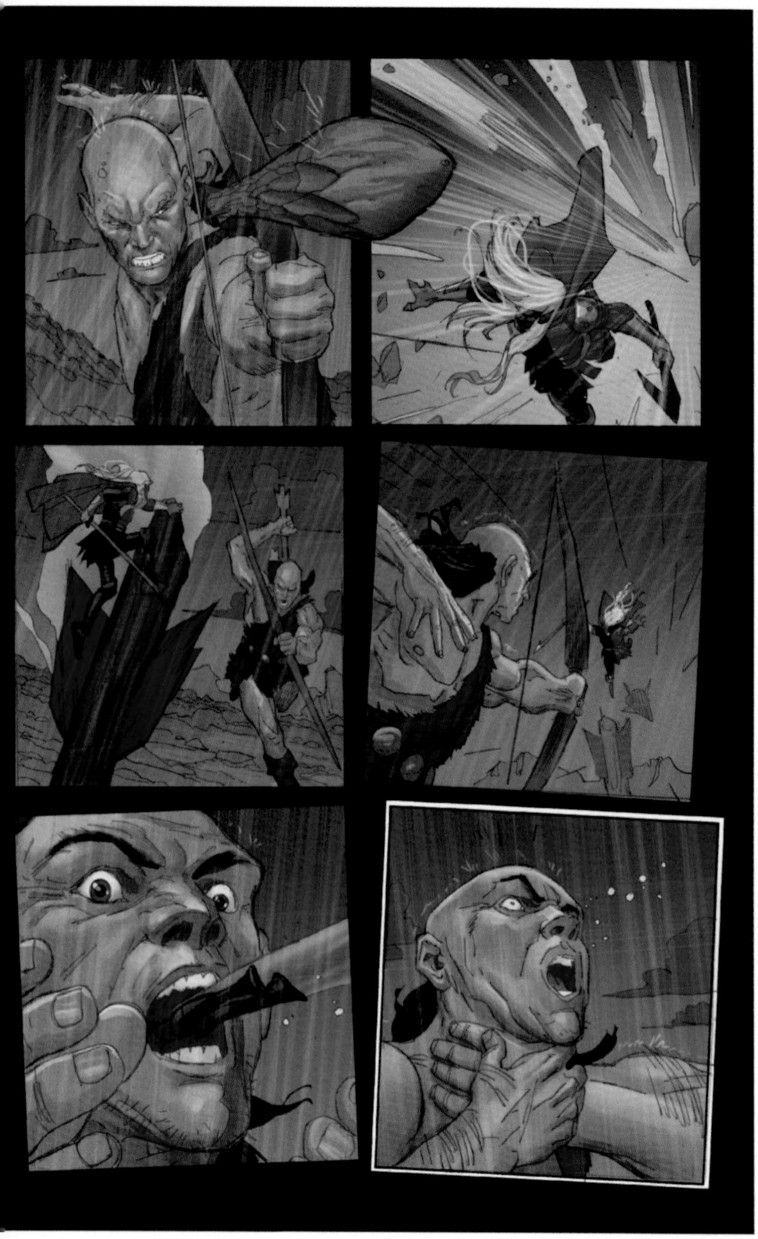

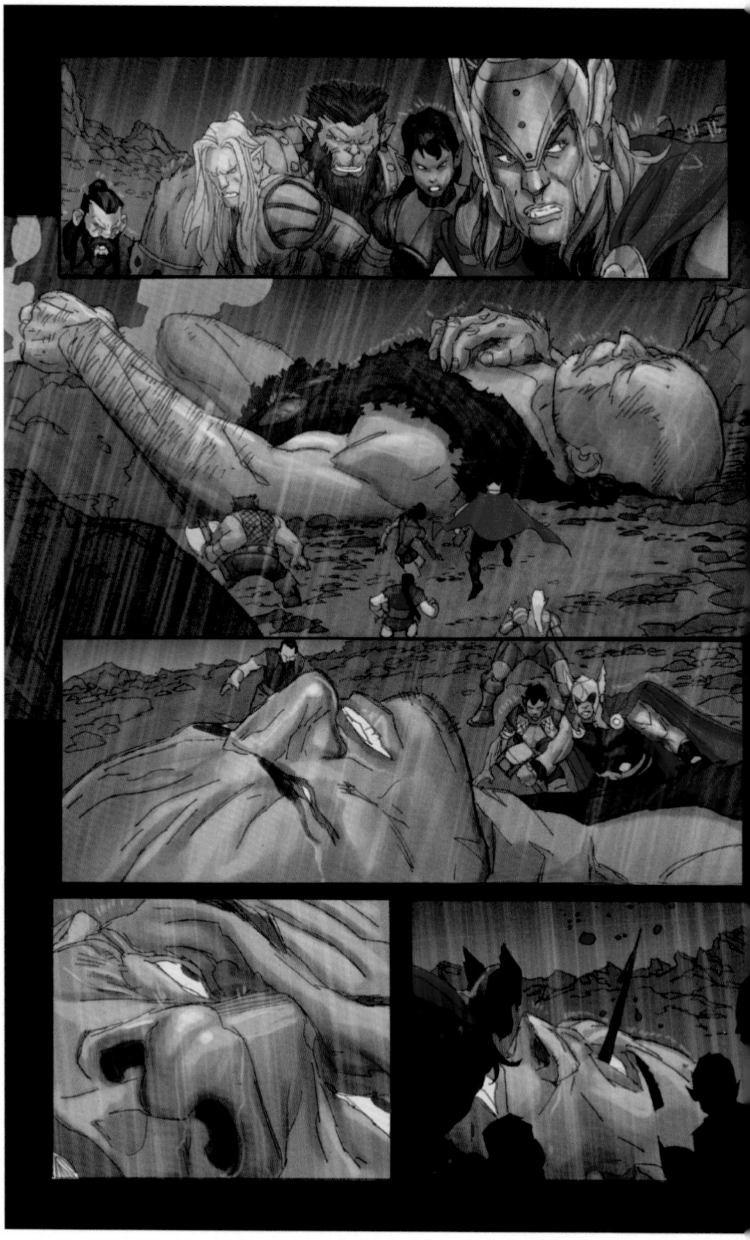

OPPOSITE: THE EFFORTS OF THOR AND THE LEAGUE OF REALMS COME TO NAUGHT AS THE GOVERNING DARK ELF COUNCIL ELECTS TO NAME MALEKITH AS SVARTALFHEIM'S KING, FREEING HIM TO PLAN A "WAR UNLIKE ANY THE NINE REALMS HAD EVER KNOWN."

***THOR: GOD OF THUNDER* #17**
INTERIOR ART BY RON GARNEY AND IVE SVORCINA, WITH LETTERING BY JOE SABINO

Epilogue.

AND THE SAGAS WOULD TELL OF FAR DARKER THINGS AS WELL.

ARE YOU CERTAIN THIS IS A GOOD IDEA?

OF A SECRET BORN IN FLAME AND FROST AND NURSED ON THE BLACKEST OF MAGIC.

RELAX, SON OF JOTUNHEIM. I KNOW WHAT I'M DOING.

YOU HAD BETTER, ELF.

KING ELF. AND AS I TOLD YOU, THE ASGARDIANS HAVE THEIR LEAGUE OF REALMS. WHY SHOULD WE NOT HAVE THE SAME?

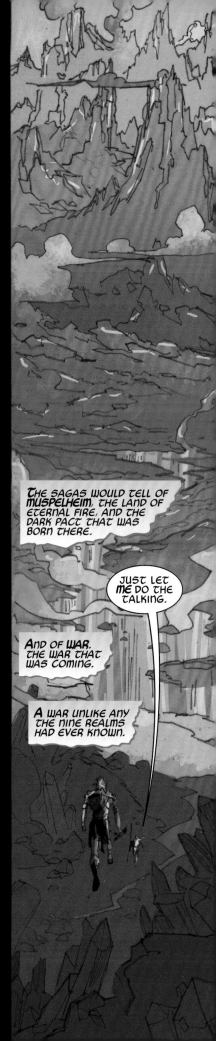

THE SAGAS WOULD TELL OF MUSPELHEIM, THE LAND OF ETERNAL FIRE, AND THE DARK PACT THAT WAS BORN THERE.

JUST LET ME DO THE TALKING.

AND OF WAR. THE WAR THAT WAS COMING.

A WAR UNLIKE ANY THE NINE REALMS HAD EVER KNOWN.

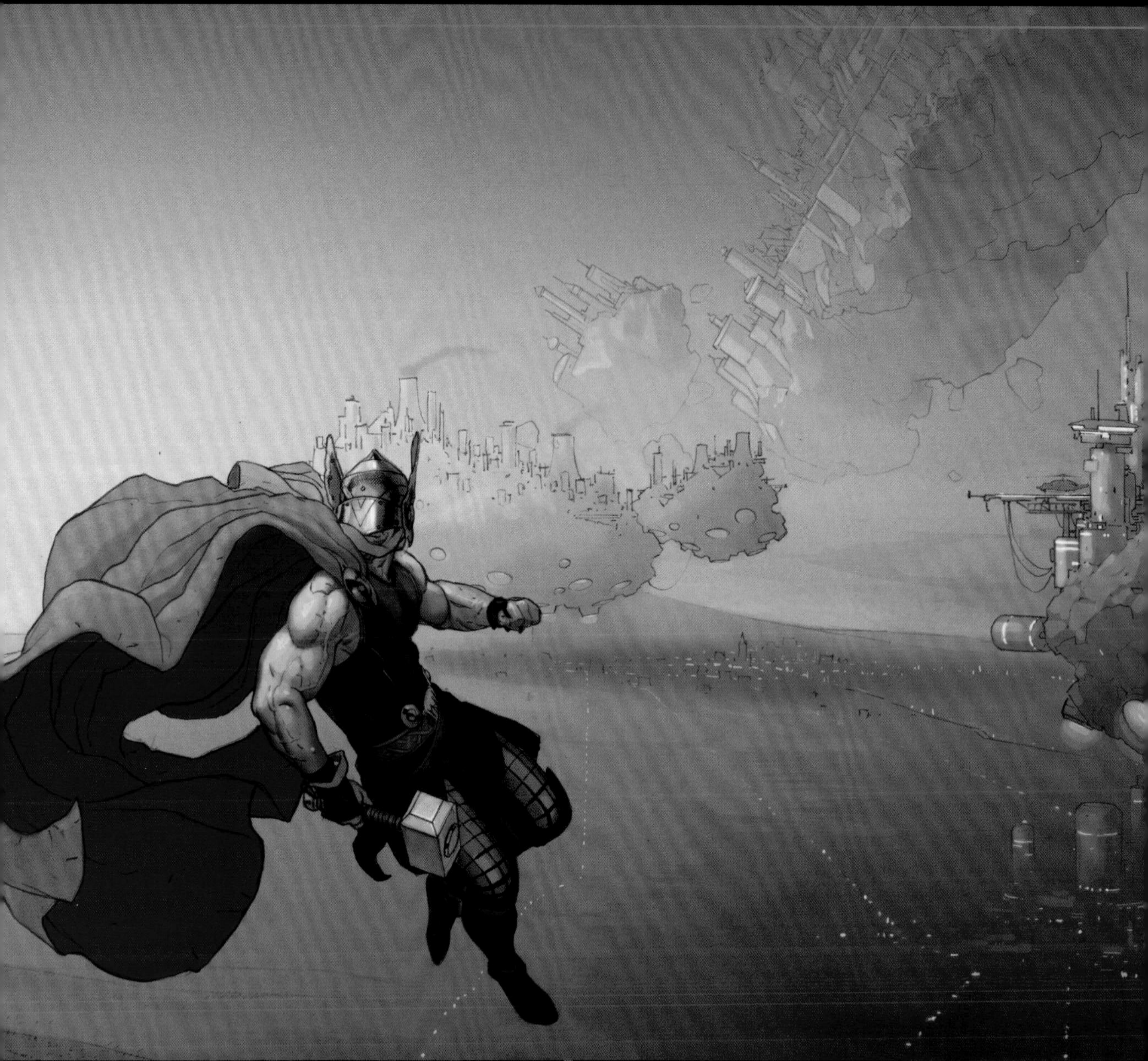
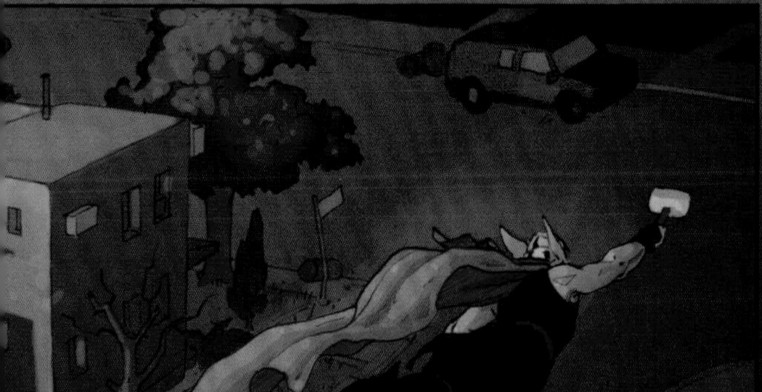
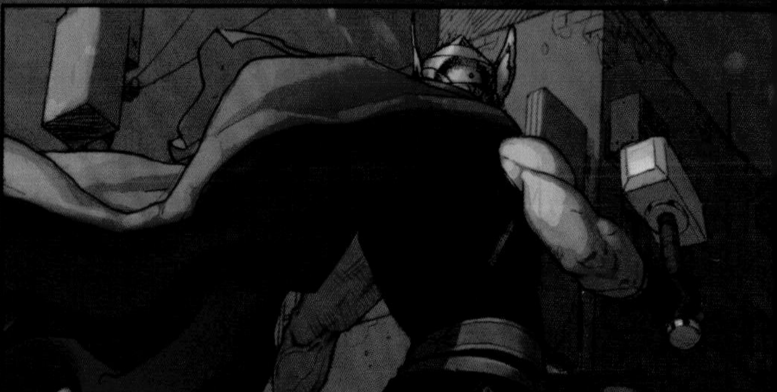

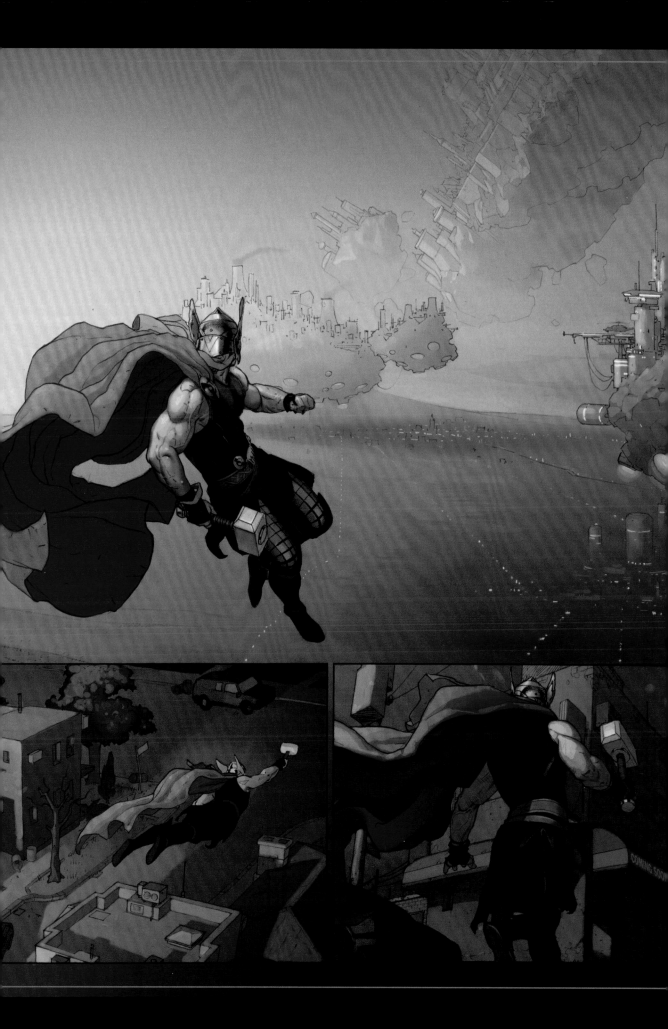

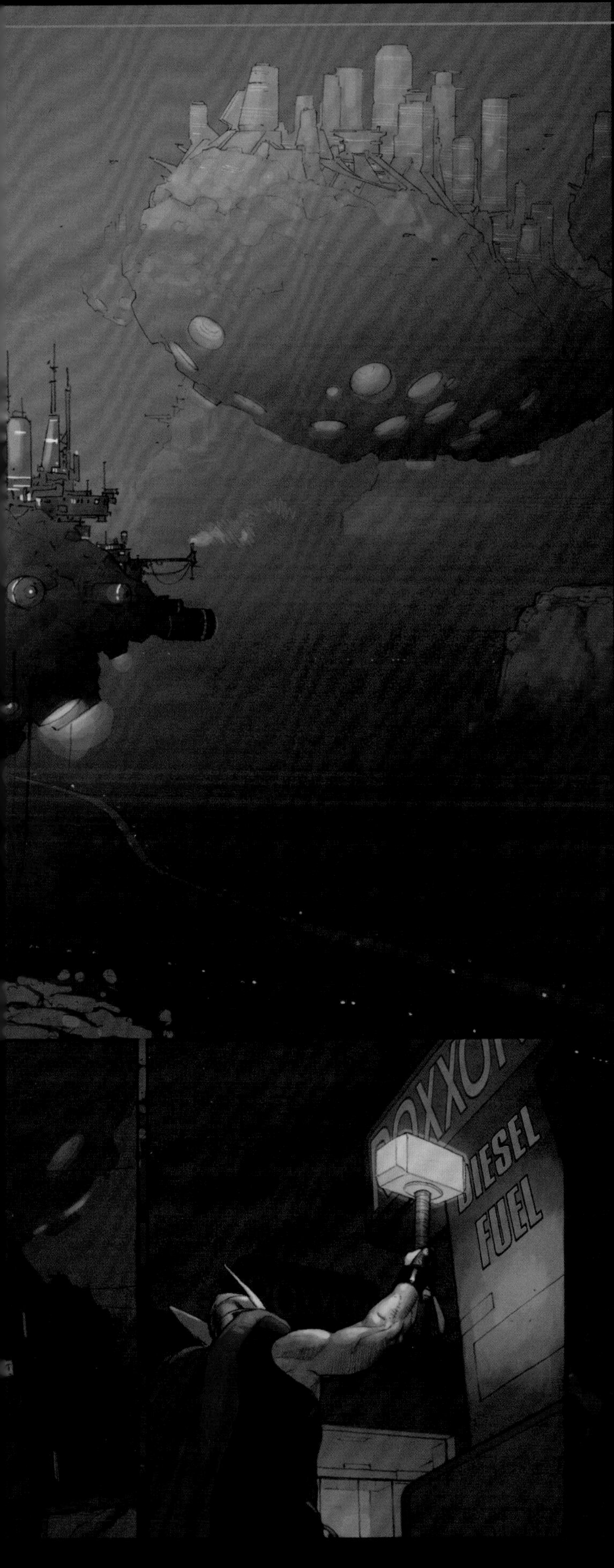
ROXXON
DIESEL
FUEL

chapter three:

THE LAST DAYS OF MIDGARD

"mark well the words of thor. anyone who threatens midgard shall come to know this **hammer** in ways they shall find most uncomfortable."
— thor

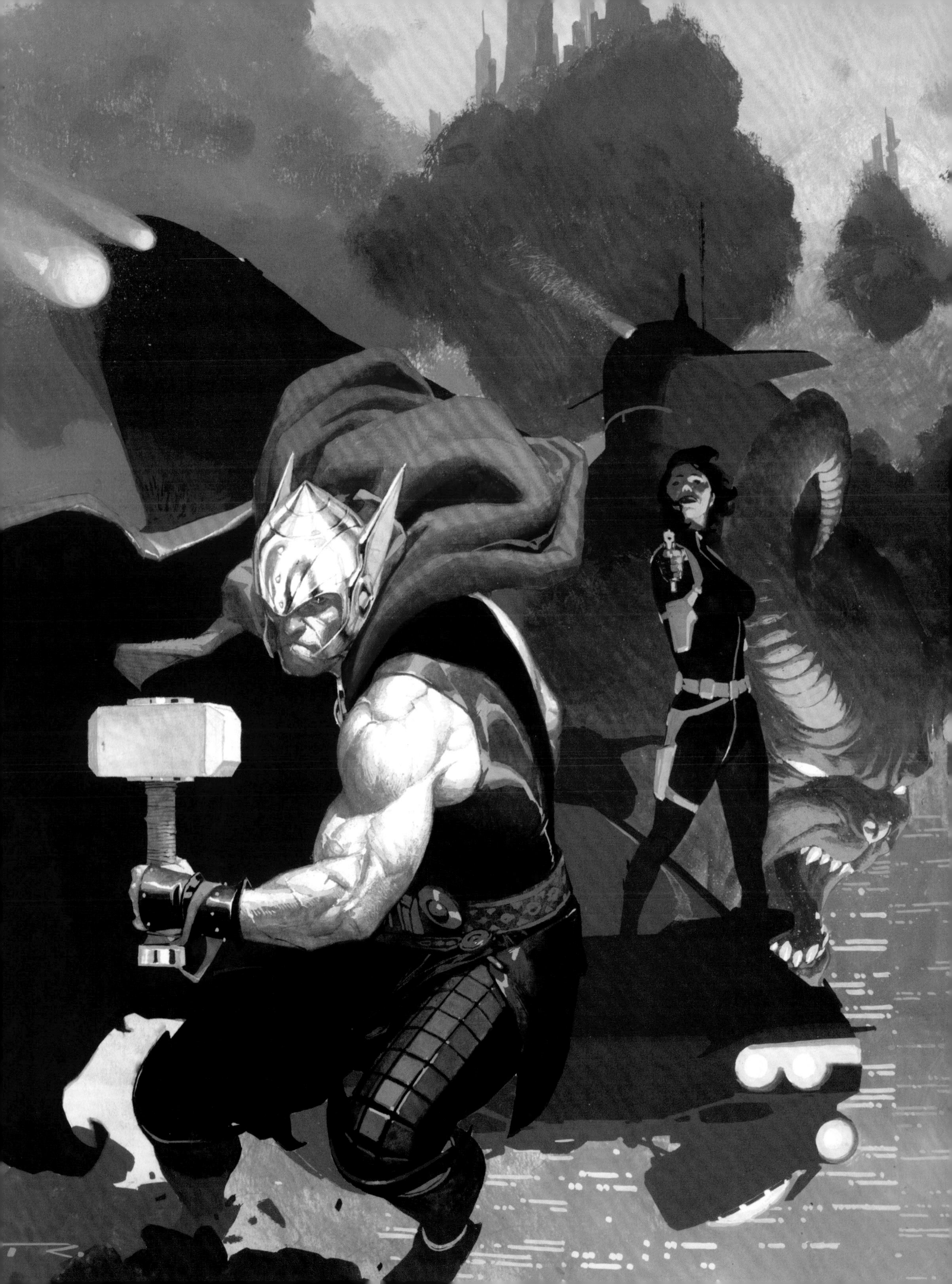

After subjecting Thor to an epic struggle across time against Gorr the God Butcher and a battle in vain against his old enemy Malekith, Jason Aaron sought to introduce a different kind of villain — one the Thunder God could not so easily hit with his hammer. And so in his next arc — "The Last Days of Midgard," its title laden with meaning — the writer and returning artist Esad Ribić pitted Thor against the notorious Roxxon Corporation.

"I didn't want every villain to be an Elf or a Frost Giant — a fantasy villain," Aaron says. "I liked the idea of mixing it up, which was how I dealt with my run on *Wolverine*. I wanted us to do a different kind of story, so I thought the idea of Marvel's mightiest god fighting the Marvel Universe's mightiest corporation would be fun and something we hadn't seen before."

Aaron intended to return Roxxon — a controversial energy corporation in the Marvel Universe since the 1970s — to its status as a major player. In doing so, he introduced new CEO Dario Agger, whom Aaron describes as the "super-arrogant, super-devious head of the company." Agger was nicknamed the Minotaur in business school — for good reason, as it soon turned out. "The idea of giving him some dark super-powers of his own was so we could have him and Thor punch each other in the face once in a while," Aaron laughs.

Under the guise of saving the planet, Agger's Roxxon is only out for profit — and its pollution-spewing flying factories soon attract the attention of S.H.I.E.L.D. environmental scientist Rosalind Solomon…and her new friend, Thor. But just as political wrangling prevented Thor from delivering justice on Malekith, legal machinations protect Agger — even after he reveals his true Minotaur form.

Agger seeks revenge on Thor by sending his factories to the Thunder God's adopted home of Broxton, Oklahoma, bringing about Asgardia's last days on Midgard. "A big part of this arc was the end of Broxton, Oklahoma, which had been the setting of Thor stories since J. Michael Straczynski," Aaron says. "This was the first time I'd come back to Broxton in the book in a big way, and I burned the whole town to the ground! Maybe it's a coincidence that the Oklahoma Sooners had just beaten my Alabama Crimson Tide in a ball game… I can't say they were unrelated, but I wanted to wrap up that part of the Thor story and move where it's going. I get the idea of grounding those characters and having them be right here outside of our window, but I wanted to put a little more distance between them. In my mind, you can do these big, grandiose, fantastic stories with Thor while still making him relatable to us on a human level."

PREVIOUS PAGES:
THOR: GOD OF THUNDER #21
INTERIOR ART BY ESAD RIBIĆ
AND IVE SVORCINA

OPPOSITE: *THOR: GOD OF THUNDER #19* COVER BY ESAD RIBIĆ

"I wanted to bring Jane back as a supporting character without making her a love interest again. After eleven issues of Thor running around through space fighting serial killers of gods and doing all these amazing things, he comes back to Earth and he still can't do anything to help someone he loves — she's going to have to fight that fight one her own. Of course, later on, that fight gets even more complicated — but I can't say I had all of that in mind when I brought her in."

— JASON AARON

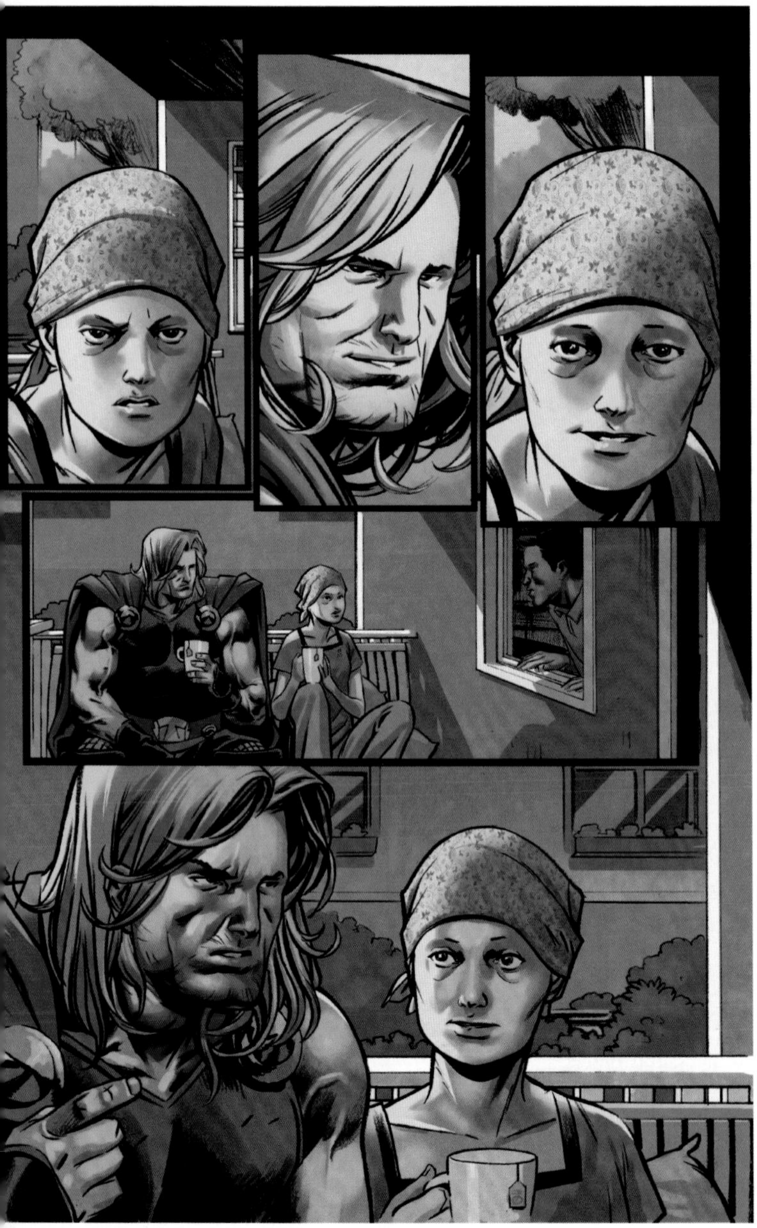

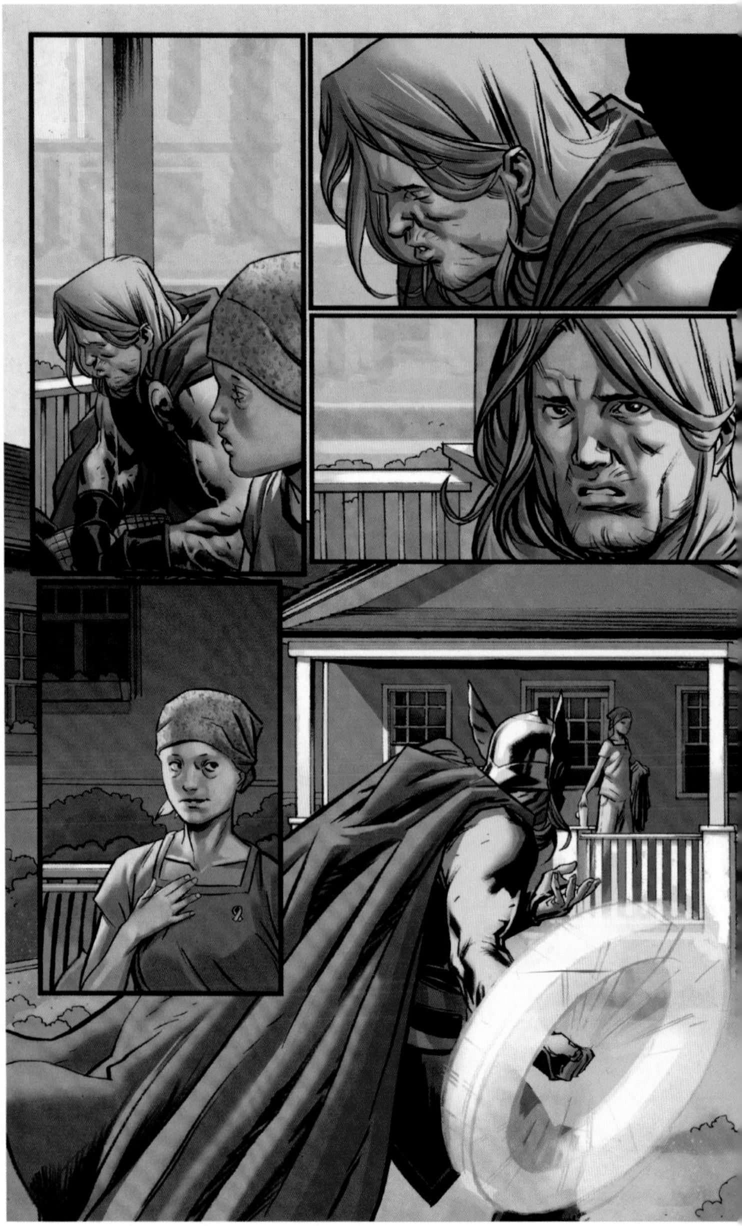

HAVING RETURNED TO MIDGARD AFTER A LONG TIME AWAY, THOR BEGINS TO RECONNECT WITH THOSE ON EARTH HE HAS SWORN TO PROTECT. VISITING HIS FORMER FLAME, DR. JANE FOSTER, HE'S SHOCKED TO LEARN SHE'S UNDERGOING TREATMENT FOR BREAST CANCER. HERE, HE TAKES HER ON A BREATHTAKING TRIP TO THE BLUE AREA OF THE MOON — AND IT WON'T BE THE LAST TIME SHE MAKES THE JOURNEY!

ABOVE AND OPPOSITE: ***THOR: GOD OF THUNDER #12*** INTERIOR ART BY NIC KLEIN

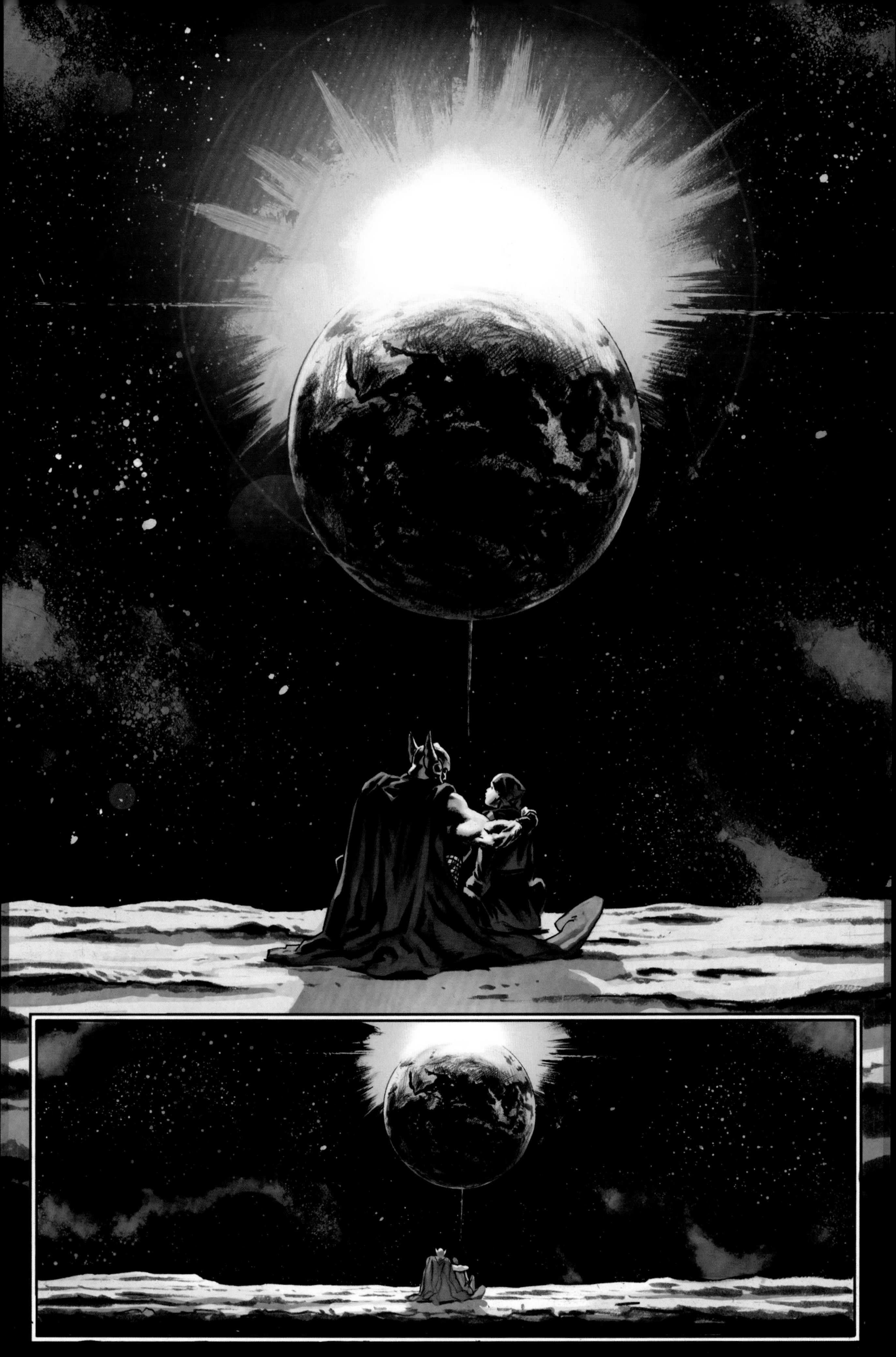

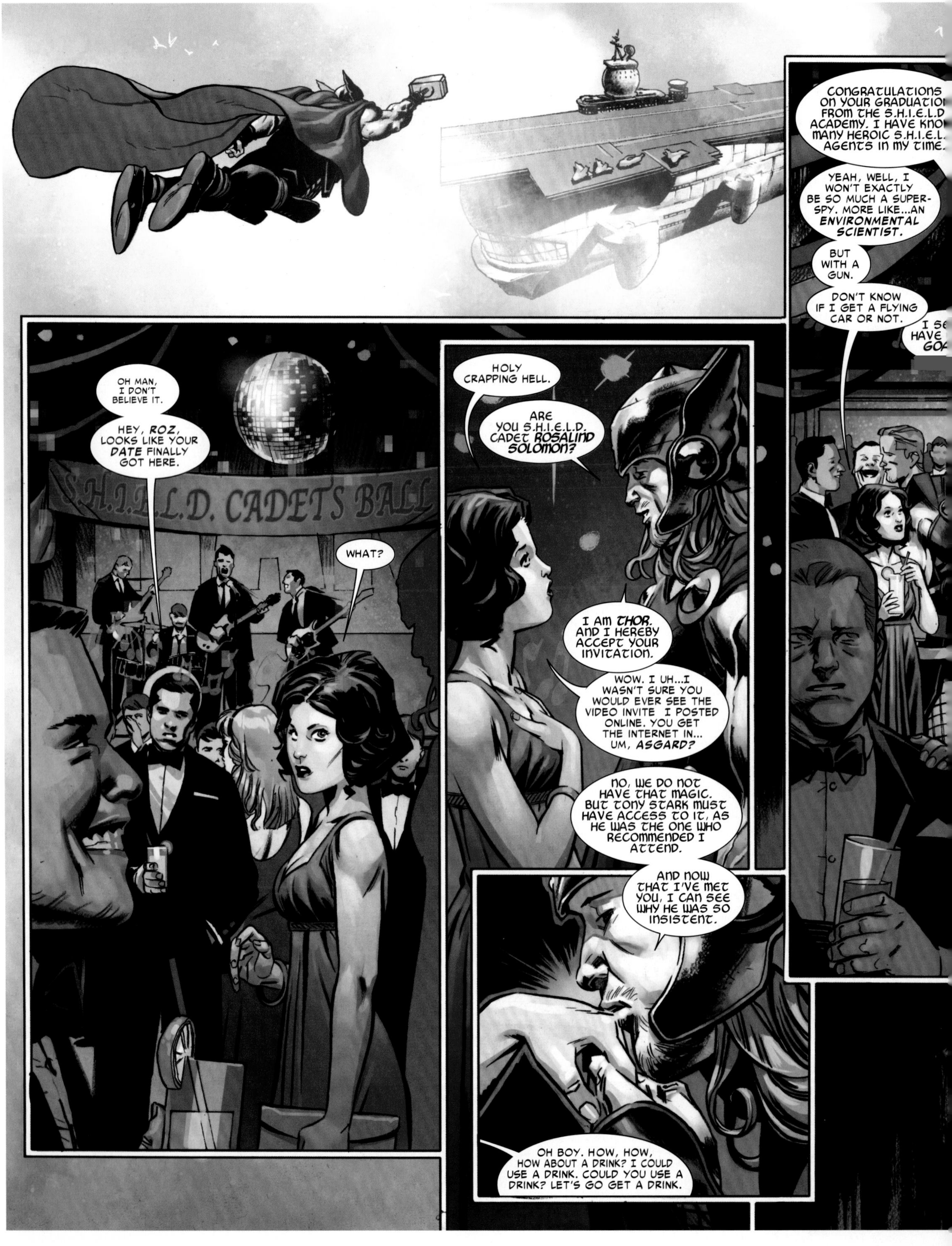

CONGRATULATIONS ON YOUR GRADUATIO FROM THE S.H.I.E.L.D ACADEMY. I HAVE KNO MANY HEROIC S.H.I.E.L. AGENTS IN MY TIME.
YEAH, WELL, I WON'T EXACTLY BE SO MUCH A SUPER-SPY. MORE LIKE...AN ENVIRONMENTAL SCIENTIST.
BUT WITH A GUN.
DON'T KNOW IF I GET A FLYING CAR OR NOT.
OH MAN, I DON'T BELIEVE IT.
HEY, ROZ, LOOKS LIKE YOUR DATE FINALLY GOT HERE.
S.H.I.E.L.D. CADETS BALL
WHAT?
HOLY CRAPPING HELL.
ARE YOU S.H.I.E.L.D. CADET ROSALIND SOLOMON?
I AM THOR. AND I HEREBY ACCEPT YOUR INVITATION.
WOW. I UH...I WASN'T SURE YOU WOULD EVER SEE THE VIDEO INVITE I POSTED ONLINE. YOU GET THE INTERNET IN... UM, ASGARD?
NO, WE DO NOT HAVE THAT MAGIC. BUT TONY STARK MUST HAVE ACCESS TO IT, AS HE WAS THE ONE WHO RECOMMENDED I ATTEND.
AND NOW THAT I'VE MET YOU, I CAN SEE WHY HE WAS SO INSISTENT.
OH BOY. HOW, HOW, HOW ABOUT A DRINK? I COULD USE A DRINK. COULD YOU USE A DRINK? LET'S GO GET A DRINK.

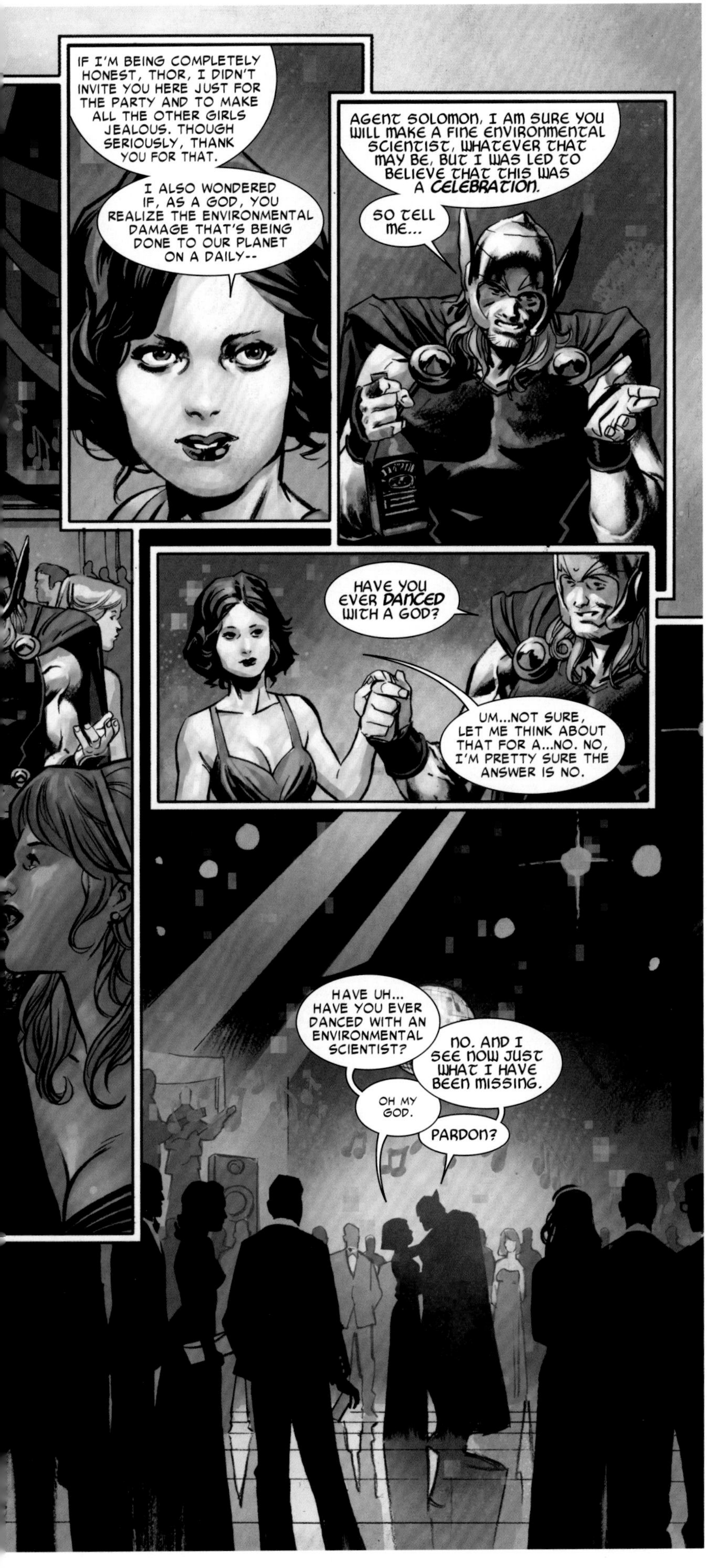
IF I'M BEING COMPLETELY HONEST, THOR, I DIDN'T INVITE YOU HERE JUST FOR THE PARTY AND TO MAKE ALL THE OTHER GIRLS JEALOUS. THOUGH SERIOUSLY, THANK YOU FOR THAT.
I ALSO WONDERED IF, AS A GOD, YOU REALIZE THE ENVIRONMENTAL DAMAGE THAT'S BEING DONE TO OUR PLANET ON A DAILY--
AGENT SOLOMON, I AM SURE YOU WILL MAKE A FINE ENVIRONMENTAL SCIENTIST, WHATEVER THAT MAY BE, BUT I WAS LED TO BELIEVE THAT THIS WAS A CELEBRATION.
SO TELL ME...
HAVE YOU EVER DANCED WITH A GOD?
UM...NOT SURE, LET ME THINK ABOUT THAT FOR A...NO. NO, I'M PRETTY SURE THE ANSWER IS NO.
HAVE UH... HAVE YOU EVER DANCED WITH AN ENVIRONMENTAL SCIENTIST?
NO. AND I SEE NOW JUST WHAT I HAVE BEEN MISSING.
OH MY GOD.
PARDON?

THOR MAKES THE ACQUAINTANCE OF A POTENTIAL NEW LOVE INTEREST, ROOKIE S.H.I.E.L.D. AGENT (AND ENVIRONMENTAL SCIENTIST) ROSALIND SOLOMON.

THOR: GOD OF THUNDER #12 INTERIOR ART BY NIC KLEIN, WITH LETTERING BY JOE SABINO

"Roz's name is a nod to Lee and Kirby. Roz was Jack Kirby's wife, and Solomon was Stan Lee's mother's maiden name. So it's a tip of the hat to those guys."
— JASON AARON

THOR AND ROZ SOLOMON ATTACK A ROXXON ATMOSPHERIC-TREATMENT FACILITY, WHILE THE GOD OF THUNDER DOES WHAT HE DOES BEST: SMITING A FROST GIANT.

RIGHT:
THOR: GOD OF THUNDER #20
INTERIOR ART BY ESAD RIBIĆ AND IVE SVORCINA

OPPOSITE:
THOR: GOD OF THUNDER #19
INTERIOR ART BY ESAD RIBIĆ AND IVE SVORCINA

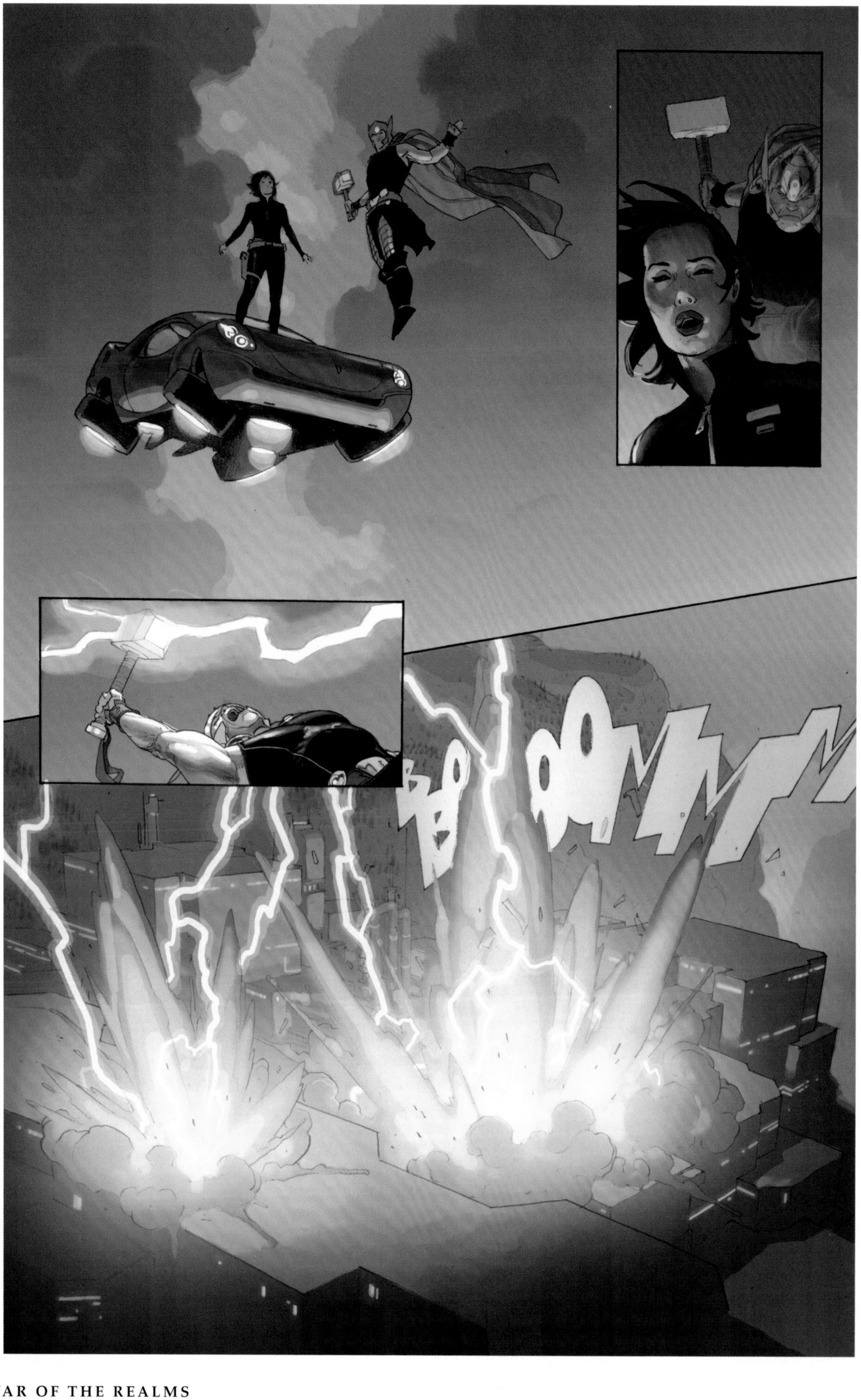

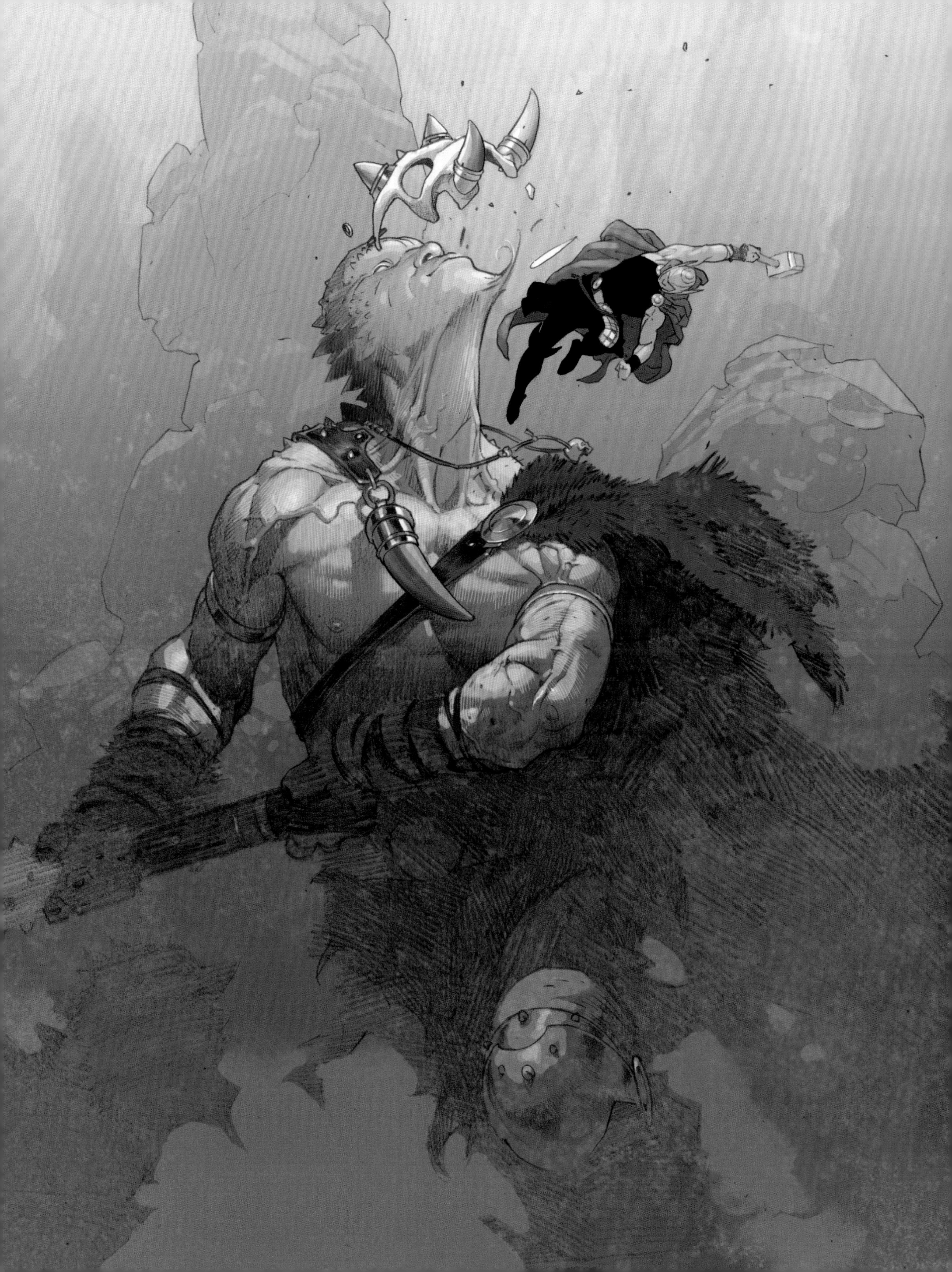

DARIO AGGER REVEALS HIMSELF TO BE A LITERAL MINOTAUR.

THOR: GOD OF THUNDER #20 INTERIOR ART BY ESAD RIBIĆ AND IVE SVORCINA

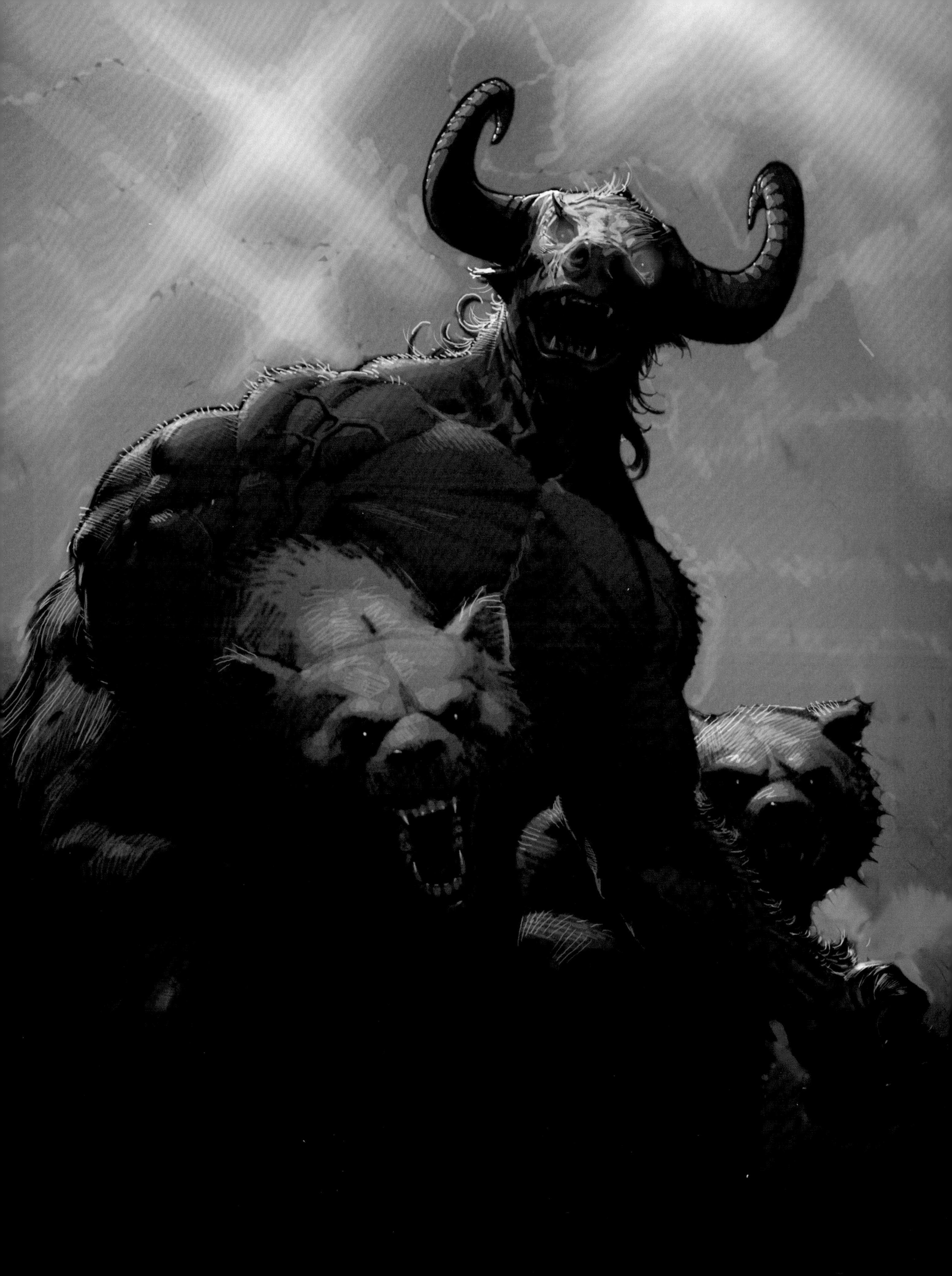

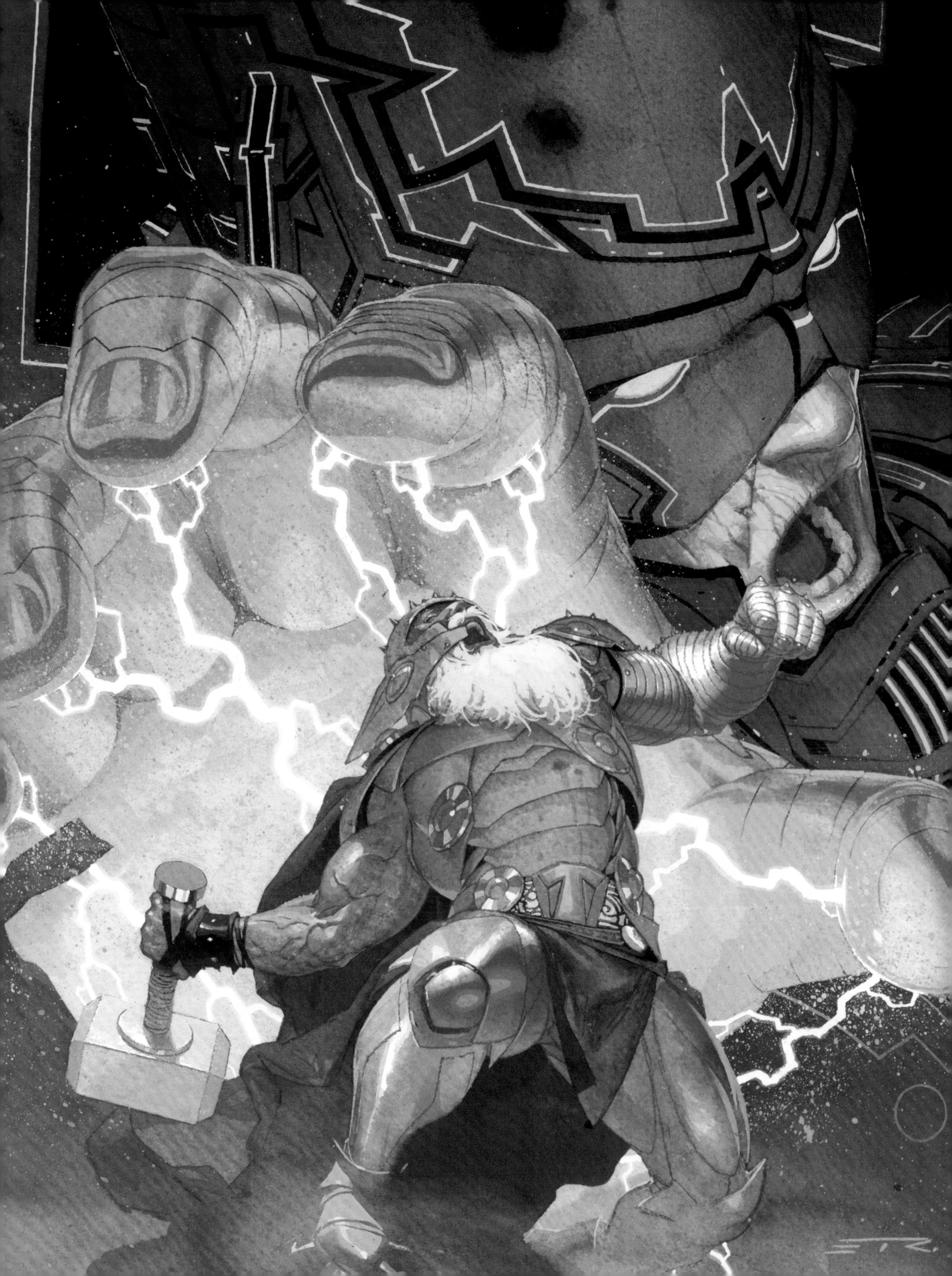

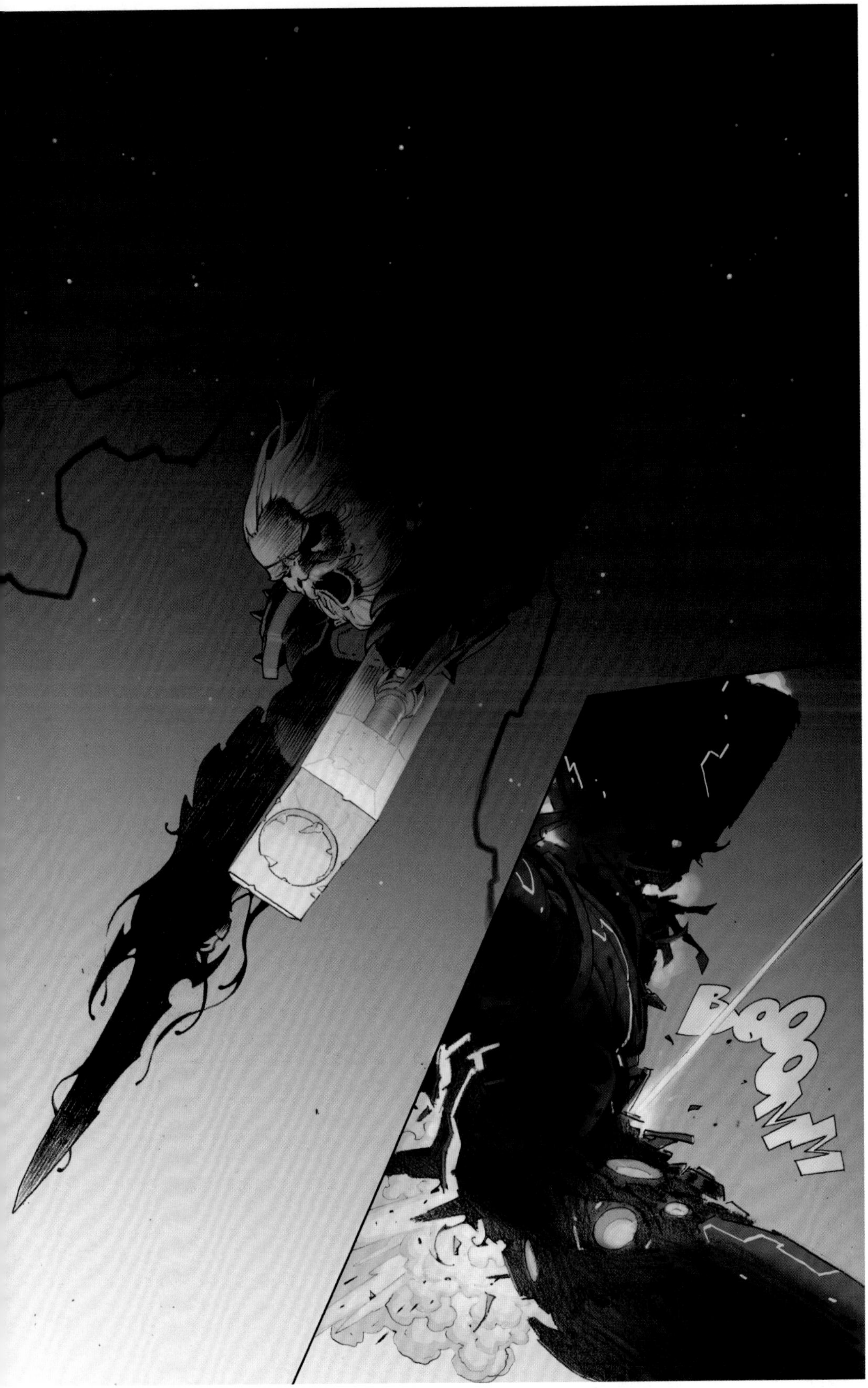
BOOOOM!

Meanwhile, at the end of time, Midgard faces its literal last days at the mercy of the world-eating Galactus — only for King Thor and the Girls of Thunder to come to its defense. In desperation, Thor retrieves the deadly weapon All-Black the Necrosword — and secures victory as All-Black the All-Father…the God of Butchers…the Necro-Thor! Galactus falls — and where Thor's blood spills, new plant life blooms on Earth. But the saga of All-Black is far from over; it has continued throughout Aaron's *Thor* run.

"I wanted to see Esad draw old Galactus and King Thor," Aaron says. "We kind of already introduced the idea that Midgard in that far future was dead — it was a lifeless husk. I liked the idea of old King Thor still going down to see it, even though there's nothing there. Then, when Galactus comes to finally, finally eat Earth — to get rid of the planet that's been such a thorn in his side — Thor still risks his life to fight for it almost on principle."

LEFT: ***THOR: GOD OF THUNDER #23***
INTERIOR ART BY ESAD RIBIĆ
AND IVE SVORCINA

OPPOSITE: ***THOR: GOD OF THUNDER #20***
COVER BY ESAD RIBIĆ

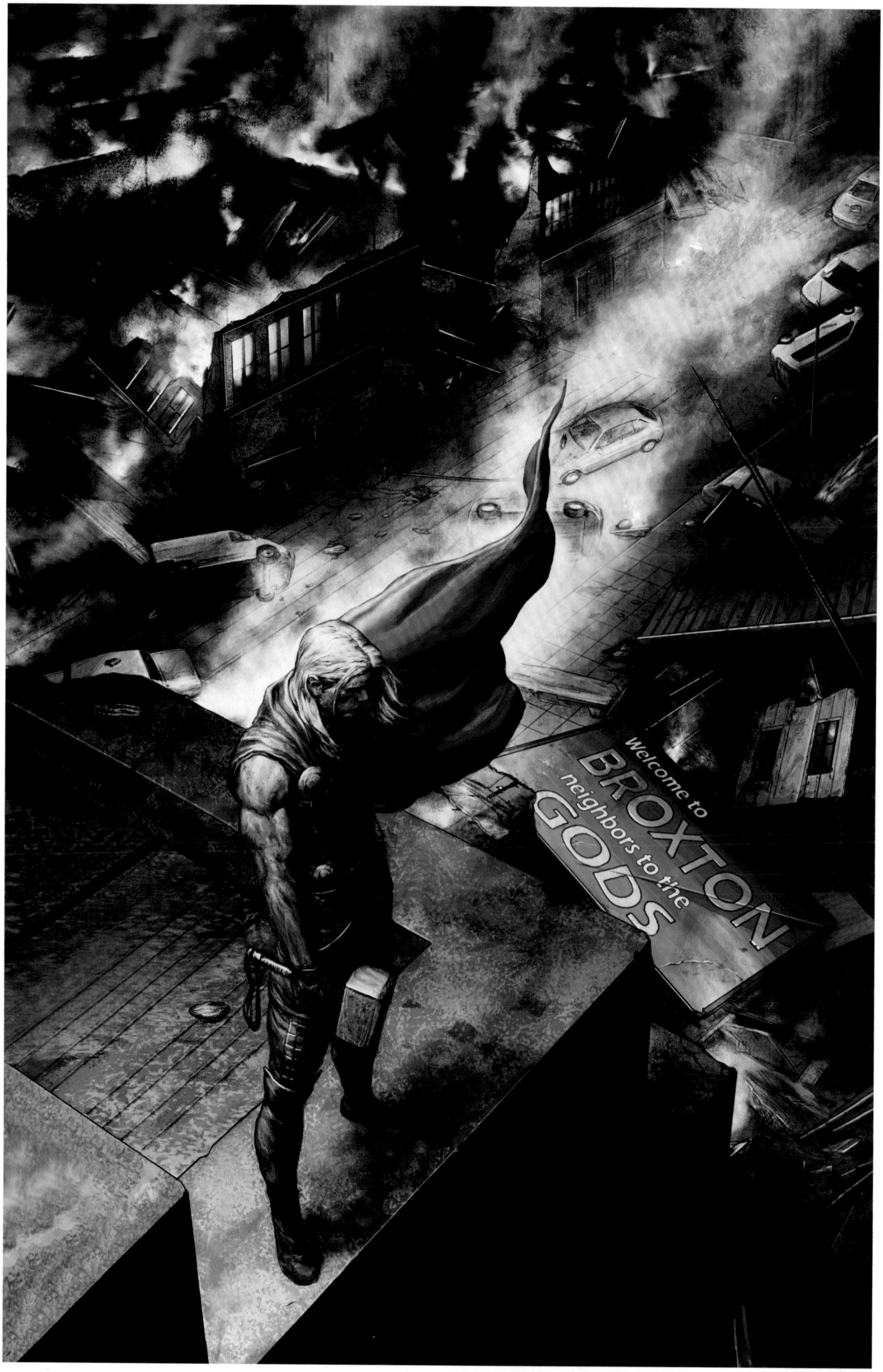
Welcome to
BROXTON
neighbors to the
GODS

AS THE ALL-MOTHER, FREYJA, RETURNED ASGARDIA TO THE STARS, THOR LEFT BEHIND HIS MAJESTIC PALACE, BILSKIRNIR, FOR THE PEOPLE OF THE BROKEN TOWN OF BROXTON.

RIGHT: *THOR: GOD OF THUNDER* #24 COVER BY AGUSTIN ALESSIO

OPPOSITE: *THOR: GOD OF THUNDER* #25 COVER BY ESAD RIBIĆ

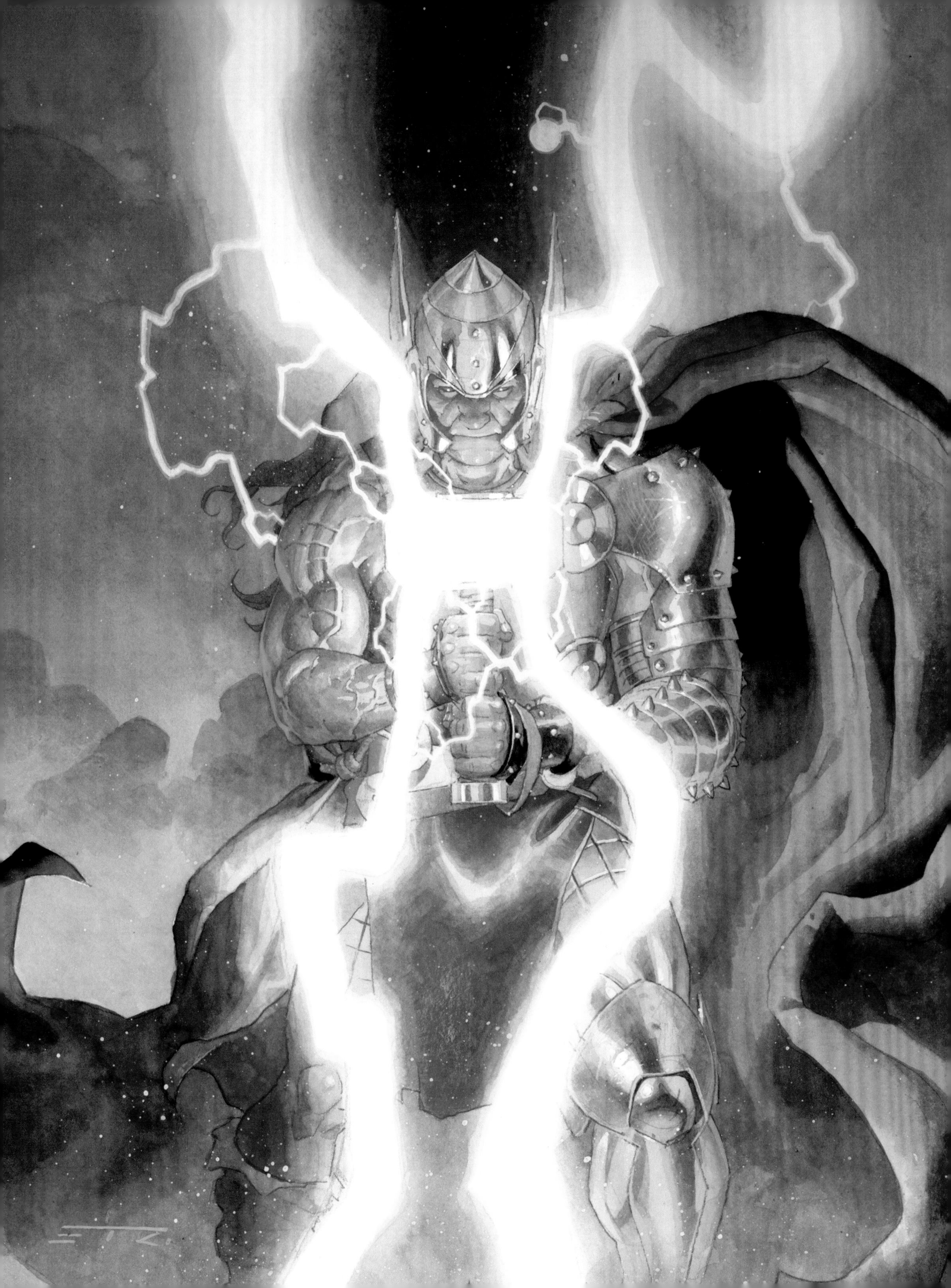

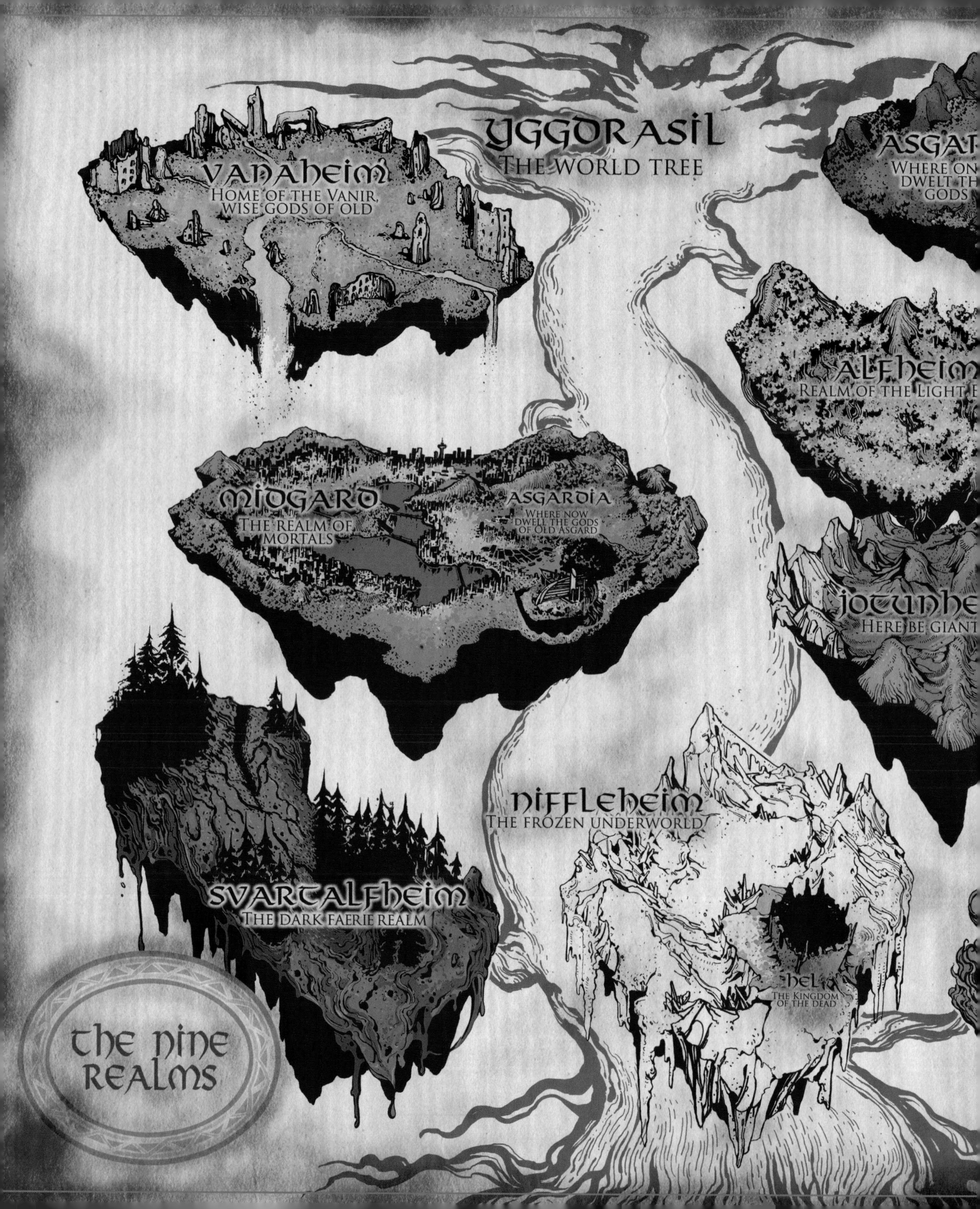
YGGDRASIL
THE WORLD TREE
VANAHEIM
HOME OF THE VANIR, WISE GODS OF OLD
ASGAR
WHERE ON
DWELT TH
GODS
ALFHEIM
REALM OF THE LIGHT E
MIDGARD
THE REALM OF MORTALS
ASGARDIA
WHERE NOW DWELL THE GODS OF OLD ASGARD
JOTUNHE
HERE BE GIANT
NIFFLEHEIM
THE FROZEN UNDERWORLD
SVARTALFHEIM
THE DARK FAERIE REALM
HEL
THE KINGDOM OF THE DEAD
THE NINE REALMS

chapter four:

THE TENTH REALM

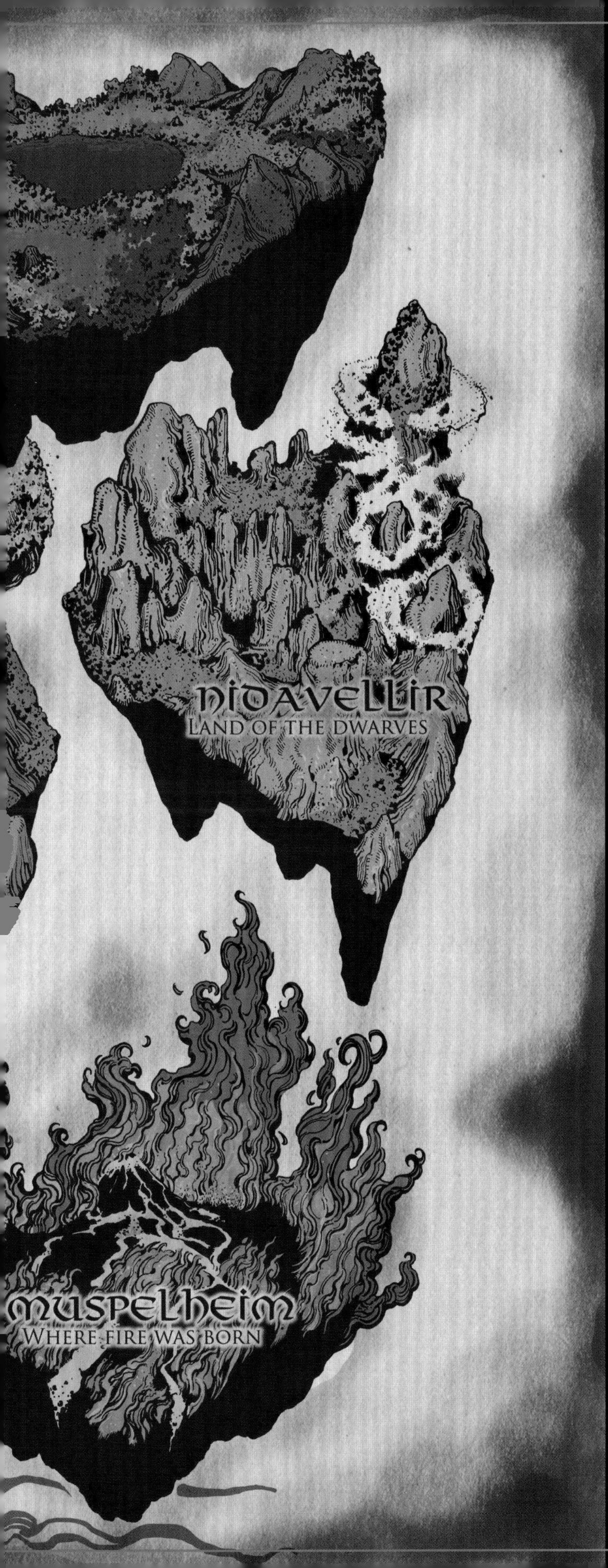
NIDAVELLIR
LAND OF THE DWARVES
MUSPELHEIM
WHERE FIRE WAS BORN

IN THE BEGINNING, THERE WAS DARKNESS. AND THEN FROM THE SOUTH CAME FIRE, AND FROM THE NORTH, COLD AND MIST. AND WHERE THE TWO FORCES MET IN THE YAWNING VOID, LIFE WAS BORN. GODS AND GIANTS. DWARVES AND ELVES. TROLLS AND MEN. AND WORLDS WERE MADE FOR EACH OF THEM. NINE IN TOTAL.

OR SO WE BELIEVED.

For decades, Thor's adventures have spread across the Nine Realms of existence, each connected by the roots of Yggdrasil, the World Tree. In these pages, you'll get a taste of the richly varied worlds on which Malekith has set his sights — and learn how Nine was revealed to be Ten.

ASGARD

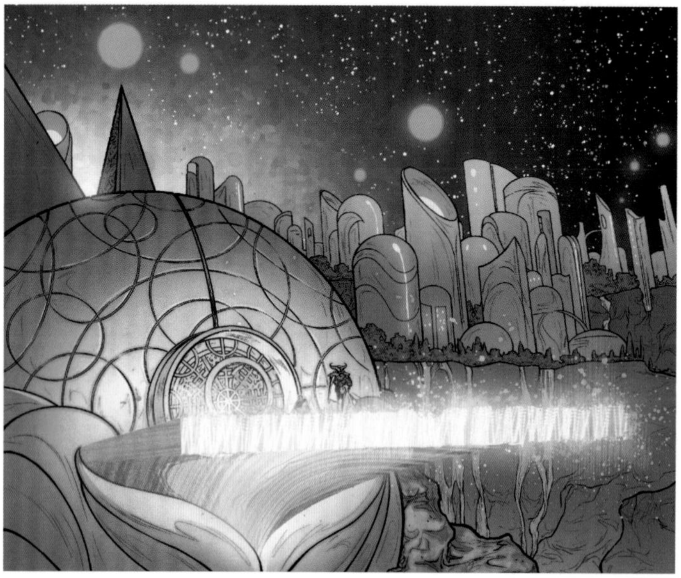

Or as it has been known since old Asgard fell, Asgardia. High on Yggdrasil, Asgard was, for centuries, the gleaming Realm Eternal — home to All-Father Odin; his son, Thor; and their fellow gods of the Aesir, including Lady Sif, Balder the Brave and the Warriors Three, all watched over by the ever-vigilant guardian Heimdall. The Asgardians have traditionally enjoyed access to the other realms via the Rainbow Bridge. Recently, Asgardia was located on Earth in the skies over Broxton, Oklahoma, prior to the events of "The Last Days of Midgard" — but in the cosmos, the ruins of Old Asgard remain.

THOR (2014) #6 INTERIOR ART BY RUSSELL DAUTERMAN AND MATTHEW WILSON

MIDGARD

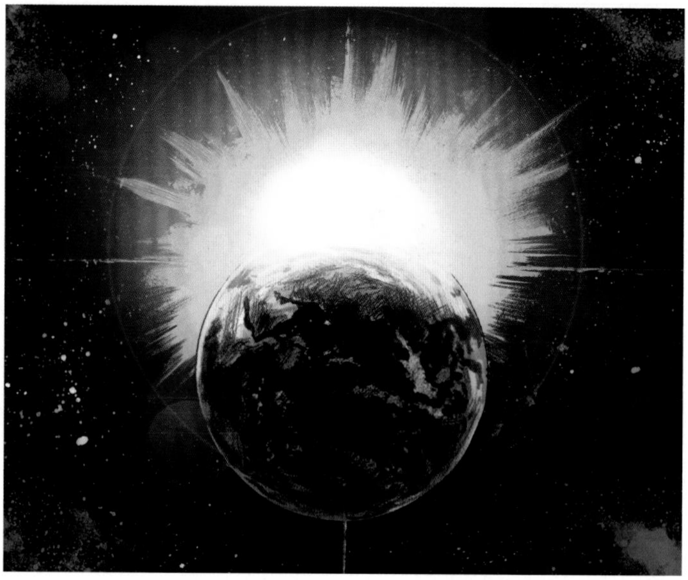

At the heart of the World Tree's trunk is the center realm of Midgard — or as we know it, Earth. Thor has been fascinated with the mortals of Midgard since the days of the Vikings who worshiped him. After being banished there by Odin to learn humility, Thor has served as Midgard's champion — and as one of Earth's Mightiest Heroes, the Avengers. With many friends, allies and loved ones on Midgard — including his former girlfriend, Jane Foster — Thor has frequently seen his loyalties torn between the land of his birth and his adopted home.

THOR: GOD OF THUNDER #12 INTERIOR ART BY NIC KLEIN

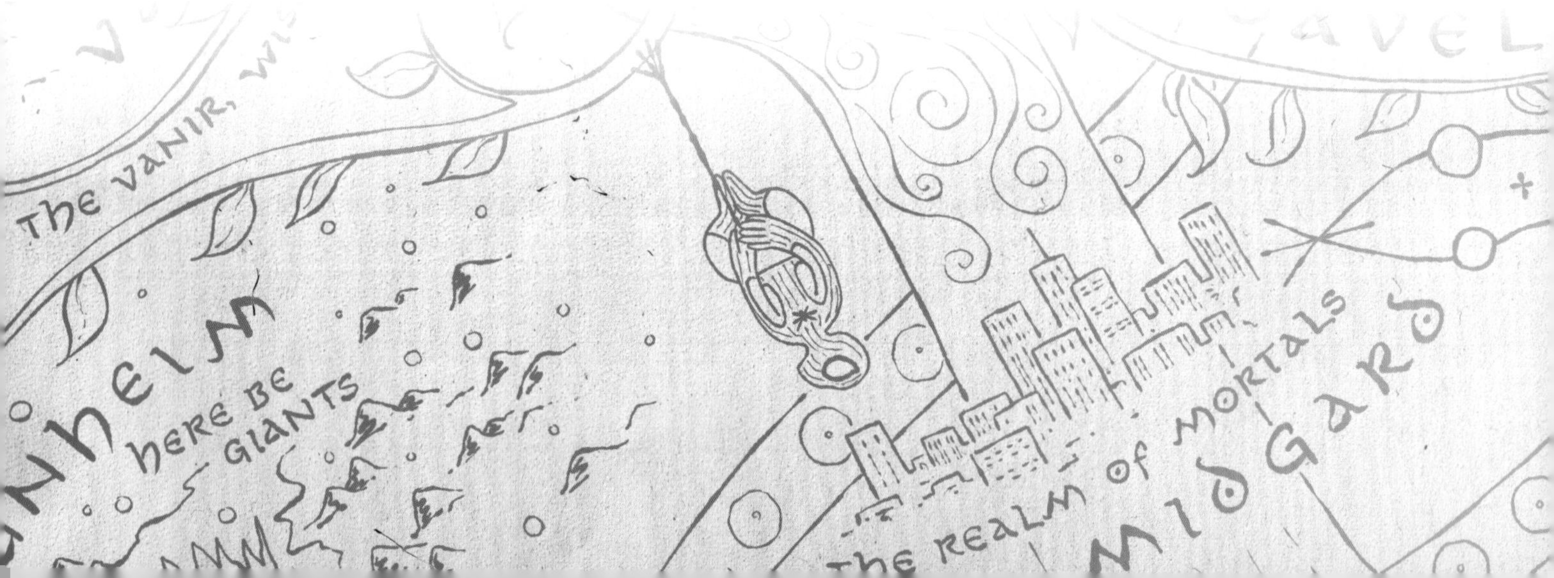
THE VANIR,
HERE BE GIANTS
THE REALM OF MORTALS
MIDGARD

ALFHEIM

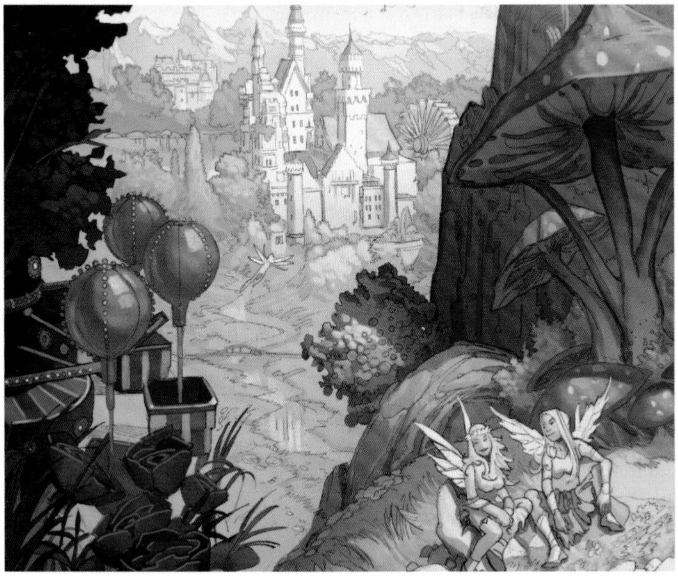

Alfheim is the realm of the Light Elves, a lush world high on Yggdrasil covered with lavish, flowery gardens. Ljosalfgard is the capital of this Faerie paradise, home to Ice Elves and Spice Elves, Air Elves in their wondrous flying machines, Sea Elves in their coral castles, triple-jointed Pleasure Elves, Elves of the Vale and Moon Elves all aglow with Firefly Wine. 'Tis a place of joy and otherworldly wonder.

***THOR: GOD OF THUNDER* #15** INTERIOR ART BY RON GARNEY AND IVE SVORCINA

JOTUNHEIM

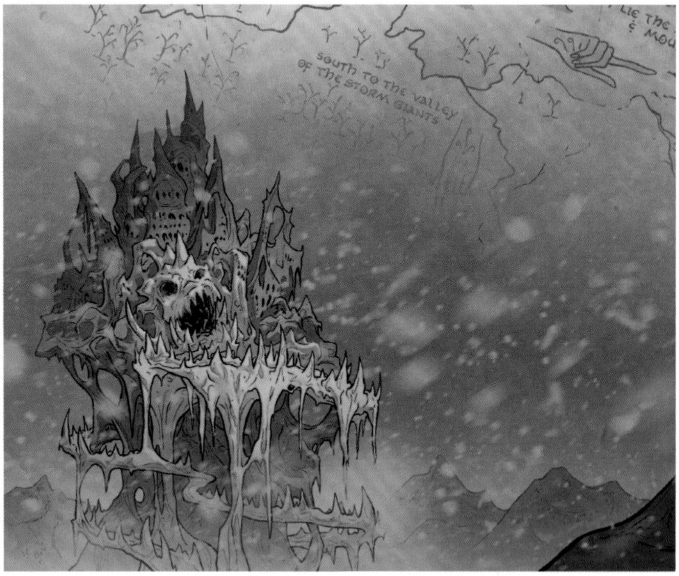
South to the valley of the Storm Giants

Here be giants. Much of Jotunheim is dominated by the frozen tundra that is home to the fearsome Frost Giants, including their icy stronghold of Utgard. But there's also the valley of the Storm Giants and the muddy peaks of the Mountain Giants. Prior to his death centuries ago, the Frost Giants were ruled by King Laufey, great enemy of Odin and father of Loki.

***THOR (2014)* #3** INTERIOR ART BY RUSSELL DAUTERMAN AND MATTHEW WILSON

SVARTALFHEIM

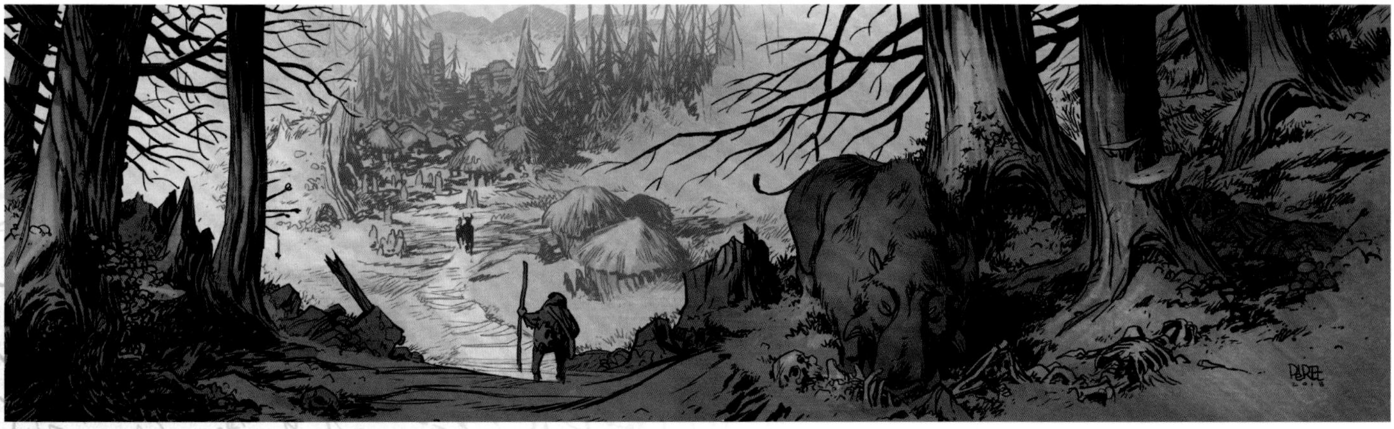

Where Alfheim is a realm of peace high on the World Tree, Svartalfheim — home of the Dark Elves — is one of war, lying low in Yggdrasil's roots. This swampy domain — dripping ooze, covered with thorns and fungus — is where a young Malekith, forged by battle and filled with bloodlust, rose to become a powerful sorcerer and king.

***MIGHTY THOR: AT THE GATES OF VALHALLA* #1** INTERIOR ART BY RAMÓN PÉREZ AND MATTHEW WILSON

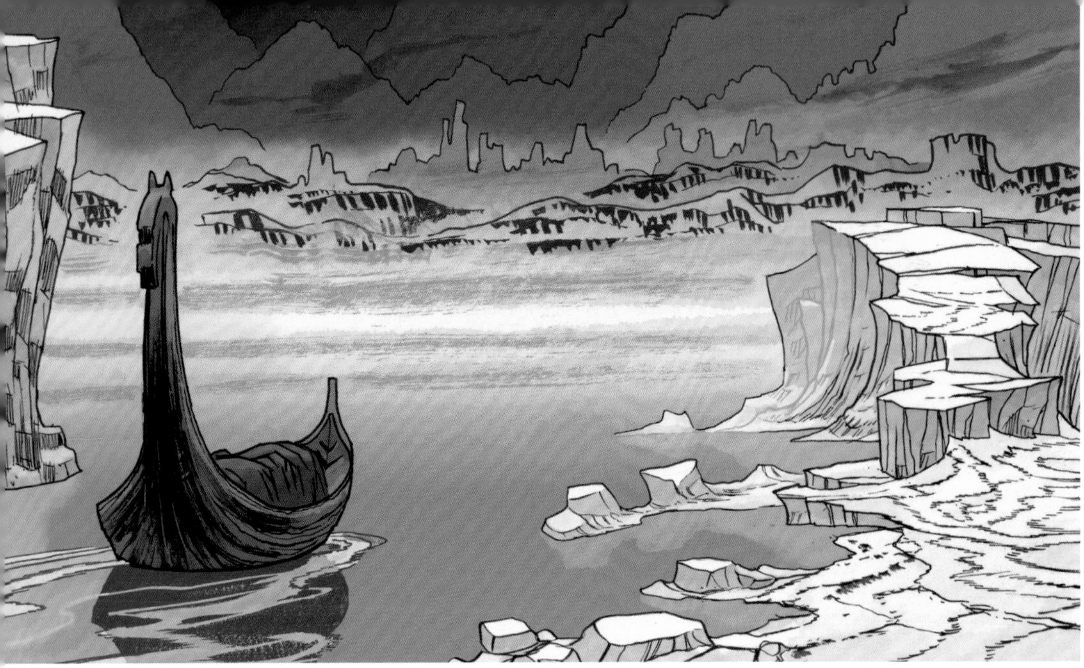

NIFFLEHEIM

Low on the World Tree is the frozen underworld of Niffleheim — where sits Hel, kingdom of the dead, and the Hall of Nastrond, eternal prison for the most fearsome of dishonored souls. But hidden within Niffleheim also lies Valhalla, land of the honored dead, whose location is known only to the All-Father and his Valkyries.

MIGHTY THOR* (2015) *#701 INTERIOR ART BY JAMES HARREN AND DAVE STEWART

VANAHEIM

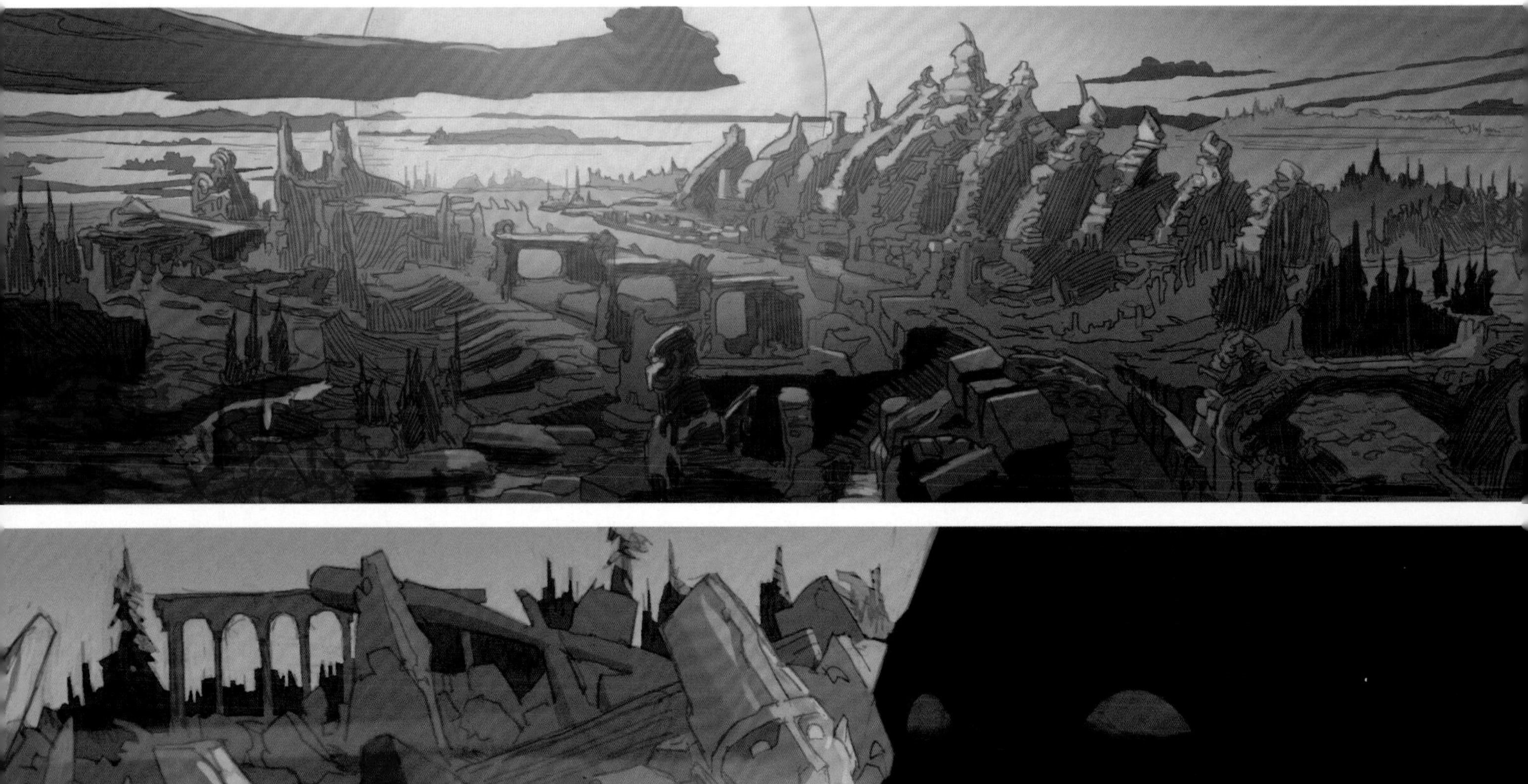

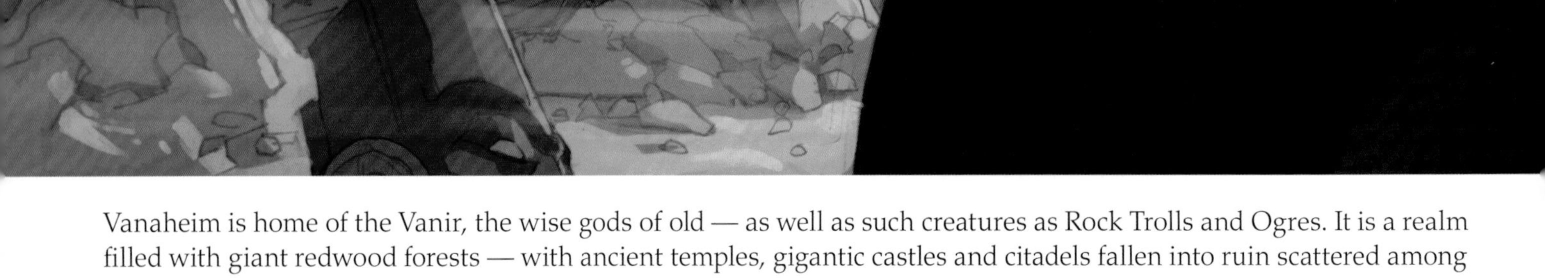

Vanaheim is home of the Vanir, the wise gods of old — as well as such creatures as Rock Trolls and Ogres. It is a realm filled with giant redwood forests — with ancient temples, gigantic castles and citadels fallen into ruin scattered among them. Long ago, the marriage of Odin and Freyja secured a union between the gods of the Aesir and the Vanir.

THOR: GOD OF THUNDER #16 INTERIOR ART BY RON GARNEY AND IVE SVORCINA

MUSPELHEIM

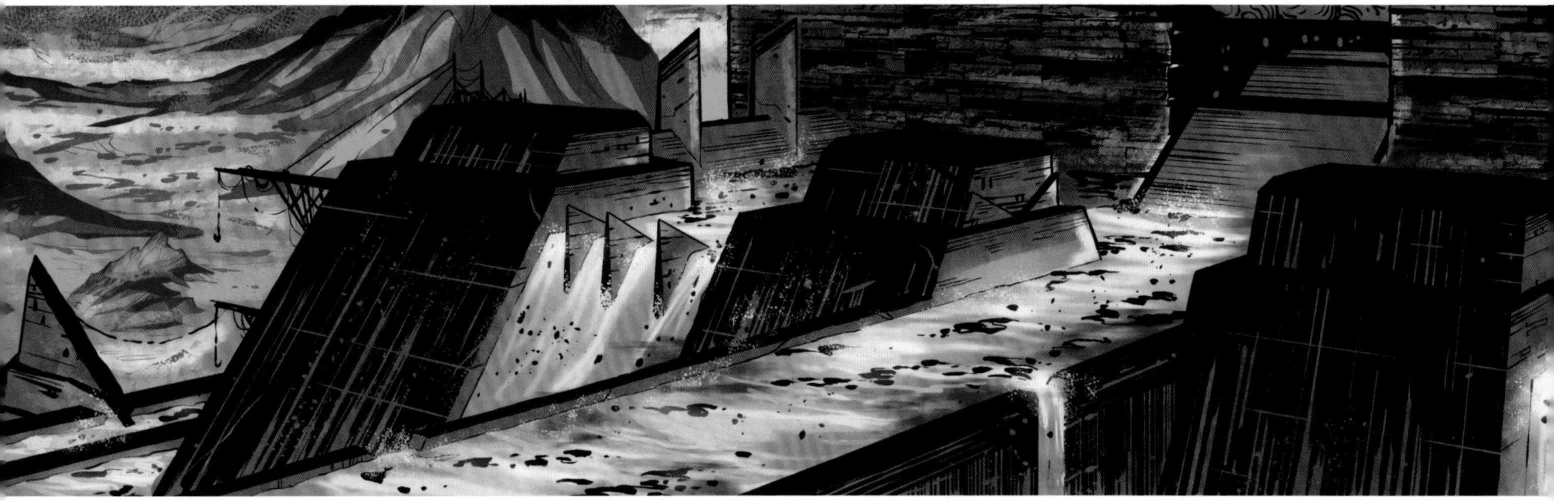

Muspelheim is where fire was born. It is a world of eternal flames and volcanos and rivers of lava, once ruled by Surtur — home to the fearsome Fire Goblins. Soon, in these pages, you will meet its new Queen.

MIGHTY THOR (2015) #22 INTERIOR ART BY VALERIO SCHITI AND VERONICA GANDINI

NIDAVELLIR

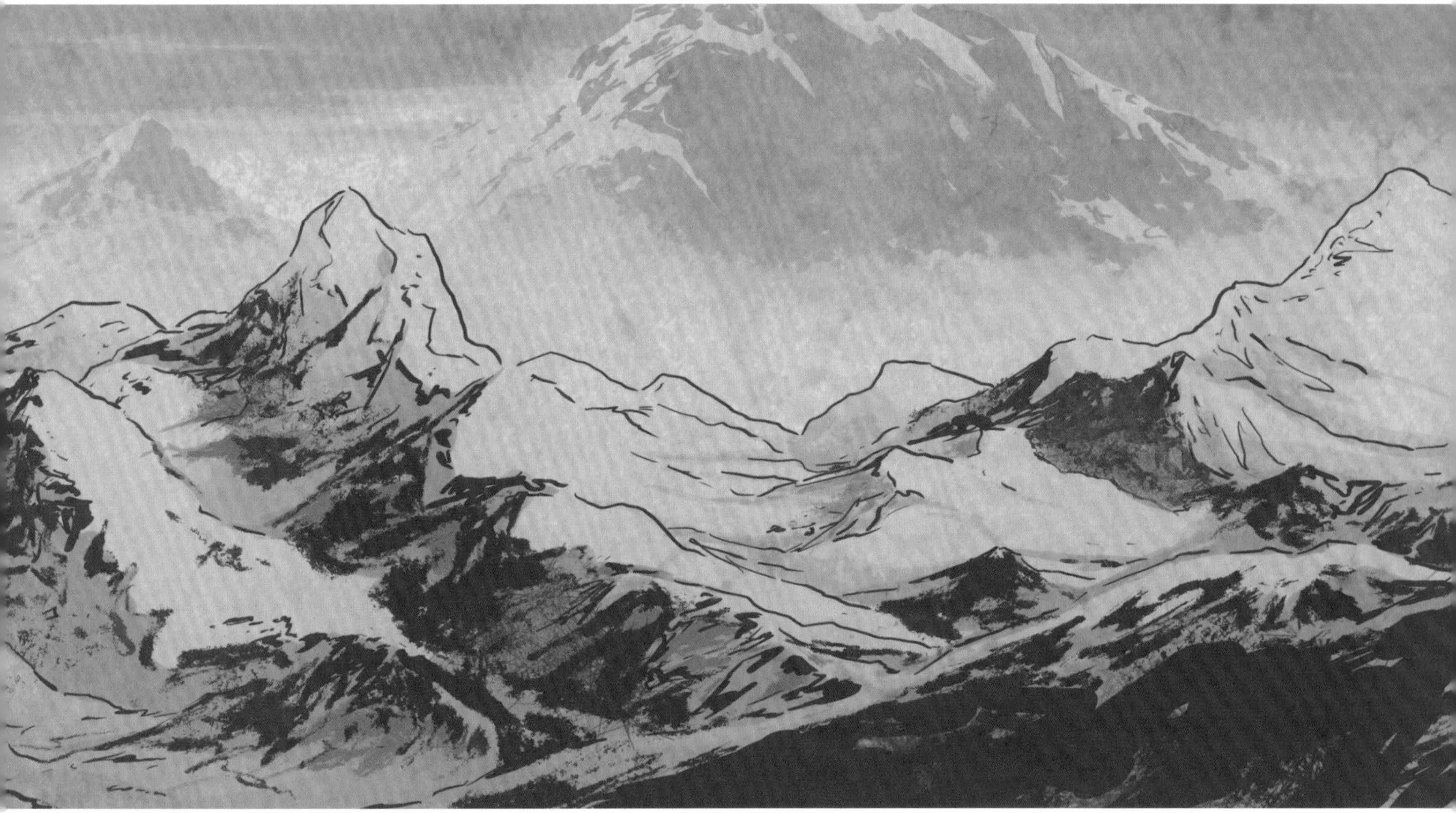

Nidavellir is the misty, mountainous land of the Dwarves, who craft the most powerful weapons in all the realms, including Mjolnir itself. It is a realm of caves and mines and epic mountains, with Hreidmar's Hol as its great cave capital.

MIGHTY THOR (2015) #13 INTERIOR ART BY STEVE EPTING AND FRANK MARTIN

HEVEN

In the 2014 series *Original Sin*, written by Jason Aaron, many of Marvel's heroes are rocked by world-changing secrets courtesy of super villain the Orb, wielding an eye stolen from the murdered Watcher. For Thor, the stunning revelation is that he has a sister. Not only that, the Thunder God learns, but "the ***foundation***, the very ***structure*** of the cosmos is a ***lie***." There is a tenth realm!

In the pages of the five-issue *Original Sin #5.1-5.5* — plotted by Aaron and Al Ewing, and scripted by Ewing — Thor seeks the truth…and learns of the realm of Heven, which long ago went to war with Asgard. The Queen of the Angels of Heven abducted the child of Odin and Freyja, named Aldrif,

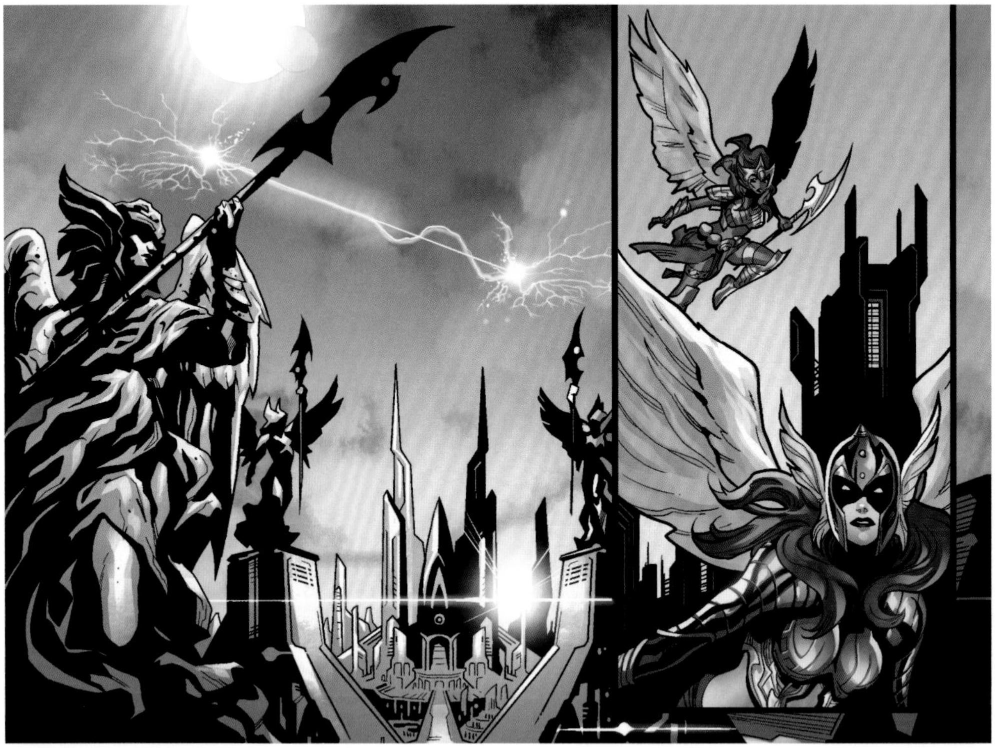

ABOVE: THE GLORY OF HEVEN!
MIGHTY THOR (2015) #23 INTERIOR ART BY VALERIO SCHITI AND RAIN BEREDO

BELOW: THOR AND LOKI ARRIVE IN THE TENTH REALM.
ORIGINAL SIN #5.1 INTERIOR ART BY SIMONE BIANCHI

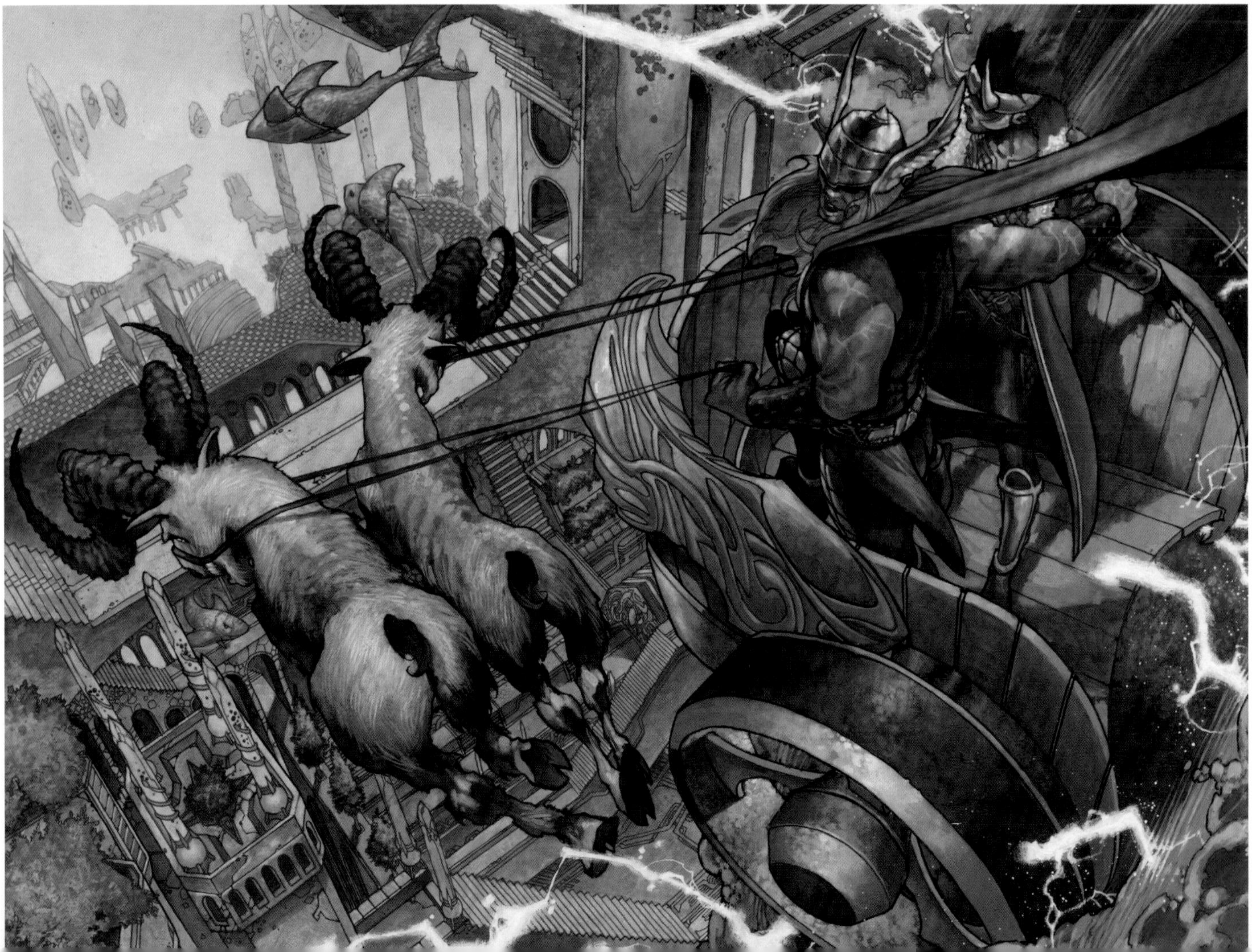

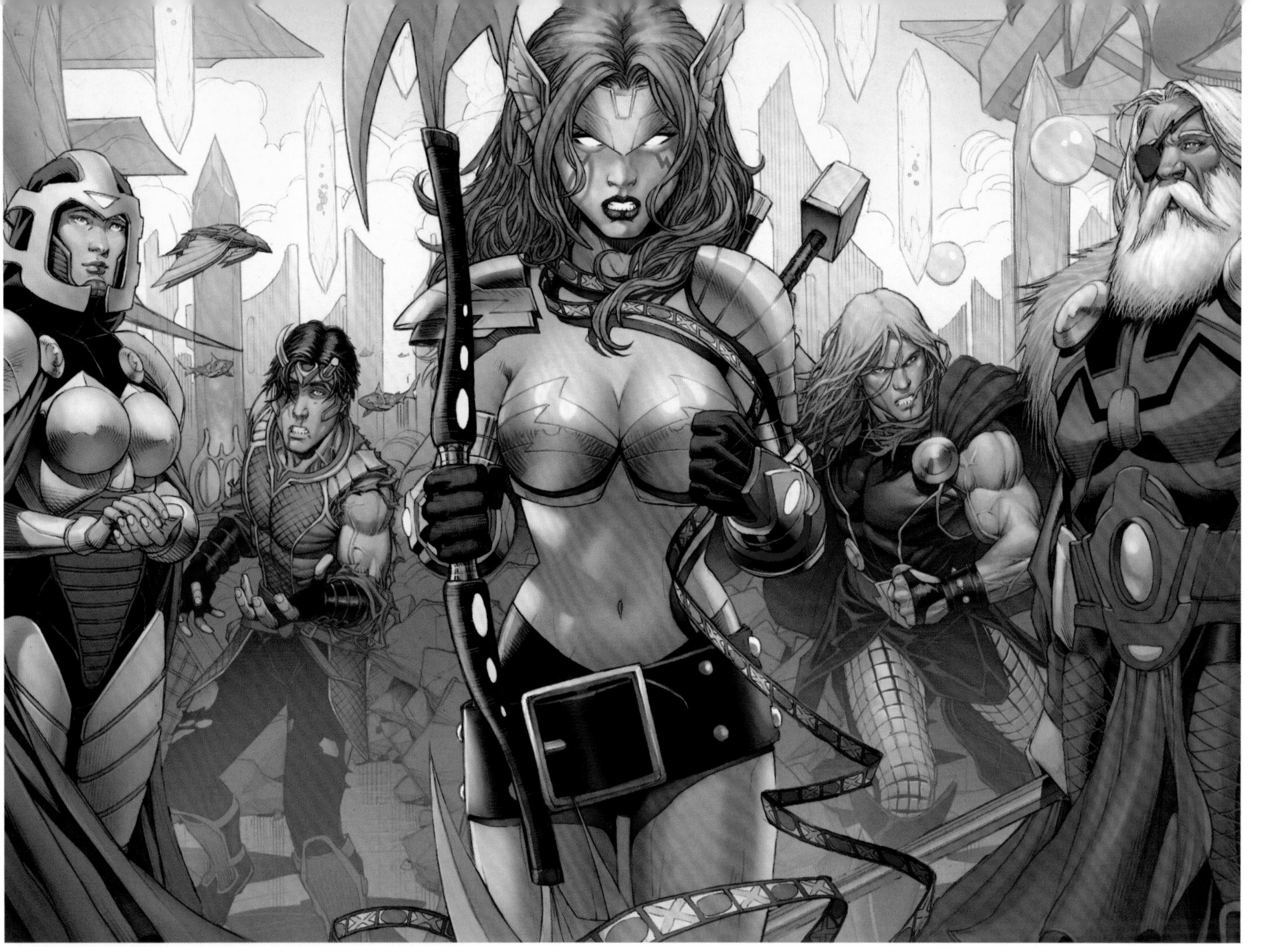

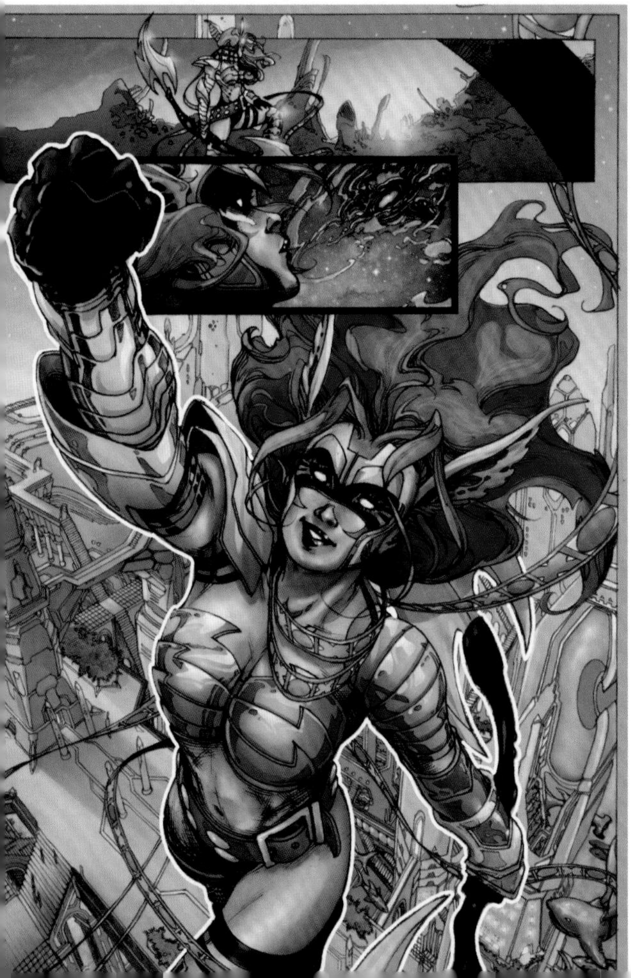

and seemingly slew her — leading the furious All-Father to exact his revenge. Odin tore Heven loose from the other realms — from the roots of Yggdrasil itself — and sealed it away, hidden far from sight and memory, wiped from Asgardian legends like a stain. A mournful Freyja still believes her daughter dead, but, thanks to the Orb, Thor knows different. Loki's magic enables him and Thor to take the ultimate journey into mystery, into the space beyond and on to Heven — the world they were never supposed to know existed!

There, Thor battles Angela, Hunt-Leader of the Angelic Armies — until her true identity is revealed…by none other than Odin! She is Thor's sister — and after she discovers the truth, she is cast out of Heven by its queen. Thor and Loki's adventure has won them a sister who, though filled with rage for now, may one day be an ally — and brought them an unexpected reunion with their father, who now returns to Asgardia. But it has also opened the door to a world filled with furious warrior Angels, who are destined to play a major part in the unfolding War of the Realms.

FOLLOWING A DIFFICULT FAMILY REUNION, ANGELA SEEKS HER DESTINY IN THE STARS.

ABOVE: *ORIGINAL SIN* #*5.1* AND #*5.2* INTERLOCKING COVERS BY DALE KEOWN AND JASON KEITH

LEFT: *ORIGINAL SIN* #*5.5* INTERIOR ART BY SIMONE BIANCHI

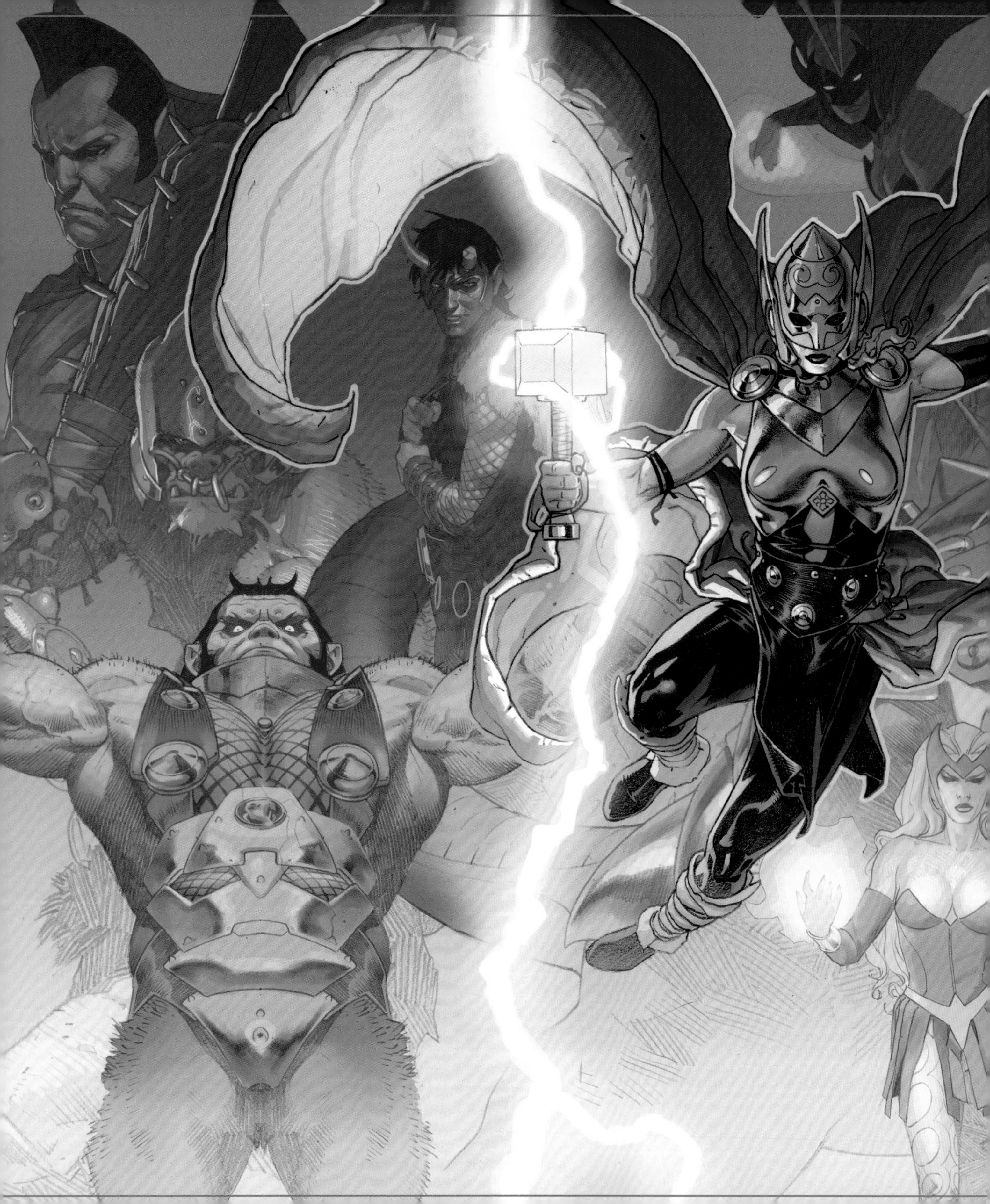

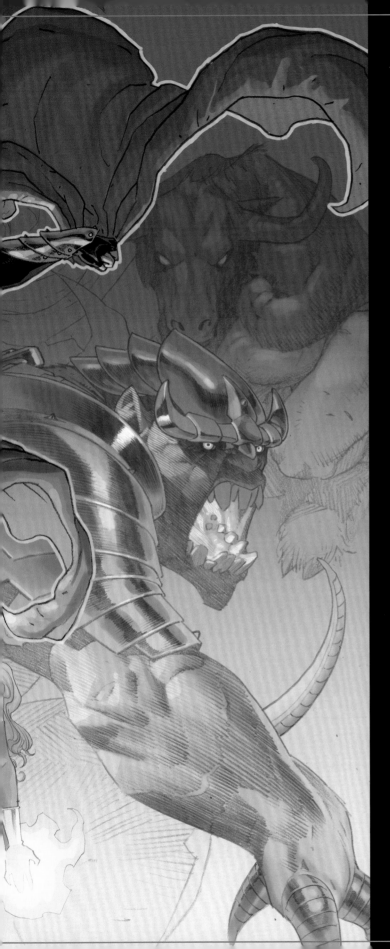

CHAPTER FIVE

WHO IS THOR?

"THERE MUST ALWAYS BE A THOR."
— THOR

"There are elements to Thor that you have to have. There was back and forth about whether she should have armor, and I decided to put that half-armor on her just to differentiate her. I added another cape around her waist so she has two capes. You cannot believe how helpful it is for the Thor character to have a cape, because that gives you physics — it helps you to express the movement or the wind. Her helmet was actually inspired by Viking helmets in existence. I have a history book that has one on the cover, so I used that helmet as a template."

— ESAD RIBIĆ

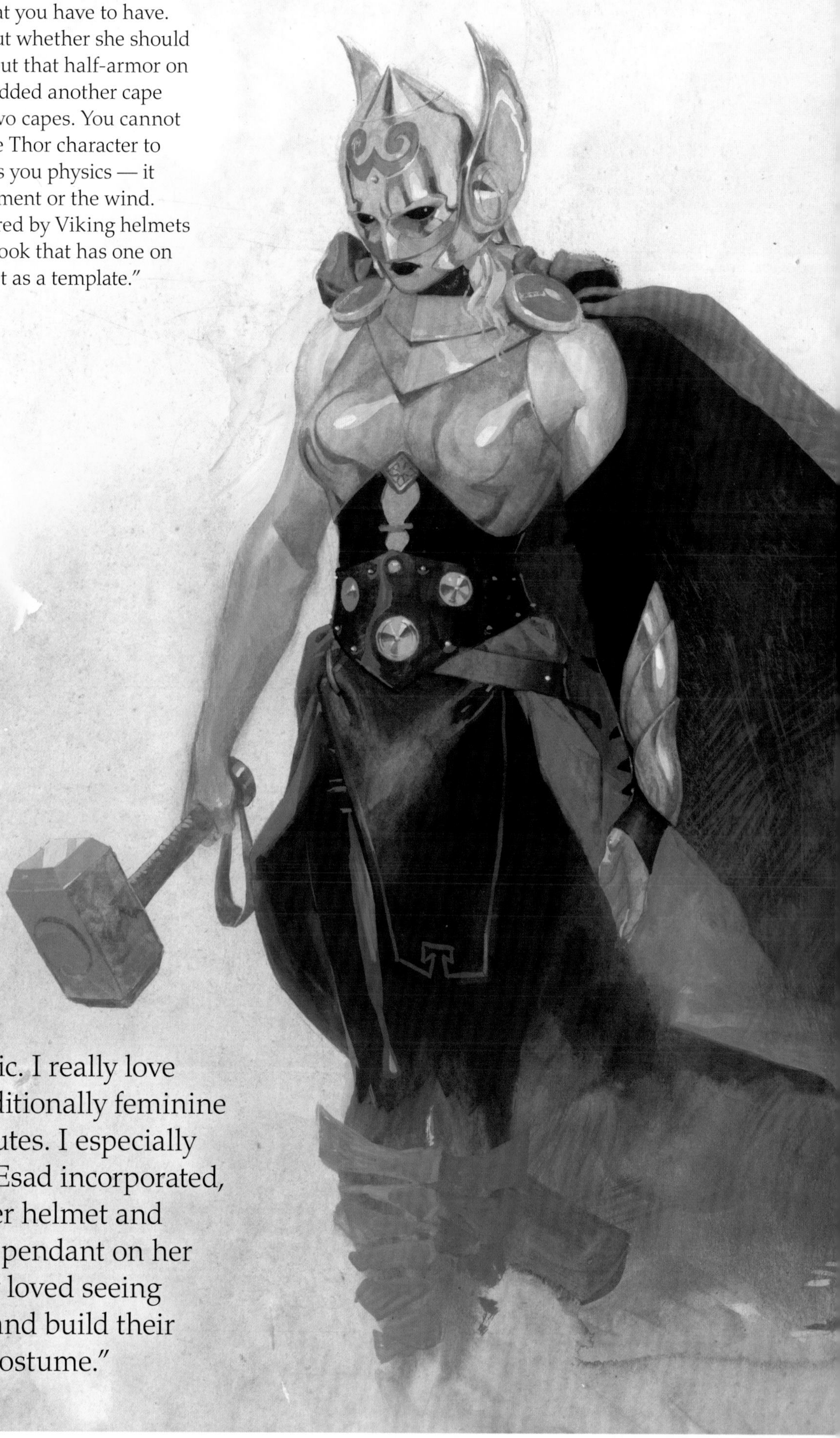

"Esad's design is terrific. I really love how it is a mix of traditionally feminine and masculine attributes. I especially love the little details Esad incorporated, like the symbol on her helmet and the diamond-shaped pendant on her chest plate. I've really loved seeing people cosplay Thor and build their own versions of her costume."

— RUSSELL DAUTERMAN

The impact of *Original Sin* was not limited to the revelations regarding Heven and Angela. In the series' climactic battle on the moon, Nick Fury — with the knowledge of the Watcher — whispers into Thor's ear…and renders him no longer worthy to wield Mjolnir!

Jason Aaron admits events lined up nicely: Marvel was looking to relaunch *Thor*, and this *Original Sin* twist offered a "great opportunity to change gears."

"I knew that Nick Fury had become imbued with the knowledge and wisdom of a Watcher," Aaron says. "In the midst of that fight, I needed him to be able to take Thor off the table. And I thought it was way more interesting to bring him down with a whisper, which again dives deep into that idea of worthiness. Fury whispers in his ear, and the main question is, 'What did he whisper?' I learned a lesson when I did *Punisher*. At one point when Bullseye whispers something to Frank that freaks him out, I wrote the actual dialogue in the script — we just printed it really tiny. It wasn't so tiny that people couldn't magnify it. I didn't want to make that mistake again, so Fury's whisper is actually just gibberish — even though, at the time, I knew what he said."

It would be some time before anyone else would learn the words Fury spoke.

With Mjolnir lying on the moon, someone needs to step forward to be Midgard's protector — especially when Malekith leads an army of Frost Giants in an assault on Earth to reclaim the skull of King Laufey, recently discovered by Roxxon!

Step forward someone does, and so a new Thor is born — this time, a Goddess of Thunder. But who is she, really? The guessing game continued for eight issues of *Thor*. Particularly keen to solve the mystery, the now-unworthy Odinson considers an array of candidates including Roz Solomon, Angela, the Enchantress and even his own mother, Freyja. He wasn't the only one, as the new female Thor quickly became a sensation.

"I was surprised by the whole thing," Aaron says. "The positive response, the negative response, how big it became… You don't ever expect any of that stuff, especially as I'd been on the book for a few years. The mystery at the time — who was this new Thor? — was a lot of fun to play with. To me, the story we did speaks directly to a core piece of Thor's mythology, going back to his first appearance in *Journey into Mystery* #83 — that first story where a doctor goes into a cave and picks up this hammer and becomes Thor. It's a very cool part of that character's mythology that doesn't always get addressed. Having someone new come along, pick up that hammer and be transformed by it, and then to follow them for a prolonged period of time, was something I was very interested in doing and, to me, in every way a Thor story."

Though he had departed as the series artist for the relaunch, Esad Ribić delivered what Aaron believes was the perfect design for the new title character. "Esad's design is the one piece of his original art I've got on my wall," Aaron says. "We wanted her to be Thor. We wanted people to look at her and think Thor. We also wanted something that covered her face to speak to the mystery of her identity."

Taking the baton from Ribić was a young artist named Russell Dauterman. And in doing so, he began a highly successful, career-making creative partnership with Aaron that, five years later, continues with *War of the Realms*.

"Working with Russell was a huge highlight," Aaron says. "Following Esad on that book gave him big shoes to fill. Before Esad you had Olivier Coipel — two gargantuan artists who had defined Thor for a long period of time. And Russell was pretty new when he got that gig. [Editor] Wil Moss called him the week he got married — he was on his honeymoon and he got the call to say, 'Hey, do you want to draw *Thor*?' But he was in every way the perfect choice. One of his strengths is how great he's been at designing all the other characters. We really ramped up starting to explore those other realms, bringing in tons of new characters and reimagining old characters. It's not just the way he draws Thor in action, which is awesome, but how great he is at the world-building part of it."

OPPOSITE: *THOR (2014)* #1 DESIGN VARIANT COVER BY ESAD RIBIĆ

PREVIOUS PAGES: *THOR: GOD OF THUNDER* #25 INTERIOR ART BY ESAD RIBIĆ AND IVE SVORCINA

"This is the first drawing I ever did of the female Thor: a layout for what became the *Thor #1* cover. Originally, this was just supposed to be a variant cover, and I didn't even have the job of drawing the interiors. I had just finished my third issue of *Cyclops*, and was about to leave for my honeymoon, when *Thor* editor Wil Moss emailed me to ask about doing the variant. I said I was interested and asked if we could talk more when I got back from my trip. Within a week of being back, I was off *Cyclops* and on *Thor*. The *Thor #1* cover is really special to me and is still one of my favorites from the series."

— RUSSELL DAUTERMAN

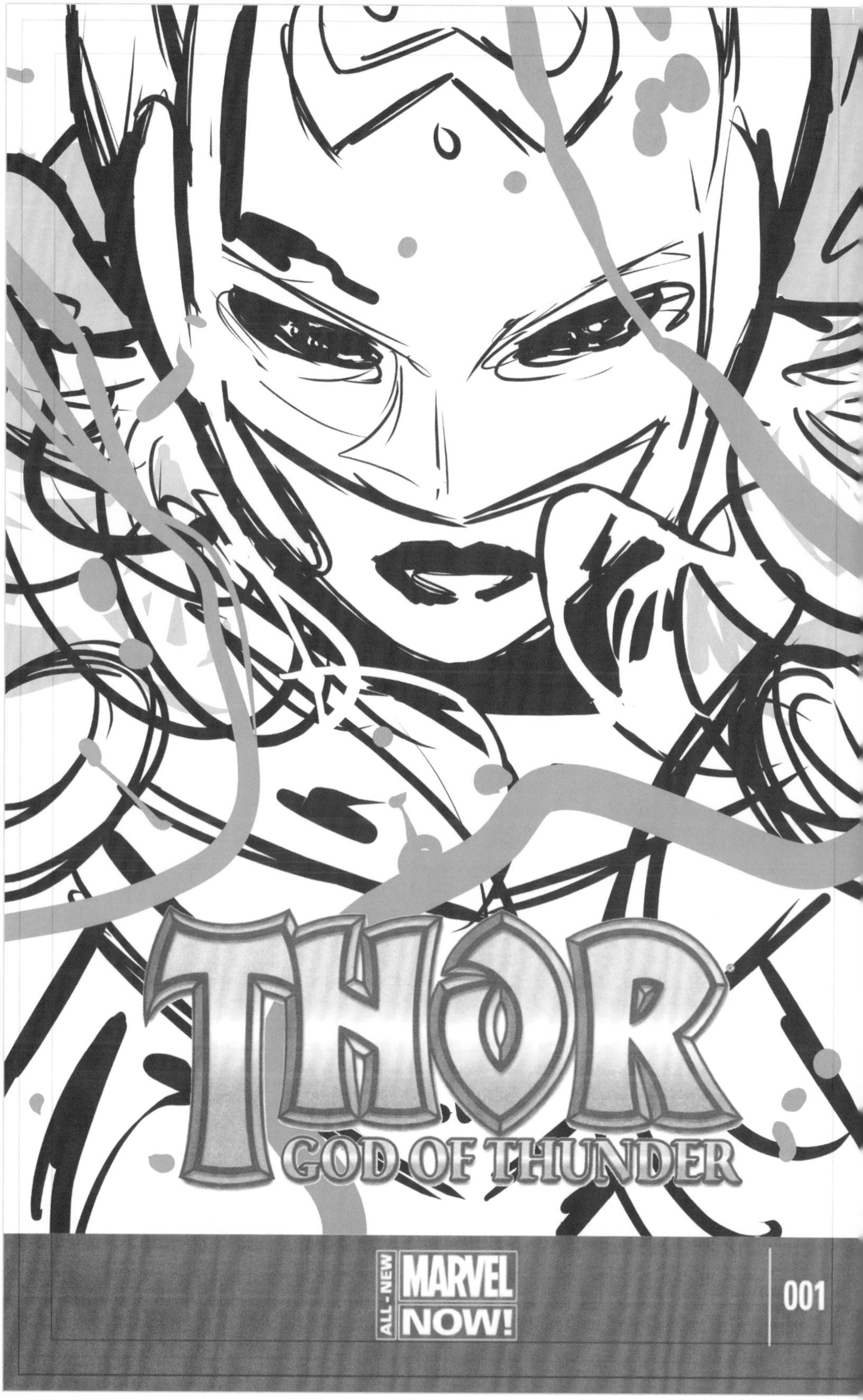
THOR
GOD OF THUNDER
ALL-NEW MARVEL NOW!
001

ABOVE AND OPPOSITE: *THOR (2014) #1* COVER ROUGH BY RUSSELL DAUTERMAN, AND FINAL ART BY DAUTERMAN AND FRANK MARTIN

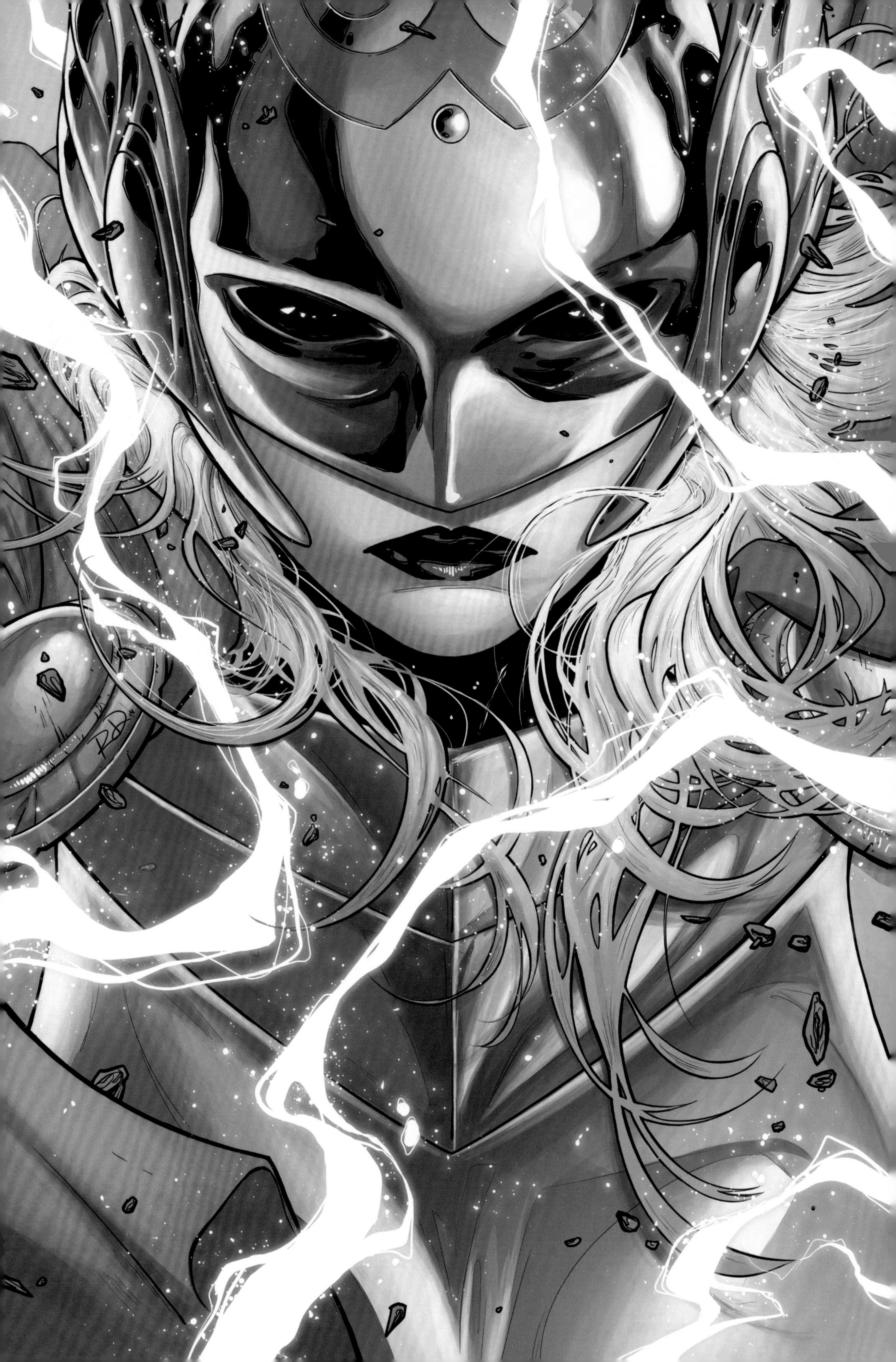

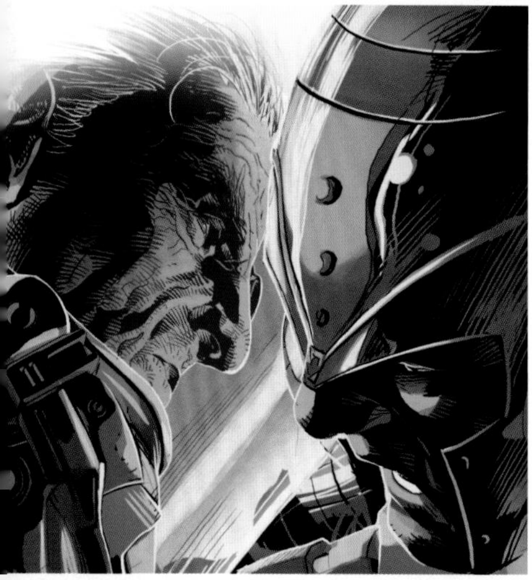

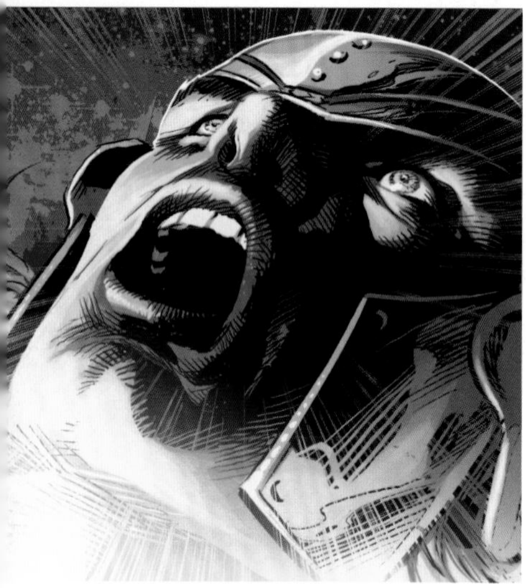

THOR IS DEFEATED WITH A WHISPER AND LEFT UNWORTHY TO LIFT MJOLNIR.

ABOVE: *ORIGINAL SIN* #7-8 INTERIOR ART BY MIKE DEODATO JR. AND FRANK MARTIN

RIGHT AND BELOW: *THOR (2014)* #1 INTERIOR ART BY RUSSELL DAUTERMAN AND MATTHEW WILSON

OPPOSITE: *THOR: GOD OF THUNDER* #25 INTERIOR ART BY ESAD RIBIĆ AND IVE SVORCINA

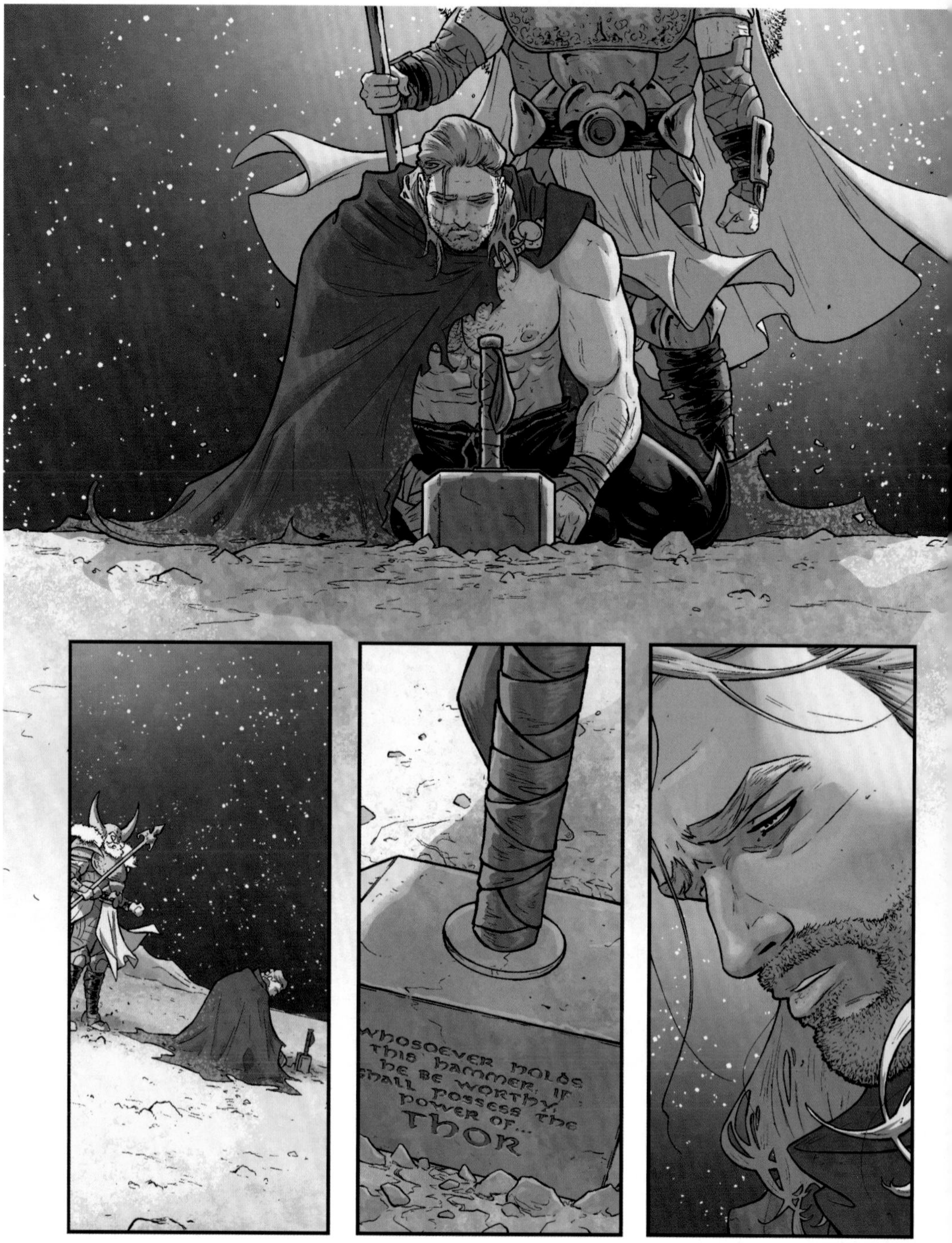
WHOSOEVER HOLDS THIS HAMMER, IF HE BE WORTHY, SHALL POSSESS THE POWER OF... THOR

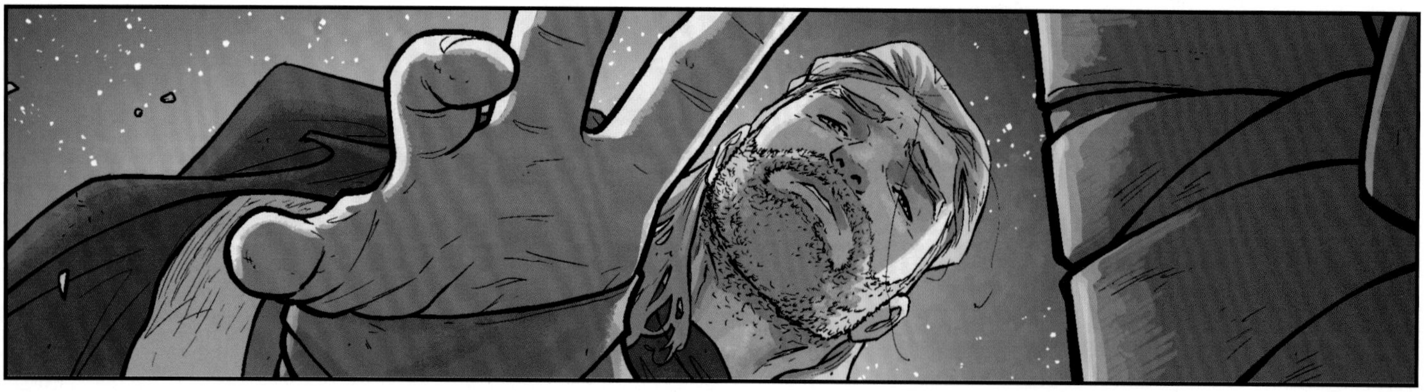

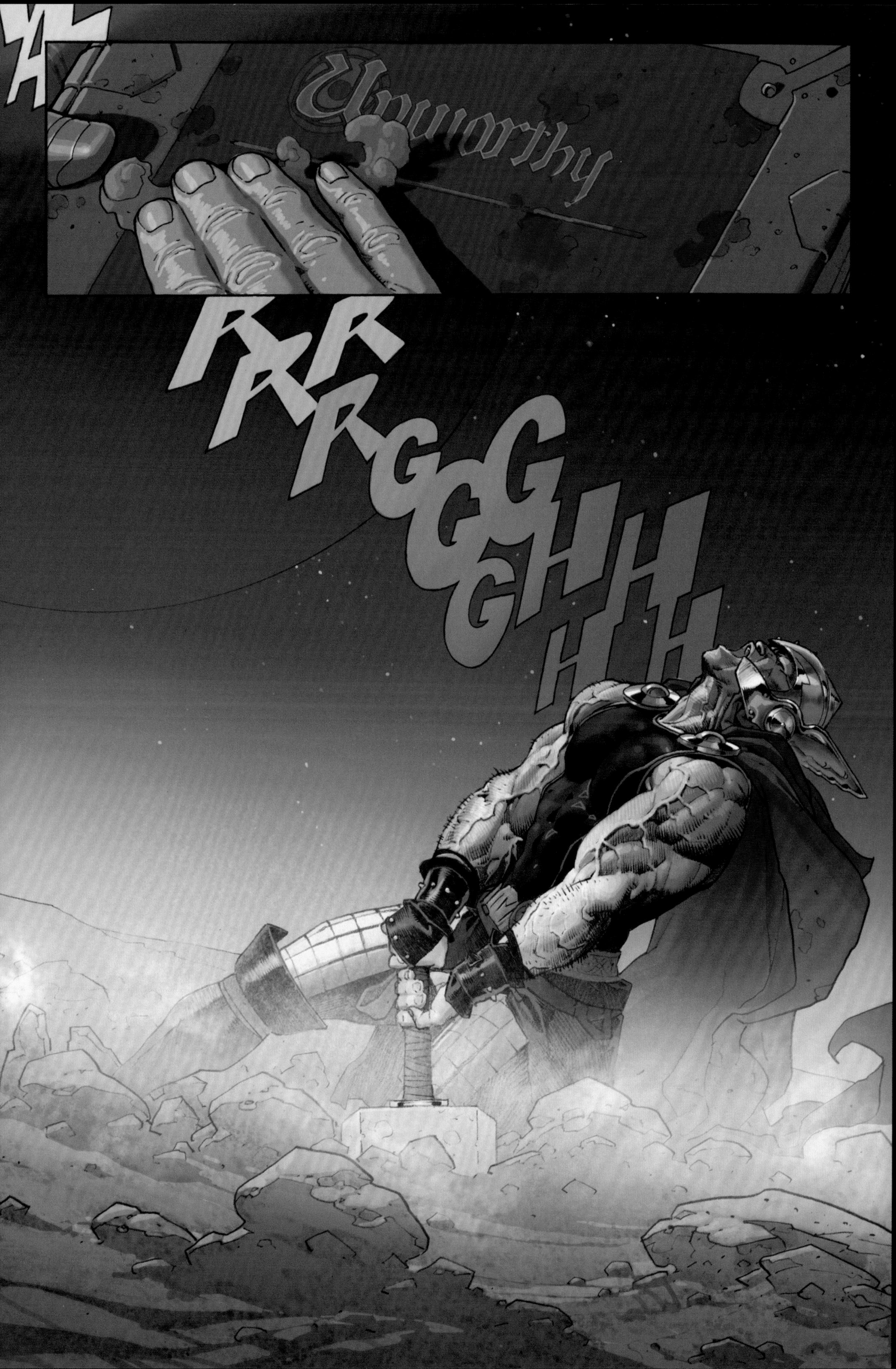
Unworthy
RRRGGGGHHHH

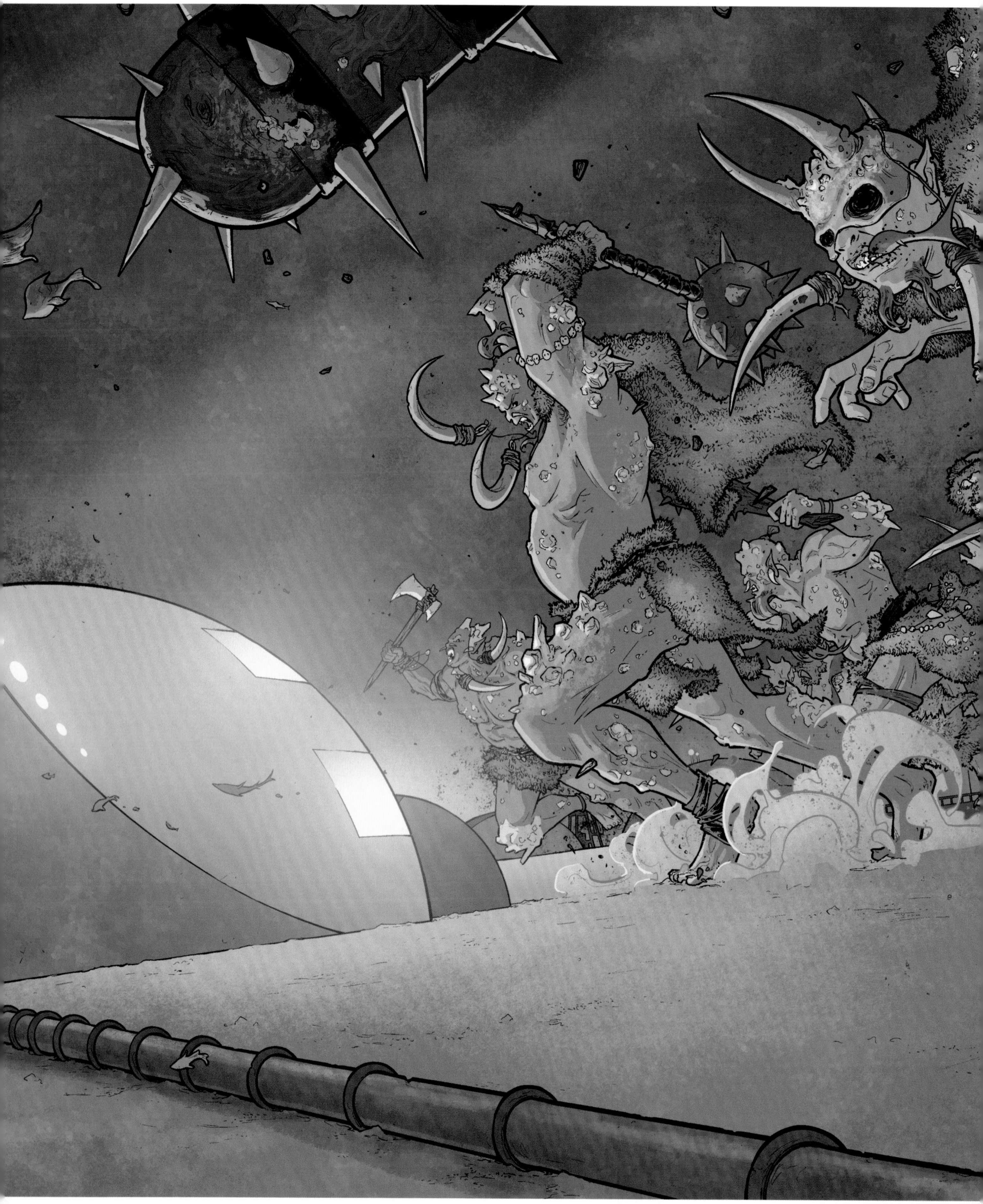

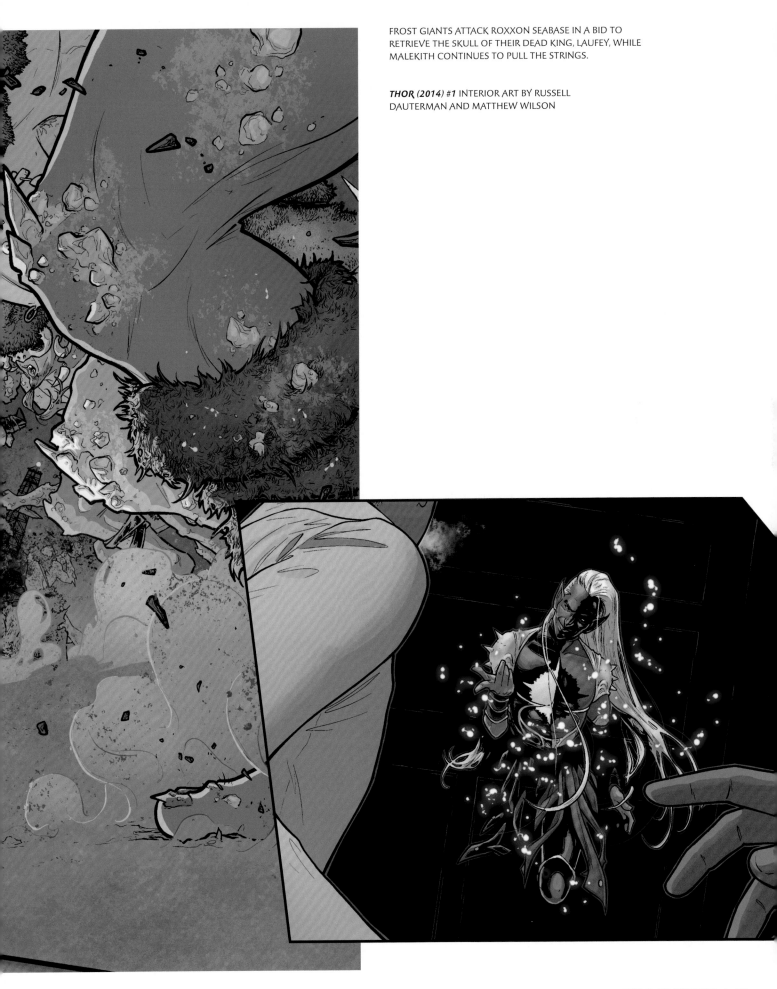

FROST GIANTS ATTACK ROXXON SEABASE IN A BID TO RETRIEVE THE SKULL OF THEIR DEAD KING, LAUFEY, WHILE MALEKITH CONTINUES TO PULL THE STRINGS.

THOR (2014) #1 INTERIOR ART BY RUSSELL DAUTERMAN AND MATTHEW WILSON

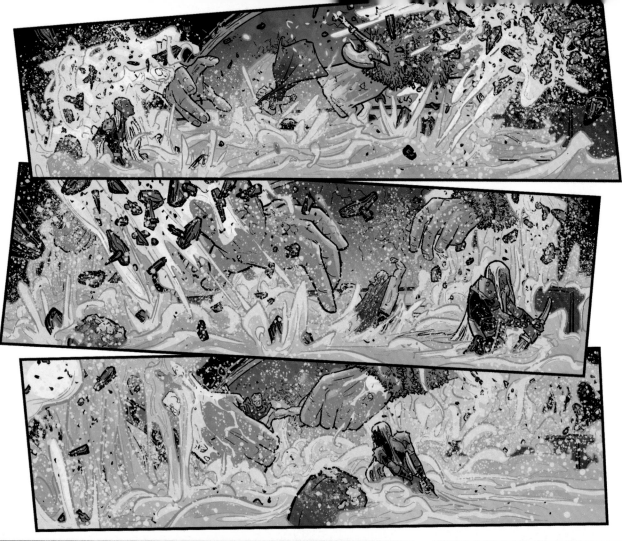

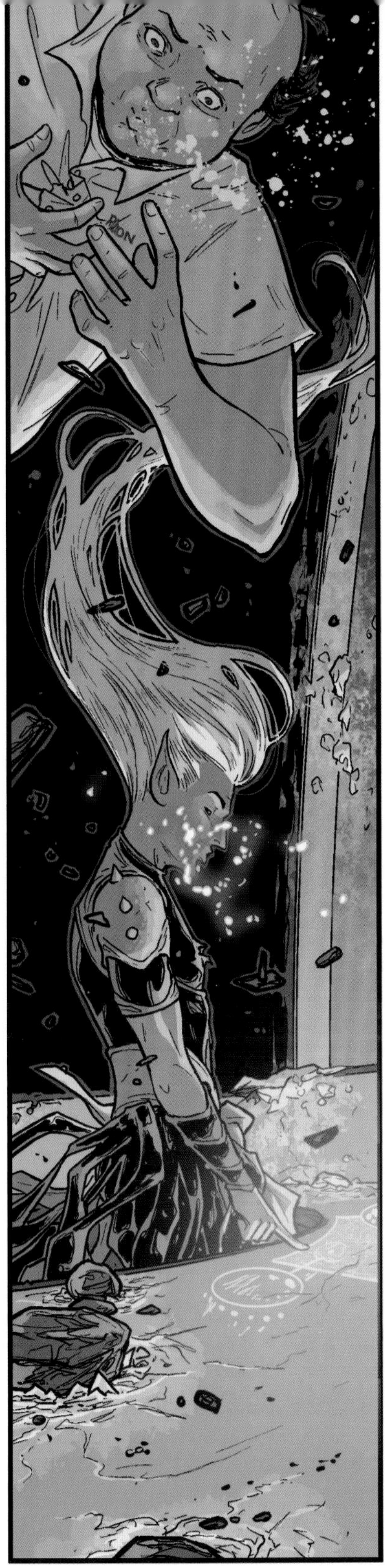

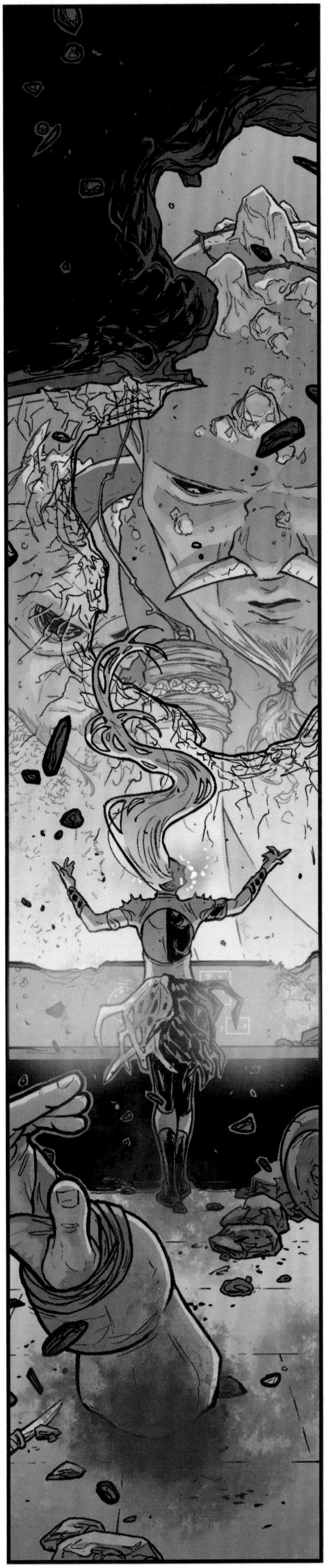

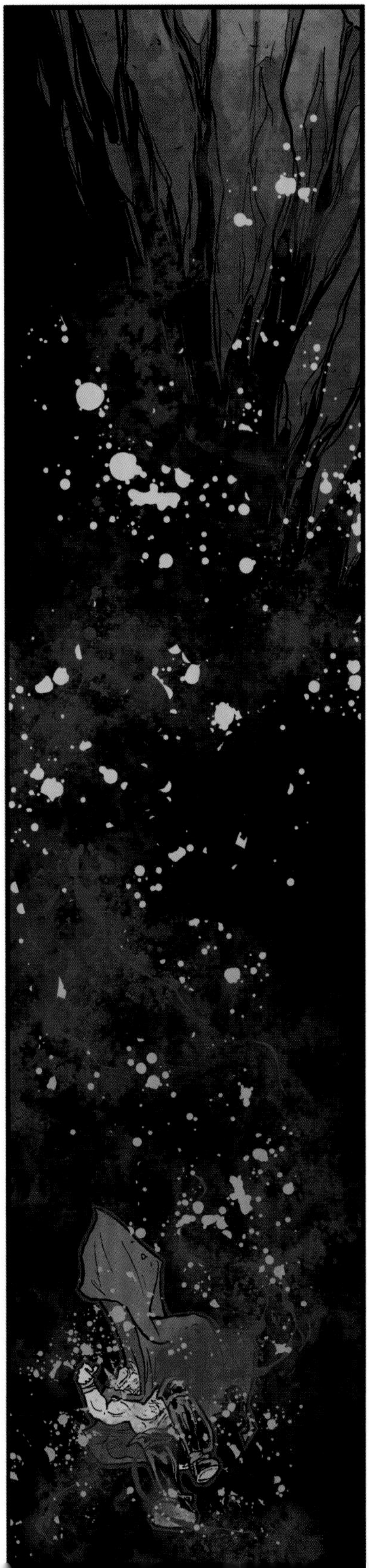

ADDING INSULT TO INJURY, MALEKITH BESTS A WEAKENED ODINSON IN BATTLE — AND TAKES HIS ARM!

THOR (2014) #1 INTERIOR ART BY RUSSELL DAUTERMAN AND MATTHEW WILSON

A NEW, WORTHY WIELDER CLAIMS THE HAMMER!

THOR (2014) #1
ART PROCESS BY RUSSELL DAUTERMAN AND MATTHEW WILSON

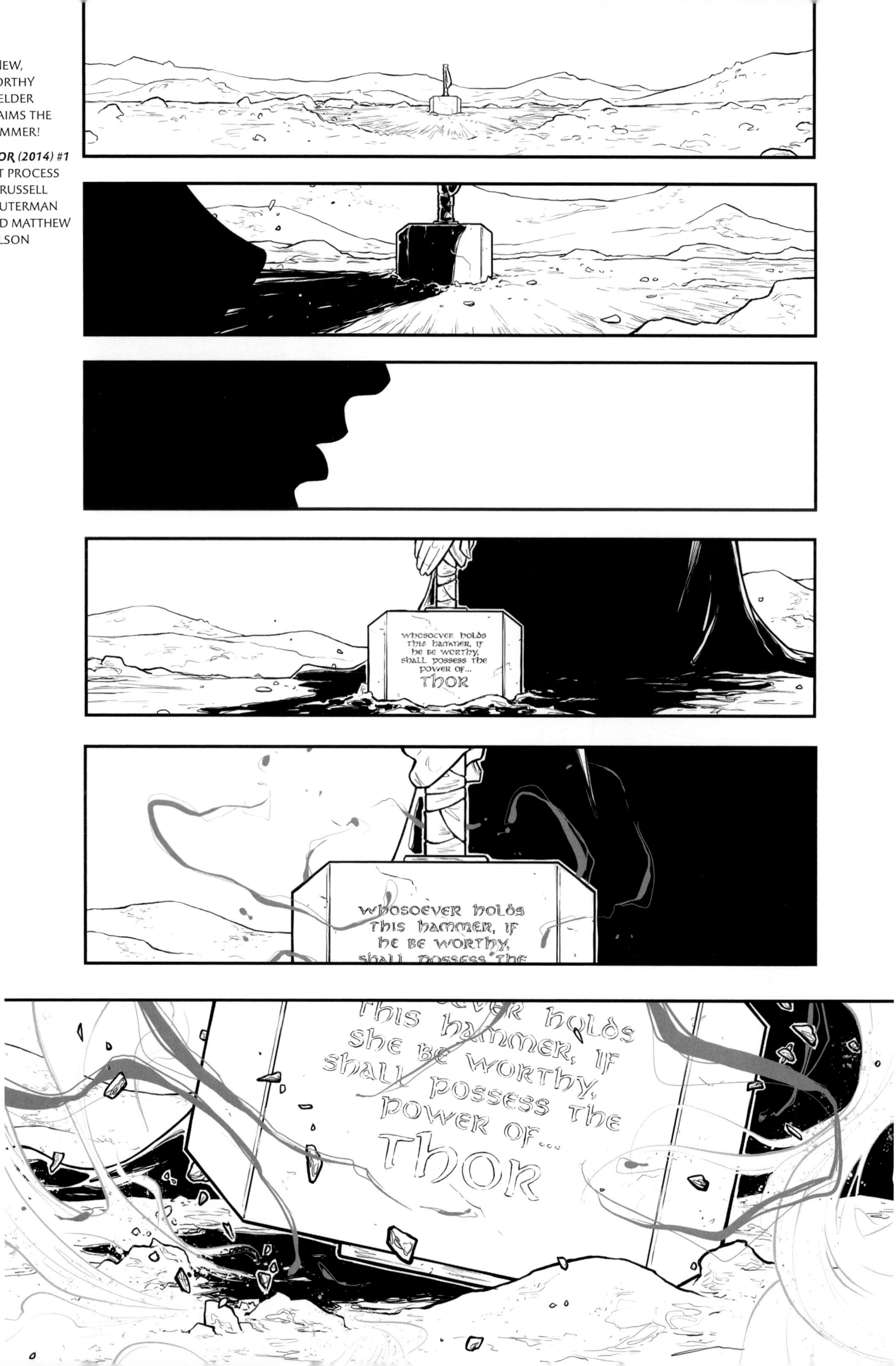
whosoever holds this hammer, if he be worthy, shall possess the power of... THOR
whosoever holds this hammer, if he be worthy,
this hammer, if she be worthy, shall possess the power of... THOR

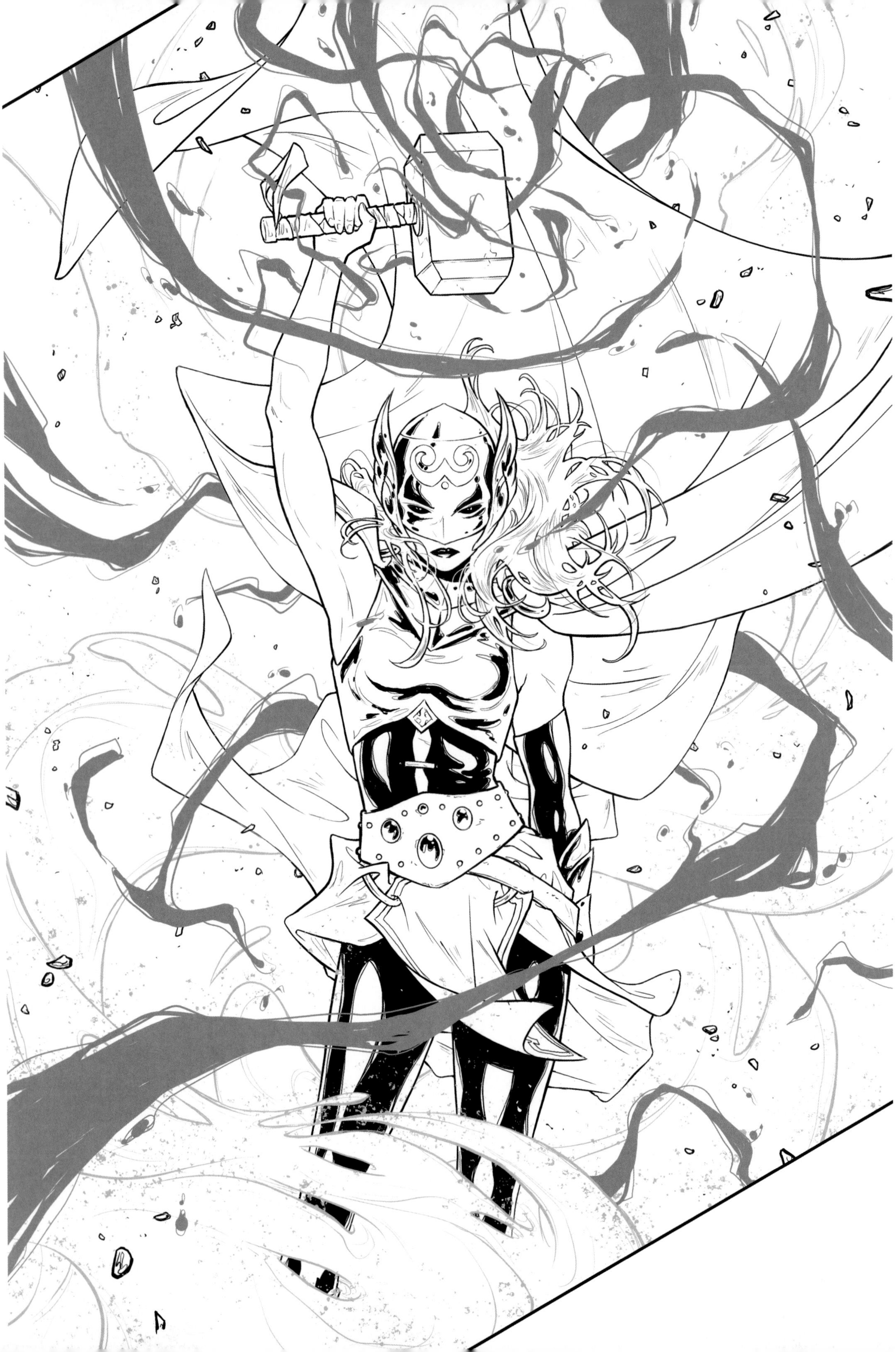

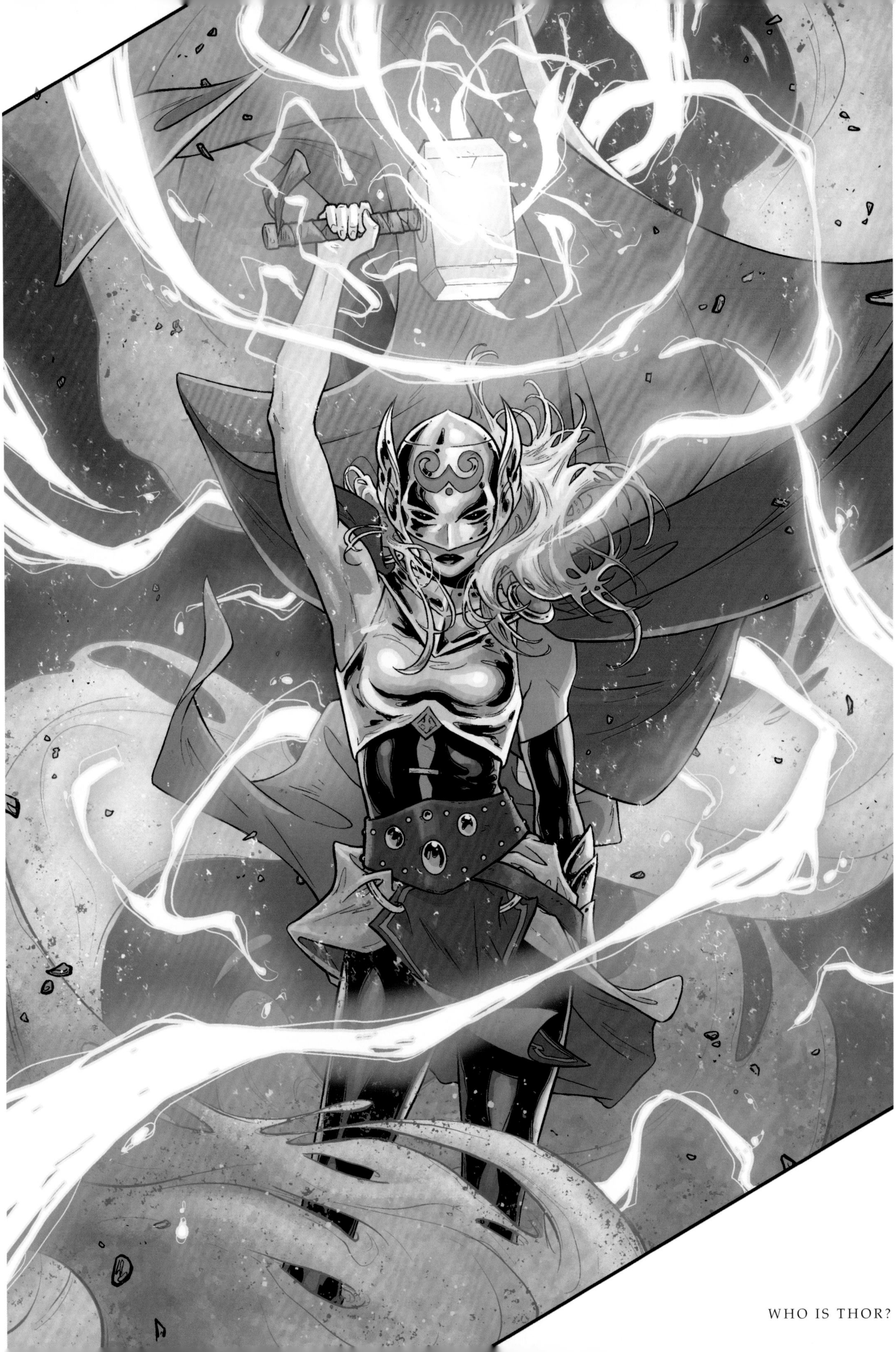

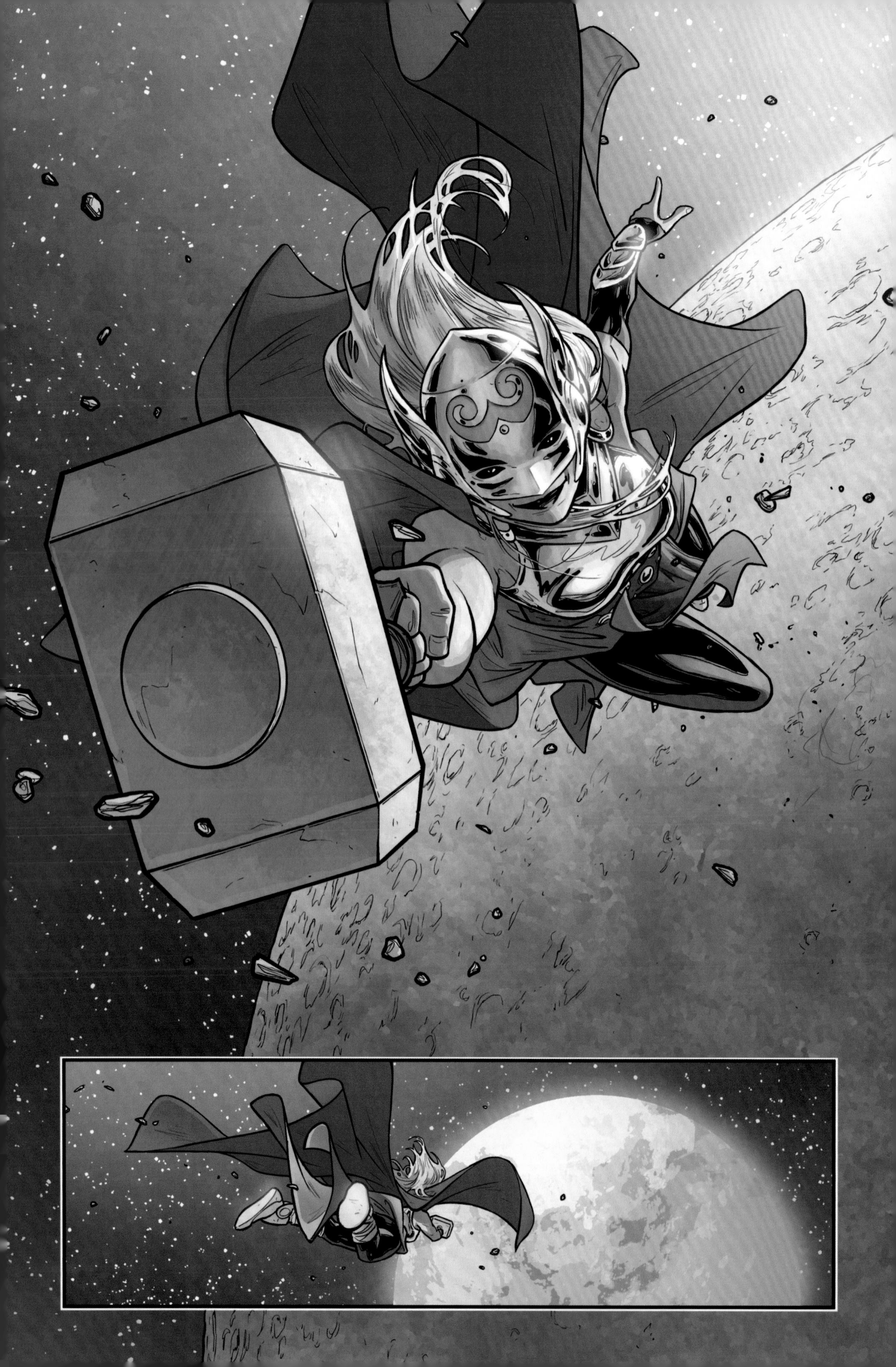

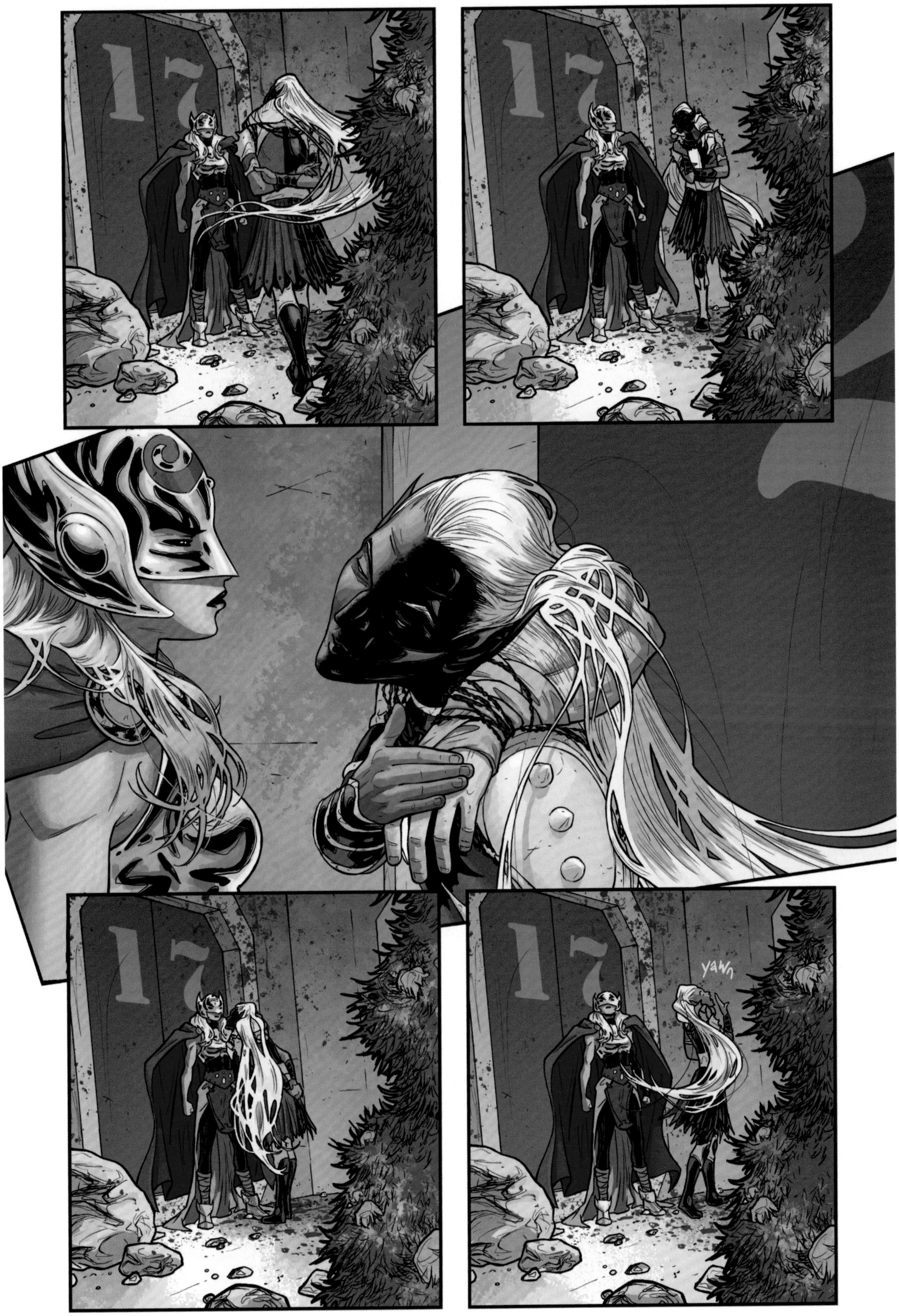
yawn

THE GODDESS OF THUNDER TAKES FLIGHT FOR THE FIRST TIME — AND MAKES A NEW ENEMY IN MALEKITH!

LEFT AND ABOVE: *THOR (2014) #2-3* INTERIOR ART BY RUSSELL DAUTERMAN AND MATTHEW WILSON

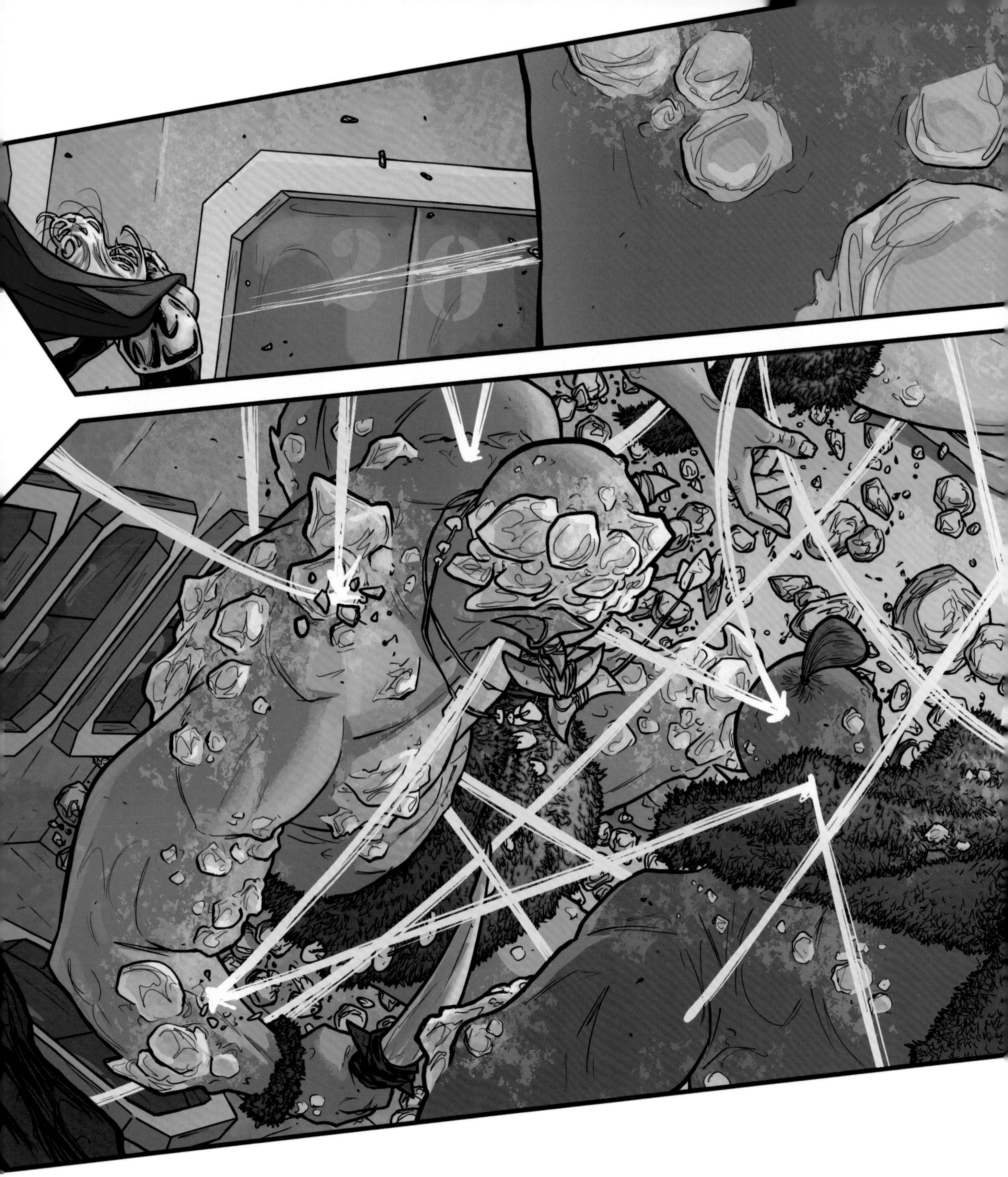

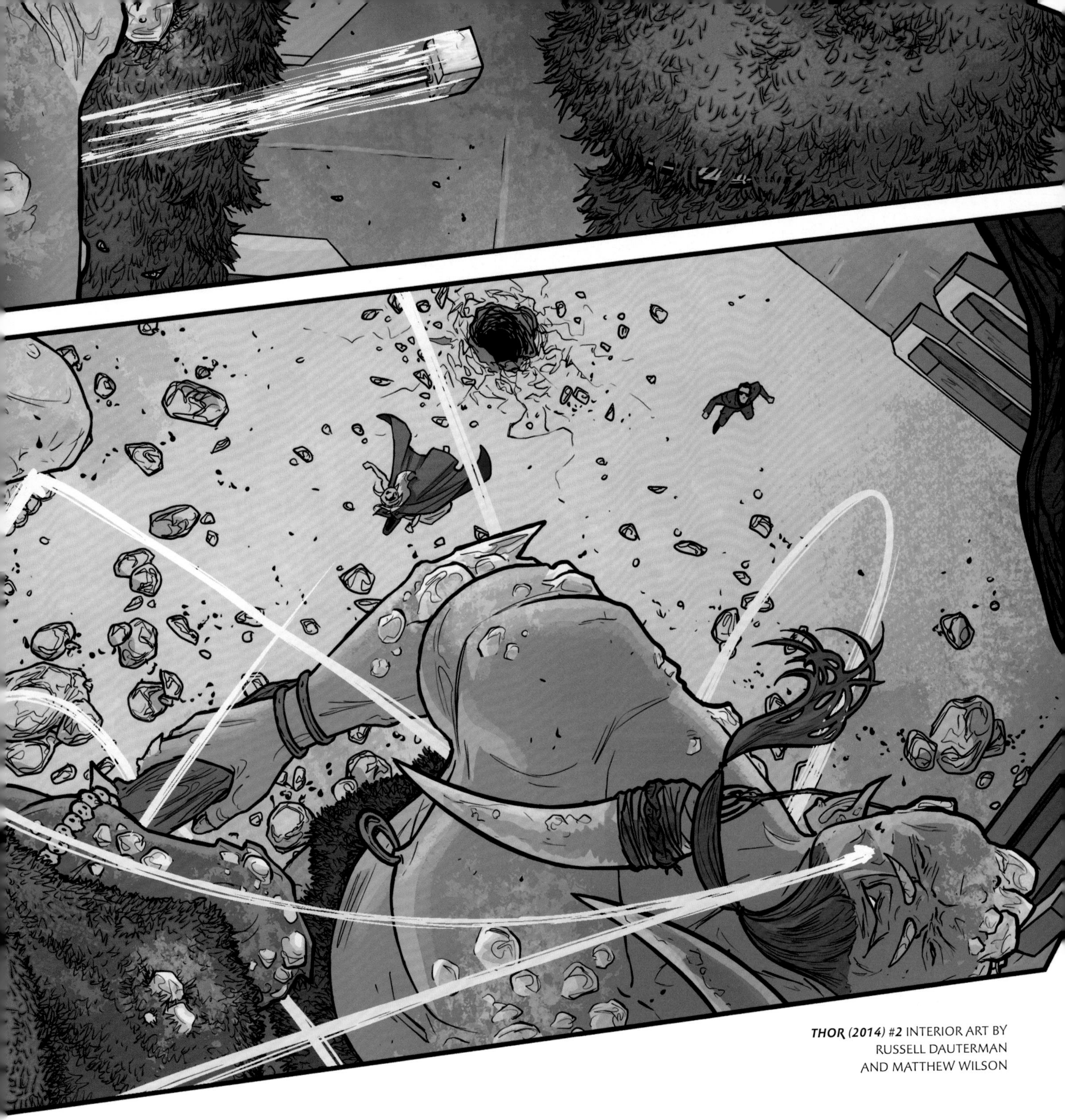

THOR (2014) #2 INTERIOR ART BY RUSSELL DAUTERMAN AND MATTHEW WILSON

"The way the hammer moves for the new Thor and reacts to her is very different. It builds up the idea of Mjolnir as a sentient being, which plays into when Thor Odinson couldn't pick it up, even Odin couldn't pick up the hammer. No one could but her. Clearly that idea of worthiness has gone beyond Odin's enchantment, and now it's almost like the hammer itself gets to choose. I really like that idea."

— JASON AARON

***THOR (2014)* #2** DESIGN VARIANT BY ESAD RIBIĆ

"The Unworthy Thor is just a stripped-down version. Half of his defining props are missing, and that is basically it."
— ESAD RIBIĆ

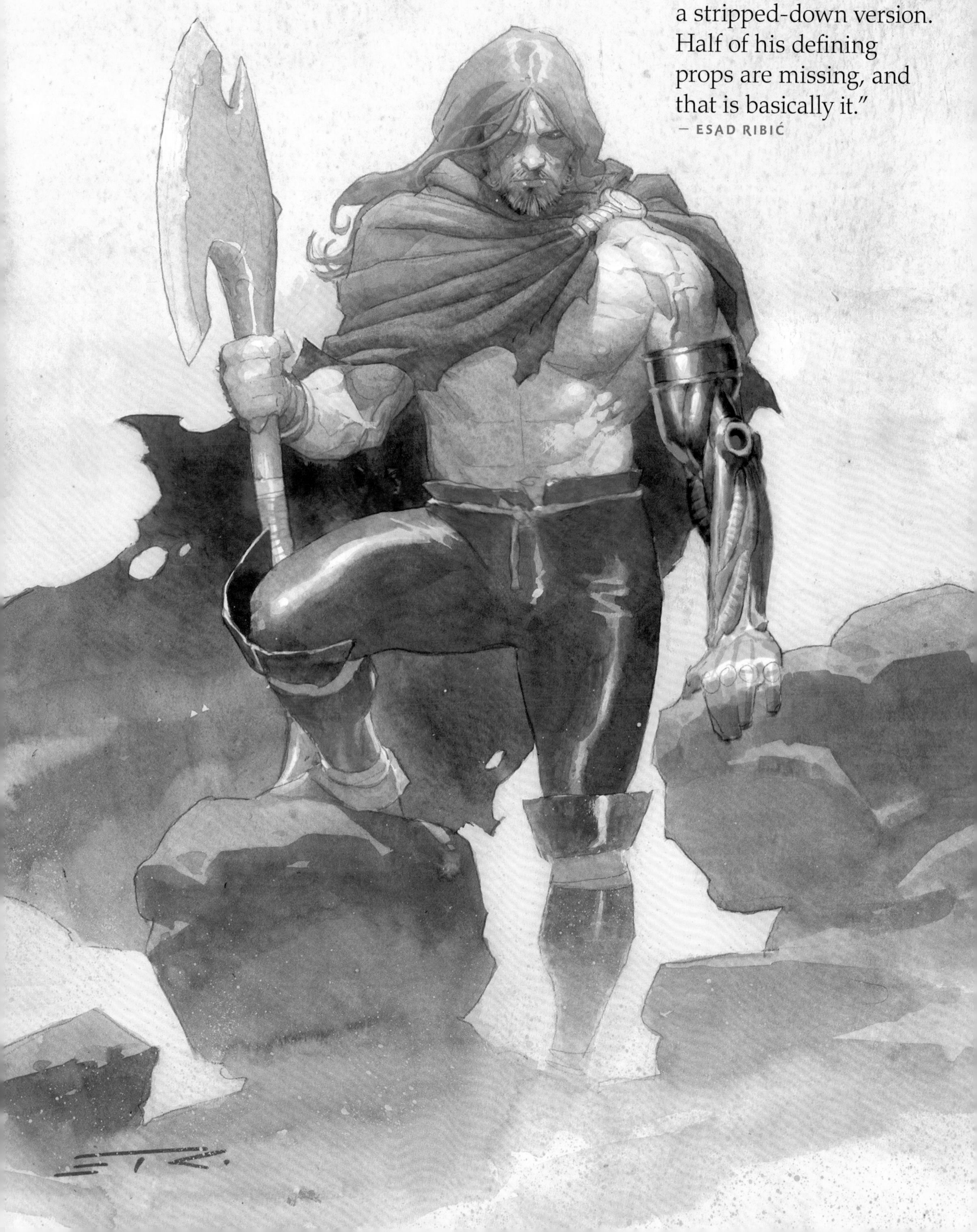

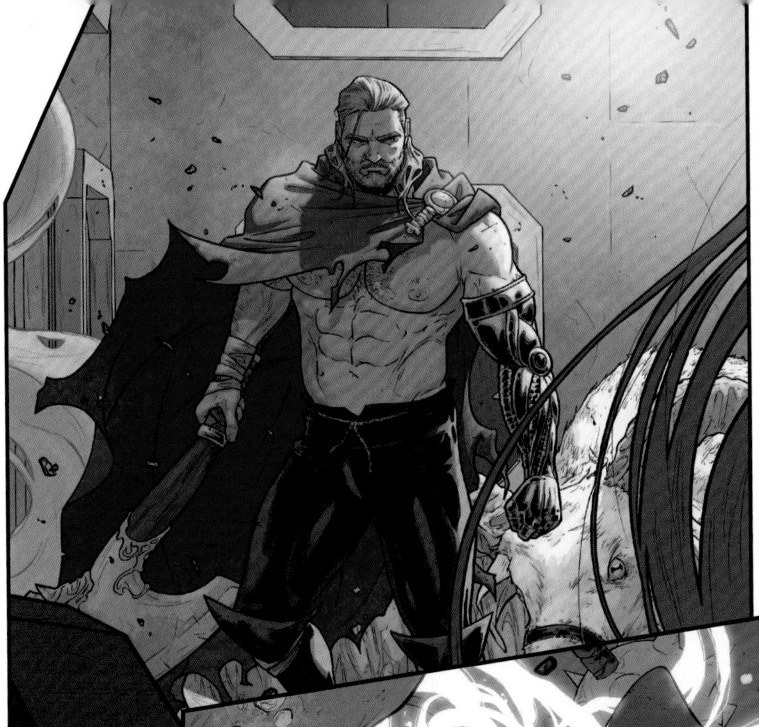

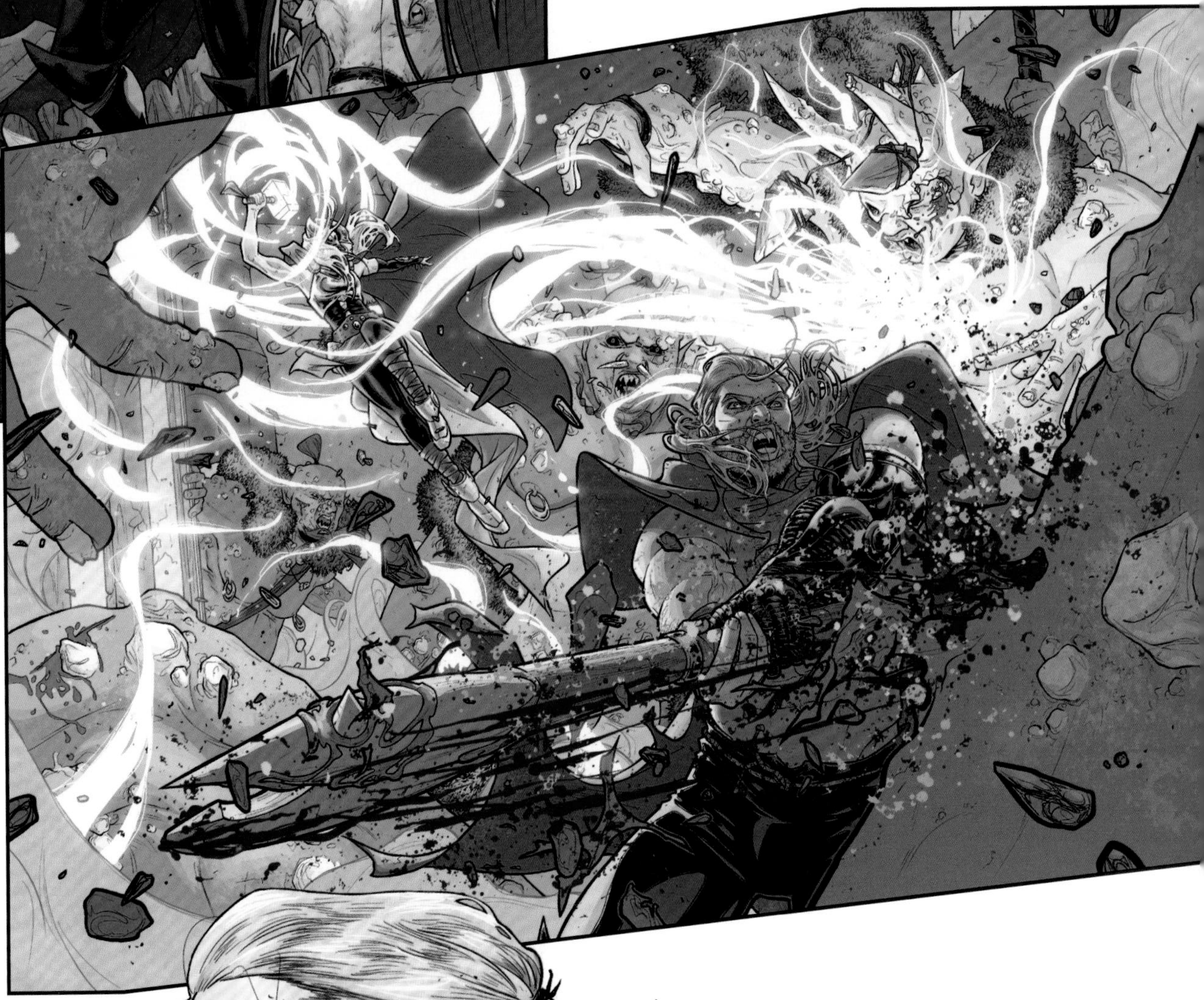

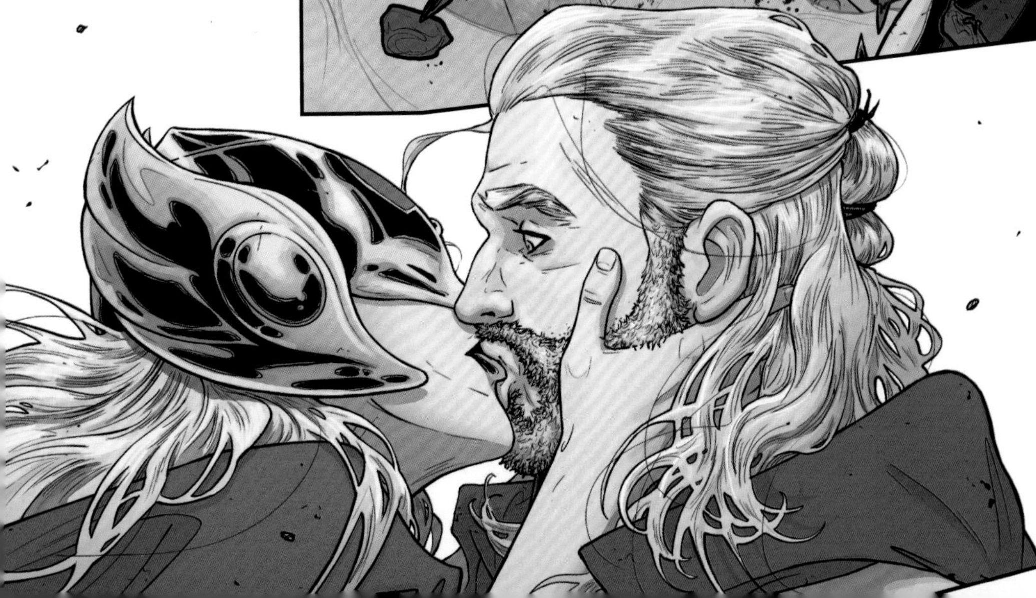

THE ODINSON, WITH A REPLACEMENT URU ARM, SHARES A BATTLE WITH THE NEW THOR — AND LEARNS SHE DEFINITELY ISN'T HIS MOTHER!

THOR (2014) #3-4 INTERIOR ART BY RUSSELL DAUTERMAN AND MATTHEW WILSON

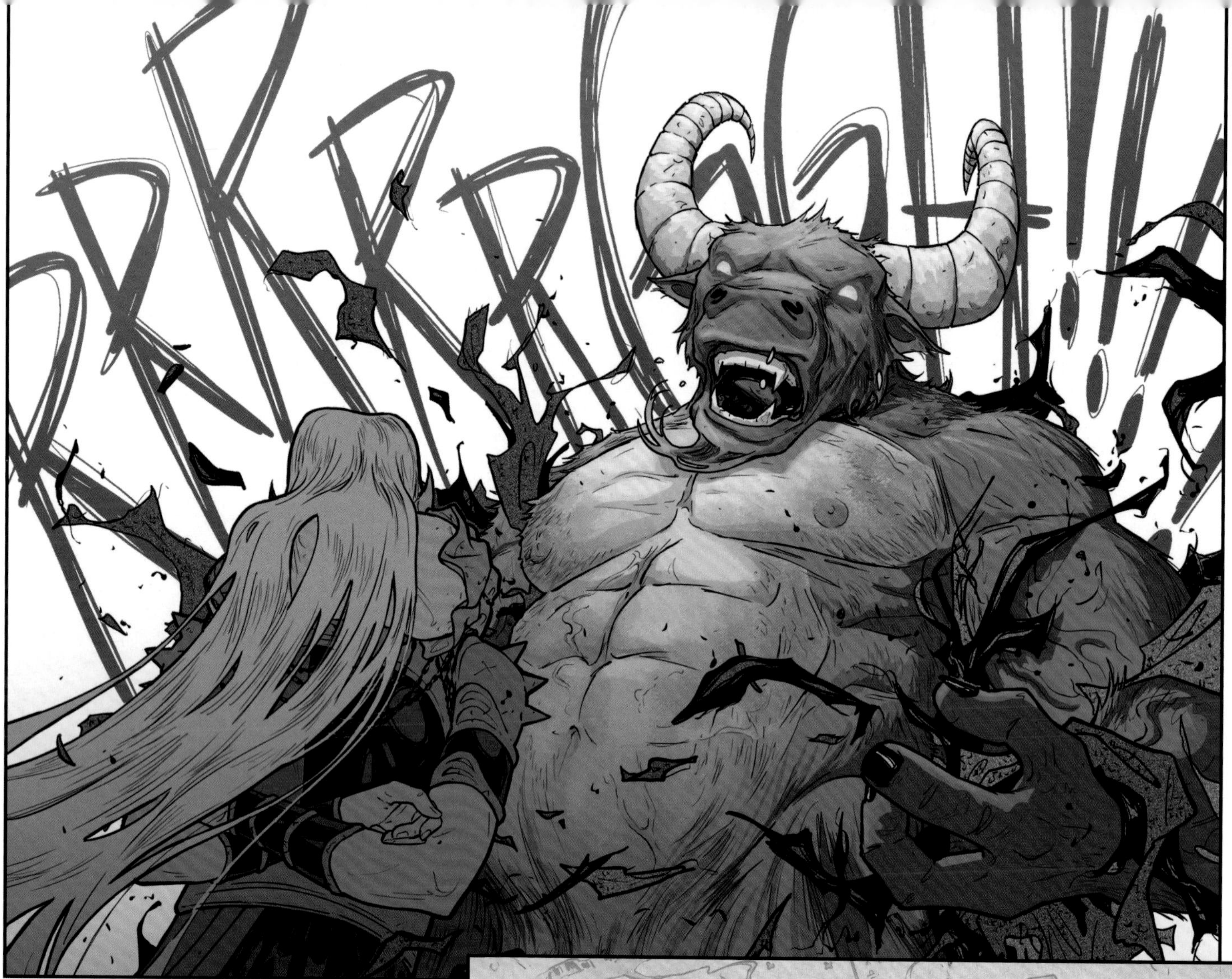

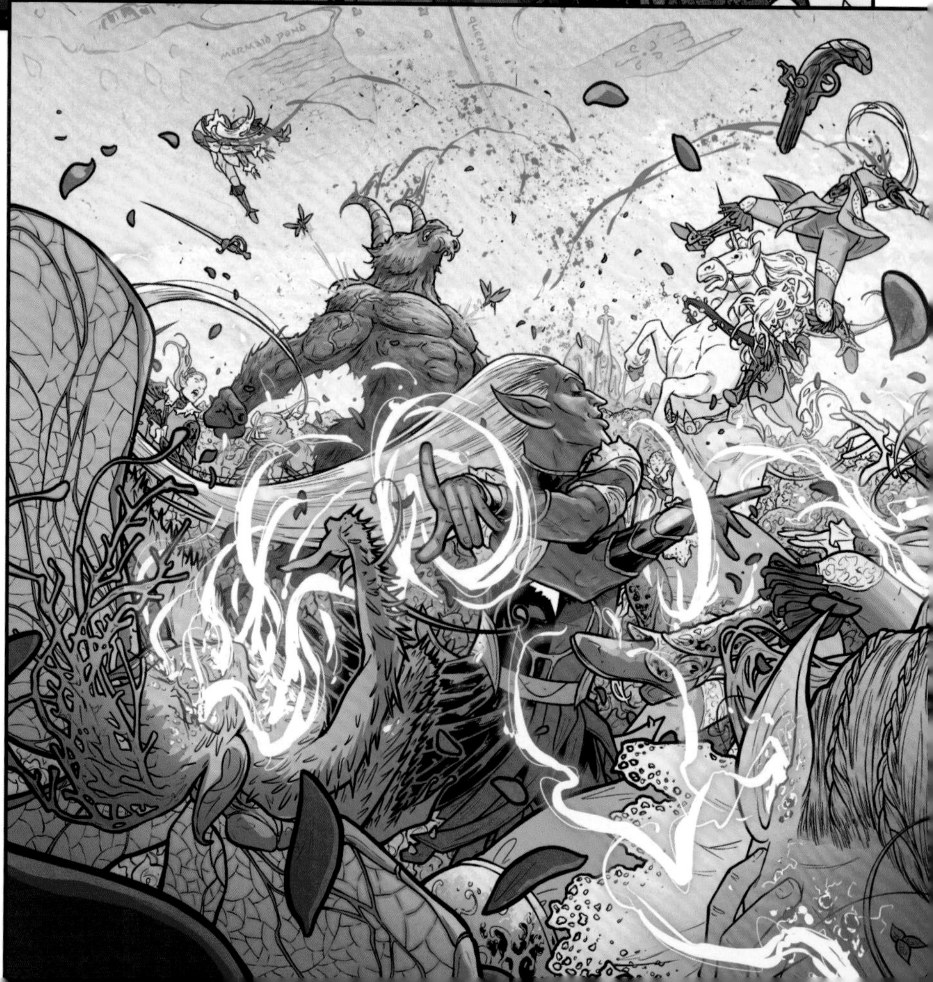

MALEKITH MEETS SOON-TO-BE-ALLY DARIO AGGER — AND THEN VIOLENTLY INTRODUCES HIM TO ALFHEIM AND THE REST OF THE TEN REALMS!

ABOVE AND RIGHT: *THOR (2014) #3* INTERIOR ART BY RUSSELL DAUTERMAN AND MATTHEW WILSON

OPPOSITE: *THOR (2014) #7* INTERIOR ART BY RUSSELL DAUTERMAN AND MATTHEW WILSON, WITH LETTERING BY JOE SABINO

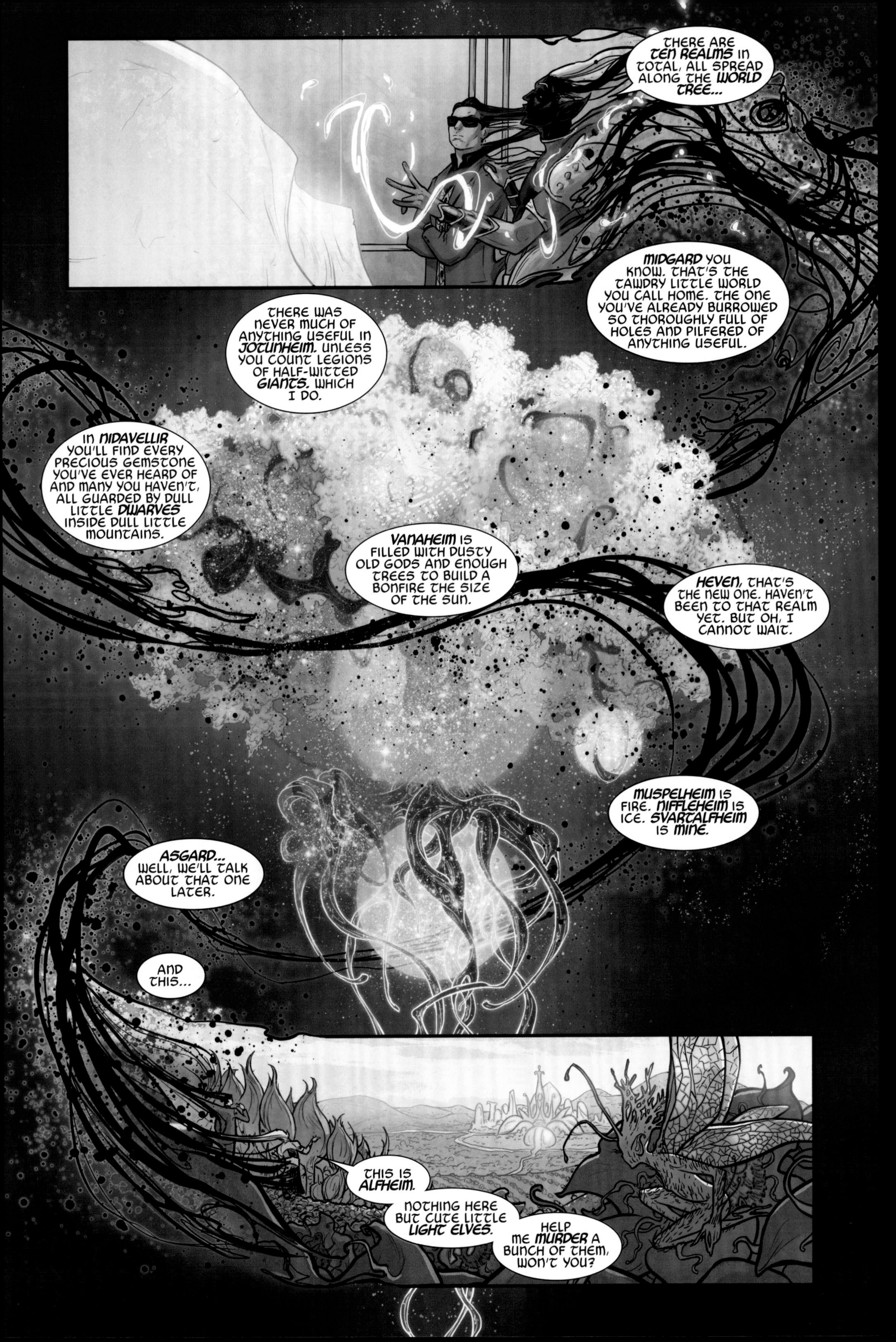
THERE ARE TEN REALMS IN TOTAL, ALL SPREAD ALONG THE WORLD TREE...
MIDGARD YOU KNOW. THAT'S THE TAWDRY LITTLE WORLD YOU CALL HOME. THE ONE YOU'VE ALREADY BURROWED SO THOROUGHLY FULL OF HOLES AND PILFERED OF ANYTHING USEFUL.
THERE WAS NEVER MUCH OF ANYTHING USEFUL IN JOTUNHEIM. UNLESS YOU COUNT LEGIONS OF HALF-WITTED GIANTS. WHICH I DO.
IN NIDAVELLIR YOU'LL FIND EVERY PRECIOUS GEMSTONE YOU'VE EVER HEARD OF AND MANY YOU HAVEN'T, ALL GUARDED BY DULL LITTLE DWARVES INSIDE DULL LITTLE MOUNTAINS.
VANAHEIM IS FILLED WITH DUSTY OLD GODS AND ENOUGH TREES TO BUILD A BONFIRE THE SIZE OF THE SUN.
HEVEN, THAT'S THE NEW ONE. HAVEN'T BEEN TO THAT REALM YET. BUT OH, I CANNOT WAIT.
MUSPELHEIM IS FIRE. NIFFLEHEIM IS ICE. SVARTALFHEIM IS MINE.
ASGARD... WELL, WE'LL TALK ABOUT THAT ONE LATER.
AND THIS...
THIS IS ALFHEIM.
NOTHING HERE BUT CUTE LITTLE LIGHT ELVES.
HELP ME MURDER A BUNCH OF THEM, WON'T YOU?

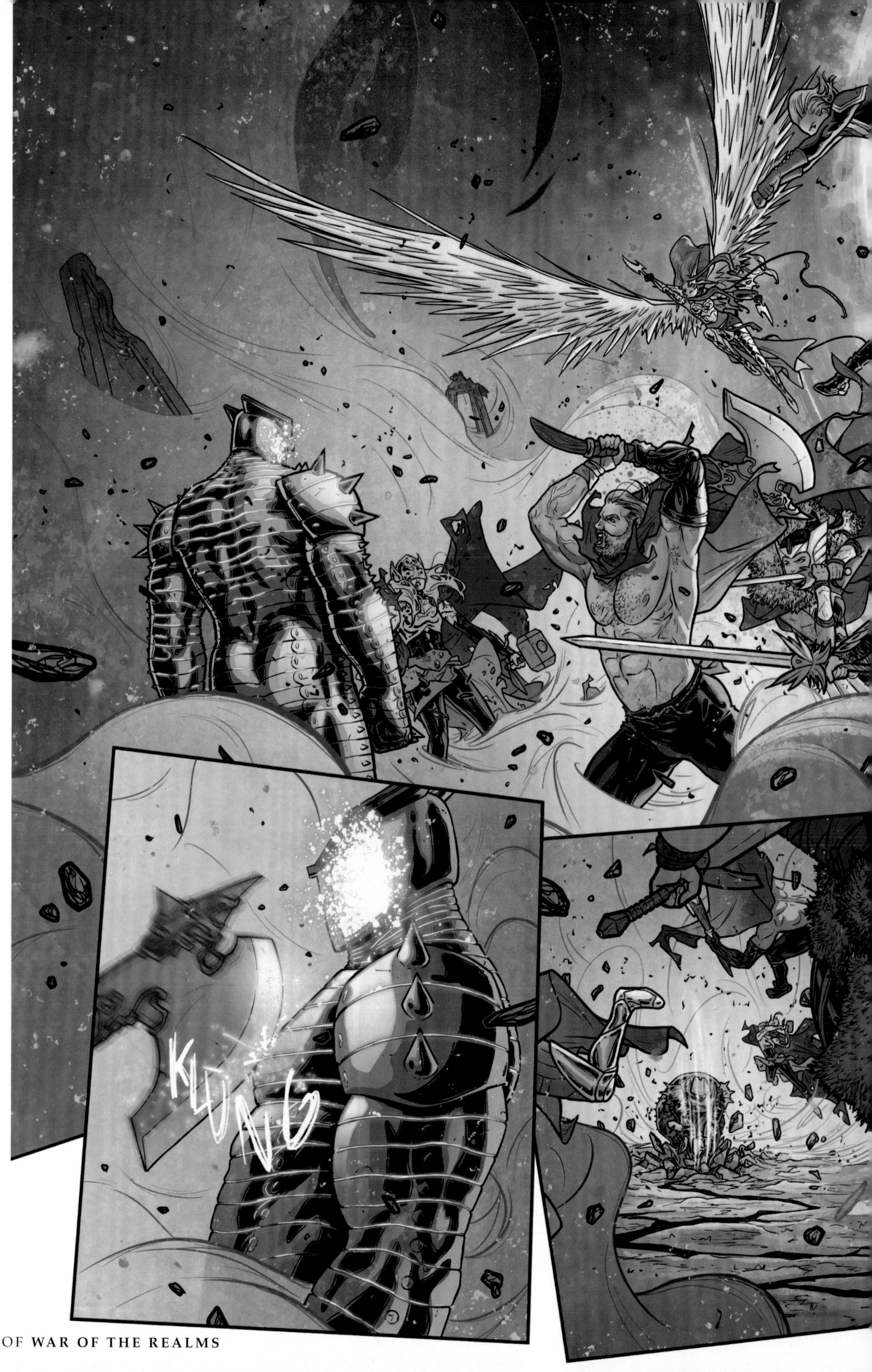
KLUNG

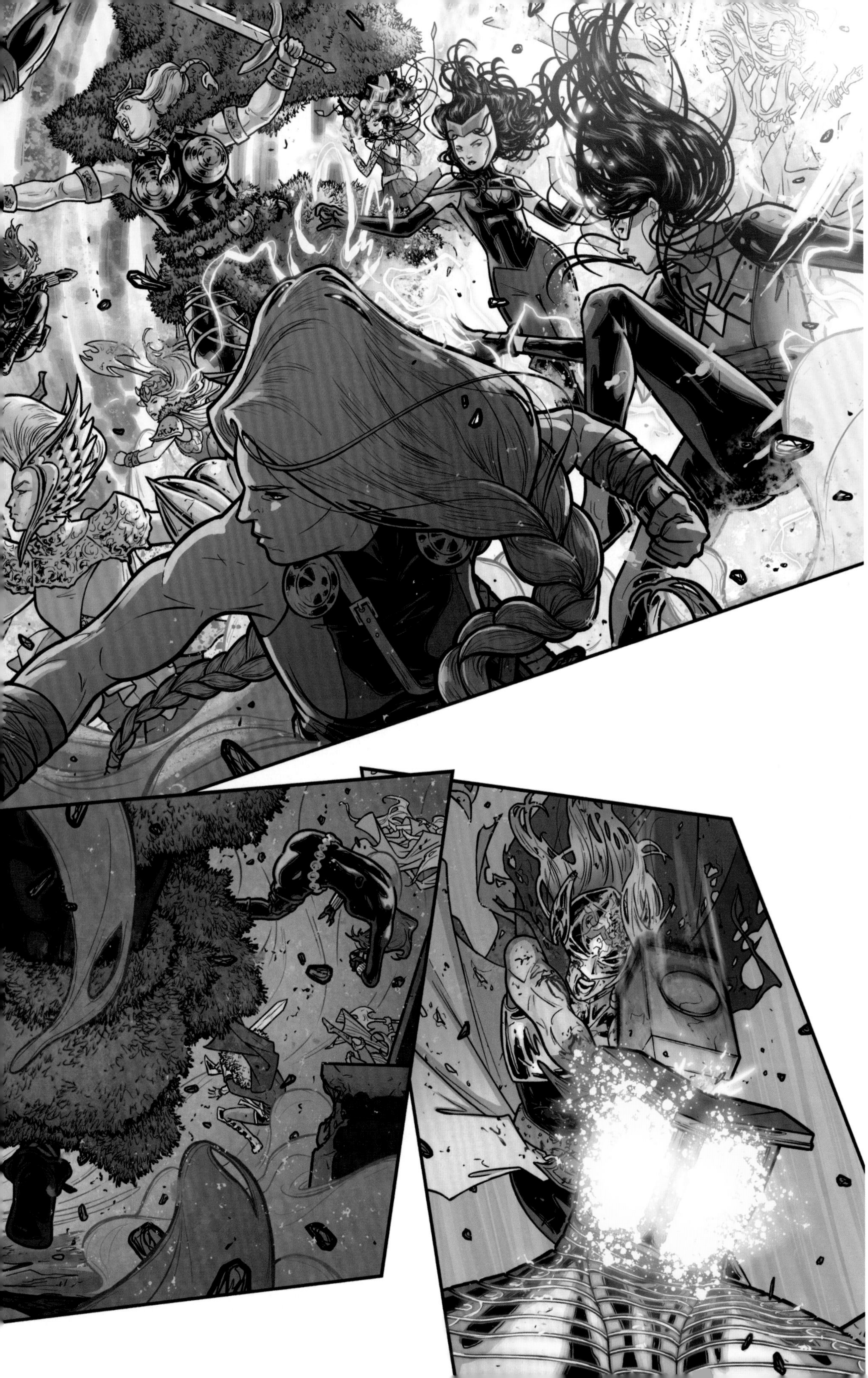

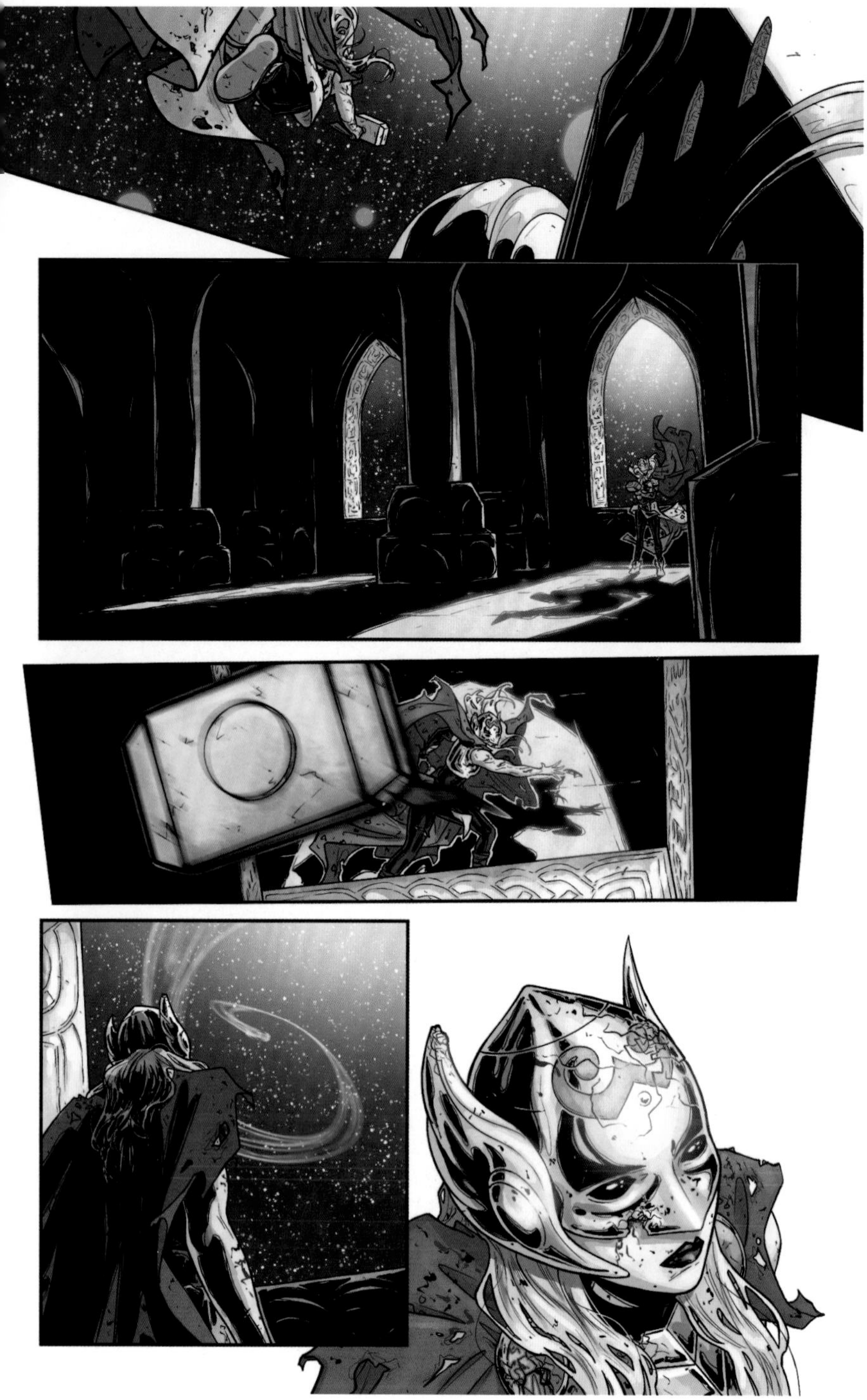

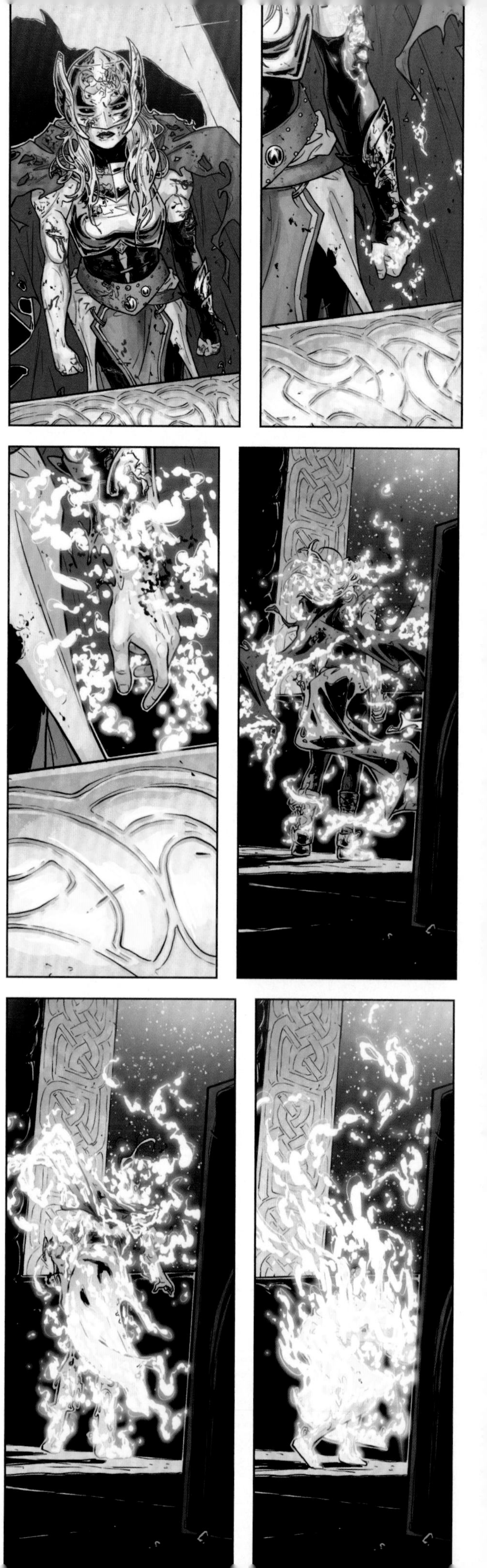

THOR JOINS ALLIES FROM ASGARD AND MIDGARD TO STAND AGAINST THE DESTROYER (PREVIOUS PAGES) — BUT THE BATTLE TAKES ITS TOLL. AS SHE RETURNS TO ASGARDIA AND RELINQUISHES HOLD OF MJOLNIR, A TRANSFORMATION OCCURS AND THE TRUTH IS REVEALED: THOR IS DOCTOR JANE FOSTER...AND IT IS KILLING HER!

THOR (2014) #8 INTERIOR ART BY
RUSSELL DAUTERMAN AND MATTHEW WILSON

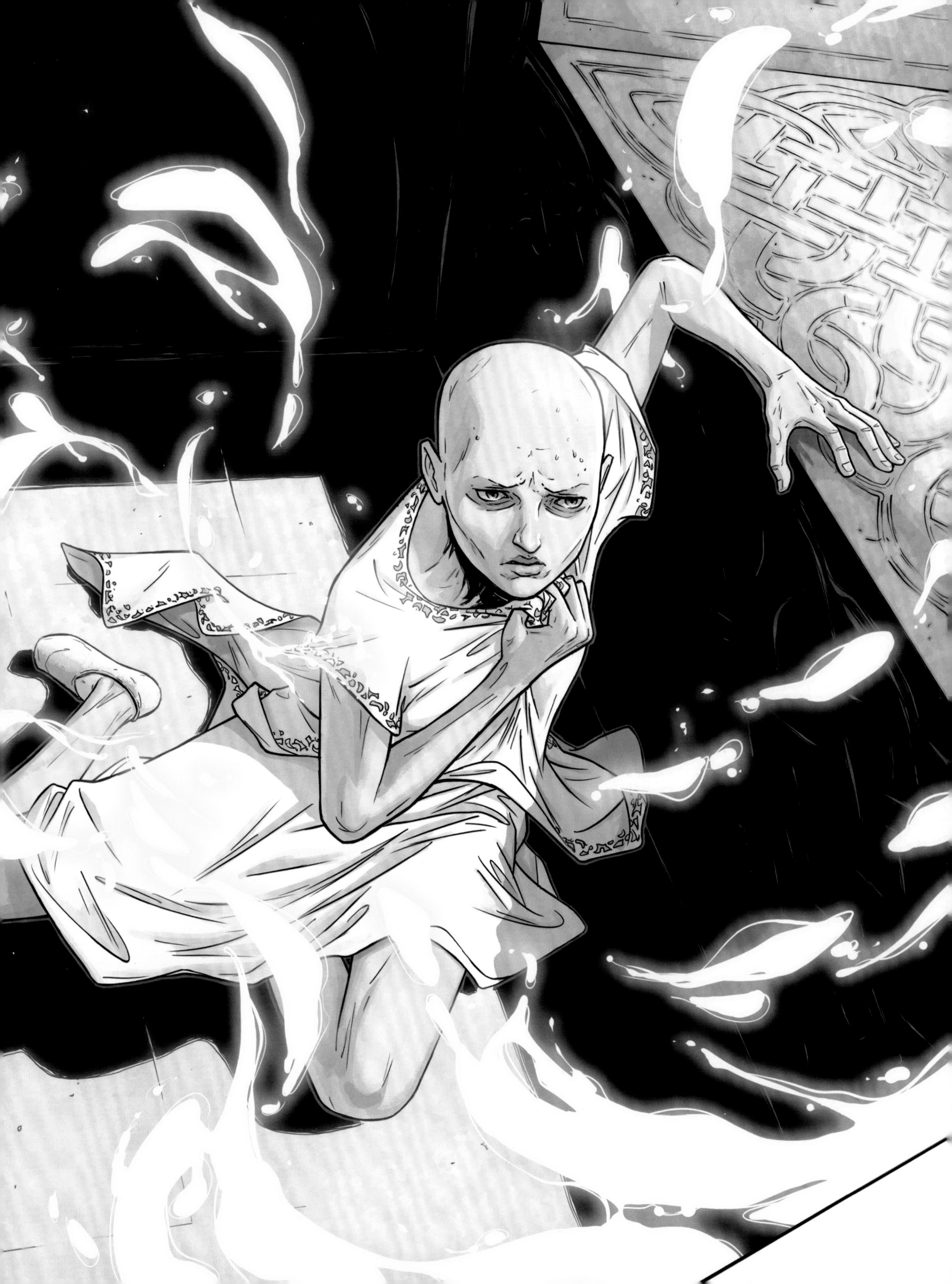

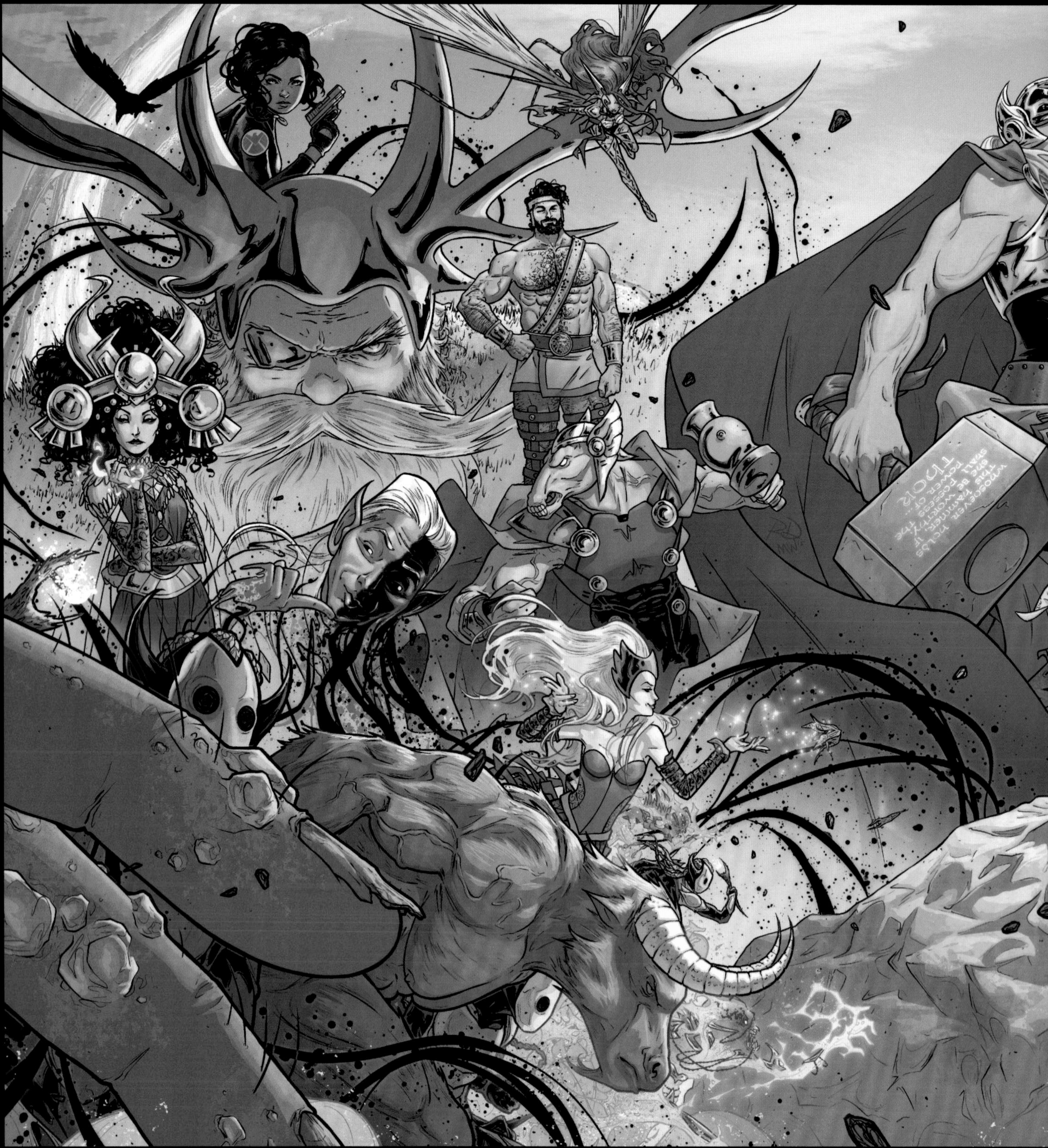

"I'm **Dr. Jane Foster**. And believe it or not, I'm also **the Mighty Thor**. Though right now I'm not feeling particularly mighty. Right now I'm just trying not to **die.**"
— Jane Foster

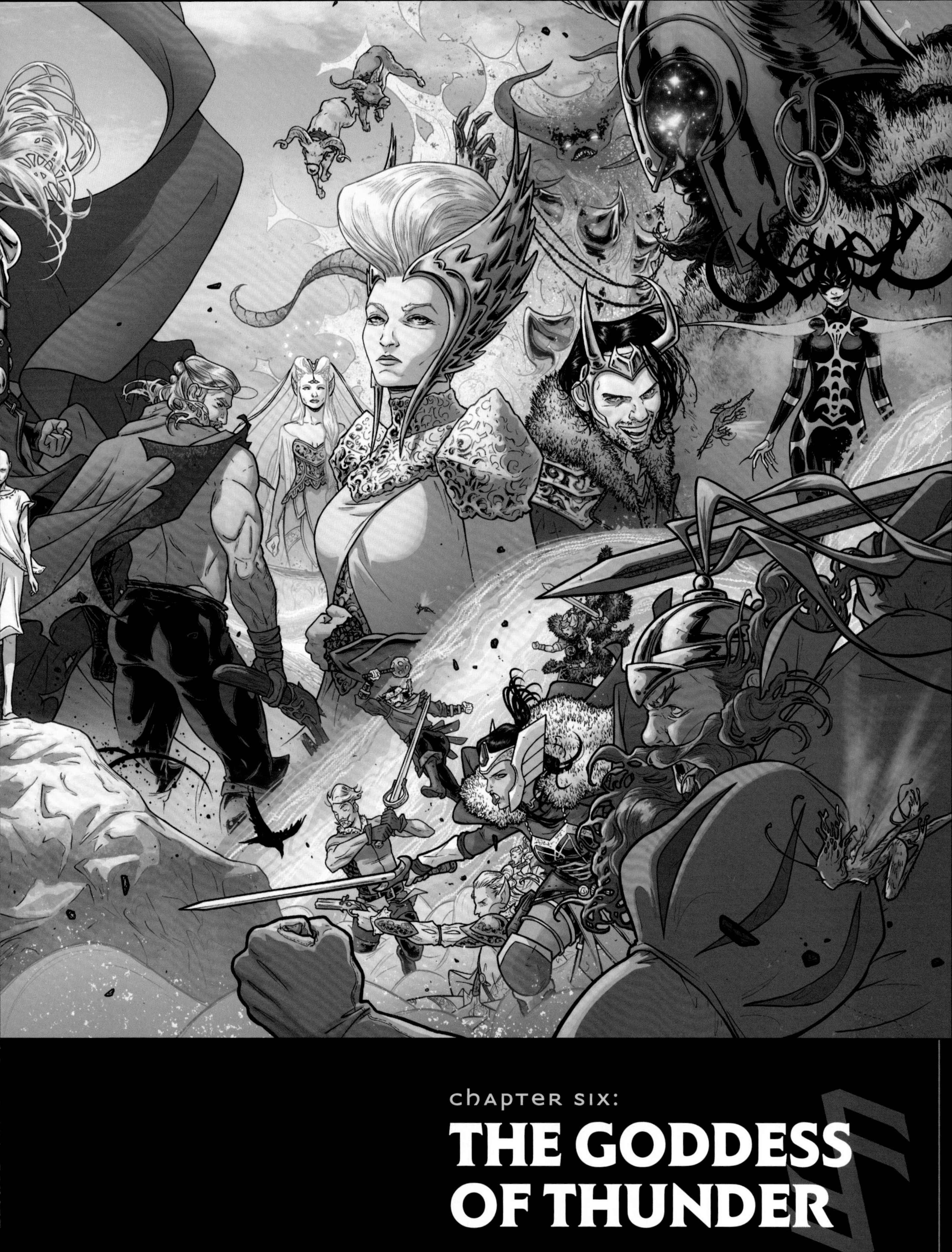

chapter six:

THE GODDESS OF THUNDER

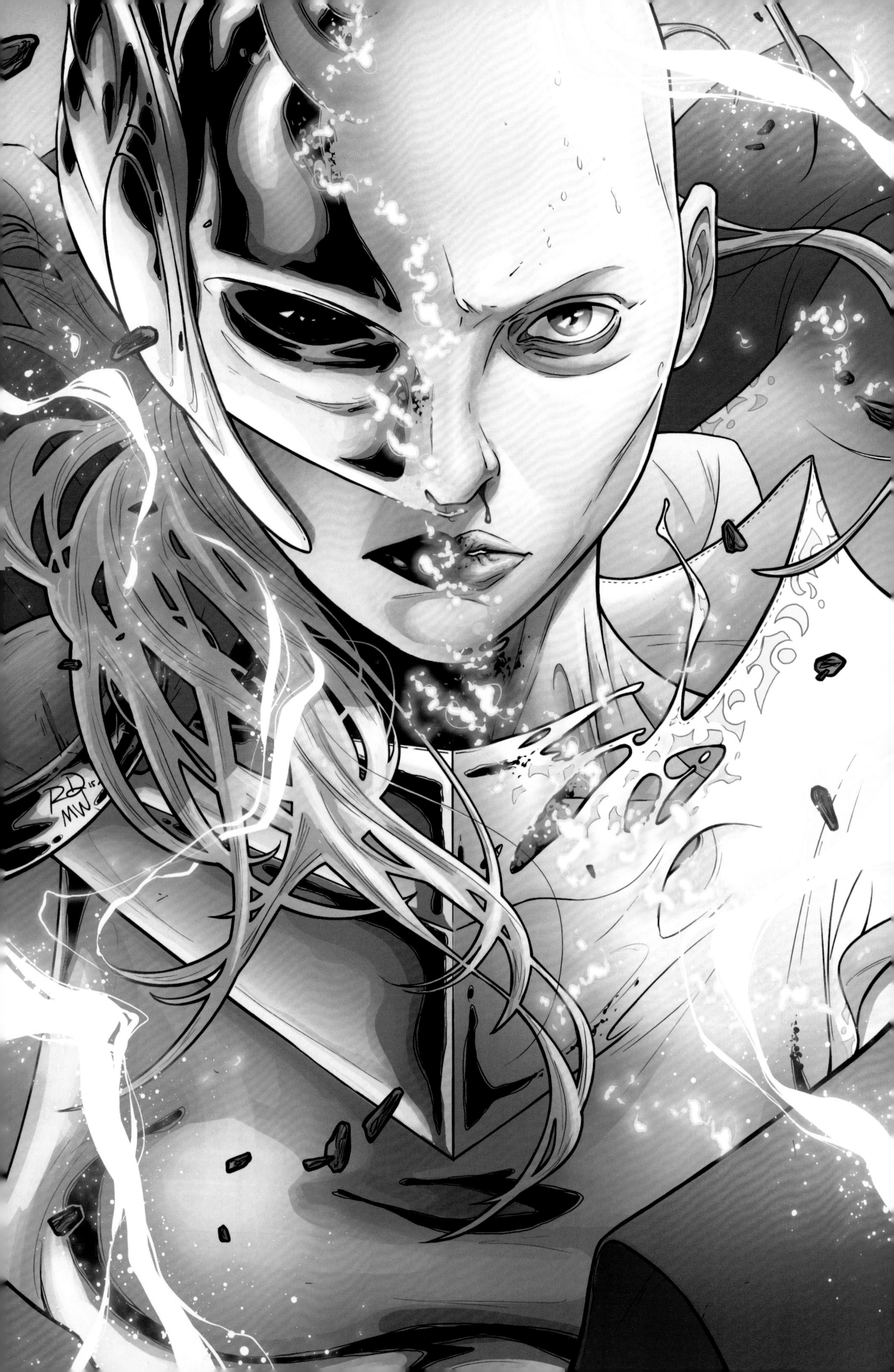

With Thor's identity revealed as Dr. Jane Foster, Jason Aaron and Russell Dauterman could finally begin the tale they really wanted to tell — of their hero battling gods, monsters, aliens, villains…and something far, far worse: cancer. Each time Jane transforms into Thor, she undoes all the good her chemotherapy treatments have been doing. "I think we knew that was a powerful story," Aaron says, "particularly powerful for people dealing with that in their own lives. It was clearly a different story from those I'd done before. And I think, in a lot of ways, it's the most Marvel of all the Marvel comics I've done. The idea of this person who is fighting this very real battle in her mortal life and, as a result, is pretty weak and frail, but she can come along and pick up the hammer and be transformed into the Mighty Thor. But at the same time, by doing that she's only making her problem worse — she's killing herself more each time. That to me feels like a very Marvel Comics idea."

While Aaron knew where he was heading with Jane's story, he did not know how long he would have to tell it. "We had no idea when the book started what the response would be; we had to be flexible," Aaron says. "Like, would we get six months with Jane as Thor? Who knows. Thankfully, the response was great — especially from a lot of people picking up the book who had never read *Thor* before — and sales went up!"

Mighty Thor is Jane's story, but it also furthers the deadly agenda of Malekith and his cabal, with the War of the Realms beginning in earnest. Aaron says he knew it was "risky" to start the new series with a war that was "not going to end for a long, long time," but he felt the moment was right. "At some point I decided I was going to be on *Thor* until they just physically took it away from me," he laughs. "So I was just writing with the confidence of someone who is just going to do it until they tell me to stop. Thankfully nobody has told me to stop. I knew that this war was going to go on a long time. It was going to travel from one realm to the next before things come to a head. The whole idea was to use that war as a way to do a travelogue of those different realms, and Russell and I pretty much redesigned all the creatures from those realms. A lot changes over the course of *Mighty Thor* — but war is still churning and churning in the background."

PREVIOUS PAGES: *MIGHTY THOR (2015)* #1 WRAPAROUND COVER BY RUSSELL DAUTERMAN AND MATTHEW WILSON

OPPOSITE: *MIGHTY THOR (2015) #1* VARIANT COVER BY RUSSELL DAUTERMAN AND MATTHEW WILSON

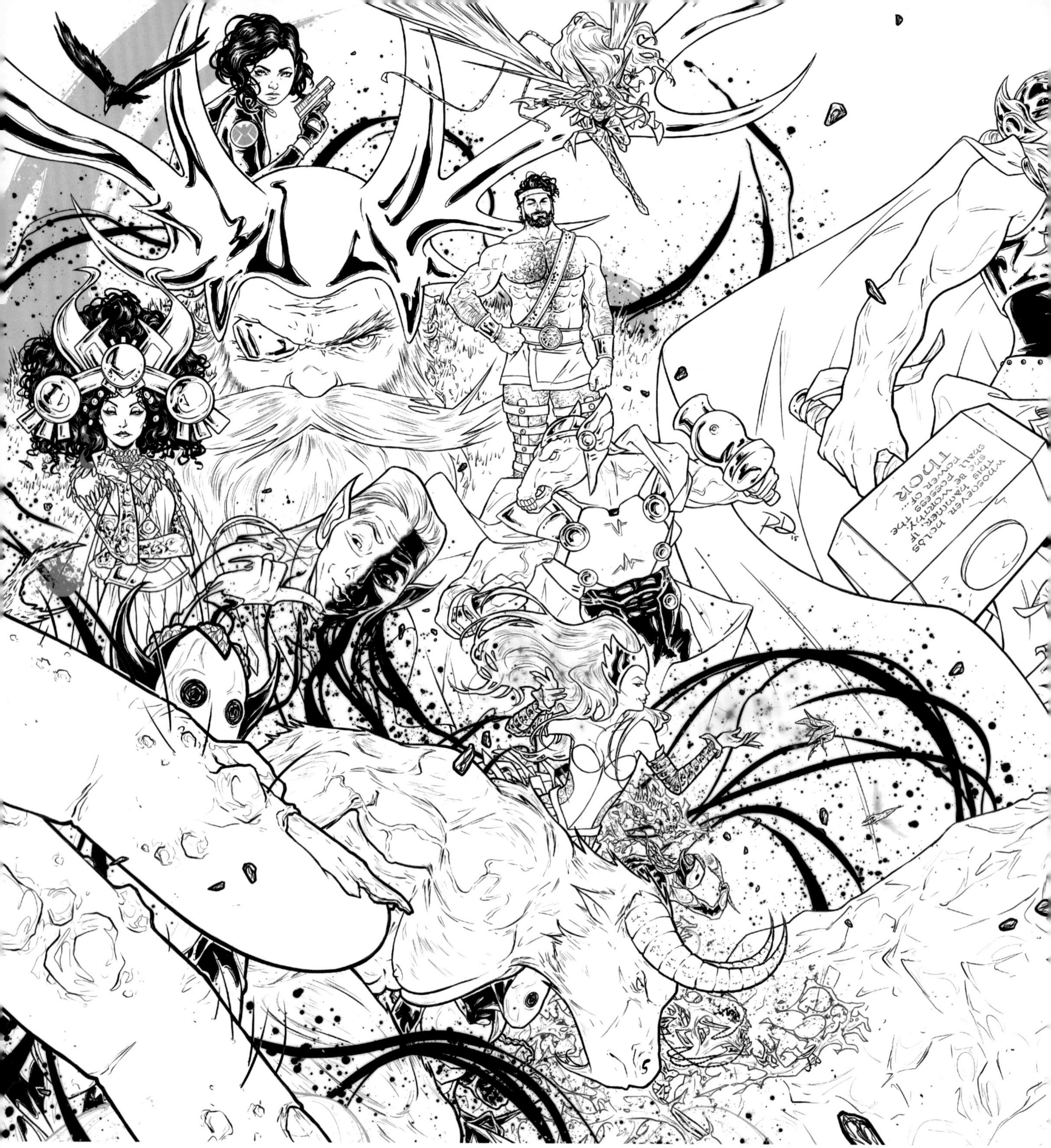
Whosoever holds
this hammer, if
she be worthy, the
shall possess
power of...
THOR

"I pushed for the chance to do the big gatefold cover for *Mighty Thor #1*. I thought we needed something special, since we were relaunching the book after *Secret Wars*. Plus, so much of our first volume was about the mystery of who Thor was, but we started to get to the meat of the story with *Mighty Thor #1*. I wanted this cover to sum up a lot of what was going to happen in that story."
— RUSSELL DAUTERMAN

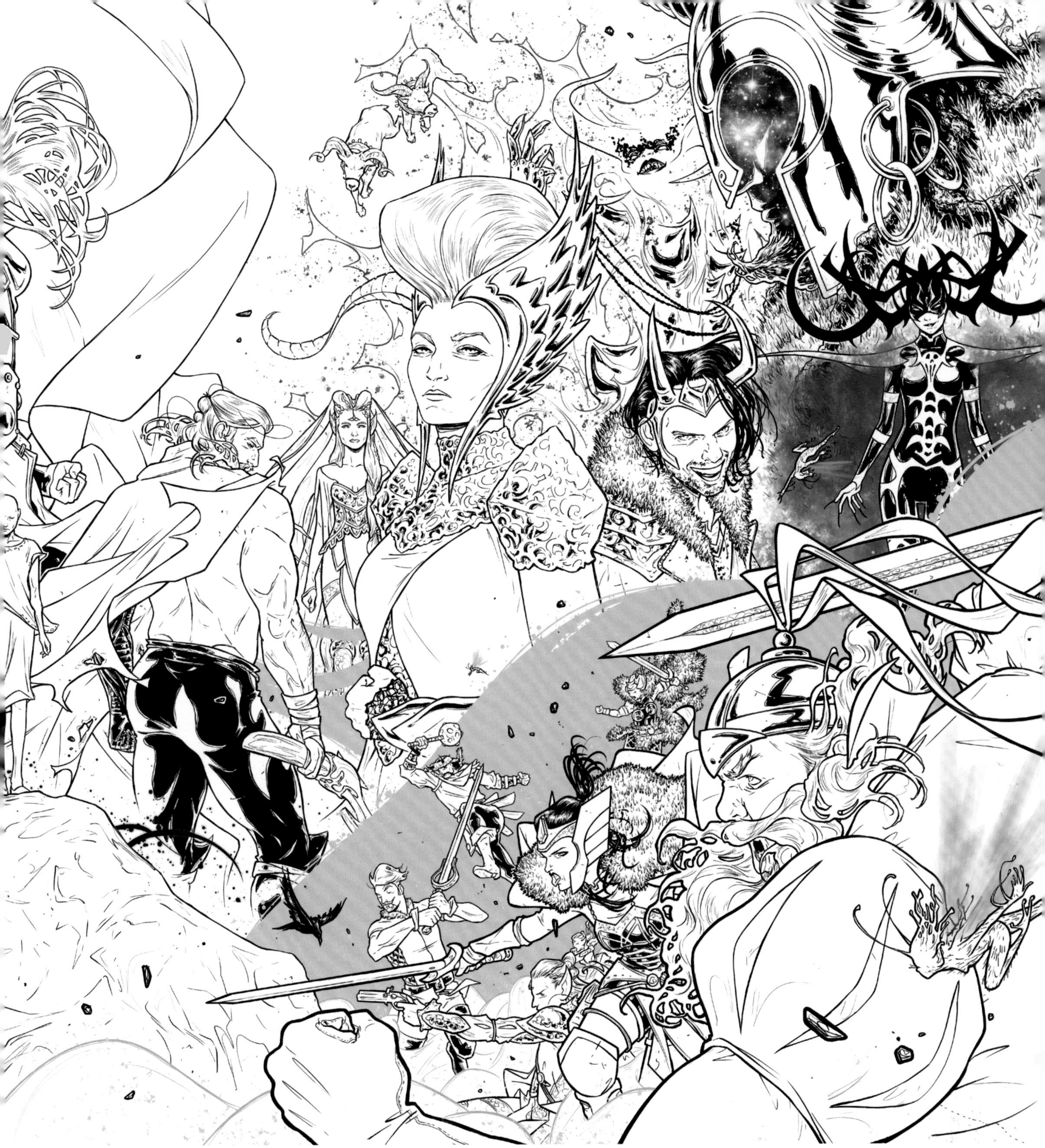

MIGHTY THOR (2015) #1 COVER INKS BY RUSSELL DAUTERMAN

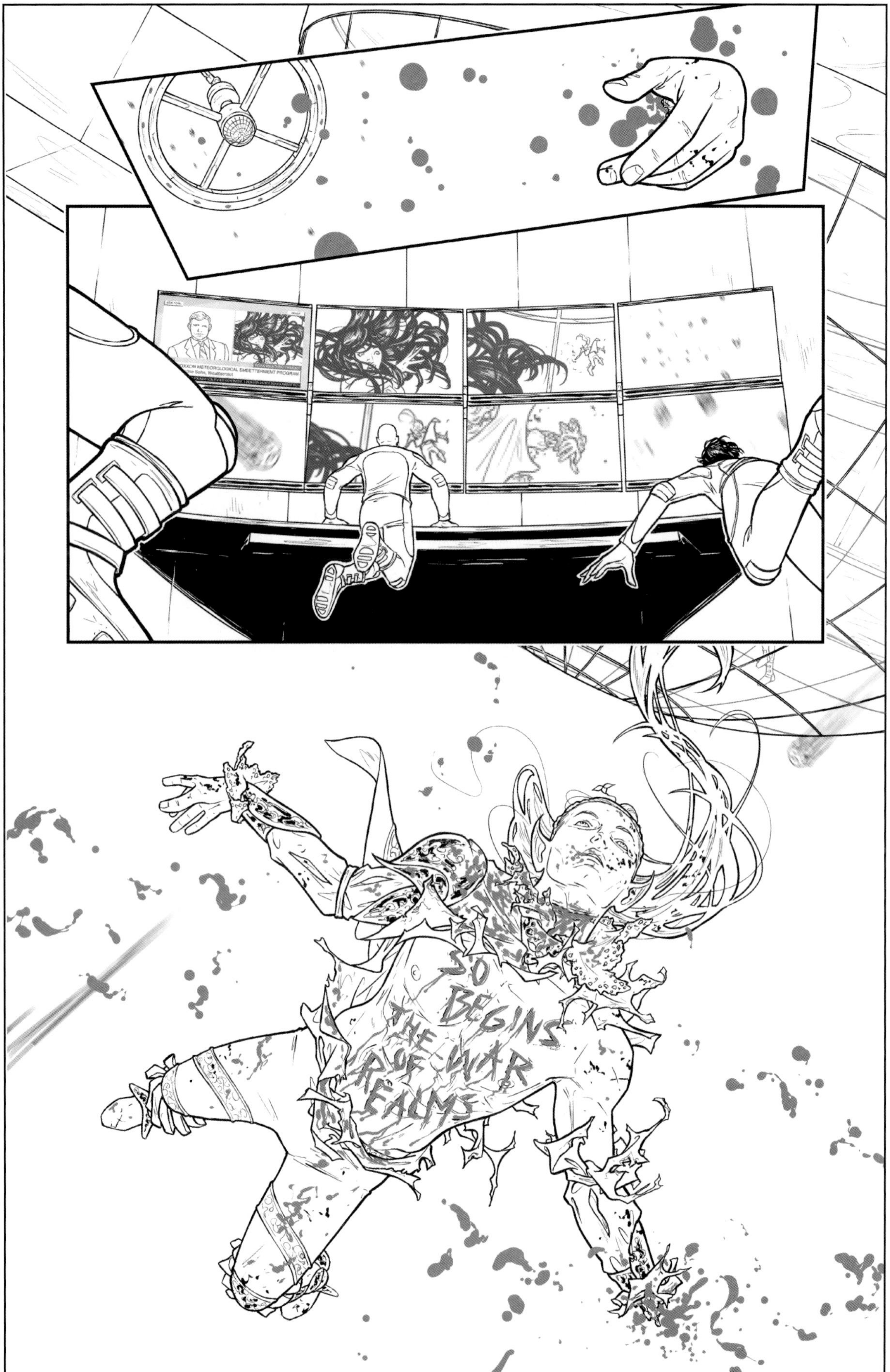
SO
BEGINS
THE
OF WAR
REALMS

SO BEGINS THE WAR OF THE REALMS! MALEKITH SENDS A POWERFUL MESSAGE AS THE CORPSES OF DEAD LIGHT ELVES RAIN DOWN ON A ROXXON METEOROLOGICAL SPACE STATION, AND SOON ITS WRECKAGE IS SENT HURTLING TOWARD EARTH!

RIGHT, OPPOSITE AND FOLLOWING PAGES: *MIGHTY THOR (2015) #1* INTERIOR INKS BY RUSSELL DAUTERMAN, AND FINAL ART BY DAUTERMAN AND MATTHEW WILSON

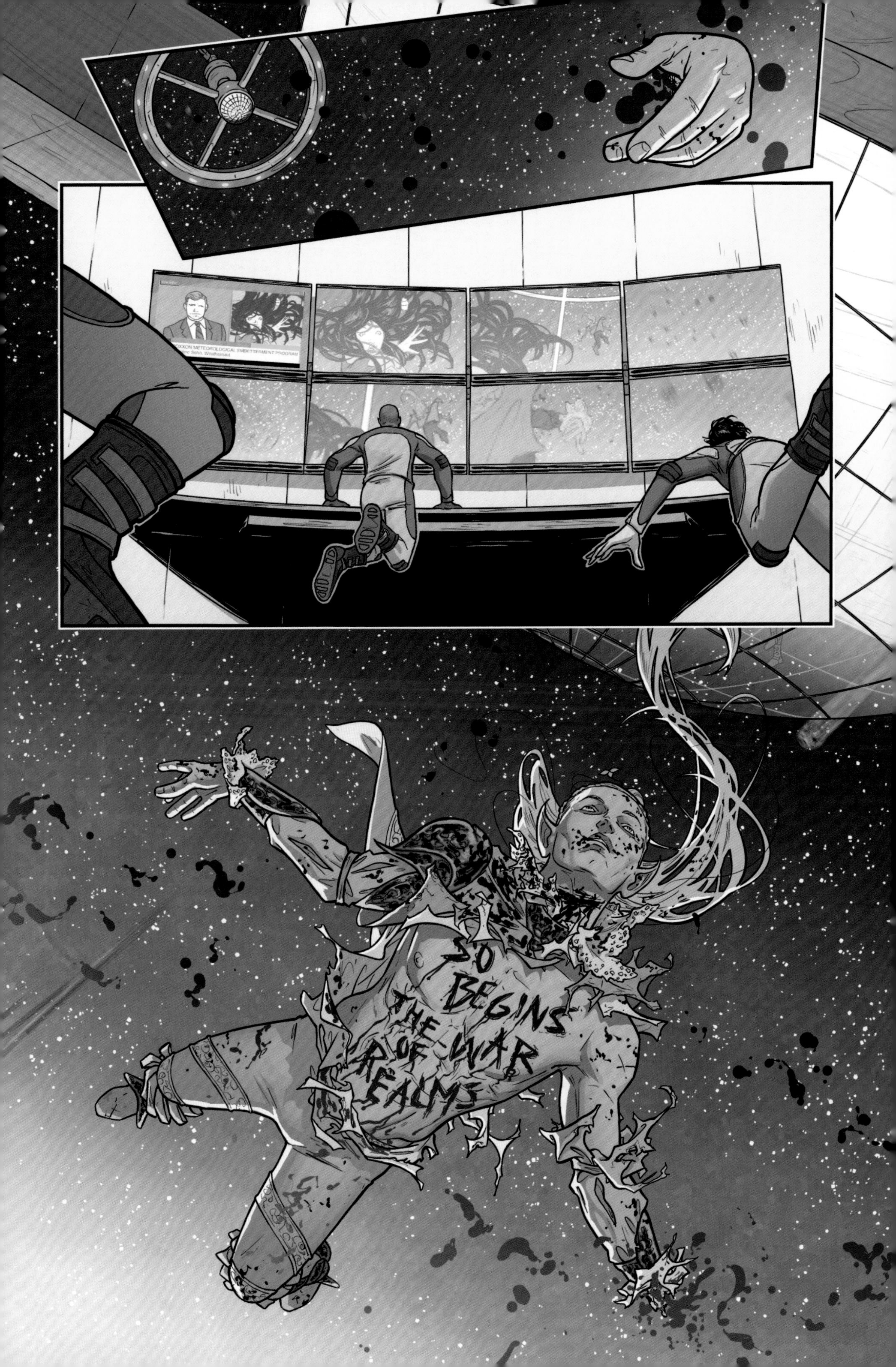
METEOROLOGICAL EMBITTERMENT PROGRAM
SO BEGINS THE WAR OF REALMS

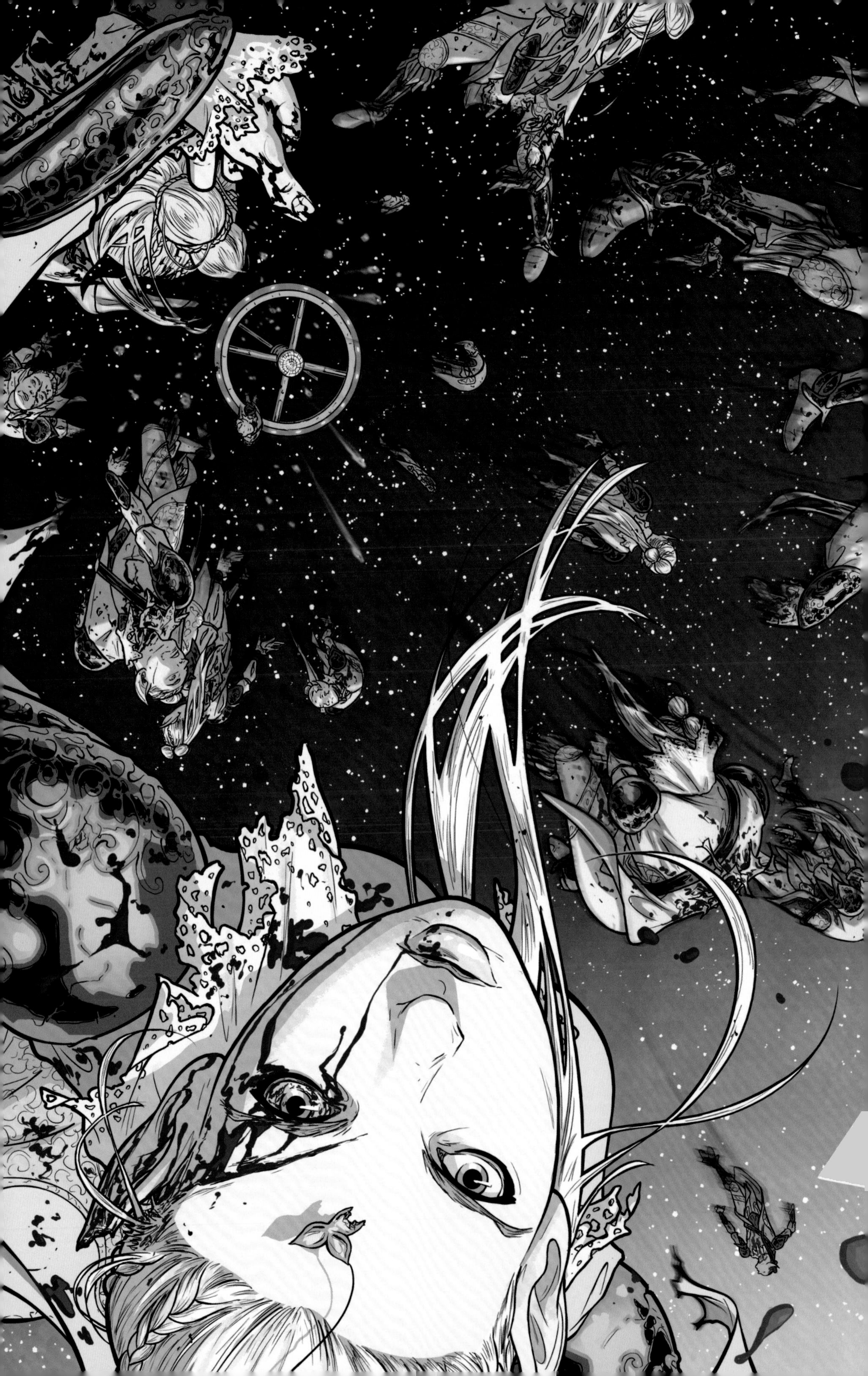

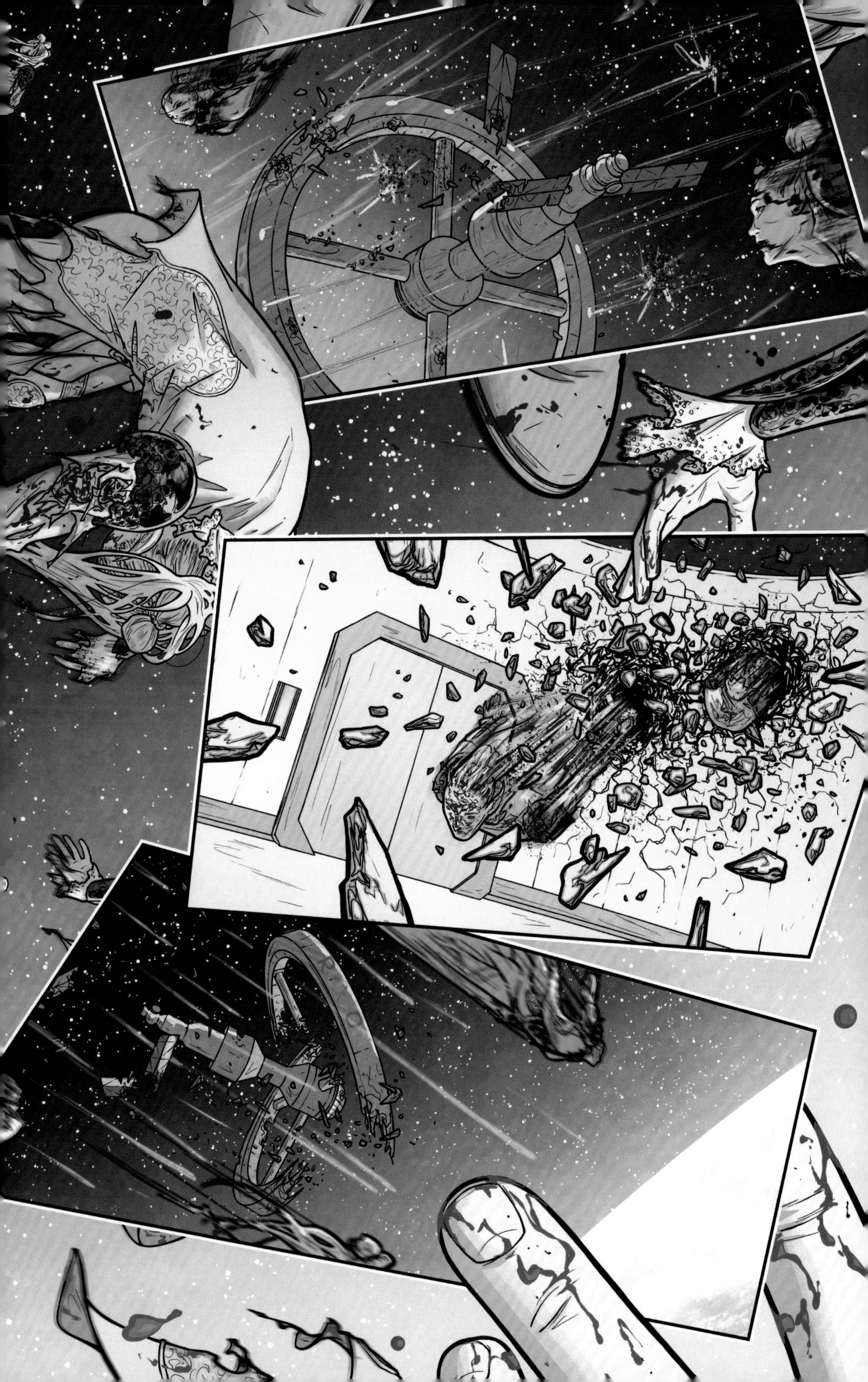

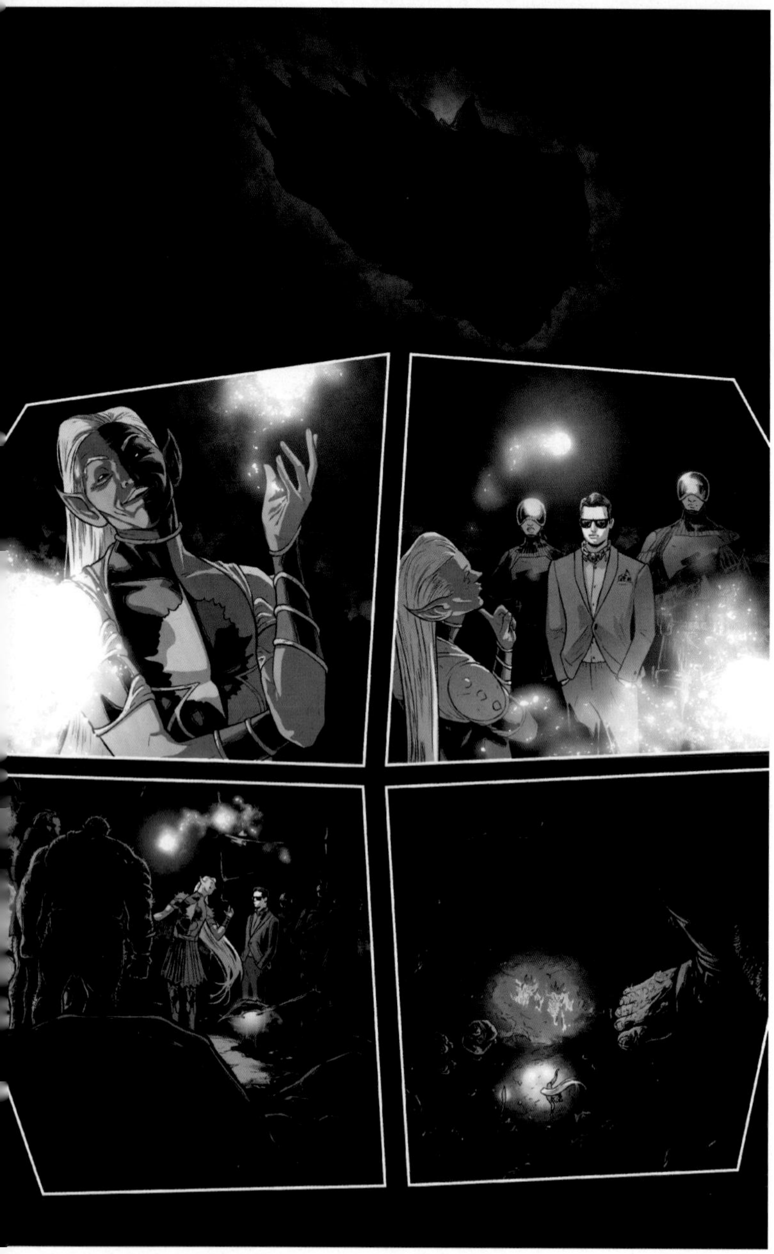

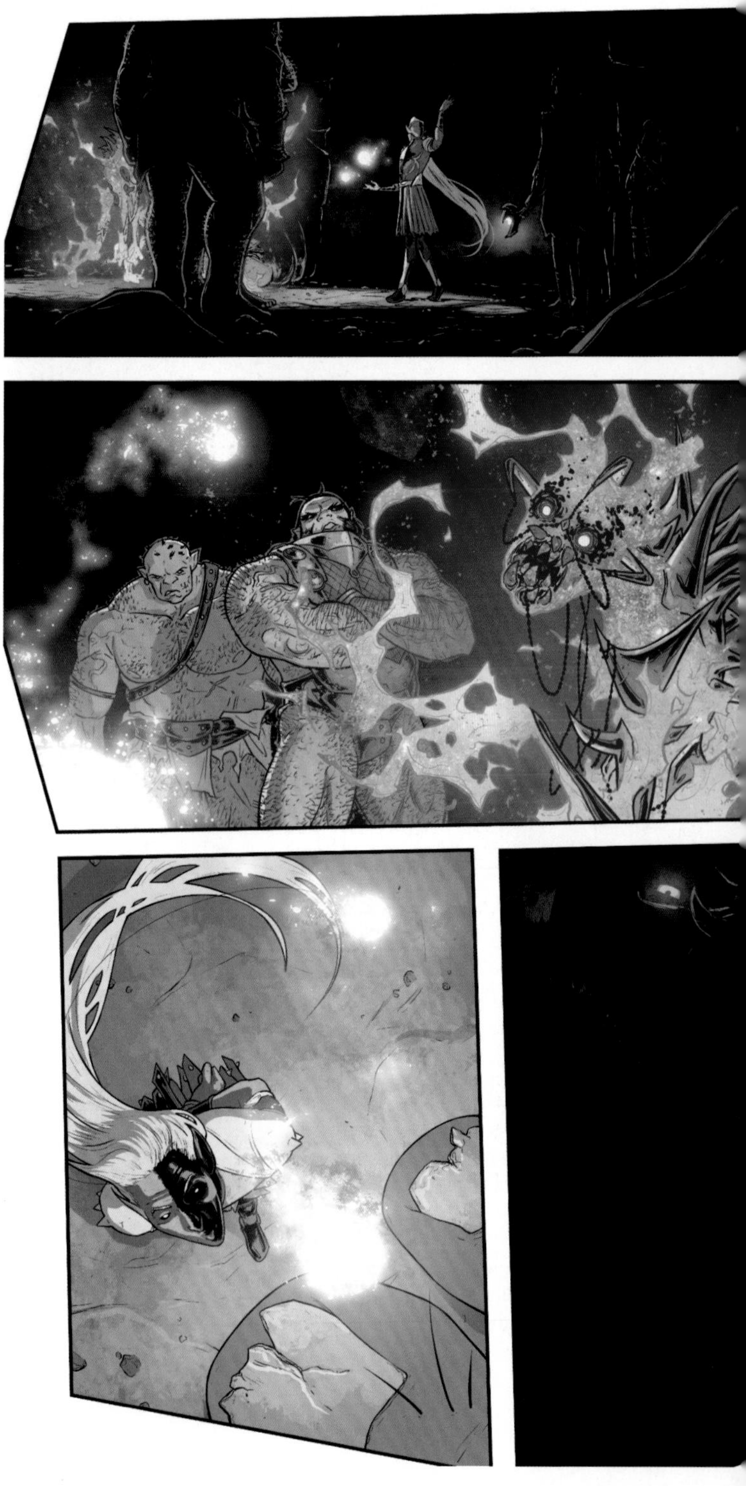

MALEKITH CONTINUES TO ASSEMBLE HIS DARK COUNCIL, INCLUDING DARIO AGGER, ULIK, A FIRE GOBLIN OF MUSPELHEIM AND LAUFEY — WHOM HE HAS MANAGED TO BRING BACK TO LIFE! AND THEN THERE'S THE NEW RECRUIT: THE FROST GIANT KING'S DEVIOUS SON, LOKI! SOON, MALEKITH WAGES A WAR OF THE ELVES IN ALFHEIM!

ABOVE, RIGHT AND OPPOSITE:
MIGHTY THOR (2015) #1-2 INTERIOR ART BY RUSSELL DAUTERMAN AND MATTHEW WILSON

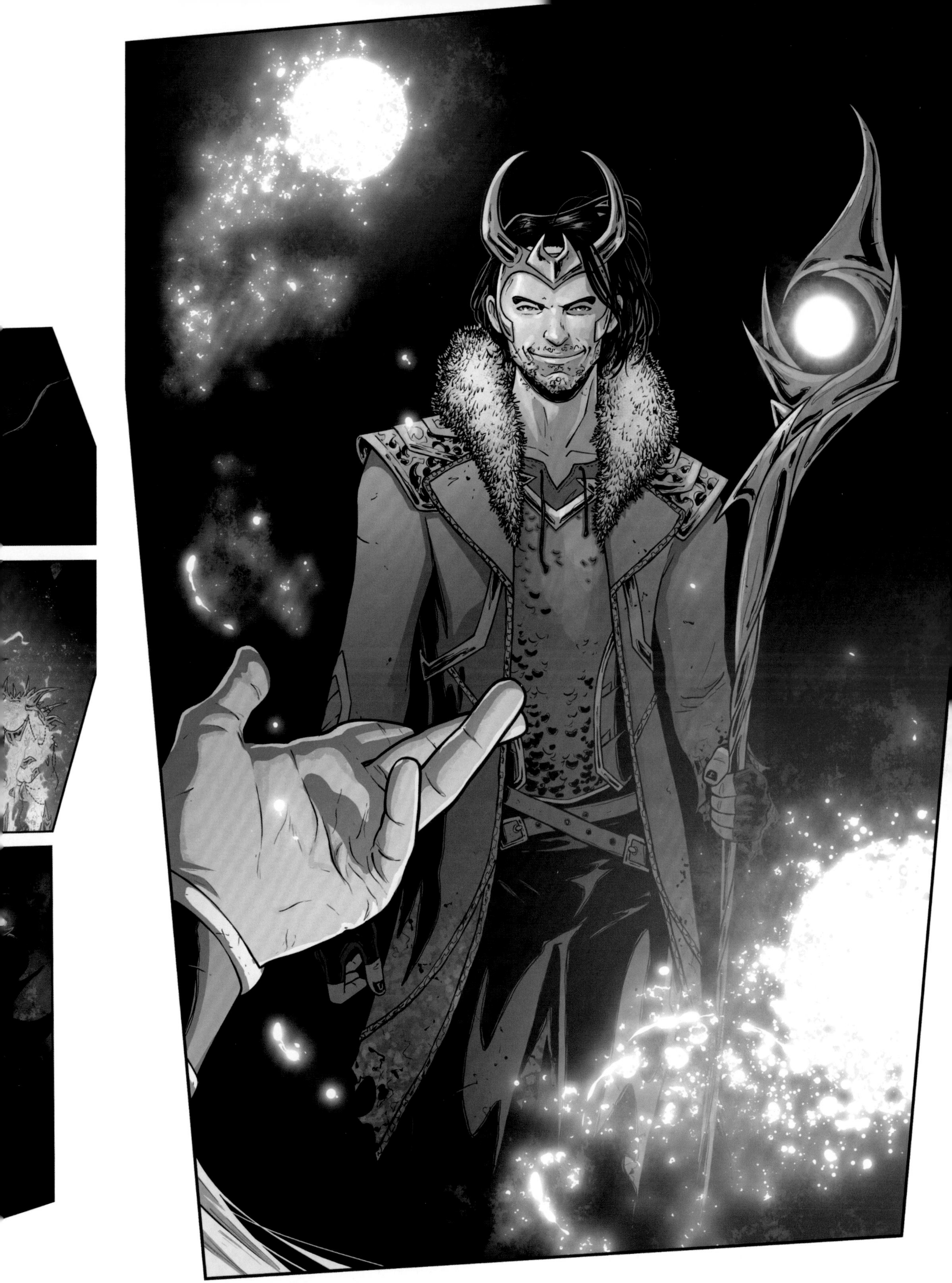

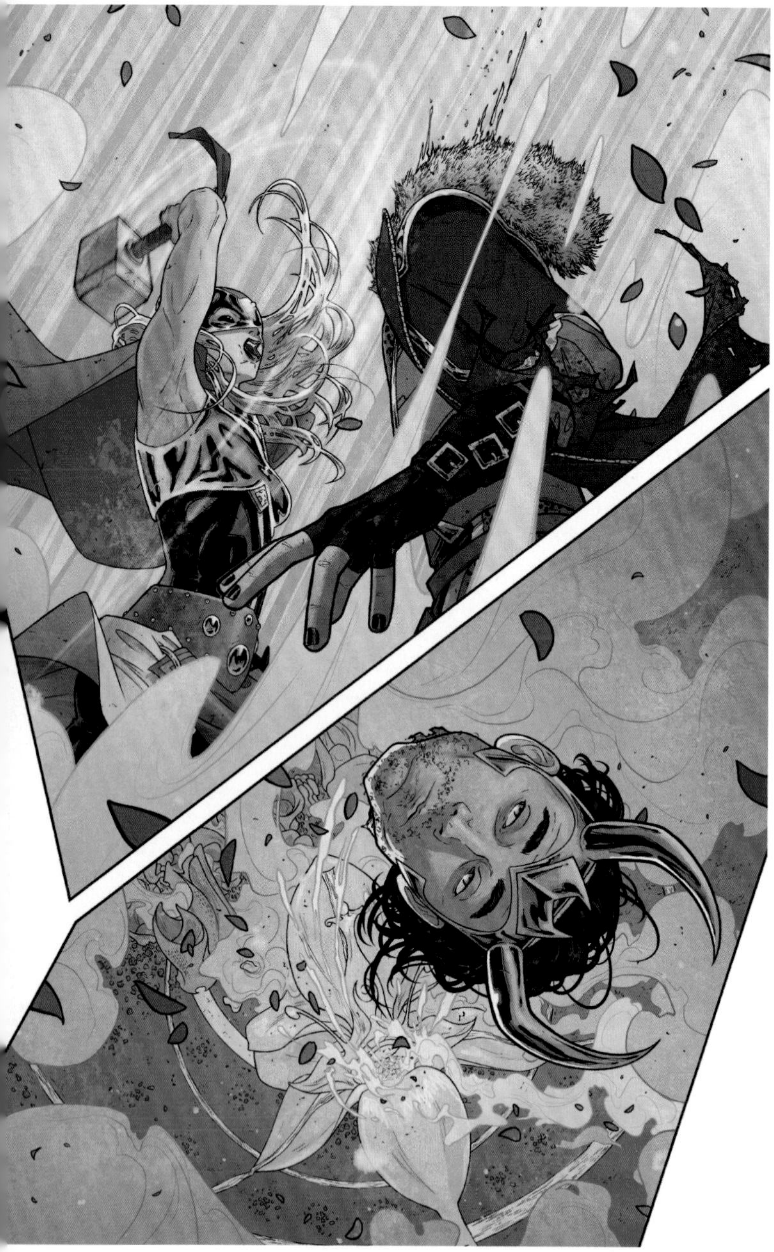

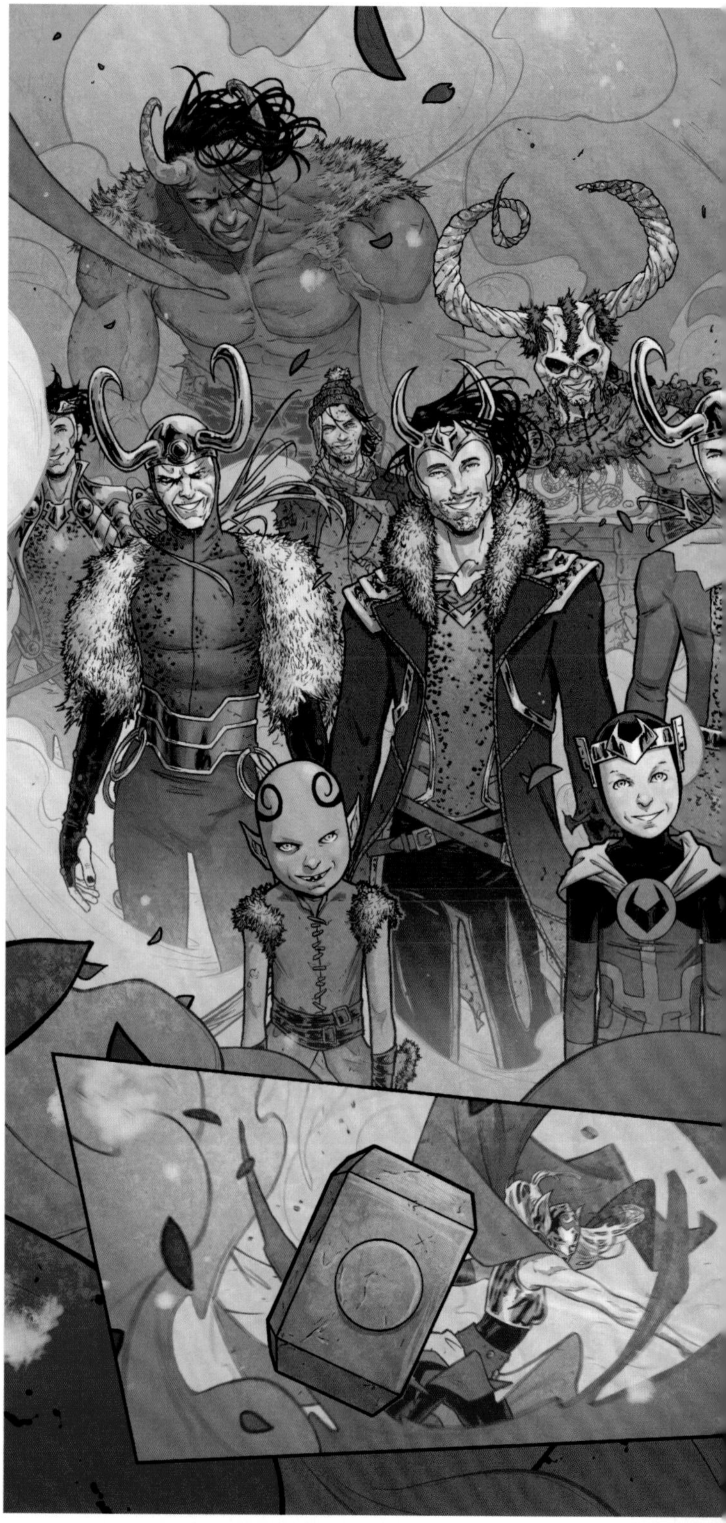

AS THOR FIGHTS TO SAVE ALFHEIM, SHE FACES HER FIRST CLASH WITH THE TRICKSTER LOKI — THEN SMITES THE ALL-FATHER HIMSELF, ODIN!

ABOVE, RIGHT AND OPPOSITE: *MIGHTY THOR* (2015) #3-4
INTERIOR ART BY RUSSELL DAUTERMAN AND MATTHEW WILSON

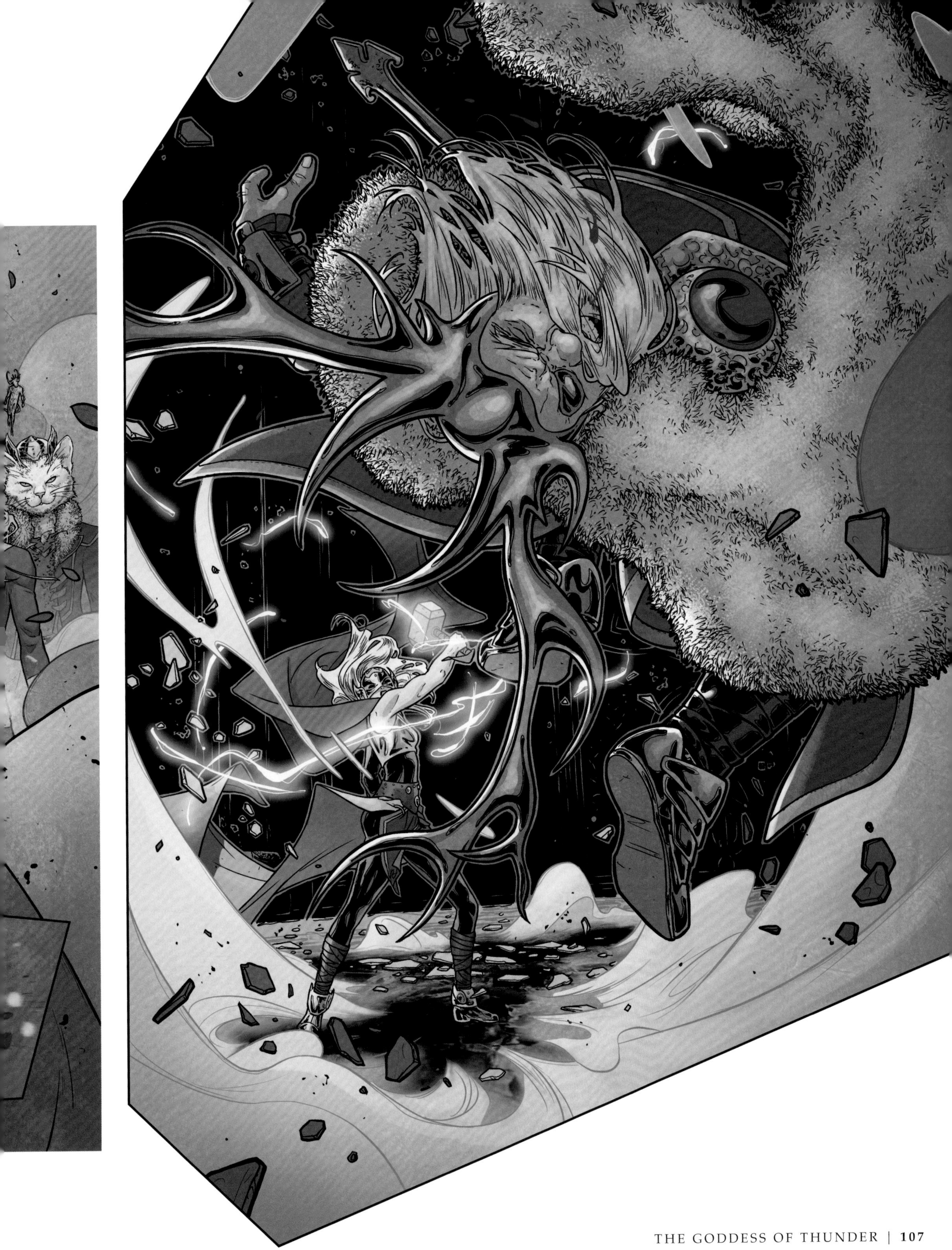

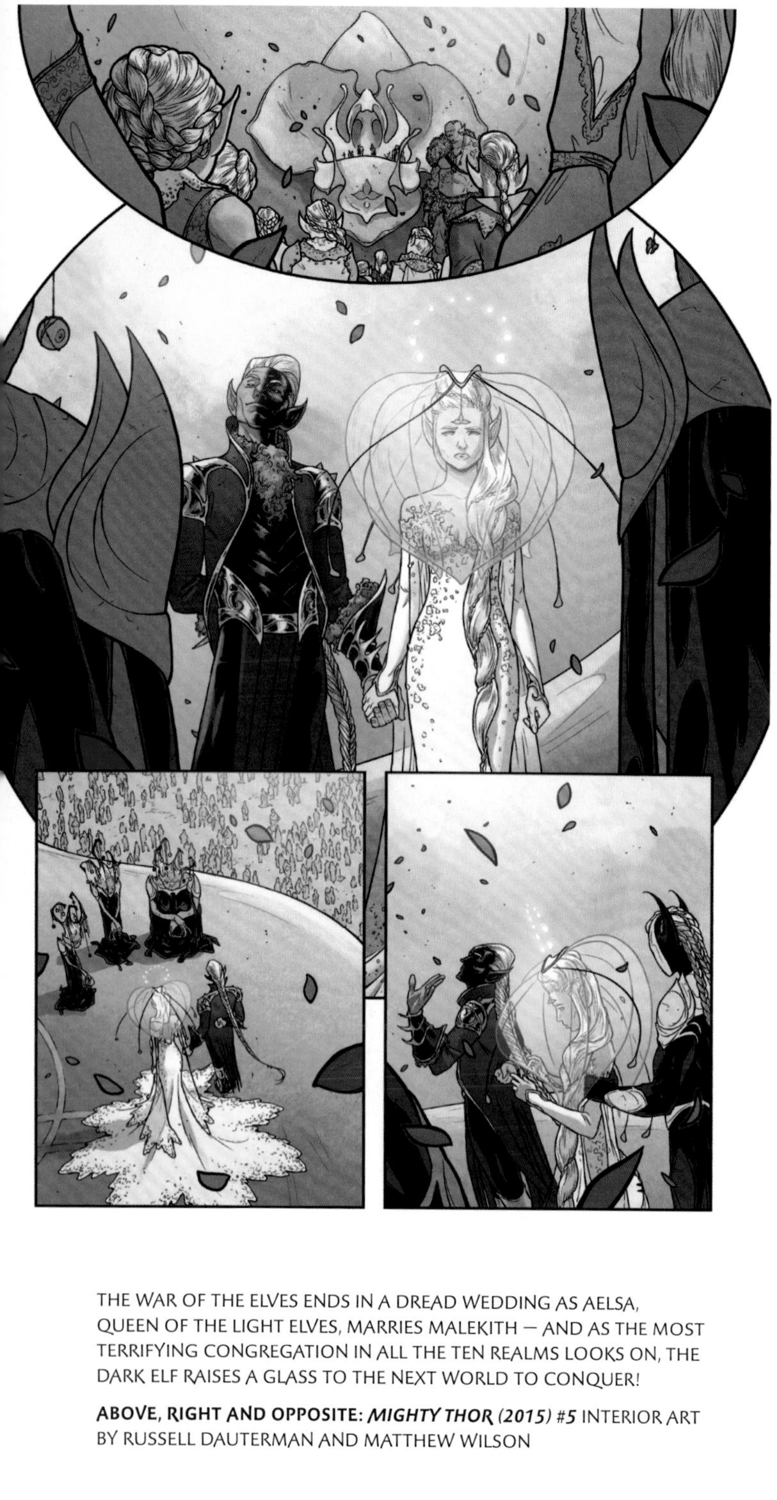

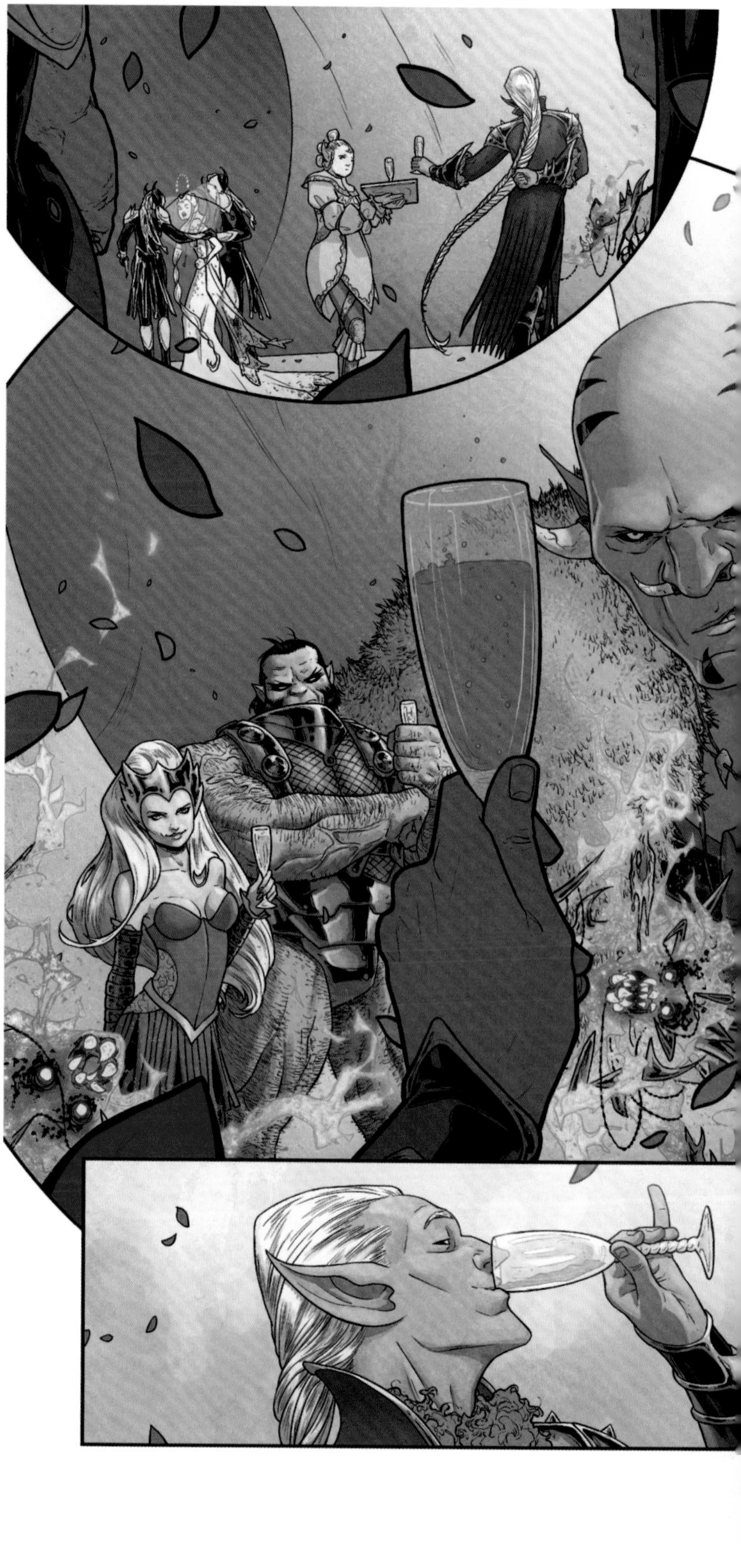

THE WAR OF THE ELVES ENDS IN A DREAD WEDDING AS AELSA, QUEEN OF THE LIGHT ELVES, MARRIES MALEKITH — AND AS THE MOST TERRIFYING CONGREGATION IN ALL THE TEN REALMS LOOKS ON, THE DARK ELF RAISES A GLASS TO THE NEXT WORLD TO CONQUER!

ABOVE, RIGHT AND OPPOSITE: *MIGHTY THOR (2015) #5* INTERIOR ART BY RUSSELL DAUTERMAN AND MATTHEW WILSON

LOKI CARRIES OUT AN ACT OF ULTIMATE BETRAYAL — STABBING HIS ADOPTIVE MOTHER, FREYJA, IN THE BACK!

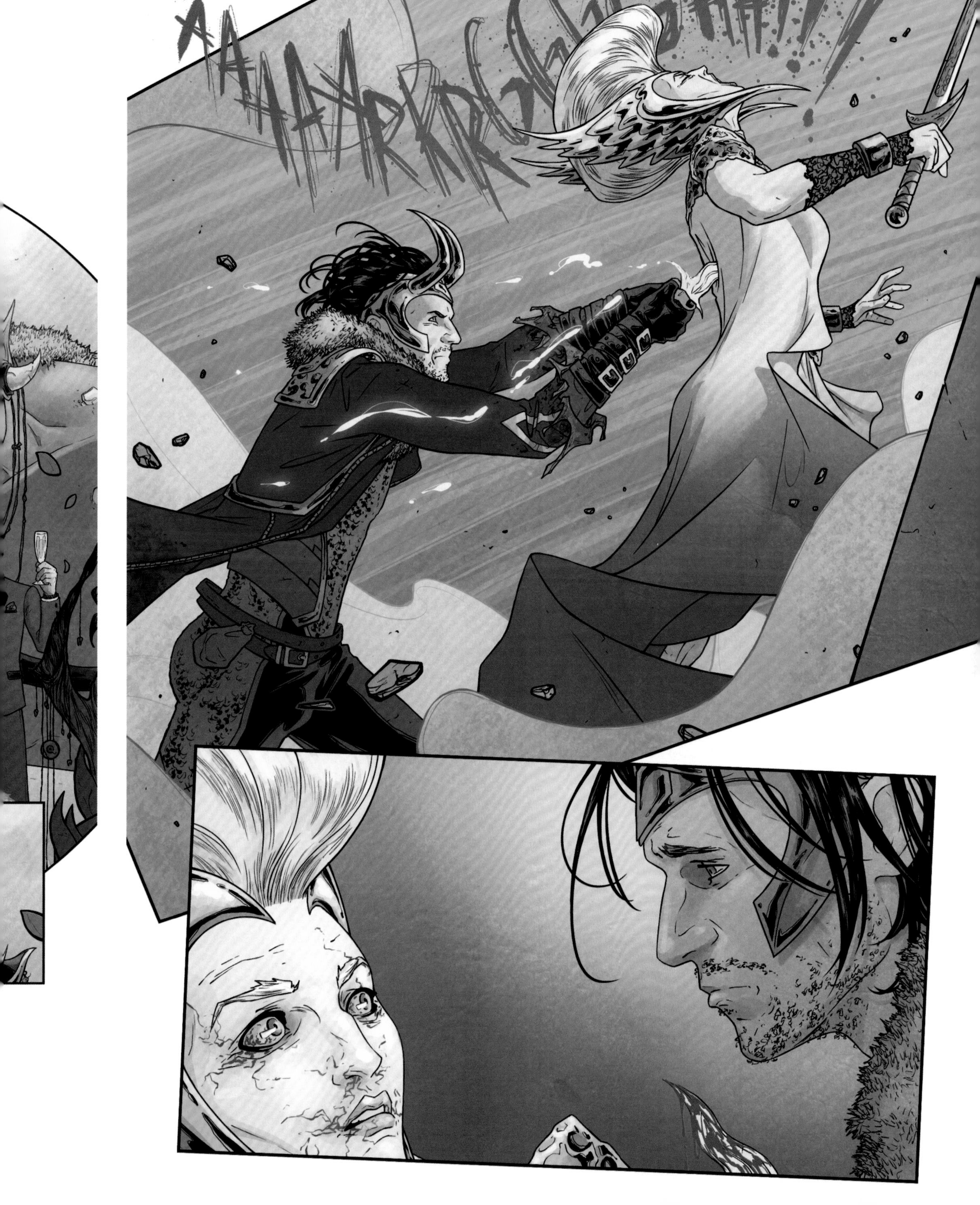
AAAARRRGGGHH!!!

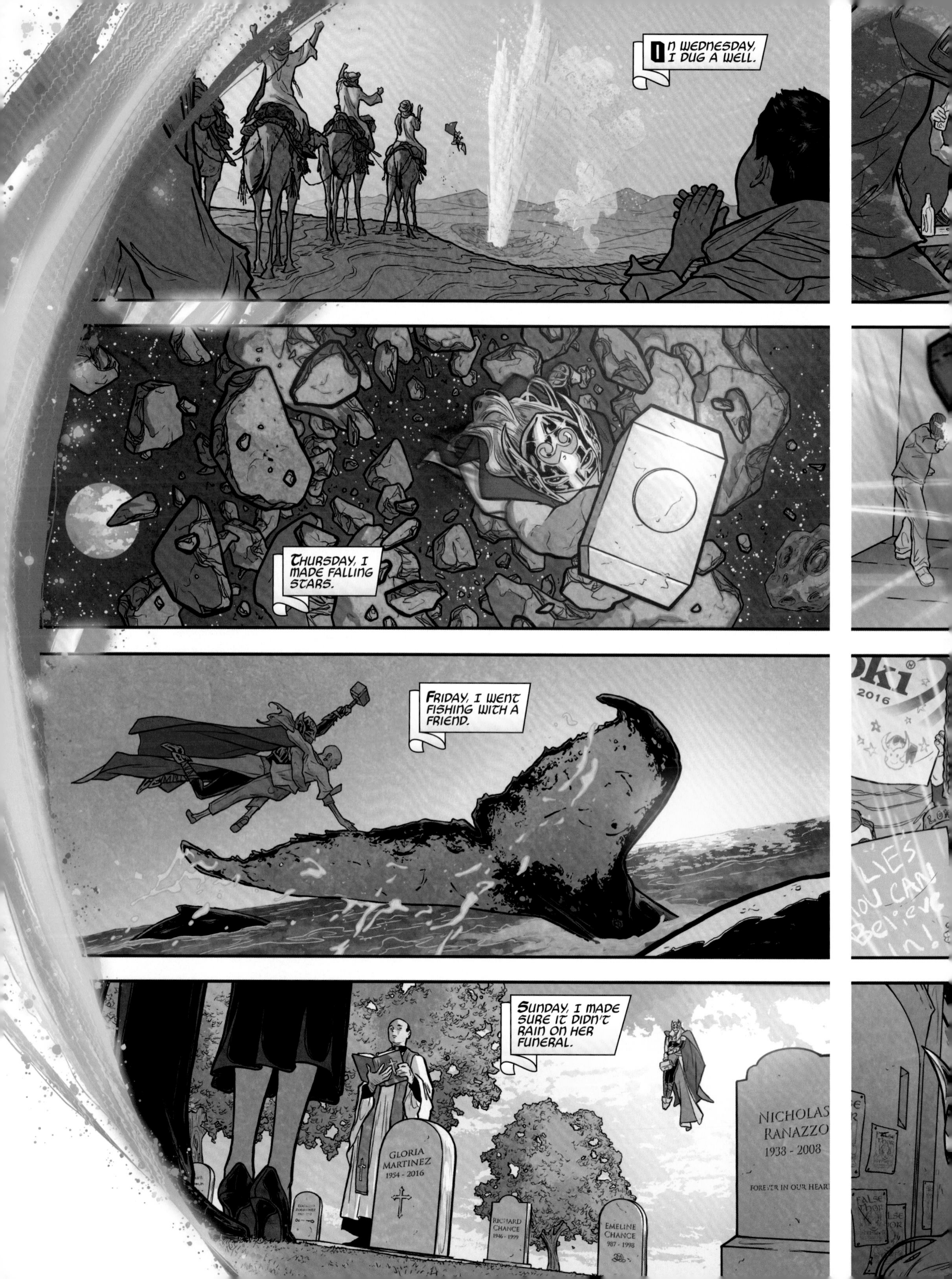
ON WEDNESDAY, I DUG A WELL.
THURSDAY, I MADE FALLING STARS.
FRIDAY, I WENT FISHING WITH A FRIEND.
SUNDAY, I MADE SURE IT DIDN'T RAIN ON HER FUNERAL.
GLORIA MARTINEZ 1954 - 2016
RICHARD CHANCE 1946 - 1999
NICHOLAS RANAZZO 1938 - 2008

"I really wanted to show Jane's fight against cancer in as realistic a way as possible. I wanted her to look like someone going through chemotherapy. I wanted her to look tired and gaunt and to be a bit hunched over as if she was weighed down by her illness. But I always tried to incorporate her inner strength — the bit of Thor that's intrinsically part of Jane — either through her eyes or facial expression."

— RUSSELL DAUTERMAN

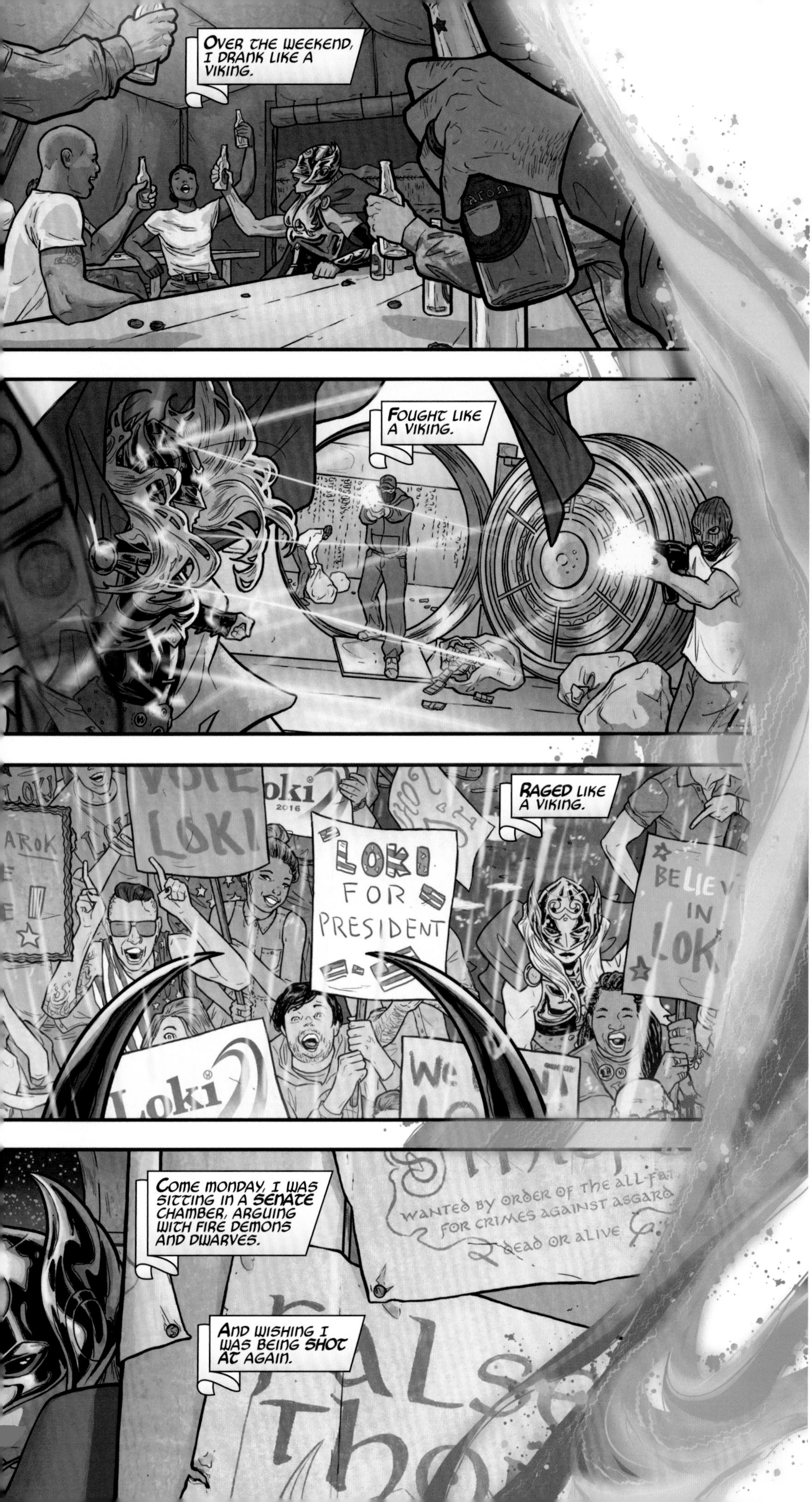

OVER THE WEEKEND, I DRANK LIKE A VIKING.
FOUGHT LIKE A VIKING.
VOTE LOKI
Loki 2016
RAGED LIKE A VIKING.
LOKI FOR PRESIDENT
BELIEVE IN LOKI
Loki
COME MONDAY, I WAS SITTING IN A SENATE CHAMBER, ARGUING WITH FIRE DEMONS AND DWARVES.
wanted by order of the all-fa
for crimes against asgard
dead or alive
AND WISHING I WAS BEING SHOT AT AGAIN.

A WEEK IN THE LIFE OF THE GODDESS OF THUNDER!

***MIGHTY THOR* (2015) #5**
INTERIOR ART BY RUSSELL DAUTERMAN AND MATTHEW WILSON, WITH LETTERING BY JOE SABINO

THOR REFLECTS ON THE FORCES MOUNTING AGAINST HER.

MIGHTY THOR* (2015) *#3 COVER BY RUSSELL DAUTERMAN AND MATTHEW WILSON

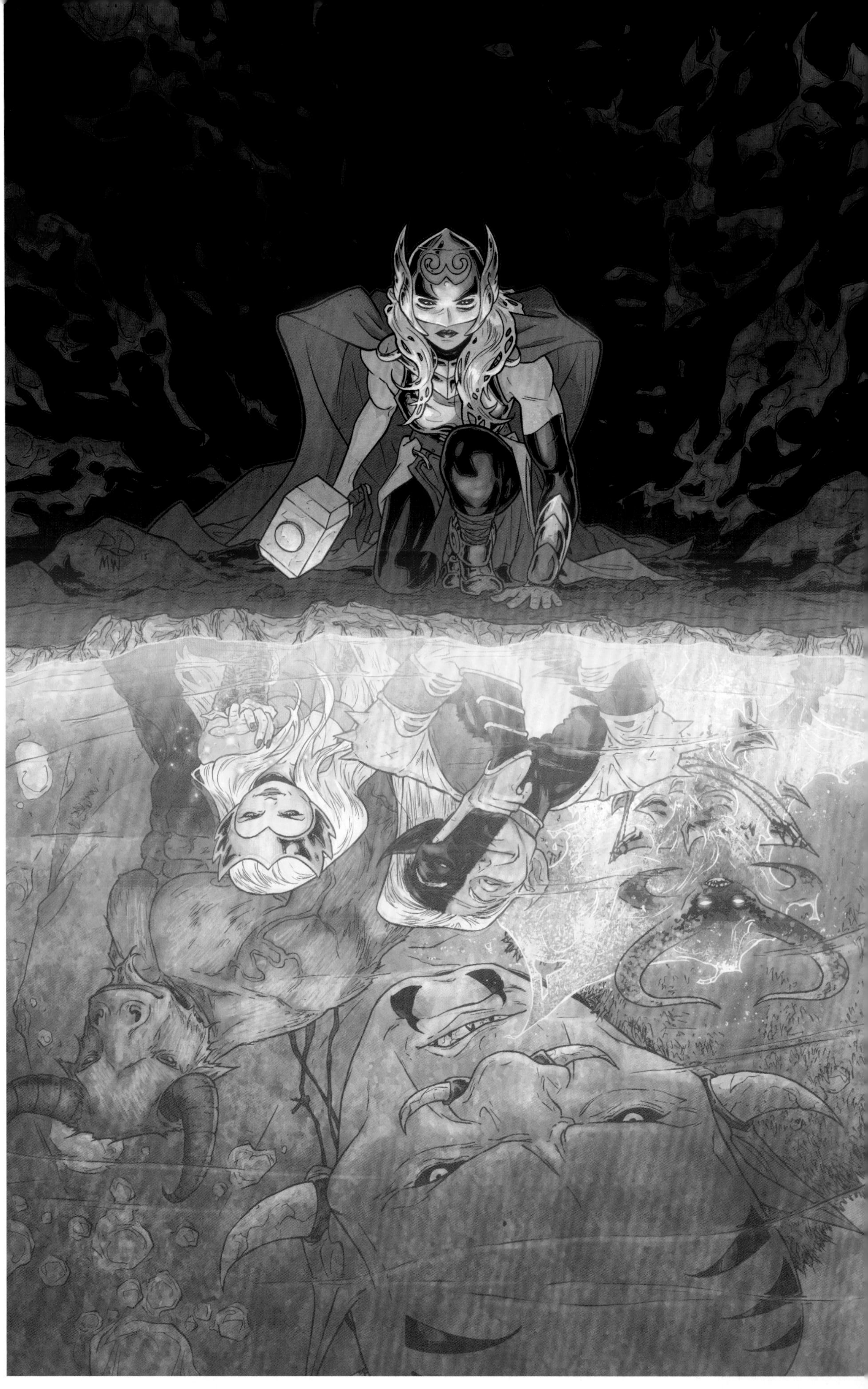

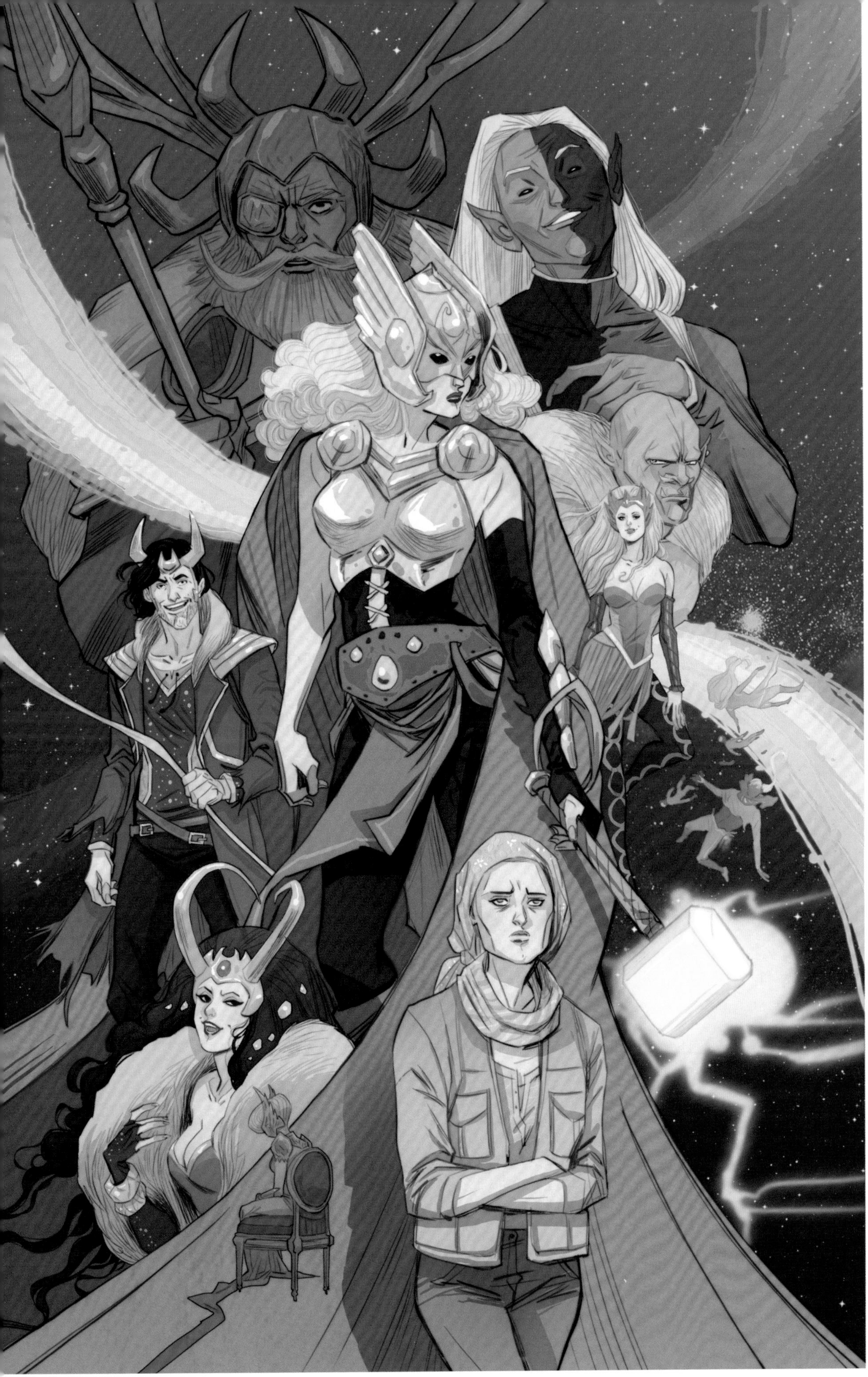

THE STORY THUS FAR!

***MIGHTY THOR* (2015) #8**
VARIANT COVER BY MARGUERITE SAUVAGE

"Whether it's the Avengers or the League of Realms, there are always challenges when drawing a team book — making sure everyone gets enough 'screen time,' showing several characters in multiple panels without making them too small, keeping the pages from being overcrowded, etc. On the other hand, you get to draw cool team action shots and a variety of characters."

— STEVE EPTING

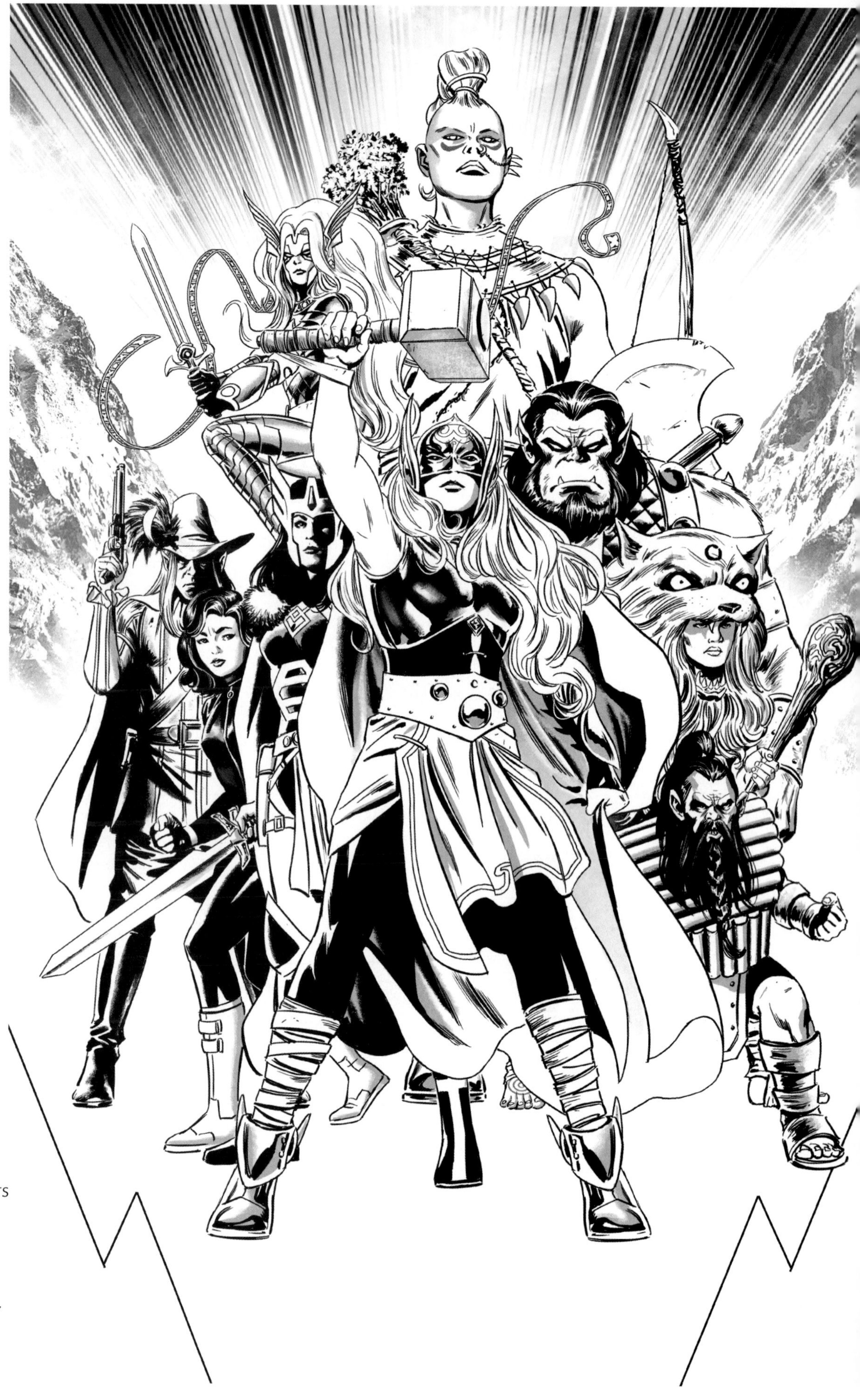

IN A BID TO LIBERATE ALFHEIM FROM MALEKITH'S GRIP, THOR ASSEMBLES A NEW LEAGUE OF REALMS! JOINING UD, SCREWBEARD AND SIR IVORY HONEYSHOT ARE NEW RECRUITS ROZ SOLOMON, SIF, ANGELA, MOUNTAIN GIANT TITANYA VAETILDA VINNSUVIUS AND RO BLOODROOT, WOOD WIZARD OF VANAHEIM.

RIGHT AND OPPOSITE: ***MIGHTY THOR (2015) #13*** INTERIOR INKS BY STEVE EPTING AND COLORS BY FRANK MARTIN

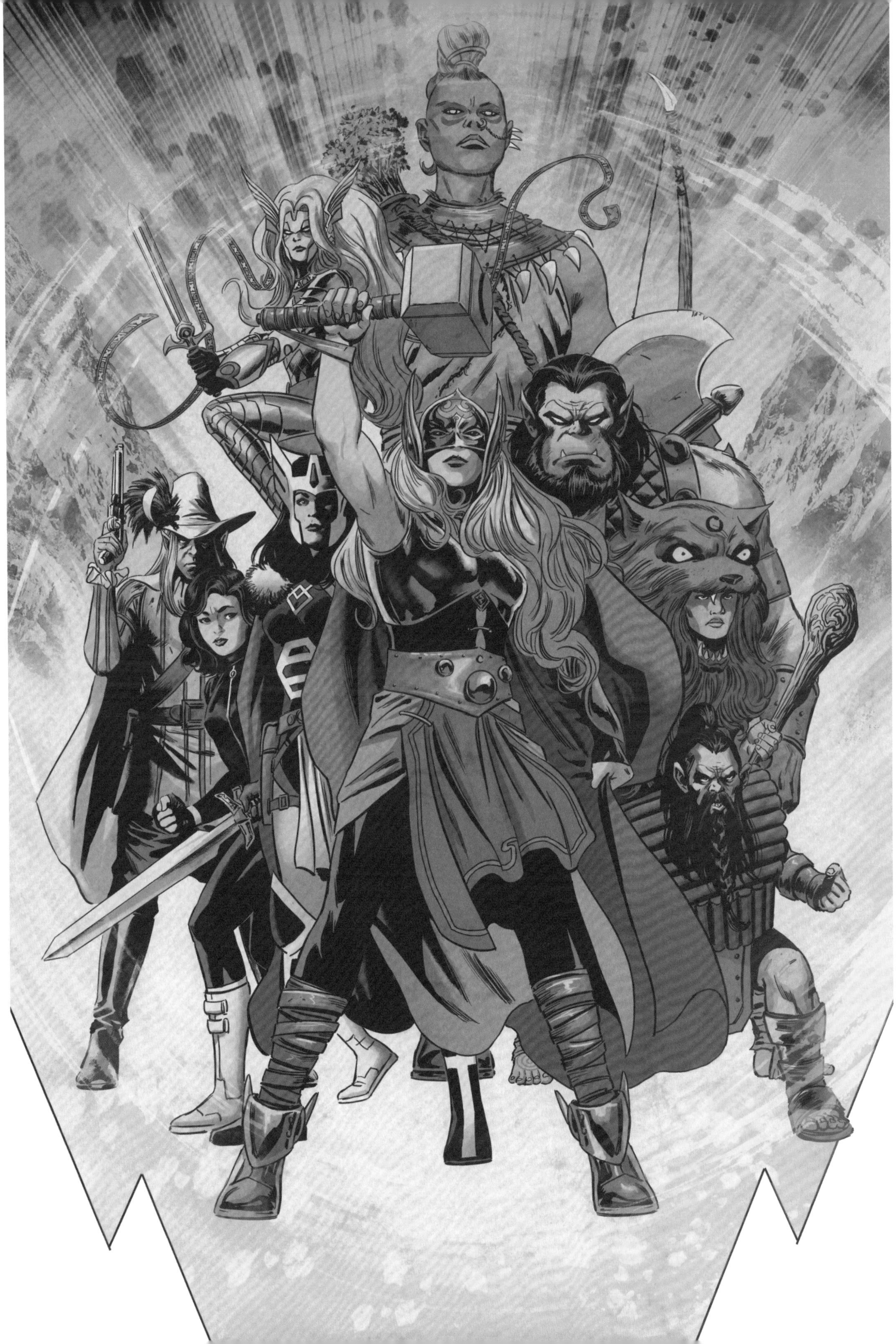

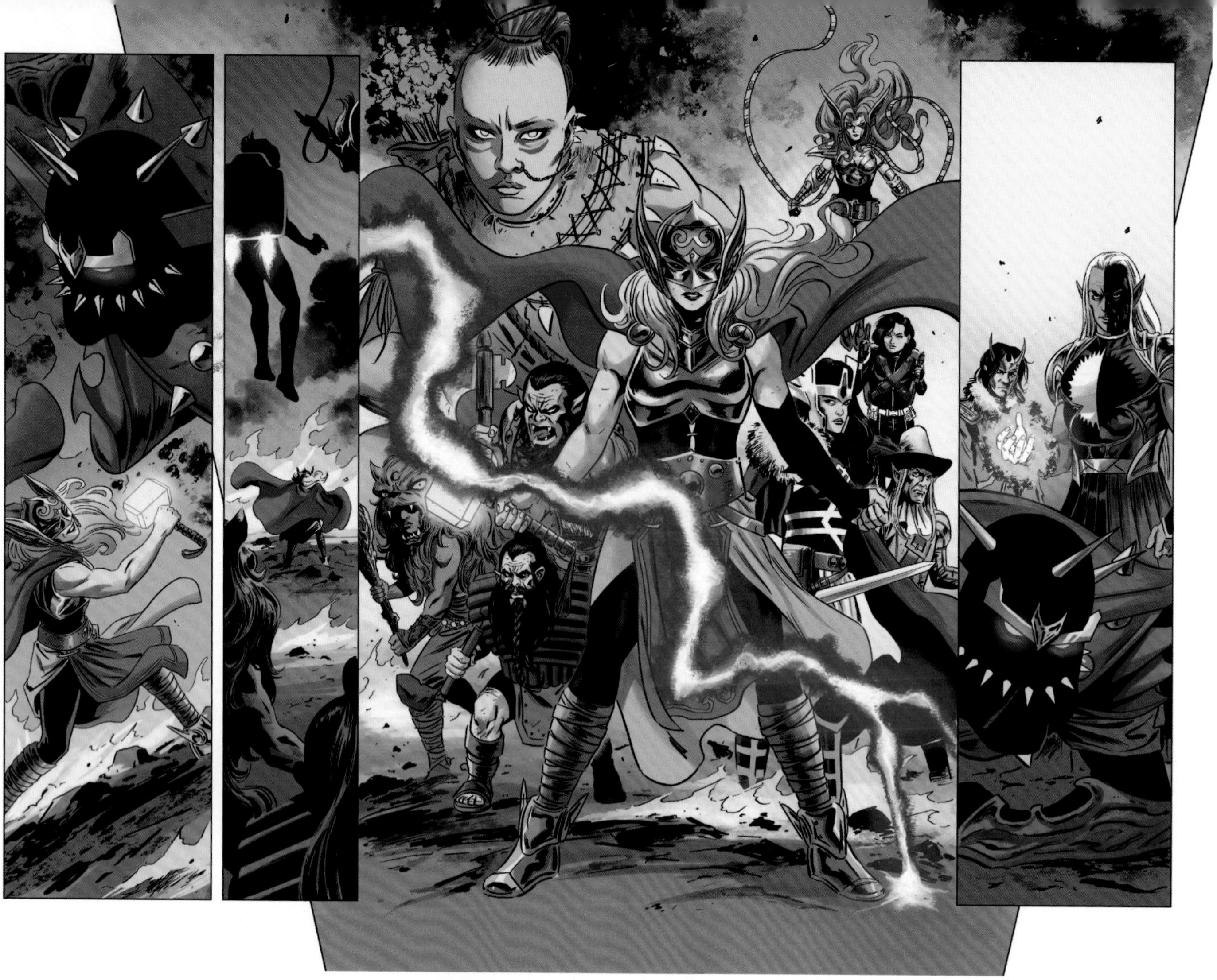

"It's always fun to draw the villains." – STEVE EPTING

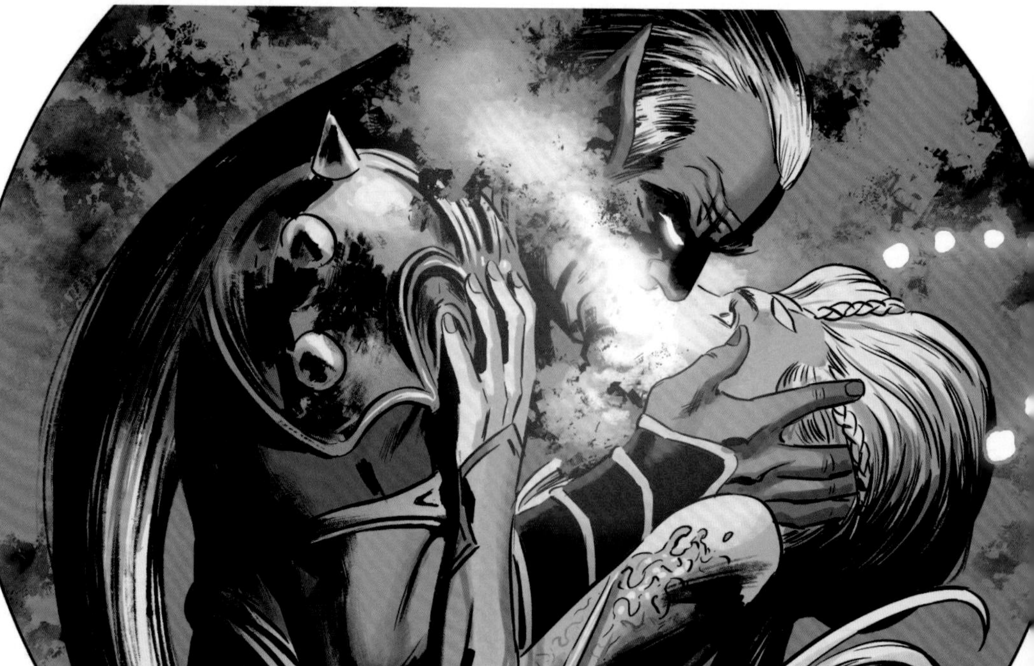

THE LEAGUE OF REALMS FACES MALEKITH AND HIS ALLIES — INCLUDING THE NEW KURSE, ONCE THE ORIGINAL LEAGUE MEMBER LADY WAZIRIA. MALEKITH ULTIMATELY TAKES HIS LEAVE OF A RAVAGED ALFHEIM AND SEALS HIS DIVORCE FROM AELSA WITH A BRUTAL KISS!

MIGHTY THOR (2015) #13-14
INTERIOR ART BY STEVE EPTING AND FRANK MARTIN

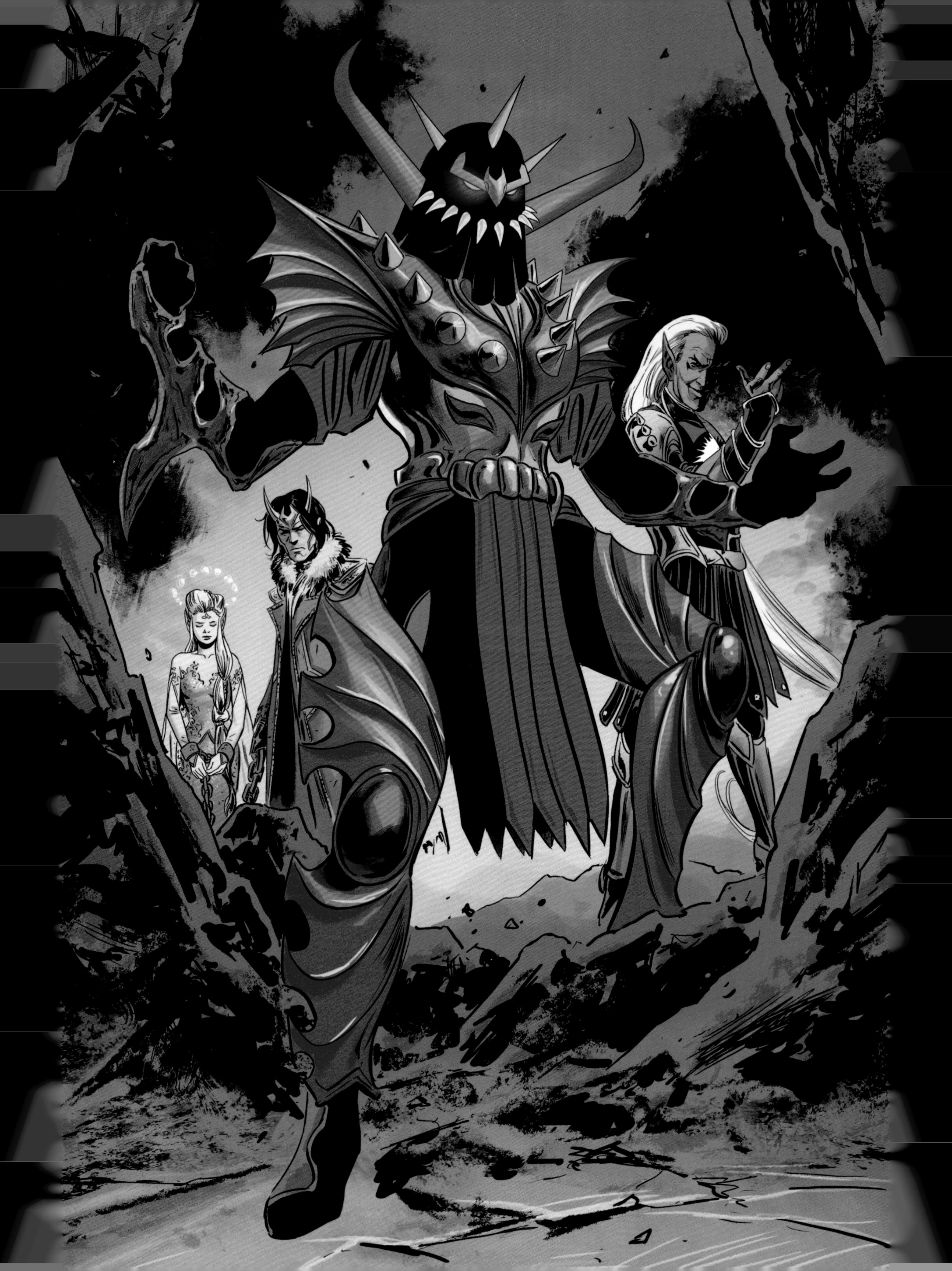

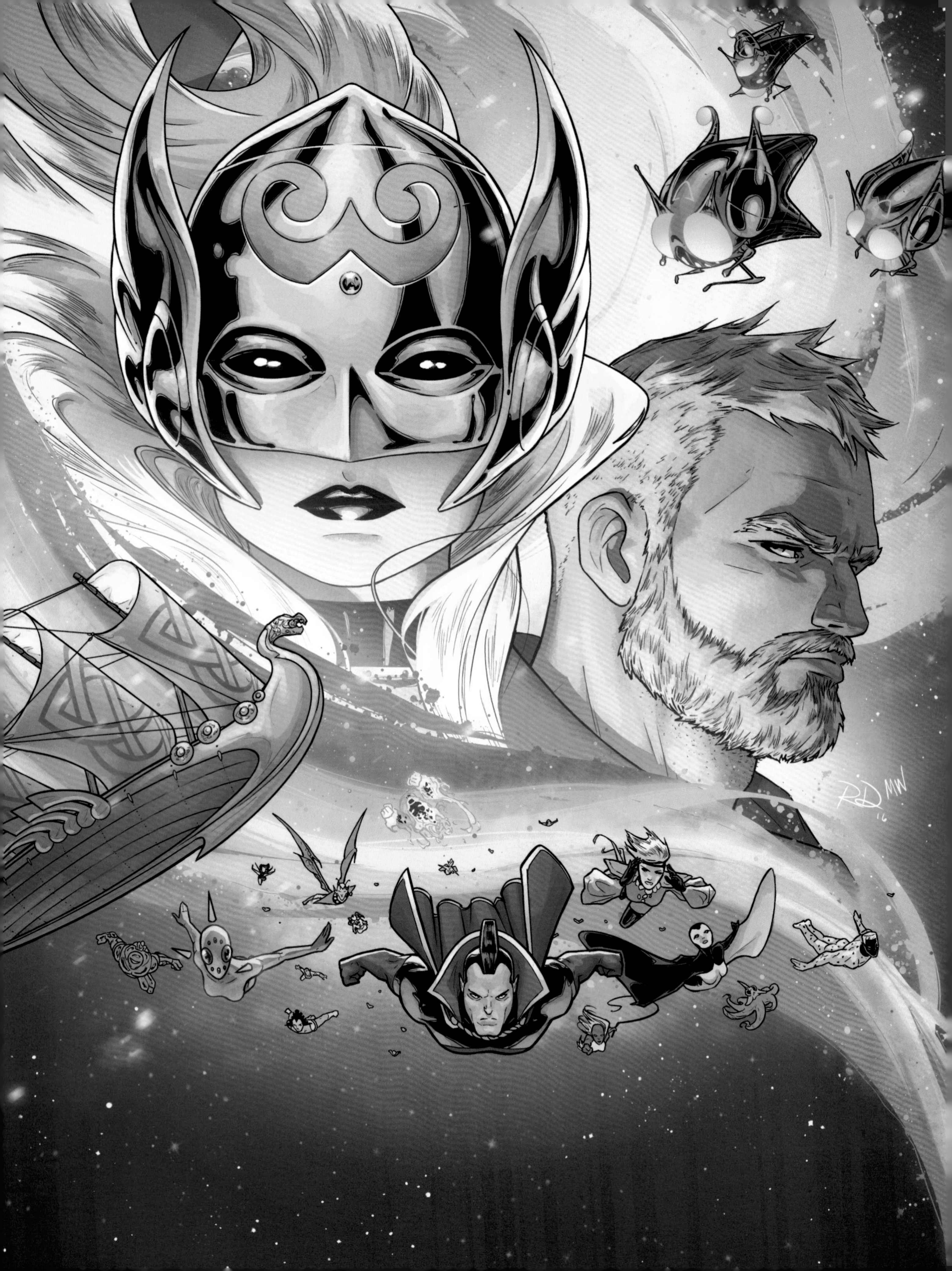

"I loved the idea of Odin coming back with this murderous brother and kind of just saying, 'He's a good guy now — I've forgiven him.' Cul's part of the court of Asgard. I'm definitely trying to play up the *Game of Thrones* aspect of having people in that throne room who have tried to murder one another." — JASON AARON

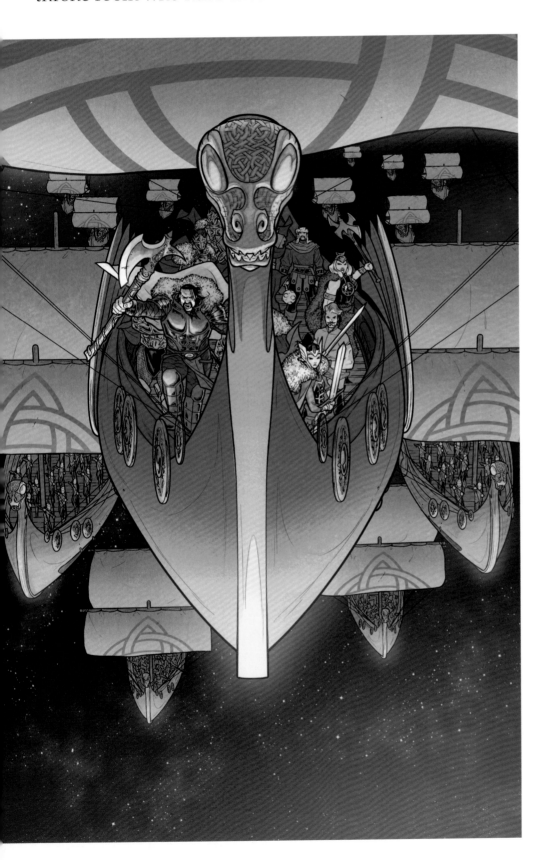

THE CAPRICIOUS ACTIONS OF THE ALIEN GODS SHARRA AND K'YTHRI TRIGGER AN ASGARD/SHI'AR WAR, REUNITING THOR AND THE ODINSON. LEADING THE ASGARDIAN ARMY IS CUL, ODIN'S BROTHER, WHO WAS THE VILLAIN OF THE 2011 CROSSOVER *FEAR ITSELF* BUT WAS WELCOMED BACK INTO THE FOLD BY ODIN FOLLOWING THE EVENTS OF *ORIGINAL SIN*.

OPPOSITE AND LEFT: *MIGHTY THOR (2015) #15* COVER AND INTERIOR ART BY RUSSELL DAUTERMAN AND MATTHEW WILSON

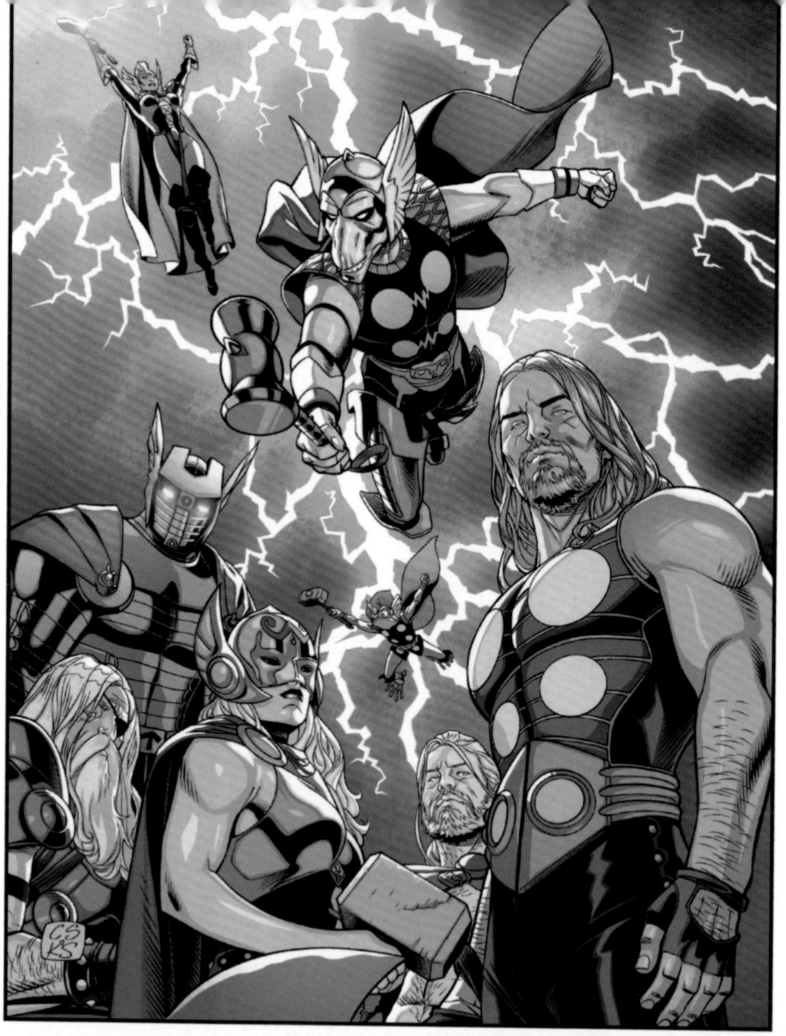

DURING 2015'S ***SECRET WARS***, JASON AARON TOLD A STORY OF MULTIPLE THUNDER GODS IN THE PAGES OF ***THORS*** — WHICH CLIMAXED WITH THE HAMMER OF ULTIMATE THOR CRASH-LANDING IN THE RUINS OF OLD ASGARD!

THORS #1 COVER BY CHRIS SPROUSE, KARL STORY AND DAVE MCCAIG; AND ***THORS*** #4 INTERIOR ART BY SPROUSE, STORY AND ISRAEL SILVA

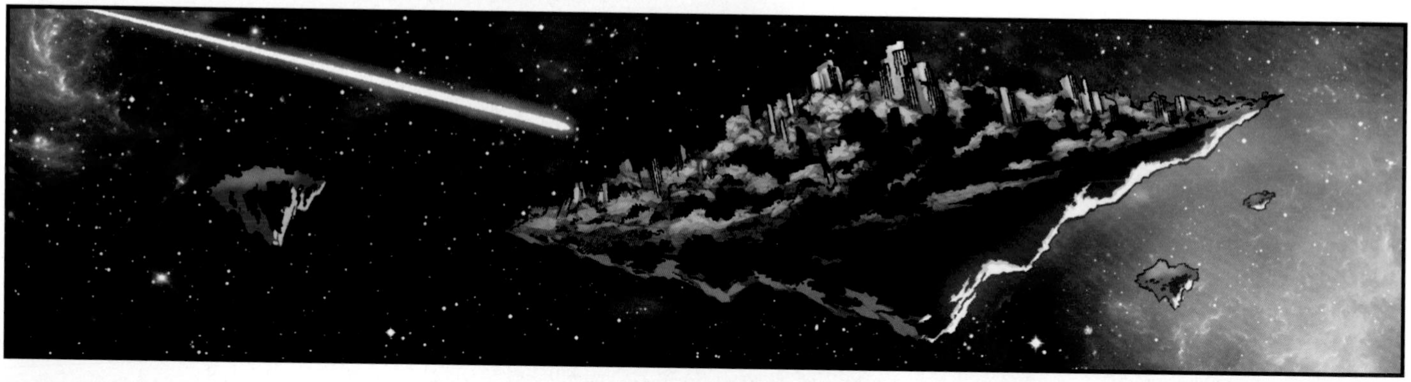

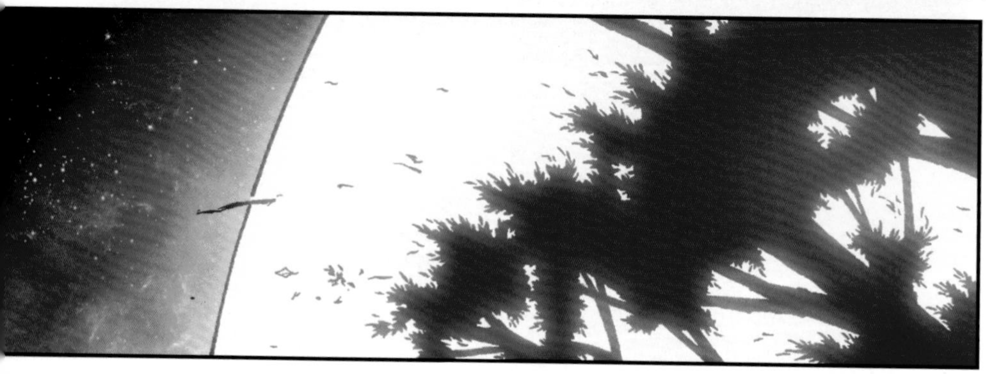

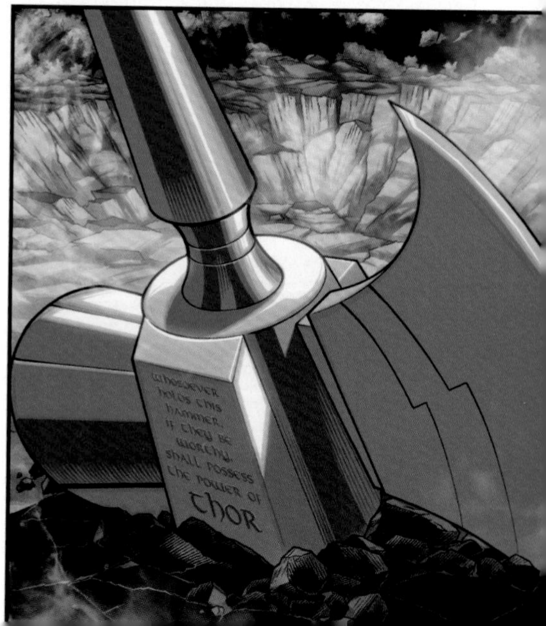
Whosoever holds this hammer, if they be worthy, shall possess the power of Thor

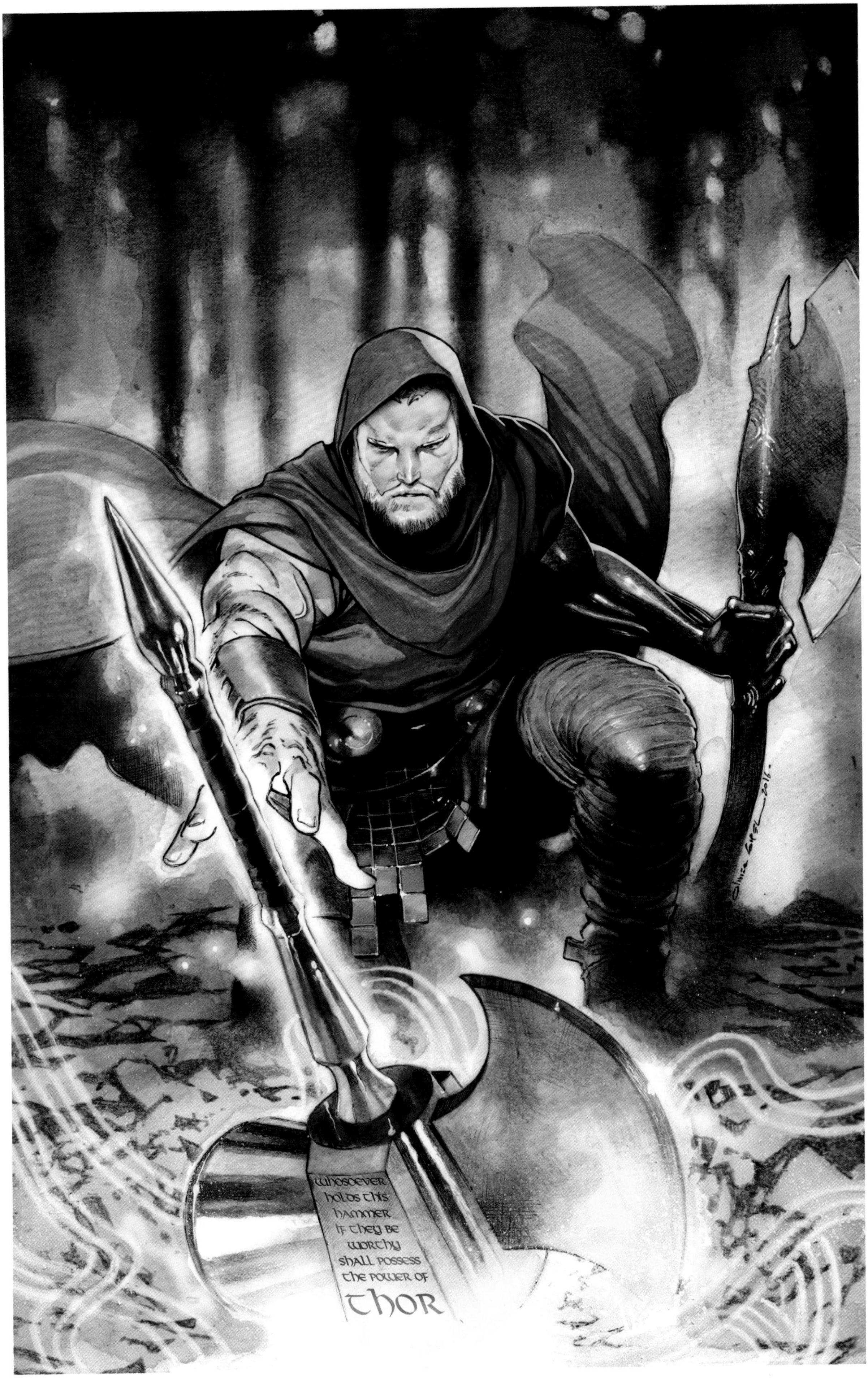
whosoever holds this hammer if they be worthy shall possess the power of
THOR

IN ***UNWORTHY THOR***, AARON AND RETURNING LEGEND OLIVIER COIPEL SET THE ODINSON ON A MISSION TO OLD ASGARD TO LOCATE THIS OTHER HAMMER — ONLY TO FIND HIS ENTIRE HOME STOLEN!

UNWORTHY THOR #1 COVER BY OLIVIER COIPEL

THE HUNT FOR THE HAMMER UNITED THE ODINSON WITH OLD FRIEND BETA RAY BILL, FAITHFUL GOAT TOOTHGNASHER AND MURDEROUS HEL-HOUND THORI TO TAKE ON COSMIC THREATS, INCLUDING THE COLLECTOR AND THANOS.

UNWORTHY THOR #3 INTERIOR ART BY OLIVIER COIPEL AND MATTHEW WILSON

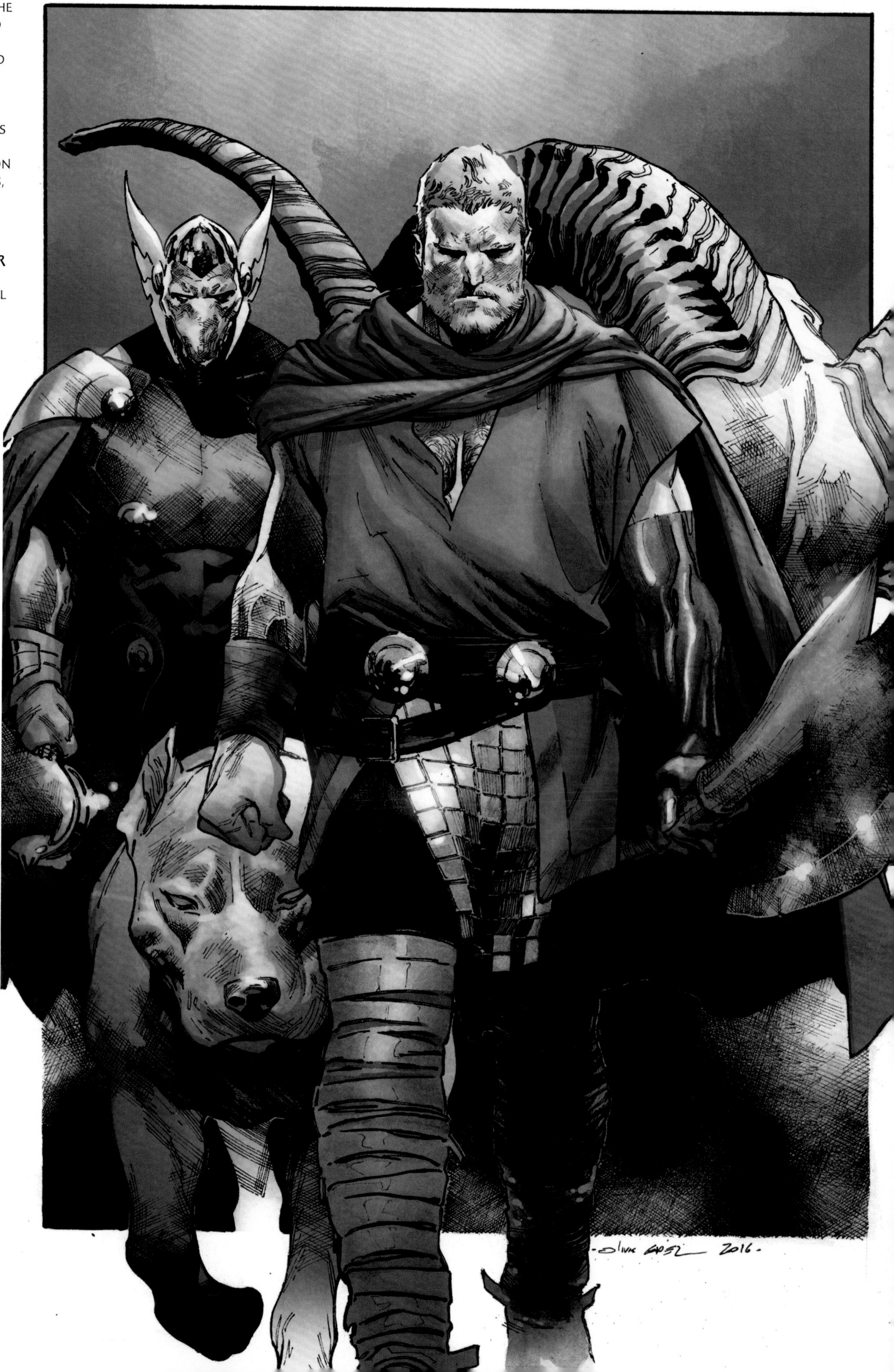
2016.

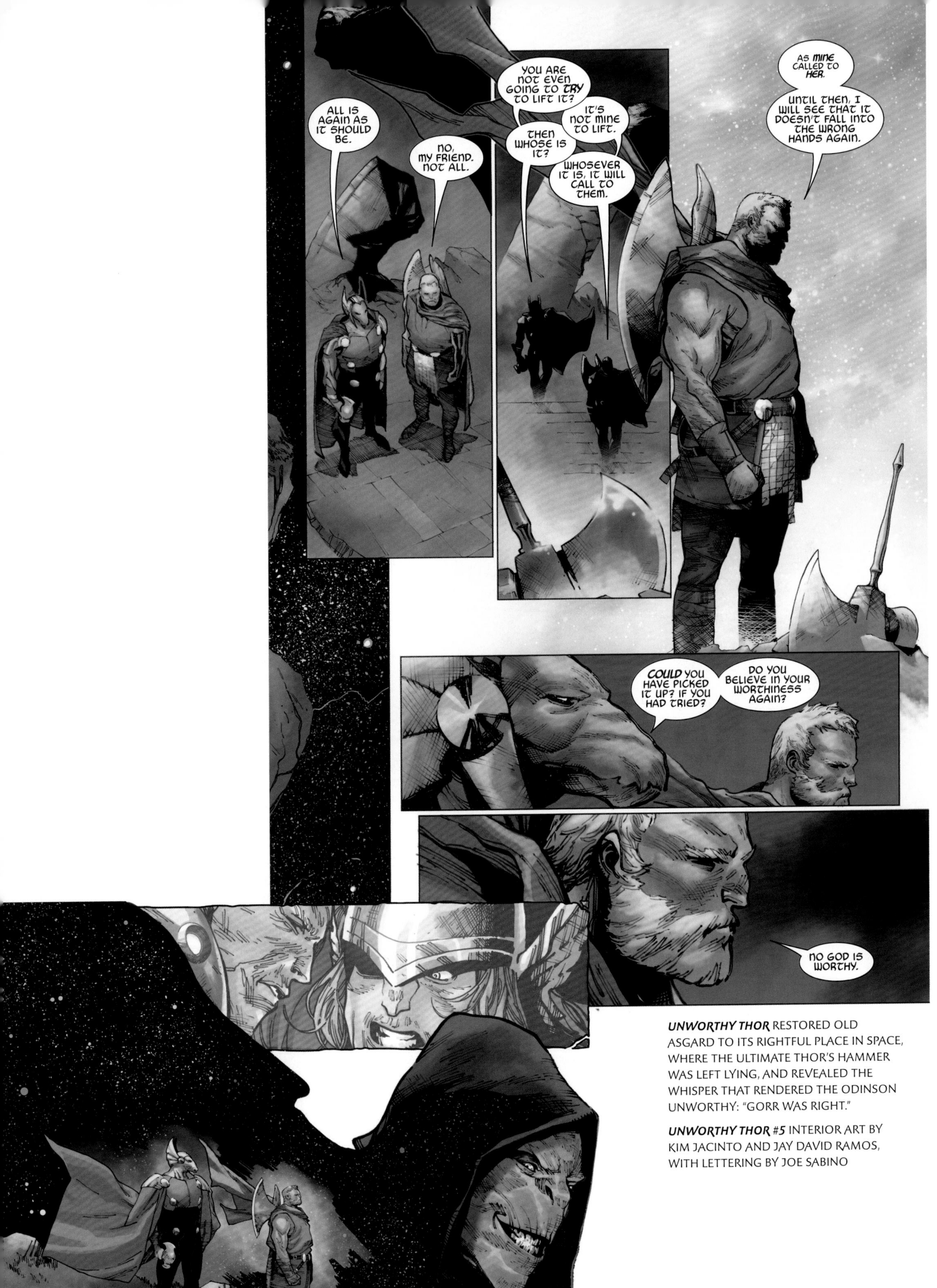
ALL IS AGAIN AS IT SHOULD BE.
NO, MY FRIEND. NOT ALL.
YOU ARE NOT EVEN GOING TO TRY TO LIFT IT?
IT'S NOT MINE TO LIFT.
THEN WHOSE IS IT?
WHOSEVER IT IS, IT WILL CALL TO THEM.
AS MINE CALLED TO HER.
UNTIL THEN, I WILL SEE THAT IT DOESN'T FALL INTO THE WRONG HANDS AGAIN.
COULD YOU HAVE PICKED IT UP? IF YOU HAD TRIED?
DO YOU BELIEVE IN YOUR WORTHINESS AGAIN?
NO GOD IS WORTHY.

UNWORTHY THOR RESTORED OLD ASGARD TO ITS RIGHTFUL PLACE IN SPACE, WHERE THE ULTIMATE THOR'S HAMMER WAS LEFT LYING, AND REVEALED THE WHISPER THAT RENDERED THE ODINSON UNWORTHY: "GORR WAS RIGHT."

UNWORTHY THOR #5 INTERIOR ART BY KIM JACINTO AND JAY DAVID RAMOS, WITH LETTERING BY JOE SABINO

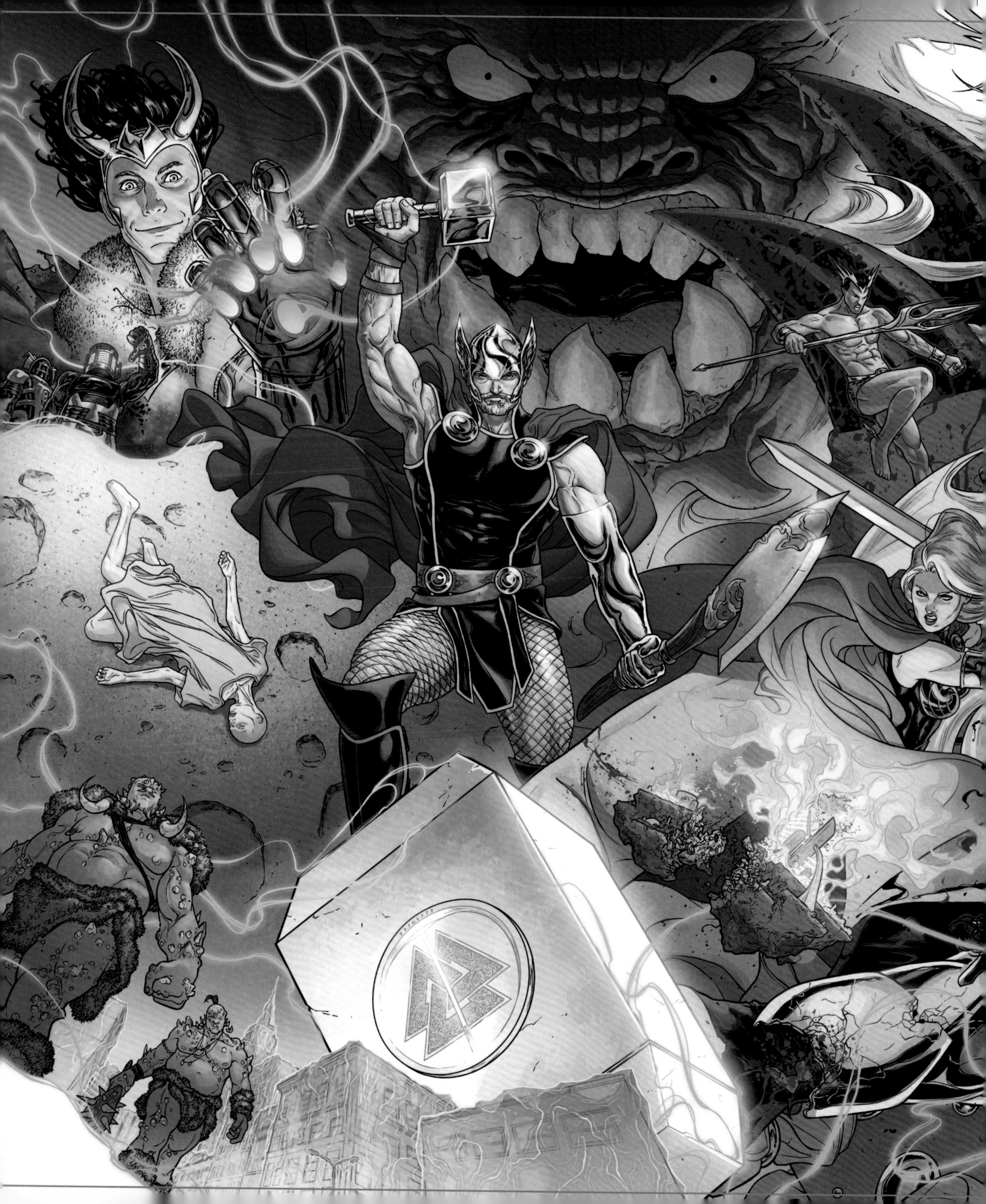

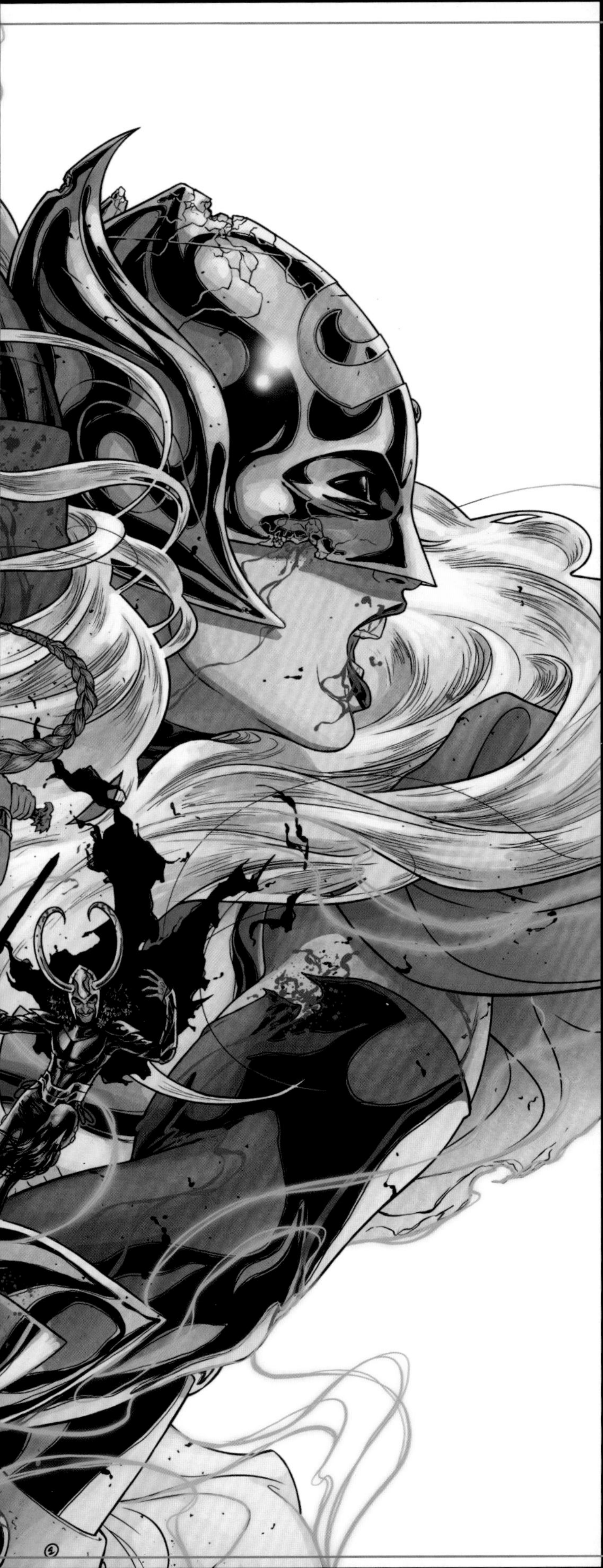

chapter seven:

THE DEATH OF THE MIGHTY THOR

"'TWAS A MORTAL. NAMED **JANE**. A WOMAN WHO GAVE UP EVERYTHING IN ORDER TO STOP YOU. **REMEMBER THAT.**"
— JANE FOSTER

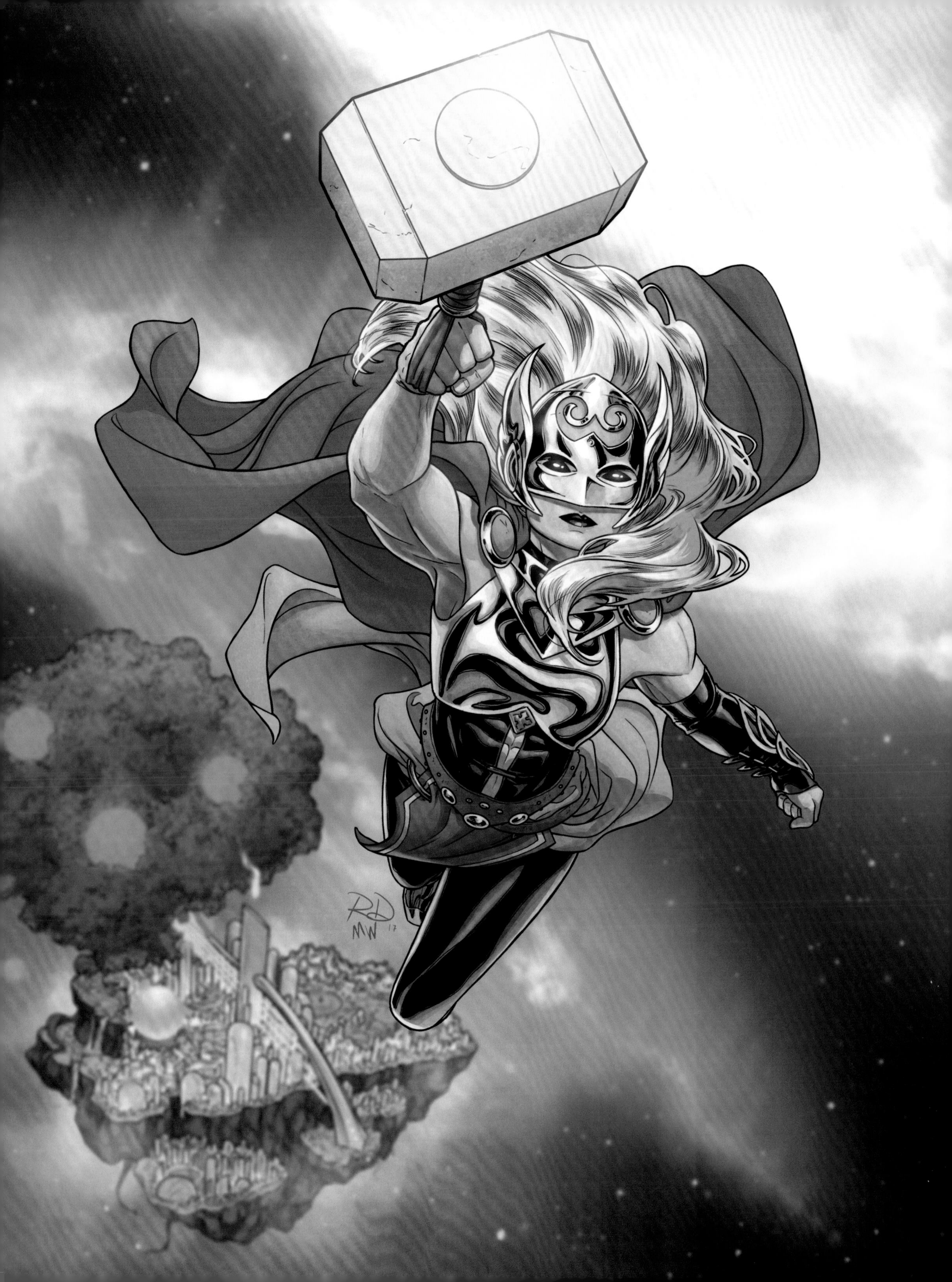

A ll good things must come to an end. And so it was with Jane Foster's time as Thor. But before she would put down her hammer for the final time, Jason Aaron and Russell Dauterman were determined to fashion an epic send-off worthy of their hero. The sprawling saga begins with Fire Goblins from Muspelheim bringing Malekith's war to Nidavellir and claiming the lives of refugee Light Elf children under Volstagg's protection. Filled with rage, Volstagg heads to Old Asgard and claims the hammer of the Ultimate Thor — becoming a vengeance-filled War Thor! This brings him into conflict with Sindr, queen of Muspelheim — and with Jane herself! But even worse is to follow. Thanks to the machinations of Malekith, the Mangog — the manifested vengeance of a billion billion souls, the ultimate judgment of the gods — arrives on Asgard's doorstep. And it comes at exactly the wrong time, just as Jane is given a terrible prognosis on Earth. Her transformations into Thor are purging her chemotherapy drugs from her system, meaning her cancer has become steadily worse — and lifting Mjolnir one more time will kill her. Both the Odinson and Odin stand in the Mangog's way, but they are not enough. Jane will join the fight, and damn the consequences!

"The whole thing was exciting and dreadful all at the same time as those pages were coming in from Russell," Aaron says. "I really wanted to stick the landing, because I had that story in my head for a long time. But I was really happy with the way it came out. She does die, she does pay the ultimate sacrifice — but that's still not the end of her story. I wasn't ready to wrap that up — I didn't want her to lose the fight in that way. I wanted her still to be a part of the Marvel Universe."

Dauterman and his colorist partner, Matthew Wilson, were charged with capturing all the action and emotion of a momentous story that destroys Asgardia, obliterates the Rainbow Bridge and ends with Thor sacrificing Mjolnir into the sun to end the threat of the Mangog — and in so doing, triggering that final transformation into Jane.

As far as Aaron is concerned, Dauterman's art "got better and better as the book went along." The writer adds: "He really nailed the last arc. Some of those pages without words were so powerful and emotional that I definitely shed some tears when I finished the script for #705 — then I think we were all shedding tears when the art came in for that issue. The last pages are some of my favorite pages from the whole run, with Odinson and the fire and the flames of Asgardia. Jane is saying her goodbye, and she takes her helmet off — we had never

shown her take her helmet off as Thor, and that was not in the script. But it's perfect — of course she takes her helmet off. It seemed like something we had planned the entire time, but we had not. That page and that kiss and the flame is one of my favorite moments probably of anything that I've been a part of."

Looking back on *Thor* and *Mighty Thor*, Dauterman remains "amazed" at the reaction to Jane Foster as Thor. "I knew the character and fantasy subject matter would be a great fit for me, and I knew that Jason and Matt were both phenomenal at what they do," Dauterman says. "But I didn't know if people would care about a Thor that wasn't Thor Odinson. And then I saw Whoopi Goldberg pointing to my art on *The View* [when the news of Jane becoming Thor was announced]. And then Thor's identity was revealed and I started getting messages from readers saying how much the new Thor meant to them. I saved a screen grab of Whoopi pointing to the issue #1 cover, and I've saved a lot of those messages from readers. Reading people's stories about their own struggles with illness or the loss of a loved one or the hope that Jane Thor has given them has really meant a lot to me. I'm surprised — and very, very glad — that this character has had an impact like that. Drawing her book was an absolute dream project and one that will always mean the world to me. I miss Jane Thor."

OPPOSITE: *INFINITY COUNTDOWN* #1 VARIANT COVER BY RUSSELL DAUTERMAN AND MATTHEW WILSON

PREVIOUS PAGES: *MIGHTY THOR (2015)* #700 INTERIOR ART BY RUSSELL DAUTERMAN AND MATTHEW WILSON

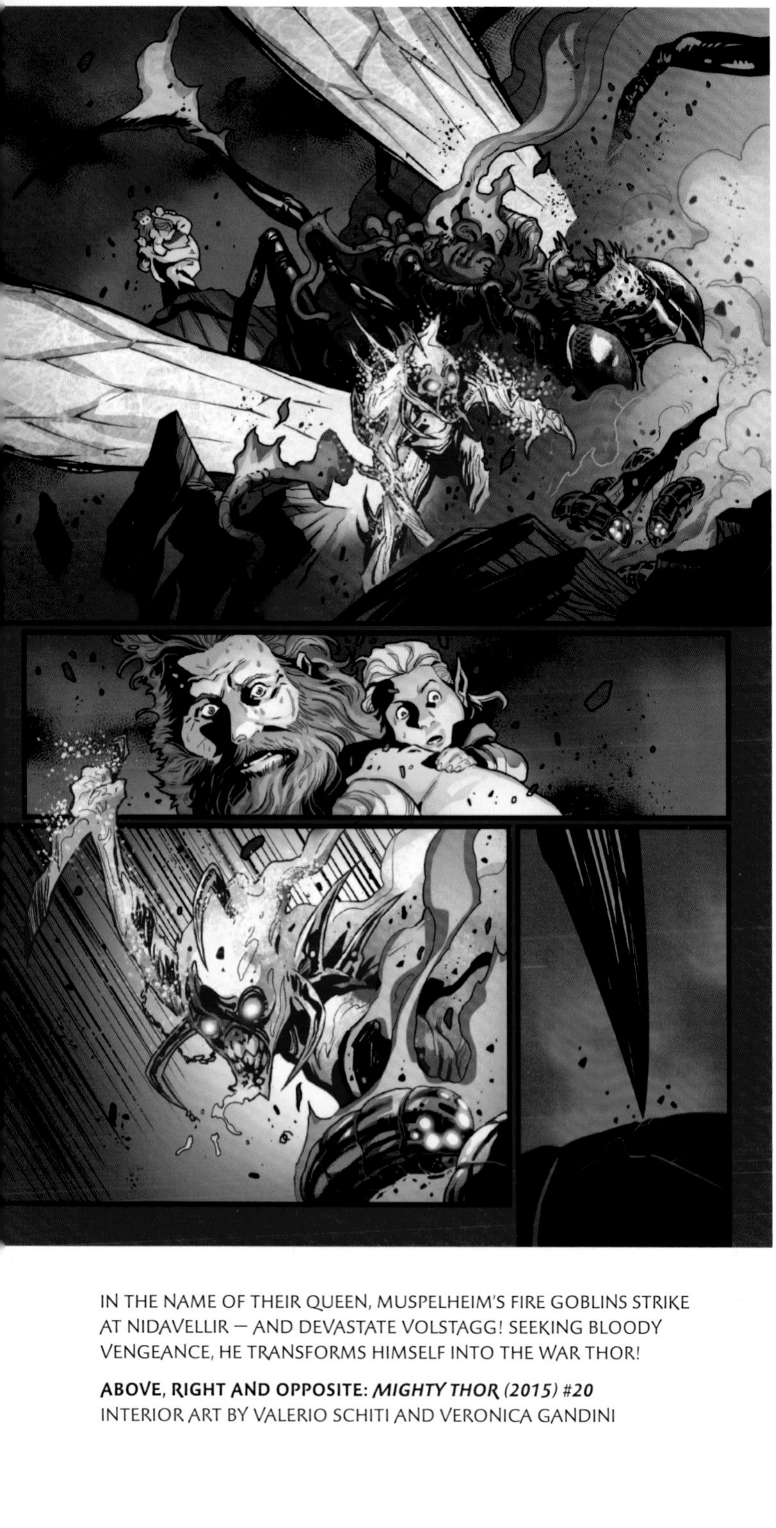

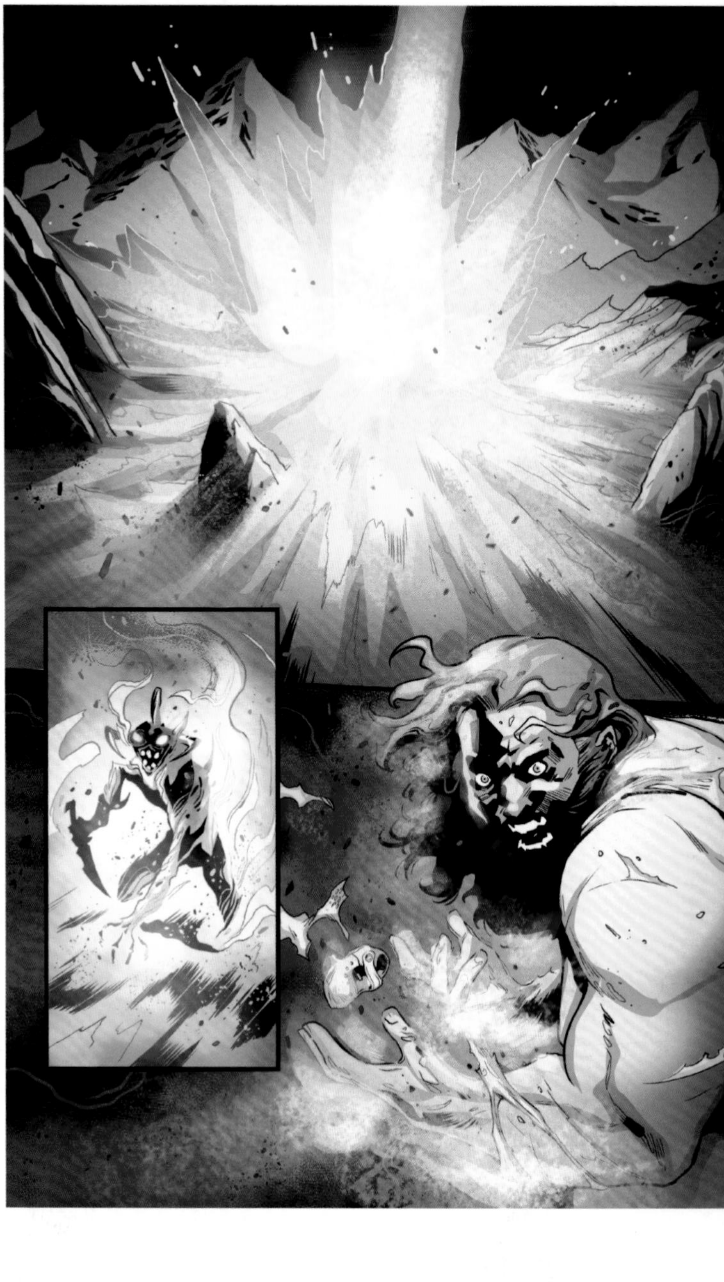

IN THE NAME OF THEIR QUEEN, MUSPELHEIM'S FIRE GOBLINS STRIKE AT NIDAVELLIR — AND DEVASTATE VOLSTAGG! SEEKING BLOODY VENGEANCE, HE TRANSFORMS HIMSELF INTO THE WAR THOR!

ABOVE, RIGHT AND OPPOSITE: *MIGHTY THOR (2015) #20*
INTERIOR ART BY VALERIO SCHITI AND VERONICA GANDINI

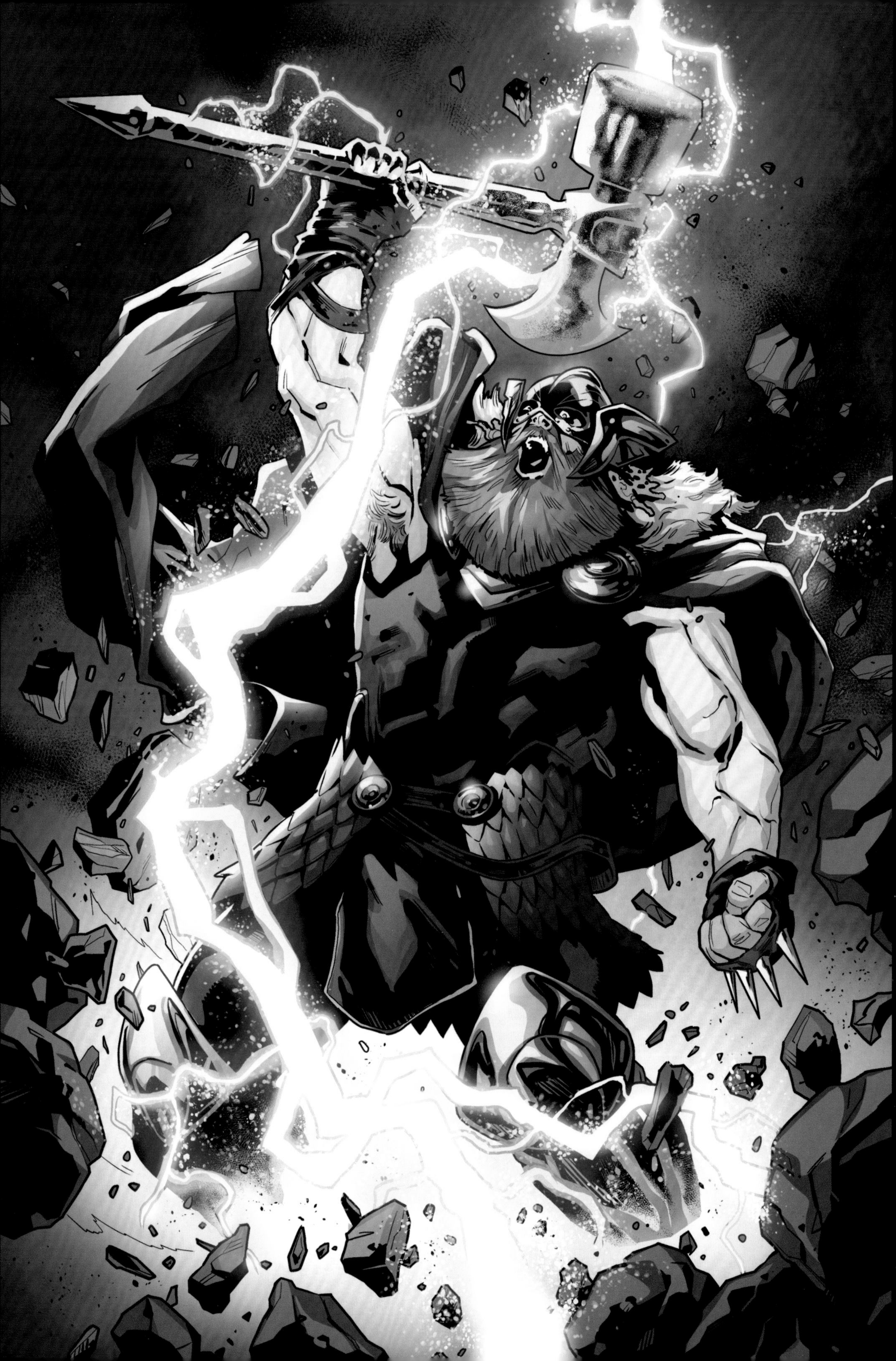

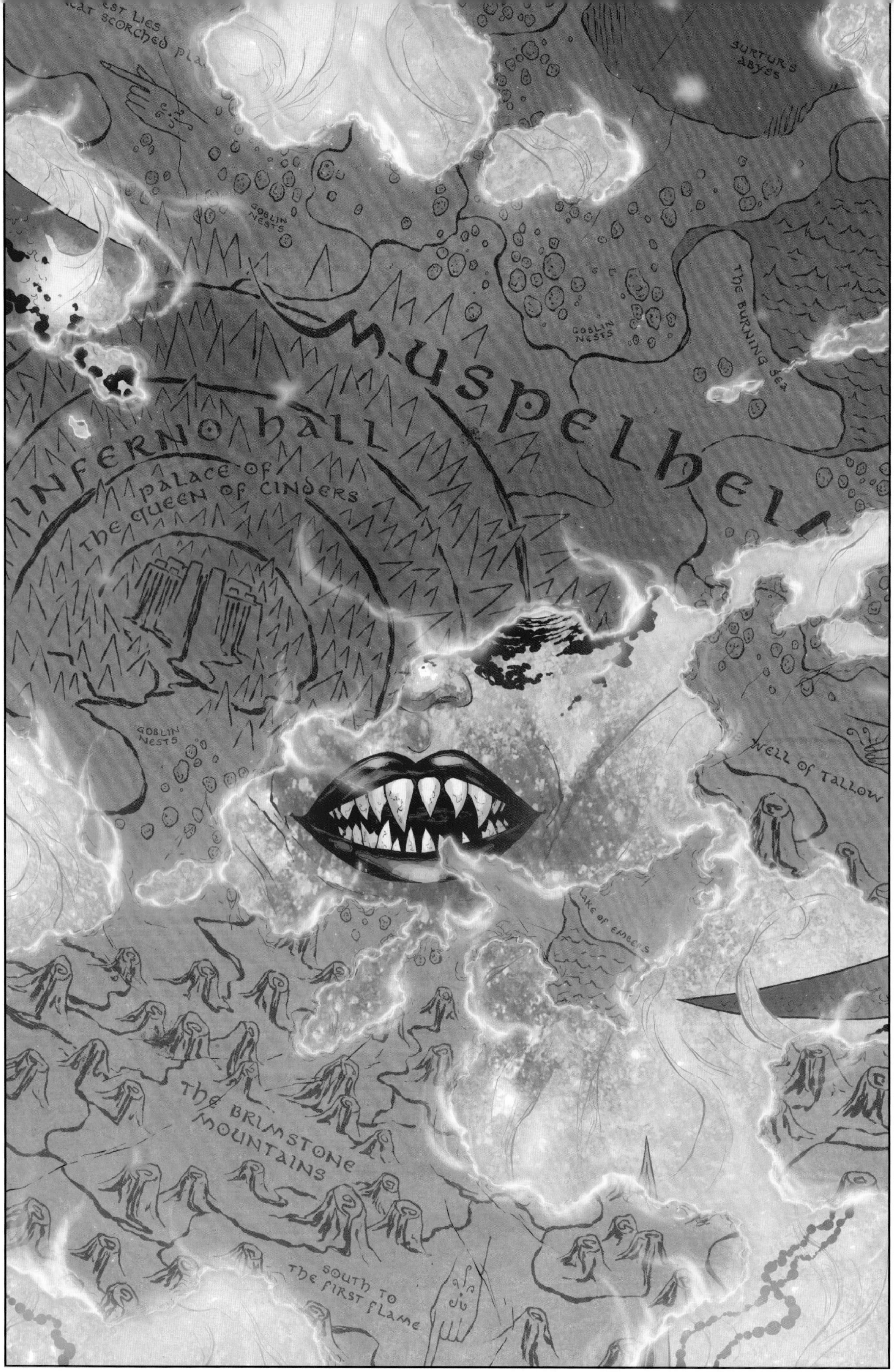
SURTUR'S ABYSS
GOBLIN NESTS
GOBLIN NESTS
THE BURNING SEA
INFERNO HALL
PALACE OF THE QUEEN OF CINDERS
GOBLIN NESTS
WELL OF TALLOW
LAKE OF EMBERS
THE BRIMSTONE MOUNTAINS
SOUTH TO THE FIRST FLAME

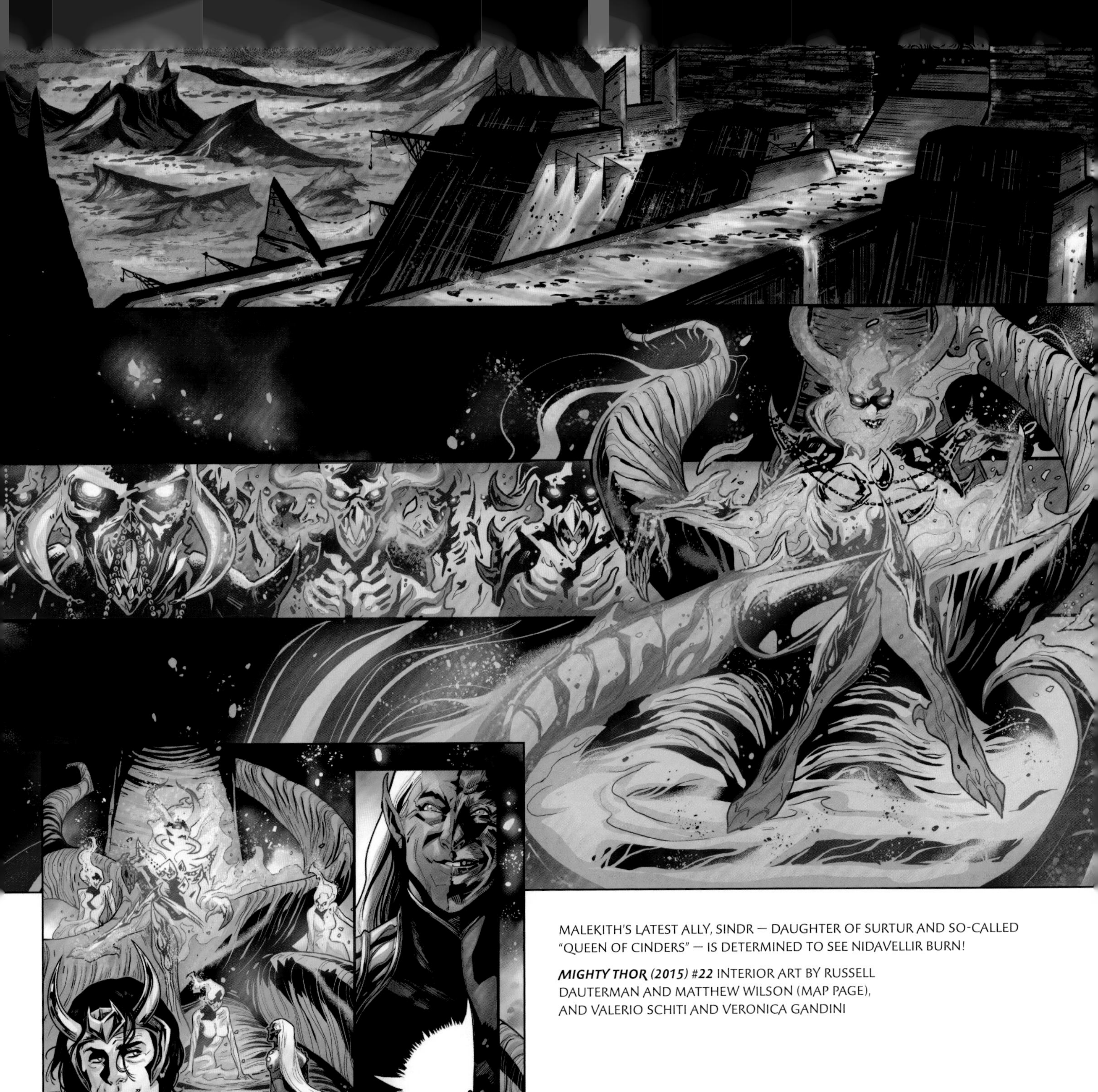

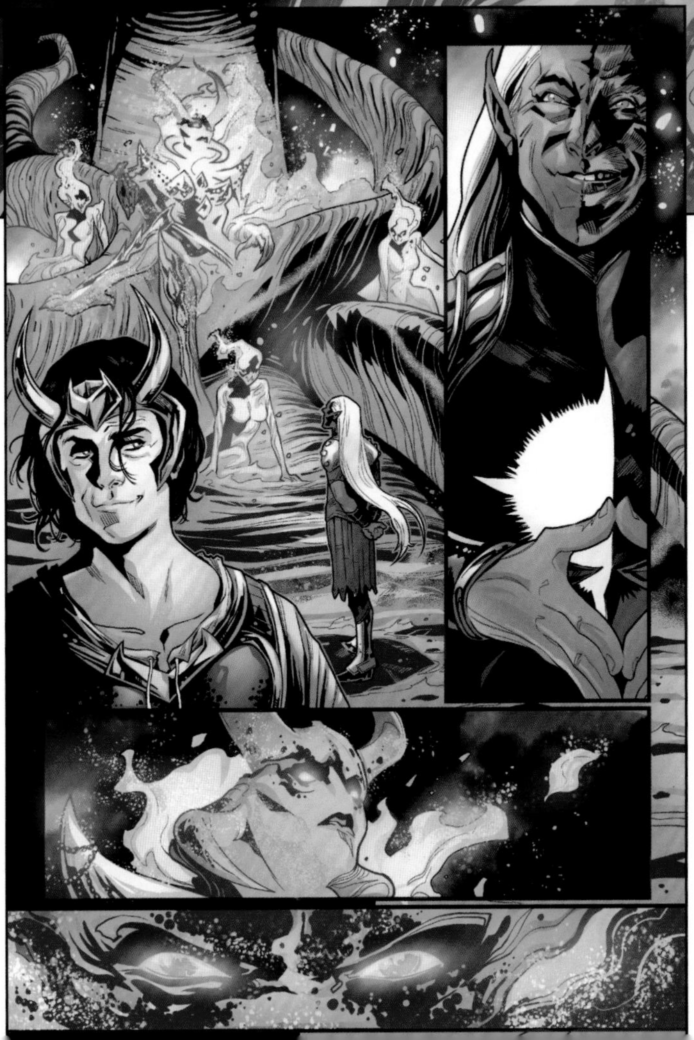

MALEKITH'S LATEST ALLY, SINDR — DAUGHTER OF SURTUR AND SO-CALLED "QUEEN OF CINDERS" — IS DETERMINED TO SEE NIDAVELLIR BURN!

MIGHTY THOR (2015) #22 INTERIOR ART BY RUSSELL DAUTERMAN AND MATTHEW WILSON (MAP PAGE), AND VALERIO SCHITI AND VERONICA GANDINI

WHEN HIS BLOODLUST OVERCOMES HIM, THE WAR THOR WOULD RAIN DEATH DOWN ON MUSPELHEIM — BUT THE REAL THOR STANDS IN HIS WAY!

RIGHT AND OPPOSITE: ***MIGHTY THOR*** *(2015)* #***22*** INTERIOR ART BY VALERIO SCHITI AND RAIN BEREDO

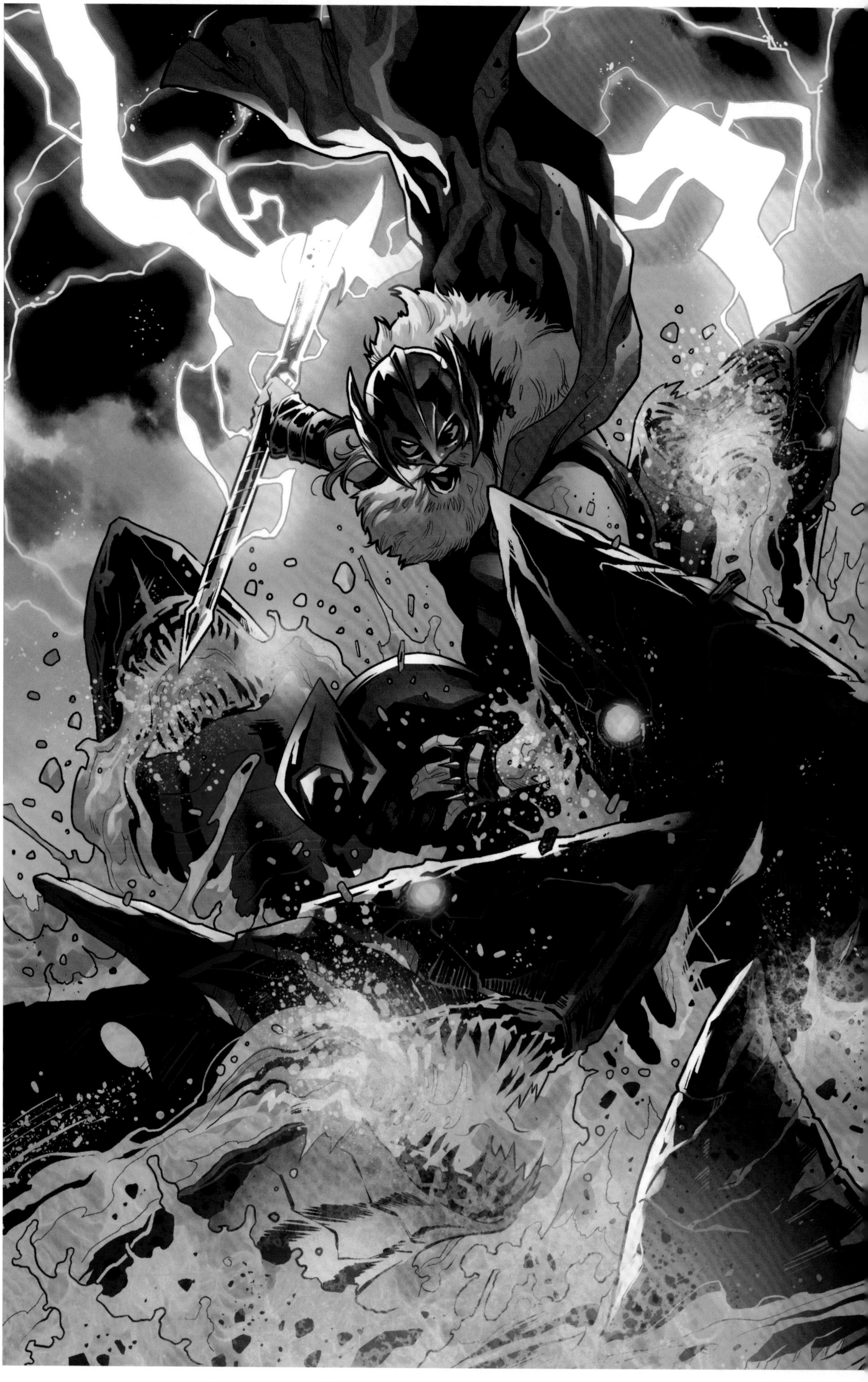

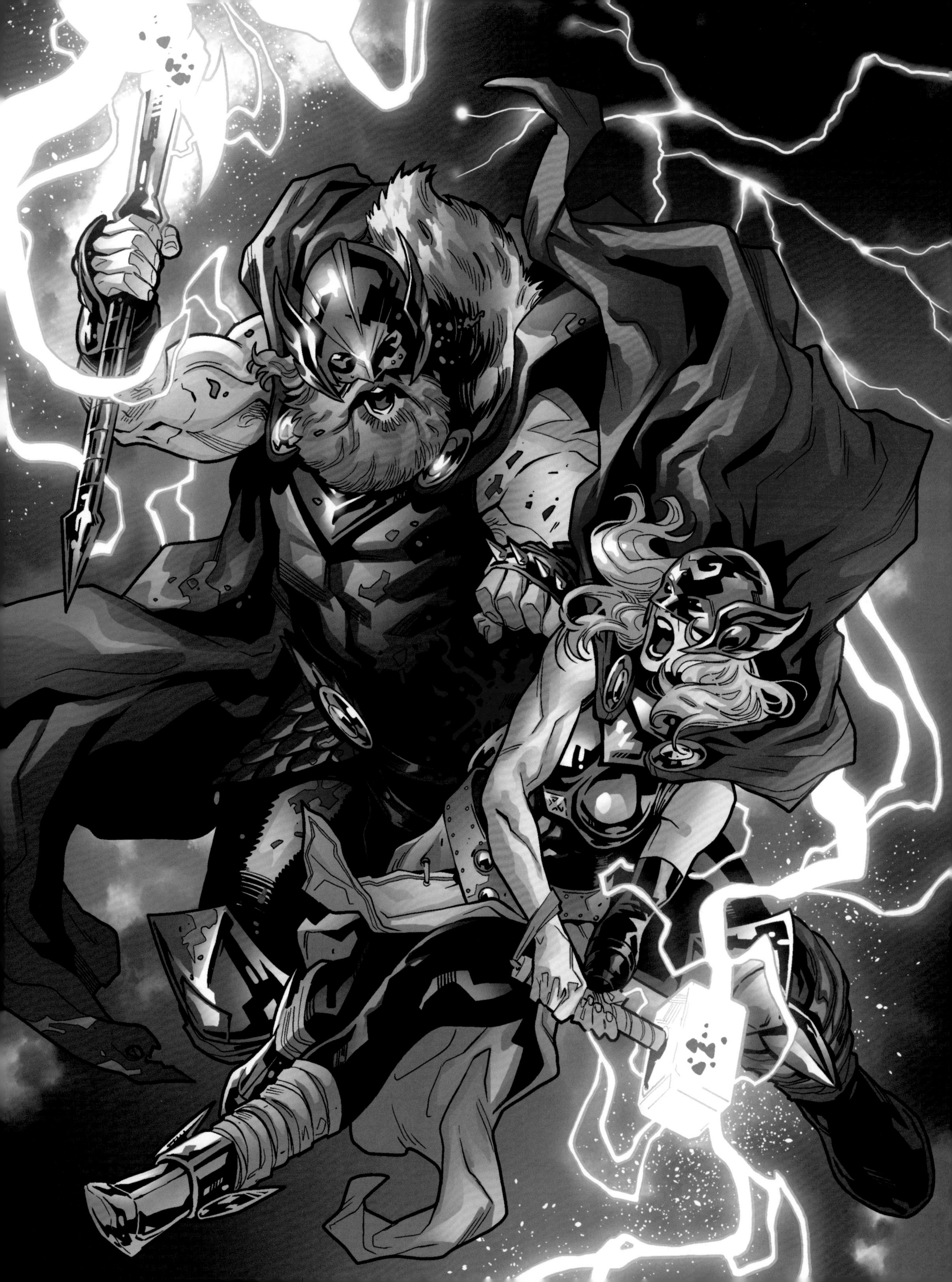

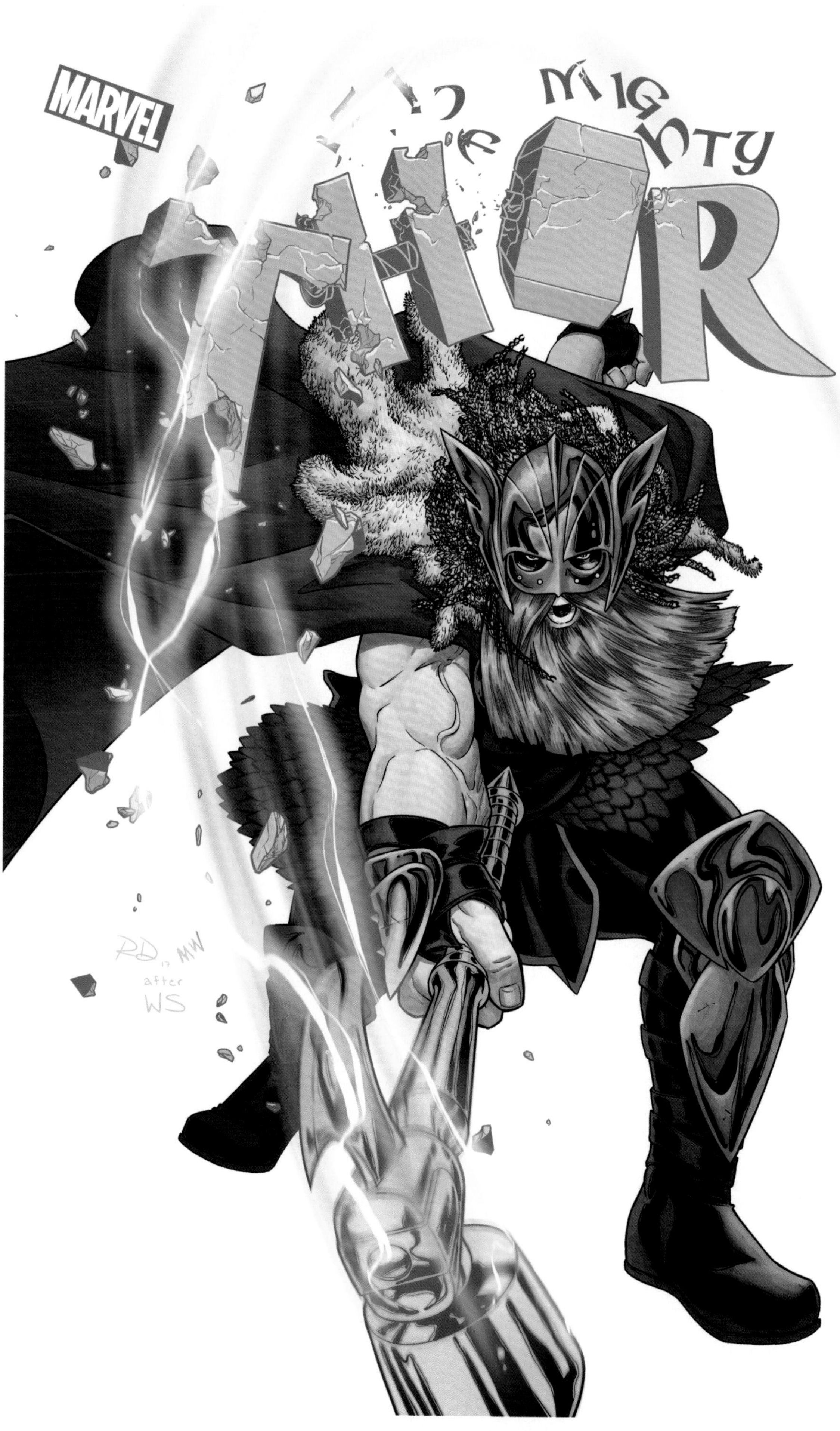
MARVEL
THOR
RD 17 MW
after
WS

RUSSELL DAUTERMAN PAID HOMAGE TO WALTER SIMONSON'S ***THOR* (1966) #337** COVER WITH HIS OWN FOR ***MIGHTY THOR* (2015) #20** — BUT JANE SOON PUTS BOTH THE WAR THOR AND THE ODINSON IN THEIR PLACE!

RIGHT: *MIGHTY THOR* (2015) #20 COVER BY RUSSELL DAUTERMAN AND MATTHEW WILSON

OPPOSITE: *MIGHTY THOR* (2015) #21 COVER BY RUSSELL DAUTERMAN AND MATTHEW WILSON

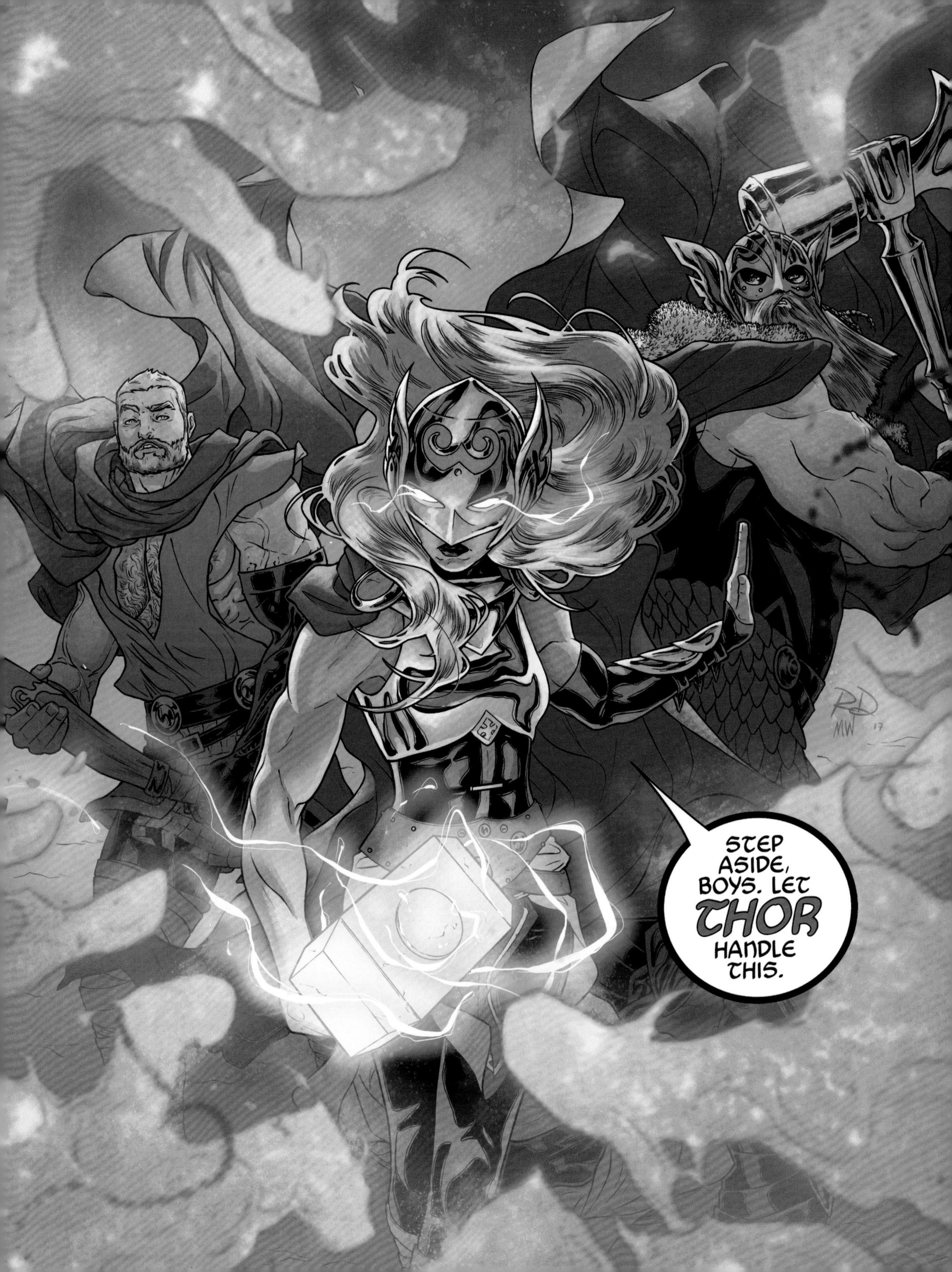
STEP ASIDE, BOYS. LET THOR HANDLE THIS.
RD MW '17

"I'm super proud of the *Mighty Thor #700* cover. I think it's a nice celebration of Thor and Jason's run in particular. And I absolutely love Matt's color palette for this one. I don't think I'd ever drawn a frog before, so that was a new challenge!"

— RUSSELL DAUTERMAN

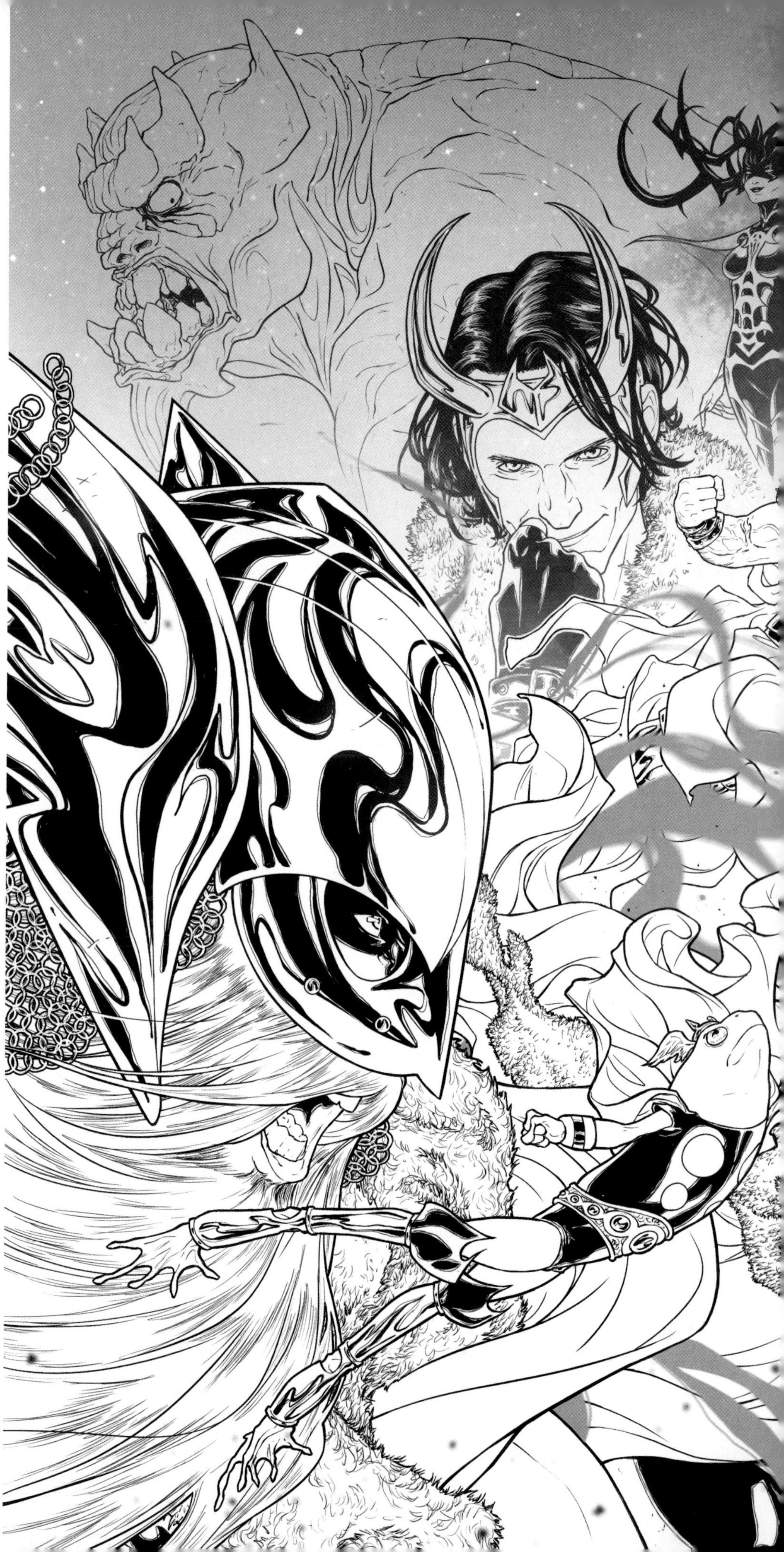

A MULTITUDE OF THUNDER GODS UNITE AS "THE DEATH OF THE MIGHTY THOR" BEGINS.

RIGHT AND FOLLOWING PAGES: ***MIGHTY THOR (2015)* #700** COVER INKS BY RUSSELL DAUTERMAN, AND FINAL ART BY DAUTERMAN AND MATTHEW WILSON

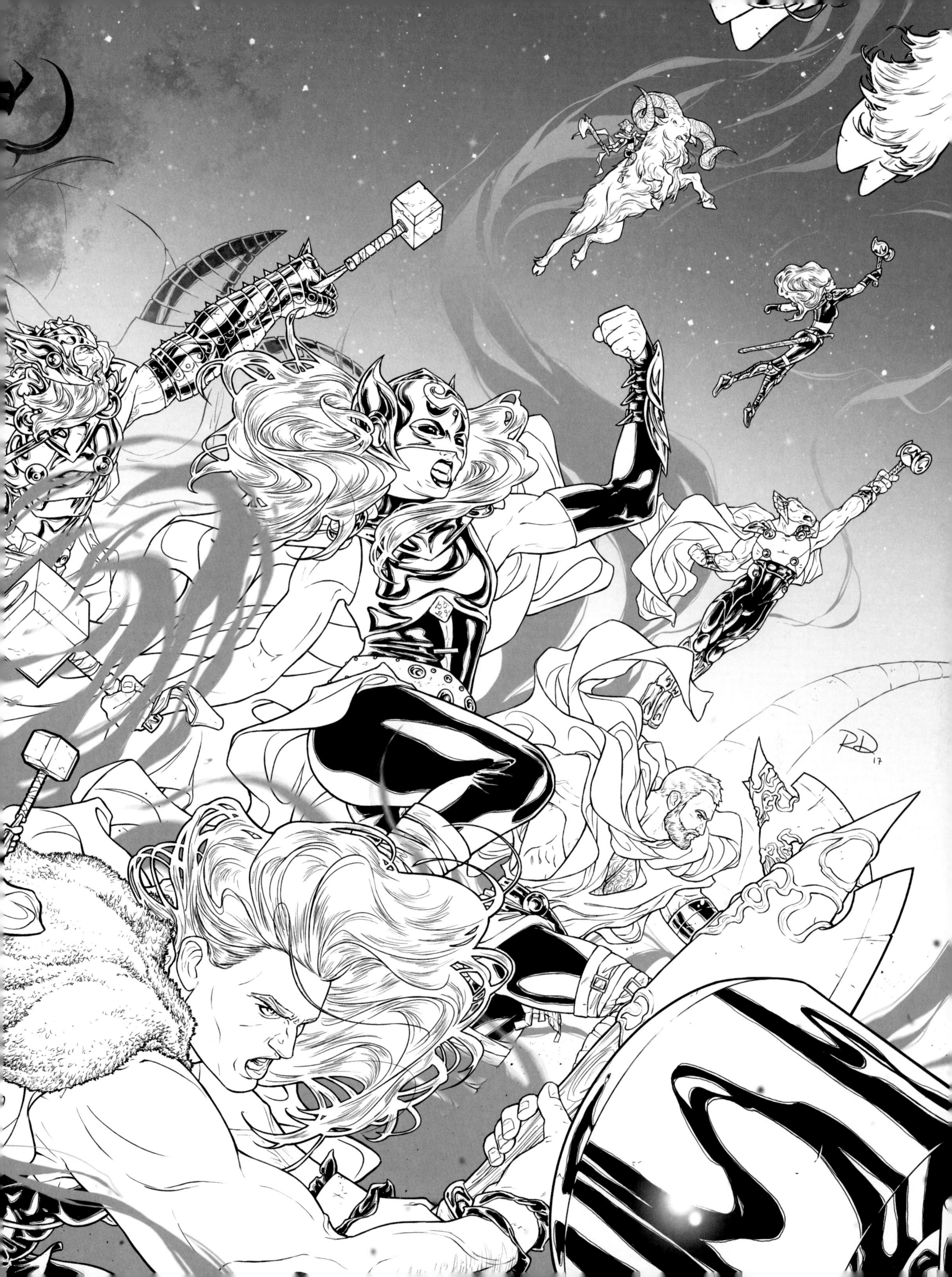

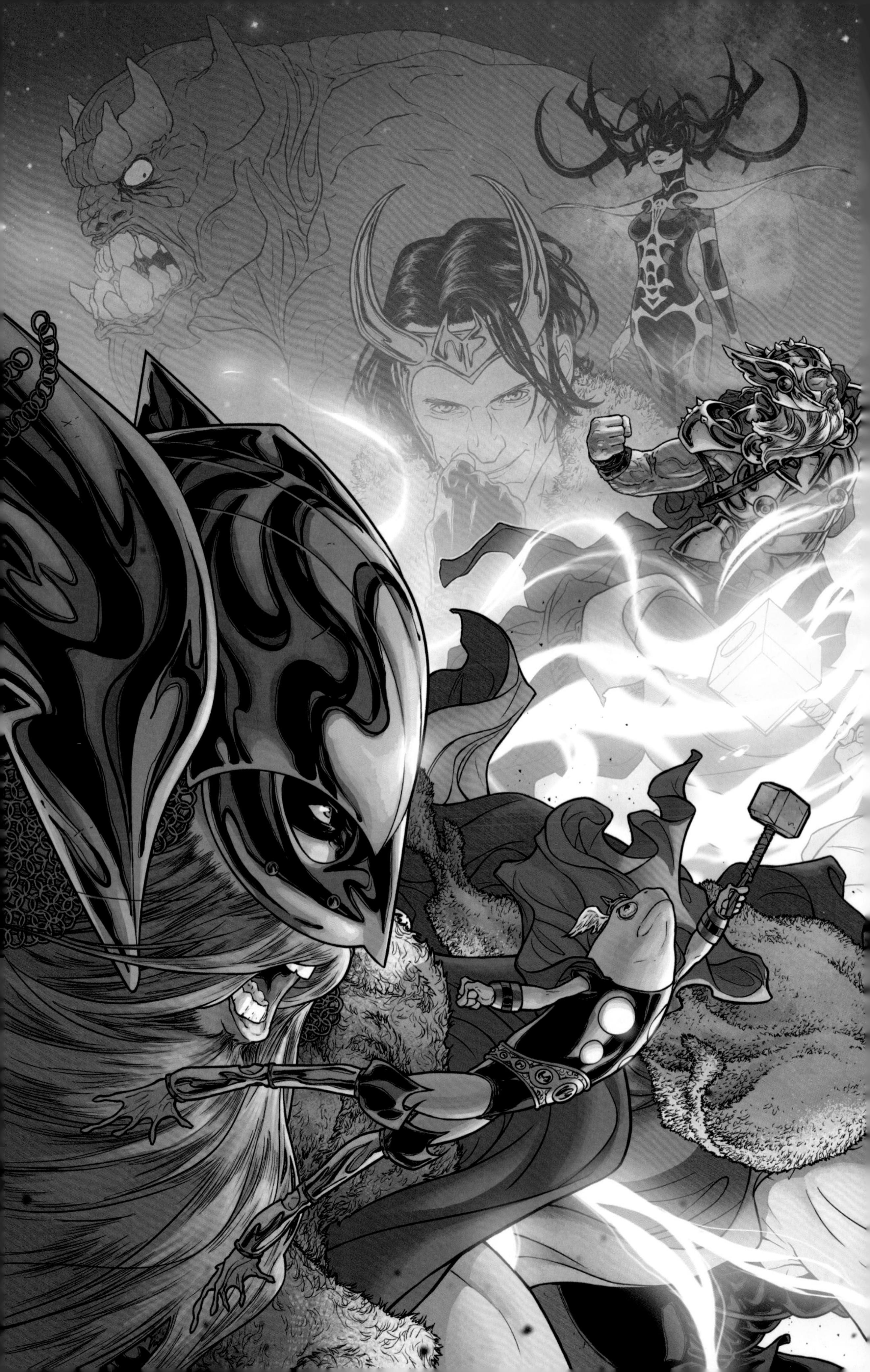

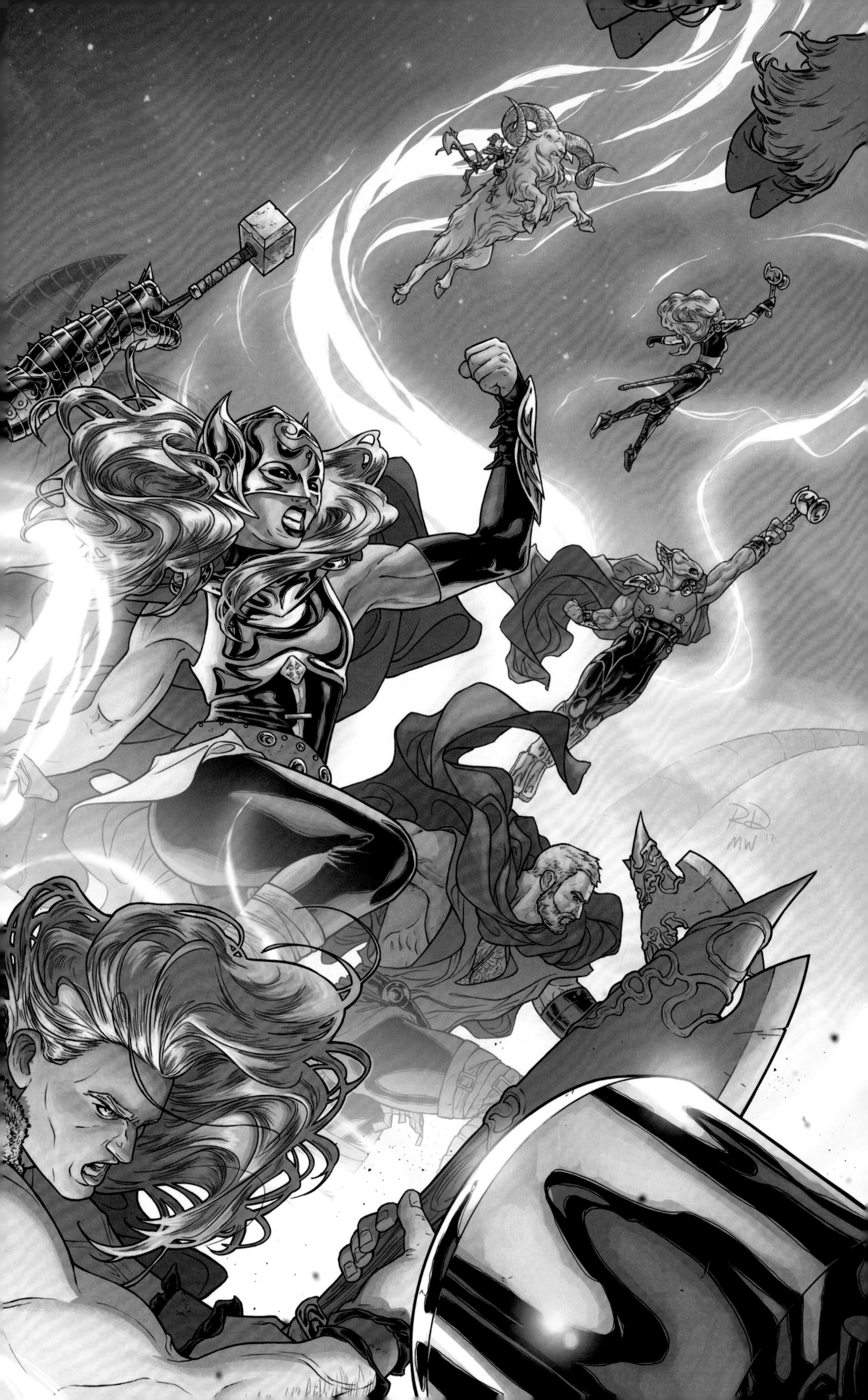

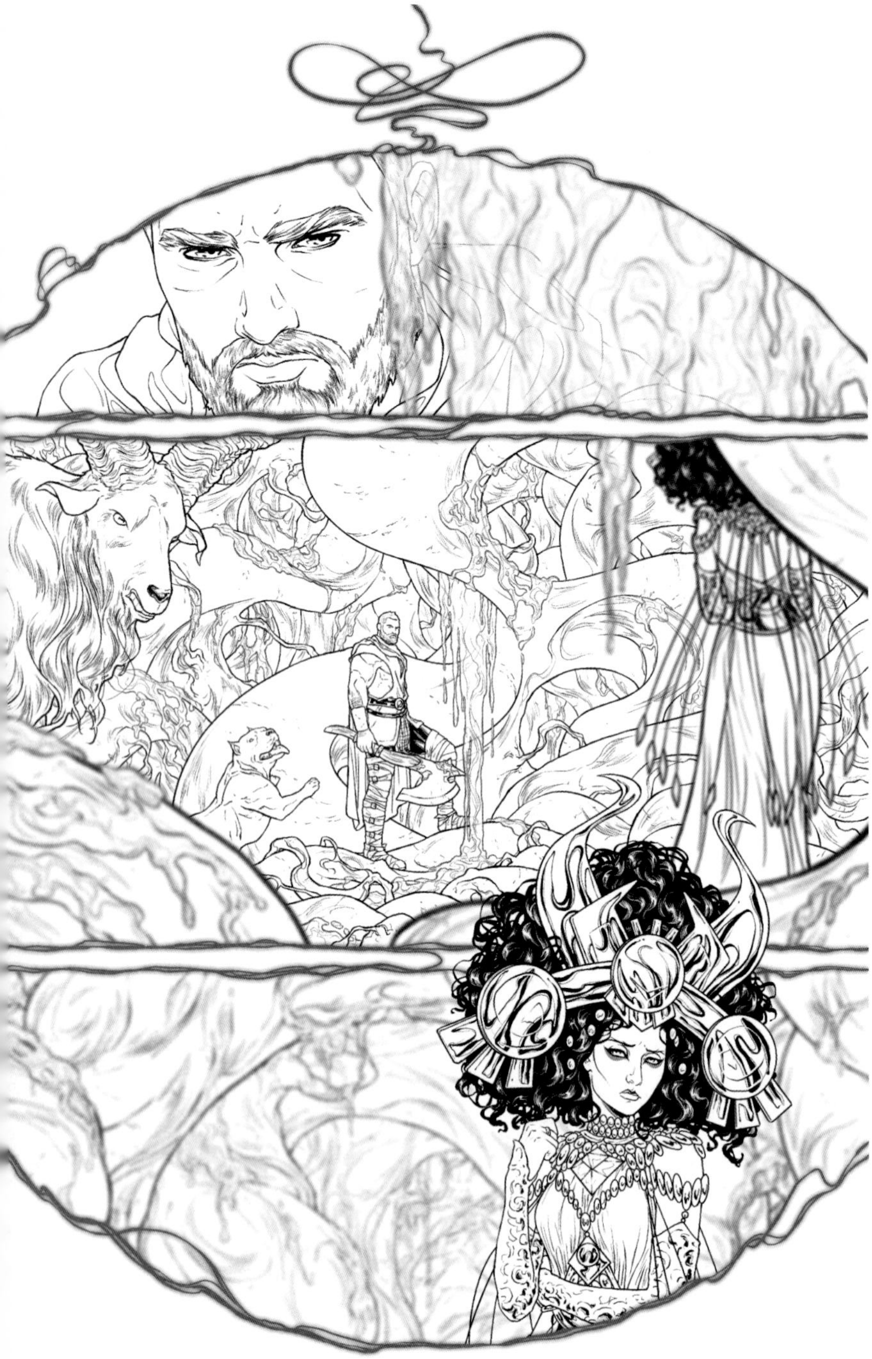

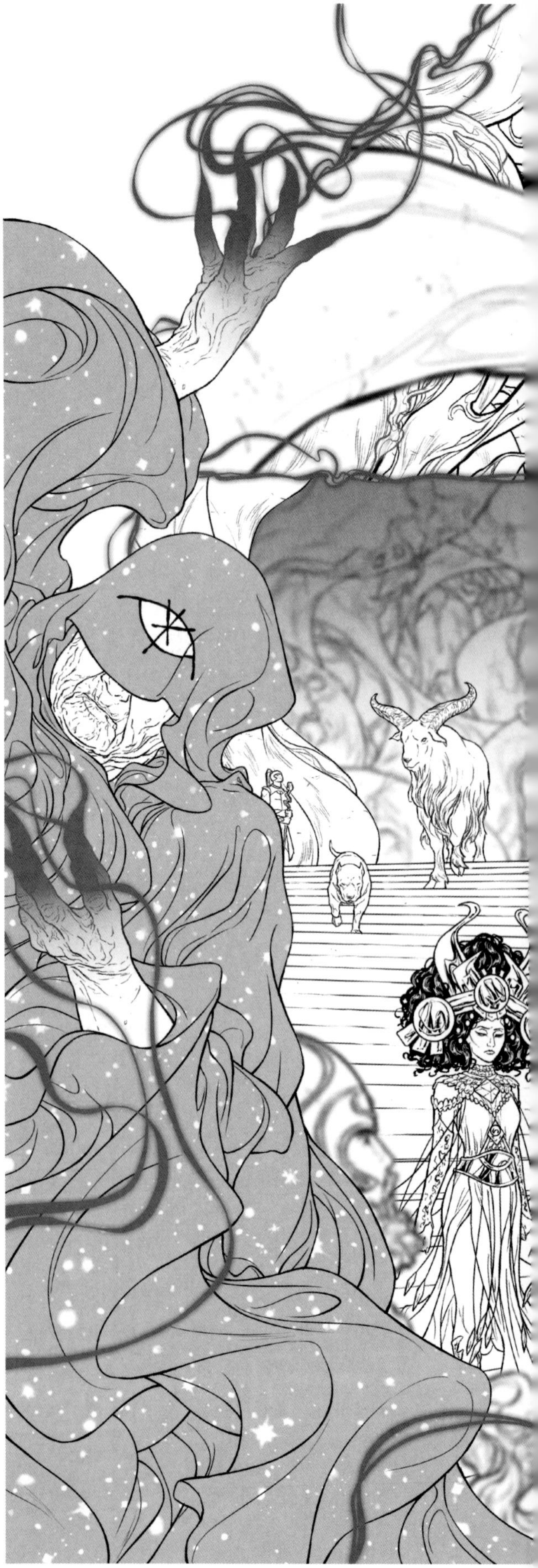

"I was excited to draw pages 2-4 from *Mighty Thor #700*. That issue had a lot of artists contributing stories, and I was drawing the sequence that framed them all. I wanted some visual clue that would differentiate the framing sequence from the other stories, and thought I could use the Norns. They're meant to be spinning the threads of fate, and I thought I'd make those magical threads coming from their fingers and use the threads as panel borders."
— RUSSELL DAUTERMAN

MIGHTY THOR (2015) #700 INTERIOR INKS BY RUSSELL DAUTERMAN

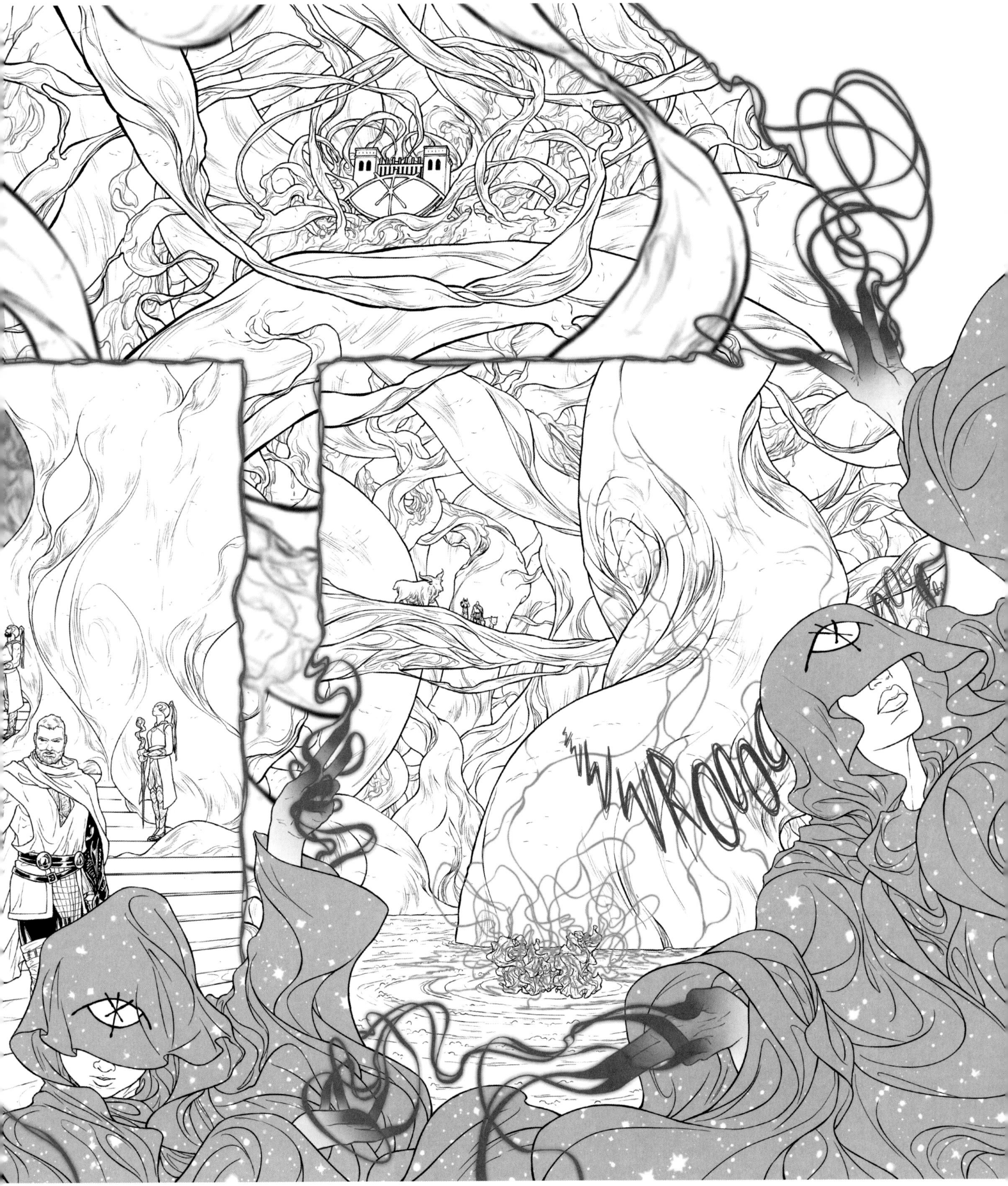
WHROOOOOM

"I'm very lucky to work with Matt Wilson. He's been so important to the success of *Thor.* I love working with him, and I can trust that he'll add something beautiful to whatever art I send him. *Mighty Thor #702* is one of my favorite covers that I've done, and one of my favorite things Matt's colored. I was thinking about all those people who'd written to say how much Jane meant to them or how they related to her battle with cancer. I wanted to do something for them that would highlight Jane's inner strength. I draw various elements on different layers in Photoshop. That way, Matt could more easily work with them, and we could achieve the effects we want. I drew Jane's line art separately from Thor's and put the magic on another layer. Matt gave each layer a different treatment and added the ripples of color. I wanted there to be an explosion of color coming from Jane, and Matt went above and beyond. He really brought the piece to life and added the perfect POW! of color that grabs your attention. The contrasting blue on Jane's face focuses your eye right there, and the blended colors are gorgeous."
— RUSSELL DAUTERMAN

"I knew showing Jane transform was an important visual for the book, so I really wanted to get it right."
— MATTHEW WILSON

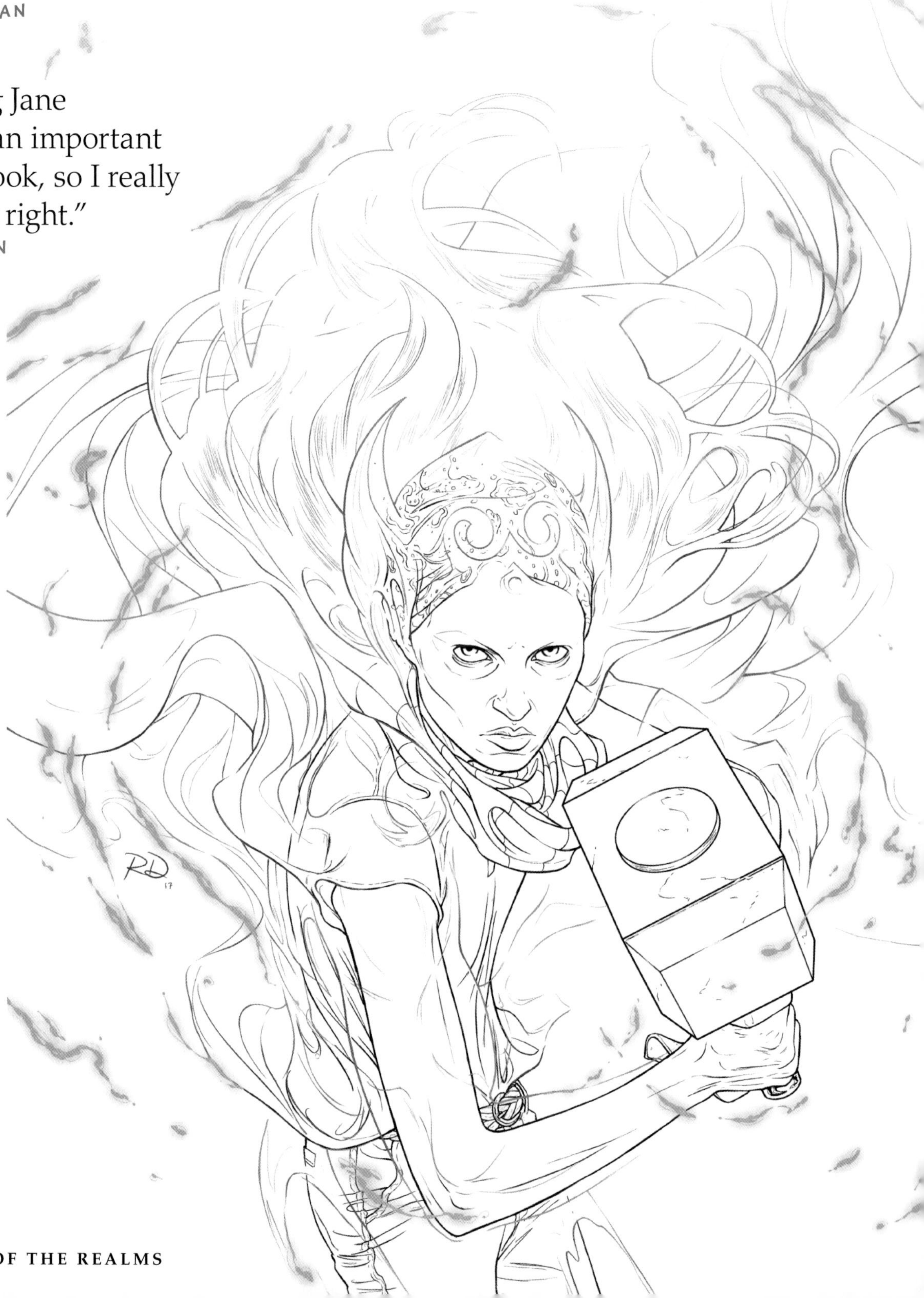
RD
17

***MIGHTY THOR* (2015) #702**
COVER INKS BY RUSSELL DAUTERMAN, AND FINAL ART BY DAUTERMAN AND MATTHEW WILSON

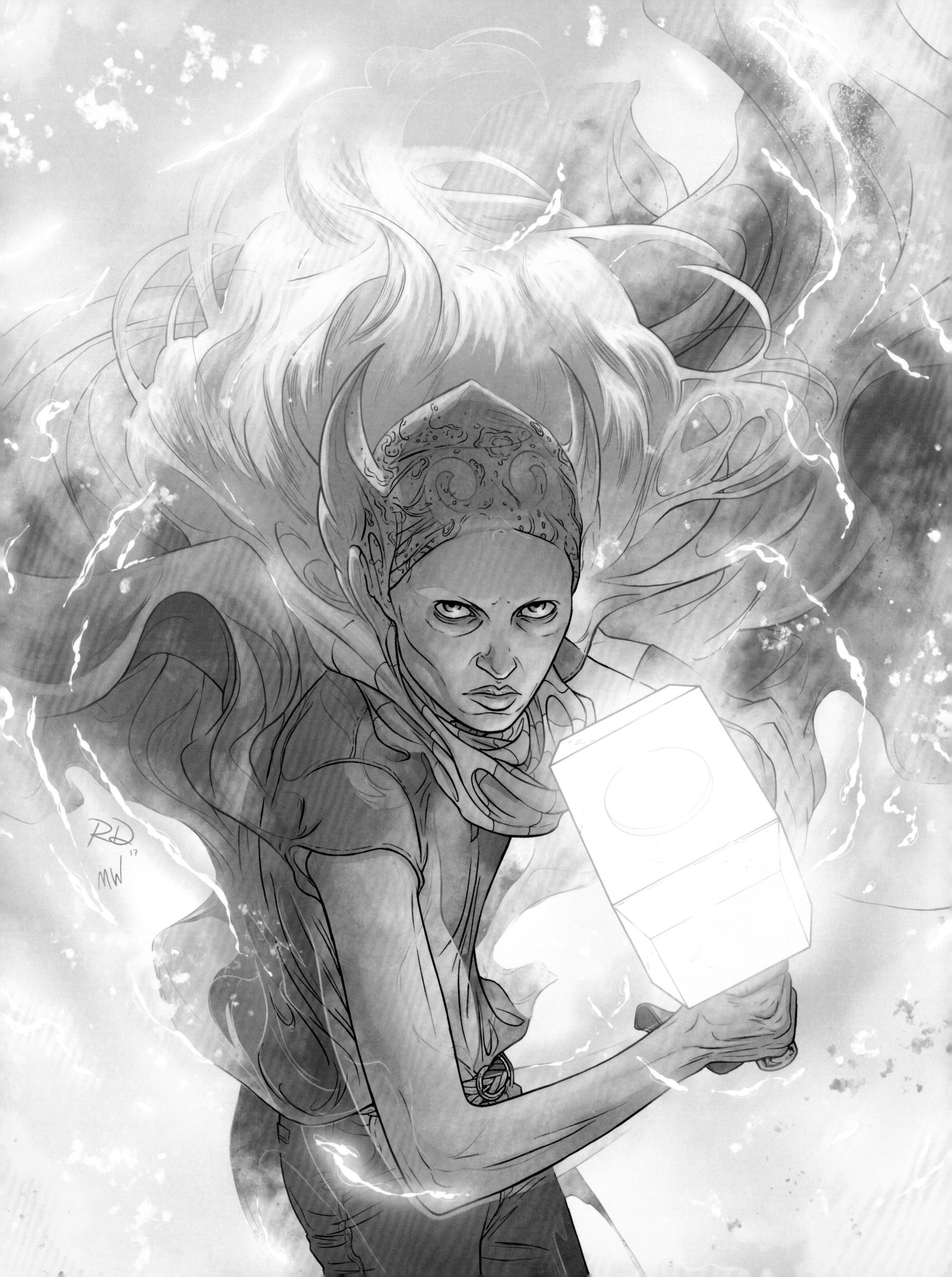

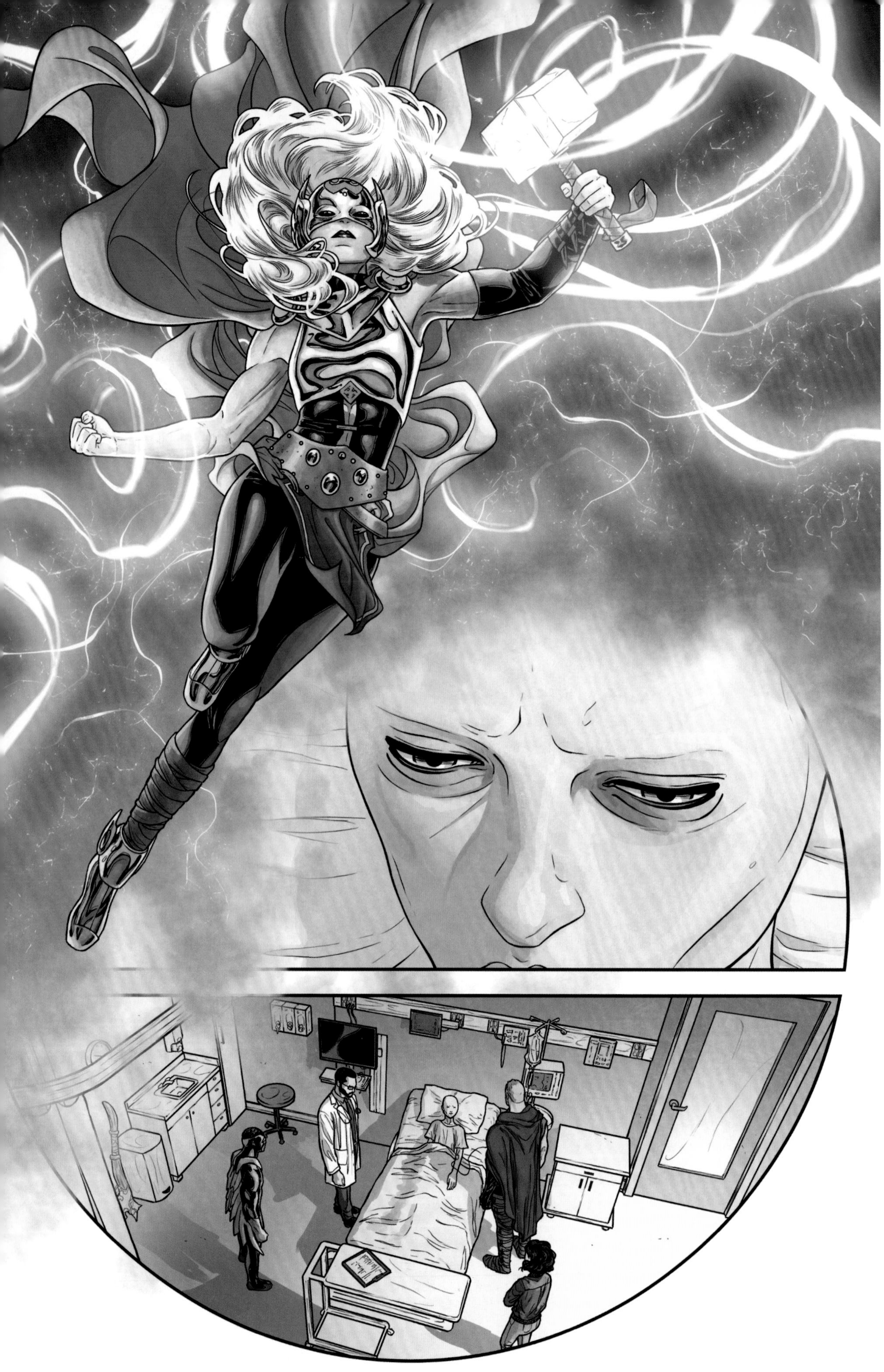

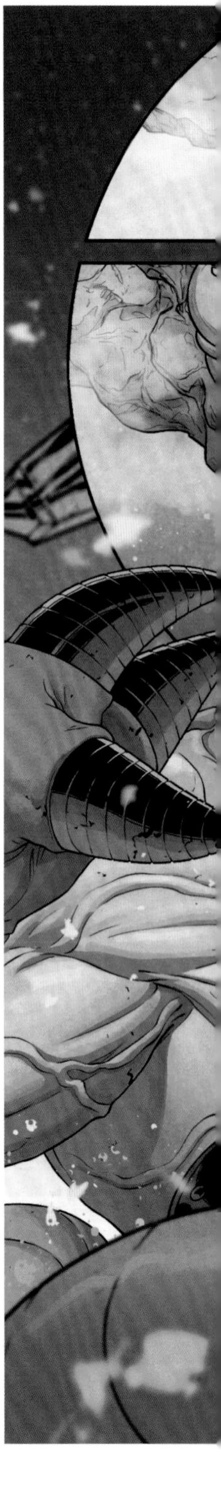

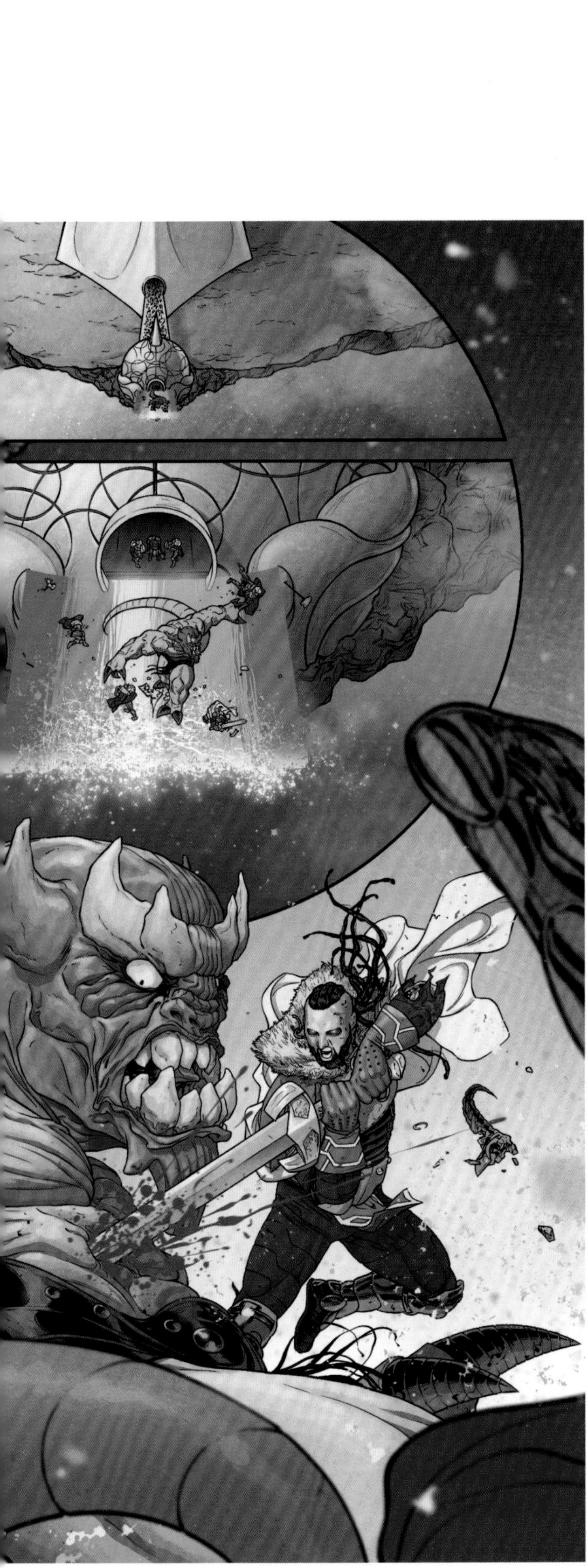

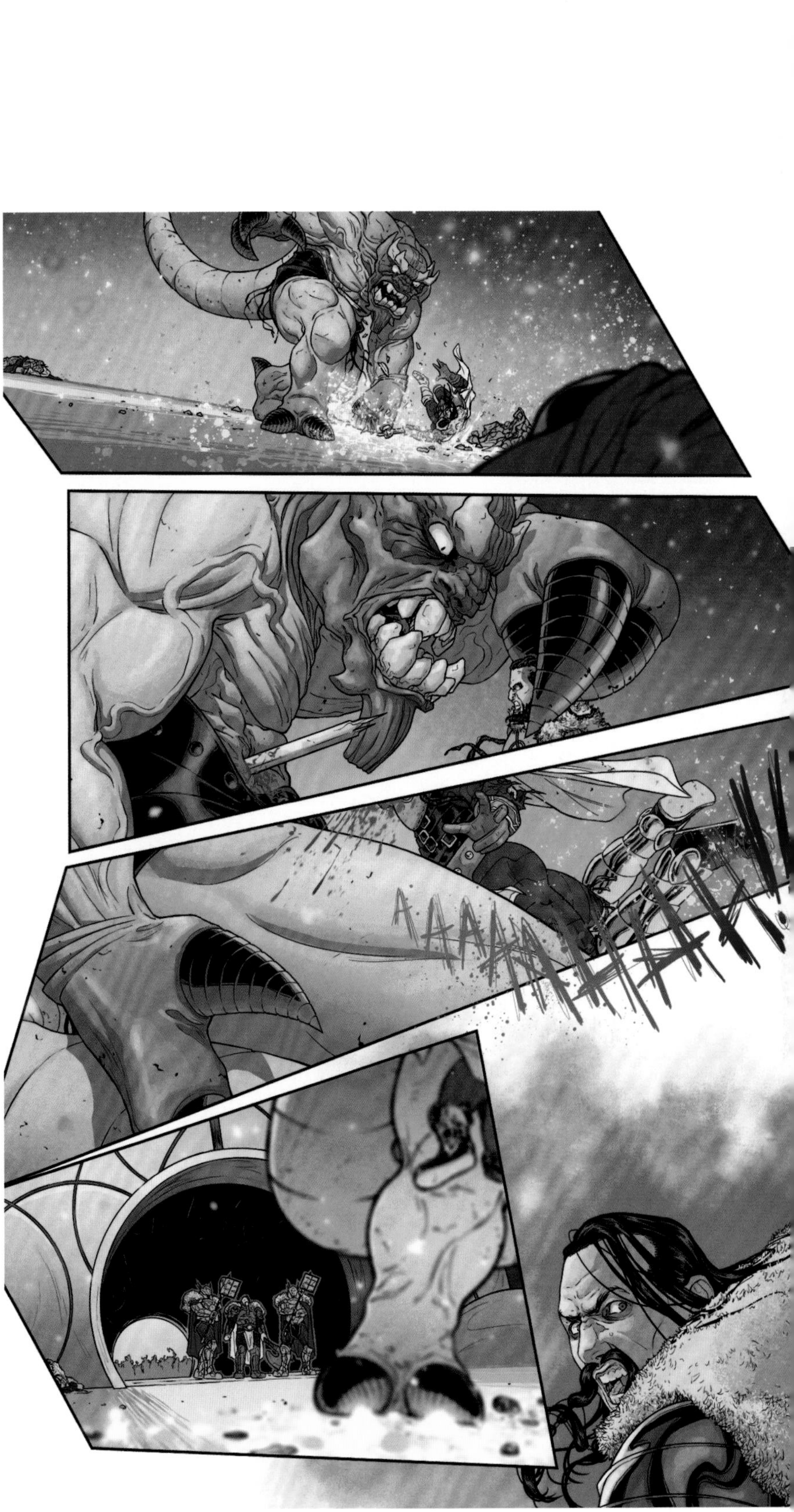

AS JANE LIES IN A HOSPITAL BED, THE MANGOG ARRIVES IN ASGARDIA — AND BRUTALLY ATTACKS HEIMDALL!

MIGHTY THOR (2015) #703 INTERIOR ART BY RUSSELL DAUTERMAN AND MATTHEW WILSON

"I started playing with panel layout a lot more during my run on *Thor*. I tried to make the panel shapes mimic what was happening within them. When the Rainbow Bridge was destroyed, I thought it'd be cool to have the panel borders crack as the bridge cracked and shatter when the bridge shattered."

— RUSSELL DAUTERMAN

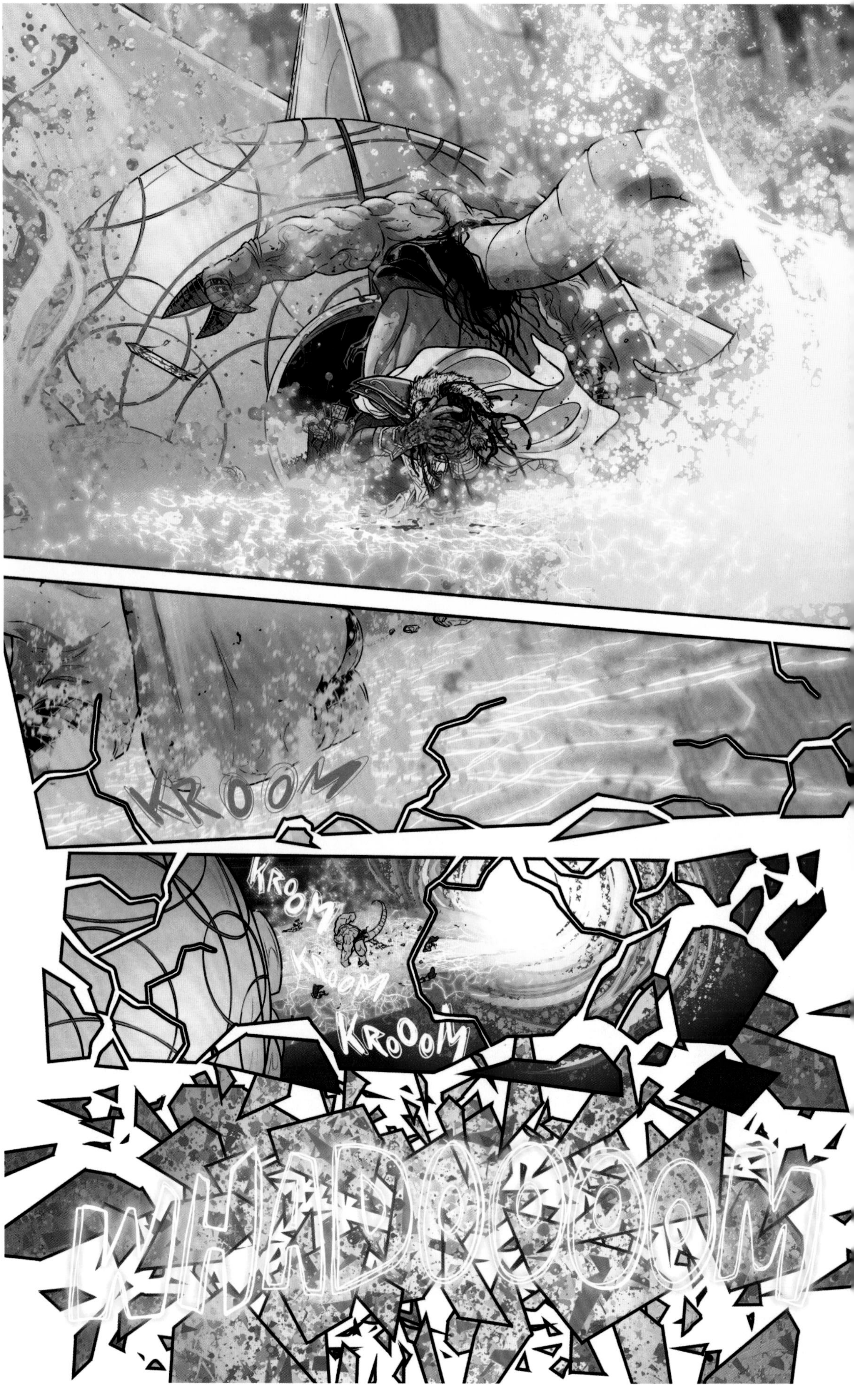
KROOM
KROOM
KROOM
KROOOM
WHADOOOOM

THE MIGHTY MANGOG DEMOLISHES THE RAINBOW BRIDGE — AND THEN BATTLES THE ODINSON AND ODIN FOR THE FATE OF ASGARDIA!

MIGHTY THOR (2015) #704 INTERIOR ART BY RUSSELL DAUTERMAN AND MATTHEW WILSON

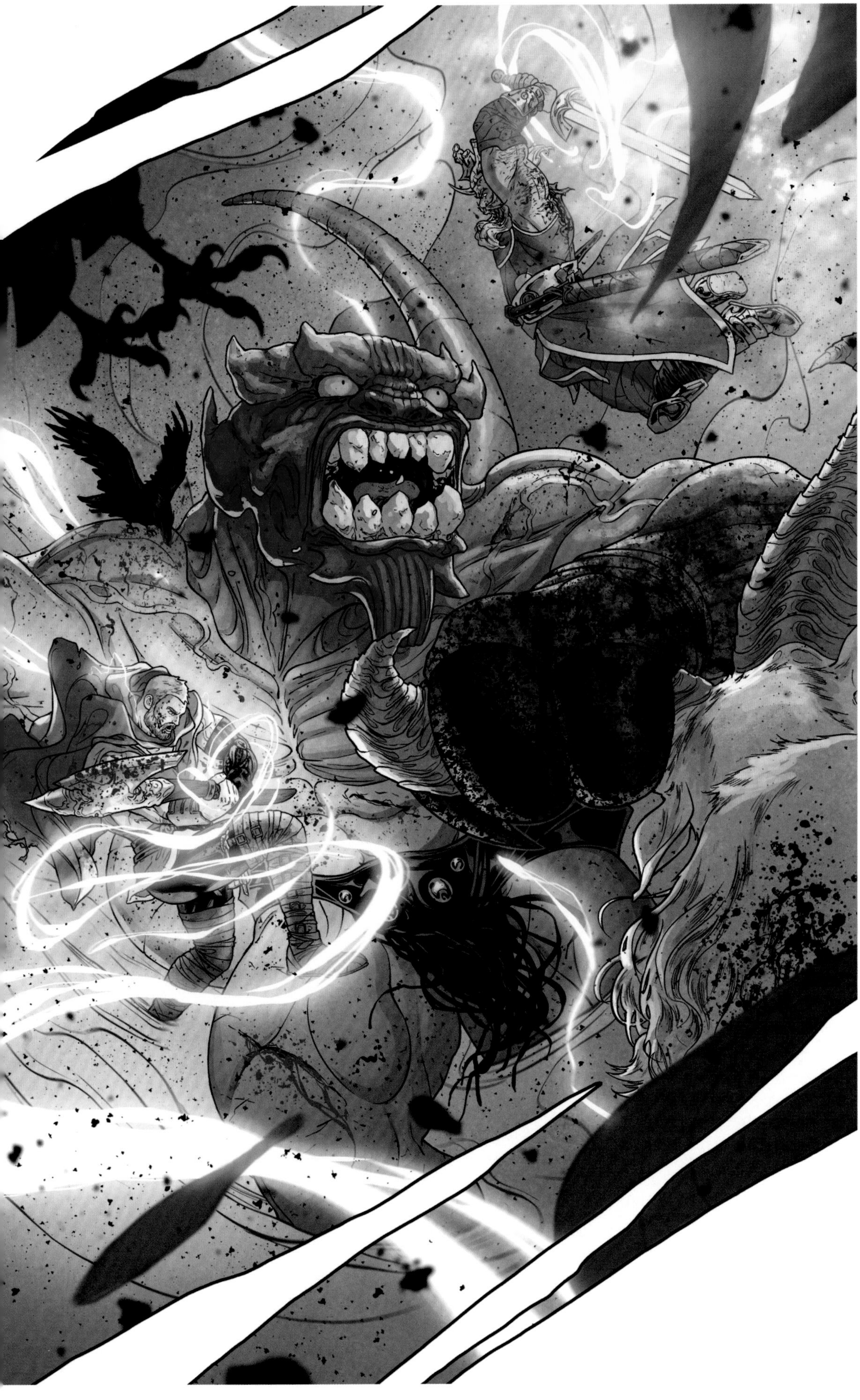

"Mangog was a character whom I'd literally had penciled in for years. He's probably my favorite villain from the Kirby Thor run. I'd dropped references to the Mangog all throughout the book. Mangog's in that big spread that Esad drew at the end of *Thor: God of Thunder*. I had had a Mangog statue sitting on my desk for years by that point staring at me, wondering when I was going to get around to his story. So I was excited to finally get there."

— JASON AARON

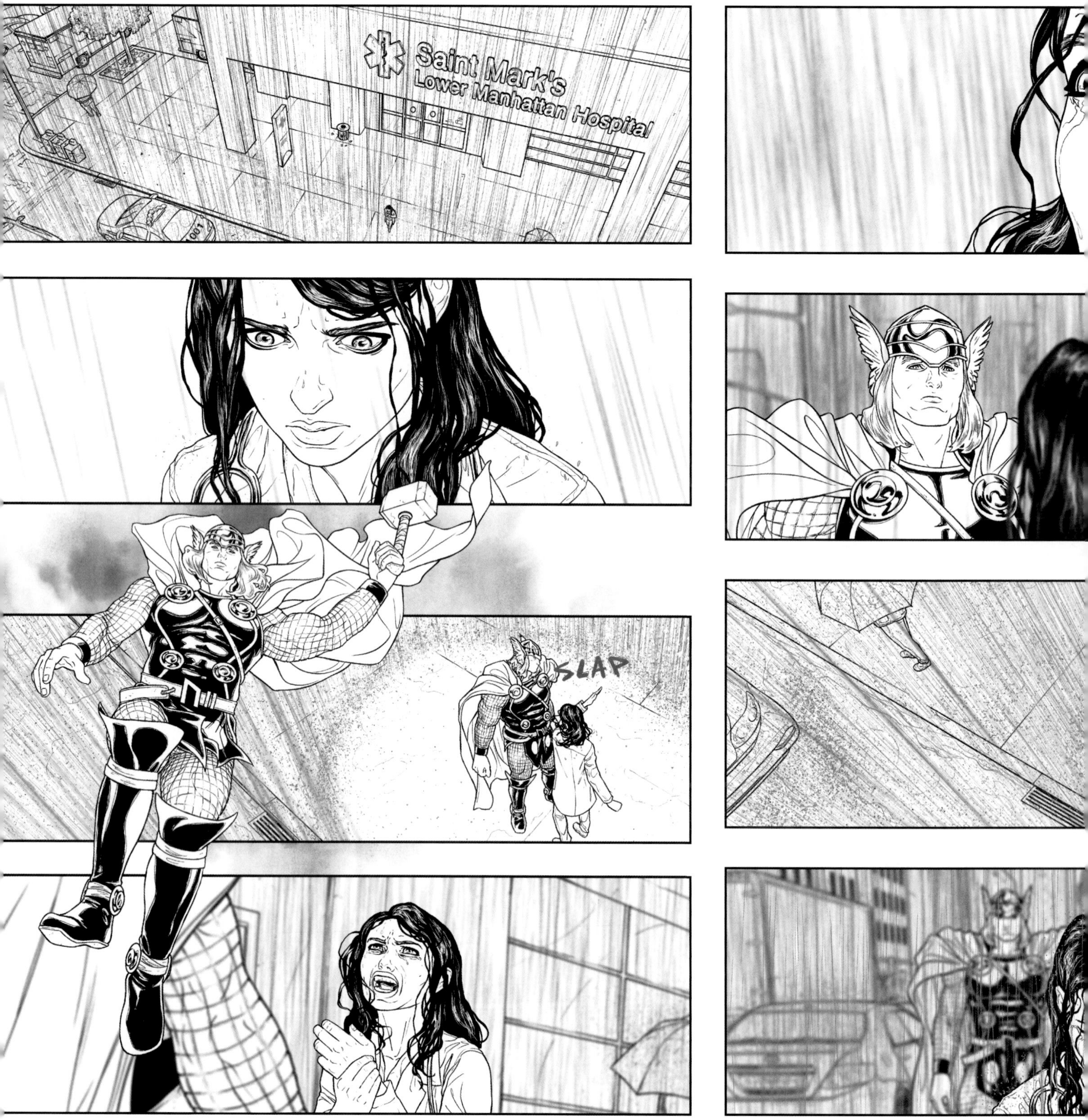
Saint Mark's
Lower Manhattan Hospital
SLAP

"The rain sequence from *Mighty Thor #704* is another favorite. I take reference photos of myself for nearly every panel. For these two pages, I would read Jason's heartbreaking dialogue, try to think of the saddest things in my own life and then take the reference photo when I was at peak sadness. That really helped me incorporate nuances into the drawings, like what a person's mouth or eyebrows do when they're really upset. That was a bummer of a day, but I do love drawing emotional moments, and I'm really happy with how those pages turned out."

— RUSSELL DAUTERMAN

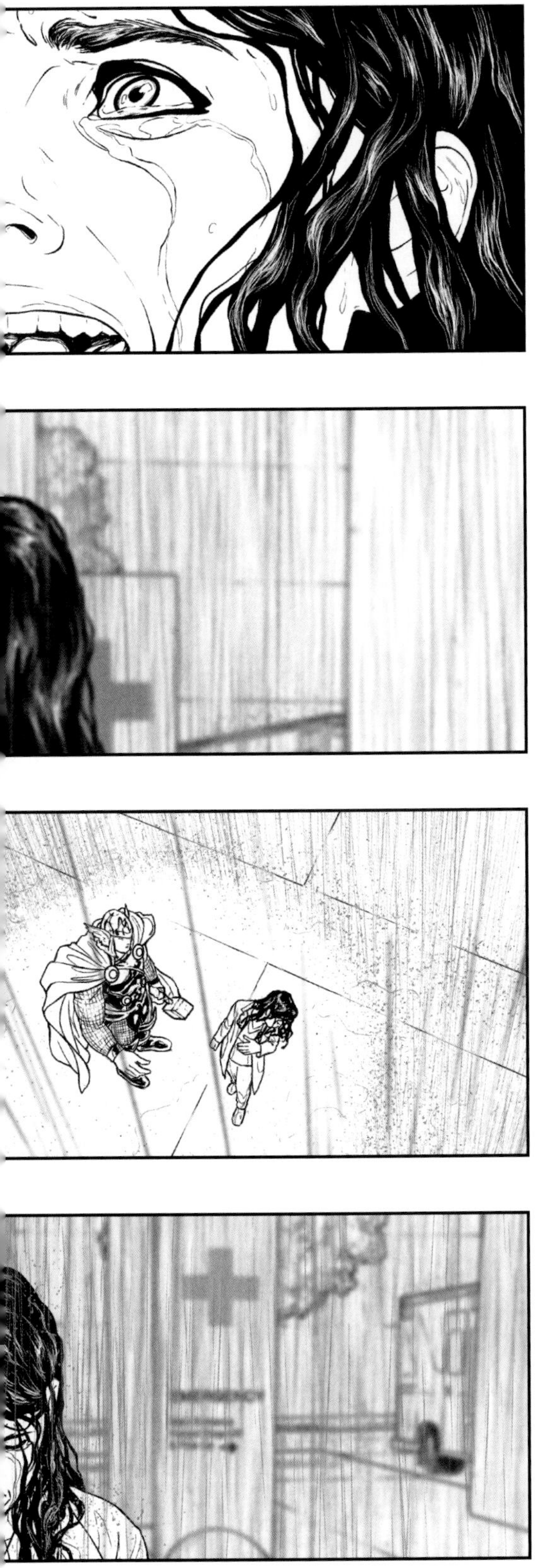

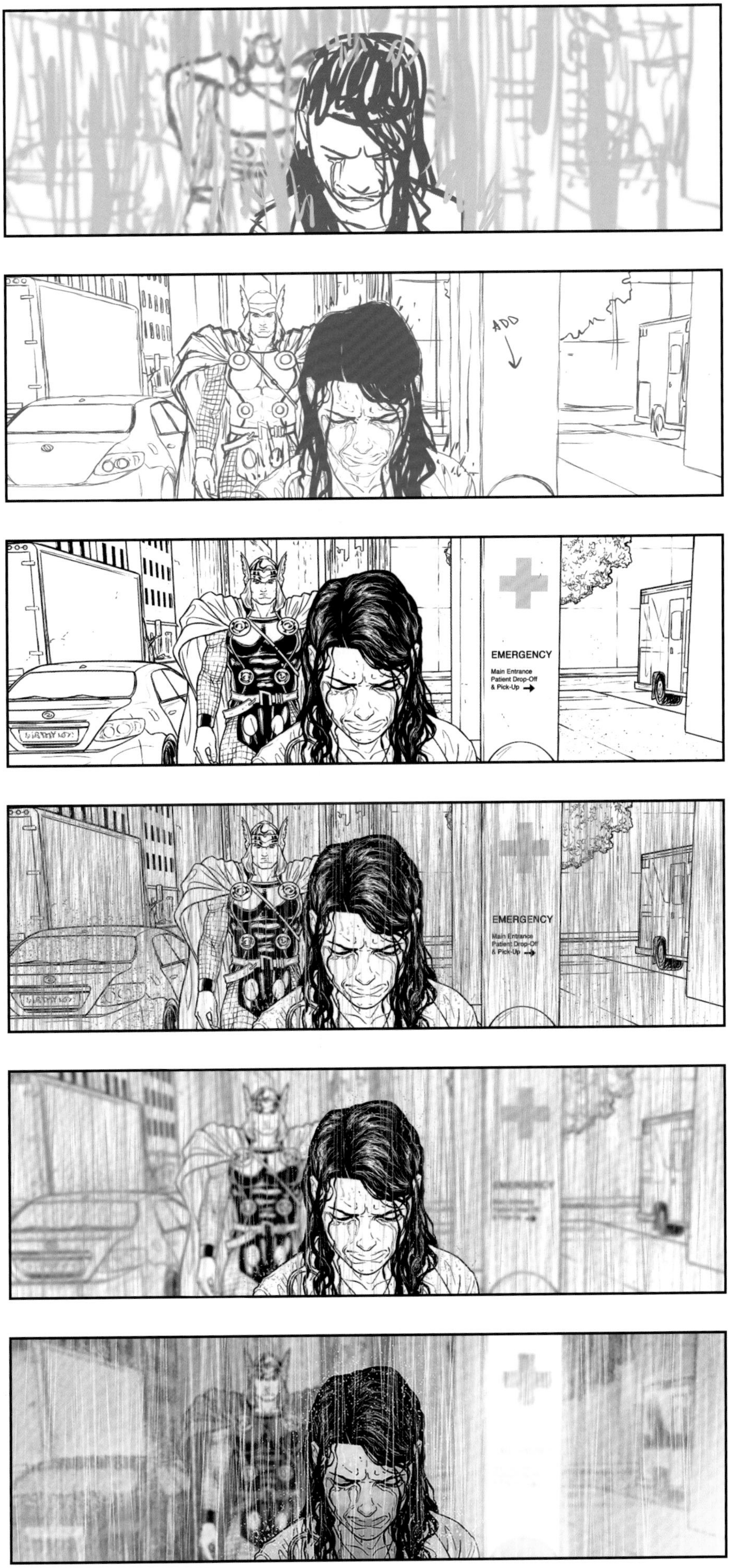
ADD
EMERGENCY
Main Entrance
Patient Drop-Off
& Pick-Up
EMERGENCY
Main Entrance
Patient Drop-Off
& Pick-Up

MIGHTY THOR (2015) #704 ART PROCESS BY
RUSSELL DAUTERMAN AND MATTHEW WILSON

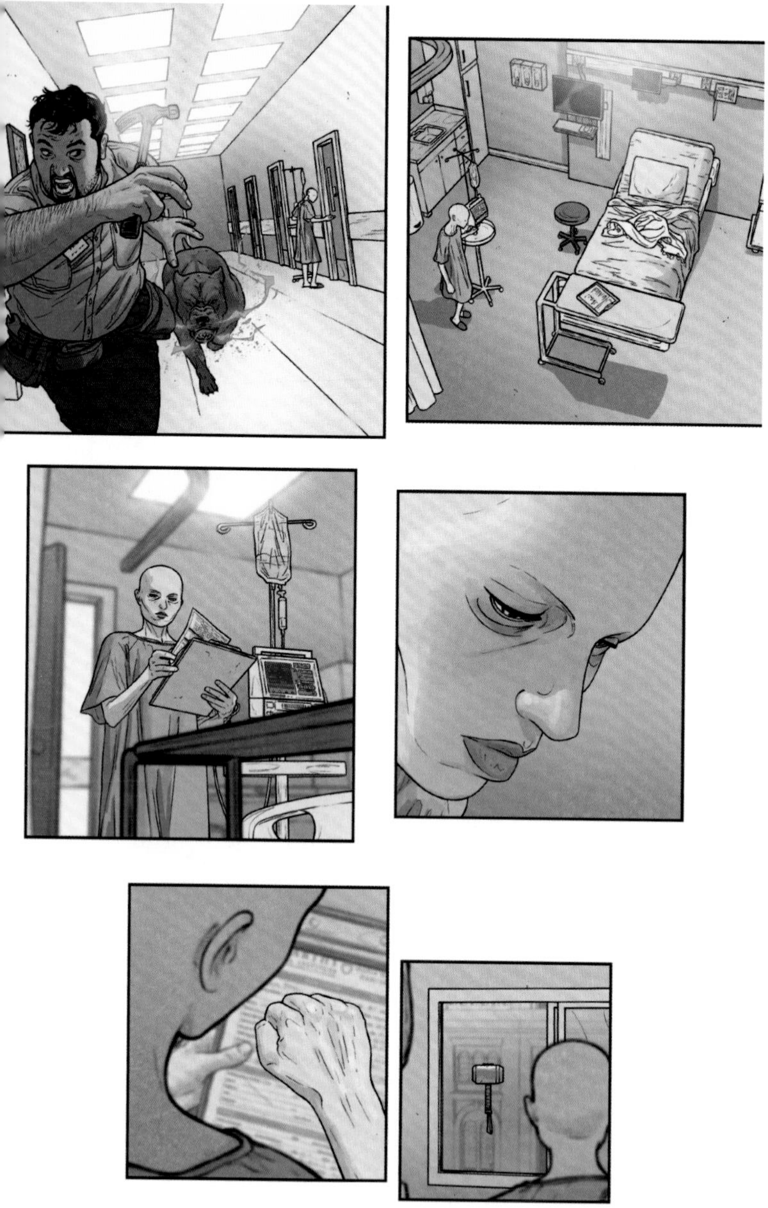

JANE FOSTER WRESTLES WITH A MOMENTOUS DECISION: UNDERGO TREATMENT AND LET ASGARDIA FALL TO THE MANGOG OR BECOME THOR ONE LAST TIME AT THE COST OF HER LIFE!

MIGHTY THOR (2015) #704 INTERIOR ART BY RUSSELL DAUTERMAN AND MATTHEW WILSON

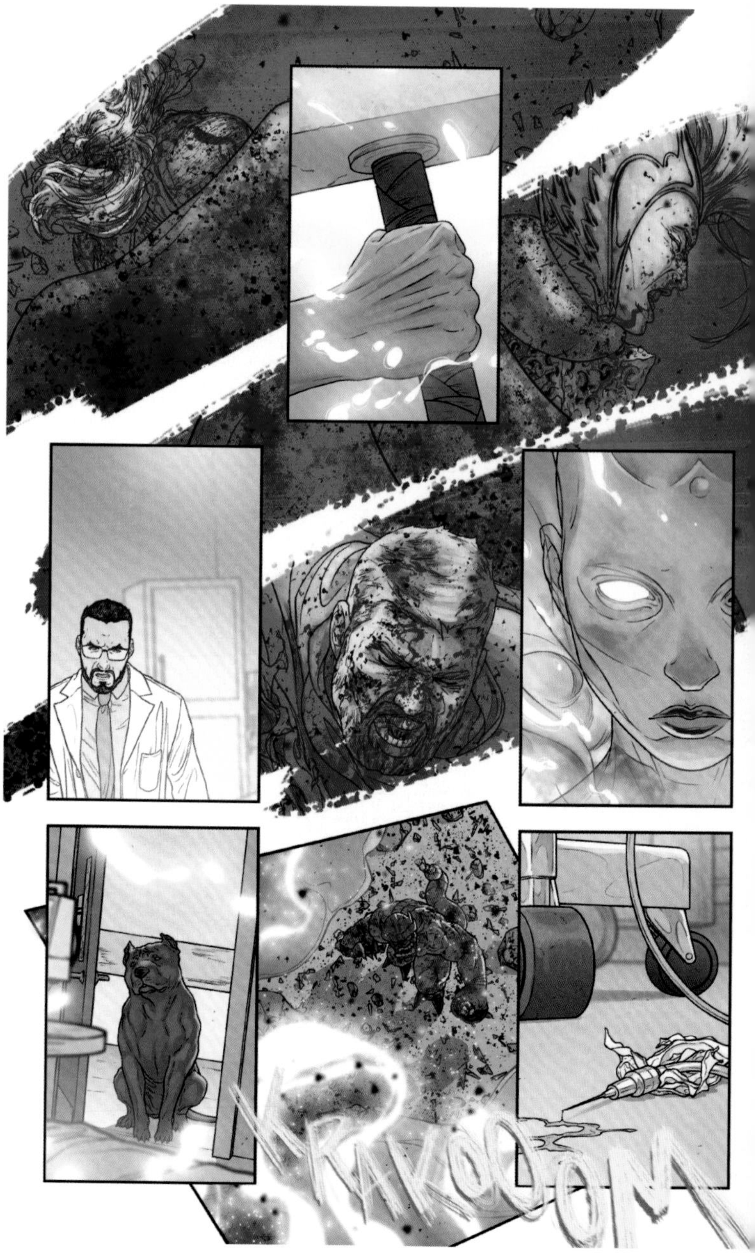
KRAKOOOM

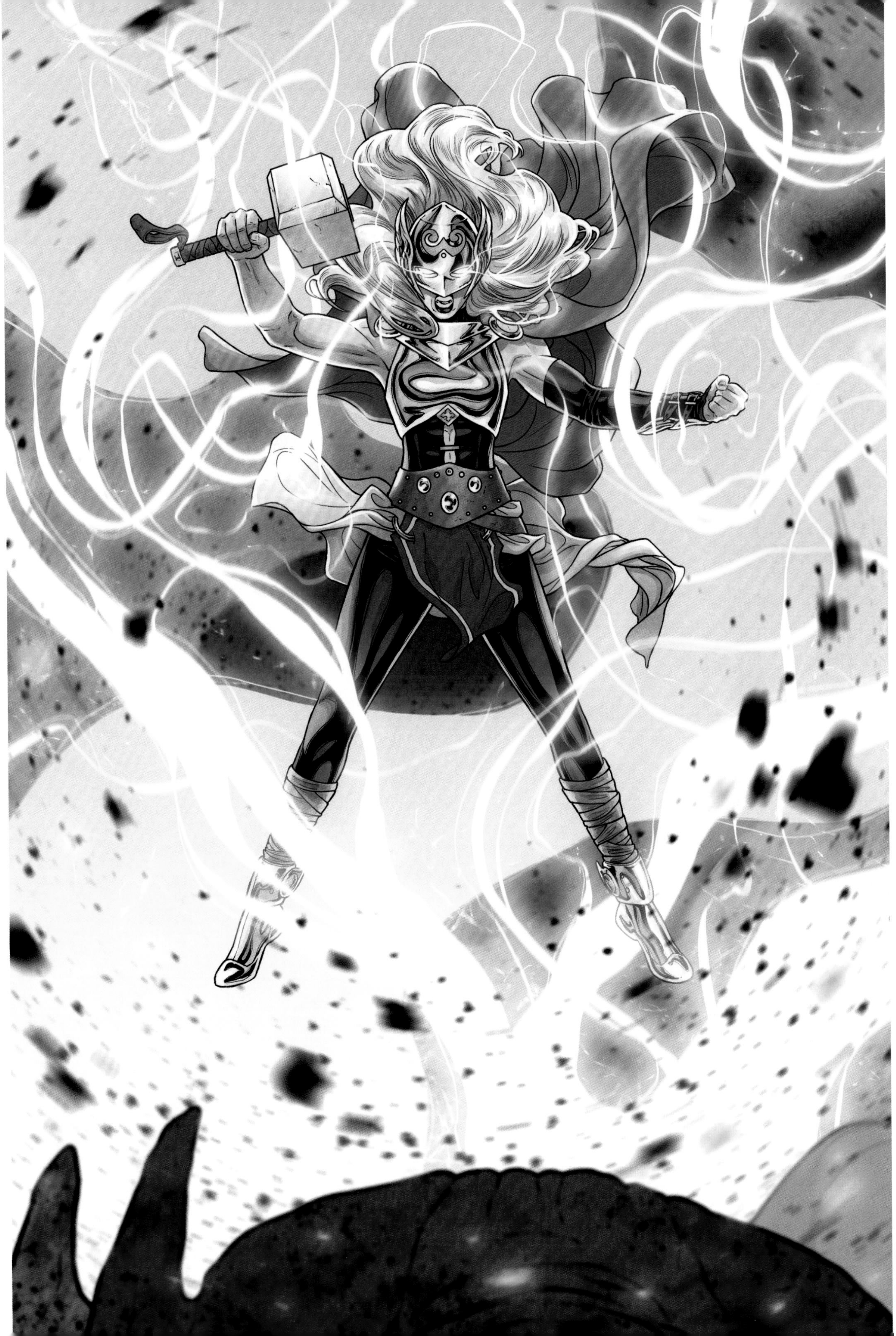

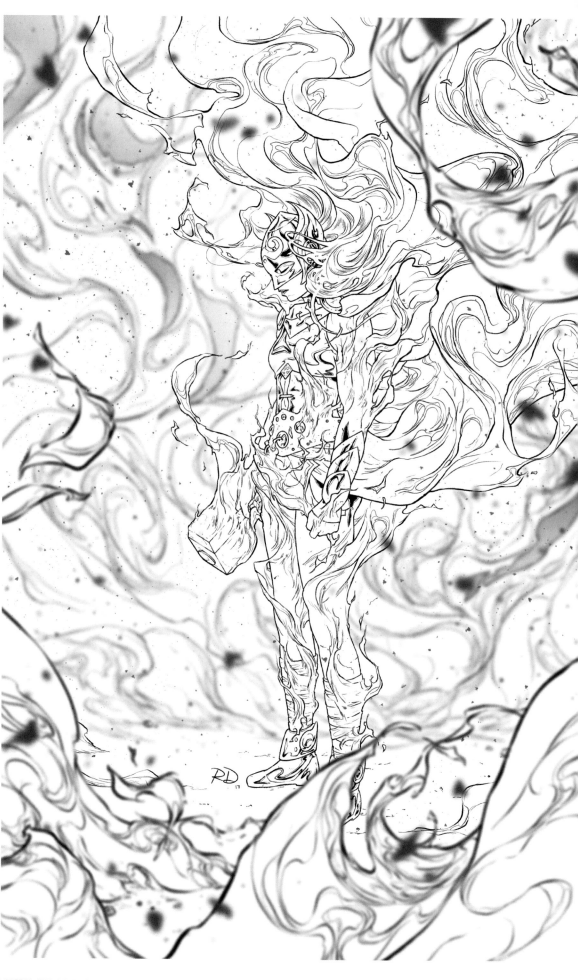

"I love the simple concept and composition of the *Mighty Thor #705* cover and really enjoyed drawing the swirling flames. This one was especially collaborative. The idea to have Thor on fire was Jason's, and Matt's colors really sell the concept. I love how the warm fire contrasts with the cool colors of Thor and the logo."

— RUSSELL DAUTERMAN

"There's always been a sense, at least to me, that Russell can probably guess what I'm going to give him. But it's also true that in nearly every issue he'll point to something I've colored as a complete surprise, and that he enjoyed being surprised by some of my choices. The result is this combination of Russell's thoughts and my own, which is an idea I quite like. It's a great representation of the collaborative nature of making comics, and a part of the job I'm really proud of when I do it well."

— MATTHEW WILSON

MIGHTY THOR (2015) #705
COVER INKS BY RUSSELL
DAUTERMAN, AND FINAL
ART BY DAUTERMAN AND
MATTHEW WILSON

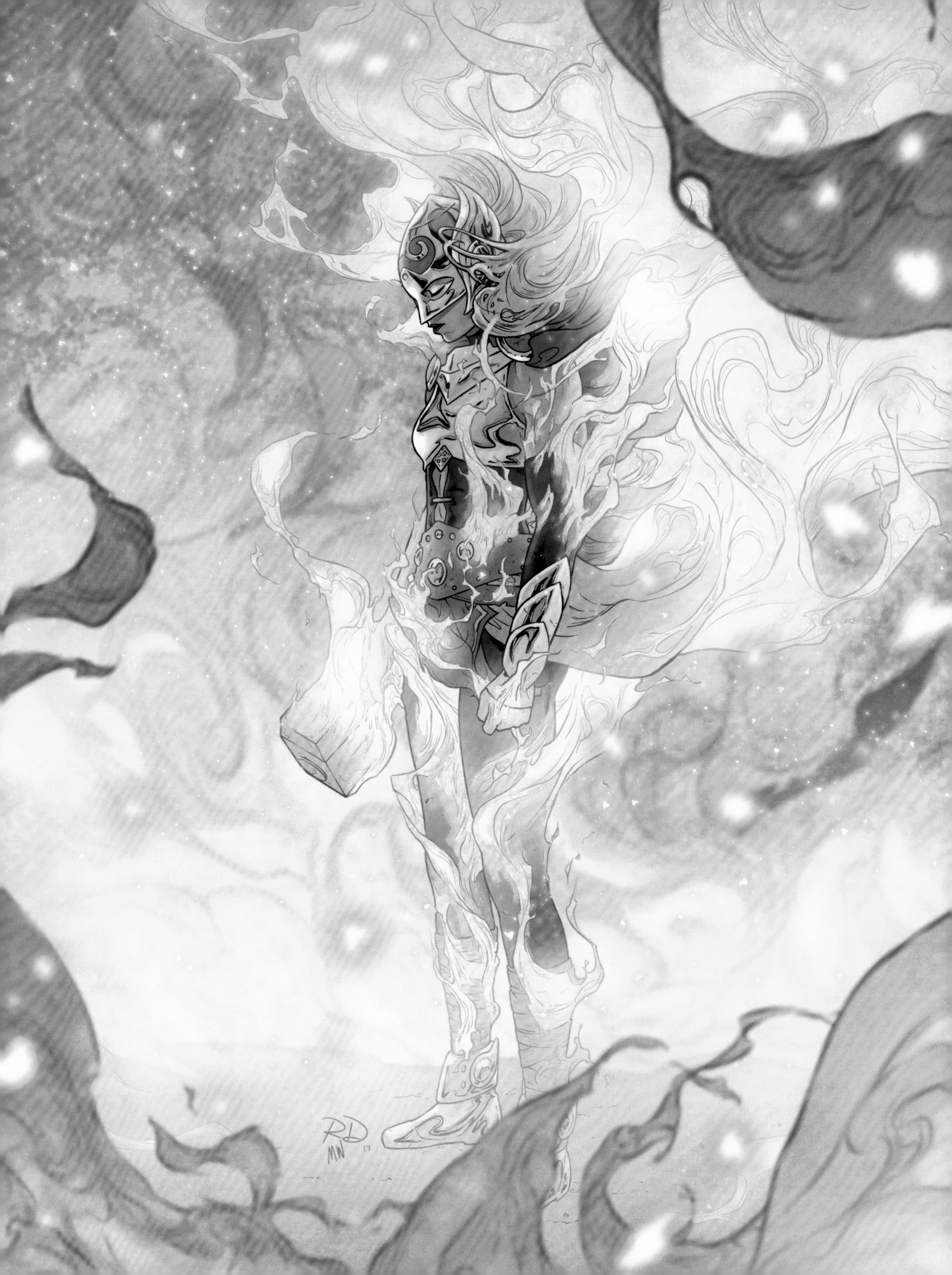

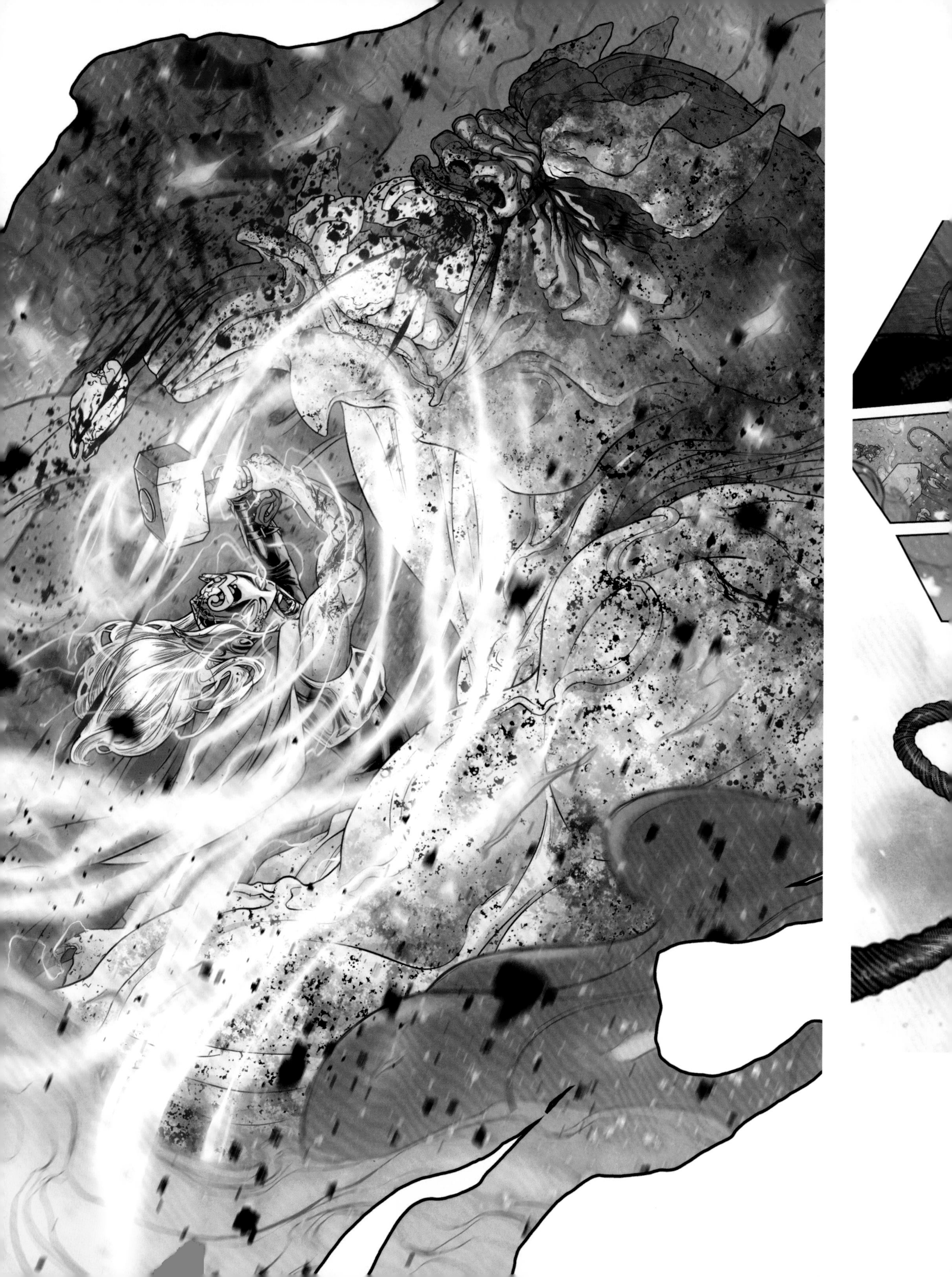

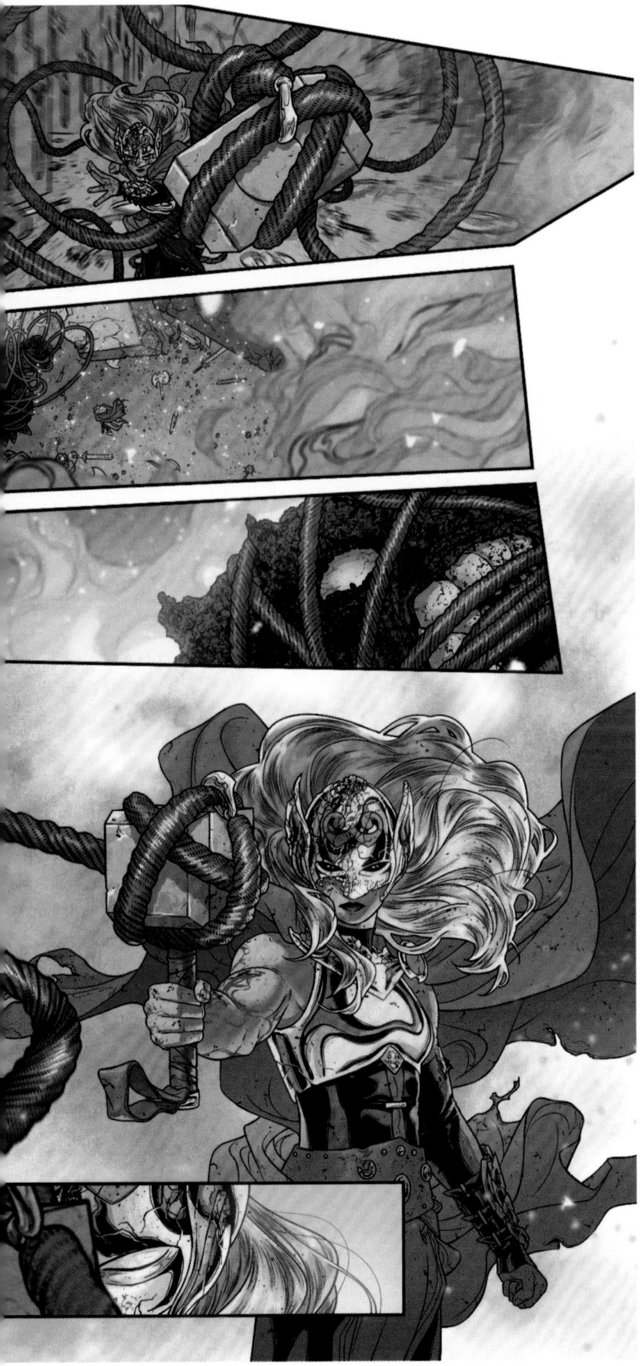

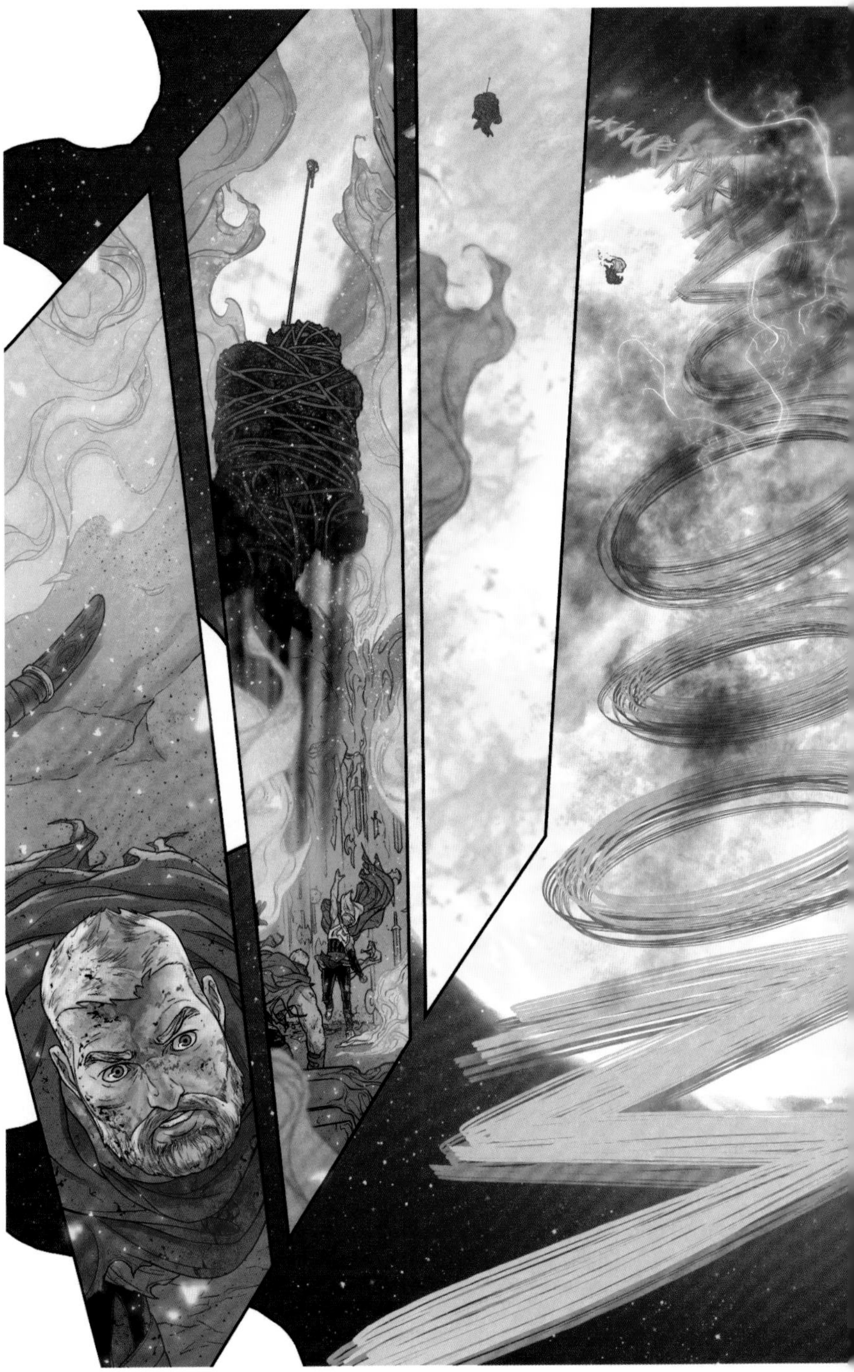

IN HER FINAL BATTLE, JANE CLASHES WITH THE MANGOG AND MAKES THE ULTIMATE SACRIFICE — MJOLNIR, THE ONLY THING KEEPING HER ALIVE— TO END HIS THREAT ONCE AND FOR ALL!

ABOVE, OPPOSITE AND FOLLOWING PAGES: *MIGHTY THOR (2015) #705*
INTERIOR ART BY RUSSELL DAUTERMAN AND MATTHEW WILSON

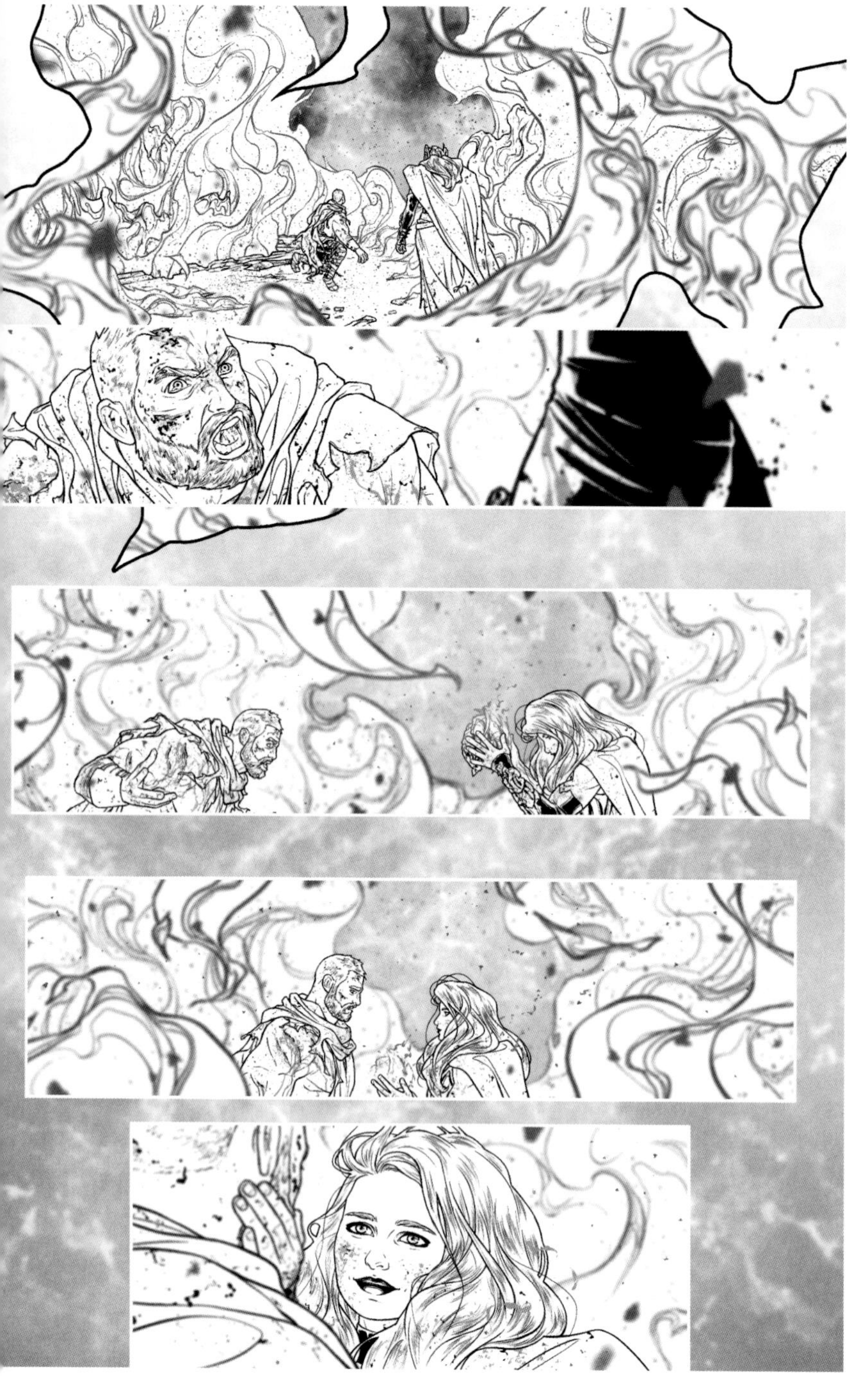

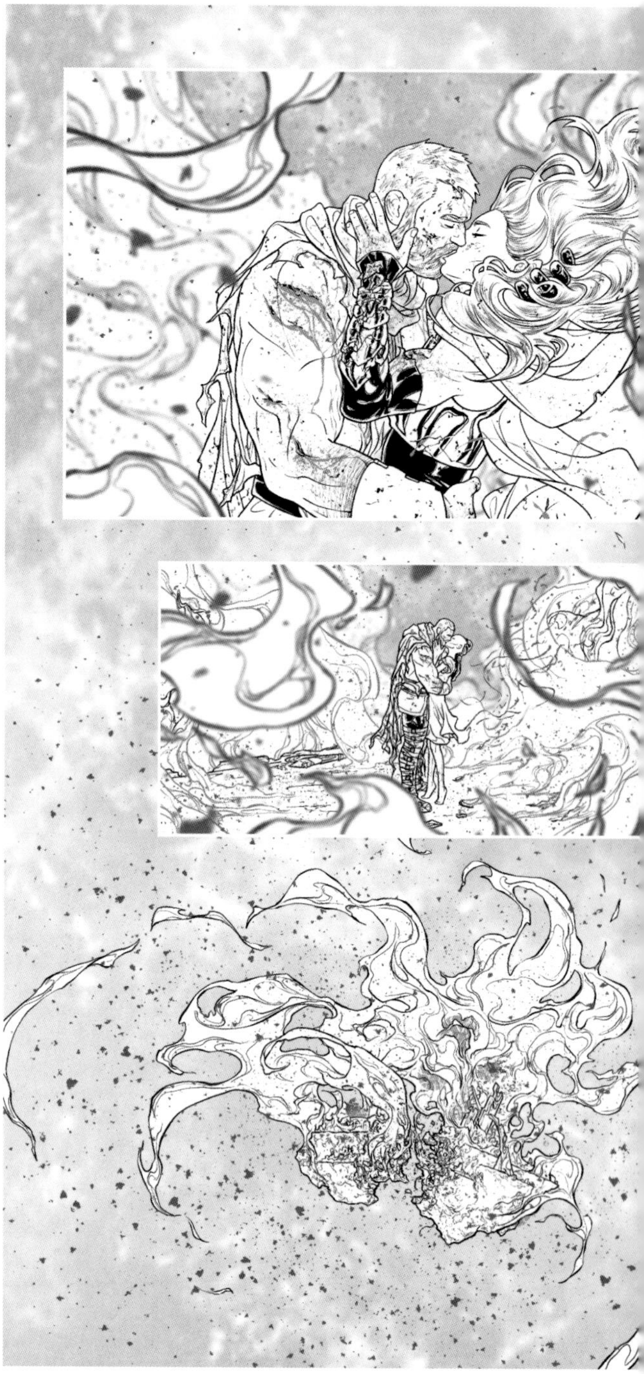

"If I had to pick one favorite page from the entire run, it would be *Mighty Thor #705,* page 18. The page is silent, with a very simple layout. I blurred most of the fire so that the focus would be on Jane and Odinson. Matt's colors are spectacular here, and I love the rainbow effect. My favorite detail is probably Jane on tiptoe in panel 2, reaching up to kiss Odinson after she's transformed."
— RUSSELL DAUTERMAN

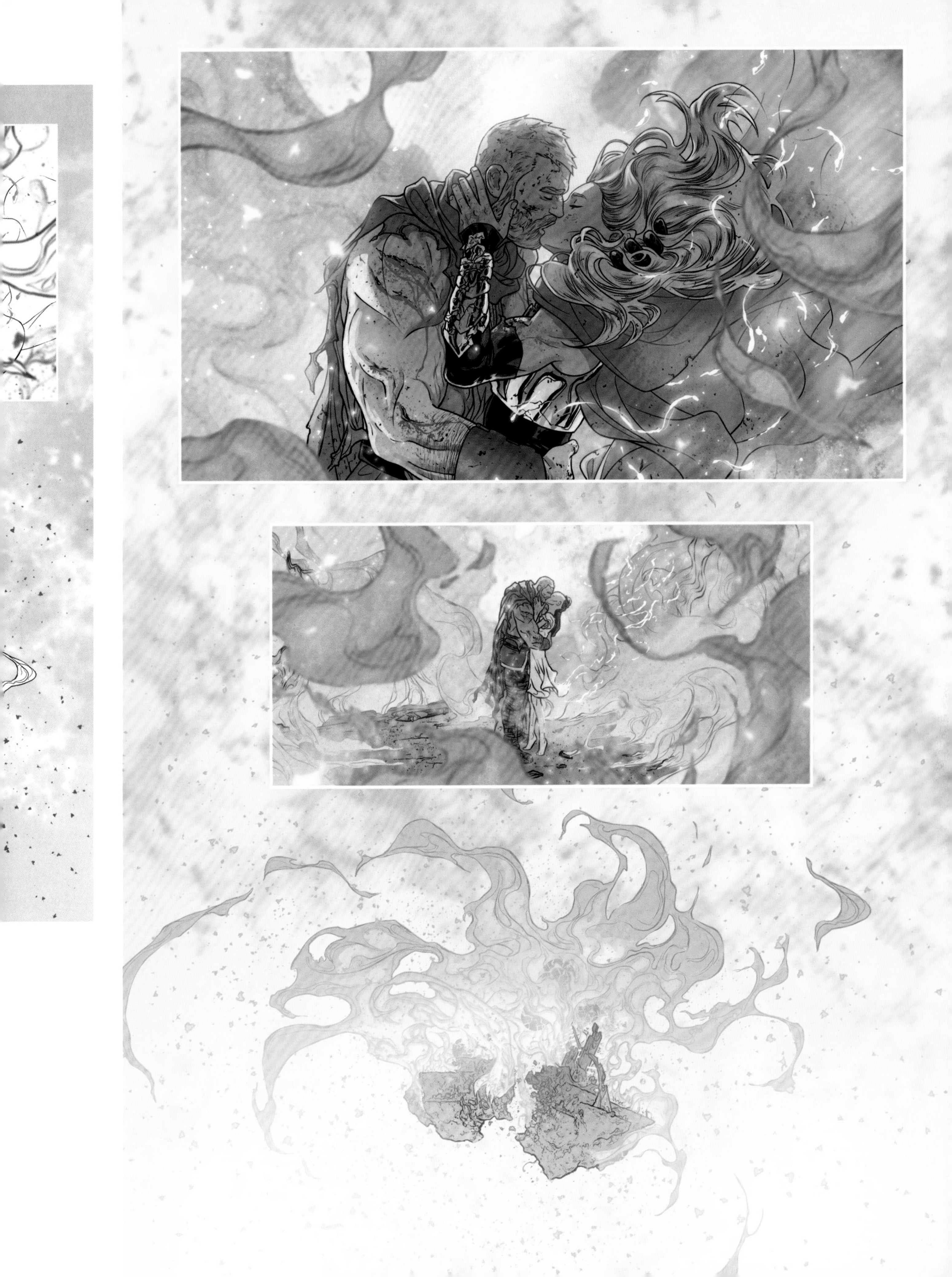

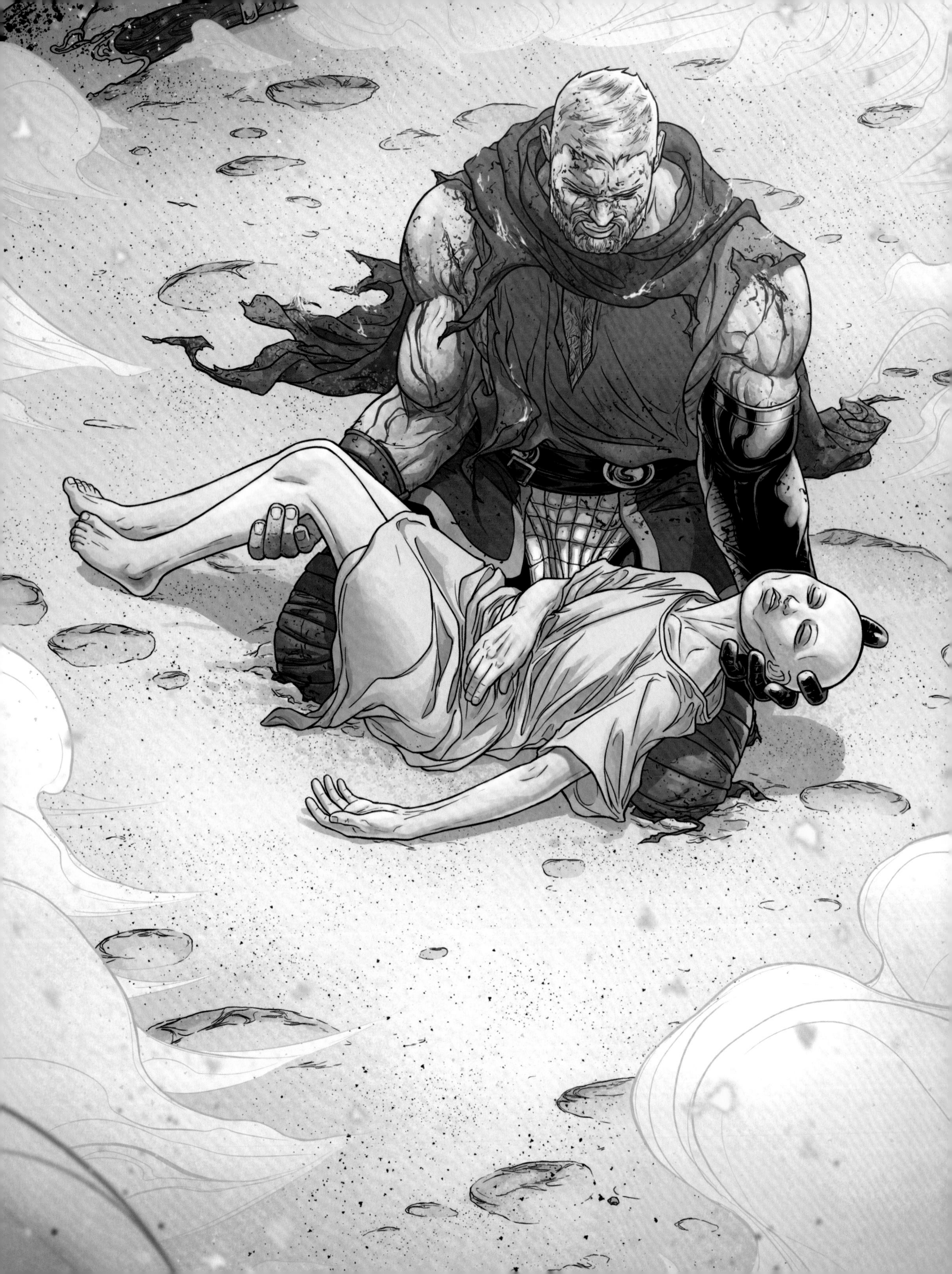

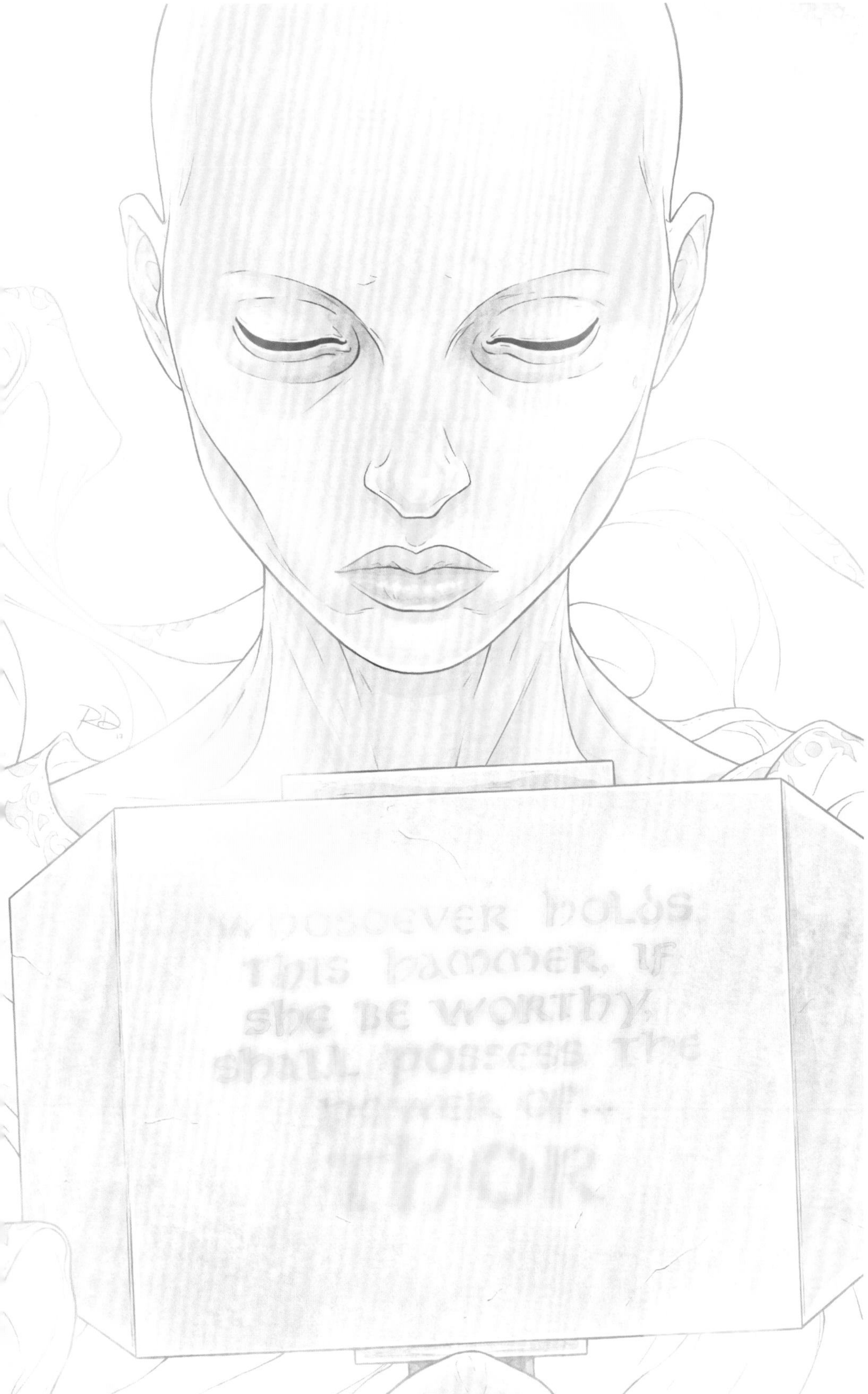
Whosoever holds
this hammer, if
she be worthy,
shall possess the
Thor

For colorist Matthew Wilson, the climax to Jane's story had personal significance: "I had colored most of the final issue of our run on the book. There were only a few pages left, about a day's worth of coloring for me, and the deadline was about a day or two away. And then, suddenly, my dad died. And he died while fighting cancer, much like the story of Jane Foster, which I had just spent the last three years coloring (roughly the same amount of time we spent dealing with his disease). It hadn't really occurred to me until then how much Jane's story ran parallel to what I was dealing with in my real life. My editors were understanding and incredibly accommodating and were able to extend my deadline because I really wanted to finish my work on our run. I also knew how proud my dad was of my career in comics and that he would've been proud of me finishing the work I had started. When I saw the final issue all put together, Marvel had put a dedication to my father in the credits page. Seeing that dedication was like a confirmation that I had done the right thing in not passing the last few pages of work off to someone else. And I know my dad would've got a real thrill from seeing his name published in a comic. So that series, and that issue in particular, will always have a very special place in my heart."

MIGHTY THOR (2015) #706
COVER BY RUSSELL DAUTERMAN
AND MATTHEW WILSON

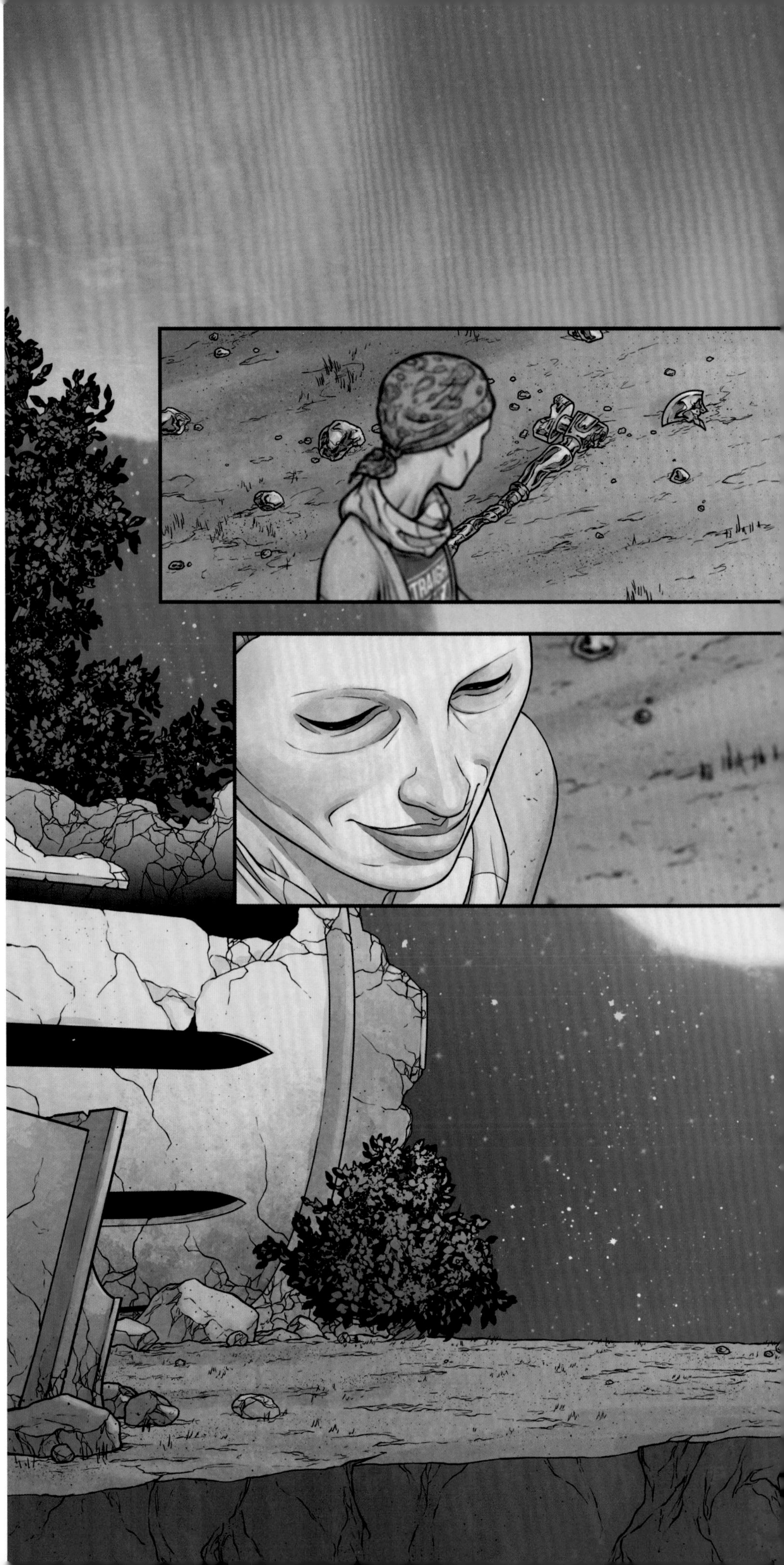

JANE MAY NO LONGER BE THOR, BUT HER STORY ISN'T OVER — SPARED FROM VALHALLA BY ODIN HIMSELF, SHE EMERGES WITH RENEWED DETERMINATION TO SURVIVE HER CANCER.

MIGHTY THOR (2015) #706 INTERIOR ART BY RUSSELL DAUTERMAN AND MATTHEW WILSON

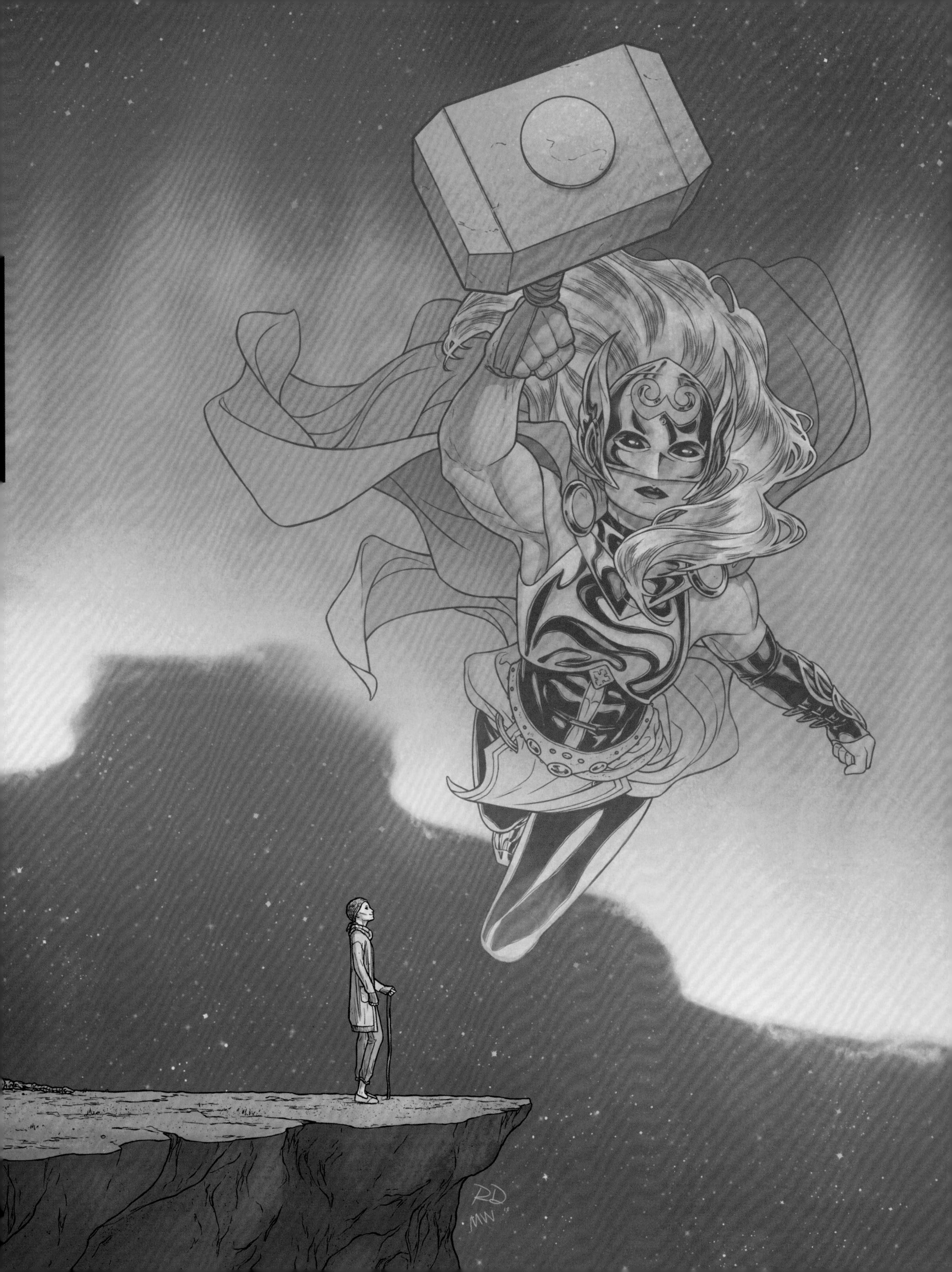

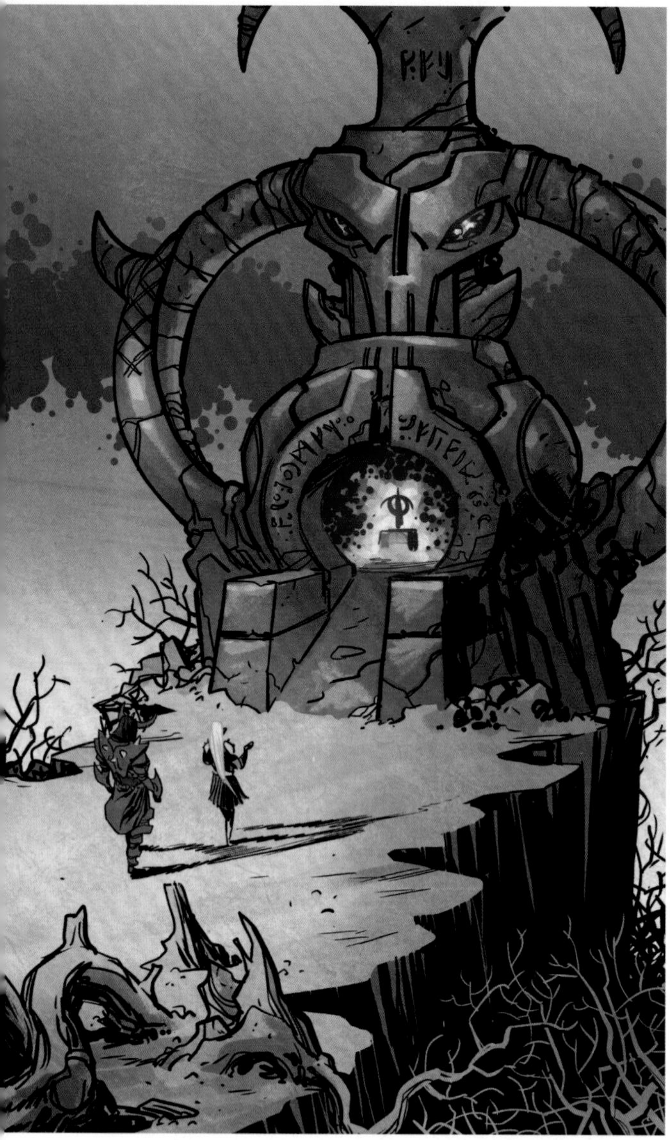

“Malekith needed his own Bifrost, and Loki was a part of helping him build it. That is the big advantage he has right now: He can hop around between all the different realms. When he decides to come here to Midgard, he can do it at the drop of a hat; there is nothing anyone can do to stop him. So that Black Bifrost is going to be a very important part of War of the Realms. Every great war story has to have a vitally important bridge.”
— JASON AARON

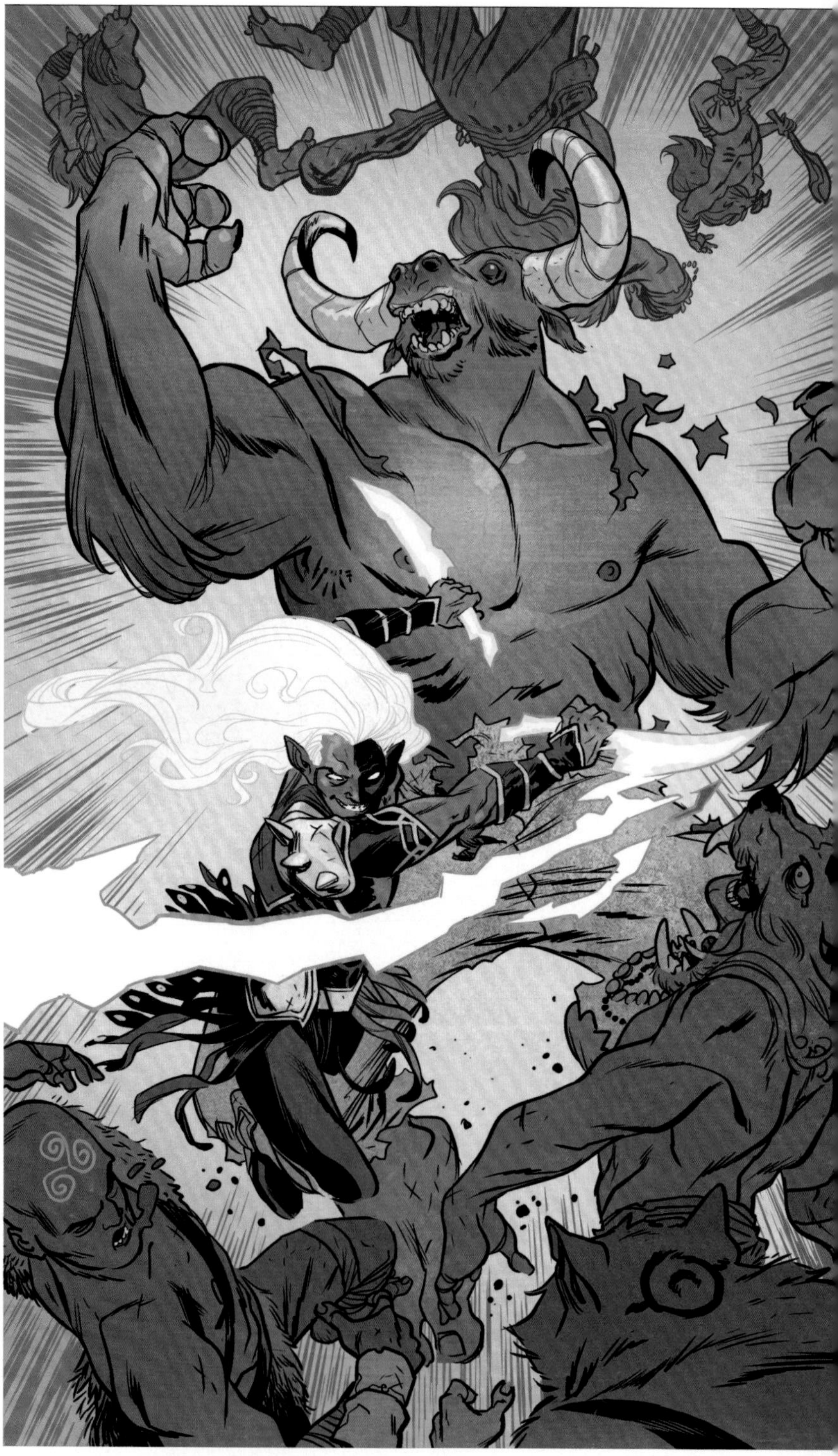

WITH THOR FALLEN, MALEKITH DECLARES HIMSELF LORD OF THE REALMS AS HE AND DARIO AGGER WREAK HAVOC ACROSS THE WORLDS, COURTESY OF THE BLACK BIFROST.

MIGHTY THOR: AT THE GATES OF VALHALLA #1
INTERIOR ART BY RAMÓN K. PÉREZ AND MATTHEW WILSON

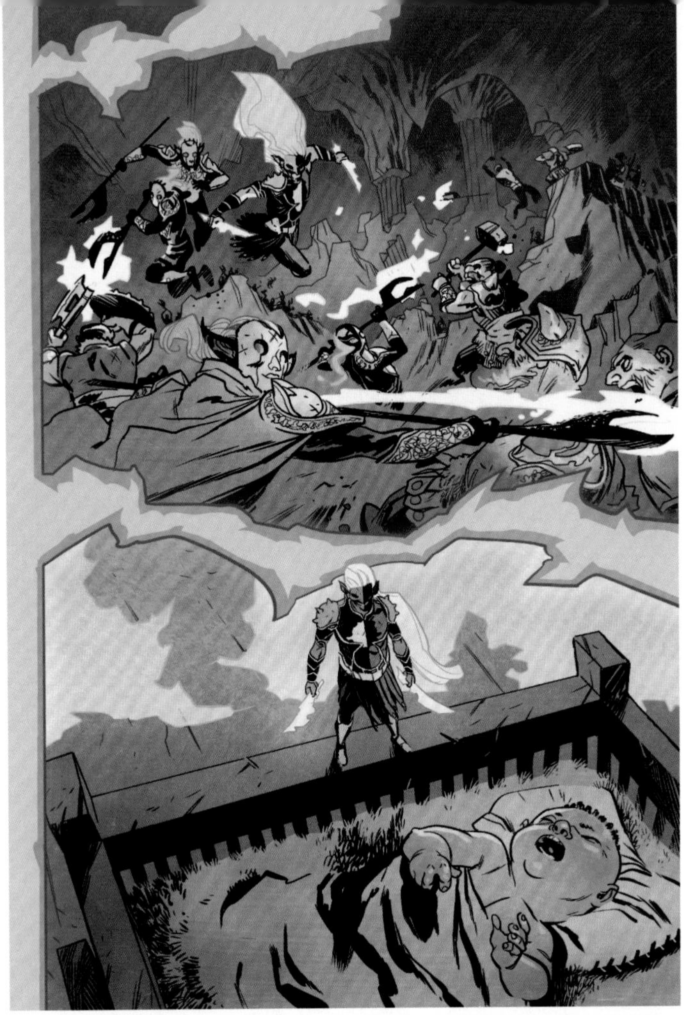
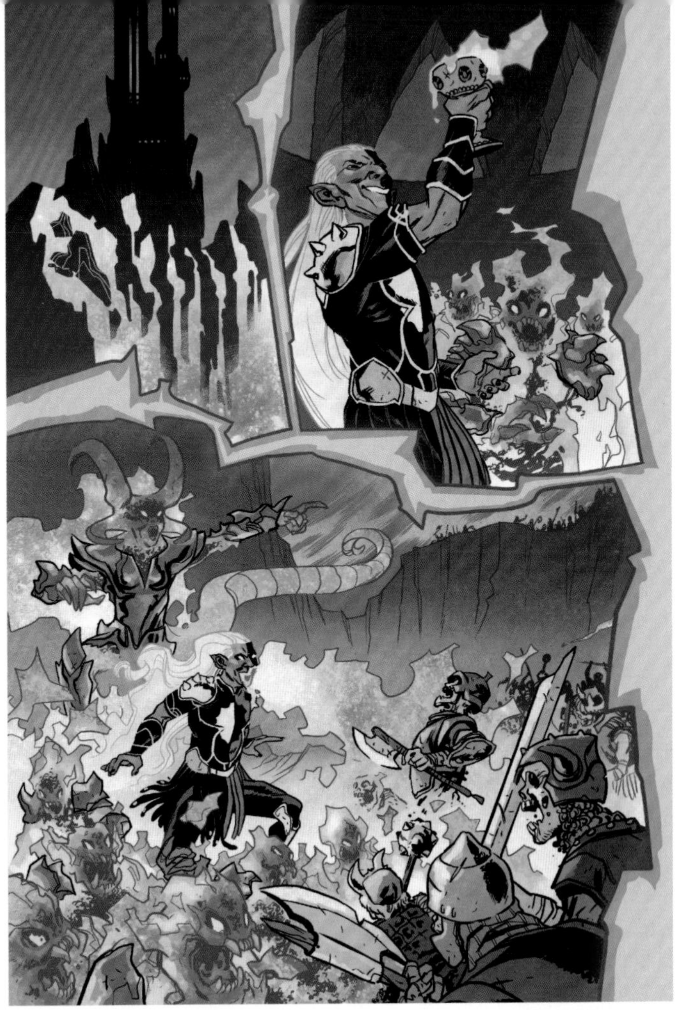
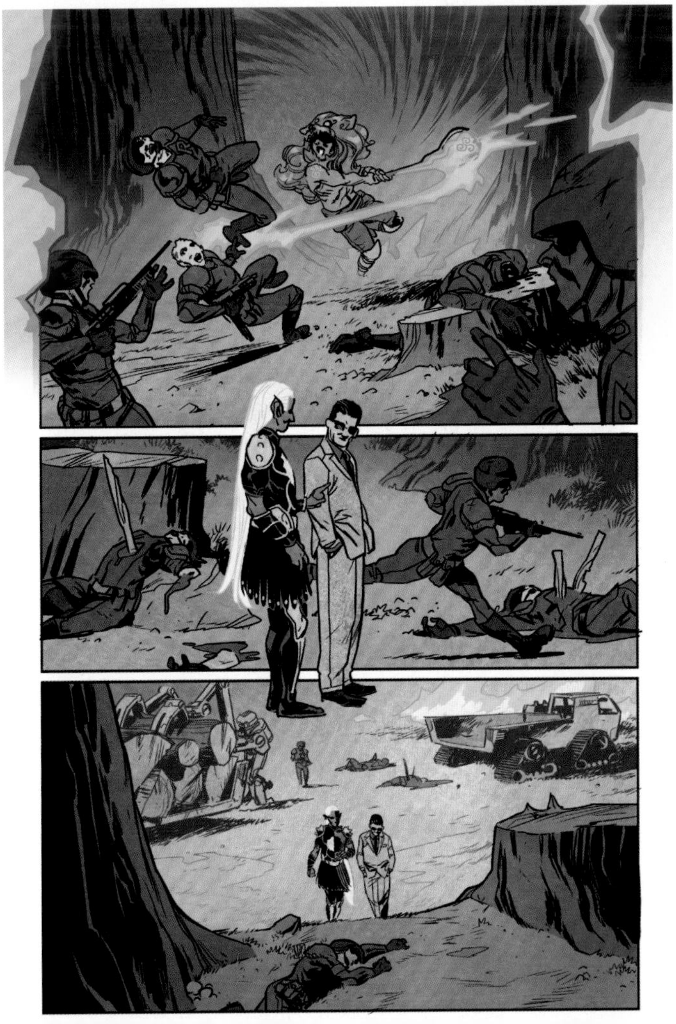
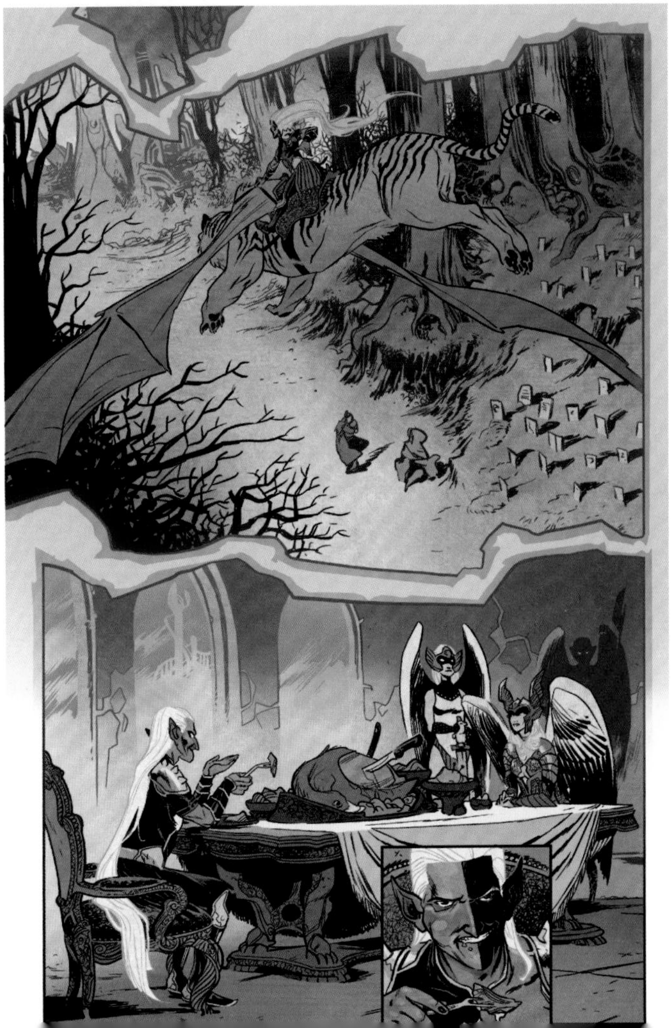

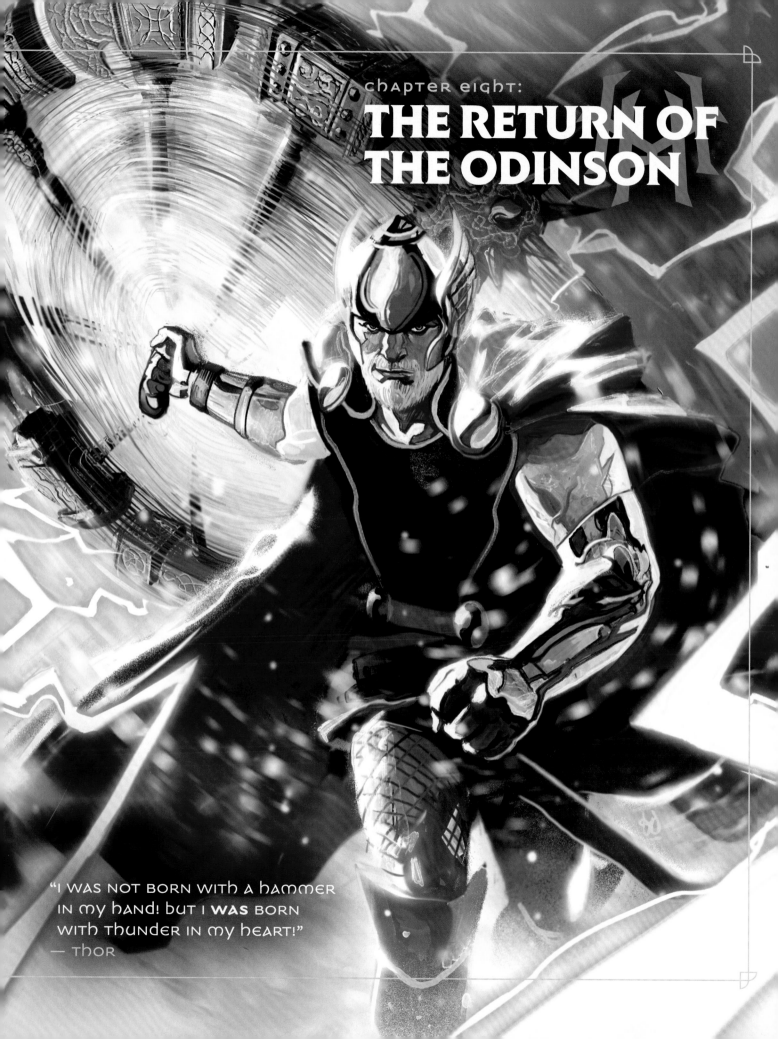

chapter eight

THE RETURN OF THE ODINSON

"I WAS NOT BORN WITH A HAMMER IN MY HAND! BUT I **WAS** BORN WITH THUNDER IN MY HEART!"
— THOR

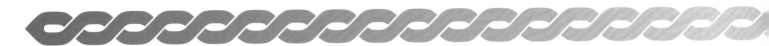

With 2018's *Thor*, Jason Aaron reinvented everything all over again. "It was about shifting gears and establishing a completely new status quo for Thor Odinson," Aaron says. "He reclaims his name, but he's not coming back to be exactly who he was before. He's still a very different Thor, in a very different place in life, so that was a lot of fun, because — even though I have been writing *Thor* for a lot of years — I don't feel like I'm repeating myself. I write different Thors, tell a lot of different kinds of stories, so this was another chance to really mix it up."

OPPOSITE: *THOR (2018) #1*
COVER BY MIKE DEL MUNDO

The story resumes with Asgardia gone, the Rainbow Bridge shattered and Heimdall blinded by the Mangog. While Freyja and many of the Asgardian gods recuperate on Midgard, a lonely Odin dwells in the ruins of Old Asgard, and Thor lives in a rusty old boat named *Toothgnasher* after his late, lamented goat — another victim of the Mangog. But for all that upheaval, the biggest change for Thor is being left without Mjolnir, the hammer sacrificed by Jane. Only the tiniest fragment remains — so what is Thor without his weapon? Aaron got creative in answering that question. Inspired by a Marvel NOW! promotional piece that Joe Quesada drew before even *Thor: God of Thunder* began, which showed Thor with some swords on his back, the writer thought it would be interesting to explore his character wielding different weapons. In the pages of *Thor*, he doesn't use swords, but instead an array of hammers forged on Old Asgard by Screwbeard and his fellow Dwarves, all enchanted by Odin and each with its own specialty.

"During the course of *Thor*, we see him with all sorts of different hammers," Aaron says. "Having Thor go into battle with hammer after hammer was a lot of fun. Smash one, call another one — I liked that a lot. It is visually stunning and also helps to highlight that there is only one Mjolnir and it's gone, so there is no easy replacement. I like watching Thor having to work harder and harder because of that."

Another major gear shift on *Thor* was Aaron's reunion with artist Mike del Mundo, with whom he had collaborated on *Weirdworld*. "Working with Mike's a total blast," Aaron says. "He brings so much energy and imagination to every page. His designs just make me so, so happy. He does the best, most creative covers in comics — they are really incredible. I've had a pretty amazing lineup of regular artists on my run: Esad, Russell and Mike, who are all very different from one another, but all work together to tell one big story."

It's a story that's only getting bigger. The latest volume of *Thor* features del Mundo's unique takes on blockbuster characters including the Juggernaut, Namor and Thanos — and that's before we get to the major players in the ongoing crisis spreading through the realms! From Sindr mounting an ultimately unsuccessful attack on Niffleheim — which leads to the return of Hela, her marriage to Karnilla and Balder the Brave being restored to life — to the Angels of Heven showing their hand as allies of Malekith, the skies continue to darken across all the worlds. As Aaron puts it, summing up the series: "We're setting the stage for war."

"I love how Jason's story leaves Thor open to drawing on new hammers and different weapons. It keeps my creative juices flowing, and I'm constantly creating. It's what I did when I was a little runt: just drawing outlandish weapons like hammers with spikes, bomb hammers, drill hammers, ax hammers, MC Hammers — it's a child's playground. Now it's real!"

— MIKE DEL MUNDO

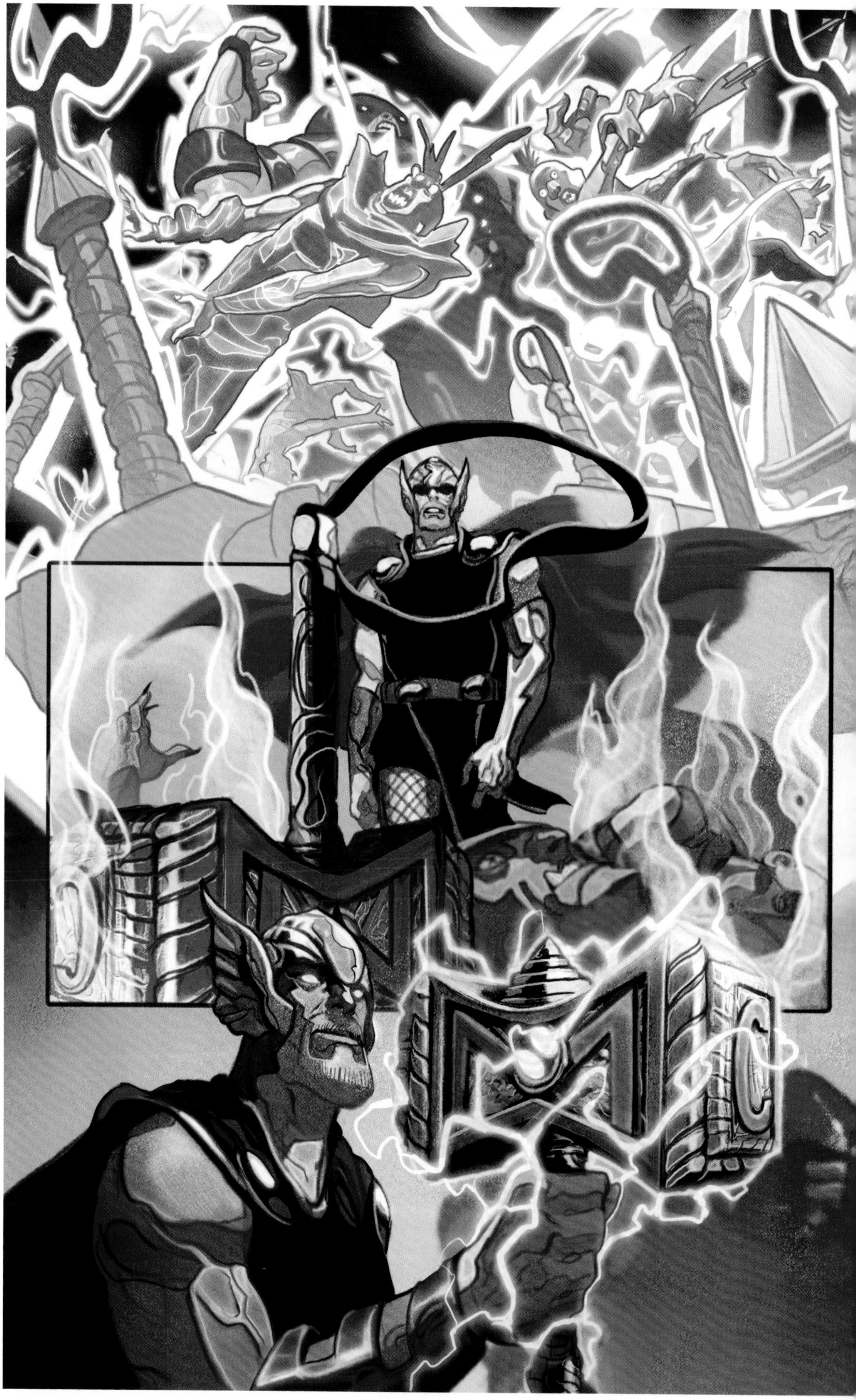

THOR CALLS DOWN A CLAMOR OF HAMMERS — AND SELECTS JUST THE ONE FOR SMITING THE JUGGERNAUT!

THOR (2018) #1 INTERIOR ART BY MIKE DEL MUNDO, WITH COLOR ASSISTS BY MARCO D'ALFONSO

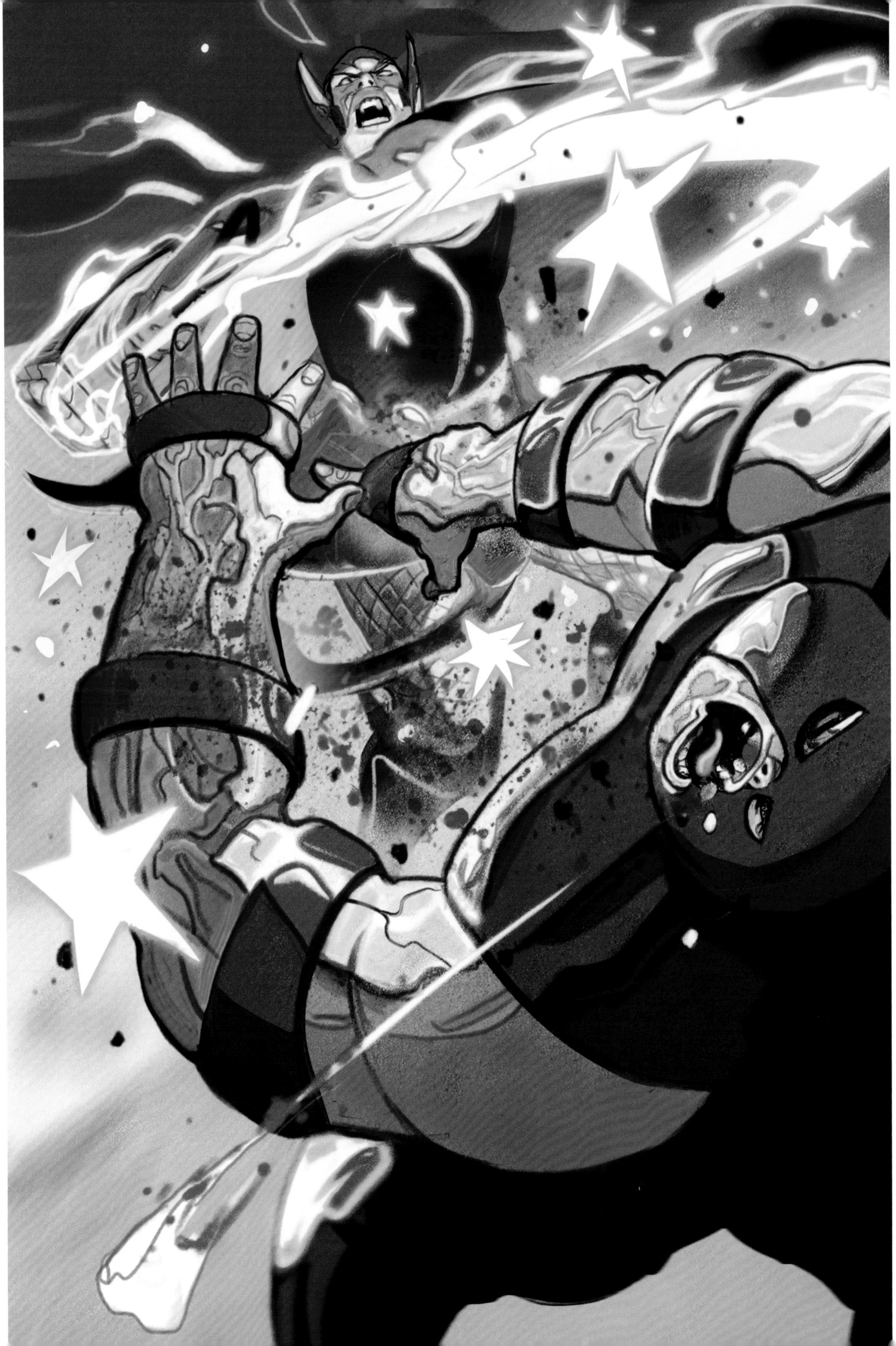

THANOS MAKES AN IMPOSING APPEARANCE.

THOR (2018) #3 INTERIOR ART BY MIKE DEL MUNDO, WITH COLOR ASSISTS BY MARCO D'ALFONSO

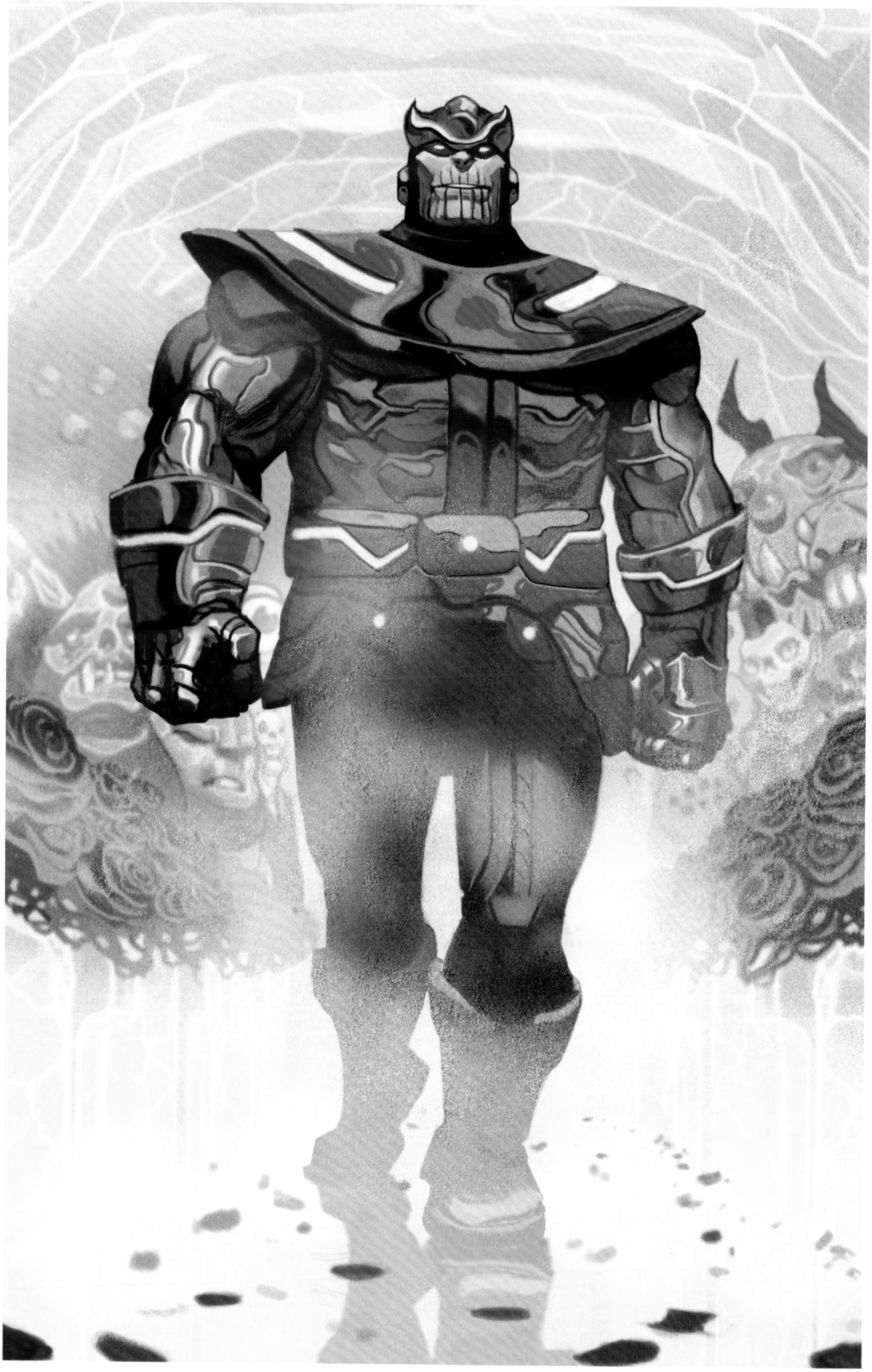

"It feels like a '90s rap cover."
— MIKE DEL MUNDO

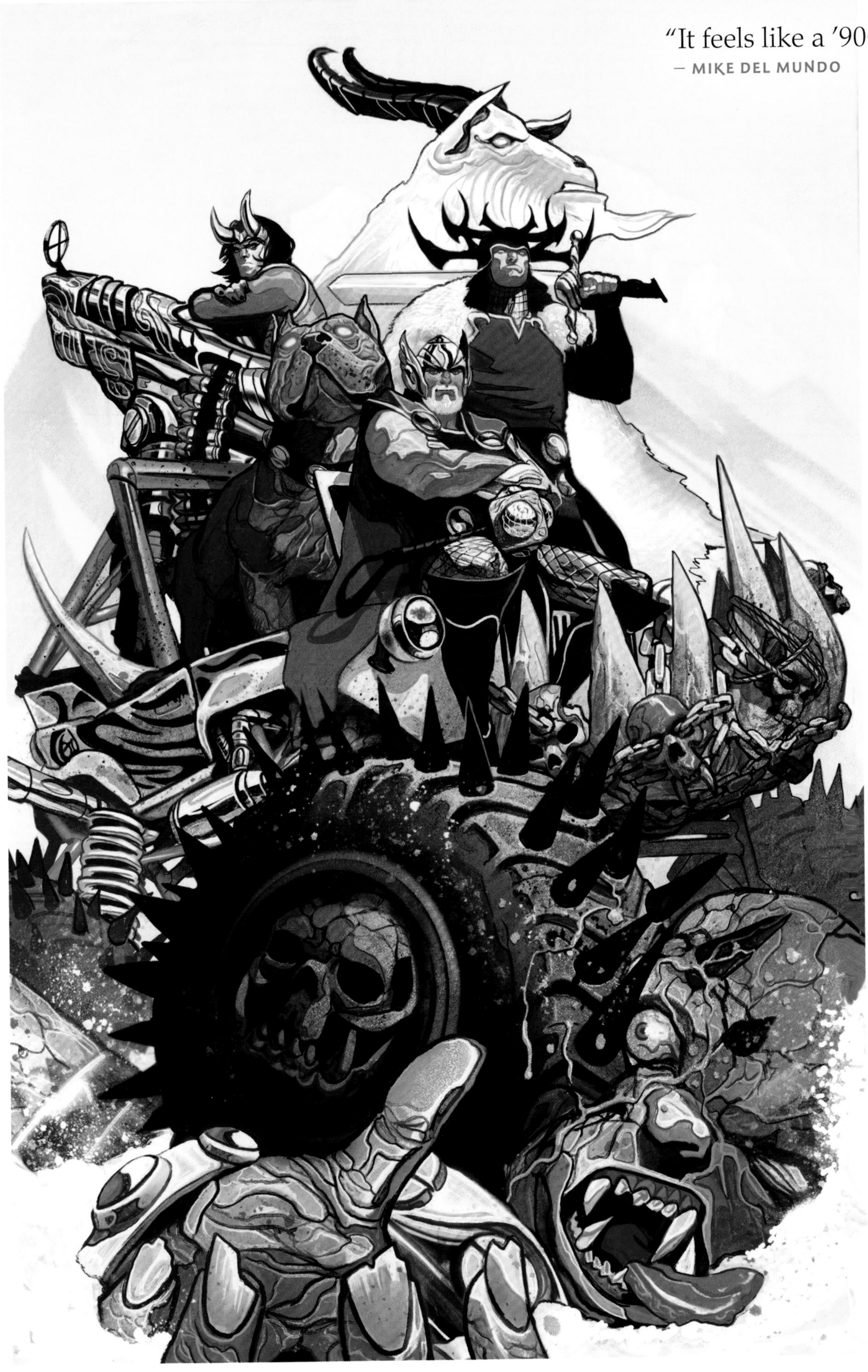

BROTHERS ARE REUNITED AS THOR, LOKI AND BALDER — PLUS THORI AND TOOTHGRINDER — STRIKE A POSE ON A MONSTER TRUCK IN HEL.

***THOR* (2018) #2** COVER BY MIKE DEL MUNDO

SINDR, QUEEN OF MUSPELHEIM, BRINGS THE WAR OF THE REALMS TO NIFFLEHEIM (ABOVE) — BUT HELA, TYR AND THE GIANT WOLF FENRIS RETURN TO RECLAIM HEL!

***THOR* (2018) #2** INTERIOR ART BY MIKE DEL MUNDO, WITH COLOR ASSISTS BY MARCO D'ALFONSO

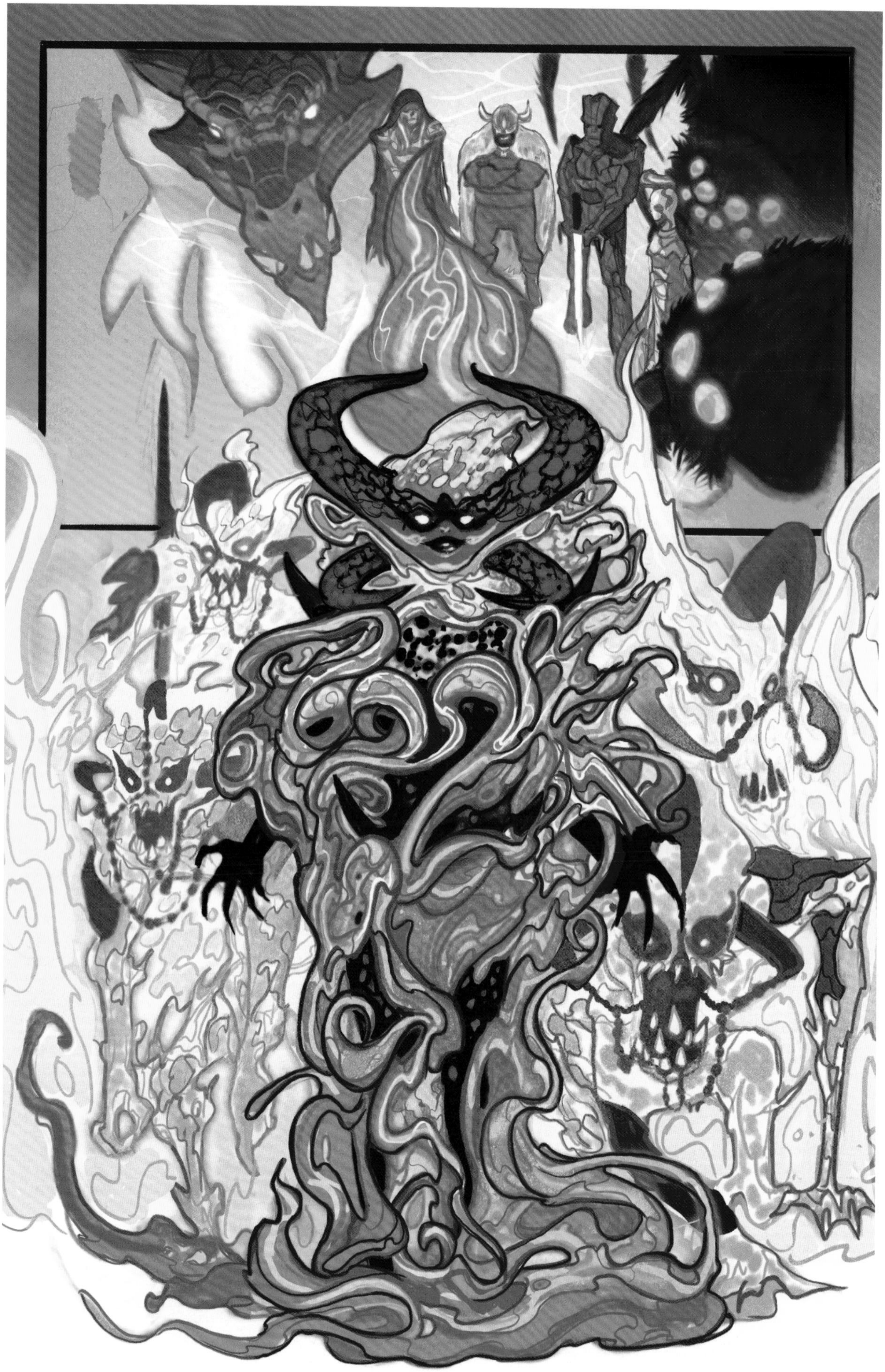

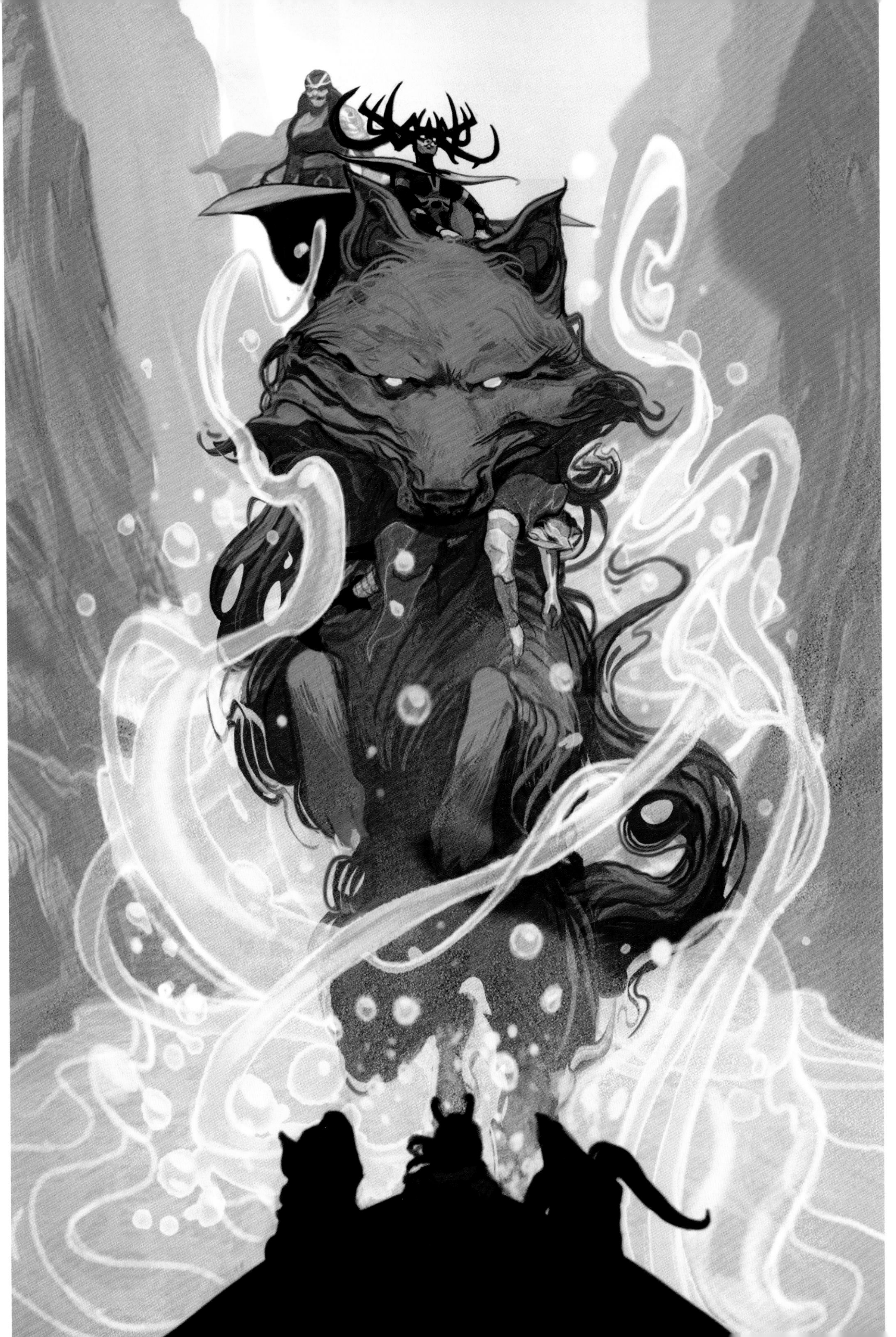

THOR LEADS BRUNNHILDE AND HER FELLOW VALKYRIES IN THE FIGHT FOR NIFFLEHEIM AGAINST SINDR.

THOR* *(2018) #4
COVER BY MIKE DEL MUNDO

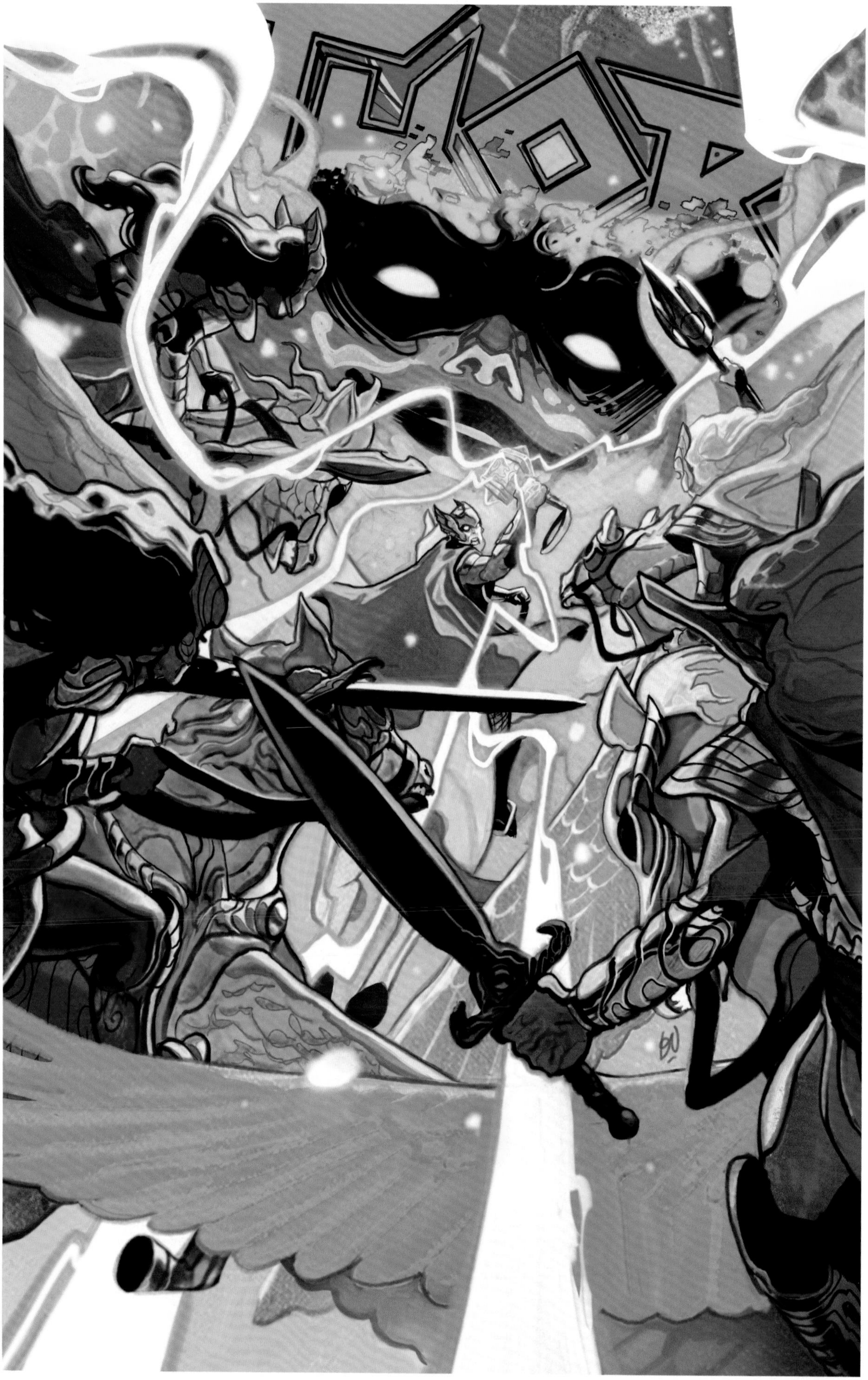

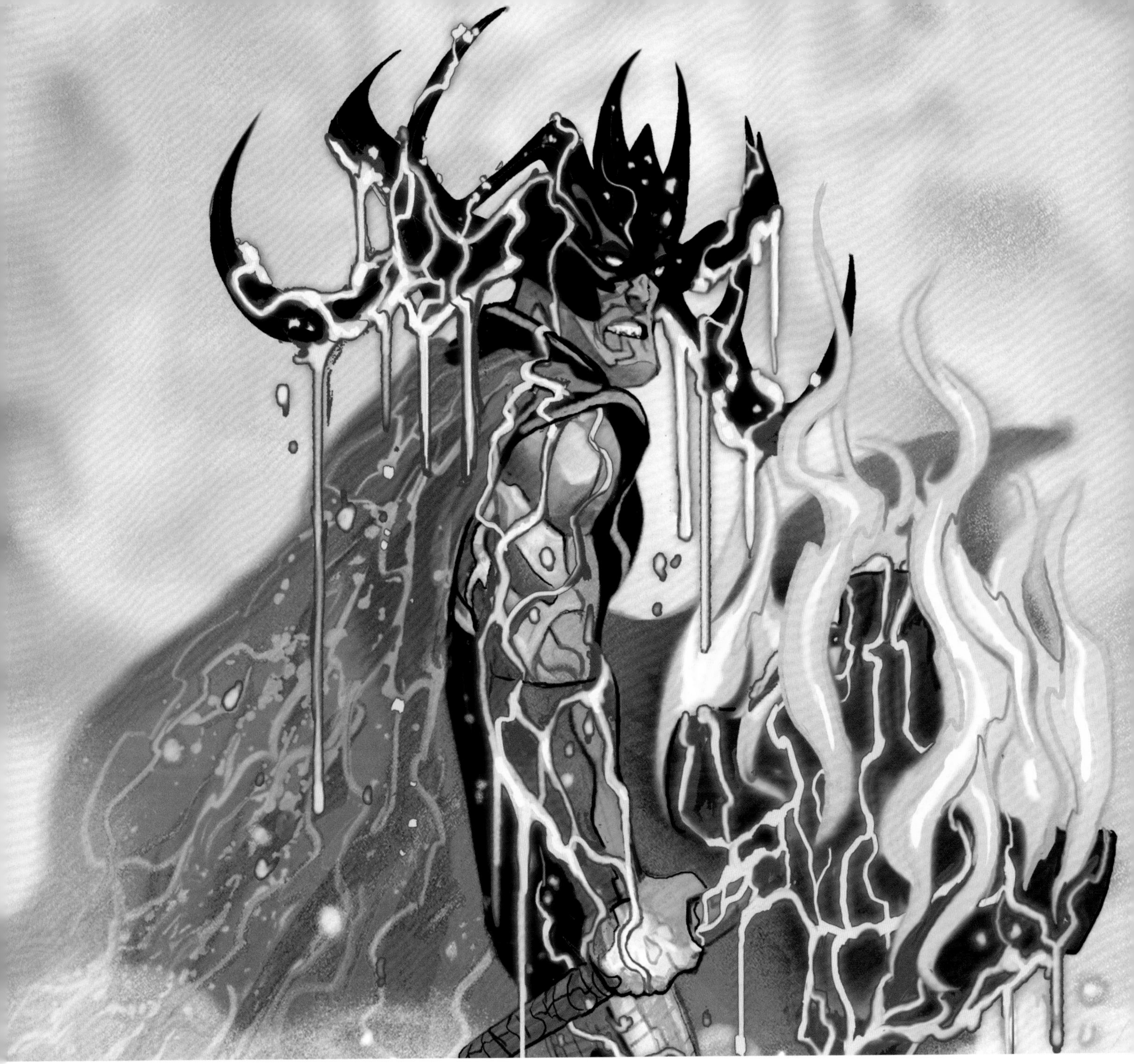

THE THUNDER GOD BRIEFLY WEARS HEL'S CROWN.

THOR (2018) #4 INTERIOR ART BY MIKE DEL MUNDO, WITH COLOR ASSISTS BY MARCO D'ALFONSO

"Niffleheim hasn't fallen, but it is definitely more chaotic than before. You've got the queens of Hel now, Hela and Karnilla, who aren't exactly the best of friends — an uneasy union ruling the land of the dead. So it certainly leaves a question mark as to which side of the war this realm would fall on. Even when Malekith doesn't completely decimate or take control, just like he never really attacked Asgard, he still manages to manipulate things to create ruin and confusion and chaos all around, just to aid his cause."

— JASON AARON

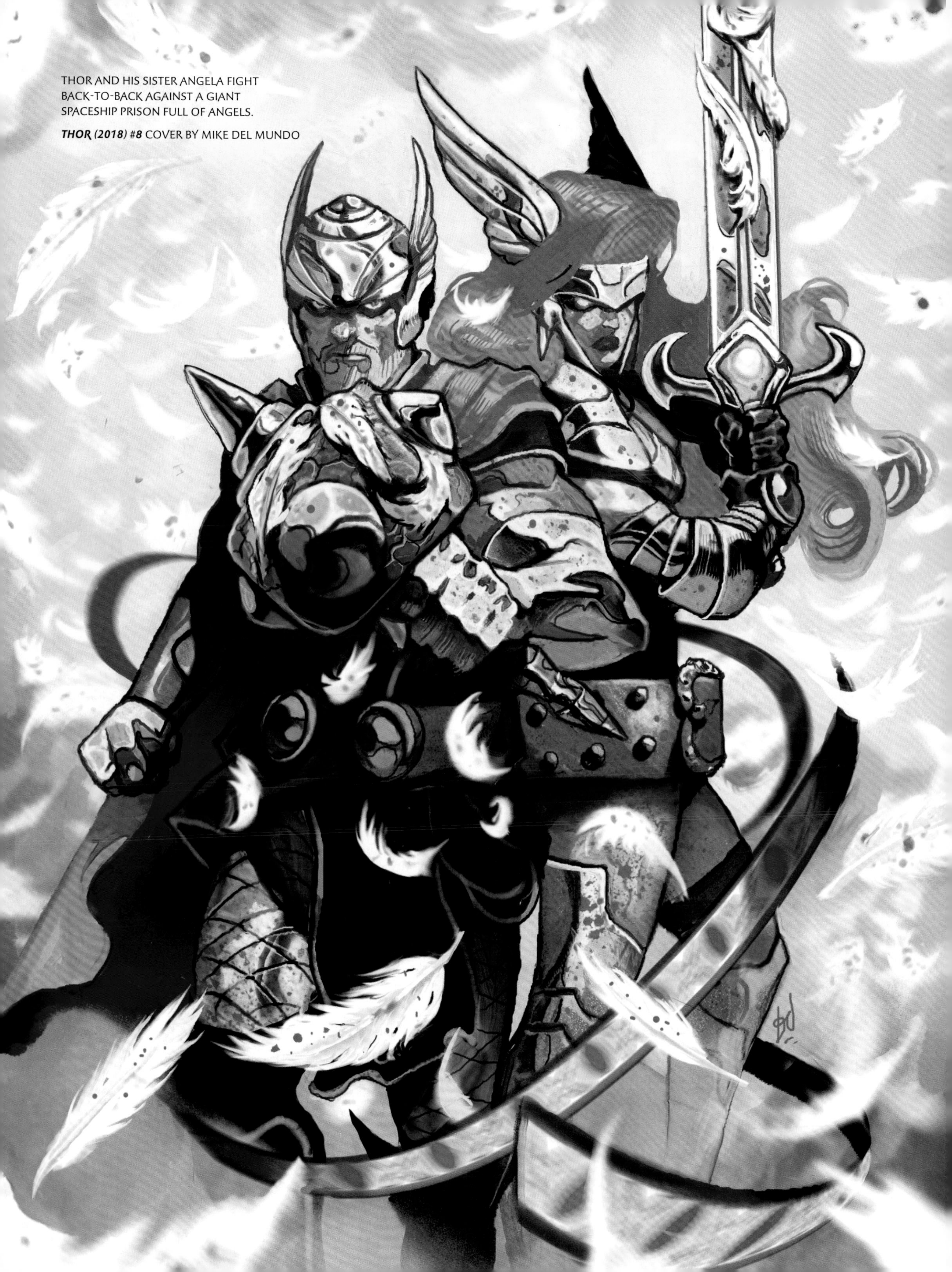

THOR AND HIS SISTER ANGELA FIGHT BACK-TO-BACK AGAINST A GIANT SPACESHIP PRISON FULL OF ANGELS.

THOR (2018) #8 COVER BY MIKE DEL MUNDO

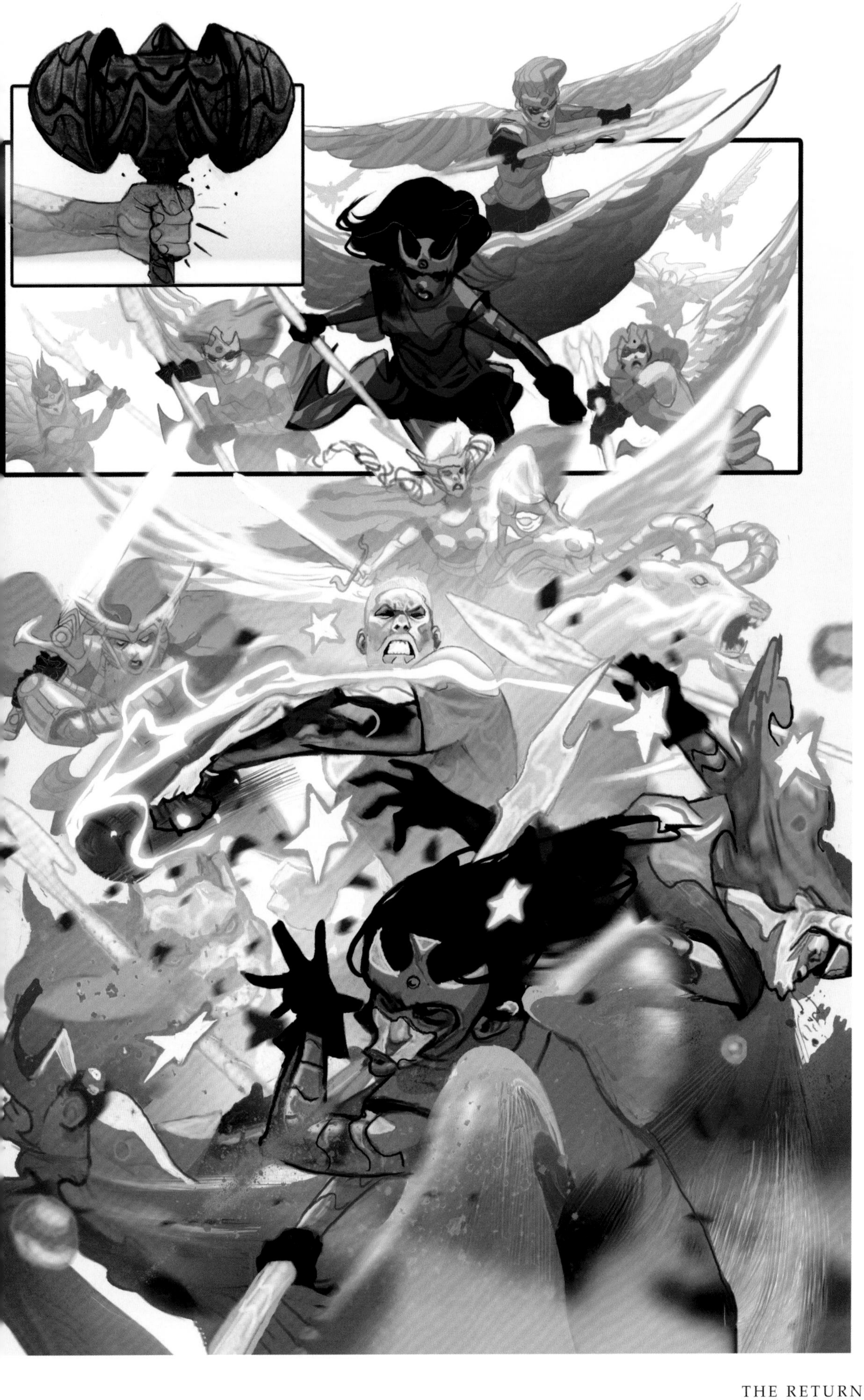

"Thor took out one crew, one big spaceship of Angels, but not the queen — not the entirety of the forces of Heven. The Angels of Heven will be a big part of Malekith's army when it hits the shores of Midgard."

— JASON AARON

VALKYRIE JOINS THE FIGHT.

THOR (2018) #8 INTERIOR ART BY MIKE DEL MUNDO

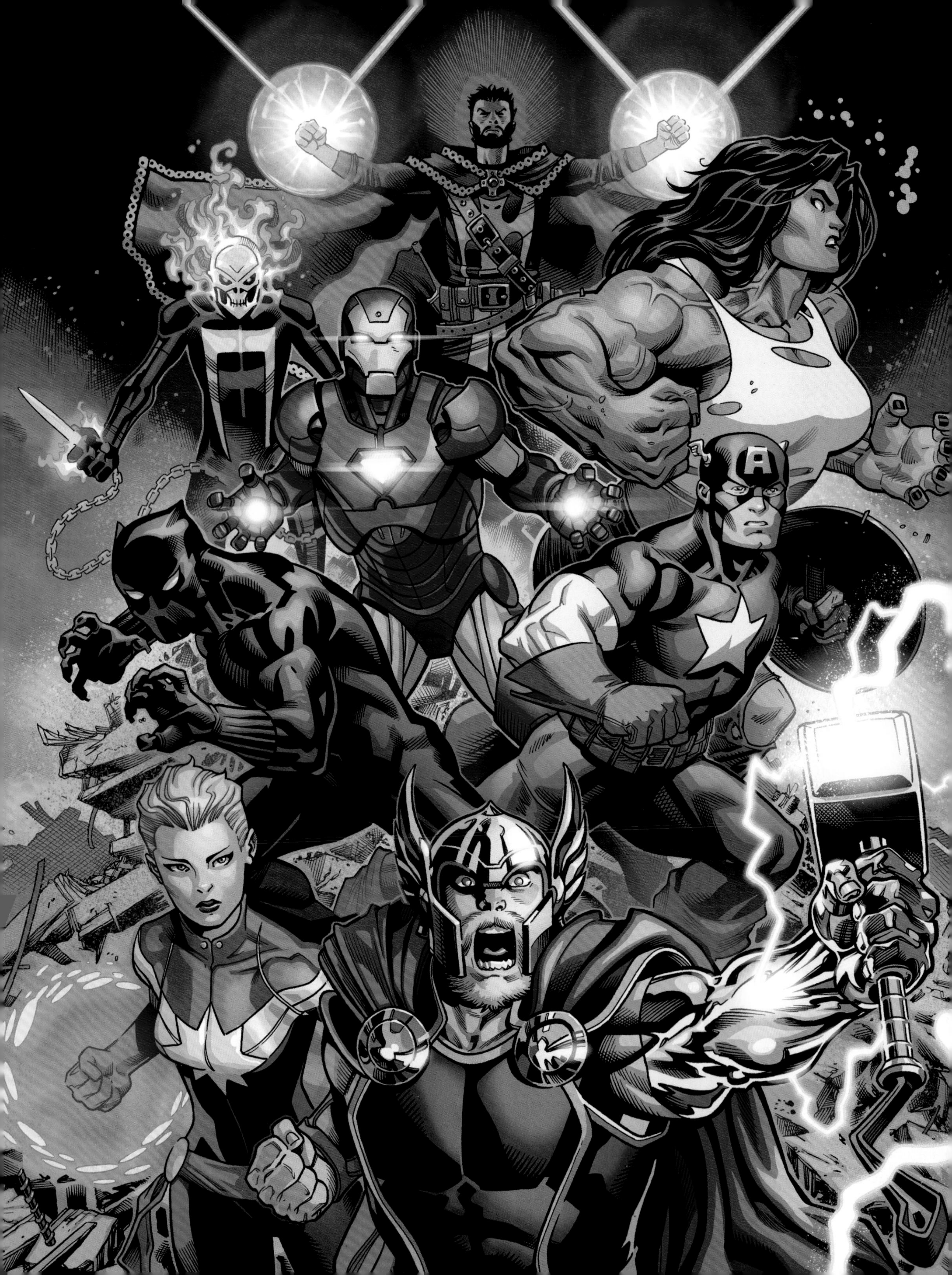

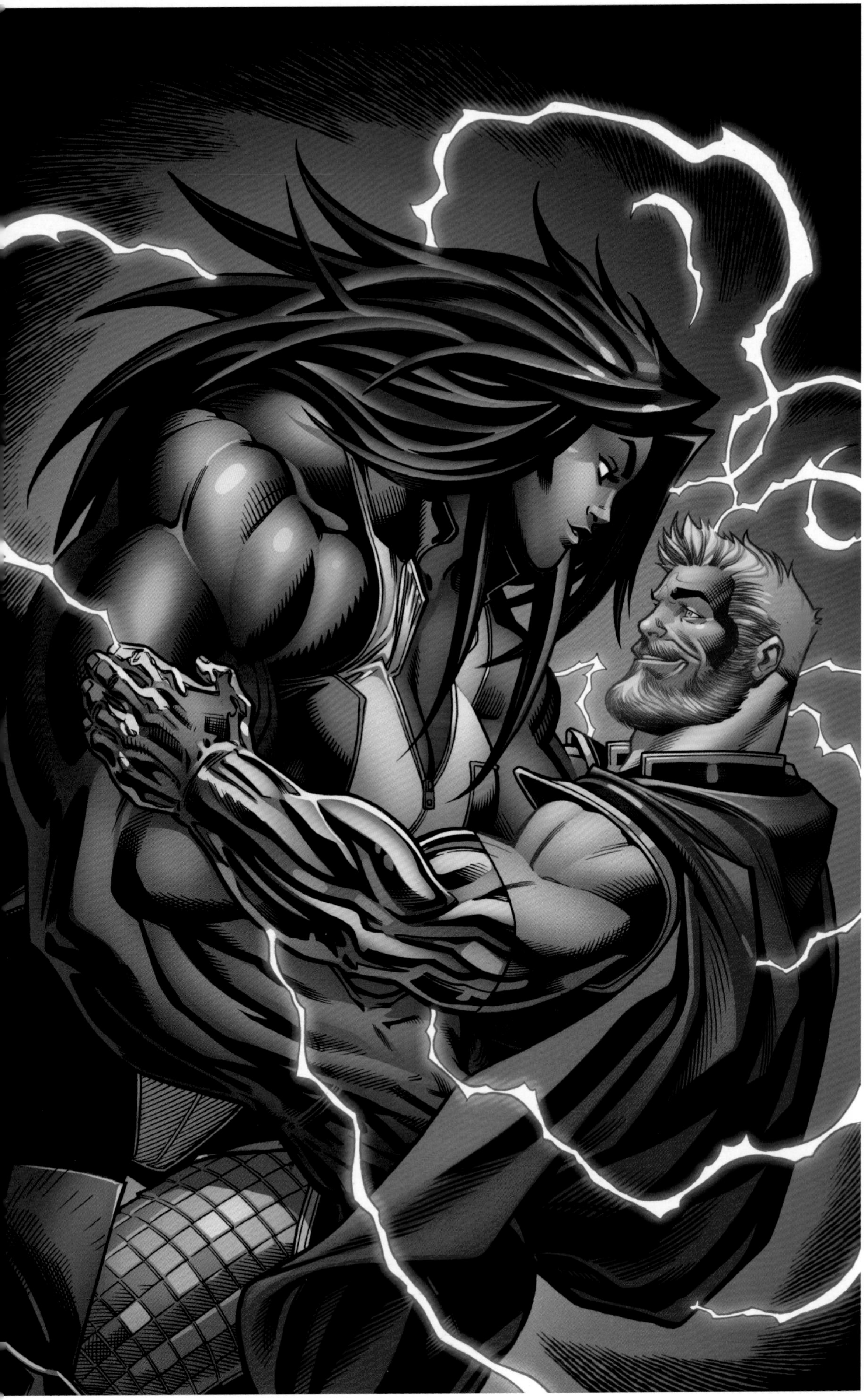

"It's a blast to work with Ed again. He does big, bombastic super heroes, so I like that it feels like a classic Thor — but with a twist. Over the course of my entire run, we've seen Thor with a lot of different love interests — I never wanted him to be a guy who settles down. So coming to *Avengers*, I got really excited about the idea of a Thor/Hulk romance. They are kind of starting that. It is not a situation where they instantly fall in love with each other and everything is rosy — it's awkward and rocky for a bit."

— JASON AARON

THANKS TO LOKI'S MACHINATIONS, THE AVENGERS REASSEMBLE — WITH THOR FRONT AND CENTER IN THE BLOCKBUSTER RELAUNCH OF THE TEAM BOOK BY JASON AARON AND ED MCGUINNESS. AND UNEXPECTED ROMANCE AWAITS IN THE ARMS OF JENNIFER WALTERS, THE HULK!

OPPOSITE AND LEFT: ***AVENGERS (2018) #1*** AND ***#11*** COVER ART PENCILED BY ED MCGUINNESS, INKED BY MARK MORALES AND COLORED BY JUSTIN PONSOR

JANE FOSTER TAKES THOR'S MURDEROUS DOG, THORI, FOR A WALK.

THOR (2018) #8 INTERIOR ART BY MIKE DEL MUNDO

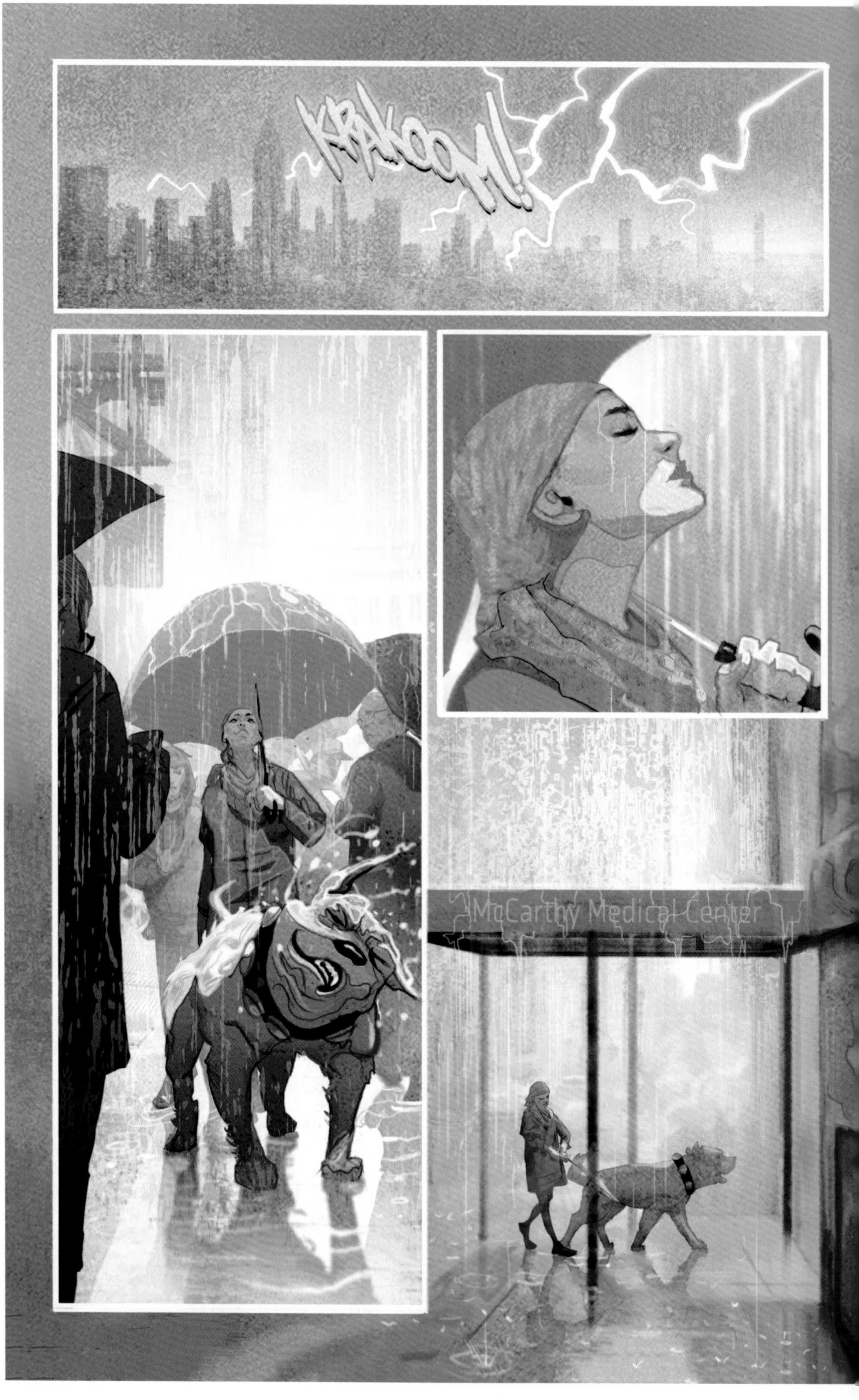
KRAKOOM!
McCarthy Medical Center

"I knew even when we got to end of the story of Jane Thor that it wasn't the end of Jane's story. Jane's not going anywhere — she will have a role to play in War of the Realms."

— JASON AARON

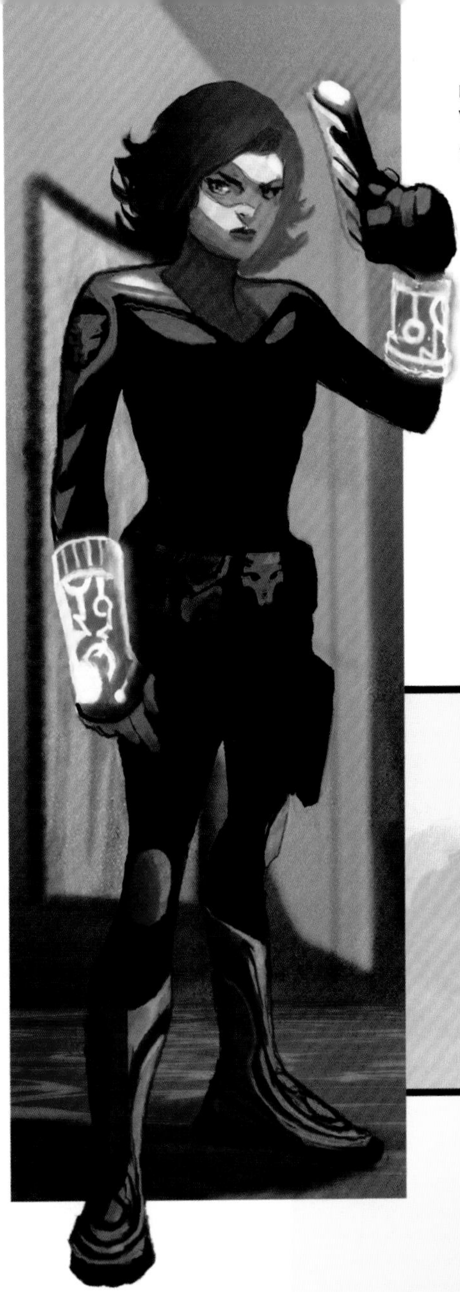

ROZ SOLOMON, AGENT OF WAKANDA — PACKING A GUN THAT FIRES VIBRANIUM BULLETS — TAKES DOWN A FROST GIANT.

THOR (2018) #9 INTERIOR ART BY MIKE DEL MUNDO

"One of the first big things we saw Roz doing in the Battle of Broxton was taking on a whole bunch of Trolls. Clearly, she is still dealing with the aftermath and ramifications of that, which has changed who she is. Roz's previous job went away when S.H.I.E.L.D. shut down. When the Black Panther, leader of the Avengers, has to build a new support network, we get the Agents of Wakanda, with Roz Solomon one of the first people recruited for that gig."

— JASON AARON

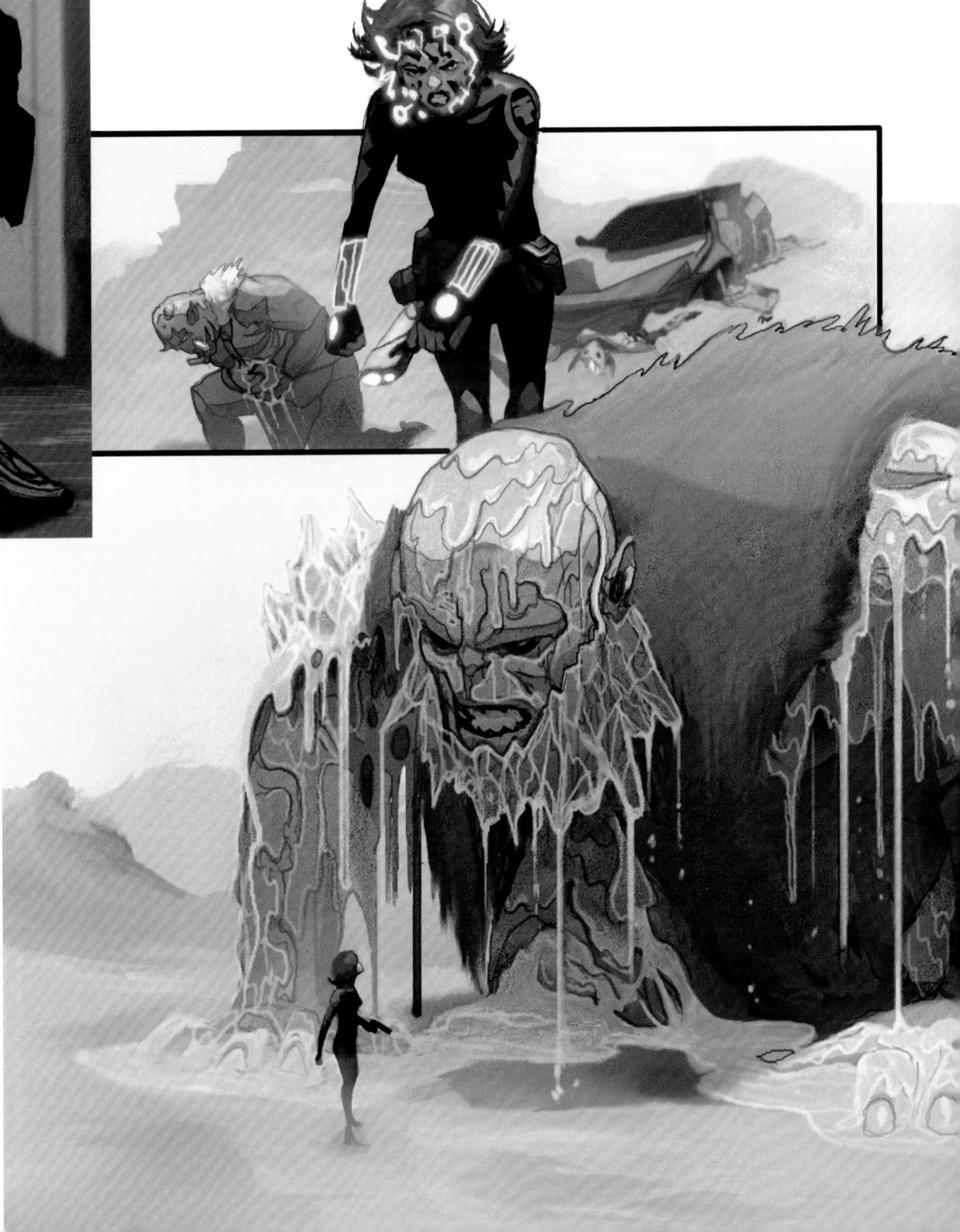

THE MAN OF LETTERS

The one constant of Jason Aaron's saga of Thor run has been its letterer — Virtual Calligraphy's Joe Sabino. Here he shares his thoughts on putting the words into the mouths of the huge cast spread across the Ten Realms!

THE RIBIĆ ERA: "My lettering on Jason's *Thor* run has basically evolved with the art. In the beginning, it was defining captions and styles for young, present and old Thor and new characters — as with any new series. I tried very hard to keep sound effects in the same style as Esad Ribić's painted ones when they needed to be added — I used one specific font for those. I wanted everything to be organic and natural to what was such an intense and epic start. For Esad's run, I'd actually do the sound effects in Adobe Illustrator, then paste them into the art in Photoshop, match colors and textures, and blend and mask them as needed. That's not something we commonly do as letterers, since it can be a bit time-consuming and we're usually racing deadlines since we're toward the end of the production process."

THE DAUTERMAN ERA: "When Russell Dauterman and Matthew Wilson came on, it was an entirely different, but still awe-inspiring, direction for the art. Basically the only things that changed for me, since most of the style template had been established, were the brighter, cleaner captions for Thor's narration — and a new, scratchy font for the sound effects and screams to match those of Russell's art. I think I really started to nail the yells and screams during Russell's run. That's when I'd get little notes back from the editors saying 'Nice, Joe!' or some positive feedback from fans."

THE DEL MUNDO ERA: "For Mike del Mundo's run, the only thing that has changed is that I'm actually lettering sound effects with the paintbrush in Illustrator when needed. That is something I never did until now — I feel like Jason's run has needed that extra little touch and effort because of its size, scope and popularity. I got a kick out of the Fire Demon train in *Thor (2018) #2*. Mike del Mundo suggested we drop in a Black Sheep reference, and I had the beat from the song 'The Choice Is Yours' in my head the entire time I was working on the book."

CHARACTER VOICES: "Gorr was the first character to get his own voice. He was such a unique, dark and formidable character that he needed it. Then there was the Minotaur; he got his own style of rough voice because of his importance and power. I think the Frost Giants were pre-established, but they're always fun because they're blue and have a rough border. I've had everything: magic styles, the Phoenix Force, Fire Demons, Norns, Fin Fang Foom, Mangog, Necro-Galactus... My template is pretty huge because of all the characters that have already

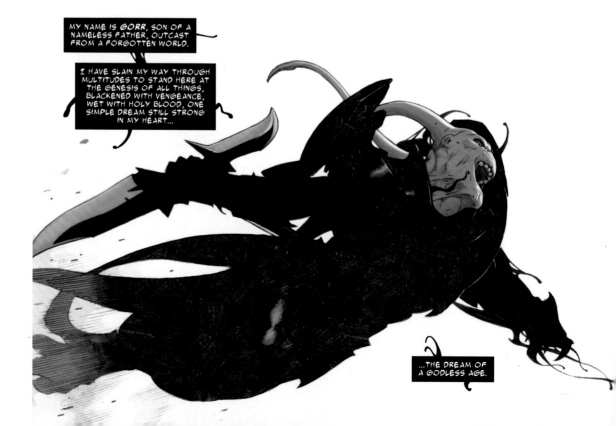

MY NAME IS GORR, SON OF A NAMELESS FATHER, OUTCAST FROM A FORGOTTEN WORLD.
I HAVE SLAIN MY WAY THROUGH MULTITUDES TO STAND HERE AT THE GENESIS OF ALL THINGS, BLACKENED WITH VENGEANCE, WET WITH HOLY BLOOD, ONE SIMPLE DREAM STILL STRONG IN MY HEART...
...THE DREAM OF A GODLESS AGE.

GORR'S INNER THOUGHTS, COMPLETE WITH TENDRILS!

THOR: GOD OF THUNDER #5 INTERIOR ART BY ESAD RIBIĆ AND IVE SVORCINA, WITH LETTERING BY JOE SABINO

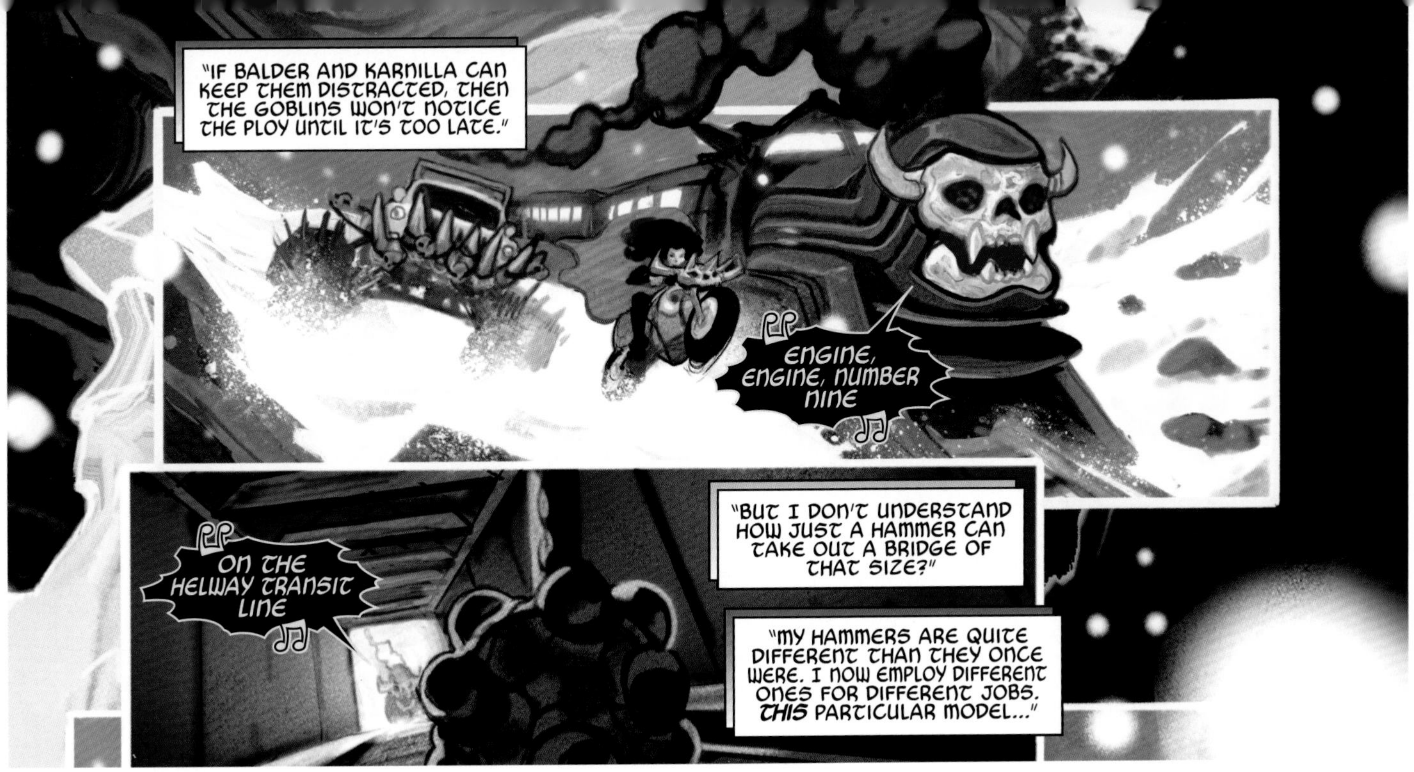
"IF BALDER AND KARNILLA CAN KEEP THEM DISTRACTED, THEN THE GOBLINS WON'T NOTICE THE PLOY UNTIL IT'S TOO LATE."
ENGINE, ENGINE, NUMBER NINE
ON THE HELWAY TRANSIT LINE
"BUT I DON'T UNDERSTAND HOW JUST A HAMMER CAN TAKE OUT A BRIDGE OF THAT SIZE?"
"MY HAMMERS ARE QUITE DIFFERENT THAN THEY ONCE WERE. I NOW EMPLOY DIFFERENT ONES FOR DIFFERENT JOBS. *THIS* PARTICULAR MODEL..."

WHO KNEW FIRE GOBLINS LIKED BLACK SHEEP?

***THOR (2018)* #2** INTERIOR ARTWORK BY MIKE DEL MUNDO, WITH LETTERING BY JOE SABINO

appeared in *Thor*. The biggest struggle is trying to remember if a random character that popped up from the realms has an Asgardian font or human font — I have to go back and check that a lot. My favorite narration captions are for Gorr in *Thor: God of Thunder #5*. I drew out and played with the tendrils from his Necrosword. I felt it was a subtle little touch that blended in nicely with Esad's art."

JANE THOR: "One of the funnier anecdotes while working on Thor is that they wouldn't tell me who the new Goddess of Thunder was, which became a dilemma in *Thor (2014) #2*. I had to ask if Thor's thought balloons should be in the human font or Asgardian. After what I assume was some internal discussion among the editors, they told me human. I was not told anything else until I started working on page 14 of #8. They kept that one a tight secret. The death of Jane Foster had me misty-eyed when I did that issue."

THE THOR TEAM: "The whole creative team was snuck into the bar in *Mighty Thor #702*, page 4. I'm the dude in the brown hoody in the back. I have to give my editors a lot of credit — they've consistently recruited top talent for Jason's *Thor*. My jaw *dropped* when the art rolled in for that first issue when Thor walks into the room with the gods on meat hooks. Even the guest artists. How insane was Ron Garney's Malekith splash?! That still haunts me years later! Bring on War of the Realms — I can't wait to see what Jason has planned for us!"

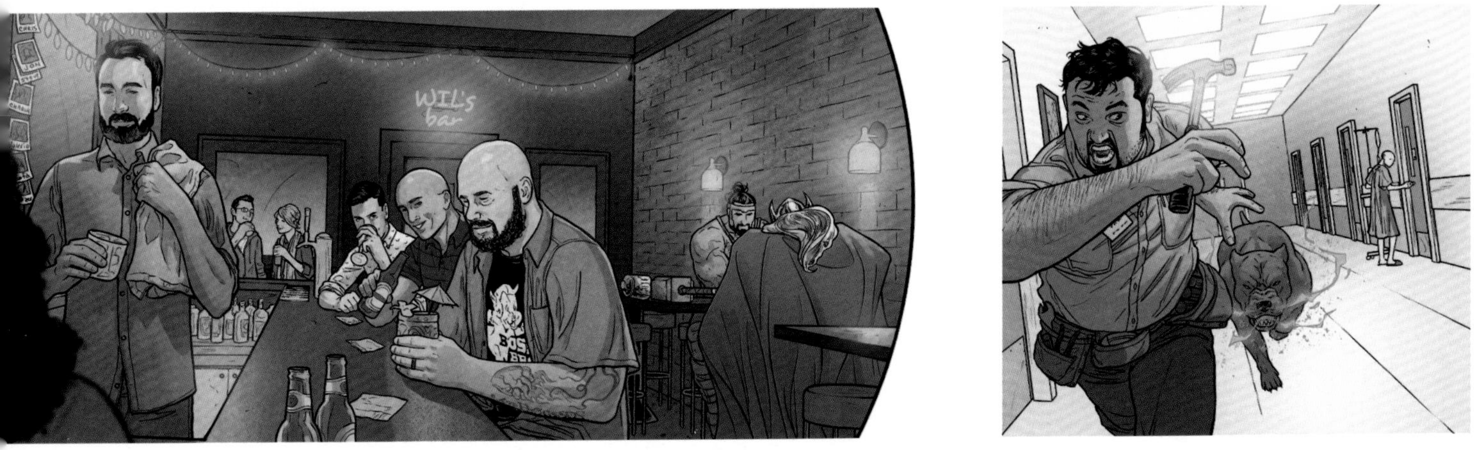
WIL's bar

"TEAM THOR" HANGS OUT AT WIL'S BAR IN ***MIGHTY THOR (2015)* #702**. FROM RIGHT TO LEFT ARE JASON AARON, MATTHEW WILSON, RUSSELL DAUTERMAN, ASSOCIATE EDITOR SARAH BRUNSTAD AND JOE SABINO, WITH EDITOR WIL MOSS TENDING BAR (AND MORE FAMILIAR NAMES NOTED ON PHOTOS BEHIND HIM). AND ESAD RIBIĆ GOT IN ON THE CAMEO ACTION IN ***MIGHTY THOR (2015)* #704**!

***MIGHTY THOR (2015)* #702** AND **#704** INTERIOR ART BY RUSSELL DAUTERMAN AND MATTHEW WILSON

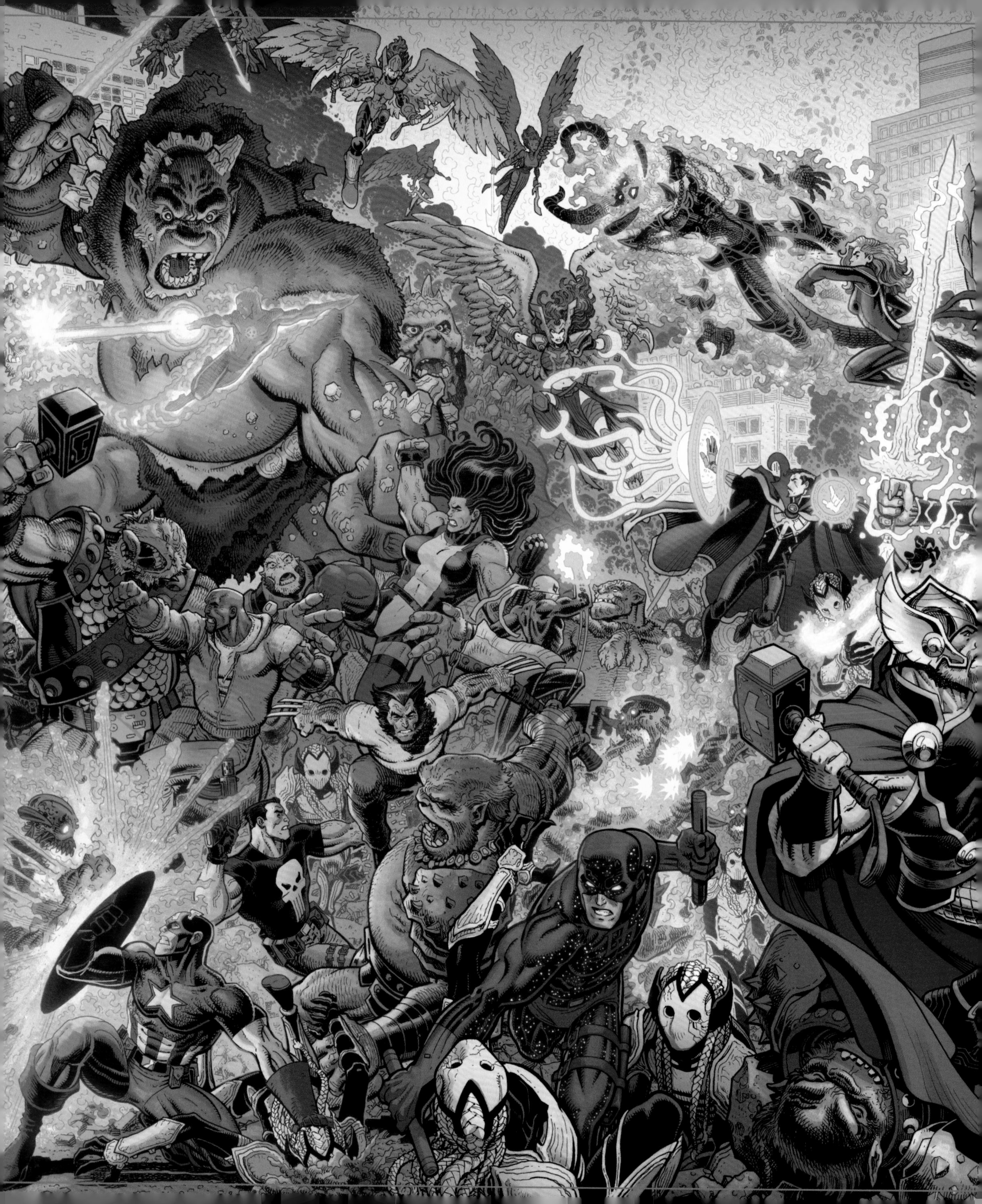

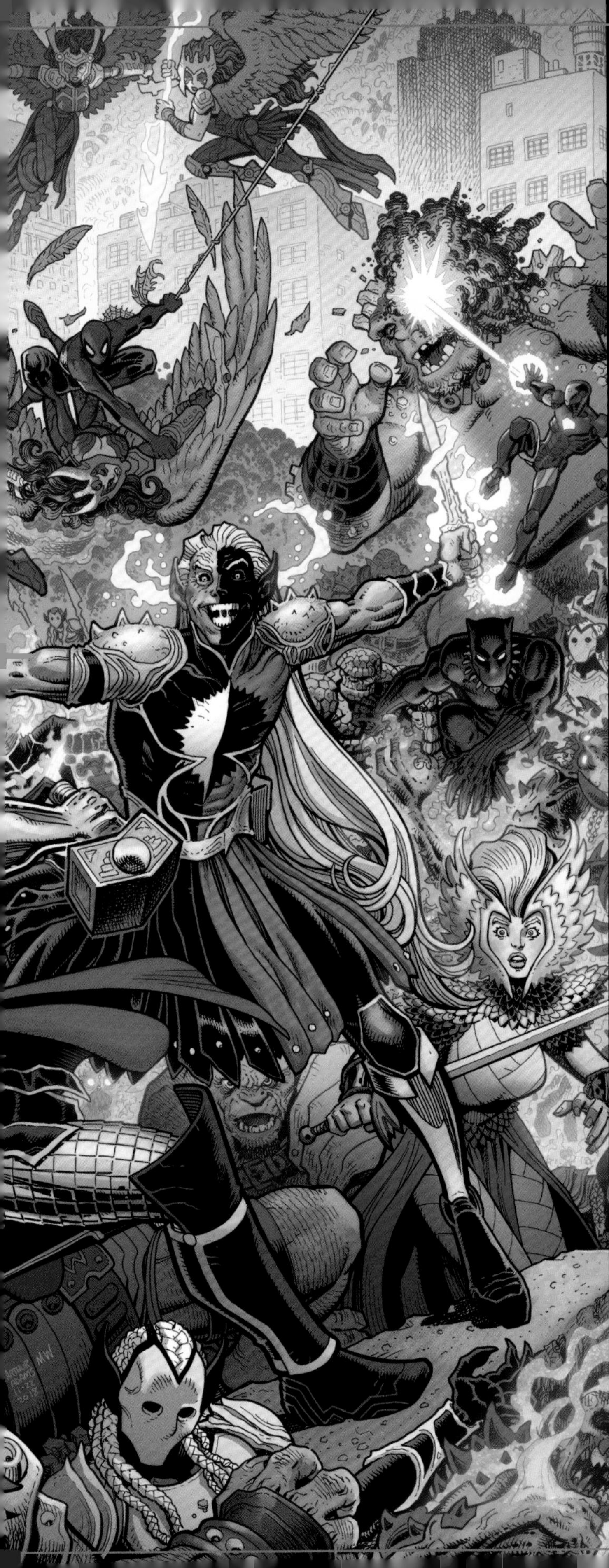

chapter nine:

THE WAR OF THE REALMS

"I am Malekith the War Messiah, who shall deliver the Ten Realms unto the salvation of blessed eternal bloodshed. Who shall lift the Dark Elves of Svartalfheim to reign supreme over all branches of the mighty World Tree."
— Malekith

And so, to war. Nine Realms have fallen — whether to Malekith, in line with him or into chaos — and now the Dark Elf is coming for Midgard!

"For six years now, we've been building toward this," Jason Aaron says. "We've seen Malekith's war spread from one realm to another, and those realms have had to join his cause or be trampled underneath his army. We are finally at the point where Midgard is the last to be affected, so it's time for an invasion by the biggest, scariest monsters from the other realms. It's where everything I've been doing comes to a head — with Thor, with Odin, with Jane — with all the characters that have been a big part of my run. And the Avengers are a big part of this. It made perfect sense to make this a bigger story than just a Thor story. Along the way, I knew we were heading toward this War of the Realms story, but I didn't know what it would be. Would it be an arc of *Thor*? An arc of *Thor* and *Avengers*? The idea of making it a bigger thing — making it an event — is a lot of fun. It's very much a big Thor story, but clearly the stakes are bigger than just Thor, so it becomes a very big Marvel Universe story. It's gonna be one of those big, old-fashioned Marvel event stories where everyone gets involved, so you get Spider-Man and Daredevil with huge roles over the course of the story."

War of the Realms renews Aaron's creative partnership with Russell Dauterman — though in truth, they've been working together on the series since right after *Mighty Thor* ended. "We knew pretty quickly we wanted Russell to draw all of *War of the Realms*," Aaron explains. "Pretty much as soon as he was done with *Mighty Thor*, he started on *War of the Realms*. That meant I had to write #1 about a year in advance. Normally that would have been really scary, but it really wasn't a big deal because I'd been laying those tracks for so long that I knew what that story was and everything I needed to do to get to that point."

"*War of the Realms* is way bigger than anything I've drawn before," Dauterman adds. "This is the storyline Jason's been building to since he started his *Thor* run, and it brings in so many Marvel characters. That's been super cool, seeing how characters like Daredevil or Punisher mesh with the sword-and-sorcery, fantasy stuff of the Ten Realms. We're getting to continue the story we were

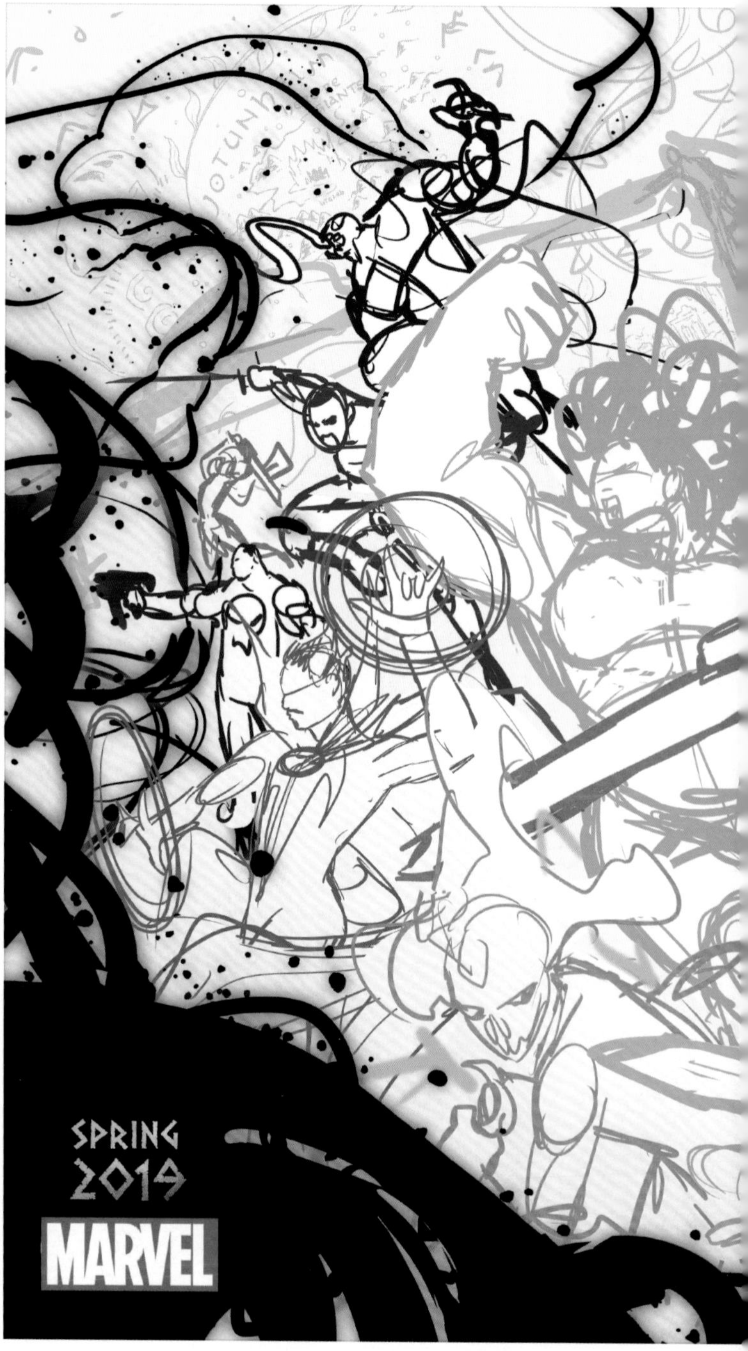
SPRING
2019
MARVEL

telling in *Mighty Thor* — but with a much bigger scope and with ramifications for the larger Marvel Universe. I'm very excited to draw something on such an epic scale."

Aaron shares that excitement every time new pages from Dauterman arrive. "I love seeing Russell draw Spider-Man," Aaron says. "I love seeing him draw Wolverine, the Fantastic Four and all these characters we've not seen him draw before. The story gives him a lot of opportunity to go crazy with

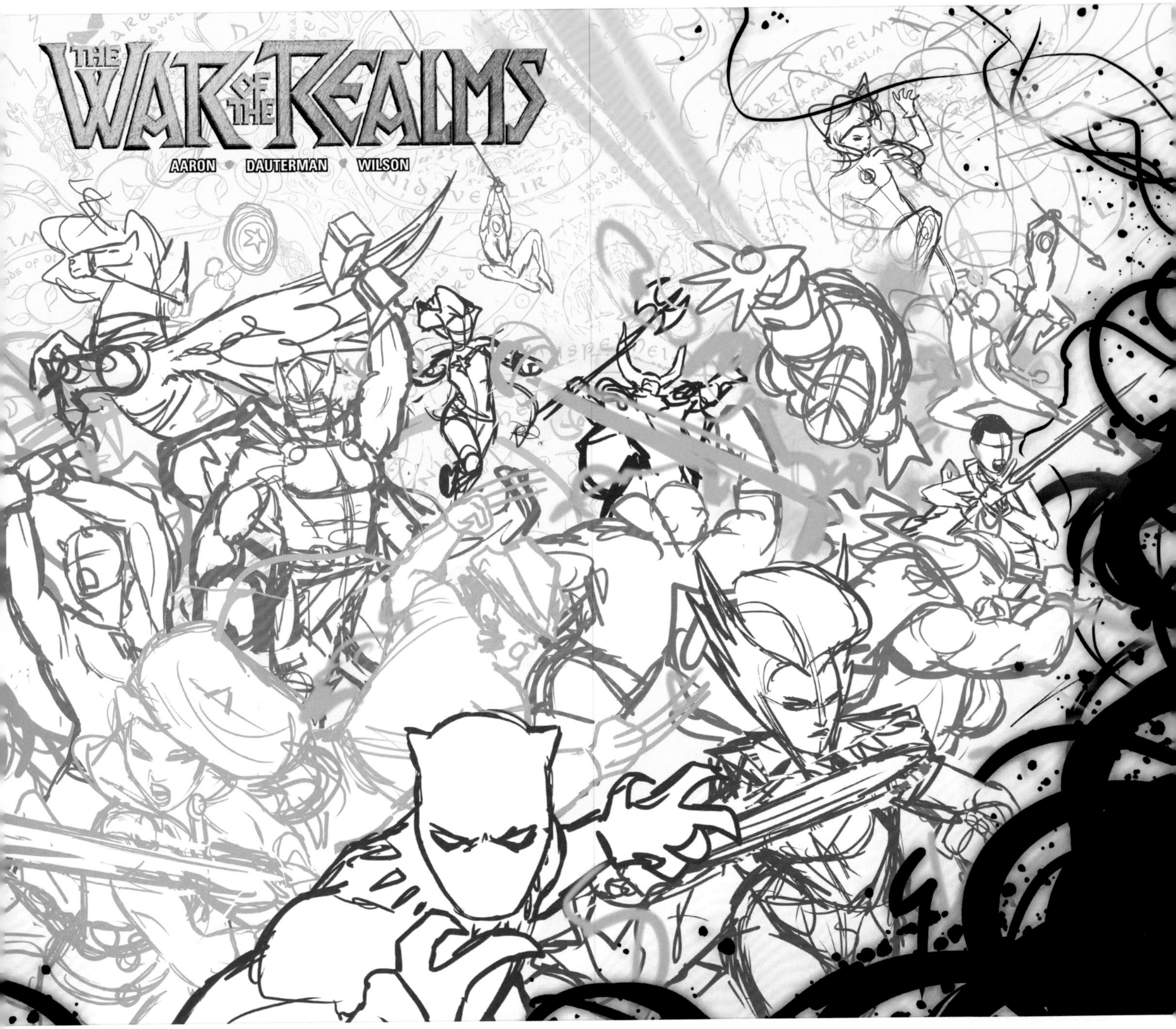
THE WAR OF THE REALMS
AARON
DAUTERMAN
WILSON

stuff — there are so many characters, so many fights and so many realms. I'm blown away with what he's doing. It's really neat to see him wanting to play with all the toys in the Marvel toy box — but also still telling this really big and important Thor story."

Over the following pages, enjoy a taste of what Aaron and Dauterman have planned as they plunge the Marvel Universe into war!

ABOVE: RUSSELL DAUTERMAN TAKES ON A GIANT CAST IN THIS ***WAR OF THE REALMS* #1** GATEFOLD VARIANT COVER – LAYOUT ABOVE, FINAL VERSION WITH COLORS BY MATTHEW WILSON ON THE FOLLOWING PAGES.

PREVIOUS PAGES: *WAR OF THE REALMS* #1 COVER BY ARTHUR ADAMS AND MATTHEW WILSON

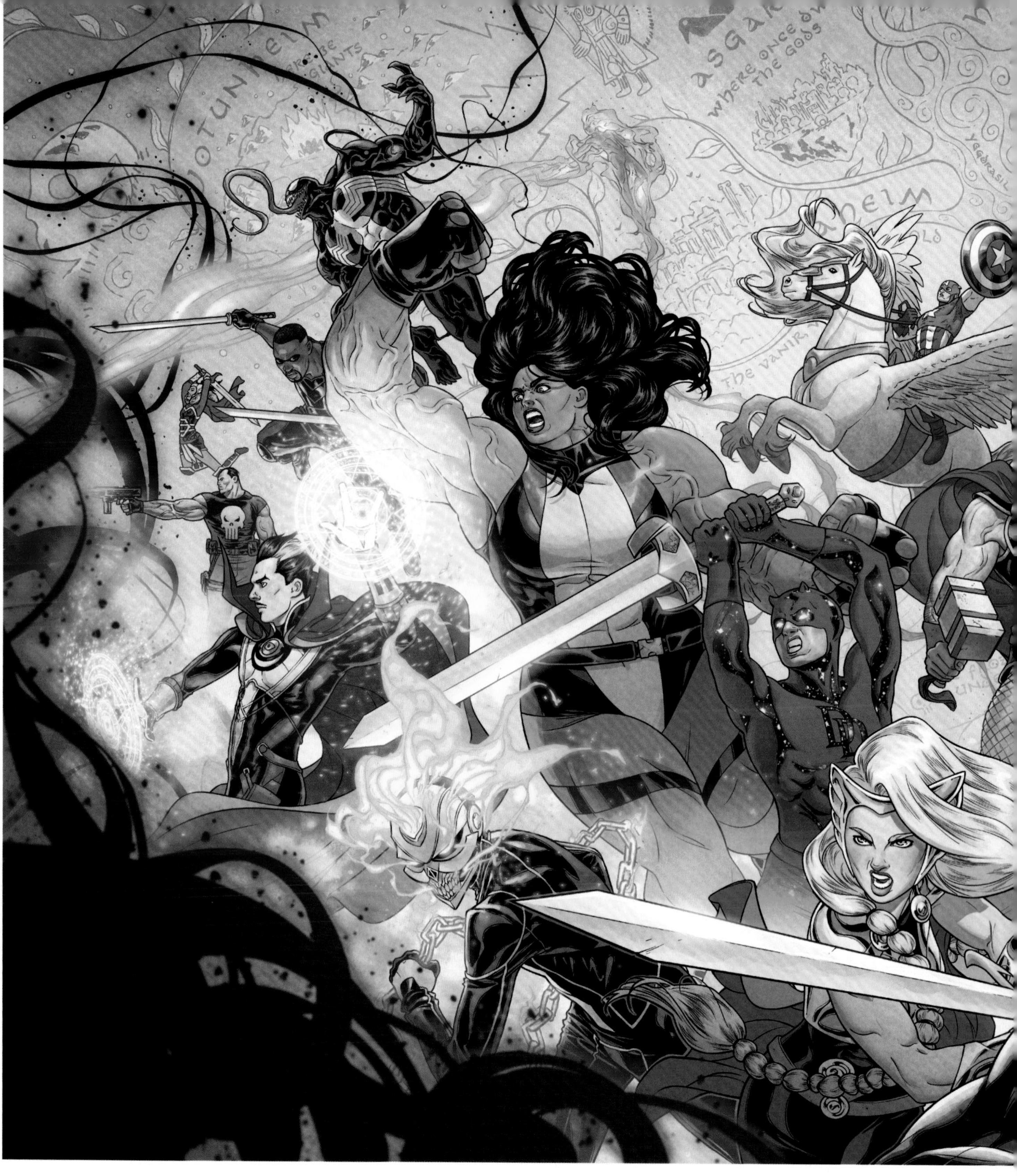
THE VANIR

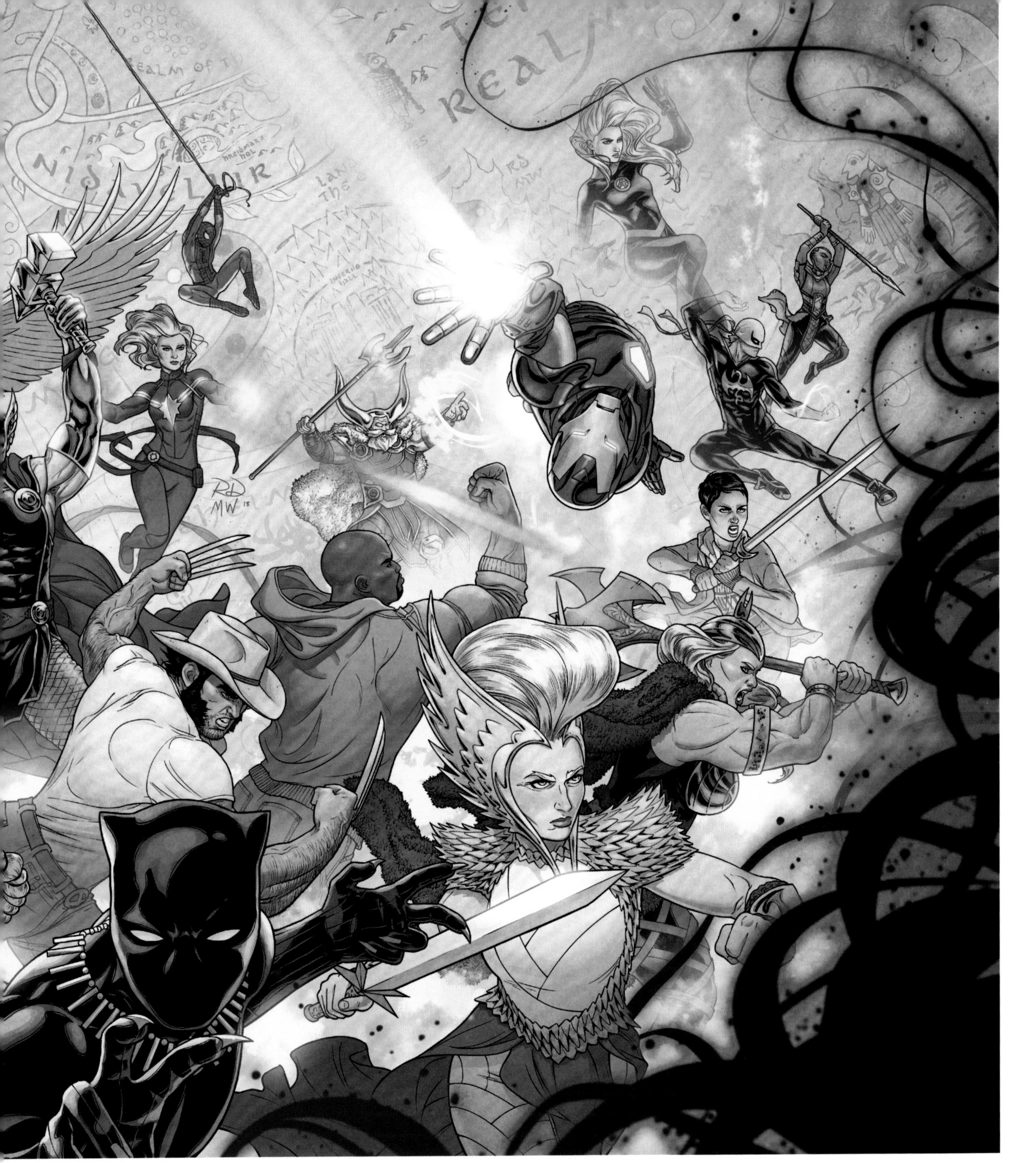

"I was thrilled that Matt and I got to do a wraparound gatefold cover for *War of the Realms #1*. I tried to fit as many characters as I could and give them each a moment. Before *War of the Realms*, I'd never drawn a lot of these big Marvel heroes, so this series — and this cover in particular — are super exciting. So far, my favorite new characters to draw are Black Panther, Captain Marvel and Wolverine."

– RUSSELL DAUTERMAN

"It is cool to see Art drawing this kind of stuff again."
— JASON AARON

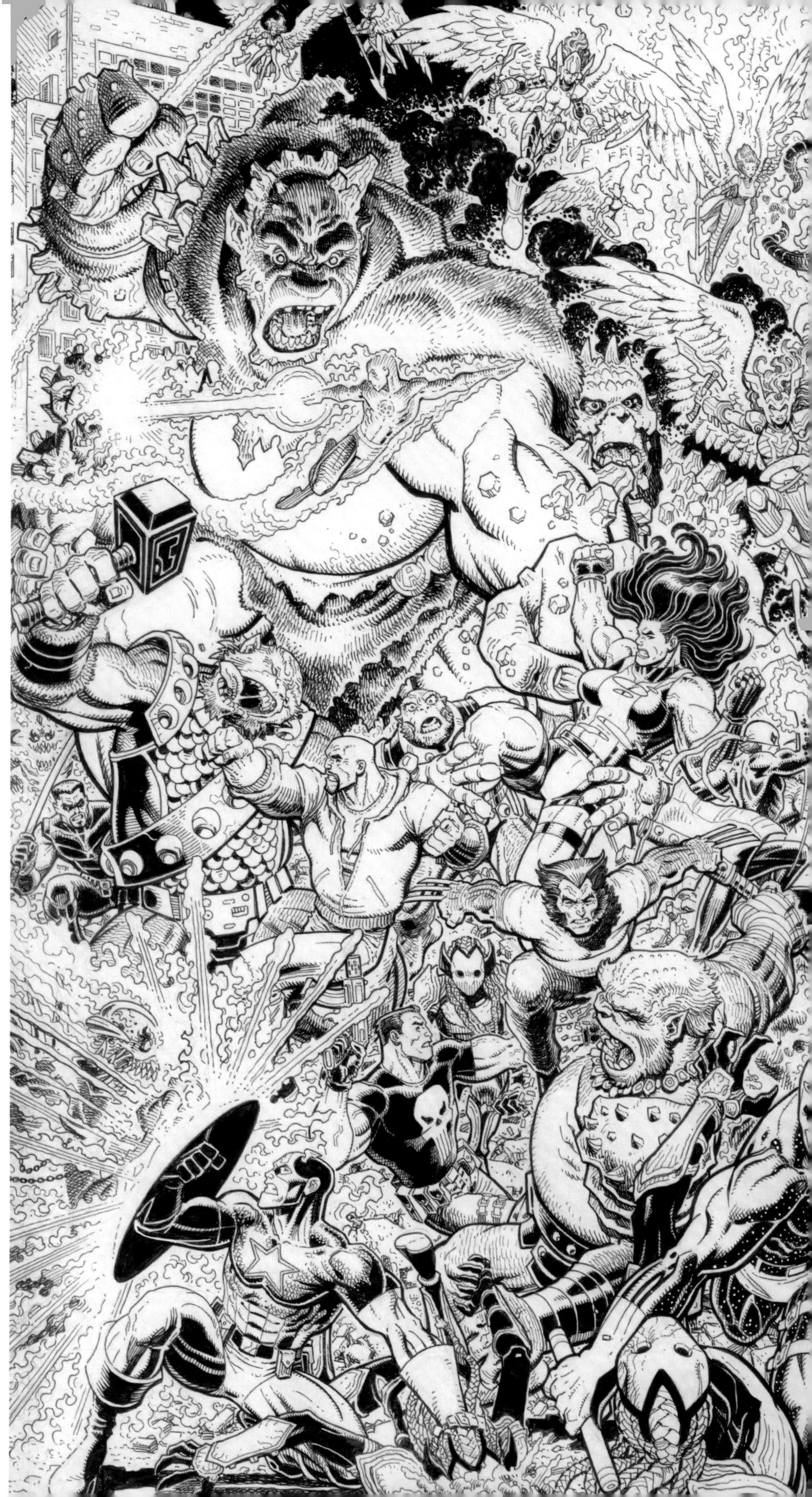

***WAR OF THE REALMS* #1** COVER
INKS BY ARTHUR ADAMS

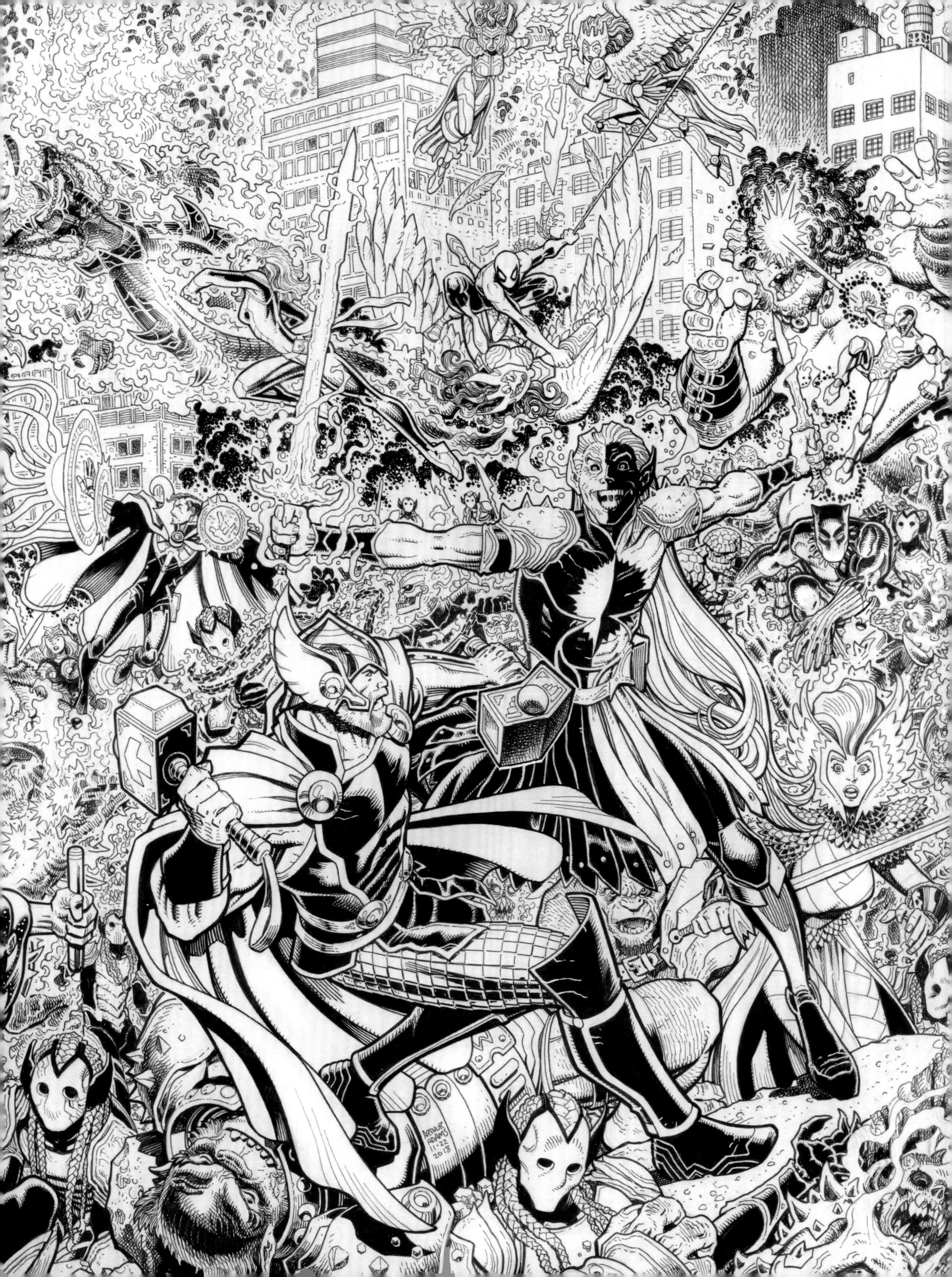
ARTHUR ADAMS
11-22
2018

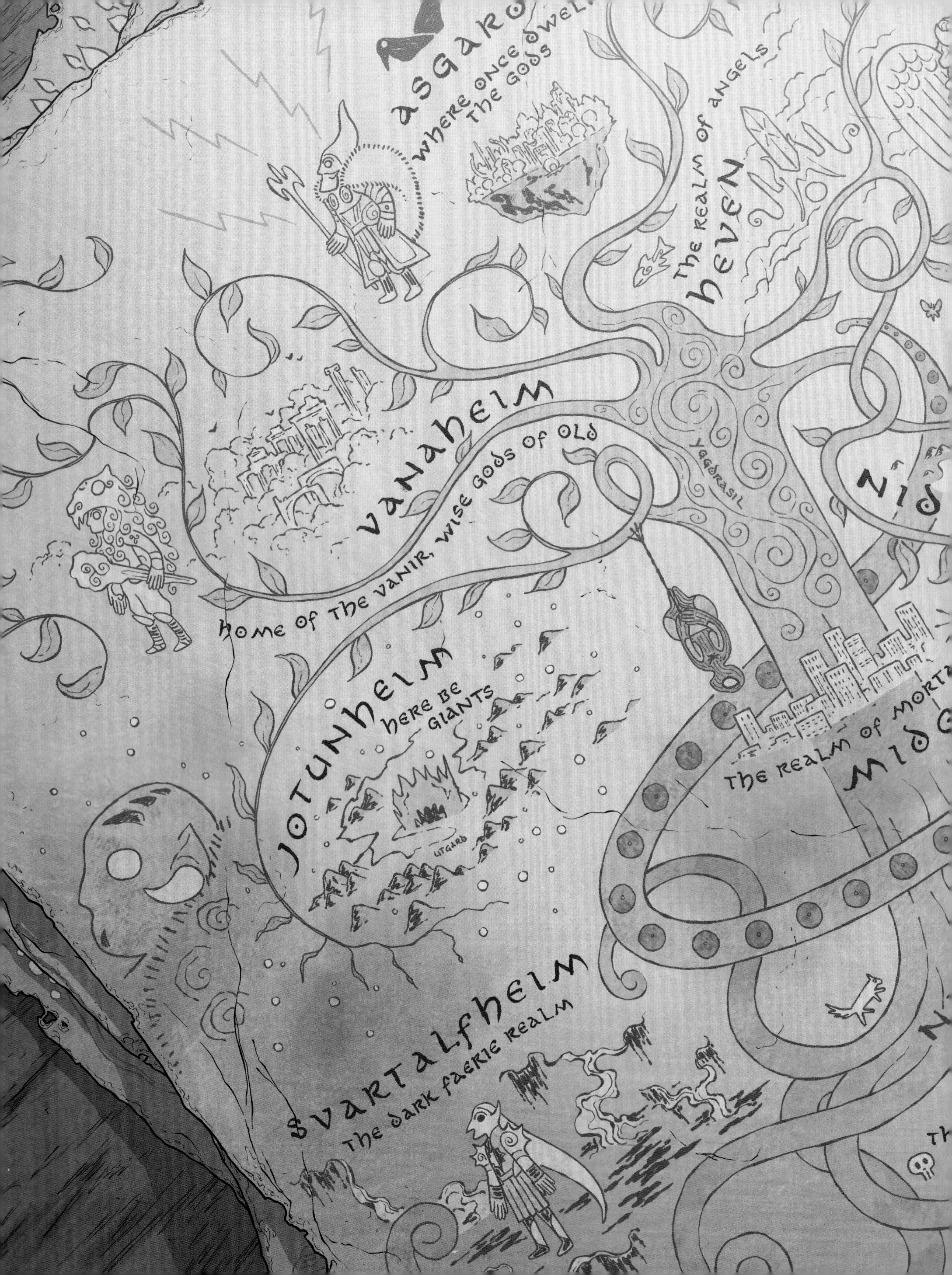
ASGAR
WHERE ONCE DWEL
THE GODS
THE REALM OF ANGELS
HEVEN
VANAHEIM
HOME OF THE VANIR, WISE GODS OF OLD
YGGDRASIL
NID
JOTUNHEIM
HERE BE GIANTS
UTGARD
THE REALM OF MORT
MIDG
SVARTALFHEIM
THE DARK FAERIE REALM

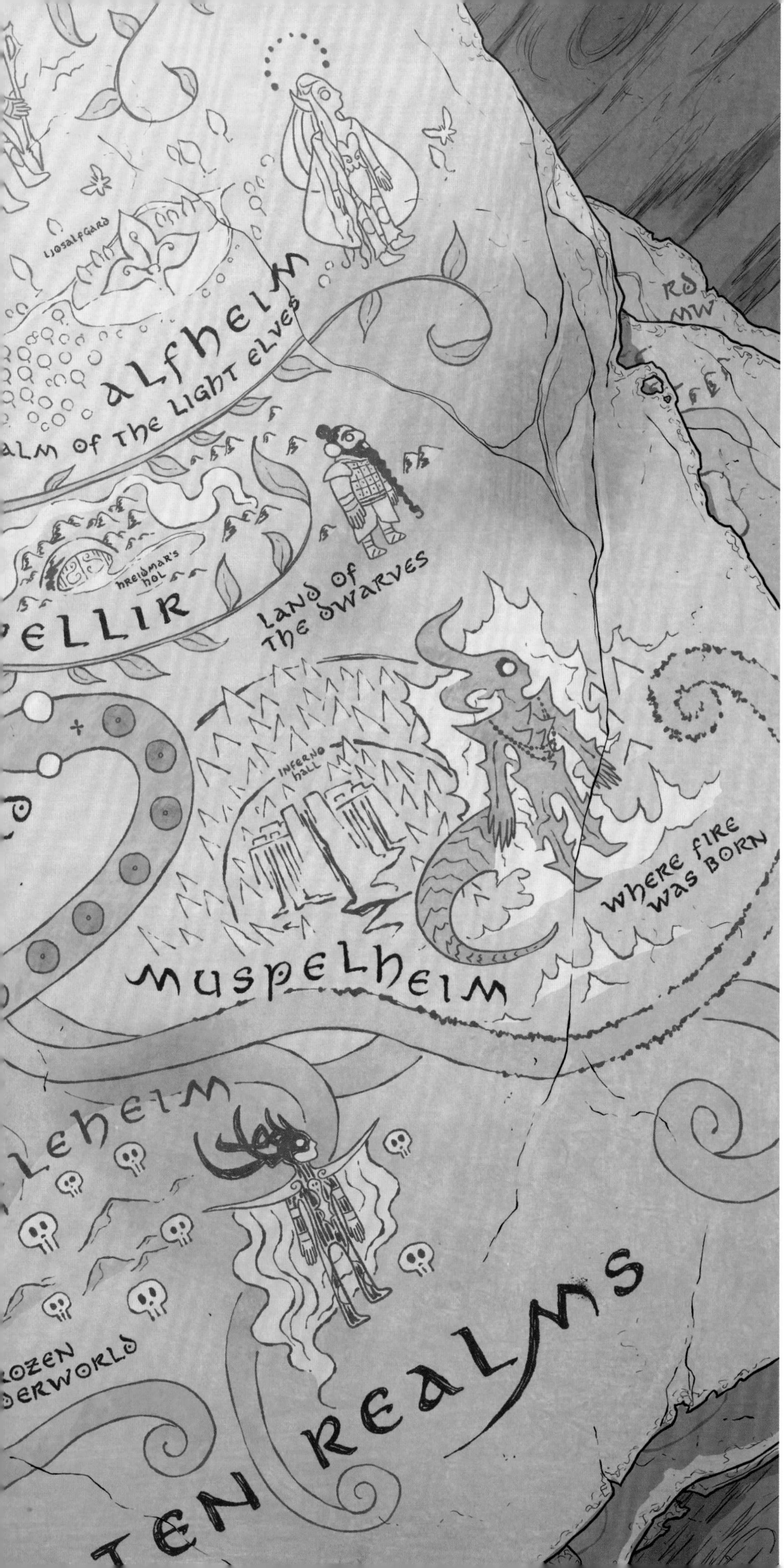
LJOSALFGARD
ALFHEIM
ALM OF THE LIGHT ELVES
HREIDMAR'S HOL
ELLIR
LAND OF THE DWARVES
INFERNO HALL
WHERE FIRE WAS BORN
MUSPELHEIM
LEHEIM
ROZEN
DERWORLD
TEN REALMS

"Like any big fantasy story, *War of the Realms #1* opens with a map."
— JASON AARON

WAR OF THE REALMS #1 INTERIOR ART BY RUSSELL DAUTERMAN AND MATTHEW WILSON

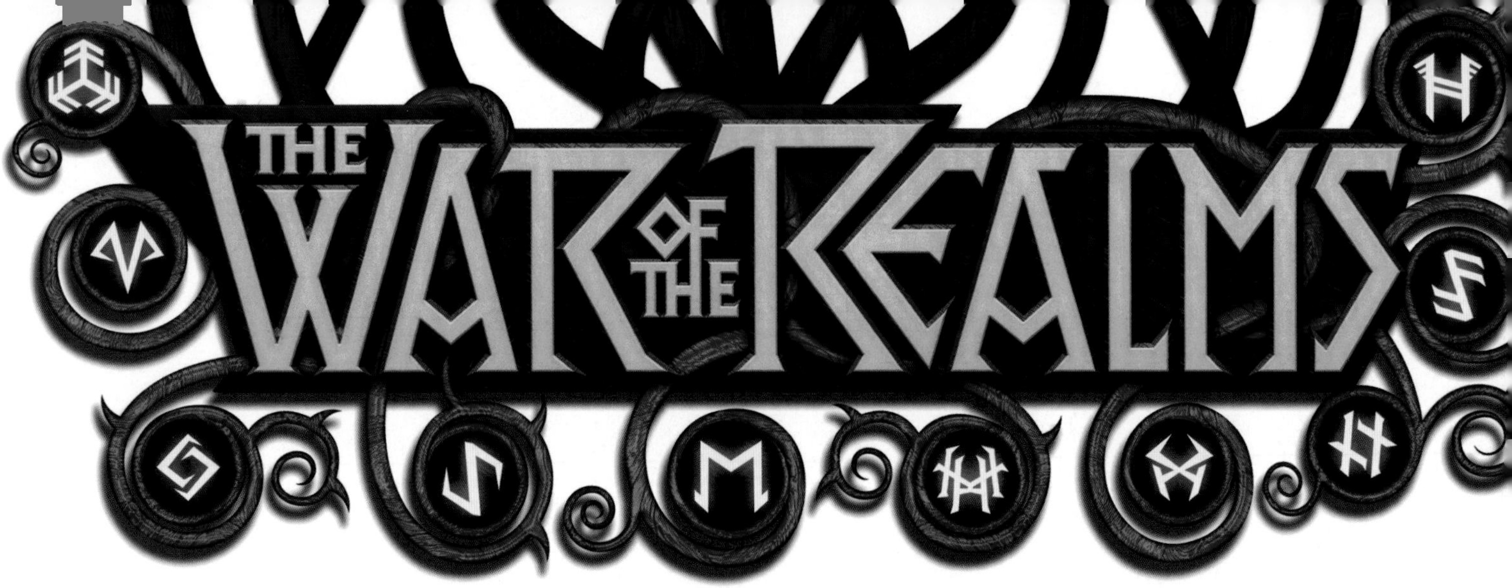
THE WAR OF THE REALMS

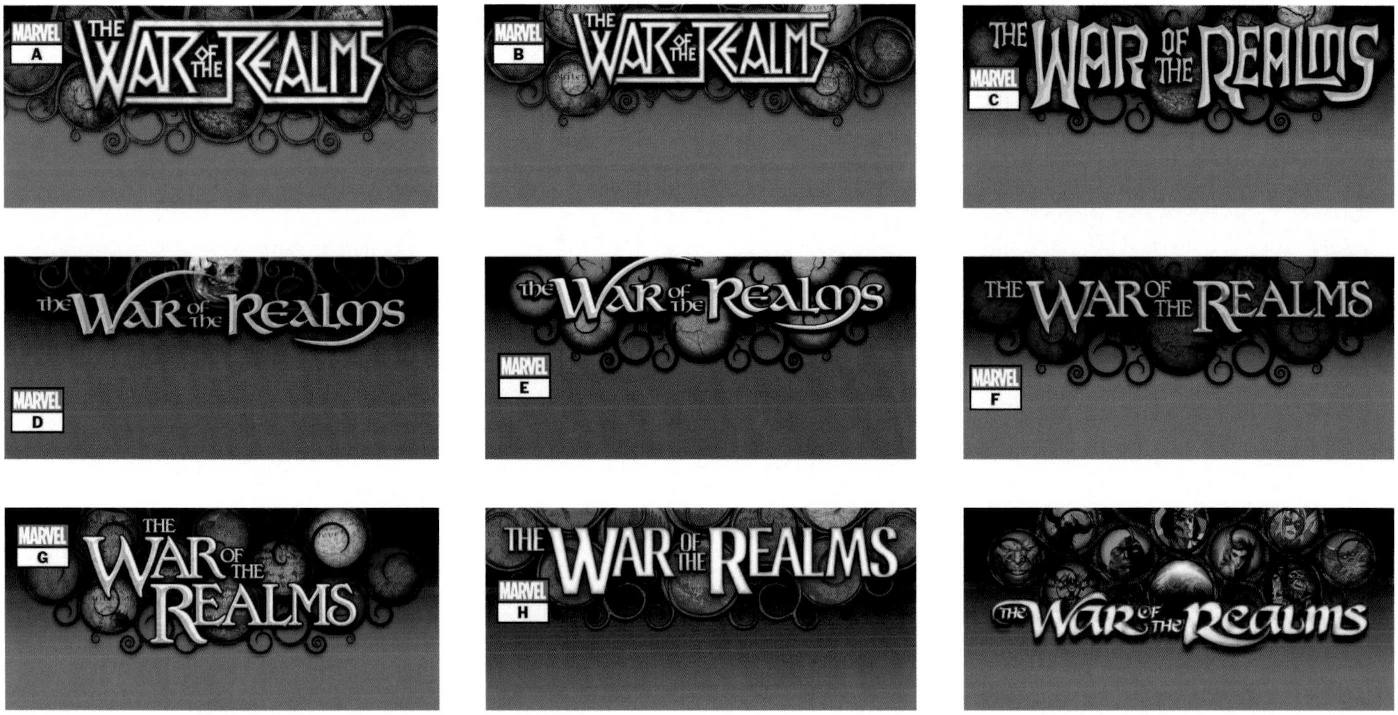
MARVEL A
THE WAR OF THE REALMS
MARVEL B
THE WAR OF THE REALMS
THE WAR OF THE REALMS
MARVEL C
the WAR of the REALMS
MARVEL D
the WAR of the REALMS
MARVEL E
THE WAR OF THE REALMS
MARVEL F
MARVEL G
THE WAR OF THE REALMS
THE WAR OF THE REALMS
MARVEL H
THE WAR OF THE REALMS

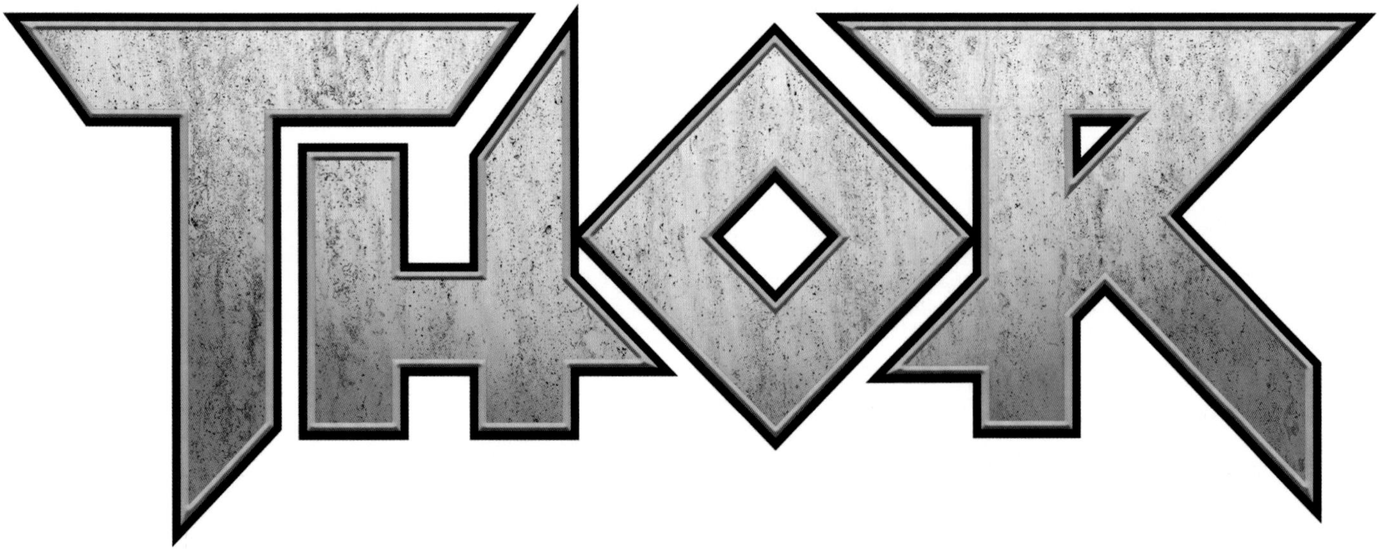
THOR

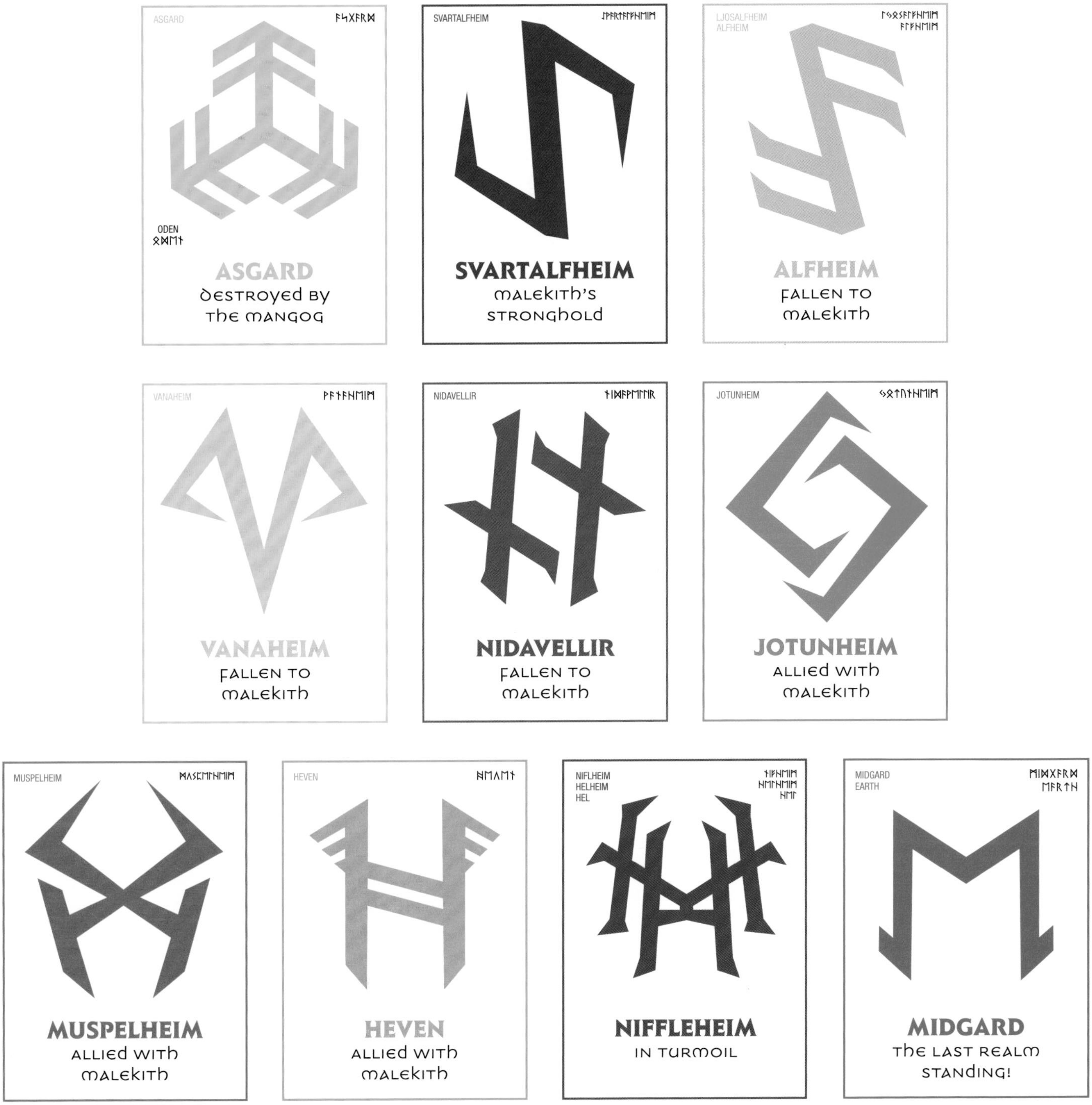
ASGARD
ODEN
ASGARD
DESTROYED BY THE MANGOG
SVARTALFHEIM
SVARTALFHEIM
MALEKITH'S STRONGHOLD
LJOSALFHEIM
ALFHEIM
ALFHEIM
FALLEN TO MALEKITH
VANAHEIM
VANAHEIM
FALLEN TO MALEKITH
NIDAVELLIR
NIDAVELLIR
FALLEN TO MALEKITH
JOTUNHEIM
JOTUNHEIM
ALLIED WITH MALEKITH
MUSPELHEIM
MUSPELHEIM
ALLIED WITH MALEKITH
HEVEN
HEVEN
ALLIED WITH MALEKITH
NIFLHEIM
HELHEIM
HEL
NIFFLEHEIM
IN TURMOIL
MIDGARD
EARTH
MIDGARD
THE LAST REALM STANDING!

"Going in, we knew we wanted the *War of the Realms* logo to take a cue from the current *Thor* logo (by Marvel designer Jay Bowen) and also incorporate, in some way, visuals that would represent the Ten Realms. And we wanted a logo that would have some real presence. Patrick McGrath from Marvel's Creative Services department took that tall order and delivered something we're all really happy with. I especially love how the World Tree frames the logo and the symbols of the realms. And speaking of the symbols, those are based on the Norse rune for the first letter of each Realm. The symbols don't match the runes exactly — it's more like the runes were jumping-off points. They also incorporate elements from Jay Bowen's *Thor* design. So it all feels of one piece, which was important to us. My favorite is the Niffleheim symbol, which resembles Hela's crown."

— EDITOR WIL MOSS

"Loki's allegiances lie with Loki. He is always going to be playing his own game. We've seen him do a lot of noble things and a lot of horrible things over the course of the last few years, and even the horrible things — in Loki's mind — he's doing for the right reasons. Outside the pages of *Thor*, we've seen him involved in one of the big stories in *Avengers*. We also saw him be a big part of *Infinity Wars*. He was even the Sorcerer Supreme for a while in *Doctor Strange*. Within all those stories, we saw references to the War of the Realms. I think everything Loki has done to try to gain more power for himself or put more players on the board on Earth has all been with an eye toward this war that he knows is coming. He knows Earth isn't ready — and in his own warped Loki way, he's doing his part to get it ready."

— JASON AARON

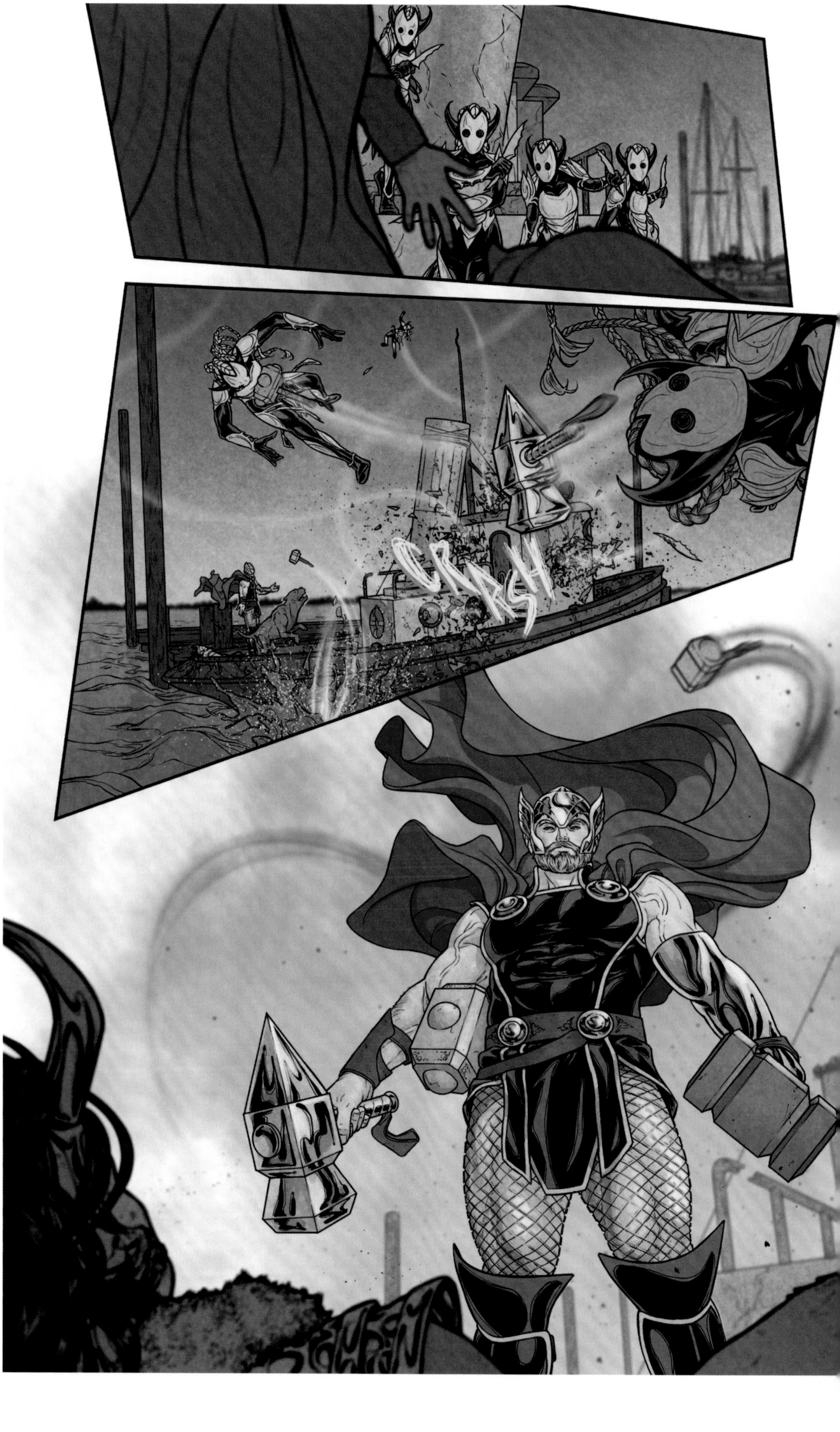
CRASH

RIGHT AND OPPOSITE:
***WAR OF THE REALMS* #2** INTERIOR ART BY RUSSELL DAUTERMAN AND MATTHEW WILSON

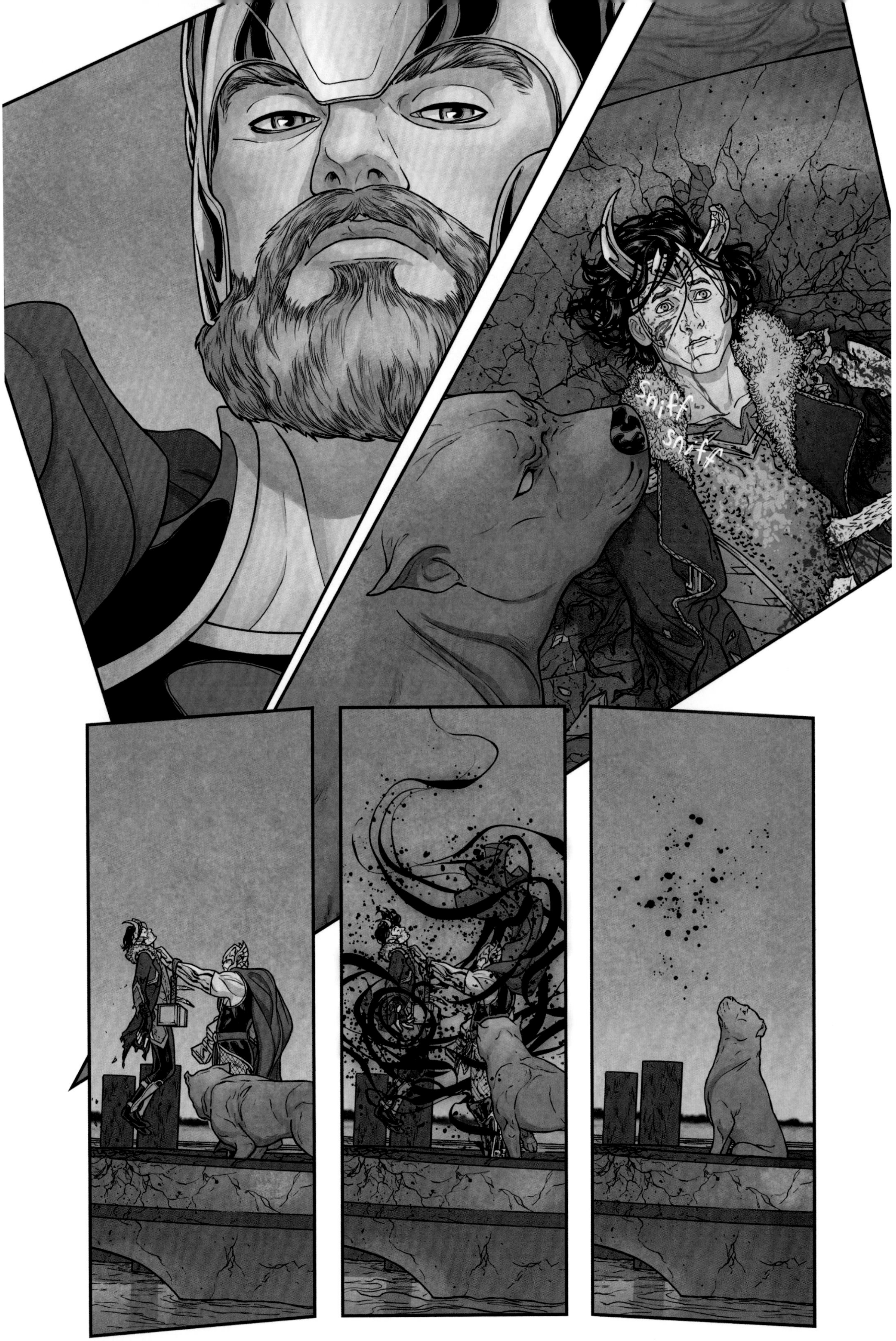
sniff
sniff

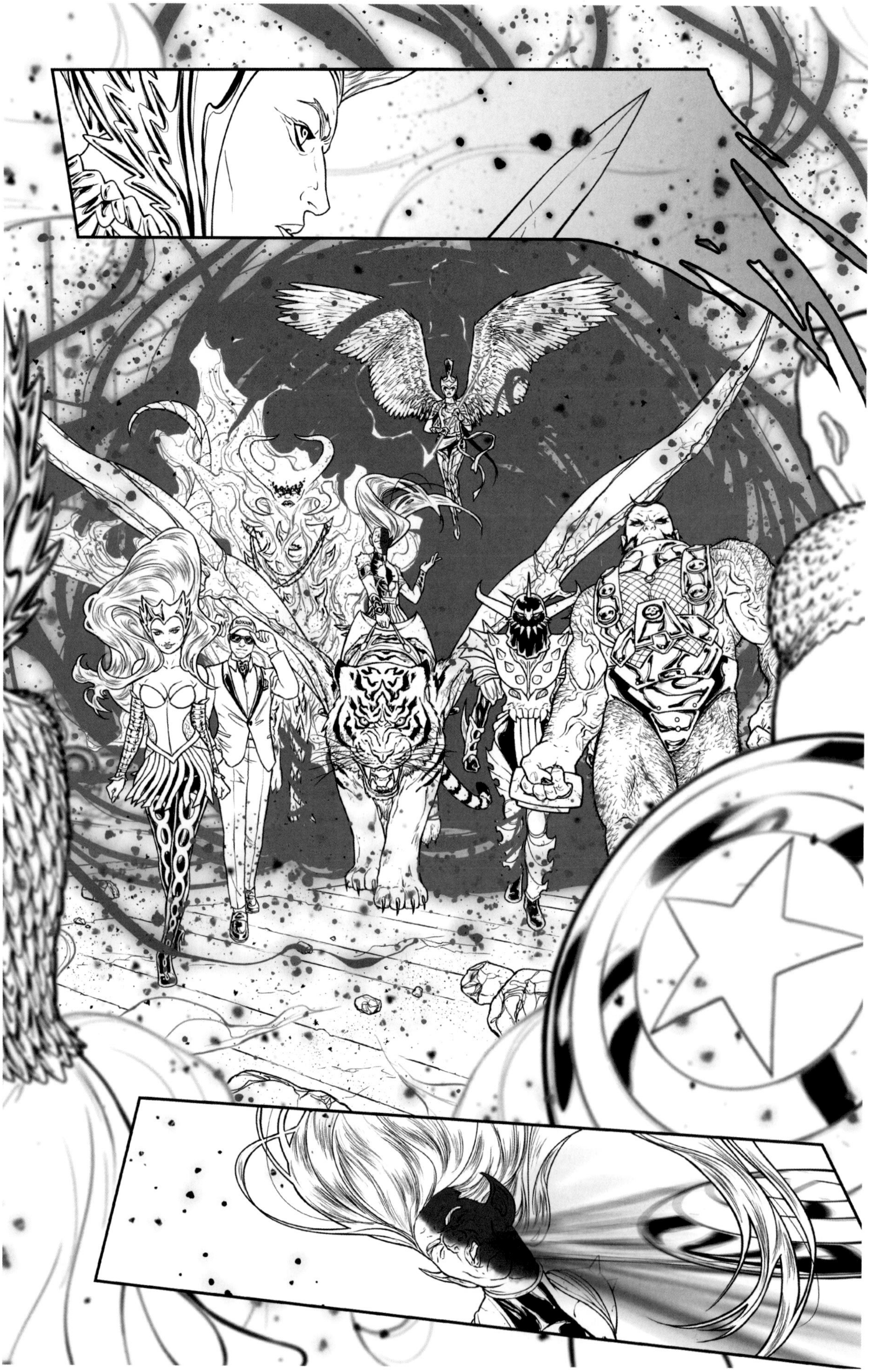

MALEKITH ARRIVES WITH HIS HEAVY HITTERS: THE ENCHANTRESS, DARIO AGGER, SINDR THE QUEEN OF HEVEN, KURSE AND ULIK. MIDGARD DOESN'T STAND A CHANCE!

WAR OF THE REALMS ***#1*** INTERIOR ART BY RUSSELL DAUTERMAN, WITH COLORS (OPPOSITE) BY MATTHEW WILSON

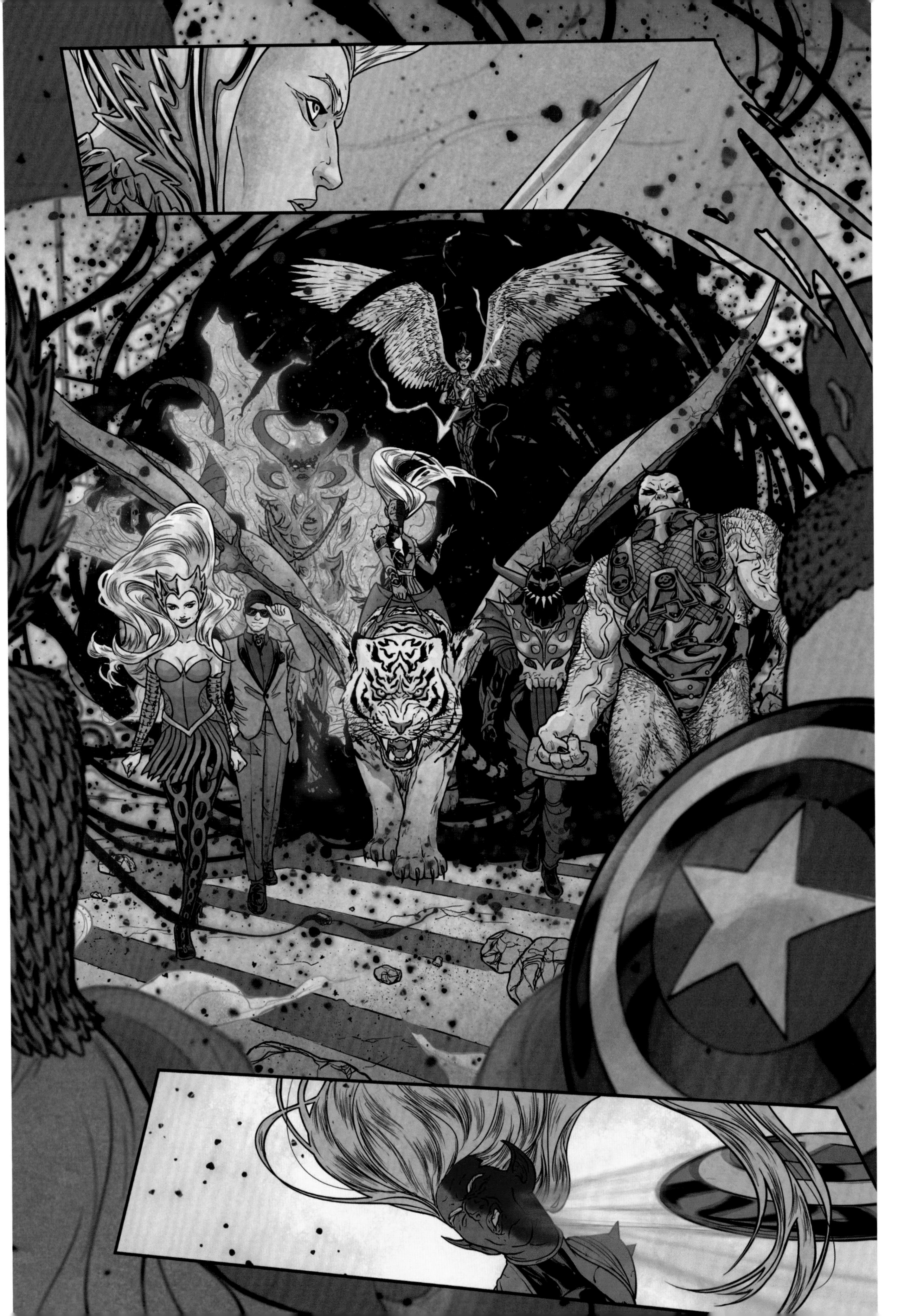

SPIDER-MAN SWINGS INTO ACTION AS EARTH'S HEROES ENTER THE FRAY — INCLUDING JASON AARON FAVORITES DOCTOR STRANGE, WOLVERINE AND THE PUNISHER.

RIGHT: *WAR OF THE REALMS* #1 INTERIOR ART BY RUSSELL DAUTERMAN AND MATTHEW WILSON

OPPOSITE: *WAR OF THE REALMS* #2 COVER BY ARTHUR ADAMS AND MATTHEW WILSON

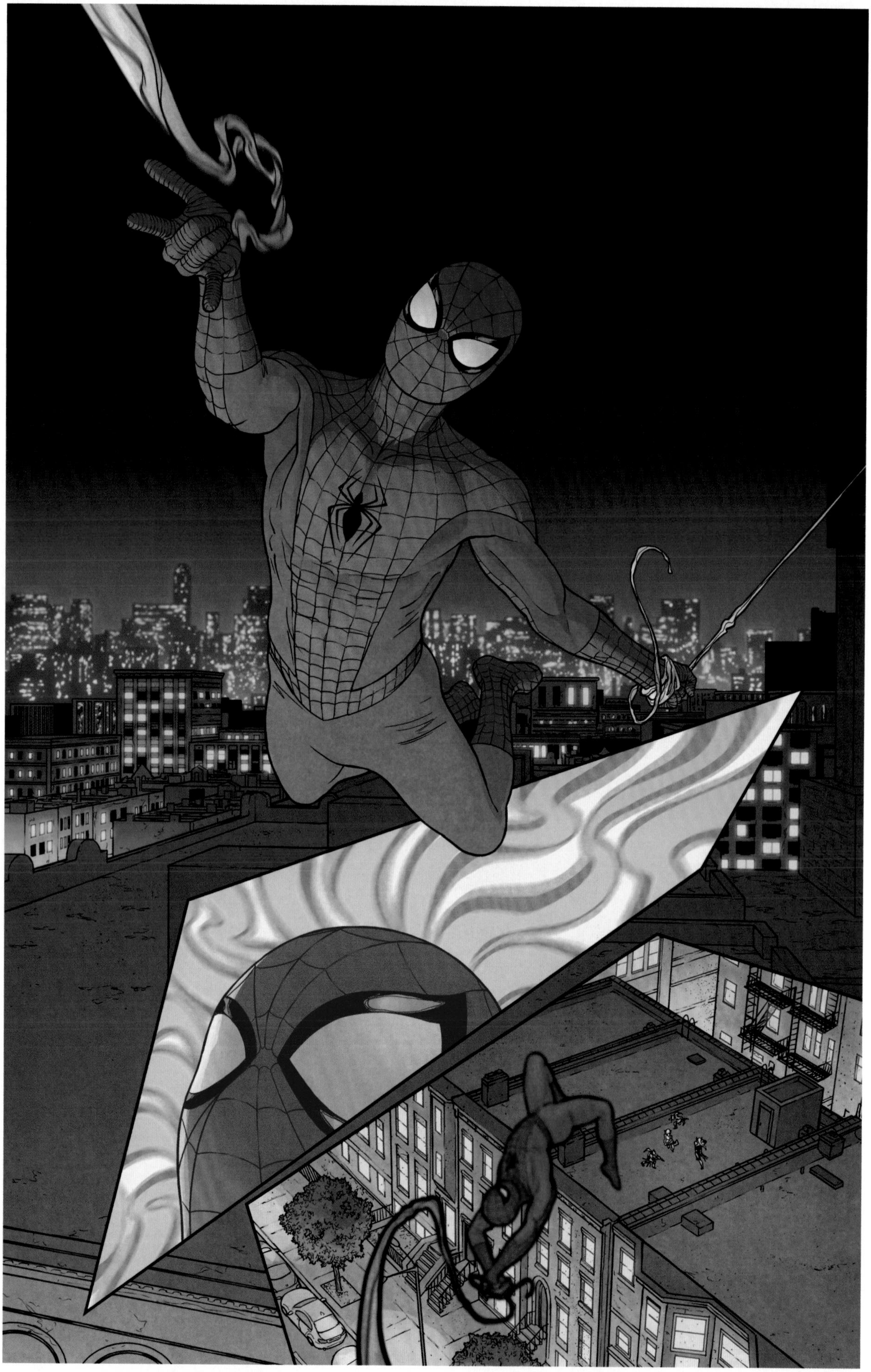

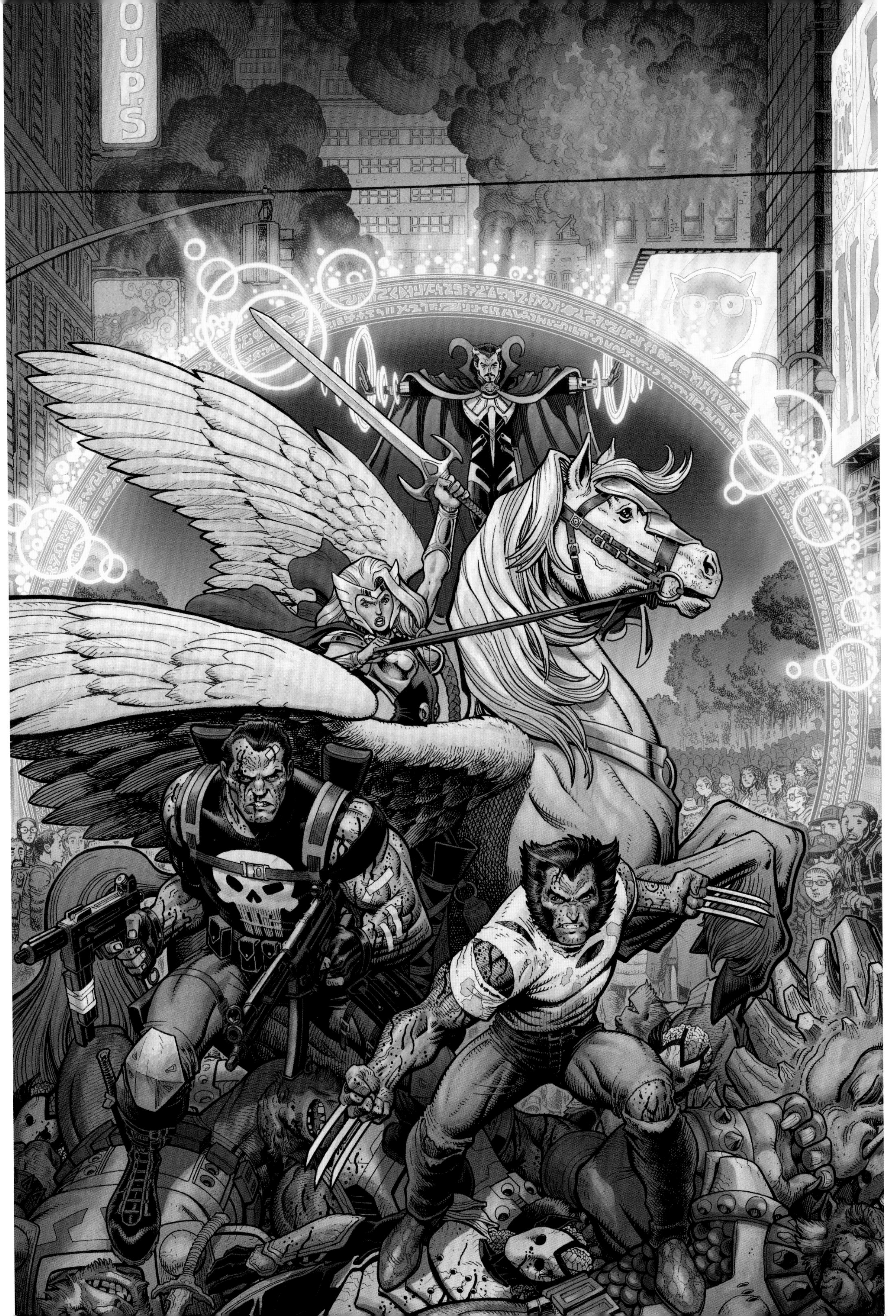

"I'm always looking for ways to make the structure of the page emulate whatever's happening in the story, whether that's with page layout and panel shapes or with drawn-in sound effects. I really like being experimental with that stuff. I started by drawing some sound effects on top of the art or intermixed. Lately, I've been using the sound effects more as graphic elements. So they might be a panel's background, or I might draw the shape of the panel as the sound effect and put the action inside it."

— RUSSELL DAUTERMAN

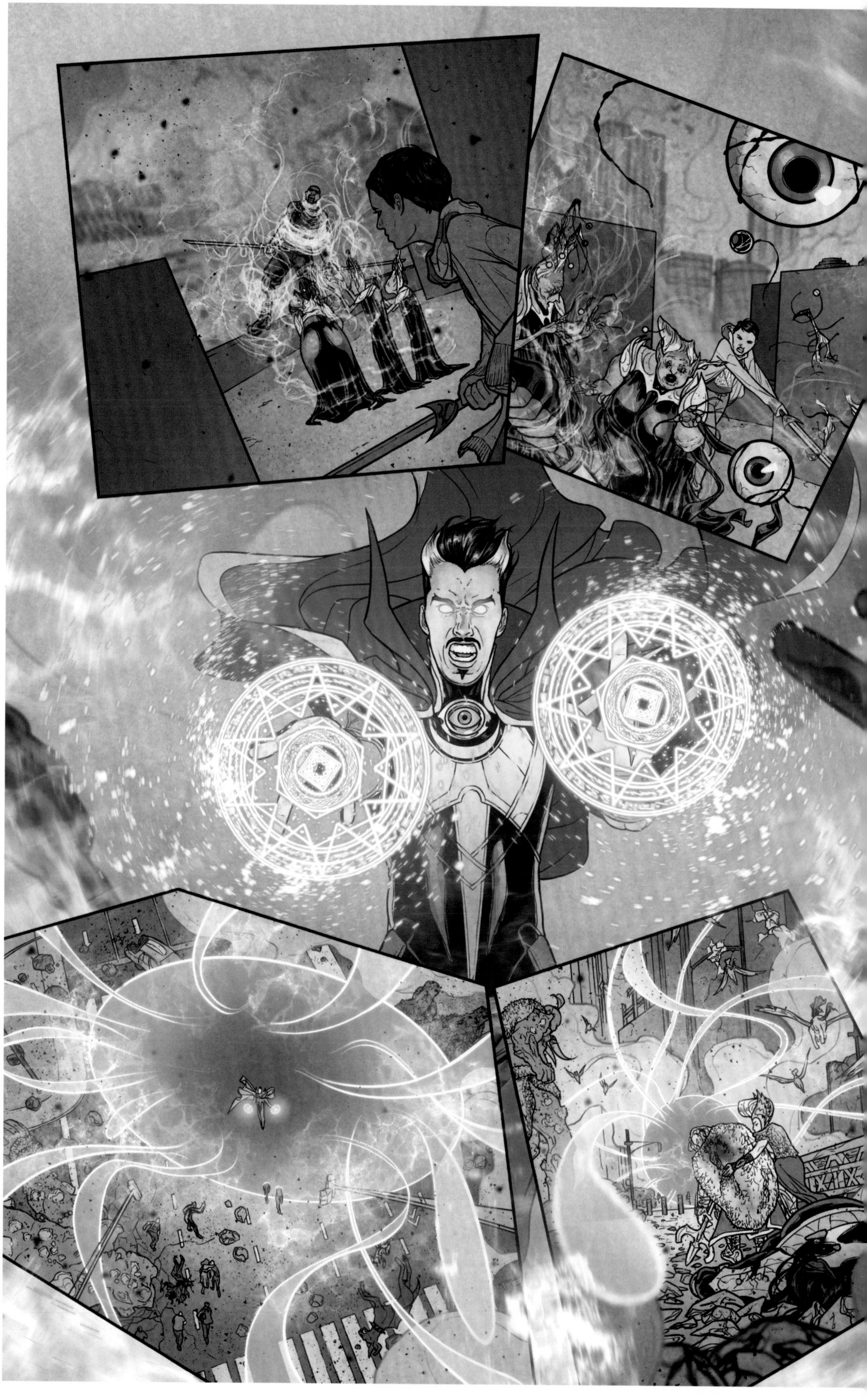

DOCTOR STRANGE AND THE AVENGERS ARE DRAWN INTO THE BATTLE.

RIGHT: ***WAR OF THE REALMS #2*** INTERIOR ART BY RUSSELL DAUTERMAN AND MATTHEW WILSON

OPPOSITE: ***WAR OF THE REALMS #1*** INTERIOR ART BY RUSSELL DAUTERMAN AND MATTHEW WILSON

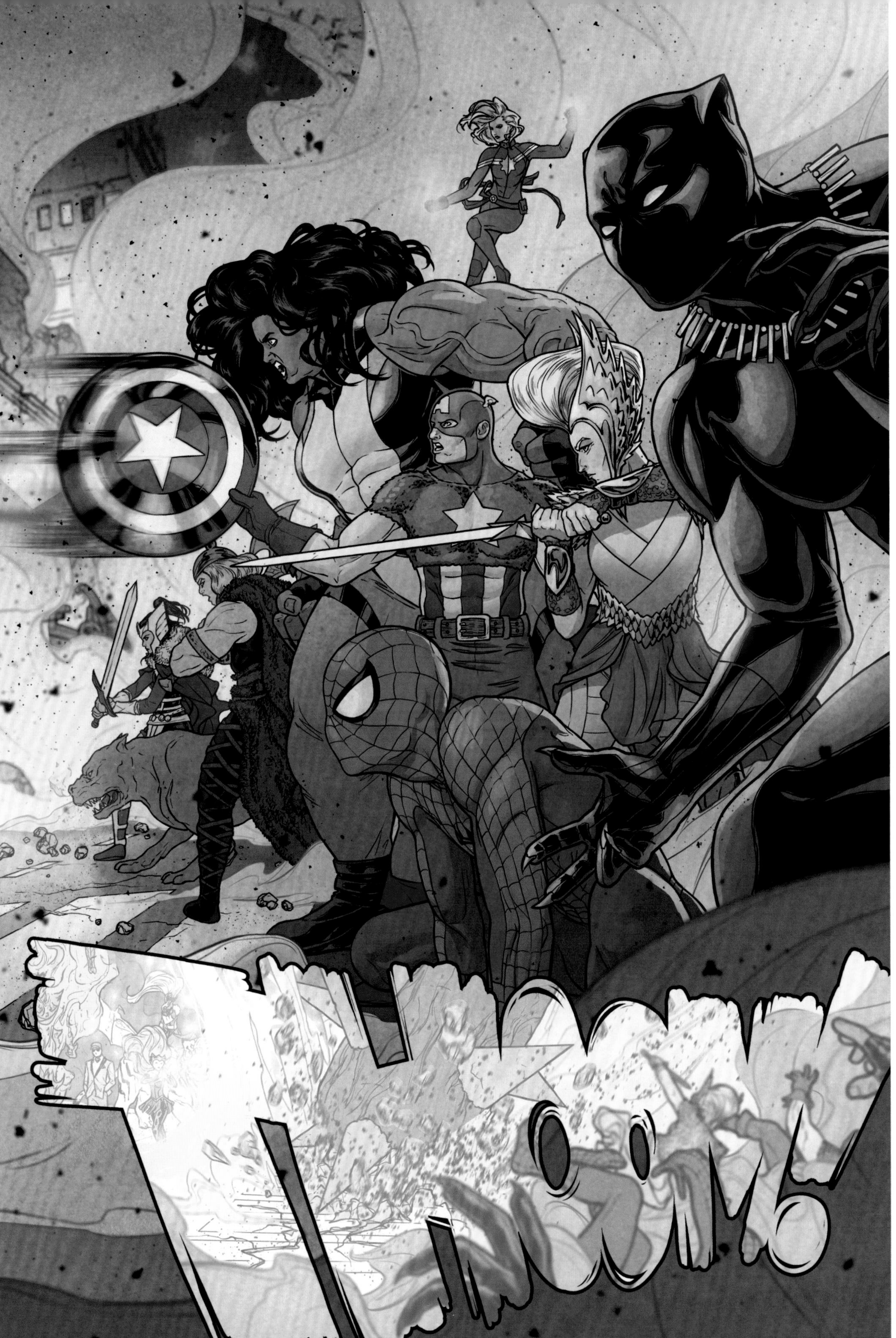
THOOM!

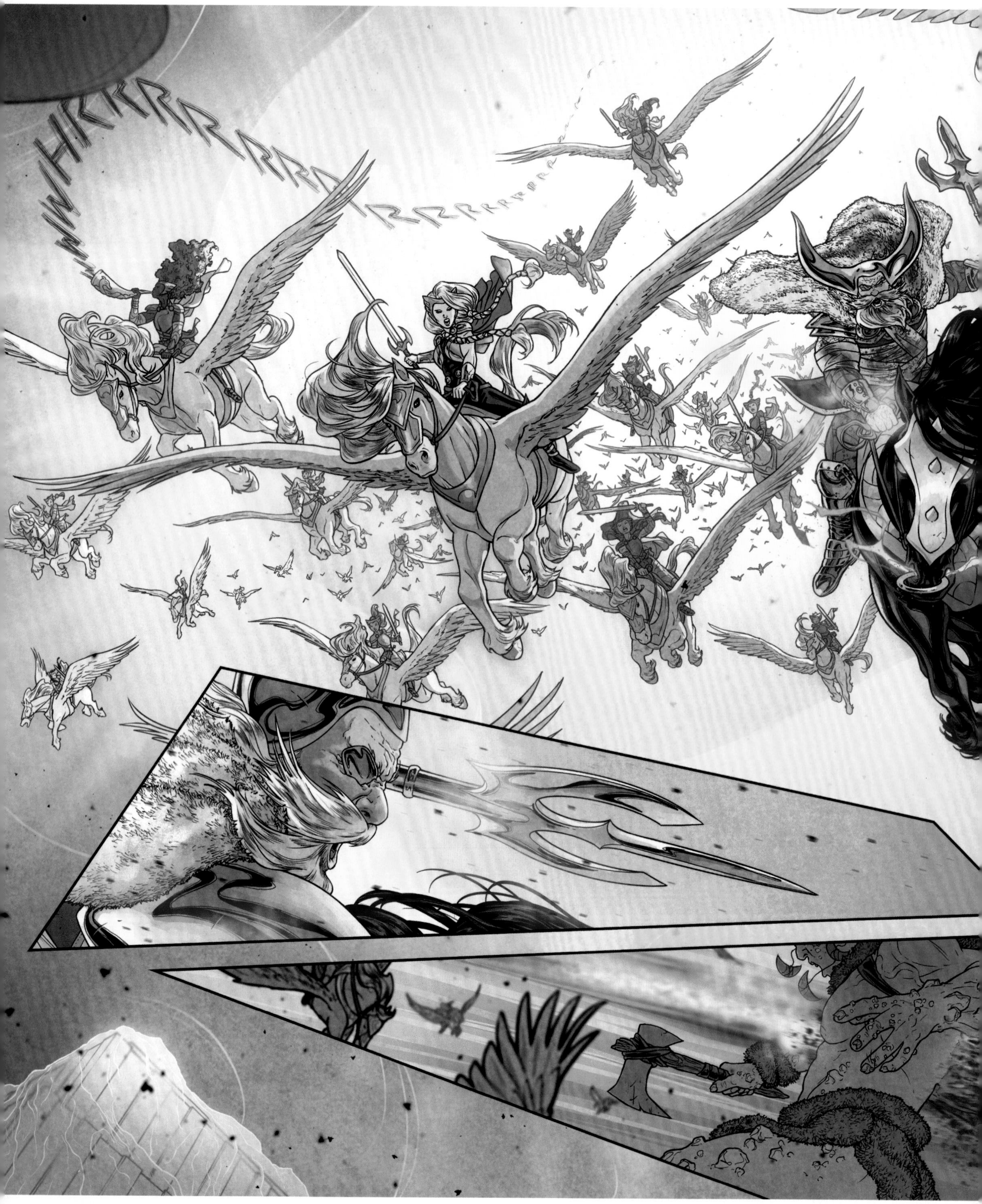
HKRRRRRRRRRRRR

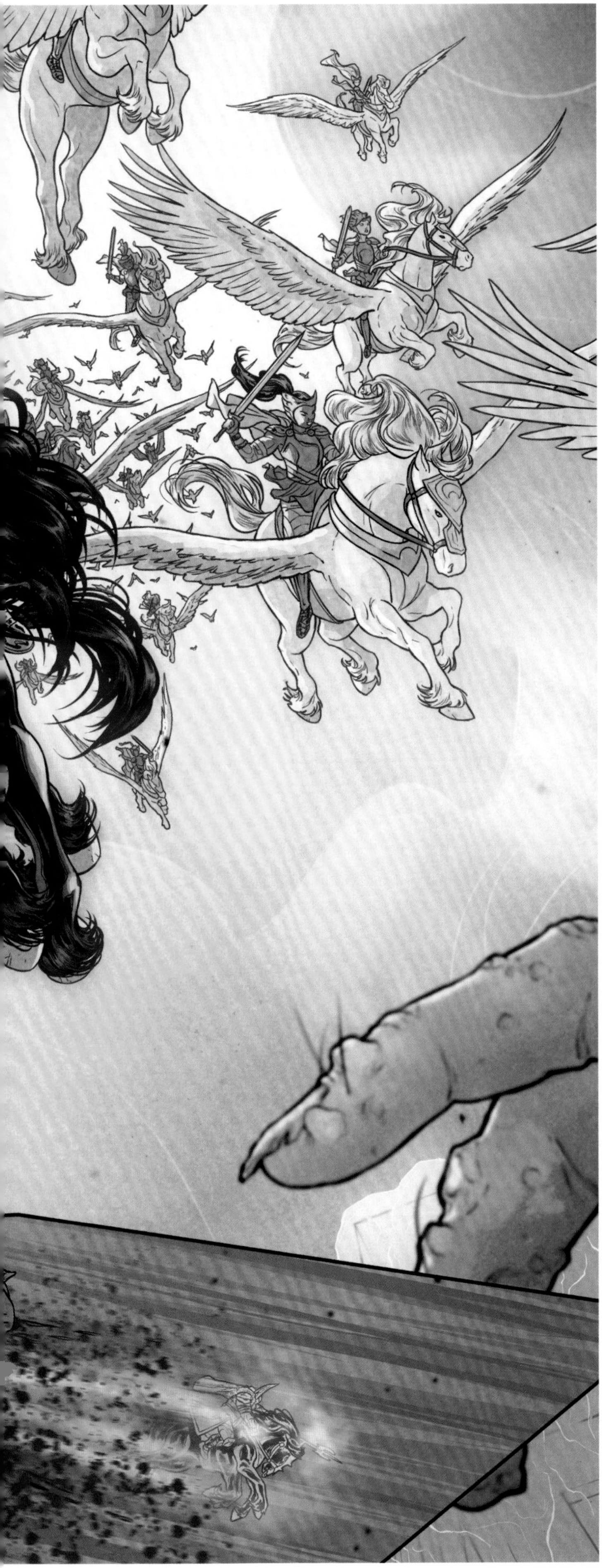

"I've been drawing Valkyrie, who I'd only drawn a few times before. I love her! I designed her a new look, and I can't wait for everyone to see this big spread with her and the Valkyries."
— RUSSELL DAUTERMAN

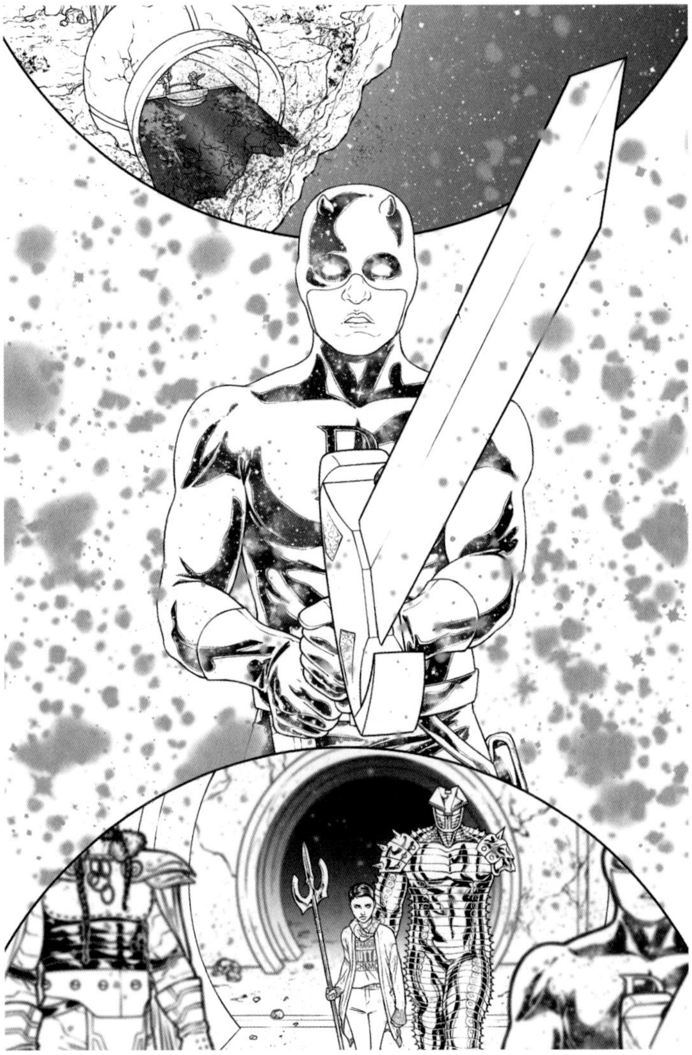

"When drawing Heimdall in *Thor*, I played up the star effect that we'd seen before in his eyes. I made all the shadows in his skin have that galaxy effect. And for the stars/nebulae that made up his eyes, I changed them depending on his mood or how much power he was using. As soon as I read that Daredevil would take Heimdall's place, I knew I wanted to incorporate that galaxy effect. I ended up just using it for his costume to imply that this power is something Daredevil is wearing — not intrinsically part of him, like with Heimdall."
— RUSSELL DAUTERMAN

ODIN, BRUNNHILDE AND HER FELLOW VALKYRIES TAKE FLIGHT, WHILE DAREDEVIL TAKES ON A NEW ROLE

LEFT: *WAR OF THE REALMS* #2 INTERIOR ART BY RUSSELL DAUTERMAN AND MATTHEW WILSON

ABOVE: *WAR OF THE REALMS* #3 INTERIOR INKS BY RUSSELL DAUTERMAN

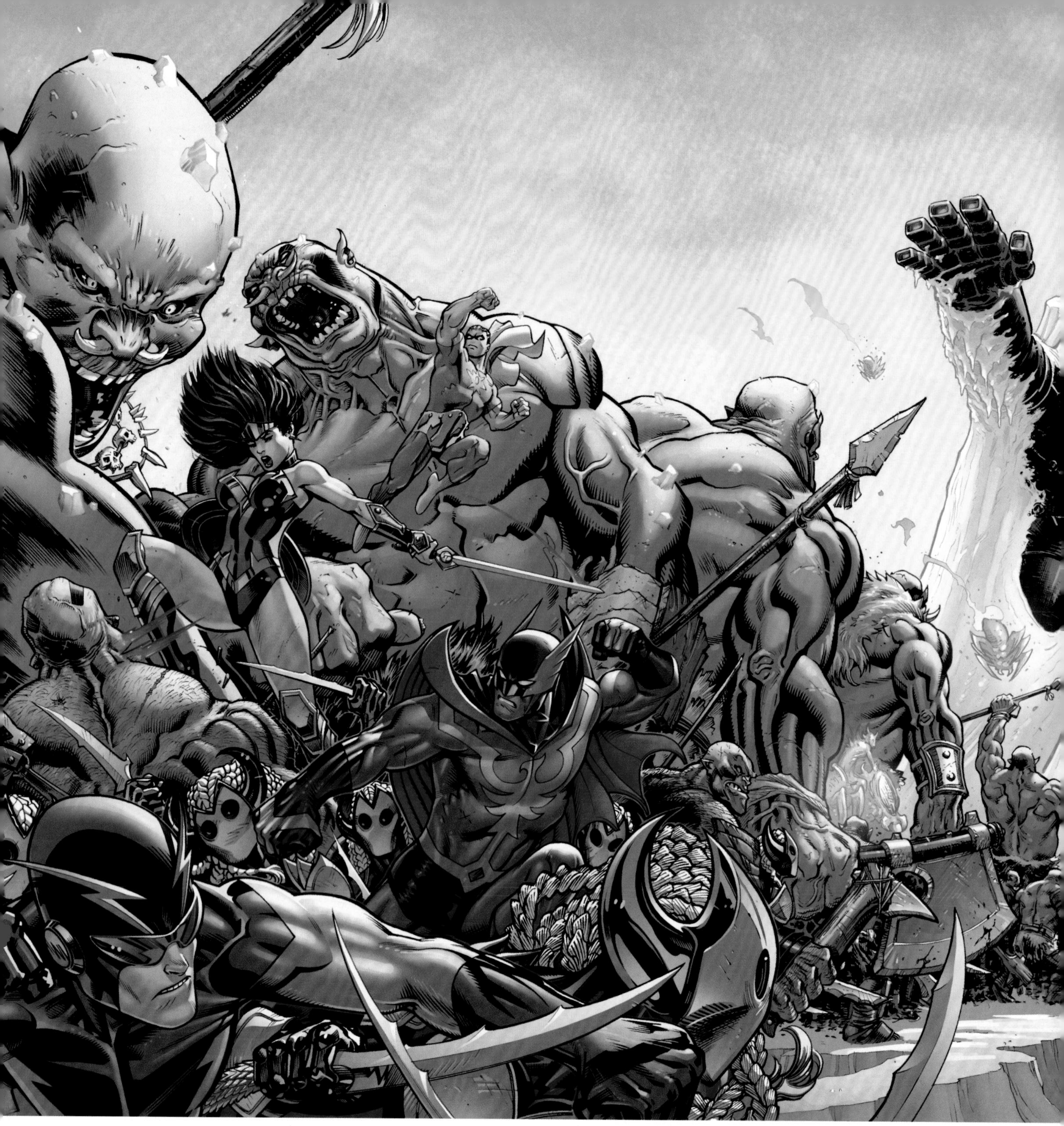

“Anytime I get to team up with Jason on anything is such a privilege! His take on these heroes is spot-on, and I love it. He really knows how to write to the individual artist, and he is constantly pushing me creatively. To put it short, I love working with Jason on anything — this guy is the landlord of the House of Ideas!”
— ED McGUINNESS

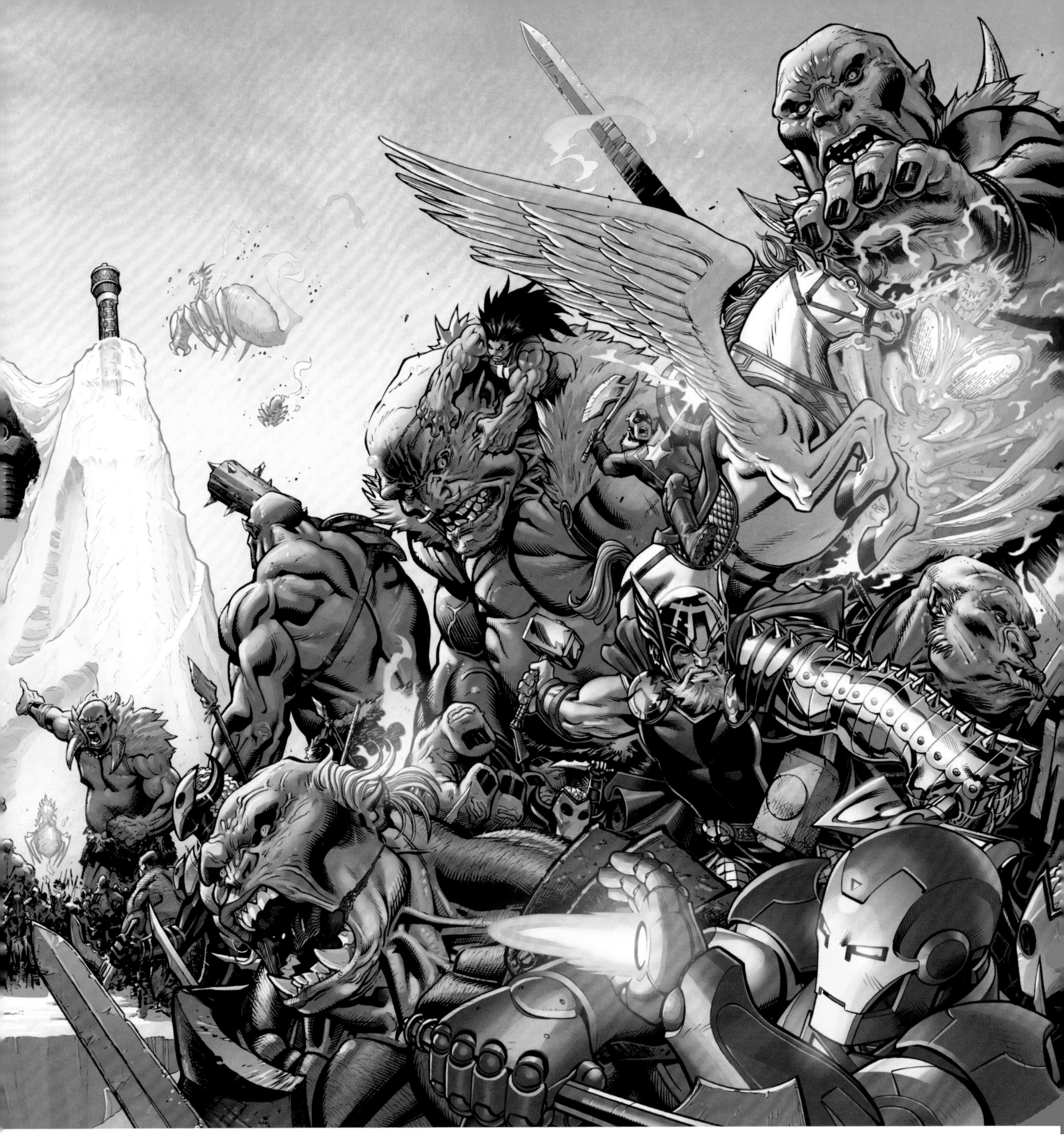

THE WAR OF THE REALMS COMES TO THE DOORSTEP OF AVENGERS MOUNTAIN — THE TEAM'S INCREDIBLE NEW HEADQUARTERS IN THE BODY OF A DEAD CELESTIAL — AND THE AVENGERS AND THE SQUADRON SUPREME OF AMERICA ARE THERE TO MEET THE INVADING FORCES!

AVENGERS (2018) #18-20 INTERLOCKING COVERS BY ED MCGUINNESS AND VAL STAPLES

"At one point in the story, Cap, Spidey, Iron Fist and a couple of other characters get sent on a mission to Jotunheim, the realm of ice and snow. Some of the characters outfit themselves with Asgardian weaponry and winter clothing. Iron Fist is especially into the sword-and-sorcery aspect of the mission and adds an Asgardian cloak and gloves to his costume. I thought Cap would be more practical, so I designed a new coat for him — basically Captain America-branded outerwear. Spidey does not prepare as well for the cold and ends up with an ill-conceived addition to his costume."

— RUSSELL DAUTERMAN

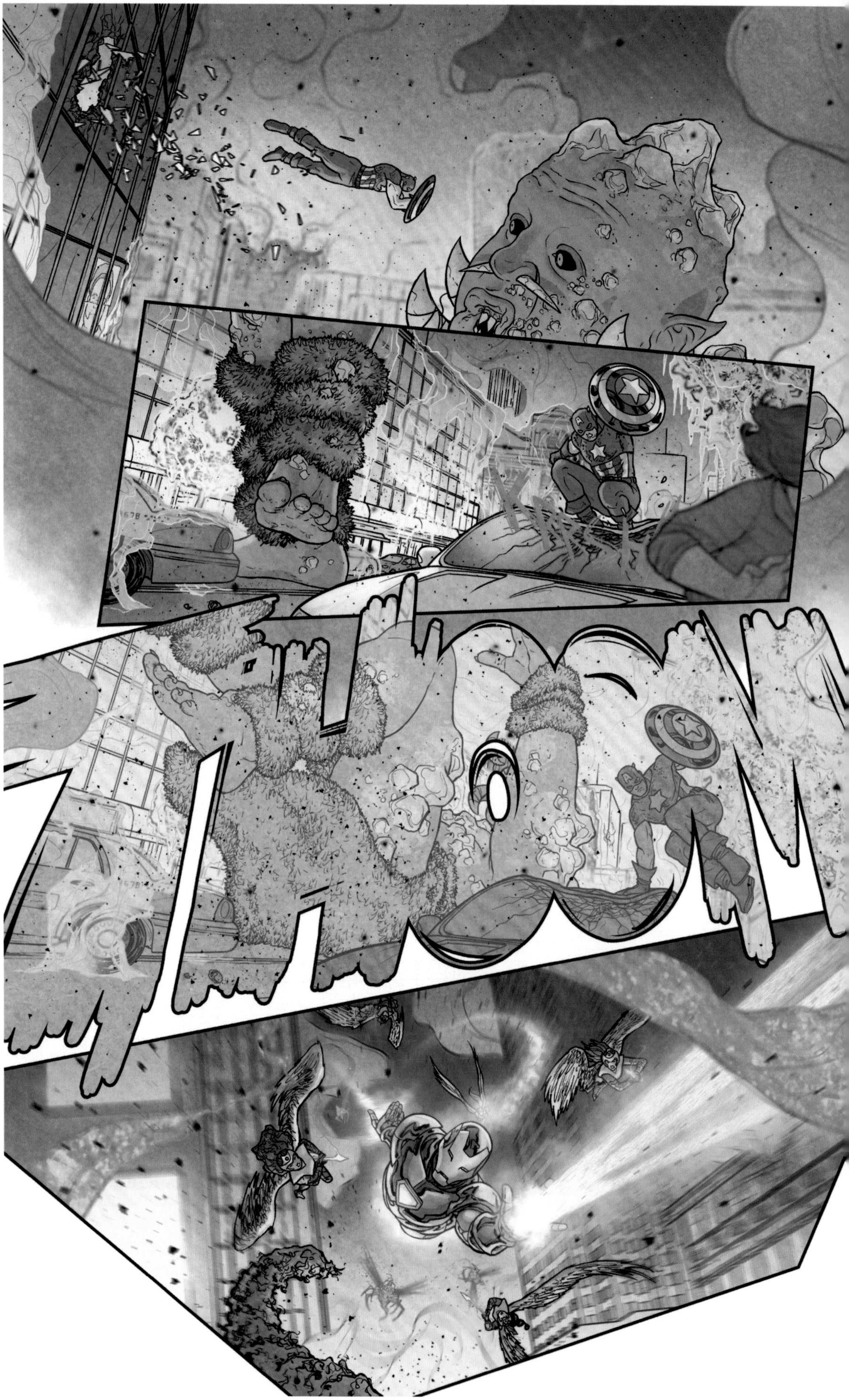

CAPTAIN AMERICA TAKES ON A FROST GIANT AS MARVEL'S HEROES SUIT UP FOR WAR. IN THE REAL WORLD, THAT BUILDING IS MARVEL'S OFFICE — AND THE SPECIFIC WINDOW HAS A GIANT PRINTOUT OF TOM BREVOORT'S HEAD FACING OUT OF IT. (IT'S A LONG STORY.)

RIGHT: ***WAR OF THE REALMS* #2** INTERIOR ART BY RUSSELL DAUTERMAN AND MATTHEW WILSON

OPPOSITE: ***WAR OF THE REALMS* #3** INTERIOR INKS BY RUSSELL DAUTERMAN

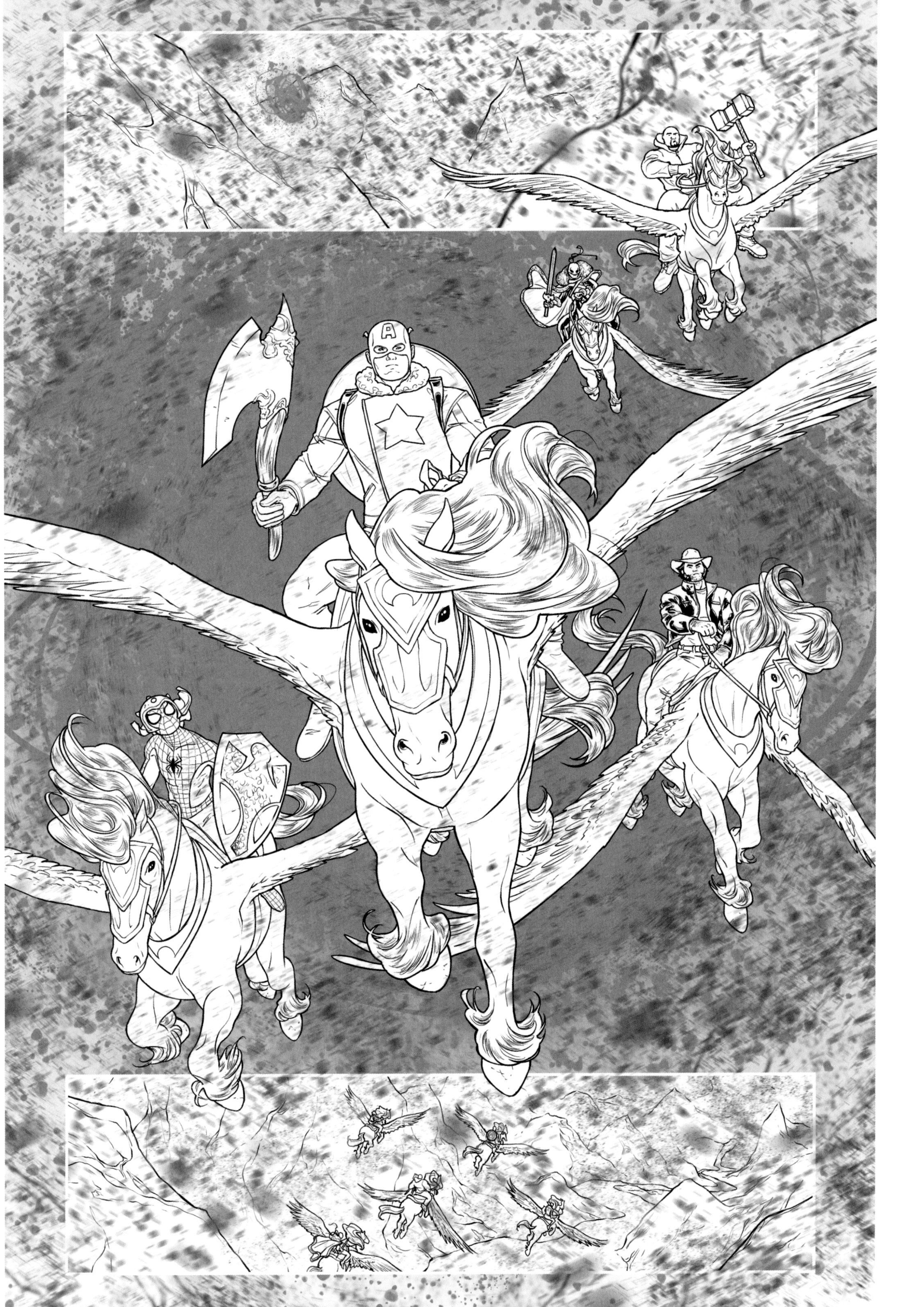

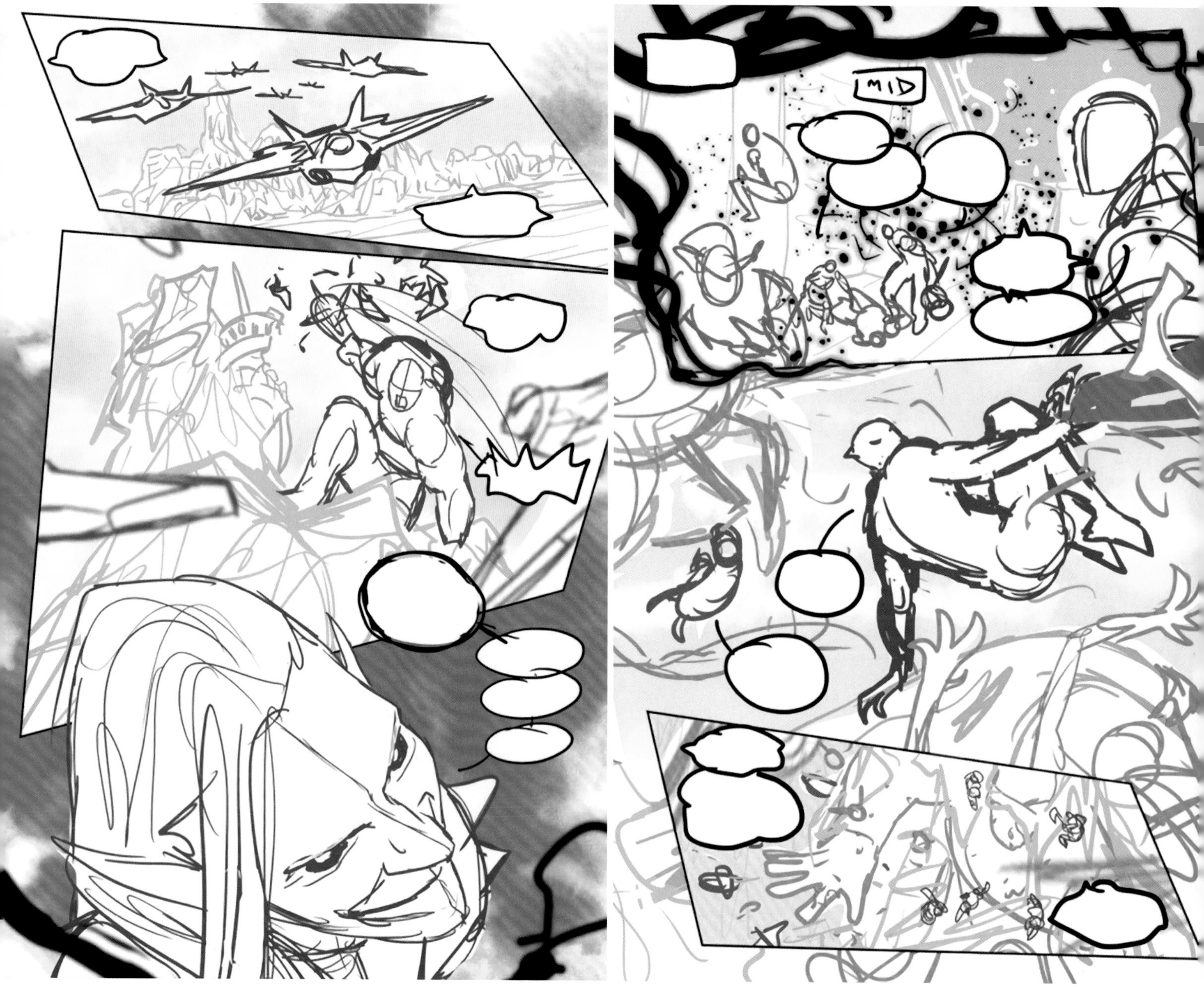
MID

"For the layouts, I'm drawing just enough detail so that my editors, Jason and I know what's what, and everything is pretty rough. I use so many colors to differentiate the various elements. Assigning a specific color to each character lets me track them more easily. With the layouts, I'm not concerned with making a good drawing. Instead, I'm putting together a puzzle. The script lays out all these different pieces — action, setting, characters, dialogue, etc. — and I need to figure out how to arrange it all so that the story flows. I'm always trying to find some 'wow!' moment for the characters in the layout stage — I think of it as the 'copy machine test.' When I was a kid, my mom worked from home and had one of those giant copy machines in our house. I used to photocopy the coolest images from my comics and collage them together. I always have that in mind when I'm doing layouts: Is this something I would've photocopied?"
— RUSSELL DAUTERMAN

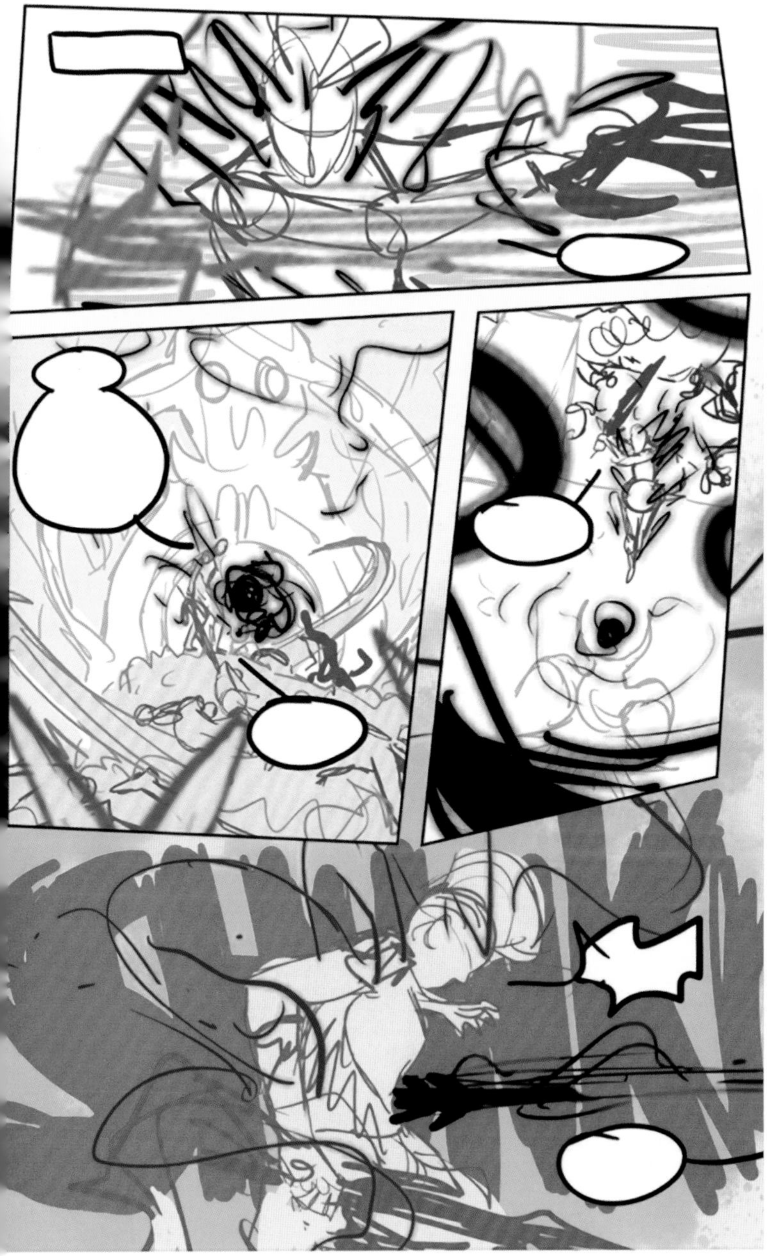

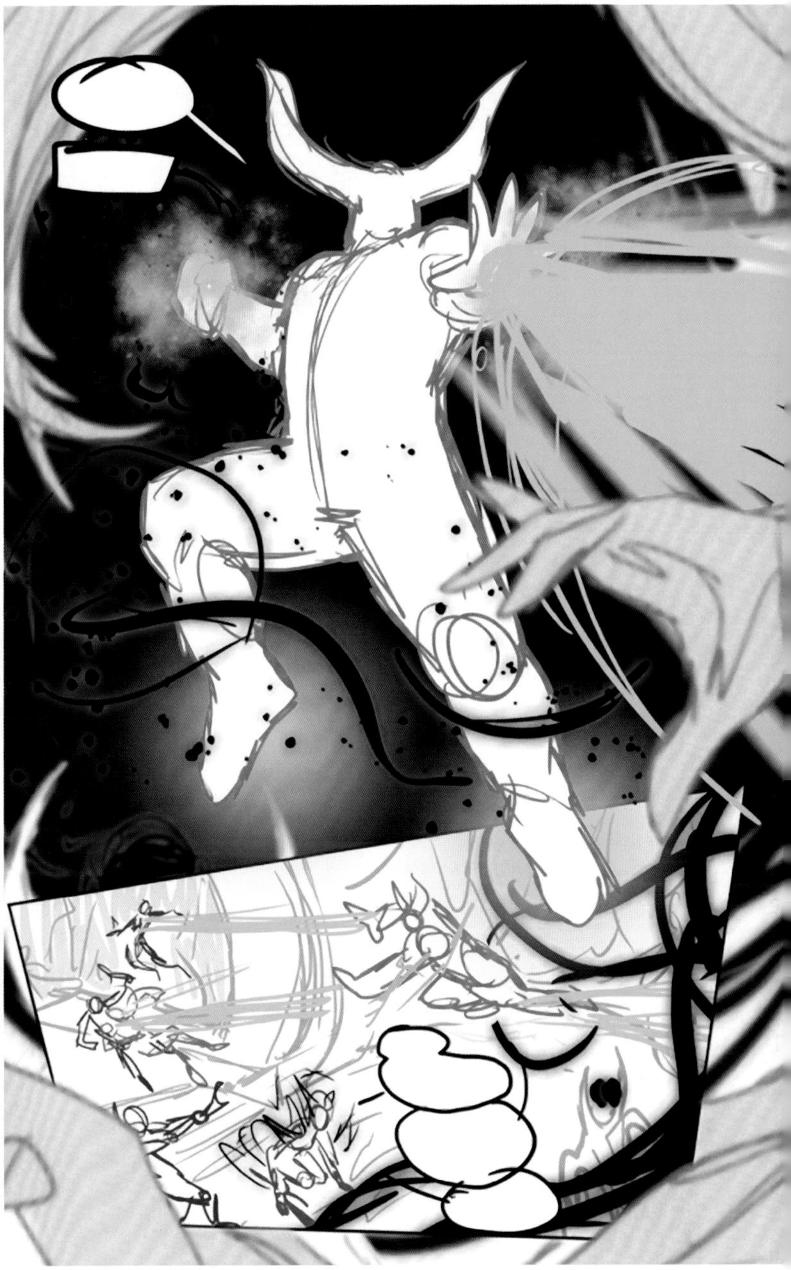

THESE LAYOUTS — MINI MULTICOLOR MASTERPIECES IN AND OF THEMSELVES — HINT AT THE SHAPE OF THINGS TO COME.

***WAR OF THE REALMS* #4** LAYOUTS BY RUSSELL DAUTERMAN

RD
2014-2018

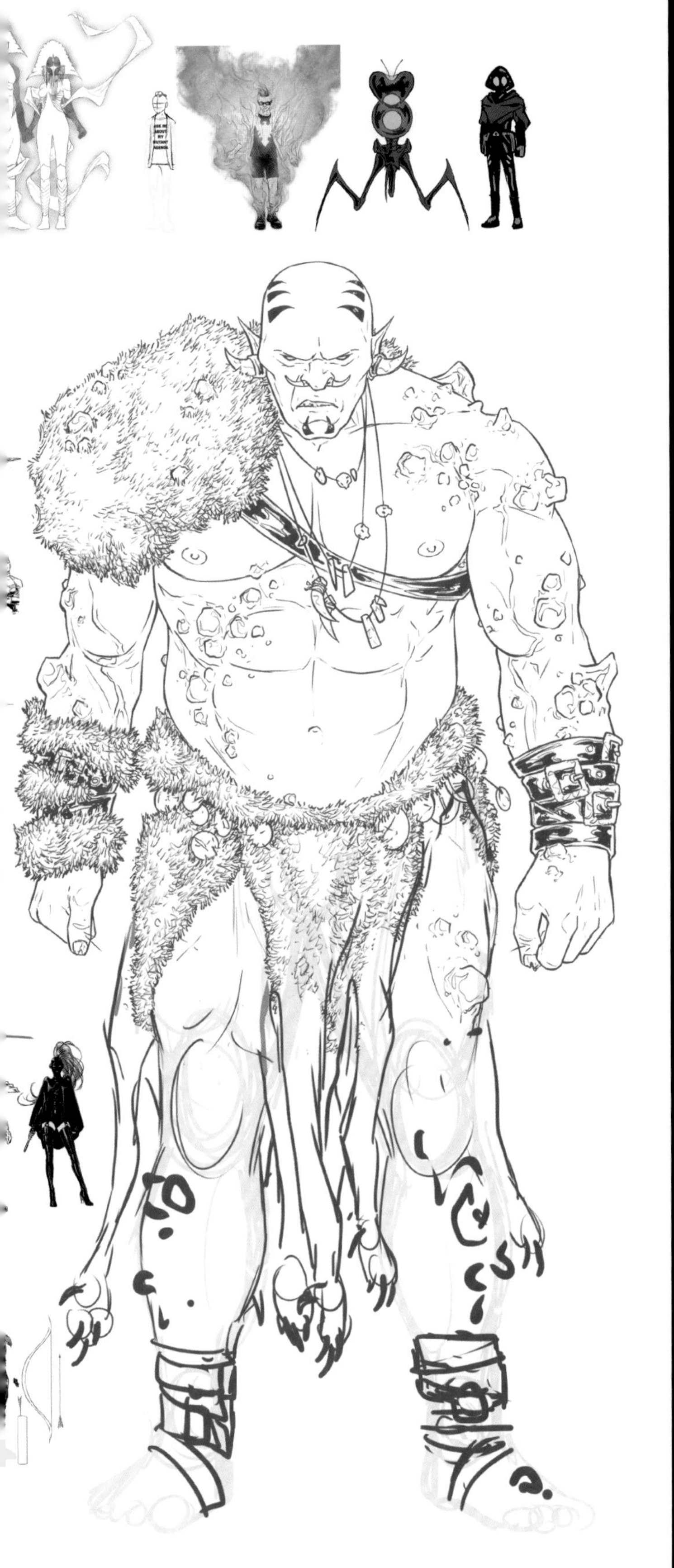

chapter ten:

DAUTERMAN DESIGNS

"I absolutely love designing characters. I went to school for that, and I always get excited when there's a new design to do."
— Russell Dauterman

JANE FOSTER THOR

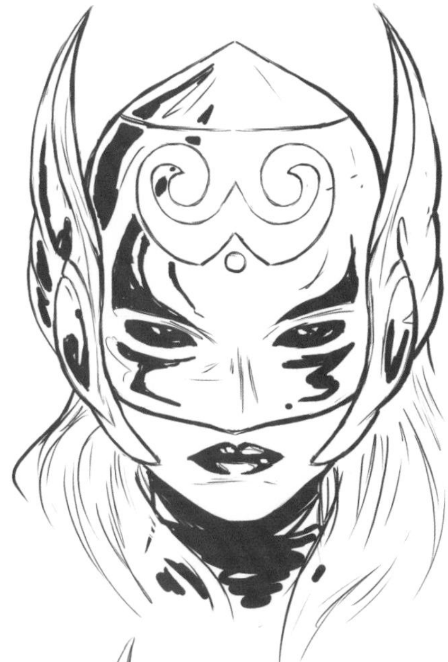

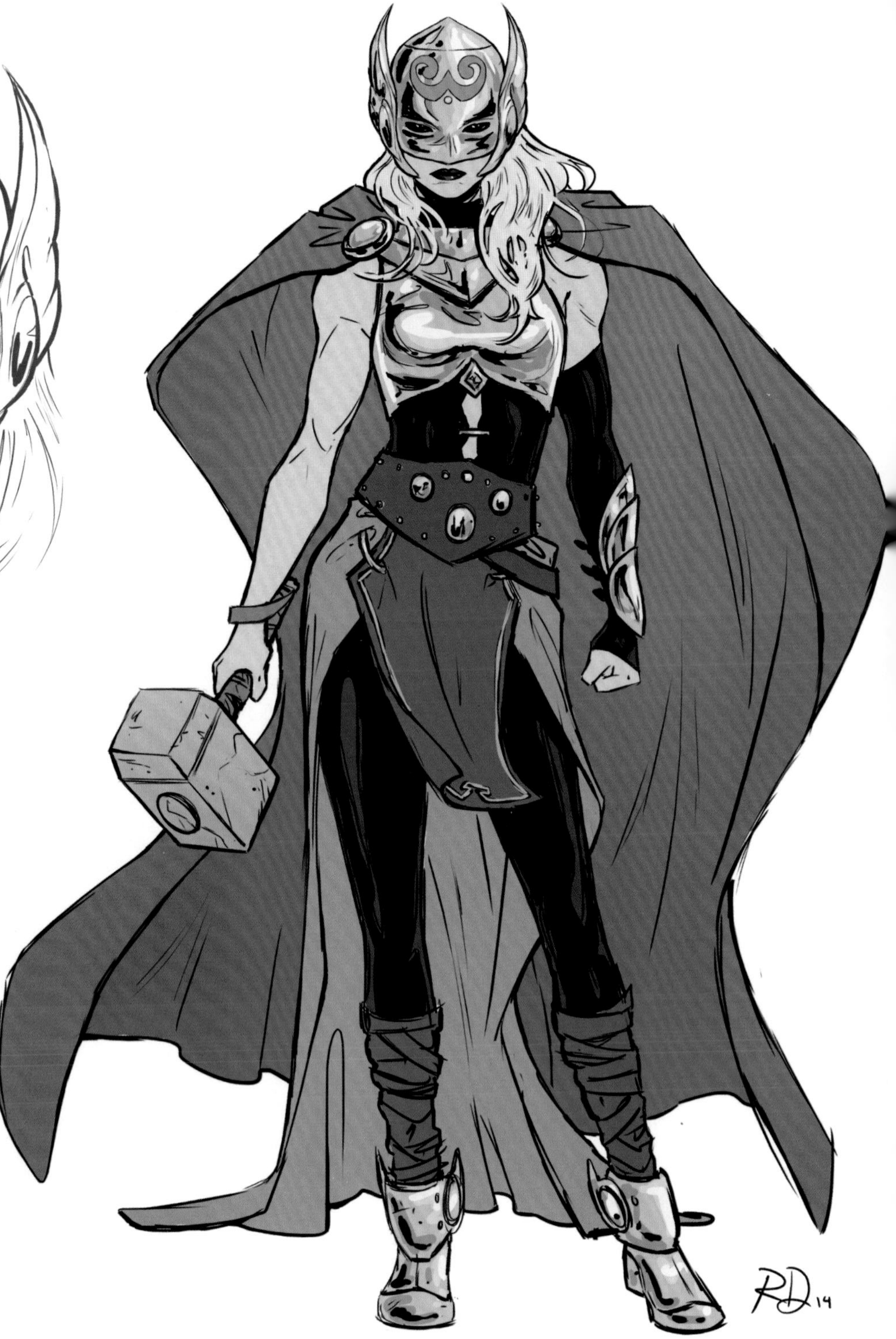

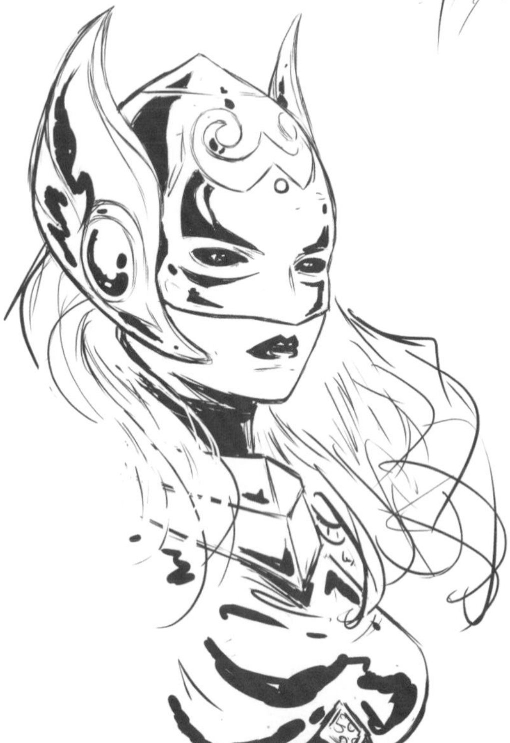

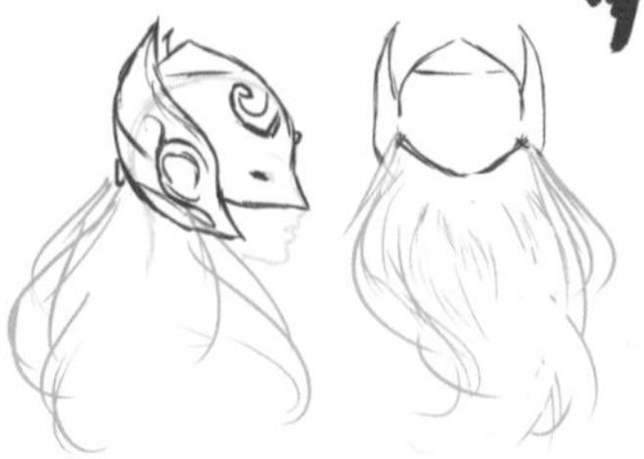

"I wanted Jane's human look to feel very familiar and to be pretty basic in comparison to her imposing Thor costume and all the dramatic fantasy costumes in the Thor world. I figured that she'd shop at J.Crew or similar practical, upscale stores; that she'd like layers because her weight loss might make her cold; and that she'd wear comfortable shoes since she's a doctor and is used to being on her feet a lot. For her head scarf, I used a paisley pattern because I thought it resembled amoeba — a subtle nod to her science/medical background."

— RUSSELL DAUTERMAN

Throughout his time working on *Thor, Mighty Thor* and now *War of the Realms*, artist Russell Dauterman has drawn meticulous character models and design sketches for all his major players. Not only that, but his computer wizardry allowed him to maintain an evolving height chart (as demonstrated across the previous pages) to keep track of their relative sizes. "I added as I went along," Dauterman says, "and referred to it for nearly every page!"

The design process — as well as his own personal refinements of pre-existing designs — is one of the parts of being a comics artist he says he most enjoys. "For characters that I'm going to be drawing a lot, I like to do a character model ahead of time — to figure out how I want to draw the character's face, body proportions, costume, etc.," Dauterman says. "The first model I did for *Thor* was of Jane Thor herself. Esad had already designed a beautiful costume, but I wanted to figure out how I would interpret it. It's one of the things I love most about comics: They combine so many different disciplines of art, from costume and set design to composition and figure drawing. I get to do a variety of things I'm interested in."

As we bring *The Art of the War of the Realms* to a close, we present a gallery of Dauterman's finest character models, including his insights on some of his favorites.

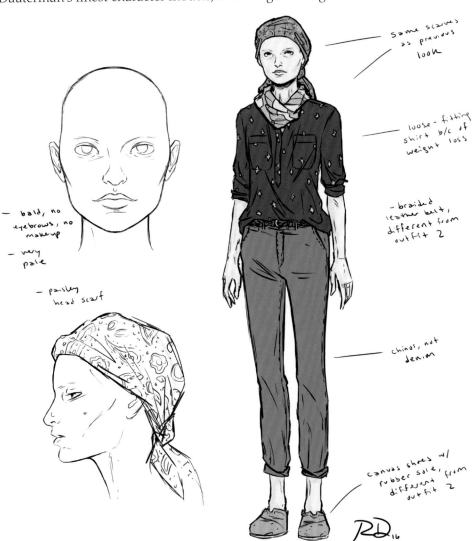

- bald, no eyebrows, no makeup
- very pale
- paisley head scarf

same scarves as previous look

loose-fitting shirt b/c of weight loss

- braided leather belt, different from outfit 2

chinos, not denim

canvas shoes w/ rubber soles from different outfit 2

THOR ODINSON

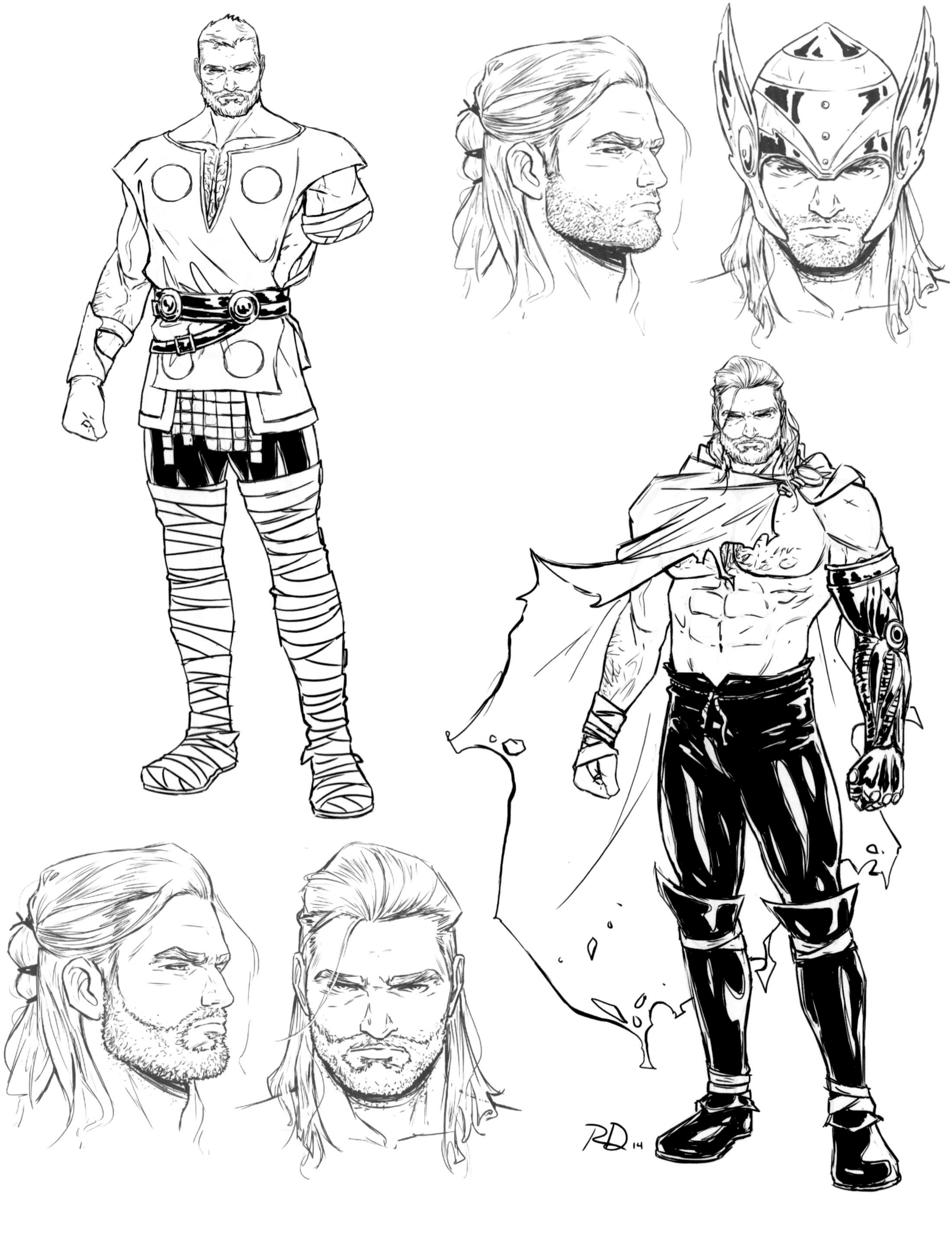

"I was really thrilled to redesign Thor Odinson. That was the first major Marvel character I'd gotten to design, in terms of creating a new super-hero costume that would be used in various books. Marvel wanted this design to be a return to the classic version of the character. I drew from the designs by Jack Kirby, Olivier Coipel and Esad Ribić, incorporating classic elements and blending them with new ones. Originally, I'd just used his black metal arm that we'd seen previously but gave him a gold hammer. The gold arm was Wil Moss' idea, which I thought was brilliant! I think adding the gold arm and changing some of the other metal bits to match helped make him feel more heroic and optimistic."

— RUSSELL DAUTERMAN

- cape is detachable

- double sword holster can be added, attached to back of costume + under cape fasteners

- Asgardian embroidery on belt

- 4 straps attaching front piece of boot

MALEKITH & LOKI

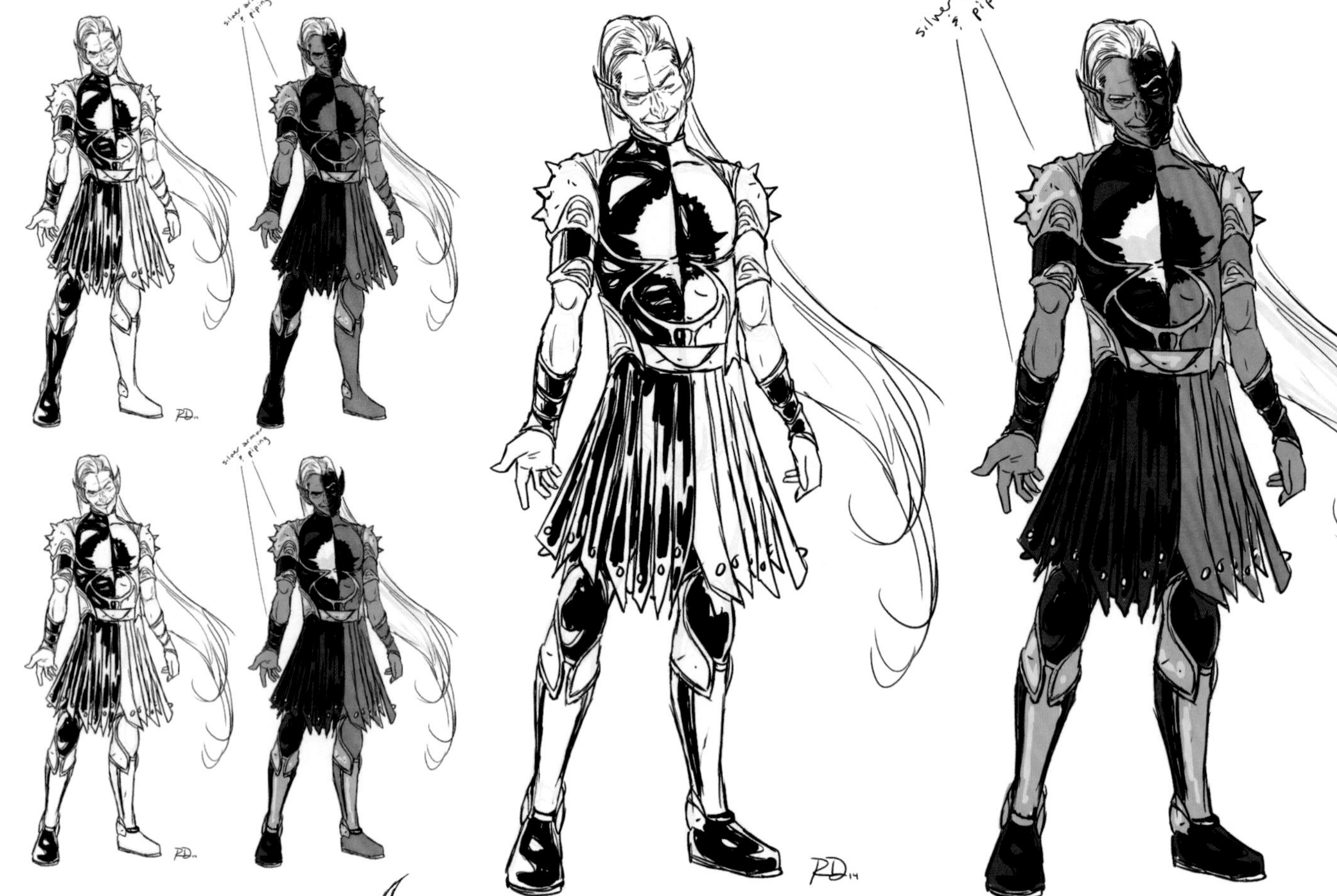
silver armor & piping
silver armor & piping
silver armor & piping

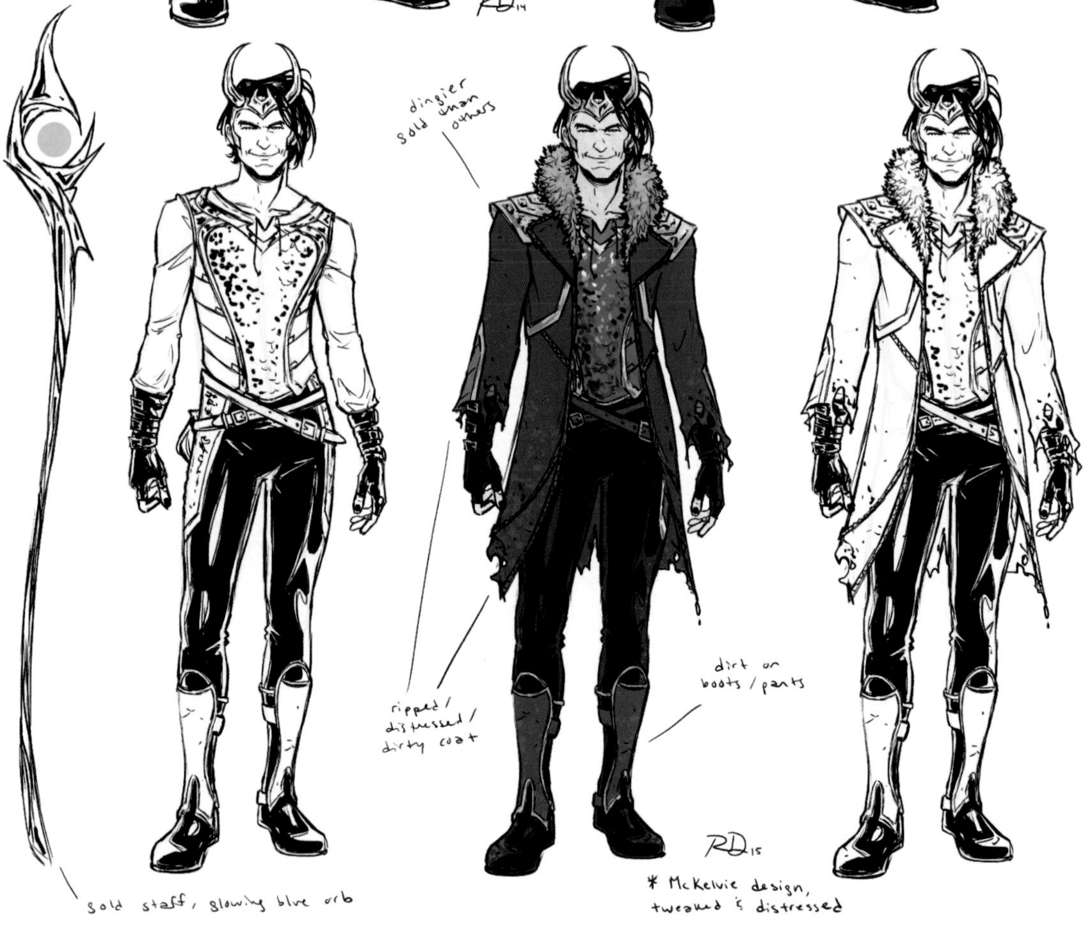
dingier gold than others
ripped / distressed / dirty coat
dirt on boots / pants
gold staff, glowing blue orb
* McKelvie design, tweaked & distressed

"I love drawing Malekith. He's fun because of how exaggerated I can make him — everything from his body language to his smile to his hair is all dialed up so that he has a very obvious presence. He slinks and slithers and flows with a perverse sort of charm, manipulating his movements like he manipulates everything around him. I try to give him this wry, smug, condescending face that you just want to punch."

— RUSSELL DAUTERMAN

ODIN & FREYJA

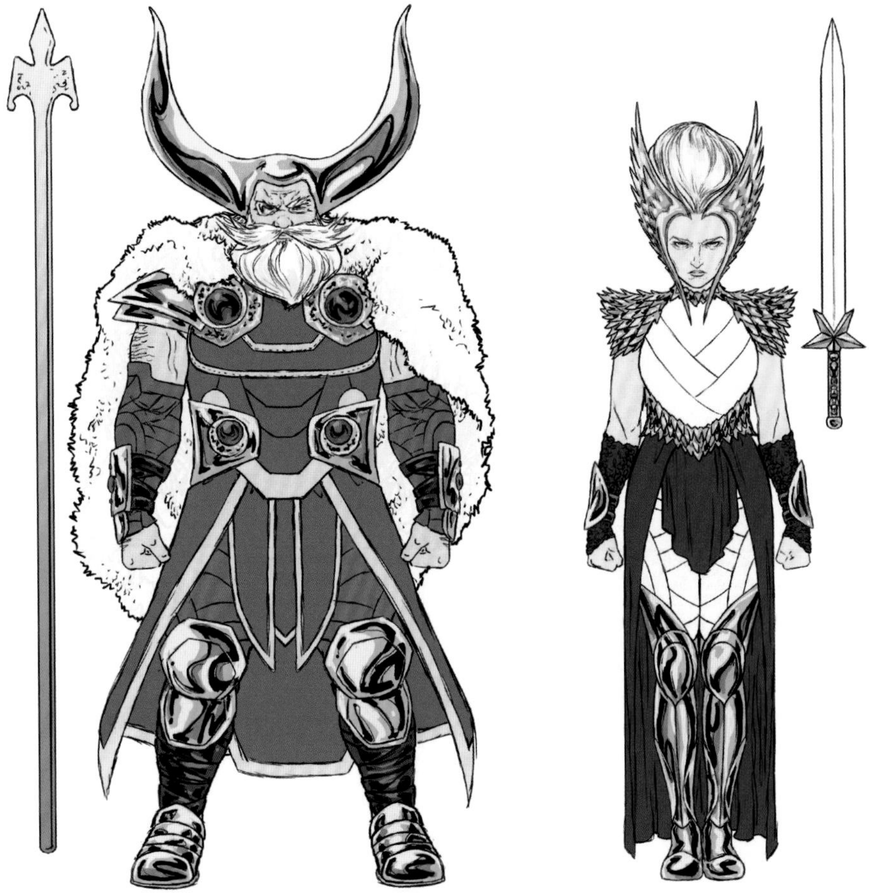

"My designs for Freyja and Odin are some of my favorites, especially the tweaked versions for *War of the Realms*. I wanted them both to look regal, so I went for lots of gold and imposing silhouettes. Odin's known for his crazy hats, and I love the idea of doing headdresses in the shape of animal horns for him — I think they suit his alpha personality. I think the mix of materials on his costume, the silhouette and the layers all help to make Odin look important — and a little pompous and pretentious.

"Freyja's winged headdress and bouffant hair came about because I wanted to give her something to increase her height, bringing her closer to Odin's stature. And I wanted to give her a signature look. I didn't think she'd wear as many heavy materials as Odin — she'd be more sleek and ready to fight. But she also needed to look intimidating and to look like royalty."

— RUSSELL DAUTERMAN

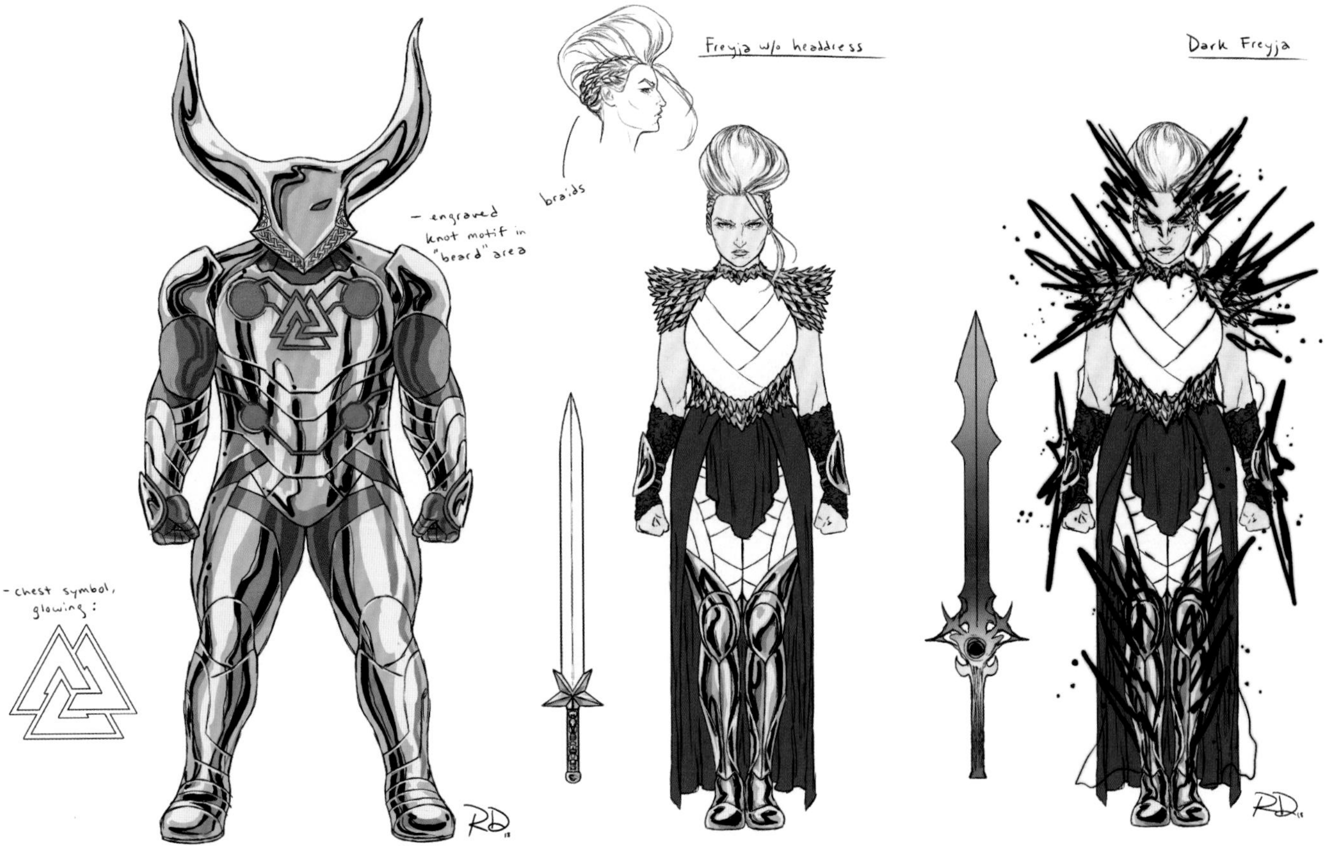
Freyja w/o headdress
Dark Freyja
braids
- engraved knot motif in "beard" area
- chest symbol, glowing:
RD

ROZ SOLOMON, THE WAR THOR & THE MANGOG

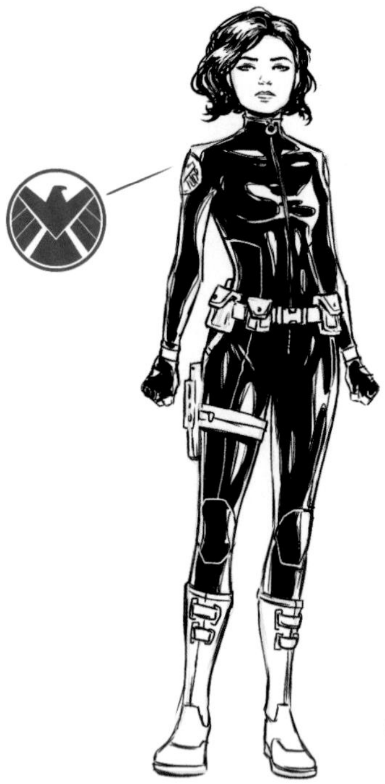

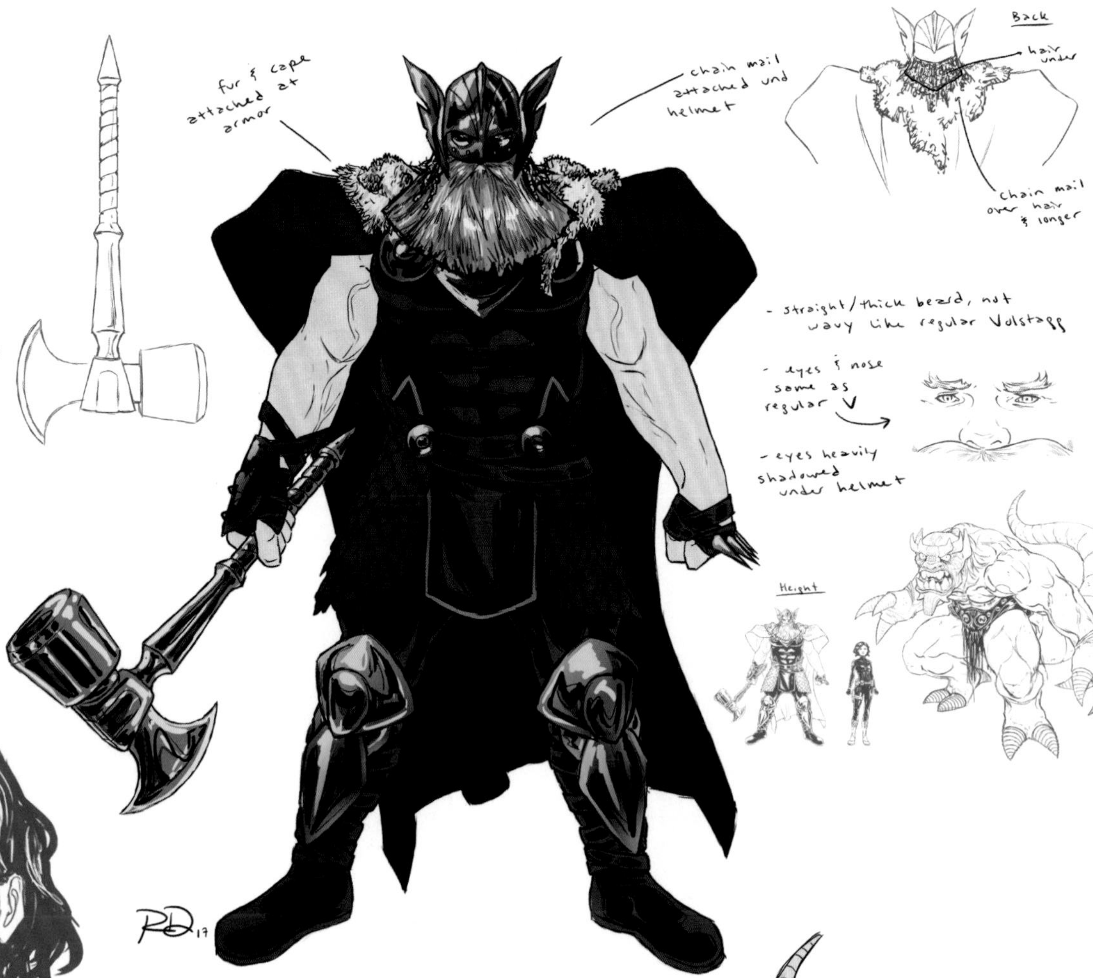
fur & cape attached at armor
chain mail attached und helmet
Back
hair under
chain mail over hair & longer
- straight/thick beard, not wavy like regular Volstagg
- eyes & nose same as regular V
- eyes heavily shadowed under helmet
Height

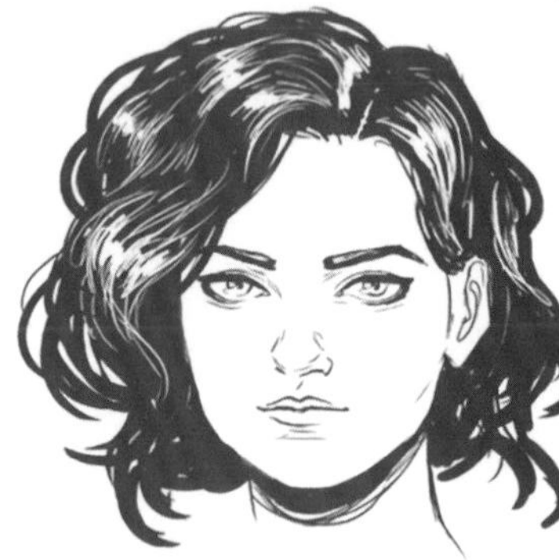

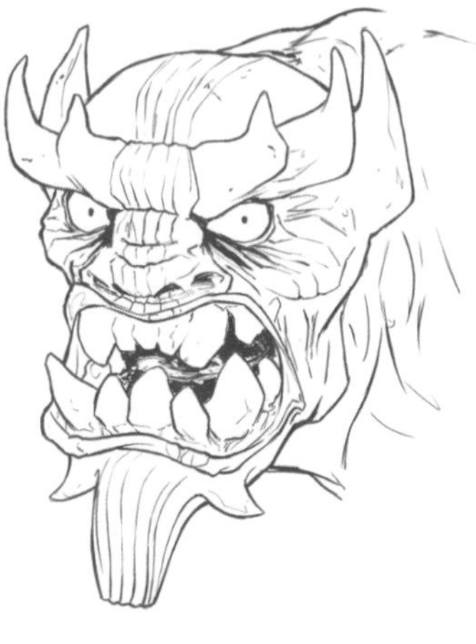

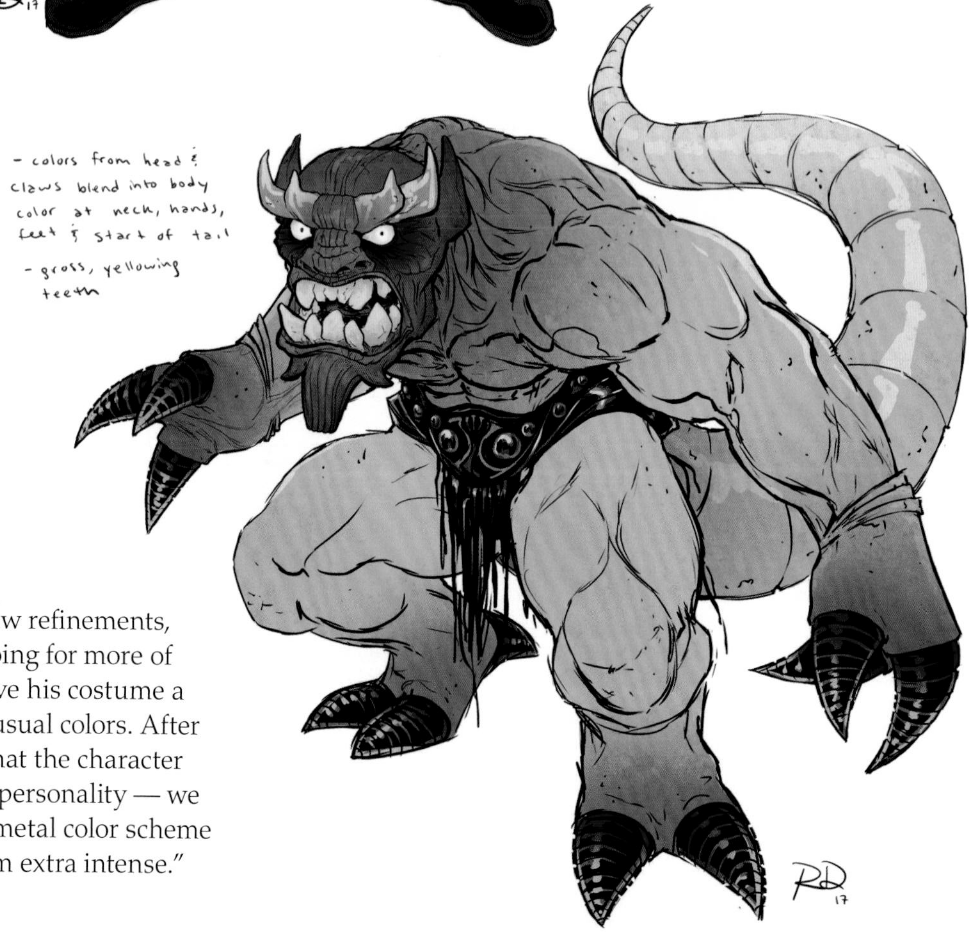
- colors from head & claws blend into body color at neck, hands, feet & start of tail
- gross, yellowing teeth

"The War Thor design went through a few refinements, mostly involving color. At first, I was going for more of a heroic, Volstagg-as-Thor look, and gave his costume a bright color scheme to echo Volstagg's usual colors. After talking with Jason — and finding out that the character would have a darker, almost villainous personality — we matched that with this black and dark-metal color scheme and added the spiked glove to make him extra intense."

— RUSSELL DAUTERMAN

SINDR & FIRE GOBLINS

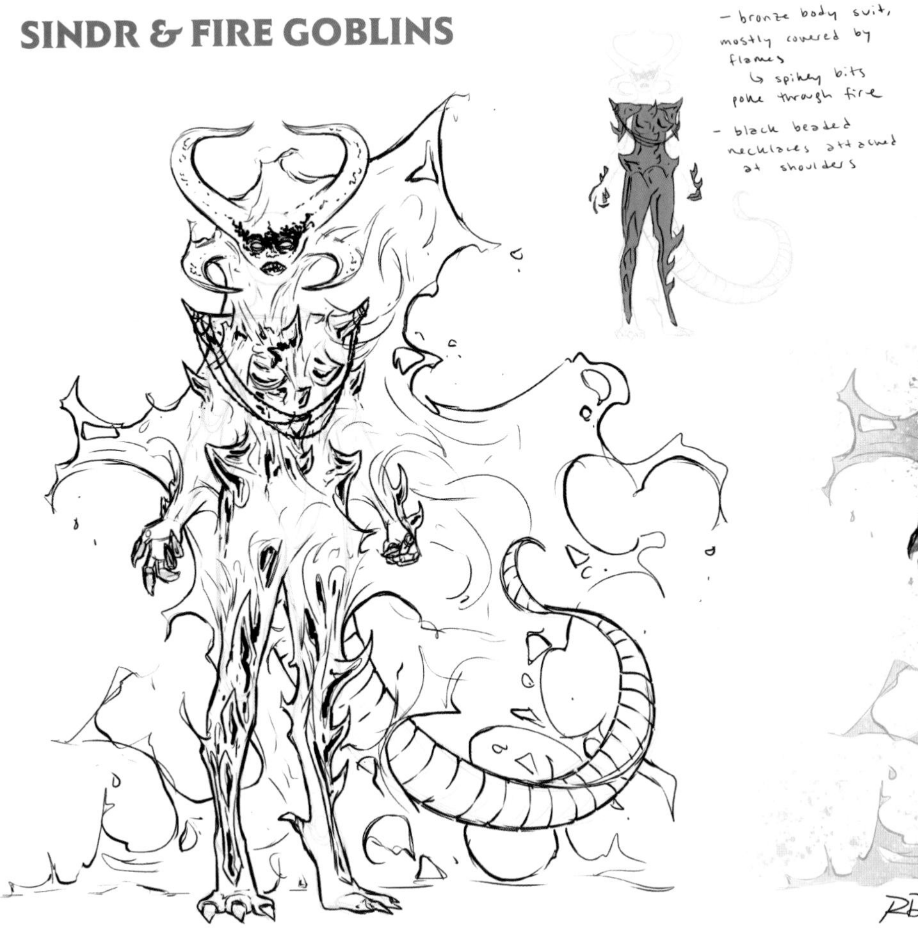
- bronze body suit, mostly covered by flames
↳ spikey bits poke through fire
- black beaded necklaces attached at shoulders

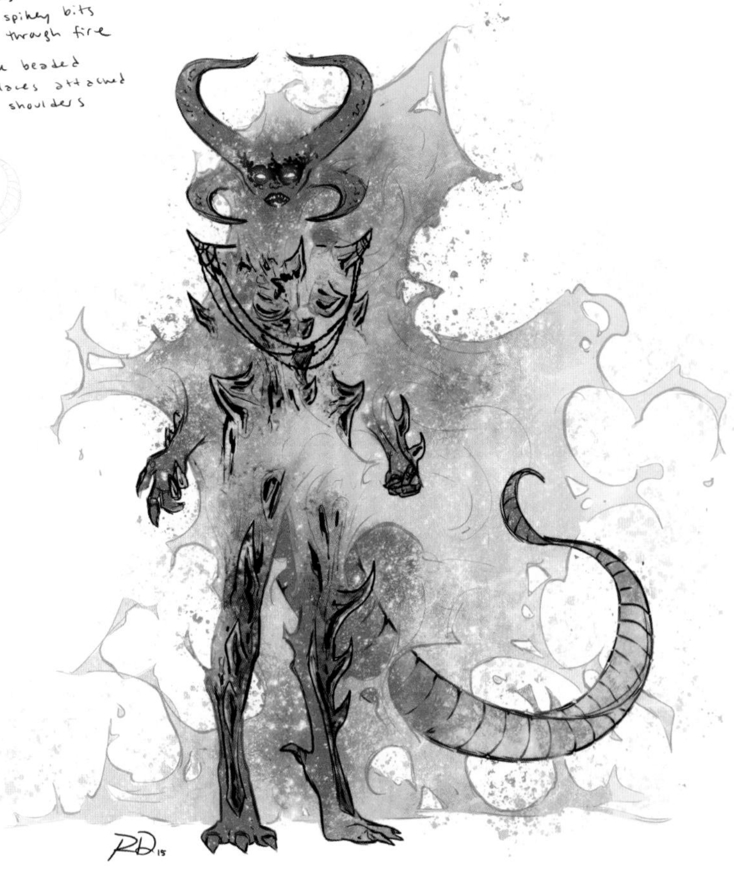

"The Queen of Cinders and her Fire Goblins were a treat to design and might be my favorite characters to draw. I love drawing the wonky anatomy on the goblins especially. For the designs, I looked at high-fashion clothes and jewelry and mixed that with Surtur's aesthetic."

— RUSSELL DAUTERMAN

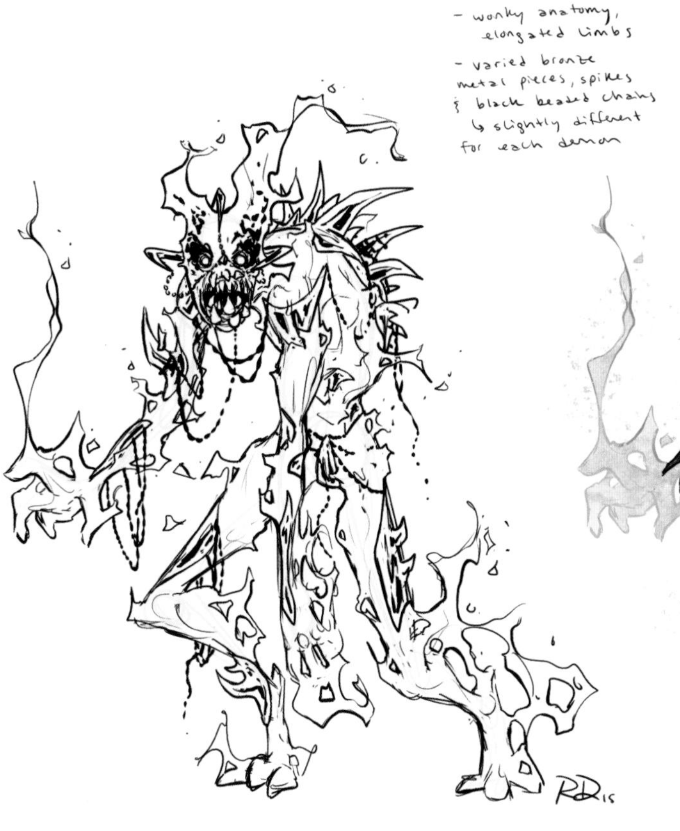
- wonky anatomy, elongated limbs
- varied bronze metal pieces, spikes & black beaded chains
↳ slightly different for each demon

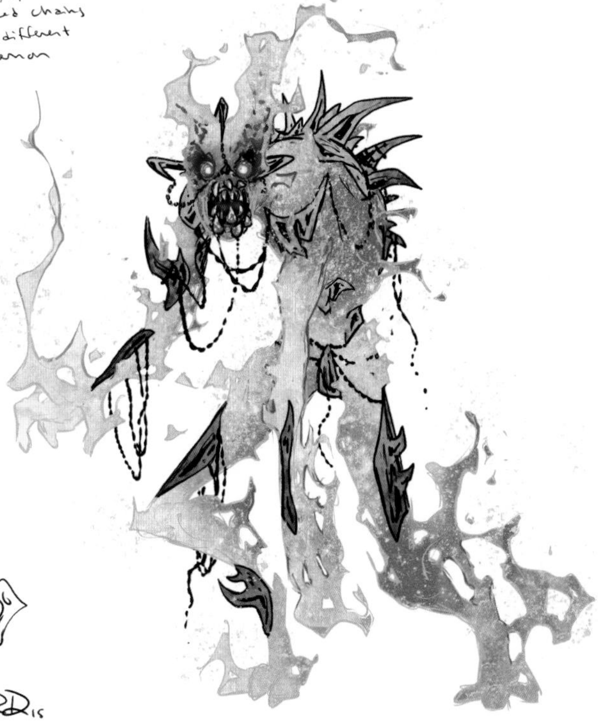

TITANYA VAETILDA VINNSUVIUS & RO BLOODROOT

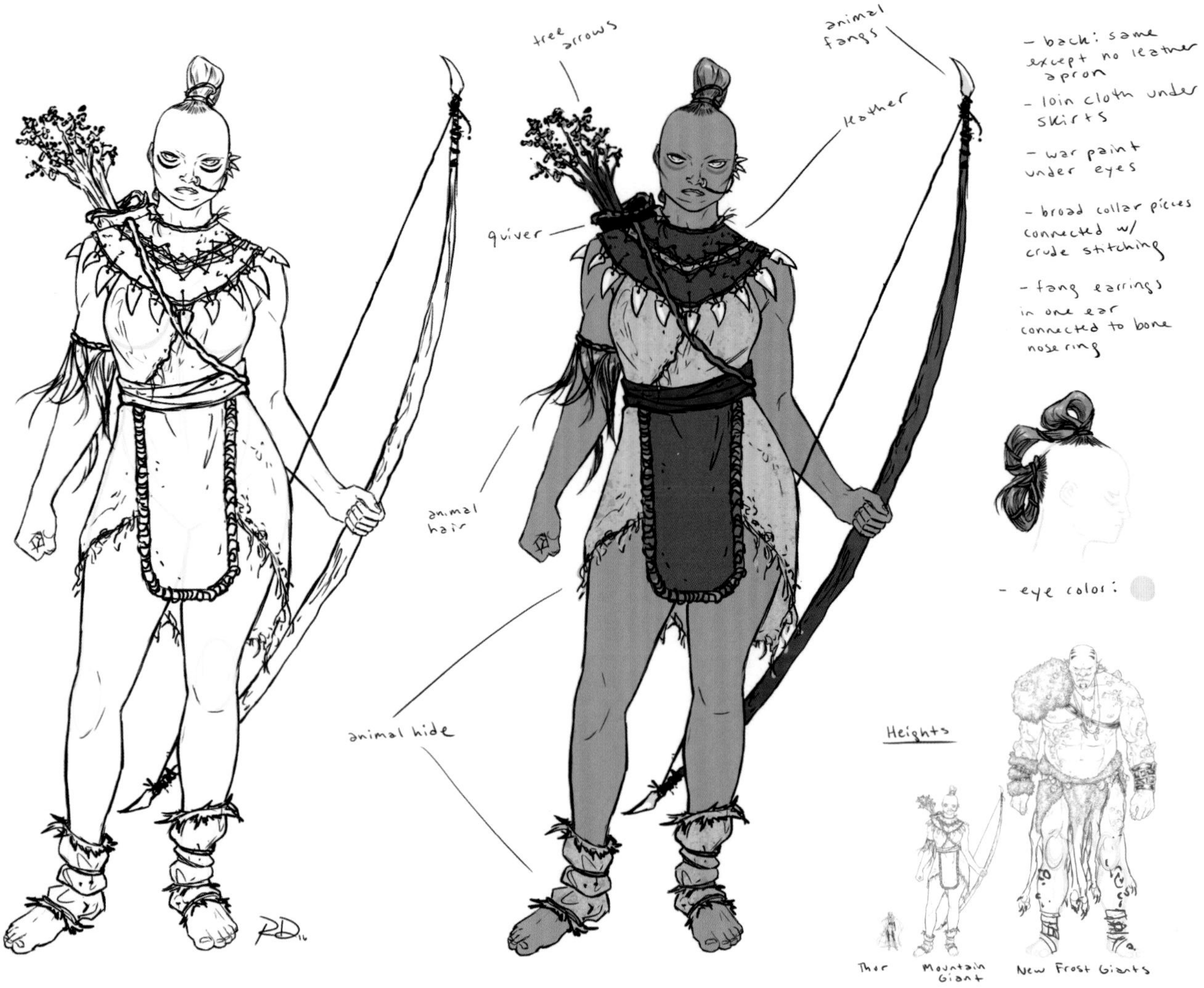
tree arrows
animal fangs
leather
quiver
animal hair
animal hide
- back: same except no leather apron
- loin cloth under skirts
- war paint under eyes
- broad collar pieces connected w/ crude stitching
- fang earrings in one ear connected to bone nosering
- eye color:
Heights
Thor
Mountain Giant
New Frost Giants

"I try to find something I love about every character and every design. Usually I build the design around that thing. For the Vanaheim wizard, Ro Bloodroot, I started with the wolf-head headdress."

— RUSSELL DAUTERMAN

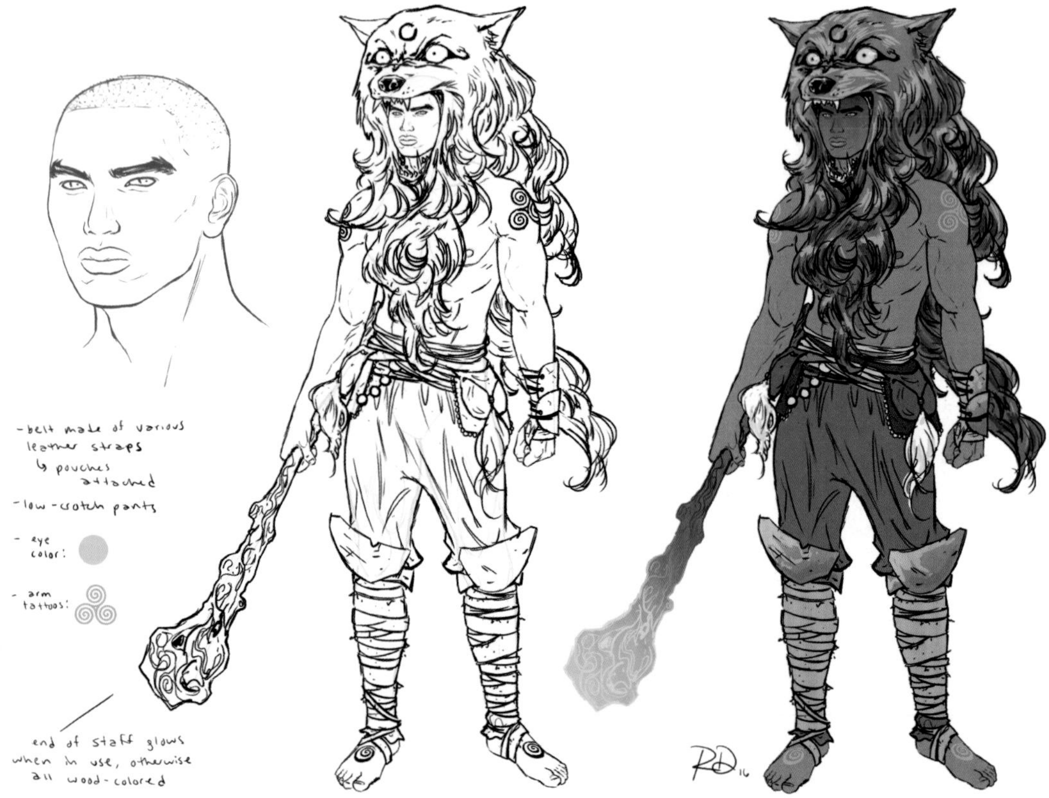
- belt made of various leather straps ↳ pouches attached
- low-crotch pants
- eye color:
- arm tattoos:
end of staff glows when in use, otherwise all wood-colored

QUENTIN QUIRE, SHARRA AND K'YTHRI

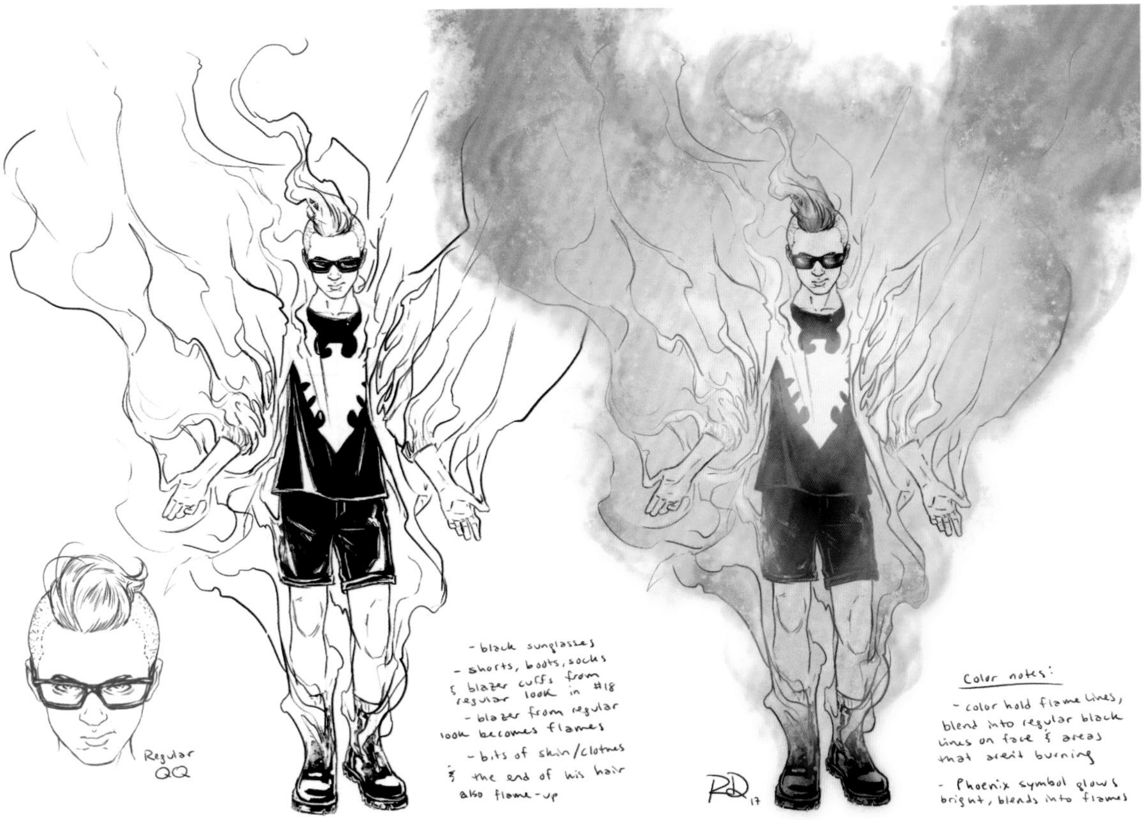

Regular QQ
- black sunglasses
- shorts, boots, socks & blazer cuffs from regular look in #18
- blazer from regular look becomes flames
- bits of skin/clothes & the end of his hair also flame-up
RD 17
Color notes:
- color hold flame lines, blend into regular black lines on face & areas that aren't burning
- Phoenix symbol glows bright, blends into flames

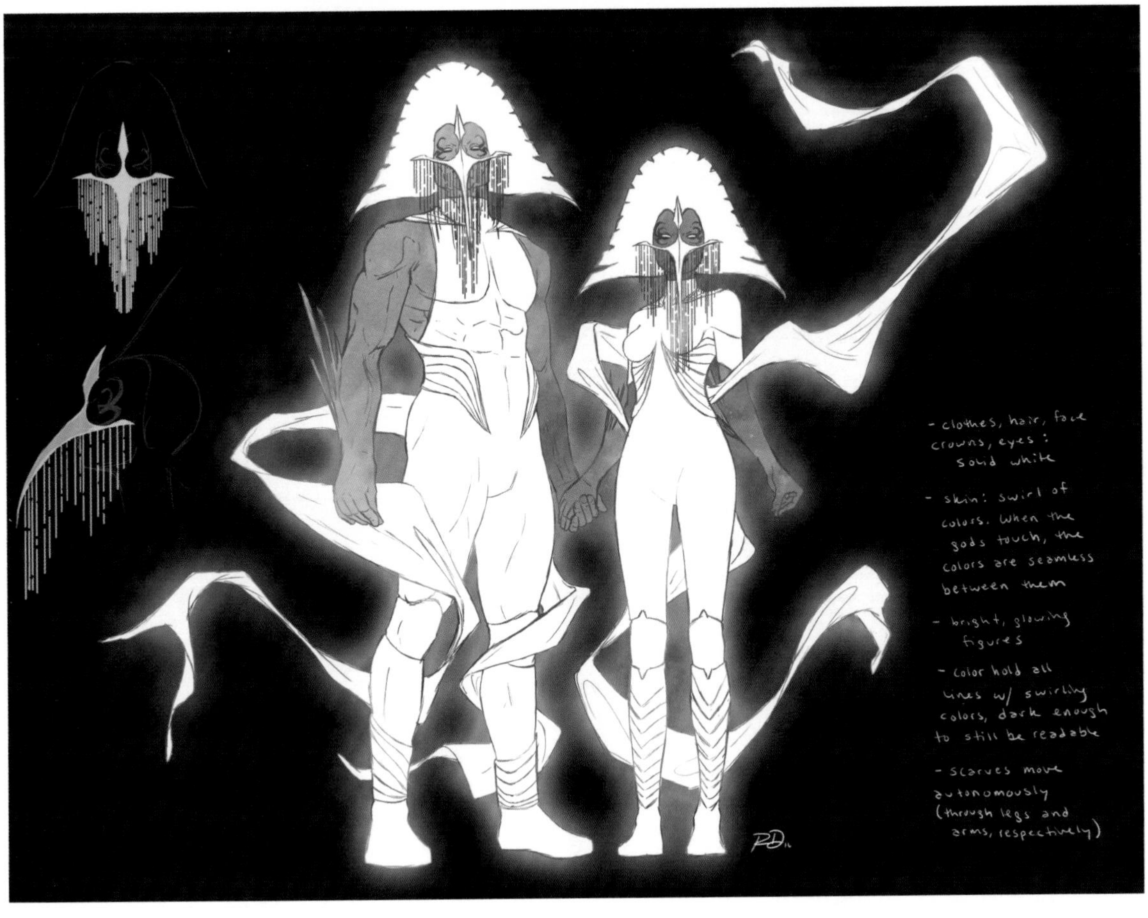

- clothes, hair, face crowns, eyes: solid white
- skin: swirl of colors. When the gods touch, the colors are seamless between them
- bright, glowing figures
- color hold all lines w/ swirling colors, dark enough to still be readable
- scarves move autonomously (through legs and arms, respectively)
RD 16

"Designing the Shi'ar gods was a fun opportunity to go a little nuts. We'd seen them in flashbacks before, with their incredible Dave Cockrum hair, but I was given free rein to reinterpret them. Jason described the gods as so bright it would hurt to look at them. I envisioned them as always showing off and reminding everyone around them of how powerful and important they are. I thought the glowing-white costumes would make them stand out and envisioned their skin to be a swirl of moving colors, like a lava lamp. I thought it'd be intimidating for them to have these Eiko Ishioka-inspired face masks and strange scarves that move around their bodies autonomously."

— RUSSELL DAUTERMAN

NORNS AND ANGELS

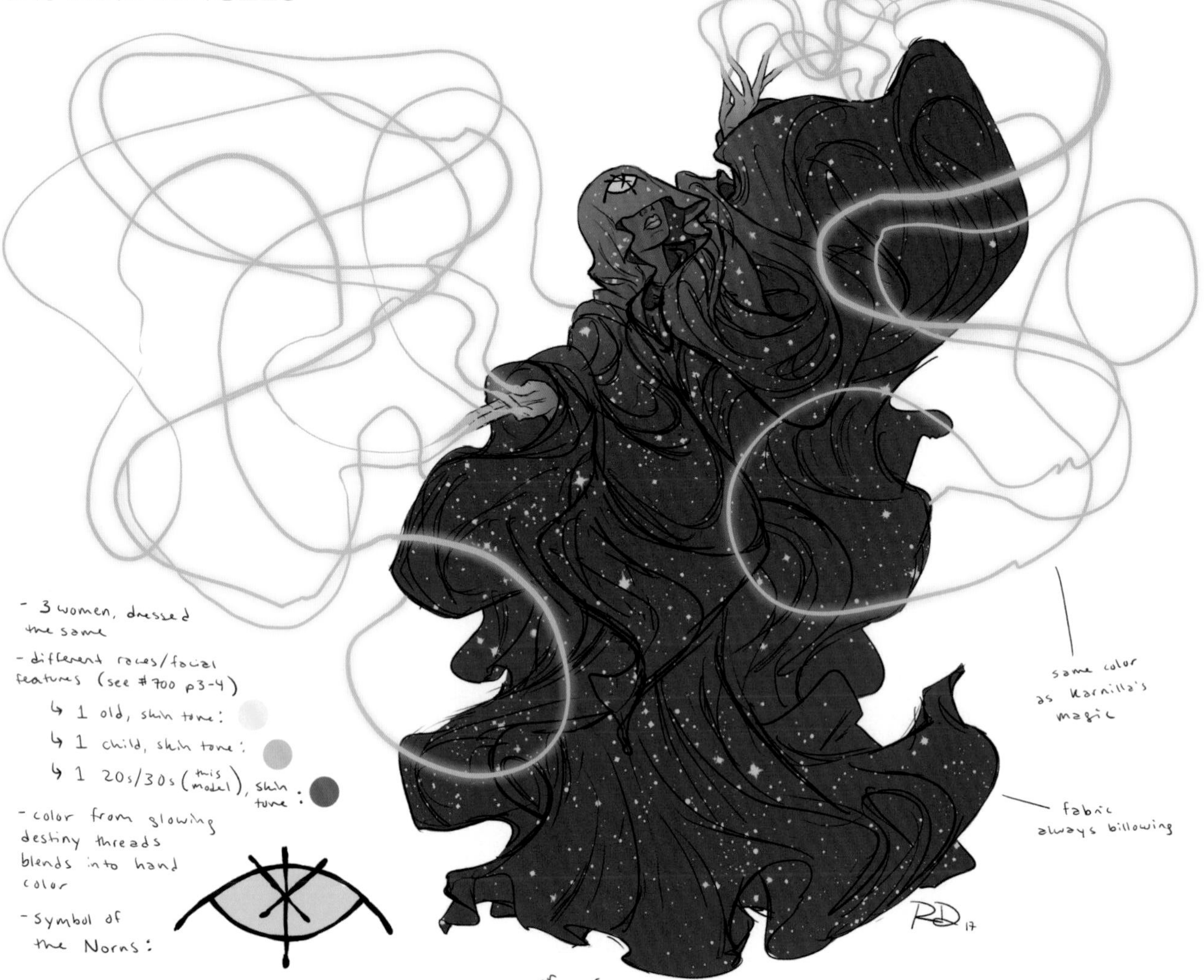

- 3 women, dressed the same
- different races/facial features (see #700 p3-4)
↳ 1 old, skin tone:
↳ 1 child, skin tone:
↳ 1 20s/30s (this model), skin tone:
- color from glowing destiny threads blends into hand color
- Symbol of the Norns:
same color as Karnilla's magic
fabric always billowing
RD 17

"For the Norns, I hit on the idea early on to have their eyes covered by some sort of eye symbol. I made that the focal point of the design and kept the rest of the look very simple."

— RUSSELL DAUTERMAN

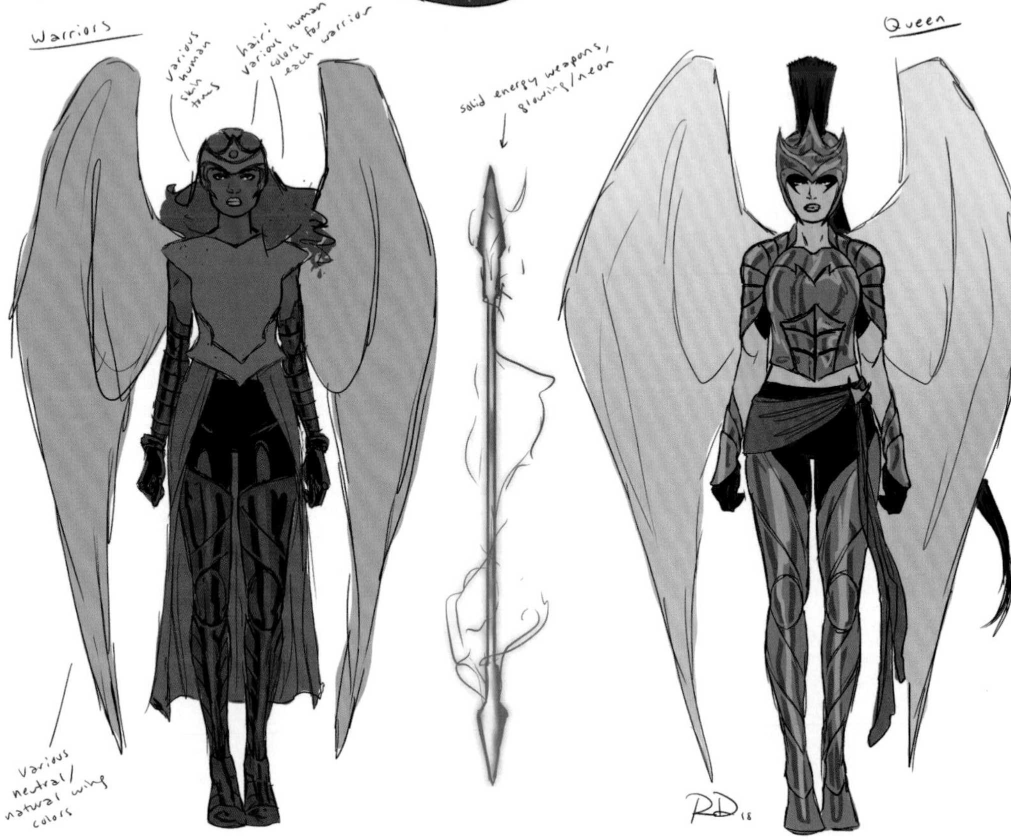

Warriors
various human skin tones
hair: various human colors for each warrior
solid energy weapons, glowing/neon
Queen
various neutral/natural wing colors
RD 18

HELA, CAPTAIN AMERICA AND VALKYRIE

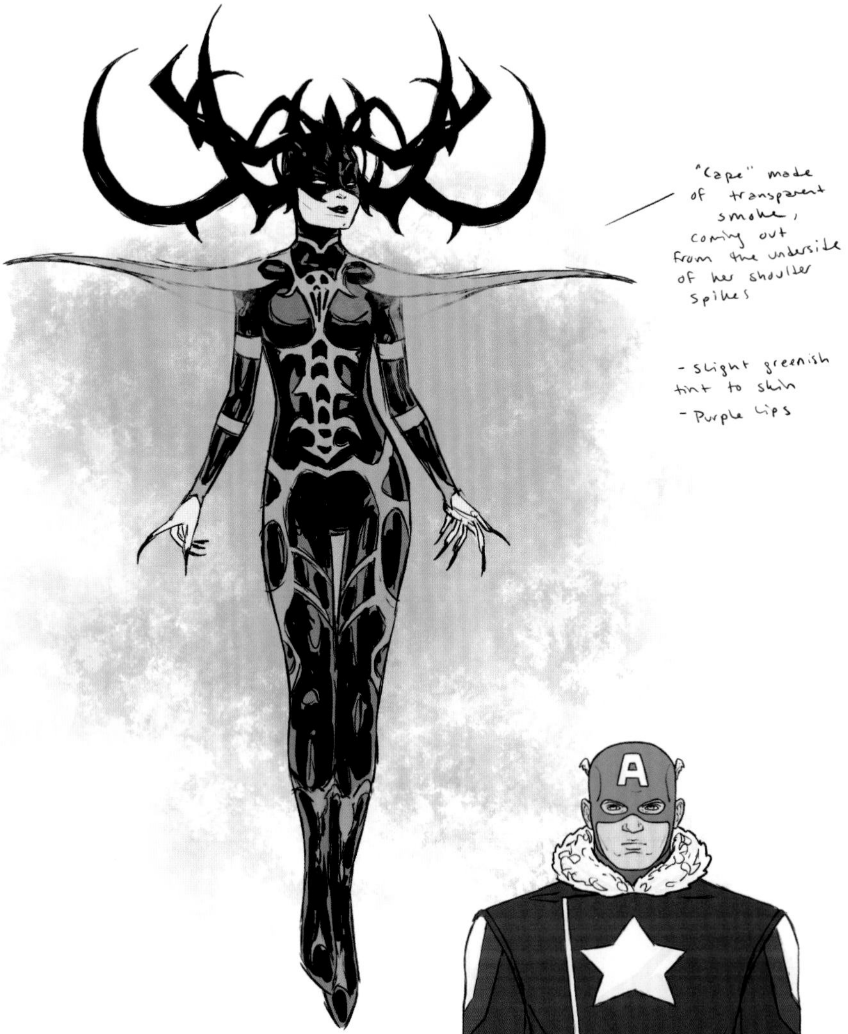
"Cape" made of transparent smoke, coming out from the underside of her shoulder spikes
- slight greenish tint to skin
- Purple lips

"Valkyrie's original costume is iconic for that character, but I thought it could use a modern update. I'd redesigned the costumes for the other Valkyries during my time on *Mighty Thor* and wanted to give Brunnhilde something that fit their new aesthetic. So I took elements from her classic look and some of her more recent ones, combined those with bits of my design for the Valkyries, and tied things together with new elements — all in trying to keep the character recognizable, but fresh."

— RUSSELL DAUTERMAN

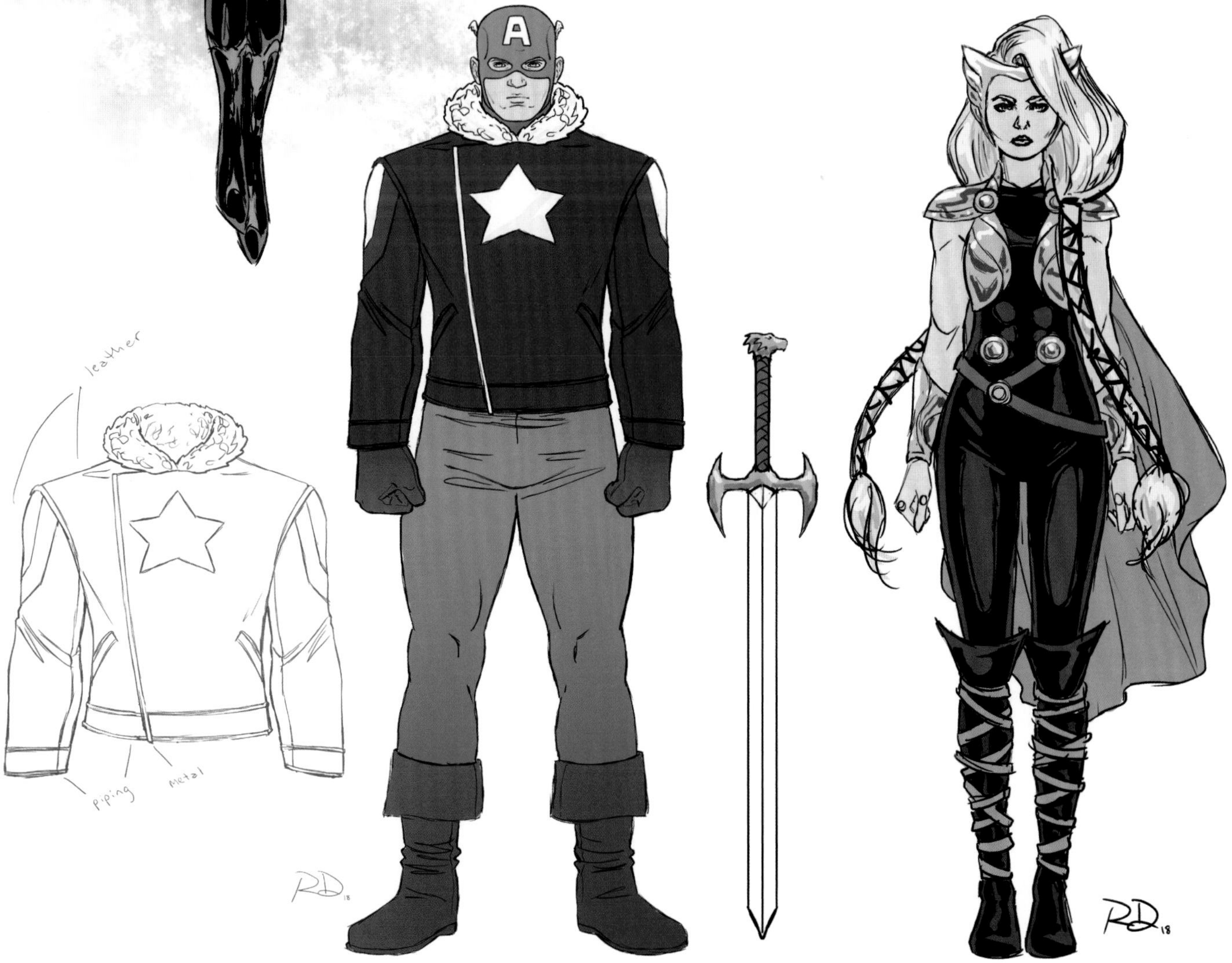
leather
piping
metal

AFTERWORD

When I first read *Thor: God of Thunder #1* in 2012, I hadn't been hired yet at Marvel or DC. To be honest, I was worried I never would be. (In hindsight, that was probably silly. I'd only been drawing comics in any sort of professional capacity for a few years at that point. But still, that's how I felt.) When I got to the page in *God of Thunder #1* in which Thor is floating in front of the sky castle, I just stared at it for a long time — the art was so incredible. And then there was the splash page with the gods on meat hooks! I was so taken with the visuals and so wowed by Jason's writing that *God of Thunder* instantly became my favorite monthly comic. And it stayed that way for its whole run. When I got to that double-page spread at the end of the "Godbomb" arc with Thor and Gorr and the two hammers, I remember thinking it was some of the best comic art I'd seen.

Fast-forward about ten months, and I'm being asked to follow that up!

I'm still amazed that I was picked to follow Esad. My art didn't really fit the aesthetic of *God of Thunder*. Looking back at all the art in this collection, though, I can see how many different flavors of art there have been in Jason's run. Each chapter feels unique, both visually and tonally through the writing. Jason has managed to play to each artist's different strengths and somehow make everything hang together to form one cohesive story about worthiness — whether he's writing about giant gods hanging from meat hooks or monster trucks in Hel or a cancer patient throwing an alien creature into the sun.

Seeing how all those stories and series are paying off in *War of the Realms*, I'm even more impressed by Jason. He's weaving together threads he's been working with for years and weaving in a ton of Marvel Universe characters to create what will hopefully be a big, exciting and satisfying end to his Thor saga.

In my farewell letter at the end of *Mighty Thor*, I wrote that drawing Jane's series was a dream project for me. I said I lucked out by getting to draw that series and by getting to work with Jason, Matt, Wil, Sarah and Joe. I still feel incredibly lucky to keep working with those amazing people, to keep drawing Jason's Thor epic and to be drawing all the characters and craziness of *War of the Realms*. I really hope you enjoy it! Thanks so much for reading.

Thank you to everyone at Marvel who put this collection together for showing off all the art. This is incredibly cool. I'm thrilled to be a part of it and thrilled to be in the company of so many incredible *Thor* artists.

KRAKATHOOOM!

RUSSELL
DAUTERMAN